114

One-Minute

D0118470

① Type *WP* then press the Ret

② **Type** your document.

    Indent with the Tab key.
    End paragraphs (not lines) and insert blank lines with the
       Return key.
    Erase mistakes with the Backspace or Del key.
    Get help with the F3 key.

③ To **print** your documents, hold down the Shift key while you press the F7 key, let go of them both, then press the 1 key on the top row of the keyboard.

④ To **save** your document, press the F10 key, type a name up to eight characters long, then press Return.

⑤ Press the F7 key, then *N* twice to clear the screen and **start over**. Repeat steps 2 to 4 to produce another document.

▼

⑥ Press the F7 key, *N*, then *Y* to **exit** WordPerfect.

WORDPERFECT®
TIPS AND TRICKS
FOURTH EDITION

Alan R. Neibauer

SYBEX®

San Francisco ■ Paris ■ Düsseldorf ■ Soest

Acquisitions Editor: Dianne King
Developmental Editor: Eric Stone
Copy Editor: Kathleen Hummel
Technical Editor: Avon Murphy
Word Processor: Deborah Maizels
Book Designer: Jeffrey James Giese
Layout Artist: Charlotte Carter
Screen Graphics: Delia Brown
Desktop Publishing Operators: Charles Cowens, Robert Myren, Daniel Brodnitz
Proofreader: Edith Rex
Indexer: Julie Kawabata
Cover Designer: Thomas Ingalls + Associates
Cover Photographer: Mark Johann
Screen reproductions produced by XenoFont

WordPerfect is a registered trademark of WordPerfect Corporation.
XenoFont is a trademark of XenoSoft.

SYBEX is a registered trademark of SYBEX Inc.

TRADEMARKS: SYBEX has attempted throughout this book to distinguish proprietary trademarks from descriptive terms by following the capitalization style used by the manufacturer.

SYBEX is not affiliated with any manufacturer.

Every effort has been made to supply complete and accurate information. However, SYBEX assumes no responsibility for its use, nor for any infringement of the intellectual property rights of third parties which would result from such use.

Library of Congress Card Number: 89-52178
ISBN 0-89588-681-2
Manufactured in the United States of America
10 9 8 7 6

To Adam and Joshua: the next generation

ACKNOWLEDGMENTS

Although only my name is on the cover of this book, a talented group of professionals at Sybex deserves much of the credit. Producing this book in a timely manner, yet accurately covering the best features of both WordPerfect 5.0 and 5.1, is a task one individual could never accomplish.

Eric Stone served as developmental editor for this edition, smoothing out the rough edges and keeping us all on time. Eric's excellent contributions as copy editor in the previous edition made our work much easier.

Serving as copy editor was Kathy Hummel. Kathy had to not only edit the manuscript but coordinate the text with the figure and the notes from the text, and make sure each piece fit together into a unified book. She did so wonderfully.

My special thanks to Joanne Cuthbertson, supervising editor, and Avon Murphy, technical reviewer. Among other things, the technical reviewer is responsible for checking the accuracy of each instruction presented.

Special recognition must also go to those who produced the finished product—word processor Deborah Maizels, indexer Julie Kawabata, desktop publishing operators Charles Cowens, Robert Myren, and Daniel Brodnitz, layout artist Charlotte Carter, and proofreader Edith Rex. The superb design of the book is the contribution of Jeff Giese.

The foundation of this edition was laid some time ago. In addition to Eric Stone, those that worked so flawlessly on the last edition include Brian Atwood, Scott Campbell, Jocelyn Reynolds, Charles Cowens, Sonja Schenk, and Jeff Giese.

A sincere thank you to Dianne King and Dr. Rudolph S. Langer.

My acknowledgments could not be complete without thanking my wife of 23 years, Barbara Neibauer. Over the years she's seen my work, my papers, and my junk slowly spread through the house, like some mysterious and uncontrollable weed in the garden. She patiently steps over the books and crumpled pages, and picks up the pens and pencils from the rug. Everything would be impossible without her.

CONTENTS AT A GLANCE

TABLE OF CONTENTS

PART 1: AN OVERVIEW OF WORDPERFECT

CHAPTER 2: CREATING AND EDITING DOCUMENTS

CHAPTER 3: FORMATTING DOCUMENTS FOR A PROFESSIONAL LOOK

CHAPTER 4: CONTROLLING THE PRINTING PROCESS

PART 2: ADVANCED FEATURES FOR SPECIALIZED DOCUMENTS

■
CHAPTER 5: CUSTOMIZING WORDPERFECT FOR THE WAY YOU WORK

CHAPTER 6: FORM LETTERS MADE EASY

CHAPTER 7: AUTOMATING YOUR WORK WITH MACROS AND BOILERPLATE TEXT

CHAPTER 8: PARAGRAPH INDENTATIONS FOR ADDED EMPHASIS AND FLEXIBILITY

CHAPTER 9: MULTICOLUMN DOCUMENTS: THE FIRST STEPS IN DESKTOP PUBLISHING

CHAPTER 10: CREATING AND EDITING TABLES

CHAPTER 11: ADVANCED TABLE MANIPULATION

CHAPTER 12: SORTING TABLES AND LISTS: EASY ACCESS TO YOUR DATA

CHAPTER 13: WORDPERFECT'S REFERENCE TOOLS

CHAPTER 14: FINISHING TOUCHES FOR MAJOR DOCUMENTS

CHAPTER 15: SPECIAL CHARACTERS FOR TECHNICAL AND FOREIGN-LANGUAGE DOCUMENTS

PART 3: WORDPERFECT AS MULTIPURPOSE SOFTWARE

CHAPTER 16: USING WORDPERFECT AS AN OUTLINE AND THOUGHT PROCESSOR

CHAPTER 17: USING WORDPERFECT AS A GRAPHICS TOOL

CHAPTER 18: ENHANCING DOCUMENTS WITH GRAPHICS

CHAPTER 19: USING WORDPERFECT AS A SPREADSHEET

CHAPTER 20: USING WORDPERFECT AS A DATABASE MANAGER

PART 4: TIMESAVING TECHNIQUES FOR CORRESPONDENCE AND RECORD-KEEPING

CHAPTER 21: STREAMLINING FORM DOCUMENTS

CHAPTER 22: USING WORDPERFECT TO AUTOMATE MASS-MAILINGS

■

CHAPTER 23: ADVANCED DOCUMENT ASSEMBLY

CHAPTER 24: COMBINING MACROS, MENUS, AND MERGES

APPENDIX A: CONFIGURING WORDPERFECT FOR YOUR PRINTER

■ APPENDIX B: INSTALLING FONTS AND TESTING YOUR PRINTER

■ APPENDIX C: USING WORDPERFECT'S DICTIONARY AND THESAURUS

INTRODUCTION

WordPerfect's enduring popularity should not surprise anyone. After all, here is a word processing program that combines the best and most powerful features needed by academic, professional, and business typists.

But rather than settle for mere acceptance, WordPerfect has listened carefully to its users, adding features and capabilities with each new release.

While WordPerfect doesn't lack even one important attribute, it is easy to learn and use—even for occasional users.

With this book you won't spend your valuable time memorizing keystrokes. Instead, you will follow practical, step-by-step techniques for conquering that mountain of paperwork quickly. You will master each feature of WordPerfect version 5.0 and 5.1 by performing a real and useful application. You will also learn many special techniques designed to streamline your work and to utilize the full potential of your computer and printer.

If you are a new WordPerfect user, this book will start you with the basic skills. But even the fundamentals are covered in a practical way designed to get you in "production" as quickly as possible. Once you have these skills, the applications that follow show you how to use your computer for typical word processing tasks.

Are you already familiar with WordPerfect? Use this book to solve the word processing problems—even the tough ones—that you are facing today.

Take a look at what this book offers.

WHAT THIS BOOK CONTAINS

This book is divided into four parts. Part 1 (Chapters 1 through 4) reviews the WordPerfect basics. These chapters explain how WordPerfect operates, how to enter and edit text, and how to format text to make your documents look good and have impact.

If this is your first experience with WordPerfect, or if you're just switching to its newest version, read Chapters 1 through 4 carefully for an introduction. If you have already begun using WordPerfect, review these chapters briefly before going on to the specific applications that follow. You'll learn how to create, edit, format, and print documents of all types—and how to master version 5.1's optional pull-down menus and mouse operations.

Part 2 presents techniques for general word processing applications and for some special WordPerfect features like sorting, index generation, special characters, and statistical typing. In Chapter 5 you will learn how to change

WordPerfect's built-in default settings, and how to use style sheets, a powerful feature that makes formatting multiple documents as easy as formatting one.

Chapters 6 and 7 present several methods for creating simple form letters and documents. Chapter 6 also explains how to display and use two documents at one time. Chapter 7 concentrates on boilerplate text and WordPerfect's powerful Macro feature. You'll see how sections of text can be quickly recalled with a few keystrokes. With boilerplate and macros, you can create a multitude of "personalized" documents from standard paragraphs and phrases. You'll also learn how to edit macros you've already created.

Chapters 8 and 9 explain special formatting applications. Chapter 8 details paragraph indentation, and Chapter 9 covers multicolumn documents such as newsletters. Unlike most word processing programs, WordPerfect lets you see multicolumn text right on the screen.

The next three chapters, 10 through 12, comprise a unit on tables and other columnar typing. Chapter 10 shows applications for creating and editing tables, and in Chapter 11 you'll see how to move and copy entire columns. Chapter 12 explains how your tables can be sorted numerically or alphabetically. If you're using version 5.1, read these chapters also to learn about this version's powerful Table Editor. You'll learn how to create spreadsheet-like tables, complete with lines, boxes, and even shaded areas.

In Chapters 13 and 14 you'll learn how to use WordPerfect to create research reports or major papers. Automatically creating an index, table of contents, or list is illustrated in Chapter 13, while Chapter 14 concentrates on footnotes, bibliographies, and other considerations of long documents. When you're done with these chapters, you'll also be able to create tables of authorities and automatic references to pages, figures, and tables in your document. Chapter 15 reveals how special characters and foreign words are created. You'll learn how version 5.1 can print over 1500 special characters on graphics printers, and how to format even the most complex mathematical equation using the remarkable new Equation Editor.

Part 3 brings out some of the best of WordPerfect. These five chapters, 16 through 20, present applications for using WordPerfect as an "integrated software" package—combining outlining and thought processing, graphics, spreadsheets, and database management into your word processing efforts.

Chapter 16 explains how to use WordPerfect as an outline processor to develop your ideas. This chapter includes details on creating custom outline styles with version 5.1.

Chapters 17 and 18 form a unit on graphics and desktop publishing. In Chapter 17 you'll learn how to add lines and boxes to your documents, while Chapter 18 shows how to use drawings and artwork to produce attractive, finished copy. If you have a laser printer or a high-quality dot-matrix printer, these chapters show you how WordPerfect takes the place of some expensive desktop publishing packages.

Chapter 19 turns WordPerfect into a spreadsheet for combining what-if problems with documents. You'll learn how WordPerfect can automatically add columns or rows of numbers, and perform four-function math. With version 5.1, you'll learn how to create complete spreadsheets with the Table Editor, and how to automatically link spreadsheets created by other programs such as Lotus 1-2-3 with your documents. Chapter 20 covers the WordPerfect database management system, and introduces programmed macros—a feature that lets you write programs for automating your database efforts.

Part 4 concentrates on more advanced document and data merging applications. Chapter 21 combines data management techniques with form letter generation. Chapter 22 shows how labels and envelopes can be printed—even on laser printers. If you have version 5.1, you'll learn how new features make it even easier to print on labels of all types. In Chapter 23 you'll learn advanced techniques for document assembly, including the creation of master documents. Chapter 24 puts it all together to show how WordPerfect can produce custom menus for high-speed document processing. These chapters also show you additional ways to harness the power of programmed macros, including the rich command language in version 5.1.

Appendices A and B concentrate on your printer. In Appendix A you'll learn the details of printer installation. Appendix B shows you how to use your printer's special features, including cartridges and soft fonts for laser printers. Appendix C explains how to operate WordPerfect's spelling checker and thesaurus.

◼ DIFFERENCES BETWEEN VERSIONS

There are some substantial differences between versions 5.0 and 5.1 of Word-Perfect. So to make this book as useful as possible to all WordPerfect users, these differences have been treated a special way.

In most cases, the text of the chapter is valid for both version 5.0 and 5.1. However, in the margins you'll see three different messages about 5.1.These are important, so make sure you understand them before going on. Following is an explanation of each of the messages:

Warning   This message means that the exact series of
             keystrokes listed in the chapter will not work with
             version 5.1. In some cases, you will be instructed to

refer to a page in the section called "Version 5.1 Features" at the end of the chapter before continuing. There you will find the exact steps to follow. In other cases, the version 5.1 keystrokes will be presented right in the margin note. Follow the instructions in the note, and then continue in the main text.

Note

This message means that some minor variation exists between versions 5.0 and 5.1, but the keystrokes presented in the chapter will perform properly. In many cases, this means that a prompt line or menu illustrated in the text will appear differently with version 5.1. If the differences are major, the version 5.1 display will be shown at the end of the chapter. Regardless of any cosmetic differences, you can still follow the instructions given in the main text to perform the operation being described.

New Feature

This message means that a new feature, related to the subject being discussed in the chapter, has been added to version 5.1. You'll be referred to the "Version 5.1 Features" section to learn about these new capabilities.

CONVENTIONS USED IN THIS BOOK

On the keyboard template that you received with WordPerfect, and in the WordPerfect manual, all function commands are given names. But if you lose your template, or just decide not to place it on your keyboard, you might have trouble remembering what keystrokes the name represents. So throughout this book, all functions are referred to by the actual keystrokes used. Instead of saying *press the Print key*, our instructions will say *Press Shift-F7*.

COMBINING KEYSTROKES

In many instances you will have to press more than one key to perform a certain task. These key combinations are of two types:

- You might have to press two or more keys at the same time.

- You might have to press several keys in sequence.

Keys that should be pressed together are separated with a hyphen. For example, if an instruction says to press Shift-F7, this means that you should press and HOLD DOWN the Shift key, then press and release the F7 key, and finally release the Shift keys. The sequence is this:

1. Press and hold down the first key listed.

2. Press and release the second key.

3. Release the first key.

Other key combinations must be pressed in sequence, one after the other. These are always separated by blank spaces. For instance, if an instruction says to press F7 N N, this means you should:

1. Press and release the F7 key.

2. Press and release *N*.

3. Press and release *N* a second time.

This might seem to be a great number of keystrokes for one command. However, as you learn commands such as these, you'll find they become almost automatic. In most cases, you don't have to pause between keystrokes, so pressing three keys will not slow your progress.

The instruction Shift-F7 2 combines both types of instructions. First do Shift-F7 by pressing and holding the Shift key while you press F7. Let go of them both, and then press *2*.

VERSION 5.1 INSTRUCTIONS

In the "Version 5.1 Features" section at the end of each chapter, the instructions also show the sequence of pull-down menu commands that you must select—either with the keyboard or with the mouse—such as this instruction to print a document:

1. Press Shift-F7 1 or select **F**ile **P**rint **F**ull Document.

This means that to print a document, use the Shift-F7 1 keystrokes or the Full Document option on the Print menu accessed from the File pull-down menu. Using the keyboard, you'd display the menu bar, then press the letters shown in boldface. With the mouse, you'd click on the menu choices or options.

For example, to select F**ile** P**rint** F**ull**, you would:

Keyboard	Mouse
Press Alt-=	Click the right button
Press *F*	Click on File with the left button
Press *P*	Click on Print with the left button
Press *F*	Click on Full Document with the left button

At the end of each chapter, under "Version 5.1 Features," you'll find the section "Mouse and Menu Equivalents." This section summarizes the pull-down menu commands equivalent to the version 5.1 keystrokes for the functions discussed in the chapter.

FOLLOWING THE INSTRUCTIONS

Most lessons in this book take you step by step through a specific task. Just follow each instruction to master the technique discussed. To differentiate between the instructions, the things you type, and things that WordPerfect displays on the screen, here are a few rules:

- When you are asked to type something in from the keyboard, what you are to type will appear in bold, like this:

  1. Type **myfirst**

- Sometimes you will be asked to type several lines of text, or even entire paragraphs. These lines will be indented and set off from the instruction, and will be in a different type, like this:

  1. Type the following:

     WordPerfect allows the creation, editing, and printing of all types of documents. They can be saved at any time.

- When WordPerfect shows something on the screen in response to something you have done, that information will also be in a different type, like this:

  1. The prompt line changes to

     Save document? (Y/N) Yes

■ When you are to actually do something on your computer, I will give you a series of numbered steps to follow:

1.

2.

3.

Read and perform each step in the order given. But be sure to read all of the text that is in the step since in a few cases, some optional instructions may be given such as:

1. If you want to accept the default value, press Return, and then skip to step 18.

In this case, you could press the Return key, and then go directly to step 18, skipping any steps in between. If you don't want to accept the default value, continue reading and following the instructions without pressing Return.

■ # HOW TO USE YOUR KEYBOARD WITH WORDPERFECT

This book explains how to use WordPerfect for specific applications. You don't have to be an expert typist, but to control the powers of this program, you do have to know how the keyboard is used.

Figures I.1 through I.3 show the three major keyboards used with IBM and IBM-compatible computers.

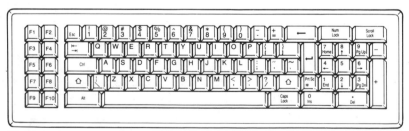

■**FIGURE I.1:** *Original IBM keyboard*

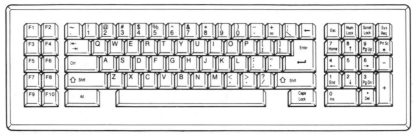

■**FIGURE I.2:** *Older IBM PC/AT keyboard*

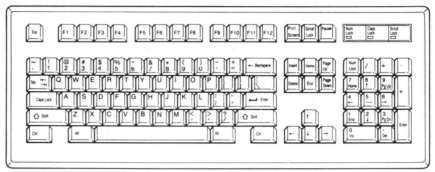

■**FIGURE I.3:** *Enhanced IBM keyboard (with PS/2 windows)*

Most of the time you will be using the middle section of the keyboard, which contains the keys for letters, numbers, and punctuation marks. If you've ever used a typewriter, you'll recognize these keys.

SPECIAL KEYS

The computer keyboard also includes some keys not found on a regular typewriter. These might be labeled with an arrow, some other figure, or an abbreviation like Alt or Ctrl. Since you will also be using these keys often, look at your keyboard for the following keys:

 This is the Tab key. When an instruction says to press Tab, press this key.

 This is the Shift key. When an instruction says to press Shift, press this key. You can press either of the two Shift keys on the keyboard.

This is the Return or Enter key—one of the most important keys you will be using. You use Return mainly to end paragraphs or to insert blank lines into the text.

This is the Backspace key. It deletes the character to the left of the cursor.

When an instruction says to press Esc, press this key, the Escape key. In WordPerfect, this key is used to repeat characters and commands automatically.

When an instruction says to press Ins, press this key. This is the Insert key, which switches between Insert and Typeover modes. In Insert mode, existing characters will move over to make room for new ones that you type. In Typeover mode, new characters will replace existing ones.

When an instruction says to press Del, press this key. This is the Delete key, used to erase the character on which the cursor is resting.

When an instruction says to press Alt, press this key, the Alternate key. It is used with the function keys described later.

When an instruction says to press Ctrl, press this key, the Control key. Like the Alt key, Ctrl is used in combination with the function keys.

CURSOR MOVEMENT KEYS

The cursor is a small blinking line or box on the screen that usually indicates where the next character typed will appear. If the cursor is at the end of your document, characters you type will be added to the end of your text. You can move the cursor anywhere in your document. If you want to add words to the middle of a paragraph, move the cursor to that spot using the *cursor movement keys*.

Most of these are located on the right side of the keyboard. If you press a cursor movement key and a number appears on the screen, press the key marked NUM LOCK.

The four most basic keys are the directional arrows.

 This is the up arrow key, designated in this book as ↑. When you press this key the cursor moves up one line.

 This is the down arrow key, ↓. When you press this key the cursor moves down one line.

 This is the right arrow key, →. It moves the cursor one character to the right.

 This is the left arrow key, ←. It moves the cursor one character to the left.

To move more than one line or character at a time, press and *hold down* the appropriate arrow key.

Other special keys are used to move the cursor more than one line or character at a time. Some are pressed individually, others in combination.

Moving Down through a Document

Home Home ↓	Moves the cursor to the end of the document.
PgDn	Moves the cursor to the top of the next page in the document.
Home ↓	Moves the cursor to the bottom of the screen or, if already there, displays the next 24 lines of text.
Esc *n* PgDn	Moves the cursor down *n* pages. Press Esc, type the number of pages to move, and press PgDn.
Esc *n* ↓	Moves the cursor down *n* lines. Press Esc, enter the number of lines to move, and press the ↓.
Ctrl-Home ↓	Moves the cursor to the bottom of the current page. The Ctrl-Home combination is called Go To.

Moving Up through a Document

Home Home ↑	Moves the cursor to the top of the document.
PgUp	Moves the cursor to the top of the previous page.
Home ↑	Moves the cursor to the top of the screen or, if already there, displays the previous 24 lines of text.
Esc n PgUp	Moves the cursor up n pages.
Esc n ↑	Moves the cursor up n lines.
Ctrl-Home ↑	Moves the cursor to the top of the current page.

Moving Left

Home ←	Moves the cursor to the left edge of the screen.
ESC n ←	Moves the cursor n characters to the left.
Ctrl-Home ←	Moves the cursor to the previous column when typing multicolumn documents.
Ctrl-Home Home ←	Moves the cursor to the first column on a multicolumn page.

Moving Right

End or Home →	Moves the cursor to the end of the current line.
Esc n →	Moves the cursor n characters to the right.
Ctrl-Home →	Moves the cursor to the next column when typing multicolumn documents.
Ctrl-Home Home →	Moves the cursor to the last column on a multicolumn page.

Moving to Specific Locations   Finally, the Go To combination (Ctrl-Home) can be used to place the cursor at a specific page or character.

Ctrl-Home *n*   Moves the cursor to the top of page *n*.

Ctrl-Home *x*   Moves the cursor to the first occurrence of the
                      character *x*. (It must occur within the nearest 2000
                      characters.) For example, press Ctrl-Home *M* to
                      place the cursor on the first letter *M* within 2000
                      characters of the cursor.

FUNCTION KEYS

Depending on your computer you may have 10 or 12 special keys, labeled F1 to F10 or F12. They are either on the left side of the keyboard or above the top row of typing characters. They operate exactly the same in either location.

These keys have been "programmed" by WordPerfect for special functions, providing quick and easy methods to perform complex tasks. Certain functions are performed by pressing a function key by itself. Other functions are accomplished by pressing them in combination with the Alt, Shift, or Ctrl key. Don't be overwhelmed by the large number of function keys available. You'll quickly learn the most important ones and before long you'll master them all. (In version 5.1, pull-down menu commands are available as alternatives to most function-key operations.)

You received two templates describing these function keys with your Word-Perfect manual. The square template with the cutout in the middle is designed for keyboards with the function keys on the side; place it over the keys and refer to it as you type. The long template is for keyboards with the function keys on the top; place it above the keys so you can refer to it when you want to use the function keys.

The template is color-coded to designate which key combination performs which function. Black functions are performed by pressing the function key alone. For other functions, you must press the function key and another key at the same time; green functions are accomplished with the Shift key, blue with the Alt key, and red with the Ctrl key.

If you have misplaced your template, here is a recap of the tasks performed by all of the function-key combinations. New key names for version 5.1 are given in parentheses.

Ctrl-F1	Shell	Ctrl-F2	Spell
Shift	Setup	Shift	Search Backward
Alt	Thesaurus	Alt	Replace
Alone	Cancel	Alone	Search Forward
Ctrl-F3	Screen	Ctrl-F4	Move
Shift	Switch	Shift	Indent—both margins
Alt	Reveal Codes	Alt	Block
Alone	Help	Alone	Indent—left margin
Ctrl-F5	Text In/Out	Ctrl-F6	Tab Align
Shift	Date/Outline	Shift	Center
Alt	Mark Text	Alt	Flush Right
Alone	List Files (List)	Alone	Bold
Ctrl-F7	Footnote	Ctrl-F8	Font
Shift	Print	Shift	Format
Alt	Math/Columns (Columns/Tables)	Alt	Style
Alone	Exit	Alone	Underline
Ctrl-F9	Merge/Sort	Ctrl-F10	Macro Define
Shift	Merge Codes	Shift	Retrieve
Alt	Graphics	Alt	Macro
Alone	End Field	Alone	Save

NUMERIC KEYPAD

On the right side of the keyboard is a group of keys called the *numeric keypad*. These keys have both numbers and arrows printed on them, and serve both as a numeric keyboard and as cursor-movement keys. To use the numeric keypad for numbers, you have to press the Num Lock key above the keypad. With the Num Lock key off, these keys are cursor movement keys; with Num Lock on, they are number keys, and the characters *Pos* blink at the bottom right of the screen (as will be explained fully in Chapter 1). With some keyboards, a small light—either in the Num Lock key itself or in the upper right corner of the keyboard—will be on when the Num Lock key is on. Simply press Num Lock if you want to turn the light and the key off.

Some keyboards have separate cursor movement keys and numeric keypad. If you have this type of keyboard, then use the keypad for entering numbers and the arrow keys to the left of the keypad for cursor movement.

HARDWARE AND SOFTWARE

This book is for users of WordPerfect version 5.0 and 5.1. It was written using both versions to ensure that the instructions were accurate no matter which version you have. I used the version of WordPerfect for the IBM PC, XT, AT, and PS/2, and compatible computers using MS-DOS, PC-DOS, or OS/2 in the DOS mode. For printing, I used a Star SG-10 dot-matrix printer, a DaisyWriter daisy-wheel printer, and a Hewlett-Packard LaserJet Plus laser printer. Word-Perfect has *driver* programs for hundreds of different printers.

Before going on, make sure that you have the proper version of WordPerfect for your computer. Then check to see that you have the minimum equipment necessary:

Equipment	Description
Computer	IBM PC, XT, AT, PS/2, or compatible computer.
Operating System	PC-DOS, MS-DOS, or OS/2.
Storage	Two floppy disk drives or one floppy drive and one hard drive. High-capacity drives are required to use version 5.1 on floppy disk systems.
Monitor	Monochrome, composite, or color monitor.

Display card	Monochrome, CGA, EGA, VGA, or compatible display adaptor; Hercules Graphic Card, Graphic Card Plus Ramfont, or InColor card, or compatible.
Printer interface	Parallel or serial, depending on your printer.
Printer	Any supported printer. You'll need the correct cable to attach your printer to the appropriate port (either parallel or serial) for your computer.

You're now ready to start WordPerfect. If you have version 5.1, however, you must run the Install program to prepare WordPerfect for use. With either version, refer to Appendices A and B to set up WordPerfect for your printer.

PART
1

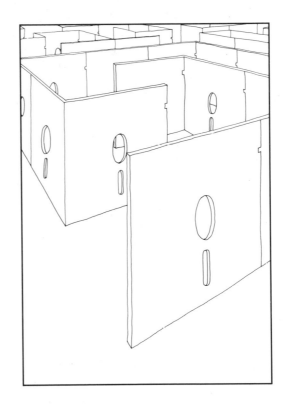

AN OVERVIEW OF
WORDPERFECT

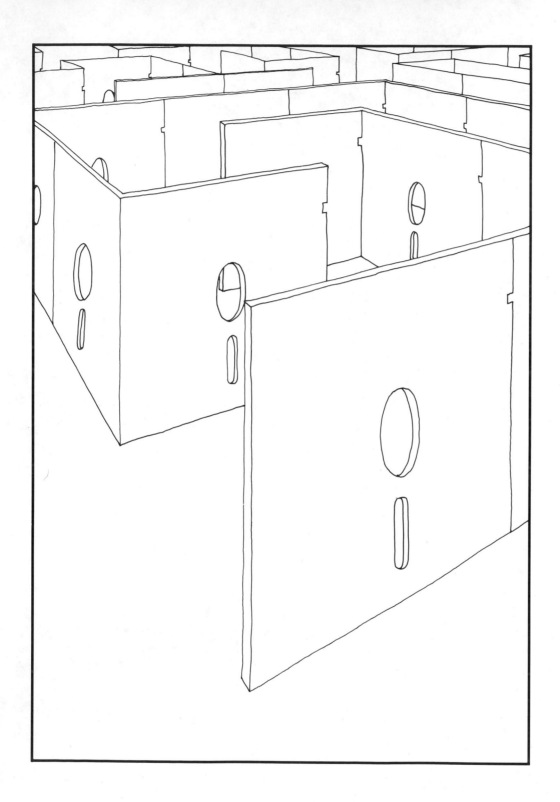

1

HOW WORDPERFECT WORKS

This chapter summarizes the basic operation of WordPerfect. It reviews how to start and use the program. Because WordPerfect is different from most commonplace word processing programs, it is important that you understand the fundamental concepts discussed here.

■ USING WORDPERFECT WITH A HARD DISK

If you are using a hard-disk drive, then you no doubt have already copied onto the hard disk all of the floppy disks supplied with WordPerfect. Following the instructions in the WordPerfect manual, you created a subdirectory to hold the WordPerfect program.

To start the program with a hard disk, follow these steps:

1. Turn on your computer, respond to the date and time prompts if they appear, and wait until the prompt

   C>>

   (or a similar prompt) appears on the screen.

2. To "log on" to the subdirectory containing the WordPerfect program, type **CD** followed by the name of your subdirectory, then press Return.

3. Type **WP** and press Return to start WordPerfect.

USING WORDPERFECT WITH FLOPPY DISKS

Note
Version 5.1 will
not run on
low-density
(360k) 5
1/4-inch
diskettes. Start
with the
WordPerfect 1
diskette, then
insert
WordPerfect 2
when prompted.

If you are using floppy disks, it's a good idea to have all of the WordPerfect disks handy while you are working with the program. Always start with the WordPerfect 1 disk (for 5 1/4-inch disks) or the WordPerfect Program disk (for 3 1/2-inch disks) in drive A and a formatted data disk in drive B. The program disk contains the WordPerfect program, the printer file for your particular printer, and some other programs that WordPerfect uses. Your own documents will be stored in the disk in drive B.

To start WordPerfect with a floppy-disk system, follow these steps:

1. Place the WordPerfect 1 or WordPerfect Program disk in drive A.

2. Turn on your computer, respond to the date and time prompts if they appear, then wait until the prompt

    A>>

    (or a similar prompt) appears on the screen.

3. Type **B:** and press Return to log onto drive B.

4. Type **A:WP** and press Return.

If you have 5 1/2-inch disks, you'll be prompted to insert the WordPerfect disk in drive A. Remove the WordPerfect 1 disk from drive A and insert the WordPerfect 2 disk. Close the disk drive latch and press any key.

THE WORDPERFECT SCREEN

The WordPerfect screen displays the document that you're working on, as well as information about the location of the cursor. During the course of your work, you will also see various prompts, selection lines, and menus.

ON-SCREEN FORMATTING

In most cases, the text appears on the screen just as it will when printed. You will see text boldfaced, centered, indented, or otherwise formatted as it will be on the printed page—even in several columns across the screen, if you have chosen that format. This lets you experiment with various formats until you see the one that you want for the printed copy.

There are a few exceptions to this "what you see is what you get" rule.

- Footnotes, which will print on the bottom of the appropriate pages, will not appear in the proper position on the screen.

- Special printer styles, such as italics or large print, may appear as regular type on the screen.

- Text will not appear justified (aligned) along the right margin, even though the default setting in printed text is for right justification.

- Depending on your video card, underlined text will appear either underlined, in reverse video (highlighted), or in a color different from the regular text.

THE STATUS LINE

When you start WordPerfect, the screen is entirely blank except for a *status line* on the bottom of the screen, which looks like this:

Doc 1 Pg 1 Ln 1" Pos 1"

This line lets you know where the cursor is located in the document. Since you can work on two different documents at one time, the status line also tells you which document you are currently editing.

The following information is normally displayed on the status line:

- The document number (Doc), which can be either 1 or 2, depending on the document you are editing. You can move back and forth between documents by pressing Shift-F3.

- The page (Pg) you are currently viewing on the screen.

- The distance of the cursor from the top of the page (Ln).

- The distance of the cursor from the left edge of the paper (Pos).

WordPerfect actually uses the position indicator to relay more information about your document's current status. *Pos* will change to *POS* if you press the Caps Lock key to type all uppercase letters, and it will blink on and off if you press the Num Lock key to type numbers using the keypad to the right of the keyboard (instead of using those keys to move the cursor). If you turn on the Bold or Underline feature, the numbers following *Pos* will appear in that style. In fact, as you move the cursor through an existing document, these numbers will appear in the same format as the character over the cursor.

The lower-left corner of the screen is usually blank when you first start WordPerfect. This indicates that you are in Insert mode. If you enter characters within existing text, words to the right will move over and down to make room for them. If you press the Ins key (the 0 key on the numeric keypad), the word *Typeover* will appear in that corner. In Typeover mode, any new characters that you type will replace existing ones.

When you recall a document, or after you name and save one, its name appears in the lower-left corner of the status line. The name includes the complete path of the file. In Typeover mode, however, the name is replaced with the word *Typeover*.

As explained in the next section, various prompts and messages appear on the status line while you are working with the program.

■   INTERACTING WITH WORDPERFECT

Note
Prompts, and many selection lines and menus, appear differently in version 5.1, although the keystrokes may be the same. Refer to "Interacting with Version 5.1," page 13 for details.

In many cases, pressing one of the function keys displays another prompt, a short list of choices on the status line, or even an entire menu of options.

PROMPTS

For example, if you press F7, the status line displays the prompt

Save Document? (Y/N) Yes

The response shown at the end of the prompt, in this case *Yes*, is the default value. You can press Return to select this value, type another choice (such as *N*—you don't have to type the whole word *No*), or press the F1 key to cancel the command. (F1 can always be used to cancel the effect of the last function key pressed.)

Note
The appearance of the version 5.1 screen is slightly different, but the steps listed here still apply.

SELECTION LINES

Other function keys display a number of choices. For example, if you press Ctrl-F9, the status line changes to

1 Merge; 2 Sort: 0

Each option on the selection line is numbered, and one character (not always the first) is bold. Press either the number or the bold letter for the desired function (such as **1** or **m** to perform a merge), or press Return to select the default *0* and cancel the action. You can also press F1 to cancel the selection line.

Your selection may perform some action immediately, or it may lead to additional selection lines. Continue picking the desired options.

MENUS

In some cases, you'll see a complete menu of options. Pressing Shift-F8, for example, will display the full-screen Format menu shown in Figure 1.1.

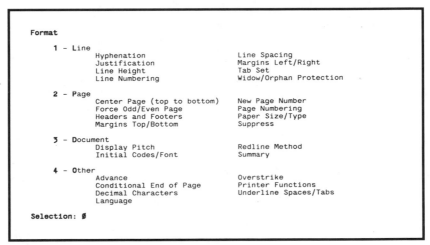

■FIGURE 1.1:   *Format menu*

Notice that the menu has four options, numbered 1 to 4, and that one letter of each choice appears in boldface. At the bottom of the screen is a prompt:

Selection: 0

You type the appropriate number or boldfaced letter to select the menu option.

You can use the default value 0 (or F1) to quickly "escape" from the menu. Press Return to accept the default value.

What happens when you select an option other than 0 depends on the selection. In this case, selecting any choice will show a new menu of additional options. With other menus, however, some setting will automatically change or you will have to type in a new setting.

■   WORDPERFECT'S DEFAULT SETTINGS

Each time you start WordPerfect, the standard page size, line spacing, and other format specifications are automatically set. These *default settings* are provided so that you can type and print most documents without worrying about such matters.

The following are WordPerfect's major default settings:

- A page size of 8-1/2 by 11 inches

- Top and bottom margins of 1 inch

- Left and right margins of 1 inch

- Single spacing, 6 lines per inch

- No paragraph indentation

- Tab stops every 1/2 inch

- Full justification

- No page numbers

These settings result in a page with 54 typed lines of text, each line about 6 1/2 inches wide. The printed text will be aligned on both the left and right margins.

In Chapter 5, you will learn how to change WordPerfect's default settings to your own specifications.

■   PAGINATION

Like most word processing programs, WordPerfect automatically divides your text into pages. When you reach the end of the page, a row of dashes will appear across the screen, and the page indicator on the status line will increase by one. If you later add or delete lines from a page, WordPerfect will adjust the text so the proper number of lines appear on each page.

In Chapter 3 you will learn how to end a page manually at any point and how to insert a *conditional* page break to keep certain blocks of text, such as tables and charts, together on one page.

SAVING YOUR DOCUMENTS ON DISK

Note
By default,
version 5.1
saves a
temporary
backup copy
every 30
minutes. Details
in Chapter 5.

As a precaution, you should save your work approximately every 15 minutes. This will prevent the loss of much of your work in the event of a power failure or other mishap. It might take a few extra seconds, but reentering twenty or so pages after you accidentally pull out the computer's plug would take a great deal more time.

To save your document and continue working on it, press F10. The prompt

Document to be Saved:

appears. Type a file name (one to eight characters with no spaces, optionally followed by a period and up to three more characters), then press Return. If you have saved the text before, its name will follow the prompt. To save the document under the same name, press Return.

Note
The appearance
of the version
5.1 screen is
slightly
different, but the
steps listed here
still apply.

You will see the prompt

Replace *FILENAME*? (Y/N) No

Press *Y* to replace the original version with the new text. If you don't want to replace the original document, press Return, then type a new document name to rename the file.

SAVING AND QUITTING

Note
The appearance
of the version
5.1 screen is
slightly
different, but the
steps listed here
still apply.

If you want to save your document and exit the WordPerfect program, press F7. The prompt

Save Document? (Y/N) Yes

appears. Press Return if you want to save the text. You will then see the same prompts that appear when you press F10 to save and continue working. Finally, the prompt

Exit WP? (Y/N) No

appears. Press *Y* to return to the operating system.

SAVING AND STARTING A NEW DOCUMENT

To save the current document on the screen and start a new one, press F7 Y, enter a document name as explained above, but press *N* in response to the Exit prompt. The current document will be removed from the screen, but you will remain in the WordPerfect program.

■   SAVING TEXT IN OTHER FORMATS

The saving techniques discussed in the previous section store your text as a WordPerfect file, complete with special formatting codes. These codes may create a problem if you plan to use the document with another word processing program, or with the PRINT command in DOS.

So WordPerfect provides several methods of converting its documents to a more general form. You can save the document as a DOS file, as a generic text file that will not contain any of the special WordPerfect codes, or in previous WordPerfect version formats. This will help people who may be using both old and new versions.

Before saving documents in these other formats, you should review some of the basic codes and concepts summarized below:

[HRt]   This invisible code is inserted into the text when you press the Return key. It stands for *hard return*.

[SRt]   When WordPerfect senses that the text will not fit on the line, it starts a new line automatically so you don't have to press Return until you reach the end of the paragraph. This is called *word wrap* and is marked by this code, a *soft return*.

CR/LF   This is an abbreviation for a *carriage return/line feed*, a generic [HRt] code used by many other word processing programs. It means that the cursor is moved to the next line and to the left margin.

Warning
Users of version 5.1 should follow the special instructions under "Saving Files in Other Formats," page 18.

Begin each of the techniques by pressing Ctrl-F5 to show the Text In/Out prompt line:

> 1 Dos Text; 2 Password; 3 Save Generic; 4 Save WP 4.2;
> 5 Comment:0

The three ways to save the file are options 1, 3, and 4. Here are the differences:

- Press **1** or **t** to save the document as a DOS text file. WordPerfect deletes all formatting codes but replaces [SRt] codes with carriage return and line feed combinations so the lines end just as they do on the screen. Use this format to later print the document from DOS using the PRINT command.

- Press **3** or **g** to save the file in a generic word processor format, which removes the [SRt] codes, making one long line out of each paragraph.

While all formatting codes are removed, most other word processing programs will be able to format the text into paragraphs.

■ Press **4** or **w** to save the file as a version 4.2 document, removing only those codes that are found in version 5 but not in the earlier version.

If you select either the generic format or the version 4.2 format, the prompt line will change to

Document to be saved:

followed by the document's name, if it already has one. Type the name you want to call the file and press Return, or just press Return to accept the name that may already be there.

If you select DOS text file format, you'll see the prompt line

1 Save; 2 Retrieve (CR/LF to [HRt]); 3 Retrieve (CR/LF to [SRt] in HZone):0

Press *1* to save the file, and respond to the Filename prompt as explained earlier.

■ RECALLING TEXT FROM OTHER FORMATS

You recall generic and version 4.2 files the same way you recall any WordPerfect document. Press Shift-F10 and enter the document's name. Since the file is not in version 5.0 format, you will see the message

Document conversion in progress

The text will appear after it has been converted to the correct format. You can recall version 5.0 documents into 5.1 the same way.

Recalling DOS text files requires an additional step. Press Ctrl-F5 1 to select the DOS Text option, then select option 2 or 3 from the prompt line.

With option 2, the carriage return and line feed combinations are replaced with [HRt] codes. The text will appear as it was when originally saved, but paragraphs cannot be reformatted easily. In fact, what appear to be paragraphs are really individual lines, each ending with a hard carriage return.

Text recalled with option 3 is much easier to reformat. The carriage return and line feed combinations are replaced with [SRt] codes if the line ends within the left and right H-Zones. Use this option if you plan to edit the document before resaving it. H-Zones are explained in detail in Chapter 3.

CONVERTING DOCUMENTS TO AND FOR OTHER WORD PROCESSORS

The Convert program provided with WordPerfect converts files created with other word processing programs to WordPerfect format and vice versa. It not only makes the files readable, but also transfers formatting codes, such as those for boldfacing and underlining, to the new document.

As an example, suppose you created a document called RESUME using WordStar.

If you have a floppy-disk system, place the Conversion disk in drive A and the disk containing the document in drive B. If you have a hard-disk system, the Convert program is already on drive C, so only insert the document disk.

From the DOS prompt, type *Convert*, then press Return. A copyright message appears, and then you see the prompt

Name of input file?

Type the drive number and the name of the file (*B:RESUME*, for example) and press Return. The prompt now reads

Name of output file?

Type the drive number and the name that you want the WordPerfect file to have, then press Return. A menu of possible input file formats will be displayed.

Press the number corresponding to the current format of the document, in this case option 4, WordStar. The program will read the document and translate it into WordPerfect format, saving it under the output file name you specified.

To convert a WordPerfect file to another format, select option 1 on the Input File Type menu. You will then see a menu of possible output file formats. From that menu, select the format for the new file.

After you've completed either type of conversion, the Convert program ends and the system prompt appears.

PROTECTING YOUR DOCUMENTS WITH PASSWORDS

Anyone with access to your disk can recall, print, or edit your documents. If you have a confidential document or text that you want to protect from prying eyes, you can lock it with a password. Once a document is locked, the password is needed to recall, edit, or print it.

Press Ctrl-F5 to display the Text In/Out prompt line, then press *2* or *p* to select the Password option. You'll see the prompt

Password: 1 Add/Change; 2 Remove:0

Press *1* or *a* to protect your document with a password. The prompt changes to

Enter Password:

Type a short, easy-to-remember password. For security, the characters will not appear on the screen. Press Return to display the prompt

Re-enter Password:

This lets you confirm the password that you just entered. Retype the same password, then press Return. When you later save the document, it will be protected by the password.

Recall a password-protected document normally, using Shift- F10 and entering its name. But before WordPerfect retrieves it, you'll see the prompt

Enter Password:

Type the password, then press Return.

To remove password protection from a document, first recall it, and then press Ctrl-F5 2 2 to select the Remove option.

Caution: If you forget your password, the document may be lost forever! Keep in mind that you must first recall a document to the screen before removing its password, so if you have forgotten the password, the Remove option will be of little use.

■ VERSION 5.1 FEATURES

INTERACTING WITH VERSION 5.1

There are two ways to communicate with WordPerfect 5.1: by the function keys or through pull-down menus. The function keys operate basically the same as with version 5.0. So in most cases, the instructions presented in the chapter apply to version 5.1 as well.

Pull-down Menus You can also select WordPerfect options for editing, formatting, and printing documents through a series of pull-down menus—using either the keyboard or a mouse. In fact, in many cases, the function keys and pull-down menus will result in displaying the same menu, prompt line, or message.

There are three basic steps to using the pull-down menus:

1. Display the menu bar.

2. Pull down the menu desired.

3. Select from the pull-down menu, and then from any additional menus that may appear.

Displaying the Menu Bar   Press Alt-= to display the Main Menu bar, as shown in Figure 1.2. If you have a mouse, click the right button to display the menu bar. To remove the menu bar, press F1 or Alt-=, or click the right button a second time.

The first option—File—is already highlighted, and all of the options have one character in boldface. Notice that the boldfaced character is not always the first, as in F**o**nt.

Pulling Down a Menu   The next step is to "pull down" a menu of options. You do this in one of three ways:

■ Press the letter that appears in boldface, such as **O** for Font, or **G** for Graphics.

■ Press the → or ← keys to highlight the choice, then press the ↓ key or Return.

■ Place the mouse pointer on the option, then click the left button.

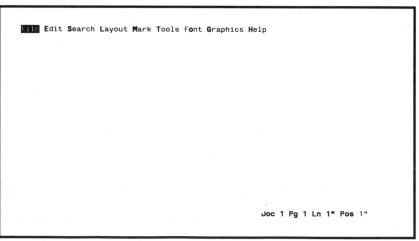

■**FIGURE 1.2:** *The menu bar*

A pull-down menu of additional options will appear on the screen as shown in Figure 1.3. As in the menu bar, each option has one character in boldface.

Some options, such as Select and Comment, have a small triangle at the right. These options have their own pull-down menus that will appear when the option is selected.

Options in brackets are unavailable and cannot be selected. Most of these are options that first require sections of text to be selected, or *blocked*. Until you block text, as you'll learn how to do later, you cannot select that option from the menu.

If you see that you've pulled down the wrong menu, press the → or ← key. The cursor moves to the next option on the menu bar and the pull-down menu automatically appears. To cancel any selection just press the Esc key.

Selecting Options   Now select an option on the pull-down menu using one of these methods:

- Press the letter that appears in boldface.

- Press the ↓ or ↑ key to highlight the choice, then press the ↓ key or Return.

- Place the mouse pointer on the option, then click the left button.

What happens next depends on the option selected. If you select an option with a small triangle, another menu appears, as in Figure 1.4. You make your selection from this new menu.

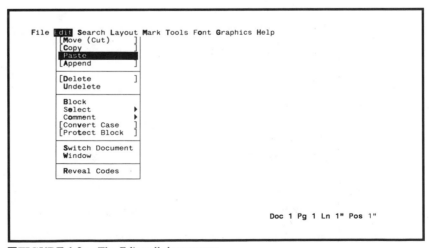

■FIGURE 1.3: *The Edit pull-down menu*

Other choices will either perform some action immediately—such as inserting a formatting code in the document—or display a prompt, selection line, or menu. In most cases, this will be the same prompt, selection line, or menu that would appear if you used the function keys.

No matter what menu is displayed, you can press the F1 key to remove it and return to the previous level. For example, if you are on the submenu shown in Figure 1.4 press Esc to display just the menu shown in Figure 1.3, Esc again to display just the menu bar, and Esc once more to clear the screen and return to the document.

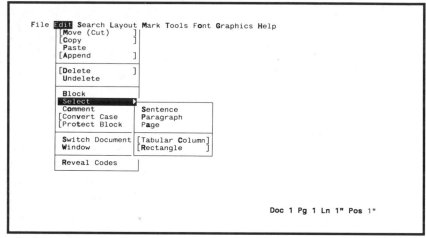

■**FIGURE 1.4:**   *The Select submenu*

USING A MOUSE WITH WORDPERFECT 5.1

If you'll be using a mouse, you'll need to be familiar with certain terminology.

Click means to quickly press and release the mouse button. For example, the instruction

> Click the left button

means to press and release the left mouse button.

Double-click means to click the mouse button twice within the double-click *interval*, which is set at about one-third of a second by default. The instruction

> double-click on the file name with the left button

means to place the pointer on the file name, then click the left button twice.

Drag means to press and hold down the button while moving the mouse pointer. So the instruction

Hold down the left button and drag the mouse

means to keep the left button held down while you move the mouse pointer.

The instructions given in this book assume that the mouse is set for right-handed operation, the default. If you are left-handed, see the section "Changing Mouse Defaults" in Chapter 5.

Here's how the mouse is used for basic WordPerfect operations:

Cursor movement	Place the pointer where you want to position the cursor, then click the left button. The cursor will appear at that position.
Vertical scrolling	Move the mouse pointer to the left edge of the screen, hold down the right mouse button, then drag the mouse in the direction you wish to scroll.
Horizontal scrolling	Place the mouse pointer at the far edge of the screen on the line you wish to scroll, hold down the right button, then drag the mouse towards the edge of the screen.
Displaying the menu bar	Click the right mouse button. Click the button again to remove the menu bar.
Pulling down a menu	Place the pointer on the menu name, then click the left button.
Selecting an option	Place the pointer on the option, then click the left button.
Selecting the default	In selection lines and prompts, clicking the right button is like pressing Return. It accepts the default value shown at the prompt line.

Selecting in lists	In lists, select an option by clicking it with the left button. Double-click with the left button to select an option and accept the default option at the same time. In List Files, for example, double-click on a file name to look at its contents.
Blocking text	Place the mouse pointer at one end of the text, press and hold down the left button, then drag the pointer to the other end of the text. Click the left button to unblock the text.

PROMPTS AND SELECTION LINES

Another change is in the format of the prompts, and many selection lines and menus. Instead of prompts appearing as this:

Save Document? (Y/N) Yes

the choices are spelled out like this:

Save Document? Yes (No)

In either case, you select the default option by pressing Return. In the version 5.0 prompt line, the letters in parentheses show the other choices—*Y* for Yes or *N* for No. In version 5.1, the options are shown as the character in bold. So if no warning note appears in the margin, indicating that the keystrokes to press are different, just follow the instructions given.

SAVING FILES IN OTHER FORMATS

When you press Ctrl-F5 in version 5.1, you'll see the prompt line

1 DOS Text; 2 Password; 3 Save As; 4 Comment; 5 Spreadsheet:0

- Press *1* or *t* to save the document as a DOS text file, as explained in the chapter.

- Press *3* or *a* to display the prompt line:

1 Generic; 2 WordPerfect 5.0; 3 WordPerfect 4.2: 0

Select the format desired, then follow the instructions explained earlier in this chapter.

MOUSE AND MENU EQUIVALENTS

Function	Keyboard	Pull-Down Menus
Save	F10	File Save
Exit	F7	File Exit
Save Other Formats	Ctrl-F5	File Text Out
Recall Other Formats	Ctrl-F5	File Text In
Password	Ctrl-F5 2	File Password

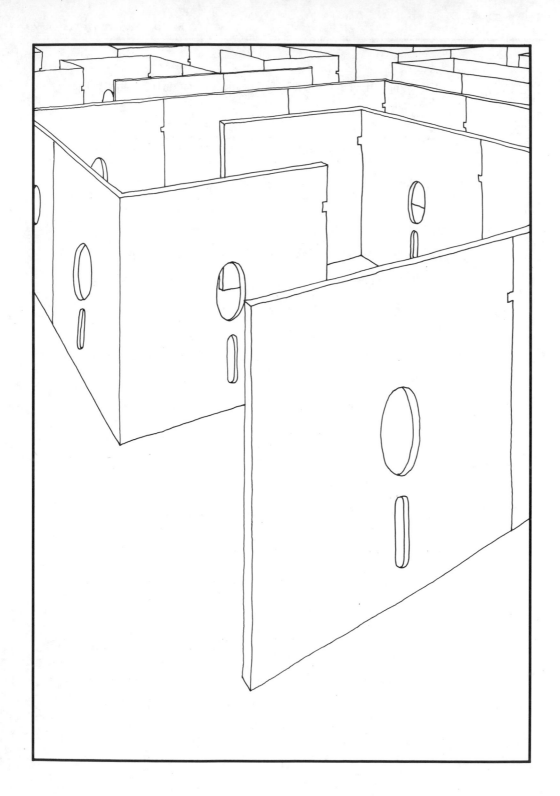

2

CREATING AND EDITING
DOCUMENTS

In this chapter, you will learn how to create and edit documents. You will first enter a new document, then learn how to delete unwanted characters and insert new ones. You will also learn some advanced editing techniques, such as manipulating large sections of text, searching your document for specific characters, and working with multiple documents.

CREATING A DOCUMENT

Creating a document with WordPerfect is a simple task. There are no special menus to read and no format settings to make because the default format is already established. You don't even have to press Return at the end of each line.

As an example, we will enter and print a typical business letter. We will use the Tab key to indent the first line of each paragraph. Make sure that you have already selected the proper printer, as explained in Appendix A, and that your printer is attached and ready.

Follow these steps to create our sample WordPerfect document:

1. Start WordPerfect as you learned in Chapter 1.

2. Type **May 2, 1991**. (Don't type the period.) If you make a mistake, press the Backspace key to erase it.

3. Press Return twice. Your screen should look like Figure 2.1.

4. Type the following inside address, pressing Return after each line:

    Sims Manufacturing Company

436 West Highland Avenue
Freemont, NY   09176

5. Press Return once more to insert a blank line.

6. Type **Dear Mr. Sims:**

7. Press Return twice—once to end the salutation, and a second time to insert a blank line.

8. Press Tab to indent the first line, then type the following paragraph. Press Return only after you have completed the entire paragraph.

All of us at Watson Metal, Inc., welcome you to our family of customers. We know that you will be happy with our prices, quality, and excellent service.

Your screen will look like Figure 2.2.

9. Press Tab to indent the first line of the second paragraph, then type the second paragraph.

If you have any questions regarding any of our services, please feel free to call me directly at (212) 555-1987.

10. Press Return four times.

11. Type **Sincerely yours,**

```
May 2, 1991

  —




                                                              Doc 1 Pg 1 Ln 1.33" Pos 1"
```

■FIGURE 2.1: *Ready to enter the address for the sample letter*

12. Press Return four times.

13. Type **William Watson.**

14. Press Return.

15. Type **President.**

Figure 2.3 shows the completed letter.

```
May 2, 1991

Sims Manufacturing Company
436 West Highland Avenue
Freemont, NY  09176

Dear Mr. Sims:

      All of us at Watson Metal, Inc., welcome you to our family of
customers. We know that you will be happy with our prices, quality,
and excellent service.
_




                                              Doc 1 Pg 1 Ln 2.83" Pos 1"
```

■FIGURE 2.2: *Ready to enter the sample letter's second paragraph*

```
May 2, 1991

Sims Manufacturing Company
436 West Highland Avenue
Freemont, NY  09176

Dear Mr. Sims:

      All of us at Watson Metal, Inc., welcome you to our family of
customers. We know that you will be happy with our prices, quality,
and excellent service.
      If you have any questions regarding any of our services,
please feel free to call me directly at (212) 555-1987.


Sincerely yours,


William Watson
President_

                                              Doc 1 Pg 1 Ln 4.5" Pos 1.9"
```

■FIGURE 2.3: *The complete sample letter*

Note
The appearance
of the version
5.1 screen is
slightly
different, but the
steps listed here
still apply.

16. Press Shift-F7 to display the Print menu (Figure 2.4). When you want to print every page of a document, press **1**; to print just the page where the cursor is located, press **2**. The rest of the options on this menu will be discussed in Chapter 4.

17. Press **1** to print the document. By default, the letter's text will be justified on both the right and left sides of the page.

If you selected manual feed when you set up your printer in Appendix A, you'll hear a short beep telling you to load the paper into the printer. When the paper is ready, press **4** to display the Printer Control menu (Figure 2.5), then **G** for the Go option.

When printing with hand-fed (manual) paper, you'll hear the beep after each page. Insert the next sheet of paper into the printer, then issue the Go command. If the Printer Control menu is already displayed, just press **G**. From the Print menu press **4 G**. If you've already returned to the document, press Shift-F7 4 G. Press F1 to return to the Print menu.

Now let's save the letter.

Note
The appearance
of the version
5.1 screen is
slightly
different, but the
steps listed here
still apply.

18. Press F7 to display the prompt

    Save Document? (Y/N) Yes

19. Press **Y** to display the prompt

    Document to be Saved:

20. Type **LETTER**.

```
Print

    1 - Full Document
    2 - Page
    3 - Document on Disk
    4 - Control Printer
    5 - Type Through
    6 - View Document
    7 - Initialize Printer

Options

    S - Select Printer          Daisywriter 2000
    B - Binding                 0"
    N - Number of Copies        1
    G - Graphics Quality        Medium
    T - Text Quality            High




Selection: 0
```

■**FIGURE 2.4:** *Print menu*

Note
The appearance
of the version
5.1 screen is
slightly
different, but the
steps listed here
still apply.

21. Press Return to store the completed letter on the disk. After the letter is saved, the prompt displays

    Exit WP? (Y/N) No

22. Press **N** to clear the screen and remain in WordPerfect.

As discussed in Chapter 1, there are several other ways to save a document. Use the one that suits your work plans.

■ BASIC EDITING TECHNIQUES

If we could type without ever making mistakes, few people would need word processors. But words are misspelled, punctuation is ignored, and information is left out or organized incorrectly. In short, much of our time at the keyboard is spent in changing what has already been typed.

RECALLING DOCUMENTS

You can edit a new document as you type it or an existing one that is already saved on the disk. Of course, to edit a saved document, you must first recall it.

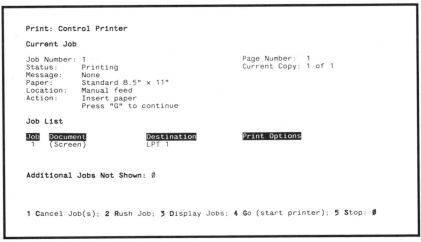

```
Print: Control Printer

Current Job

Job Number: 1                        Page Number:  1
Status:     Printing                 Current Copy: 1 of 1
Message:    None
Paper:      Standard 8.5" x 11"
Location:   Manual feed
Action:     Insert paper
            Press "G" to continue

Job List

Job  Document              Destination       Print Options
 1   (Screen)              LPT 1


Additional Jobs Not Shown: Ø


1 Cancel Job(s); 2 Rush Job; 3 Display Jobs; 4 Go (start printer); 5 Stop: Ø
```

■FIGURE 2.5:   *Printer Control menu*

If you know the name of the existing document that you want to edit, press Shift-F10. The prompt

Document to be Retrieved:

appears on the status line. Type the name of the document, then press Return. Thus, to recall the document that we just created you would press Shift-F10, type *LETTER*, and press Return. If you saved the document with a password, you'll see the prompt

Enter password:

Type the password, then press Return.

Note
The appearance of the version 5.1 screen is slightly different, but the steps listed here still apply.

If you are not sure of the document's name, press F5. The letter of the current drive and the name of the current directory appear on the status line. Press Return if that is the disk drive containing the document, or type the letter of another drive followed by a colon, then press Return. A directory of the disk appears on the screen, as shown in Figure 2.6. Use the cursor movement keys to highlight the name of the document that you want to recall, then press *1*.

THE INSERT AND TYPEOVER MODES

You can insert new characters within existing text in a document by simply moving the cursor to the point of insertion and typing. The words to the right of the cursor will move over (and down, if necessary) to make room for the new ones. This is the default *Insert* mode.

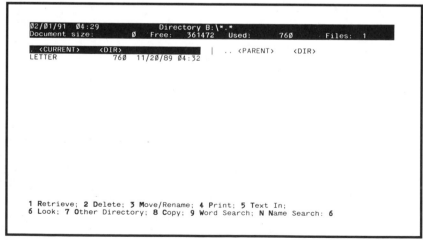

■FIGURE 2.6:   *A sample directory listing*

WordPerfect also has a *Typeover* mode. In this mode, the new characters replace the existing ones. That is, each new character you type takes the place of the one already there. To enter Typeover mode, press the Ins key and you'll see

Typeover

on the status line. Now one character will be deleted for every one you type.

The Ins key is a *toggle* key. You press it once to turn on a function; press it again to turn off the same function. So, to get back into Insert mode from Typeover, press Ins again.

Although Typeover mode offers a fast way to change mistakes, it has limited value. You must be careful not to erase words accidentally as you continue typing. It is safest to use this mode only when you are replacing characters with the same number of new ones.

DELETING TEXT

The most basic and common editing function is deleting characters. Use the Backspace and Del keys for simple character deletions.

The Backspace key deletes characters to the left of the cursor. To erase several characters, hold the Backspace key down. Press the Del key to erase the character at the cursor position.

To delete several characters to the right of the cursor, hold the Del key down. Just be careful not to hold down Del too long—with key repeat, you'll delete more characters than you want.

You can also delete characters by the word, line, or page. Press Ctrl-Backspace to delete the word on which the cursor is placed. Press Ctrl-End to delete the current line, from the cursor to the right margin.

Note
The appearance of the version 5.1 screen is slightly different, but the steps listed here still apply.

To delete all of the current page, from the cursor position down, press Ctrl-PgDn. The message

Delete Remainder of Page? (Y/N) No

appears on the status line. Press *Y* to delete the page. Only text on the current page will be deleted. If you decide not to delete the page, press Return to accept the default response (N).

To delete from the cursor position to the start of the word, press Home Backspace (one after the other, not together). If the cursor is between words you'll delete the word on the left.

If the cursor is in a word, press Home Del to delete from the cursor position to the end of the word. If the cursor is between words this will not erase the word to the right, only the blank space at the cursor position.

MOVING, COPYING, AND DELETING TEXT

To move, copy, or delete an entire sentence, paragraph, or page, place the cursor anywhere within that text and press Ctrl- F4. The prompt

Move: 1 Sentence; 2 Paragraph; 3 Page; 4 Retrieve: 0

appears on the status line. Press *1* to move, copy, or delete the sentence, *2* for the paragraph, or *3* for the entire page. Press Return to turn off the function if you change your mind.

After you make your selection, the sentence, paragraph, or page is highlighted (displayed as dark letters on a light background), and the prompt changes to

1 Move; 2 Copy; 3 Delete; 4 Append: 0

Press *1* to move the text to another position, *2* to make a copy of it elsewhere, or *3* to delete it.

If you press *1* or *3*, the highlighted text will disappear from the screen. When you move or copy text, the status line changes to

Move cursor; press Enter to retrieve

Move the cursor to where you want the text to appear, then press Return.

Press *4* to copy the selected text to the end of a document already stored on disk. The prompt will change to

Append to:

Type the name of the stored document, then press Return. The highlighted text will be added to the stored document. The text on the screen will be unaffected.

WORKING WITH BLOCKS OF TEXT

When your editing requires you to manipulate larger amounts of text that do not divide neatly into the text portions described above, you can work with *blocks* of characters. First highlight the text, then perform the action. You can highlight any amount of text, from a single character to an entire document. Once text has been designated as a block, it can be deleted, moved, or copied.

HIGHLIGHTING BLOCKS

To highlight a block, place the cursor at either the beginning or the end of the text that you want to manipulate, then press Alt-F4. The words

Block on

flash on the status line. Now, use the cursor movement keys to place the cursor at the other end of the block of text. As you move the cursor, the text becomes highlighted on the screen. If you mark too much text, move the cursor in the opposite direction to erase the highlighting. If you change your mind altogether, press Alt-F4 again. Since Alt-F4 is a toggle, this turns off the Block function.

DELETING, MOVING, AND COPYING BLOCKS

Note
The appearance of the version 5.1 screen is slightly different, but the steps listed here still apply.

To delete a block of text, highlight it and press Del. The message

Delete Block? (Y/N) No

appears on the status line. Press Y to delete the block. If you change your mind, press Return to accept the default response and leave the block intact.

To move or copy text from one location to another, press Alt-F4 to highlight it, then press Ctrl-F4. The prompt

Move: 1 Block; 2 Tabular Column; 3 Rectangle: 0

appears. Press *1* to select Block. Options 2 and 3 of this prompt are useful for moving and copying tables. See Chapter 9 for details. The prompt line changes to

1 Move; 2 Copy; 3 Delete; 4 Append: 0

Now move, copy, delete, or append as you learned above.

You can also move or copy text without inserting it immediately at its new location. Just press F1 when you see the prompt

Move cursor; press Enter to retrieve

The prompt will disappear. Now when you want to insert the text, press Ctrl-F4 4—the Retrieve option—to display

Retrieve: 1 Block; 2 Tabular Column; 3 Rectangle: 0

Press *1*. You can only store one copied or moved block of text in the *retrieval area*—an area in the computer's memory set aside to store text. But as long as it is in the retrieval area, you can insert it as many times as you want by pressing Ctrl-F4 4 1. It will remain in the computer's memory until you highlight and move or copy another block of text, or exit WordPerfect.

■   CHANGING INVISIBLE CHARACTERS

Some keys that you press—such as the space bar, Tab, and Return—do not leave characters on the screen. You can delete and insert spaces that were created by pressing the space bar in the same way that you delete and insert other characters. The Tab and Return keys, however, actually insert invisible codes. In fact, WordPerfect uses invisible codes for many of its functions. Although you don't have to make these visible to delete them, it is easier to edit complex documents if you can see the various codes.

REVEALING CODES

To display the invisible codes on the screen, press Alt-F3. A *scale line* showing the positions of the tab stops and margins appears in the middle of the screen. Above the scale line are eleven lines of text, the one containing the cursor and ten lines before it.

Beneath the scale line are also eleven lines of text, two above the cursor position and eight below, but with symbols showing the invisible codes. The position of the cursor is shown highlighted. The codes are surrounded by brackets. Figure 2.7 shows a sample screen with the codes revealed.

Note
In version 5.1, the tab code appears as [Tab].

Hard carriage returns (created by pressing the Return key) are represented by [HRt], soft carriage returns (added by word wrap) are [SRt], and tab stops are [TAB]. Table 2.1 shows some of the most common codes.

```
       May 2, 1991

       Sims Manufacturing Company
       436 West Highland Avenue
       Freemont, NY  Ø9176

       Dear Mr. Sims:

           All of us at Watson Metal, Inc., welcome you to our family of
       customers. We know that you will be happy with our prices, quality,
       and excellent service.
C:\WP5Ø\LETTER                                   Doc 1 Pg 1 Ln 1" Pos 1"
{     ▲    ▲    ▲    ▲    ▲    ▲    ▲    ▲    ▲    ▲    ▲   }    ▲    ▲
May 2, 1991[HRt]
[HRt]
Sims Manufacturing Company[HRt]
436 West Highland Avenue[HRt]
Freemont, NY  Ø9176[HRt]
[HRt]
Dear Mr. Sims:[HRt]
[HRt]
[Tab]All of us at Watson Metal, Inc., welcome you to our family of[SRt]
customers. We know that you will be happy with our prices, quality,[SRt]

Press Reveal Codes to restore screen
```

■**FIGURE 2.7:**   *A WordPerfect screen displaying the codes and scale line*

■**TABLE 2.1:** *Common WordPerfect Codes*

Code	Meaning
[Algn][c/a/flrt]	Begin and end tab align or flush right
[BOLD][bold]	Begin and end boldface
[Cntr][c/a/flrt]	Begin and end centering
[Center Pg]	Center page within top and bottom margins
[CndlEOP:n]	Conditional end of page (*n* lines to keep together]
[Col Def:]	Column definition
[Col On]	Column mode turned on
[Col Off]	Column mode turned off
[Date:*n*]	Date/time function using format *n*
[Form: *size,,type*]	Page size and form type
[Hdr/Ftr:*n,,n;text*]	Header or footer definition, *n* is type and occurrence number followed by the *text* of the header or footer
[HPg]	Hard page break inserted by operator
[HRt]	Hard return inserted with Return key
[-> Indent]	Beginning of left indent
[-> Indent <-]	Beginning of left and right indent
[<- Mar Rel]	Margin released *n* positions
[L/R Mar:*n,,n*]	Left and right margin settings
[Pg#:n]	Page number set to *n*
[Pg# Pos:*n*]	Position of page number at position *n*
[Rt Just On]	Right justification on
[Rt Just Off]	Right justification off
[Ln Spacing:*n*]	Line spacing set at *n* lines
[SPg]	Soft page break inserted by program
[SRt]	Soft carriage return inserted by word-wrap
[SUBSCRPT]	Subscript
[SUPRSCRPT]	Superscript
[TAB]	Tab

■**TABLE 2.1:**   *Common WordPerfect Codes (continued)*

Code	Meaning
[Tab Set:]	Tab stops reset by user
[T/B Mar:*n*",,*n*"]	Top and bottom margin settings in *n* inches
[UNDRLN][undrln]	Begin and end underlining

Note
Some codes are different in version 5.1. Refer to "Version 5.1 Codes," page 46.

Displaying the codes at the bottom of the screen just gives you two views of the same document. You can leave the codes revealed and continue writing or editing in the upper portion. However, you'll only be able to see eleven lines of your text in the top window and seven below, divided by the scale line and three duplicated lines.

So it's much easier to press Shift-F3 and reveal the codes when needed, then press Shift-F3 again to return the screen to normal for writing and editing.

Revealing codes is one of the best ways to locate and solve formatting problems. When the document appears incorrectly on the screen or in print, it may be that you accidentally entered or deleted a format code. Move the cursor to the position where the problem seems to start, then reveal the codes. Look carefully for formats that do not belong, or to make sure that your format changes are in the proper location.

■

DISPLAYING THE SCALE LINE

Note
The appearance of the version 5.1 screen is slightly different, but the steps listed here still apply.

Sometimes it is helpful to have the scale line displayed as you type. Press Ctrl-F3 to display the prompt line

   0 Rewrite; 1 Window; 2 Line Draw: 0

Press *1* to select the Window option and display the prompt

   Number of lines in this window: 24

Type *23*. The scale line now appears at the bottom of the screen. As you scroll through your document, the scale line will change to reflect the different margins and tab stops used to format the text. To remove the scale line, press Ctrl-F3 1, then enter *24* at the prompt.

■ DELETING TAB STOPS

To delete a tab stop, position the cursor in the blank space of the tab area, then press Del. If you have pressed Alt-F3 to reveal the codes, move the cursor until it highlights the Tab code, then press Del. The [TAB] code will disappear in the text below the scale line, and the text will shift five spaces to the left in the display above the scale line.

■ CHANGING RETURNS—SPLITTING AND COMBINING PARAGRAPHS

You press the Return key to begin a new paragraph or to insert blank lines in the text. It inserts the Hard Carriage Return code [HRt] in the text. You can divide and combine paragraphs by inserting and deleting this code.

To split one paragraph into two, position the cursor at the beginning of the sentence that will start the new paragraph, then press Return. The text of that paragraph, from the cursor position downward, will move down to the next line. Insert a tab stop, press Return again to double-space between paragraphs, or otherwise adjust the spacing, if necessary.

To combine two paragraphs, position the cursor immediately after the first paragraph that you want to combine, then press Del. The paragraph below will move up one line. If you double- spaced between paragraphs by pressing Return twice, you must press Del twice. Also, if the second paragraph was indented, you must delete the tab stop.

If you have revealed the codes by pressing Alt-F3, place the cursor on the [HRt] code, then press Del.

■ RESTORING DELETED TEXT

The Cancel command, activated by the F1 key, can be used to restore deleted text and to quickly copy text from one location to another.

If you change your mind after deleting some text, press F1. The prompt

Undelete 1 Restore; 2 Previous Deletion: 0

appears on the status line, and the last characters deleted reappear highlighted at the position of the cursor. Press *1* to restore the deleted text at that location on the screen.

WordPerfect "remembers" the last three deletions made. Press F1 to show the last deletion, then *2* to reveal the one before, and *2* again to show the deletion before that. Whatever text is highlighted will be restored when you press 1 at the Undelete prompt. Keep pressing *2* to cycle among the three previous deletions.

Since the Undelete command will restore text at the position of the cursor, it can be used as a quick way of moving words or phrases. Delete the text using any method you've learned, then move the cursor to the location where you want the text to appear and press F1 1.

■ REPEATING COMMANDS

You may want to quickly delete a certain number of characters or words or to type one character several times, such as a hyphen to create a dashed line across the screen. WordPerfect uses the Esc key for such repeated actions.

Press Esc, and the prompt

    Repeat Value = 8

appears on the status line. The default value of 8 indicates that the next nonnumeric keystroke that follows will be executed eight times. Type a new number if you want to repeat the action a different number of times, then enter the keystroke to be repeated. You cannot repeat numbers this way.

For example, to print a line of dashes across the screen, press Esc, type *64*, then press –. To delete the next ten words, press Esc, type *10*, then press Ctrl-Backspace.

■ SEARCHING FOR AND REPLACING TEXT

Have you ever misspelled the same word several times in a letter or paper or realized that you entered the wrong information in several places? WordPerfect allows you to correct this type of error quickly and easily. You can simply have WordPerfect automatically locate any text and replace it with something else, no matter how many times it appears. On the other hand, you may just want to search through a document to see if a certain word or phrase has been used or to locate a specific reference.

The text to be searched for can be from 1 to 58 characters, including letters, numbers, spaces, and punctuation marks. It can even include invisible codes such as carriage returns, tab stops, indentations, and format changes.

SEARCHING FOR TEXT

WordPerfect allows you to search either forward or backward through a document for specific text. To search forward through a document (from the cursor position to the end of the document) press F2. The prompt

> -> Srch:

appears on the status line. Type the characters that you are searching for, then press F2 again. WordPerfect scans the document, starting at the position of the cursor, and places the cursor just past the first occurrence of those characters. To search for the next occurrence of the same characters, press F2 twice. The characters will automatically appear at the prompt, and the search will begin. To search for different characters, press F2, enter the new characters, and press F2 a second time.

If no match is found, the message

> * Not Found *

appears on the status line for a few seconds, and the cursor remains in its original position.

To search backward through a document (from the cursor position to the beginning of the first page), press Shift-F2. The prompt

> <- Srch:

appears on the status line. Type the search characters, then press Shift-F2 again or just press F2.

SEARCHING FOR CODES

The text that you are searching for can include invisible codes. When the Search prompt appears, press the appropriate function key or combination. In some cases, the code will appear at the prompt, and you need only press F2 to proceed. In other cases, a special prompt line will appear with additional search choices.

For example, if you want to search forward to locate a place in the text where you marked a word to include in a table of contents, press F2, then press Alt-F5. (Tables of contents are discussed in Chapter 13.) The status line shows:

> 1 ToC/List; 2 EndMark; 3 Index; 4 ToA; 5 Defs and Refs;
> 6 Subdocs:0

Press *1* to search for a table of contents entry. The status line shows

> ->Srch: [Mark]

Press F2 to begin the search.

SEARCH HINTS

Searches always start at the position of the cursor. So to search the entire document, first move the cursor to either the start or the end. For a complete forward search, press Home Home ↑ to reach the first page before pressing F2. Backward searchers should press Home Home ↓ before pressing Shift-F2.

The search locates the occurrence of the exact characters typed, whether or not they make up a whole word. Therefore, a search for *mis* will locate *missile*, *mischief*, and even *alchemist*. To ferret out only whole words, press the space bar once before and once after typing the search word. The only problem with this solution is that WordPerfect will not locate the word if it begins a paragraph or is followed by a punctuation mark.

Also consider the case of the characters. Lowercase letters in the search string will match either lowercase or uppercase characters in the document, but uppercase characters will only match their exact counterparts. For example, a search for *alan* will find *Alan*, but one for *Alan* will not match *alan*.

WordPerfect also lets you use a *wild-card* character. The Ctrl-X character (displayed as ^X) will match any character. For example, searching for *r^Xd* will match *rad*, *red*, *rid*, and *rod*. Note that you cannot use Ctrl-X as the first character of the search word. If you try this, WordPerfect will stop at every word. To enter Ctrl-X into the search string, first press Ctrl-V to show the prompt

Key =

Then press Ctrl-X.

REPLACING TEXT

Note
The appearance of the version 5.1 screen is slightly different, but the steps listed here still apply.

When you want to search for text and replace it with other text, press Alt-F2. The status line reads

w/Confirm? (Y/N) No

Press Return if you want WordPerfect to make the replacements without stopping for confirmation (the default is No). If you press *Y*, the program will stop at each match, and you must press *Y* to make the replacement.

After you press Return or Y, the status line changes to

-> Srch:

The right arrow indicates a forward search and replace. To replace backward through the text (like a backward search) press ↑ and change the prompt to

<- Srch:

You can press ↓ to return the search and replace to forward.

Type the characters that you want to replace, then press F2. The prompt

> Replace with:

appears. Type the characters that you want to place in the document, then press F2. If you selected the default (no confirmation), the message

> * Please Wait *

appears on the status line as WordPerfect makes all of the replacements. When the replacement operation is completed, the cursor will be located at the last replacement or, if there were none made, at its original position.

Note
The appearance of the version 5.1 screen is slightly different, but the steps listed here still apply.

If you elected to confirm each replacement, the cursor will appear at each occurrence of the search word, and the prompt

> Confirm? (Y/N) No

will appear. Press *Y* to make the change, or press Return to select the No default. After each selection, the search continues.

To stop the search process at any time, press F1.

You can use the Replace command to delete characters or codes, "replacing" them with nothing, by just pressing Return at the *Replace with* prompt.

When replacing characters, WordPerfect follows the same rules as with searches. Starting at the position of the cursor, lowercase characters will match uppercase or lowercase ones, but uppercase characters will only match uppercase ones. However, if the old word starts with an uppercase letter, the replacement will be uppercase as well, no matter which case you typed.

But beware—characters will be found and replaced even if they match just part of a word. When you replace *his* with *her* without confirmation, *History* will be changed to *Hertory* and *this* to *ther*. Use unconfirmed replacement with care.

REPLACING IN BLOCKS

You can streamline the replacement operation and avoid some unwanted replacements by limiting the search area to blocks of text that you know contain the search phrase. Press Alt-F4 and designate the block area, then begin the search and replacement process. Only text in the highlighted block will be searched for possible replacement.

EXTENDING SEARCH AND REPLACE

By pressing the Home key before F2, Shift-F2, or Alt-F2, you can extend the search to include headers and footers (discussed in Chapter 9), and footnotes and endnotes (Chapter 14). For example, press Home F2 to display the prompt

-> Extended Srch

If the text is found in one of these areas, the specific area is shown, such as the footnote or header typing window.

■ COMBINING DOCUMENTS AND SAVING BLOCKS

WordPerfect enables you to combine documents that are stored separately on the disk. With this capability, you can write and store long documents in sections.

To add a document to the one currently on the screen, place the cursor where you want to add the text, then press Shift-F10. The prompt

Document to be Retrieved:

appears. Type the name of the document that you want added, then press Return. A copy of that document will be recalled from disk and inserted at the position of the cursor.

To create a new document from a block of text, first mark the block with Alt-F4, then press F10. The prompt

Block Name:

appears. Type a new document name, then press Return.

■ WORKING WITH MULTIPLE DOCUMENTS

As mentioned in Chapter 1, WordPerfect allows you to work with two documents at one time. To open a second document, press Shift-F3. The screen clears, and the status line changes to

Doc 2 Pg 1 Ln 1" Pos 1"

You can type a new document or retrieve an existing one from disk in the usual ways. To switch between the two documents, press Shift-F3. This keystroke toggles between document 1 and document 2.

With two documents in memory, you can move or copy text easily from one document to another. Press Alt-F4 to highlight the text in one document, then press Ctrl-F4 1 and select either Move or Copy. Press Shift-F3 to display the second document, move the cursor to the location where you want to insert the text, then press Return.

DISPLAYING TWO DOCUMENTS

Working with two documents is easier if you can see both of them on the screen at the same time. To display both documents, use the WordPerfect Window command.

With one of the documents displayed, press Ctrl-F3 1 to select the Window option and display

Number of lines in this window: 24

The default value of 24 indicates that the current document will use all 24 available lines of the screen; the status line uses the twenty-fifth line. Type a number less than 24, then press Return or press ↑ or ↓ until the screen is divided properly between the two documents, as shown in Figure 2.8. Move the cursor back and forth between the two document windows by pressing Shift-F3.

MOVING TEXT TO A NEW DOCUMENT

You can use the Switch feature to transfer highlighted text to a new document. Remember that the Append command will only add text to an existing file, and

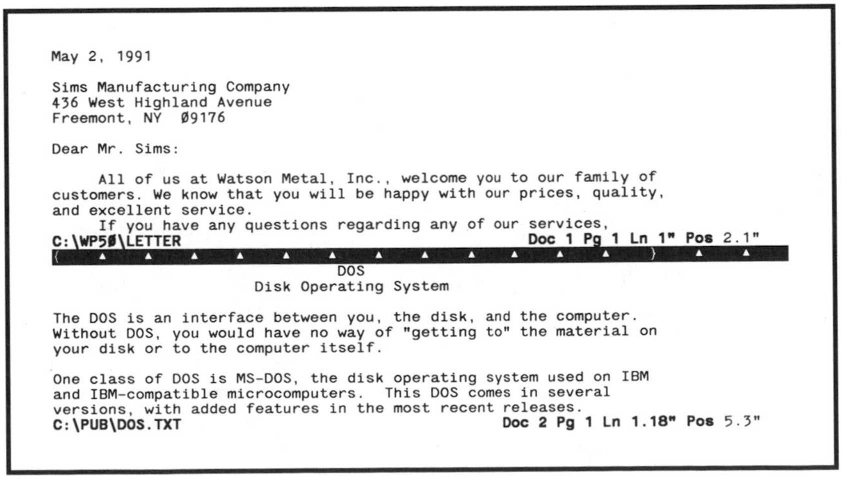

```
May 2, 1991

Sims Manufacturing Company
436 West Highland Avenue
Freemont, NY  Ø9176

Dear Mr. Sims:

     All of us at Watson Metal, Inc., welcome you to our family of
customers. We know that you will be happy with our prices, quality,
and excellent service.
     If you have any questions regarding any of our services,
C:\WP5Ø\LETTER                              Doc 1 Pg 1 Ln 1" Pos 2.1"
                              DOS
                       Disk Operating System

The DOS is an interface between you, the disk, and the computer.
Without DOS, you would have no way of "getting to" the material on
your disk or to the computer itself.

One class of DOS is MS-DOS, the disk operating system used on IBM
and IBM-compatible microcomputers.  This DOS comes in several
versions, with added features in the most recent releases.
C:\PUB\DOS.TXT                           Doc 2 Pg 1 Ln 1.18" Pos 5.3"
```

■**FIGURE 2.8:** *A screen divided into two document areas*

saving a block writes it to a new file on the disk. If you want to create a new document with text from the one on the screen and begin editing it immediately, follow these steps:

- Press Alt-F4 to highlight the block, then cut or copy the text that you want to move to a new document.

- Press Shift-F3 to switch to a new, empty document, then Return to insert the text.

- Press F10, then enter a name to save the second document.

After you have created and edited your document, you will probably want to format it, then see a printed copy. Chapter 3 reviews formatting and Chapter 4 covers printing techniques.

■ DOCUMENT SUMMARY AND COMMENTS

If you write or type a lot, or work in a busy office, keeping track of documents can be a horrendous task. Who wrote this document? Who typed that one? What the heck is REPORT.TXT?

The eleven-character document name (eight characters plus the three-letter extension) doesn't go too far in answering these questions. While the directory shows the date and time it was last edited, there is no clue to who wrote or typed it, or when it was originally created, let alone some other useful information and hints about it.

With WordPerfect, however, you can attach to the document a summary of such information, including up to seven lines of text describing the contents of the document.

In addition, you can add any number of personal comments to the document. Like the summary, comments will not be printed with the text but can be displayed on the screen for your information. Use them to write notes and reminders that you'll need when working on the document but that you do not want printed.

DOCUMENT SUMMARY

To add a summary to your document, press Shift-F8 to display the Format menu, which you saw in Figure 1.1. Notice the Summary option under Document, option 3.

Warning
Users of
version 5.1
should follow
the special
instructions
under
"Document
Summary,"
page 44.

Press *3* to select Document and display the Format Document menu, shown in Figure 2.9. Most of the options on this menu are for more complex formatting tasks that we'll discuss later, but a document summary is created using option 5.

Press *5* or *s* to display the Document Summary screen, shown in Figure 2.10.

The name of the document, if it already has one, and the date it was created are already displayed. You can also add a descriptive file name and subject, up to 40 characters each, and the names of the author and typist. The first 400 characters of the document automatically appear in the comment area near

```
Format: Document

    1 - Display Pitch - Automatic        Yes
                        Width            Ø.1"

    2 - Initial Codes

    3 - Initial Font                     Courier 1Ø

    4 - Redline Method                   Printer Dependent

    5 - Summary




Selection: Ø
```

■**FIGURE 2.9:** *Format Document menu*

```
Document Summary

        System Filename          (Not named yet)

        Date of Creation         May 1, 1991

    1 - Descriptive Filename

    2 - Subject/Account

    3 - Author

    4 - Typist

    5 - Comments
    ┌──────────────────────────────────────────┐
    │                                          │
    │                                          │
    │                                          │
    └──────────────────────────────────────────┘

Selection: Ø
```

■**FIGURE 2.10:** *Document Summary screen*

the bottom of the screen. You can add to or edit the text in the comment area without changing the text in the document itself. To do so, press *5* or *c* to place the cursor in the comment area, edit the comments, then press F7. The comments can be up to 780 characters.

Press Return once to return to the typing area.

You won't see the summary information on the screen, and it won't be printed along with the document. However, it will appear when you look at a document from the directory listing using the F5 key, and you can always refer to it, or edit it, by pressing Shift-F8 3 4.

COMMENTS

Comments usually relate to a specific section of text, unlike a summary, which refers to the entire document. When you enter a document comment, first place the cursor where you want the comment to appear in the text. Then press Ctrl-F5 to display the Text In/Out prompt line.

Warning
Users of version
5.1 should
follow the
special
instructions
under
"Comments,"
page 46.

Press *5* or *c* to select the Comment option and display the prompt line

    Comment: 1 Create; 2 Edit; 3 Change to text: 0

Press *1* or *c* to create a comment and display the Comment window (Figure 2.11)

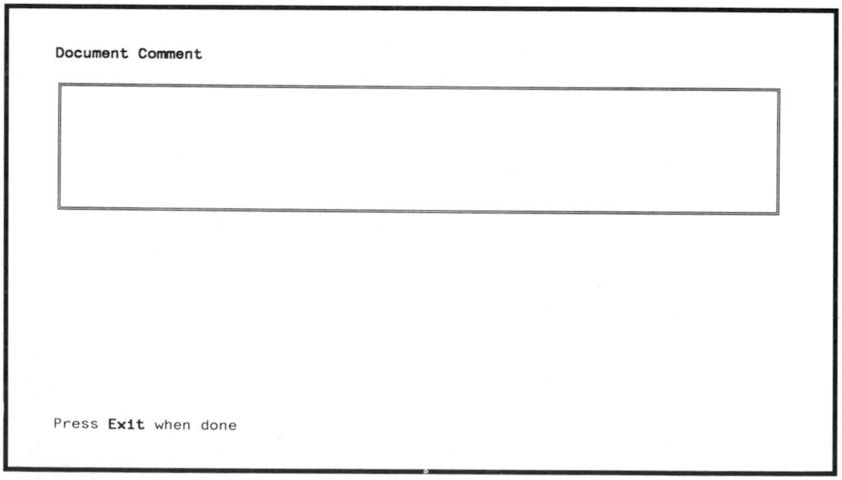

■**FIGURE 2.11:**   *Document Comment window*

Enter the text of the comment (up to 1,024 characters) then press F7. The comment appears in the text surrounded by a box, as shown in Figure 2.12.

Editing and Printing Comments   While the comments appear on the screen, they will not be printed along with the document, and you cannot edit them as you would edit normal text. To print them, you must first convert the comment to regular text. To edit them, you must redisplay the Comment screen. Start by pressing Ctrl-F5 5 to reveal the Comment prompt line.

- To edit a comment press *2* or *e*. WordPerfect will display the first comment above the cursor position. Edit the comment, then press F7.

- To convert a comment to regular text, press *3* or *t*. The box surrounding the first comment above the cursor position will disappear, but the text will remain. Since it is now regular text, it will be printed along with your document. Later you'll learn how to convert regular text into a nonprinting comment.

- Finally, to delete a comment, place the cursor just before it and press Del, or following it and press Backspace. You'll see the prompt

  Delete [Comment] (Y/N)? No

  Press *Y* to delete the comment from the document.

Note
The appearance of the version 5.1 screen is slightly different, but the steps listed here still apply.

```
May 2, 1991

Sims Manufacturing Company
436 West Highland Avenue
Freemont, NY  Ø9176

Dear Mr. Sims:

     All of us at Watson Metal, Inc., welcome you to our family of
customers. We know that you will be happy with our prices, quality,
and excellent service.

 ┌──────────────────────────────────────────────────────────────┐
 │ Send follow-up letter in two weeks.                            │
 └──────────────────────────────────────────────────────────────┘

     If you have any questions regarding any of our services,
please feel free to call me directly at (212) 555-1987.


Sincerely yours,


C:\WP5Ø\LETTER                          Doc 1 Pg 1 Ln 2.99" Pos 1"
```

■**FIGURE 2.12:**   *Comment shown in the text*

■ VERSION 5.1 FEATURES

DOCUMENT SUMMARY

To add a summary to your document, press Shift-F8 3 5 to display the Document Summary screen shown in Figure 2.13.

The date the document was created and the last time it was updated are already displayed. You can add a descriptive file name, file type, and the author's and typist's names, account name, and keywords—words or phrases that identify the document.

While you could also enter text at the Subject and Abstract prompts, you can have WordPerfect use text from the document. Press Shift-F10 to display the prompt:

Capture Document Summary Fields? No (Yes)

Press *Y*. By default, if the characters *RE:* occur in the first 400 characters of the document, the text following them on that line will appear at the Subject prompt. About the first 550 characters of the document appear in the Abstract prompt. The default subject phrase can be changed using the Document Management/Summary option in the Setup Environment menu. Setup is discussed in Chapter 5.

Once inserted, select Subject or Abstract to edit or add text.

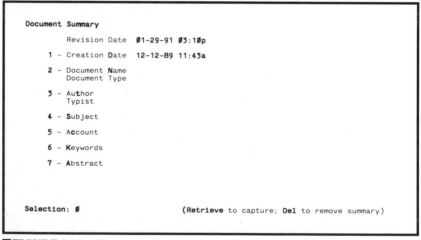

■**FIGURE 2.13:** *Document Summary screen for version 5.1*

The summary will be stored with the document when saved. To delete the summary, display it by pressing Shift-F8 3 5, then press Del to display the prompt

Delete Document Summary? No (Yes)

Press *Y*.

You won't see the summary information on the screen, and it won't be printed along with the document. However, once the document is saved, the summary will appear when you look at a document from the directory listing using the Look option of the F5 key (Figure 2.14). The name and file type you entered in the summary will appear at the top of the screen.

Notice the command line options at the bottom to display other files, display the text, print the summary, or save it as a separate disk file. If you select *Look at text*, the text of the document appears along with the usual Next and Previous options. A Look at Document Summary option will then be available to return to the summary screen.

You can also print the summary or save it as a file from the Summary menu. Save it as a separate file by pressing F10. The prompt

Enter filename:

will appear. Type the name for the file, then press Return. From the Summary menu, press Shift-F7 to print the summary.

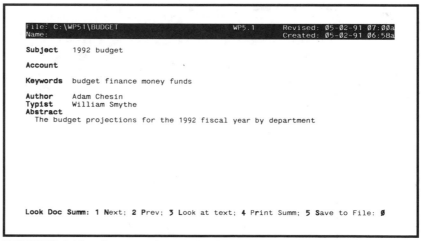

■**FIGURE 2.14:** *Summary shown in file directory*

COMMENTS

To insert a comment into the document, press Ctrl-F5 4 1, which displays the Comment window. Type up to 1,024 characters, then press F7 to return to the document. The comment appears in the text, surrounded by a box, as you saw in Figure 2.12.

Editing and Printing Comments   Although the comments appear on the screen, they will not be printed along with the document, and you cannot edit them as you would edit normal text. To edit them, you must redisplay the Comment screen. To print them, you must first convert the comment to regular text.

To edit a comment, press Ctrl-F5 4 2. WordPerfect will display the first comment above the cursor position. Edit the comment, then press F7.

To convert a comment to regular text, press Ctrl-F5 4 3. The box surrounding the first comment above the cursor position will disappear, but the text will remain. Since it is now regular text, it will be printed along with your document.

Finally, to delete a comment, place the cursor just before it and press Del, or just following it and press Backspace. You'll see the prompt

Delete [Comment]? No (Yes)

Press *Y* to delete the comment from the document.

VERSION 5.1 CODES

A number of the codes that were shown in Table 2.1 appear differently in version 5.1. Table 2.2 shows some common WordPerfect 5.1 codes.

■**TABLE 2.2:**   *Common WordPerfect Codes*

Code	Meaning
[Center]	Center (ends at carriage return)
[Flsh Rgt]	Flush Right (ends at carriage return)
[Footer *n:n;text*]	Footer definition n is the type and occurrence followed by the text of the footer
[Header *n:n;text*]	Header definition
[Just:*type*]	Justification followed by Full, Left, Right, or Center
[Paper Sz/Typ]	Paper size and type
[Pg Num:*n*]	New page number

■**TABLE 2.2:** *Common WordPerfect Codes (continued)*

Code	Meaning
[Pg Num Style:*text*]	Page number style
[Pg Numbering:*n*]	Page numbering
[SUBSCPT]	Subscript
[SUPRSCPT]	Superscript
[Tab]	Tab
[UND]	Und

MOUSE AND MENU EQUIVALENTS

Function	Keyboard	Pull-Down Menus
Append Block	Ctrl-F4 1	**Edit** Append
Block	Alt-F4	**Edit B**lock
Comment	Ctrl-F5 4	**Edit C**omment
Copy Block	Ctrl-F4 1 2	**Edit C**opy
Delete Block	Ctrl-F4 1 3	**Edit D**elete
Extended Search	Home F2	**Search E**xtended
Move Block	Ctrl-F4 1 1	**Edit M**ove
Next Search	F2 F2	**Search N**ext
Previous Search	Shift-F2 F2	**Search P**revious
Print	Shift-F7	**File P**rint
Replace	Alt-F2	**Search R**eplace
Retrieve	Shift-F10	**File R**etrieve
Retrieve Block	Ctrl-F4 4	**Edit P**aste
Reveal Codes	Alt-F3	**Edit R**eveal Codes
Search Backward	Shift-F2	**Search B**ackward

Function	Keyboard	Pull-Down Menus
Search Forward	F2	**Search F**orward
Select	Ctrl-F4	**Edit S**elect
Summary	Shift-F8 3 5	**Layout D**ocument **S**ummary
Switch Window	Shift-F3	**Edit S**witch Document
Undelete	F1	**Edit U**ndelete
Window	Ctrl-F3 1	**Edit W**indow

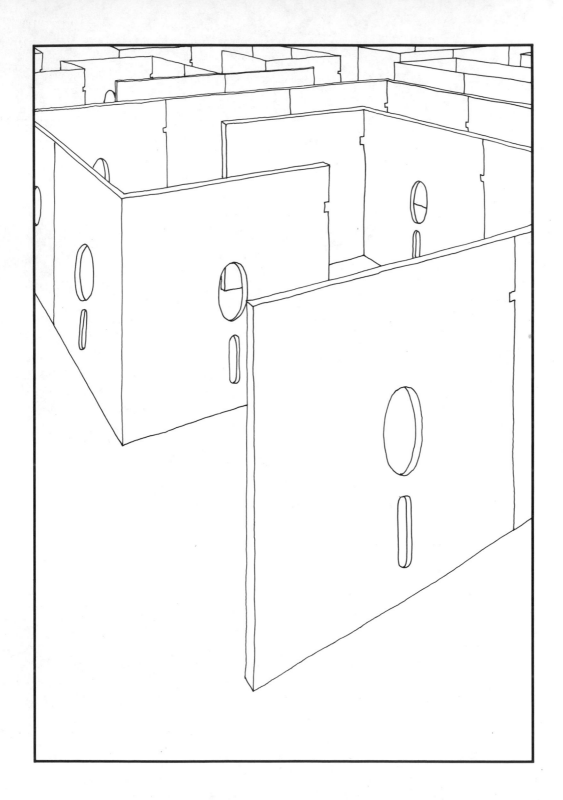

3

FORMATTING
DOCUMENTS FOR A
PROFESSIONAL LOOK

You know what they say about first impressions—they mean everything. This is as true with printed documents as with personal relationships. With documents, the first impression someone gets is from its look, not its contents. Is it neat and easy to read? Does it appear professionally done?

Let's face it, editing takes care of what you're trying to say. It is formatting that determines how the document looks—a critical step if you really want your text read.

Since WordPerfect is a screen-oriented program, you can adjust the appearance of your text on the screen until you are pleased with it and print out your document only when you are sure that its format is correct.

In this chapter, you will learn how to control page breaks, add character styles, hyphenate at the ends of lines, and set new tab stops and margins.

PAGE BREAKS

You already know that WordPerfect automatically paginates documents as you type. Using the default settings, a new page starts after every 54 lines. However, you might want to end one page before it is filled, as when typing a short cover memo or title page. To insert a page break manually, press Ctrl-Return. A double line of dashes appears across the screen, and the page indicator on the status line increases by one. To delete the page break, place the cursor after it and press Backspace, or before it and press Del.

KEEPING TEXT TOGETHER

One problem with automatic pagination is that WordPerfect might break a page in the middle of a chart, list, table, or other block of text that should be kept together. You can ensure that the text is not divided by using either of the following procedures.

Note
The appearance of the version 5.1 screen is slightly different, but the steps listed here still apply.

Block Protect   Use the Alt-F4 key to highlight the text you wish to keep together, then press Shift-F8 to see the prompt

>   Protect block? (Y/N) No

Press *Y*. The highlighting will disappear but WordPerfect will surround the block with the invisible codes [Block Pro: On] and [Block Pro: Off]. Now, no matter what changes you make to the text, that block of text will not be divided between pages.

Conditional End of Page   This procedure is slightly longer, but it reintroduces the Format menu that you'll be using often in this chapter and whenever you use WordPerfect.

Type the section of text that must be kept together on a page, then count the number of lines that the text contains. Place the cursor at the beginning of the section, then press Shift-F8 to display the Format menu.

For now, look under option 4—Other. We're interested in the Conditional End of Page format.

Press *4* or *o* to select Other and display the Format Other menu (Figure 3.1). Press *2* or *c* to select the Conditional End of Page option. The prompt changes to

>   Number of Lines to Keep Together:

Enter the number of lines you counted, and press Return three times to return to your document.

WordPerfect will print the specified number of lines on the same page, even if extra blank lines must be inserted on a previous page.

Keeping Words Together   You can also keep groups of words together on the same line by pressing Home followed by the space bar rather than pressing the space bar alone. This inserts a *hard space*. You may want to use hard spaces to keep together text such as first and last names, phone numbers, and formulas. The following text, for example, appears awkward because of the way that the lines broke:

>   The formula for calculating degrees
>   when given the Fahrenheit is C = (F
>   − 32) 5/9.

```
Format: Other

      1 - Advance

      2 - Conditional End of Page

      3 - Decimal/Align Character    .
          Thousands' Separator       ,

      4 - Language                   EN

      5 - Overstrike

      6 - Printer Functions

      7 - Underline - Spaces         Yes
                        Tabs         No




   Selection: 0
```

■**FIGURE 3.1:** *Format Other menu*

Hard spaces ensure that the formulas are kept together:

> The formula for calculating degrees
> when given the Fahrenheit is
> $C = (F - 32)\ 5/9$.

Think of the text that should be kept together as a single unit. Instead of pressing the space bar anywhere between the first and last characters of the text, press Home then the space bar. A hard space (the code [ ]) will be inserted. So, with the codes revealed, the formula above would appear as

C[ ]=[ ](F[ ]–[ ]32)[ ][ ]5/9

Since hard spaces indicate characters that must stay together on a line, they cannot be used with a unit of text longer than one line.

■

CONTROLLING THE APPEARANCE
OF CHARACTERS

WordPerfect gives you many of the powers of desktop publishing and page composition. It allows you to add lines, boxes, and graphics to a document, produce newsletters and other columnar documents, and take full advantage of today's powerful printers.

These are sophisticated features that just can't be described in one chapter. So in this chapter I'll cover the fundamental ways of changing the appearance of characters. These include underlining, boldfacing, overstriking, superscripts and subscripts, printing different size and color characters, and converting lowercase letters to uppercase. You can change the appearance of characters either as you type them or after they are entered. Character styles can be combined by pressing two or more keys or kestroke combinations (such as pressing F6 F8 for boldfaced underlined text).

By the way, depending on your computer, boldfaced and underlined characters may appear different on the screen from normal characters. You can adjust how these characters are displayed by customizing WordPerfect through the Setup menu. This is described in detail in Chapter 5. For now, keep in mind that boldfaced and underlined characters may appear in different colors or shades on your screen depending on the monitor and graphics card you're using.

BOLDFACING

To boldface characters as you type them, press F6 to turn on boldfacing, type the characters, then press F6 again to turn off the function. To boldface characters already on the screen, first highlight them as a block by pressing Alt-F4, then press F6 once.

If you press Alt-F3 to reveal the codes, boldfacing on appears as [BOLD], and boldfacing off appears as [bold]. When boldfacing is turned on, the position indicator on the status line may also appear boldfaced. Figure 3.2 shows a sample of boldfaced text with the codes revealed.

If you have a color or graphics monitor, boldfaced characters either appear in a different color or actually appear brighter than the surrounding text.

UNDERLINING

You can underline characters using the F8 toggle key. Press F8 before typing the characters to be underlined, then F8 again to turn underlining off. To underline characters already typed, press Alt-F4 to highlight them as a block, then press F8.

The codes appear as [UND] for underlining on and [und] for underlining off. When underlining is turned on, the Pos indicator on the status line will look the same as the underlined text characters. Depending on your computer, underlined characters may appear on the screen underlined, in color, or in reverse video.

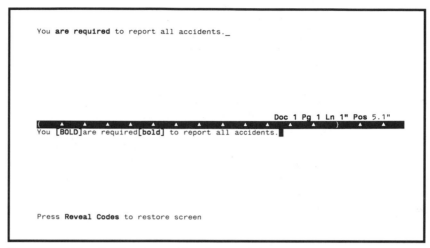

■FIGURE 3.2:   *Boldfaced text with codes revealed*

By default, WordPerfect uses a single continuous underline under both letters and spaces between words, but not under tab areas. You can change the underline style to noncontinuous using the Format Other menu. To do this, press Shift-F8 4 to display the menu, then *7* to select the Underline option. If you want to underline only words, not spaces, press *N*. The cursor moves to the Tabs option. To underline tab spaces press *Y*. Press Return twice to return to the document.

All the styles appear the same way on the screen, but they will be printed as you've selected.

OVERSTRIKING

Overstriking, performed from the Format Other menu, prints two or more characters in the same position. It is used to create special symbols not available in the IBM character set or in your printer. (Chapter 15 discusses foreign and special characters in detail.)

To overstrike characters, press Shift-F8 4 for the Format Other menu, then press *5* or *o* for Overstrike. The prompt line changes to

1 Create; 2 Edit:0

Press *1* for the prompt

[Ovrstk]

Type the characters that you want printed at the same position, then press Return three times to return to the document. You'll only see the last character you typed on the screen, but they will all be printed.

If you want to change the overstrike characters, select *2* or *e* from the Overstrike prompt line. WordPerfect will search backward through the text and display the first Overstrike code and the characters it affects. Edit the characters then press Return.

TYPING SUPERSCRIPTS AND SUBSCRIPTS

To superscript or subscript press Ctrl-F8 to see the prompt

> 1 Size; 2 Appearance; 3 Normal; 4 Base Font;
> 5 Print Color:0

Press *1* for the prompt line

> 1 Suprscpt; 2 Subscpt; 3 Fine; 4 Small; 5 Large;
> 6 Vry Large; 7 Ext Large:0

Press *1* to enter superscript characters, *2* for subscripts. You'll learn about the other options on these lines shortly. The prompt line disappears and the Pos indicator on the status line will change color or appearance as a reminder that you're in this mode. Now type the characters. They won't appear above or below the line on the screen unless you have a special graphics card. When you want to stop entering superscripted or subscripted characters, press the → key. This moves the cursor off the code and returns the Pos indicator to normal.

You can also return to normal by pressing Ctrl-F8 3 to select the Normal option.

To subscript or superscript characters after you've typed them, highlight them as a block by pressing Alt-F4, press Ctrl-F8 1, then *1* or *2* as appropriate. Chapter 15 includes more information about using subscripts and superscripts.

CONVERTING CHARACTERS TO UPPERCASE
OR LOWERCASE

To change all uppercase letters to lowercase, or vice versa, first highlight the text by pressing Alt-F4, then press Shift-F3 to show the prompt

> 1 Uppercase; 2 Lowercase: 0

Press *1* to make the highlighted block all uppercase characters, *2* for lowercase. Note that Shift-F3 is used for case conversion when the Block function is on, and for switching between documents when the Block function is off.

REMOVING BOLD AND OTHER STYLES

You can delete the character styles with the codes either invisible or revealed. When the code is revealed, position the cursor on the code then press Del.

When the code is invisible, place the cursor on the first character of the text in the special format. If the Pos indicator on the status line is in the same format (such as boldfaced or underlined) press the ← key once. The cursor will stay on the first letter, and the position number will remain the same. However, the Pos indicator will return to the color or format of normal text.

Press Del. You'll see the prompt

Delete [Bold]? (Y/N) N

Press *Y* to cancel the code.

Another method for deleting character styles is to use the Replace command. For example, suppose that you used the F6 key to boldface text in many places. After printing a draft copy, you decide that the extra emphasis isn't required and that all of the text should be printed in normal type. You can quickly make the change by deleting all the Boldface codes in one fell swoop.

To do this press Home Home ↑ to place the cursor at the start of the document. Press Alt-F2 N for replacement without confirmation, then F6 as the code you'd like to delete. The status line will show

-> Srch: [Bold]

Press F2 to show the prompt

Replace with:

Press F2 without entering any replacement characters. WordPerfect will "replace" all boldfacing codes with nothing, deleting them and printing all text in normal density.

A word of caution: You cannot use the Replace command to change all boldfacing to underlining. Entering F8 for the replacement of F6 will underline the entire document, starting at the first boldfaced characters. This is because WordPerfect replaces the first occurrence of the boldfacing code with the underlining code, but it never inserts an end-of-underlining code.

■ ADVANCED CHARACTER FORMATTING

These techniques are called advanced only because some printers will not be able to produce the effects discussed. These include printing text in different sizes and typefaces, italics, outline letters, and color.

Start by pressing Ctrl-F8 to display the prompt line

1 Size; 2 Appearance; 3 Normal; 4 Base Font; 5 Print Color: 0

Let's review these options:

- **Size** controls the size of the characters and can also be used to create superscripts and subscripts.

- **Appearance** determines the character shape and other factors. You'll soon learn all of the choices under this option.

- **Normal** cancels any of the other selections, just like pressing F6 toggled boldfacing off.

- **Base Font** determines the family, or type style, your printer will use.

- **Print Color** changes the color of the printed character. Of course you must have a color printer for this to work.

CHARACTER SIZE

This option lets you print characters as subscripts and superscripts, and in fine, small, large, very large, and extra large sizes as discussed in Appendix B. But except for superscripts and subscripts, which most printers can do, many printers will not be able to print in the different sizes and styles that we discuss here. And remember, all characters appear the same size on the screen.

Changing Sizes As You Type   When you want to enter characters a different size from normal, press Ctrl-F8 1 to select Size.

Press the appropriate number or letter to select the size desired, type the characters, then press Ctrl-F8 3 or the → key to return the characters to normal.

When you select a new size, WordPerfect automatically computes the proper margins and line spacing for you.

Changing Font Families   You can have more than one type style in a document if your printer is capable. When you want to print a character not in the current base font, change to the base font containing the desired style.

Press Ctrl-F8 4 to see the possible base fonts available on your printer.

The one marked with an asterisk is the default font assigned to your printer. All of the font sizes are determined from the base font. For example, Figure 3.3 shows the base fonts available for a laser printer containing downloaded fonts. These are type styles that are stored on a disk and loaded into the printer when needed.

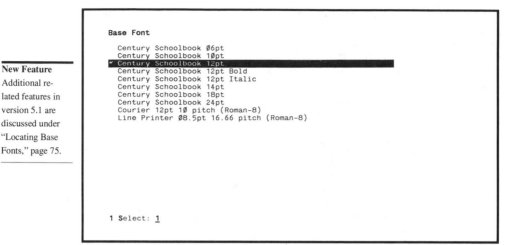

New Feature
Additional re-
lated features in
version 5.1 are
discussed under
"Locating Base
Fonts," page 75.

■**FIGURE 3.3:**   *Sample base fonts*

In this case, the base font is called Century Schoolbook 12 pt. The large font in this typeface is the next size, 14 pt., the very large is 18 pt., and the extra large is 24 pt. However, if you changed the base font to 10 pt., everything would shift down—large would be 12 pt., very large 14 pt., and extra large 18 pt.

What sizes would be available if the base font were changed to Courier 12 pt.? None, because there are no other sizes in that typeface.

Move the highlight with the arrow keys to the font desired, then press Return F7.

Changing the Size of Existing Characters   To change the size of text you've already entered, place the cursor at the start of the text you wish to change then press Alt-F4. Move the cursor to the end of the text then press Ctrl-F8 to see the prompt

Attribute: 1 Size; 2 Appearance: 0

Press *1* or *s* to show the Size prompt line then select the style desired. All of the highlighted characters will be formatted.

To return formatted characters to normal, display the codes and delete the Appearance codes in the text.

CHANGING CHARACTER APPEARANCE
AS YOU TYPE

To change the appearance of characters press Ctrl-F8 2 to select Appearance and display the prompt line

Note

The appearance
of the version
5.1 screen is
slightly dif-
ferent, but the
steps listed here
still apply.

1 Bold 2 Undrln 3 Dbl Und 4 Italc 5 Outln 6 Shadw
7 Sm Cap 8 Redln 9 Stkout: 0

Press the number or letter corresponding to the appearance desired, type the characters, then press Ctrl-F8 3 or the → key to return the characters to normal.

Pressing *1* or *2* would boldface or underline your text, just like pressing F6 or F8. So to boldface you could press F6 or Ctrl-F8 2 1, and to underline press F8 or Ctrl-F8 2 2. To stop boldfacing or underlining, press F6 or F8, press the → key, or select Ctrl-F8 3, Normal.

Option 3 prints a double underline; 4, italic printing; 5, outline letters; 6, shadow characters; and 7, small capital letters.

Redline printing, option 8, is used to print text that you'd like to add to the document; Strikeout, option 9, is for text you'd like to delete. Use these options when making tentative changes to a document, or when working with another individual.

CHANGING THE APPEARANCE OF EXISTING CHARACTERS

To change the appearance of text you've already entered, highlight it as a block then press Ctrl-F8 for the prompt

Attribute: 1 Size; 2 Appearance: 0

Press *2* or *a* to show the Appearance prompt line, then select the style desired. All of the highlighted characters will be formatted.

To return formatted characters to normal, display the codes then delete the Appearance codes in the text.

COLOR

If you have a color printer, you can set the color in which your text will be printed. Press Ctrl-F8 5 to select the Color option and display the Color menu (Figure 3.4).

The possible colors and their mix are displayed on top, and the color currently in use is at the bottom. Press the number or letter for the color in which you want to print.

If you can mix your own colors on your printer, press *O* for Other. The cursor moves to the current color prompt line. Type the percentage of red, press Return, type the percentage of green, press Return, type the percentage of blue, and press Return twice. The [Color:] code will be inserted into the text. Delete the code to return the color to normal—black.

```
Print Color

                            Primary Color Mixture
                          Red      Green      Blue

        1 - Black          0%        0%        0%
        2 - White        100%      100%      100%
        3 - Red           67%        0%        0%
        4 - Green          0%       67%        0%
        5 - Blue           0%        0%       67%
        6 - Yellow        67%       67%        0%
        7 - Magenta       67%        0%       67%
        8 - Cyan           0%       67%       67%
        9 - Orange        67%       25%        0%
        A - Gray          50%       50%       50%
        N - Brown         67%       33%        0%
        0 - Other

        Current Color      0%        0%        0%



    Selection: 0
```

■**FIGURE 3.4:** *Color menu*

COMBINING STYLES

When you are done entering characters in one size or appearance, return the style to normal before selecting the next one. This way, the characters are formatted in only one way— either italic or underlined, for example.

If you don't revert back to normal, the styles will be combined. For example, to double-underline italic characters, press Ctrl-F8 2 4 then Ctrl-F8 2 3, type the text, then return to normal. Depending on your printer, some combinations may not be possible, such as italic small capitals. You'll just have to experiment with possible combinations.

To combine styles for characters already typed, highlight the block using Alt-F4 then press the keystrokes necessary for the first of the formats. The highlighting will disappear. Press Alt-F4 to return to Block mode then press Ctrl-Home twice. The cursor will move directly to the other side of the block and become highlighted. Press the keystrokes for the other format.

With Block on, press Ctrl-Home twice to quickly rehighlight the block.

REMOVING REDLINE AND STRIKEOUT

While you can remove the Redline and Strikeout codes in the same way, these serve special purposes. You strike out text to show that you'd like to delete it from the document, and you redline text that you'd like to add. That way, when you're working on a document with another individual, both of you can easily identify changes the other would like to make. So if you really want to make these changes you can have WordPerfect do the final editing for you.

Before printing the document, follow these steps. You'll be using the Mark Text command, Alt-F5, a powerful command that's also used to create a table of contents, an index, and other reference sections.

- To remove redline and strikeout, press Alt-F5 to display the prompt

    1 Auto Ref; 2 Subdoc; 3 Index; 4 ToA short form; 5 Define; 6 Generate: 0

Note
In version 5.1, the first option on this prompt line is Cross-Ref.

- Press *6* to display the menu shown in Figure 3.5.
- Press *1*. The prompt line changes to

    Delete redline markings and strikeout text (Y/N)? No

- Press *Y*.

Any text that has been formatted as strikeout will be deleted and the redline markings will be removed.

CHANGING THE APPEARANCE OF PARAGRAPHS

Line formatting affects the placement of entire paragraphs on the screen and on the printed page. Just like character styles, line formats can be changed either

```
Mark Text: Generate

     1 - Remove Redline Markings and Strikeout Text from Document

     2 - Compare Screen and Disk Documents and Add Redline and Strikeout

     3 - Expand Master Document

     4 - Condense Master Document

     5 - Generate Tables, Indexes, Automatic References, etc.




Selection: 0
```

■**FIGURE 3.5:** *Mark Text Generate menu*

before or after entering the text. These commands affect only the text below the cursor position where you issued them. So to format an entire document you must always place the cursor at the start.

Press Shift-F8 to display the Format menu then *1* for the Format Line menu (Figure 3.6).

Let's see how to use each of these commands.

HYPHENATING TEXT

Word wrap lets you type without pressing Return at the end of each line. But at times, such as when long words are carried to the next line, a right-justified paragraph can have extra spaces between words, which are very unattractive. For example, without hyphenation the following paragraph has many noticeable gaps:

Wordwrap
automatically
returns   the
carriage   to
the   left.

While you can hyphenate as you type, this slows your typing. Instead, select either manual assisted or automatic hyphenation.

- With manual assisted hyphenation, WordPerfect will suggest possible hyphenation positions and give you the chance to confirm or change the hyphen's location.

- With automatic hyphenation, WordPerfect will actually insert the hyphen when it determines that a word should be hyphenated.

Warning
Users of version 5.1 should follow the special instructions under "Hyphenating Text," page 76.

To turn hyphenation on or off, press Shift-F8 1 1 to select the Hyphenation option on the Format Line menu. The prompt line will change to

1 Off; 2 Manual; 3 Auto:0

Press *1* or *f* if you don't want any help with hyphenation.

Press *2* or *a* to turn on assisted hyphenation. The word *Manual* replaces the word *No* at the Hyphenation option, and the [Hyph On] code is inserted in the text. As you type, WordPerfect will sense when word wrap may leave too

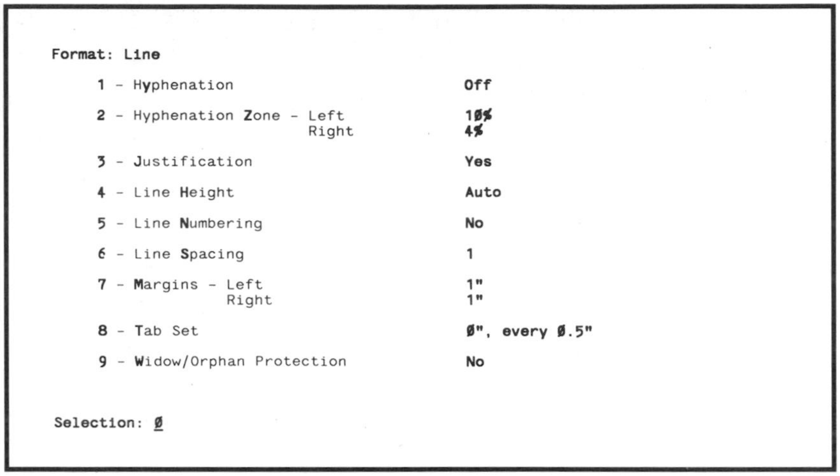

```
Format: Line

      1 - Hyphenation                       Off

      2 - Hyphenation Zone - Left           10%
                            Right           4%

      3 - Justification                     Yes

      4 - Line Height                       Auto

      5 - Line Numbering                    No

      6 - Line Spacing                      1

      7 - Margins - Left                    1"
                    Right                   1"

      8 - Tab Set                           0", every 0.5"

      9 - Widow/Orphan Protection           No


  Selection: 0
```

■**FIGURE 3.6:**   *Format Line menu*

many spaces between words. Instead of carrying the word to the next line, the program will display

Position Hyphen, Press ESC

If necessary, use the cursor movement keys to move the hyphen to an appropriate place, then press Esc.

Press *3* or *a* to turn on automatic hyphenation. The word Auto appears at the Hyphenation option and the [Hyph On] code is inserted in the text. Now as you type, WordPerfect will automatically insert a soft hyphen where appropriate, without stopping for you to position the cursor. If WordPerfect's rules of hyphenation don't apply to the word, you will be placed in manual assisted hyphenation for that word only. If you later want to delete or change the hyphen, delete the – character and edit accordingly.

The Hyphenation Zone option (2) on the Format Line menu determines the maximum number of extra spaces allowed, as a percentage of total line length, before WordPerfect suggests hyphenating. A hyphenation zone smaller than the default 10 percent (about seven characters) will result in fewer extra spaces, but more suggestions for hyphenation.

To change the hyphenation zone setting, press *2* from the Format Line menu. Type the left zone desired (in percent), then press Return. Type the setting for the right zone, then press Return. Press Return twice more to return to the document.

JUSTIFICATION

Warning
Users of version
5.1 should fol-
low the special
instructions
under "Justifica-
tion," page 76.

When you print your document in the default format, all of the lines in the paragraph except the last will be right-justified. That is, they will be even on both the left and right sides. While this gives your document a professional look, unless hyphenated it can result in extra spaces as discussed above, and it tells the reader that the document was produced by a word processor, not typed by hand. If you want your reader to feel that you personally typed the letter or other document, or want to avoid the need to hyphenate, then turn off justification in the Format Line menu.

From the Format Line menu, press *3* or *j* to select the Justification option, then press *N*. Press Return twice to return to the document. To return the entire document to the default setting, delete the [Just Off] code in the text.

LINE HEIGHT

This option, also called *leading,* determines the number of lines that are printed in each inch of space. Using the default Auto, WordPerfect adjusts the spacing to accommodate whatever size type your printer is using. However, to squeeze a few more lines on each page—or to space lines farther apart—you can enter your own fixed line measurement.

Press *4* or *h* from the Format Line menu to see the prompt

> 1 Auto; 2 Fixed: 0

Press *2* or *f* if you want to set your own line height. The cursor moves to the Line Height option on the menu and the word *auto* is replaced by some measurement. The measurement depends on the type size you're currently using, but the standard 6 lines per inch is spaced approximately .17 inches. Type the setting desired then press Return. Press Return twice more to return to the document. If you're using a standard typeface, for example, 8 lines per inch would be a setting of .13".

LINE NUMBERING

There are instances when you might want to print line numbers in the left margin. Many legal documents, for example, require line numbers—even on blank lines—that are used to refer to specific citations at some later date. You might even be using WordPerfect to write source code for computer programs. Even if the numbers are not required by the language you are using, such as Pascal or COBOL, they are useful when reading and editing your programs later on.

To include line numbers in your document, place the cursor where you want numbering to start, press Shift-F8 1 for the Format Line menu, then press *5* or *n* to select Line Numbering. Press *Y* to display the Format Line Numbering menu (Figure 3.7).

Press Return to accept the default options and return to the Format Line menu, or make selections regarding the placement of the numbers, then press Return. The code [LinNum:On] will be in the text. No numbers appear on the screen but all lines after the code are printed with line numbers. So to number the entire document, make sure the cursor is at the start of the document when you turn the option on.

To number certain lines, place the cursor on the first line to be numbered, then turn numbering on. Move the cursor past the last line you want numbered and press Shift-F8 1 5 N to select No for line numbering, and press Return three times. Numbers will be printed only next to the lines between the [LinNum:On] and [LinNum:Off] codes.

LINE SPACING

To change the line spacing, press *6* or *s* from the Format Line menu, enter the value for the new line spacing, then press Return. You can use half-line increments, such as 1.5, but the text will not appear half-spaced on the screen.

CHANGING LEFT AND RIGHT MARGINS

You can make quick margin setting changes by pressing *7* or *m* from the Format Line menu. Type the new left margin and press Return, or simply press

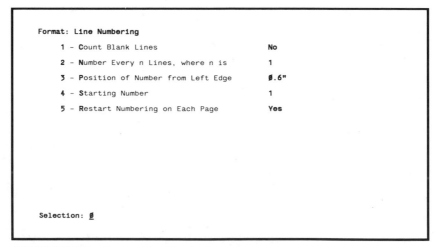

```
Format: Line Numbering

     1 - Count Blank Lines                    No

     2 - Number Every n Lines, where n is     1

     3 - Position of Number from Left Edge    0.6"

     4 - Starting Number                      1

     5 - Restart Numbering on Each Page       Yes




     Selection: 0
```

■**FIGURE 3.7:** *Format Line Numbering menu*

Return to accept the left margin. Type the new right margin and press Return, or simply press Return to accept the right margin setting. Just type the numbers; WordPerfect will add the inches sign (") for you. Then press Return twice to return to the document.

SETTING AND DELETING TAB STOPS

New Feature
Additional re-
lated features in
version 5.1 are
discussed under
"Setting Tabs,"
page 77.

To set or delete tab stops, press *8* or *t* from the Format Line menu. The bottom of the screen will change to a Tab Selection form, as shown in Figure 3.8.

The ruler line represents positions starting at the left margin of the page, in this case the default 1 inch. Half-inch positions are marked by the ^ character and each of the default left-aligned tabs is represented with an *L*. Below the ruler line are instructions for setting and clearing tab stops.

You can set four different types of tab stops, each indicated by typing a letter when you set it, as explained below. Tab types, and their letters, include the following:

L   Left-aligned tab, operates as a normal tab. This is the default tab type.

R   Right-aligned tab. Text shifts to the left from the tab stop position, aligning on the right.

D   Decimal tab, used for entering columns of numbers. Numbers shift to the left until the decimal point is entered, then to the right.

Note
The appearance
of the version
5.1 screen is
slightly dif-
ferent, but the
steps listed here
still apply.

```
L....L....L....L....L....L....L....L....L....L....L....L....L....L....L....
 !    ^    !    ^    !    ^    !    ^    !    ^    !    ^    !    ^
 1"       2"        3"        4"        5"        6"        7"        8"
Delete EOL (clear tabs); Enter Number (set tab); Del (clear tab);
Left; Center; Right; Decimal; .= Dot Leader
```

■**FIGURE 3.8:** *Tab stop selection display*

C   Center tab. Text is centered on the tab stop position.

Dot leader tabs appear in reverse.

To set a tab, move the cursor to the desired location, then enter the type of tab. To add dot leaders to left, right, and decimal tabs, press the period key after the tab type. The letter representing the tab type will appear on the ruler line.

You can also set a tab by typing its position, then pressing Return. Only left-aligned tab stops can be set this way.

Here are some more rules for setting and deleting tabs:

- To set evenly spaced tabs, type the starting position number, a comma, then the spacing. For example, type *1,.5* to enter tab stops every ten spaces starting at the 1-inch margin.

- To set evenly spaced center, right-aligned, or left-aligned tab stops, move the cursor to the starting position and enter the tab stop. Then type the starting position number, a comma, and the spacing, followed by Return.

- To delete a tab stop, type its position number, press Return, then press Del.

- To delete all tab stops, press Ctrl-End.

Press F7 to return to your document.

WIDOW AND ORPHAN LINES

A *widow line* is the first sentence of a paragraph by itself on the bottom of a page. An *orphan line* is the last line of a paragraph appearing alone at the top of a page. To avoid such lines during printing, place the cursor at the start of the document, then press Shift-F8 1 9 to select the Widow/Orphan option, press *Y,* then press Return. Press Return twice again to return to the document. Now WordPerfect will not print the first or last line of a paragraph by itself.

CENTERING TEXT

Note
The appearance of the version 5.1 screen is slightly different, but the steps listed here still apply.

To center a heading between the left and right margins, press Shift-F6, type the heading, then press Return. To center more than one line at a time, type the text, press Alt-F4, use the cursor movement keys to highlight it, press Shift-F6, then press *Y* in response to the prompt

[Center]? (Y/N) N

Each line in the highlighted block will be centered on the screen and in the printed version.

INDENTING

To indent text on the left, press F4. Each time you press F4, the left margin will shift to the right five spaces. To indent text on both sides, press Shift-F4. This indents both the right and left margins five spaces at a time. The indentation stays in effect until you press the Return key. To indent the next paragraph, press F4 or Shift-F4 again.

RIGHT-ALIGNING TEXT

To align text on the right margin, such as:

WordPerfect certainly
has many useful
formatting features!

Note

The appearance of the version 5.1 screen is slightly different, but the steps listed here still apply.

press Alt-F6, type the line, and press Return. To right-align more than one line at a time, type the text, then press Alt-F4 to highlight it. Press Alt-F6, then press *Y* in response to the prompt

[Flsh Rt]? (Y/N) No

■ CHANGING PAGE FORMATS

Page formats affect the overall appearance of the page. They include changing the top and bottom margins, adding page numbers, and using headers and footers. Specific applications for various page formats are covered in detail in later chapters.

TOP AND BOTTOM MARGINS

Press Shift-F8 2 to display the Format Page menu (Figure 3.9).

These options control the arrangement of text and other elements on the page. You'll learn about most of these settings in other chapters. But now notice that option 5 sets top and bottom margins. Press *5* or *m* to move the cursor to the top margin setting. Type the size of the top margin in inches, then press Return. WordPerfect adds the inches sign (") for you. If you just want to change the

```
Format: Page

     1 - Center Page (top to bottom)        No

     2 - Force Odd/Even Page

     3 - Headers

     4 - Footers

     5 - Margins - Top                       1"
                   Bottom                    1"

     6 - New Page Number                     1
         (example: 3 or iii)

     7 - Page Numbering                      No page numbering

     8 - Paper Size                          8.5" x 11"
               Type                          Standard

     9 - Suppress (this page only)

Selection: 0
```

■**FIGURE 3.9:** *Format Page menu*

bottom margin, simply press Return at this prompt, then type the size of the bottom margin and press Return. If you just want to set the top margin, accepting the default bottom, simply press Return. Press Return twice to return to the document. The [T/B Mar:] code is inserted in the text.

PAGE SIZE

WordPerfect collects information about the size of your pages in *forms*. Each form contains the size, the type of paper, the direction you print on it, and, for one category of paper, the paper feed. You might have one form designed for plain 8 1/2 by 11 inch paper, another for legal size, and one for envelopes. When you want to print on one of these types of paper, you only have to tell WordPerfect what form you're using, rather than change the margins or other settings.

Because paper size is somewhat dependent on the type of printer you have (you can't print on paper larger than your printer can handle), WordPerfect stores the information about forms in the printer definition. All printers come with something called the *standard form* already defined. That's plain paper, 8 1/2 by 11 inches. Most printers also have a form defined, called All Others. This form is used to quickly change to nonstandard sizes. Other printers have envelopes, legal-sized paper, or other forms defined already.

When you want to change paper size you have several possible paths. If the form is already defined, you just have to tell WordPerfect to use it. If the form isn't defined, then you have to add its definition to your printer's file. If the size you want to print on is neither wider nor longer than the All Others form (or the standard form if All Others is not defined your printer), then you just enter the new page length or width.

If you set up WordPerfect for your printer using Appendix A, you saw the forms that were already defined for your printer. So I'll start by showing you how to select one of these predefined forms. You've seen most of the menus discussed in this chapter in Appendix A. So if you're unsure of what they look like, refer to the figures in the appendix.

Selecting a Predefined Form   Follow these steps when you want to select a form that's already defined for your printer:

1. Make sure the cursor is at the start of the document, then press Shift-F8 2 to display the Format Page menu.

2. Press **8** or **s** to select Paper Size and display the Paper Size options (Figure 3.10).

3. Press the number or letter corresponding to the page size you want. The list of paper types will appear (Figure 3.11).

4. Press the number or letter corresponding to the paper type you want.

   If you select a form size and type that hasn't been defined, WordPerfect will use Standard in its place and display the message *requested form is unavailable* in the menu.

5. Press Return twice to accept the page size change. The code [Paper Sz/Typ: (*size and type*)] is inserted in the text. To return to the default form, delete the code.

```
Format: Paper Size

        1 - Standard              (8.5" x 11")
        2 - Standard Landscape    (11" x 8.5")
        3 - Legal                 (8.5" x 14")
        4 - Legal Landscape       (14" x 8.5")
        5 - Envelope              (9.5" x 4")
        6 - Half Sheet            (5.5" x 8.5")
        7 - US Government         (8" x 11")
        8 - A4                    (210mm x 297mm)
        9 - A4 Landscape          (297mm x 210mm)
        0 - Other

   Selection: 0
```

■**FIGURE 3.10:** *Paper Size options*

Defining New Forms   If you use a paper size that's not defined for your printer, you have to create the form first. Here are the steps:

1. Press Shift-F7 S to choose the Select Printer function. The list of available printers is displayed. Make sure your printer is selected. If there isn't an asterisk next to it, highlight the name and press Return S.

2. Press **3** or **e** to edit the printer definition. The Printer Selection Change Settings menu appears.

3. Press **4** or **f** for the Forms option, displaying a list of defined forms for your printer.

4. Press **1** or **a** to add a new form definition and display

   Select Printer: Form Type
   1 - Standard
   2 - Bond
   3 - Letterhead
   4 - Labels
   5 - Envelope
   6 - Transparency
   7 - Cardstock
   8 - [ALL OTHERS]
   9 - Other

5. Press the number or letter corresponding to the type of form. The Printer

```
Format:  Paper Type
        1 - Standard

        2 - Bond

        3 - Letterhead

        4 - Labels

        5 - Envelope

        6 - Transparency

        7 - Cardstock

        8 - Other




Selection: 0
```

■**FIGURE 3.11:**   *Paper Type options*

Selection Forms menu is displayed.

6. Press **1** or **s** to set the form size. You'll see the Page Size Selection menu, Figure 3.12.

7. Press the number or letter for the size of the form. The Forms menu will be redisplayed.

8. Press **4** or **l** if the paper location (feed) is incorrect. The prompt line changes to

   Location: 1 Continuous; 2 Bin Number; 3 Manual: 0

   Press the number corresponding to the paper source.

9. Set the form at Initially Present if it is not already set there. Press **3** then **Y** to change the setting.

10. Check the settings for orientation and page offset.

    ■ Orientation is used primarily for laser printers. *Portrait* orientation is normal printing, with characters across the width of the page. In *landscape* orientation, characters print down the length of the page.

    ■ Page offset sets any additional margin space at the top or left of the form. For example, multipart 8 1/2 by 11-inch forms often have a narrow area before the perforation at the top margin. The total form length is actually 8 1/2 by 11 1/2 inches. A top page offset of 1/2 inch and a top margin of 1 inch would advance the form 1 1/2 inches

```
Select Printer: Form Size
                                   Inserted
                                   Edge

        1 - Standard              8.5"    x    11"

        2 - Standard Wide         11"     x    8.5"

        3 - Legal                 8.5"    x    14"

        4 - Legal Wide            14"     x    8.5"

        5 - Envelope              9.5"    x    4"

        6 - Half Sheet            5.5"    x    8.5"

        7 - US Government         8"      x    11"

        8 - A4                    210mm   x    297mm

        9 - A4 Wide               297mm   x    210mm

        0 - Other

Selection: 1
```

■**FIGURE 3.12:** *Page Size Selection menu*

before printing. Left offsets can be used with continuous form paper to accommodate the tractor holes.

Change either of these settings if appropriate.

11. Press Return. The new form will be added to the list of those already defined.

12. Press F7 four times to return to the typing window.

Now that you've created the form, you can use it like any of the forms that came predefined.

Entering Smaller Sizes Without Defining Forms   You can use a page size that's not defined as a form as long as it's no larger than the All Others or standard form, whichever is larger; that is, no longer than 11 inches and no wider than 8 1/2. This is convenient when working with smaller forms, such as 3 by 5-inch index cards.

Here's how:

1. Press Shift-F8 2 to display the Format Page menu.

2. Press **8** or **s** to select Paper Size and display the Form Size options.

3. Press **O** to select Other. The prompt changes to

    Width: 8.5"

4. Type the width of the form, not larger than 8.5", then press Return to see the prompt

    Height: 11

5. Type the height, or length, of the form (not larger than 11"), then press Return to display the Paper Type list.

6. Press **1** for Standard.

7. Press Return twice to return to the document.

Keep in mind that changing the page size does not change the top and bottom margins, so the default 1-inch margins are still in force. If you're using a small sheet, these margins might now be too large. For instance, with 3 by 5-inch index cards you'd now have only 1 inch, or six lines, of typing per page. To fit more on the page, change the top and bottom margins.

FORMS AND PAGE FEED

If you have a laser printer, use continuous feed for paper that's loaded in the tray. Even though they are individual sheets of paper, laser printers treat them as continuous feed.

But what about printers that handle both single sheets and continuous paper? You might use continuous paper for some jobs but change to single sheets for letterhead or special paper. In this case, define two forms. Define and use the standard size and standard type as continuous paper. But also define a standard size and letterhead or bond type with manual feed (location). When you're ready to print, place the cursor at the top of the document and select the form type desired. The standard type will use continuous paper, the letterhead or bond type will use manual.

SOME HINTS ON CHANGING FORMATS

The page format settings and the use of forms control the text from the cursor position down, so you must place the cursor at the start of the text to format the entire document. To format a specific page, make your selections at the start of that page and remember to return the settings to normal for the next page.

For example, suppose that you just typed three pages using the default page formats. Now you want the fourth page printed on 14-inch paper with 2-inch left and right margins. At the top of that page, select the legal size form and change the right and left margins. If you want the fifth page on standard size paper, reset the standard size and type at the top of that page.

Resetting the format is particularly important if you are reformatting text already on the screen. When you change the margins to indent just one paragraph on the page, all text after that point will be indented. To avoid this, after you set the margins for the indented paragraph, place the cursor after that paragraph and reset the margins to the original settings.

■ VERSION 5.1 FEATURES

LOCATING BASE FONTS

The Base Font menu (Ctrl-F8 4 or Font Base Font) now includes two options:

1 Select; N Name search: 1

Use the Name Search option to quickly locate a font, particularly with long font lists. Press *N* to see the prompt

(Name Search; Enter or arrows to Exit)

Start typing the name of the font you want to select. WordPerfect will automatically locate the first font starting with the characters you enter. For example, if you start by pressing *t*, the first font starting with "t" will be highlighted. If you then type an *a*, the first font starting with "ta" will be highlighted.

HYPHENATING TEXT

To turn on automatic hyphenation, press Shift-F8 1 1 or select Layout Line Hyphenation. The Hyphenation option appears as:

1 - Hyphenation   No (Yes)

Press *Y* to turn on automatic hyphenation (or *N* if you later want to turn the feature off). Press F7 to return to the document.

If you're typing a long word that you do not want WordPerfect to hyphenate, regardless of its position at the end of a line, press Home / before the word. A [/] code is inserted to prevent automatic hyphenation from taking place—for that word only. You can also enter this code to cancel a hyphenation already inserted. Place the cursor on the first character of the word, press Home / and then delete the hyphen. The word will wrap to the next line.

JUSTIFICATION

To justify your document, press Shift-F8 1 3 or select Layout Line Justification, displaying the prompt line

Justification: 1 Left; 2 Center; 3 Right; 4 Full

Select the type of justification desired—Left turns off the default Full justification setting—then press F7 to return to the document. A [Just:*type*] code is inserted into the text. All text following the code—until the next [Just:] setting, if any—will automatically conform to your selection.

The Center and Right justification options are most useful for formatting an entire document. While you can also use them for a section of text already typed, you'll have to insert a [Just:Full] or [Just:Left] code where you want the previous justification to continue.

SETTING TABS

The Tab Set option on the Line menu appears like this:

8 - Tab Set Rel: -1", every 0.5"

Rel means that the tabs are relative to the left margin, not the edge of the page. A tab at one inch, for example, will always be 1 inch from the *margin*. If you change the left margin, the tab will move along with it. The notation *−1", every 0.5"* means that tabs are set every 1/2 inch starting at the *−1"* position, or 1 inch to the left of the left margin.

You can change the tabs to absolute—measured from the left edge of the paper. In this mode, a tab set at 1 inch will always be 1 inch from the left of the page. Changing the margin will have no effect on the tab stop.

Press *8* or *t* to see the Tab Selection form shown in Figure 3.13.

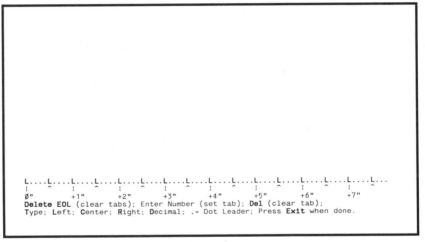

```
    L....L....L....L....L....L....L....L....L....L....L....L....L....L....L...
    !    ^    !    ^    !    ^    !    ^    !    ^    !    ^    !    ^
    Ø"       +1"      +2"      +3"      +4"      +5"      +6"      +7"
    Delete EOL (clear tabs); Enter Number (set tab); Del (clear tab);
    Type; Left; Center; Right; Decimal; .= Dot Leader; Press Exit when done.
```

■**FIGURE 3.13:**   *Version 5.1 Tab Selection form*

The ruler line represents positions starting at the left margin of the page. The plus (+) signs in front of the positions indicate that relative tabs are being used.

Since tabs are set as relative, the 0" position represents the left margin, +1" is 1 inch from the margin, and so on. If you pressed the ← key, the line would shift and the −1" position would appear—1 inch to the left of the default margin.

While you set and delete tabs as explained for version 5.0, the relative status of default tabs will affect the specific positions.

For example, suppose you clear all of the default tabs and set a new tab at the +2" position on the Tab Set form. If you press the Tab key when typing, the cursor moves to the 3" position as indicated on the status line.

Why 3" when you set the tab at the +2" position on the ruler? Remember, by default, tab stops—and thus the measurements on the Tab Set ruler—are relative to the left margin. But the position counter on the status line is referenced from the left edge of the page. Using the default 1" margin, the 2" position on the Tab Set ruler is actually the same position as the 3" measurement on the document's status line.

If you want the ruler line and position indicator to be the same, set the tab as absolute. When the Tab Selection form is displayed, press *T*. The prompt line changes to:

Tab Type: 1 Absolute; 2 Relative to Margin: 0

Press *1* or *A*. (To later change to relative tabs, press *2* or *R*.)

The scale line will change so the 1" measurement indicates the margin position, the 0" represents the left edge of the paper. The plus signs disappear, showing that absolute tabs are being used.

Throughout this book, tab stop positions that you should set are shown in the version 5.0 format—as absolute tabs. If you set the tabs using these positions, but you keep the default relative type, all of your settings will be off by 1 inch and your documents will not appear as they should. To use these same positions with version 5.1, first set the tab type to absolute. If you prefer to use relative tabs, subtract 1 inch from each position shown.

PAGE SIZE

The concept of using forms to define page sizes is the same in version 5.1. What differs is the way in which forms are added and edited. In this version, all work with forms is performed through the Page Size option on the Format Page menu.

Selecting a Predefined Form   Follow these steps to select one of the forms that are already defined for your printer:

1. Press Shift-F8 2 7 or select **L**ayout **P**age Paper **S**ize to display a list of defined forms (Figure 3.14).

2. Press the ↓ key to highlight the form you want to use, then press Return three times.

Defining New Forms   To use a paper size that's not defined for your printer, you have to create the form first. Here's how:

1. Press Shift-F8 2 7 or select **L**ayout **P**age Paper **S**ize to display the list of defined forms.

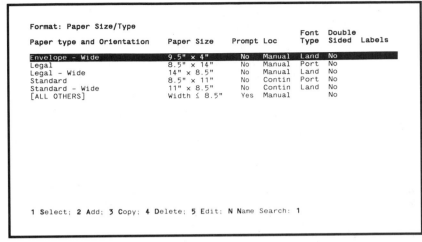

```
Format: Paper Size/Type
                                                        Font  Double
Paper type and Orientation     Paper Size    Prompt Loc Type  Sided  Labels

Envelope - Wide                9.5" x 4"     No     Manual Land  No
Legal                          8.5" x 14"    No     Manual Port  No
Legal - Wide                   14" x 8.5"    No     Manual Land  No
Standard                       8.5" x 11"    No     Contin Port  No
Standard - Wide                11" x 8.5"    No     Contin Land  No
[ALL OTHERS]                   Width ≤ 8.5"  Yes    Manual       No




1 Select; 2 Add; 3 Copy; 4 Delete; 5 Edit; N Name Search: 1
```

■**FIGURE 3.14:**   *Paper Size/Type list*

2. Press **2** or **A** to see the list shown in Figure 3.15.

3. Press the number or letter for the type of form. The Edit Paper Definition menu is displayed (Figure 3.16).

4. Press **1** or **S** to set the form size. You'll see the Paper Size menu, similar to Figure 3.10.

5. Press the number or letter for the size desired. The Edit Paper Definition menu will be redisplayed.

```
Format: Paper Type
        1 - Standard

        2 - Bond

        3 - Letterhead

        4 - Labels

        5 - Envelope

        6 - Transparency

        7 - Cardstock

        8 - [ALL OTHERS]

        9 - Other



Selection: 1
```

■**FIGURE 3.15:**   *Paper Type options for version 5.1*

```
Format: Edit Paper Definition

        Filename                HPLASERJ.PRS

    1 - Paper Size              8.5" x 11"

    2 - Paper Type              Standard

    3 - Font Type               Portrait

    4 - Prompt to Load          No

    5 - Location                Continuous

    6 - Double Sided Printing   No

    7 - Binding Edge            Left

    8 - Labels                  No

    9 - Text Adjustment - Top   Ø"
                         Side   Ø"


Selection: Ø
```

■**FIGURE 3.16:**   *Edit Paper Definition menu*

6. Look at the Location option. If it says Continuous then WordPerfect assumes you're using continuous feed paper, and it won't stop to let you insert individual sheets into the printer. If the location is correct, then skip to step 10. Otherwise continue here.

7. Press **5** or **l** for the prompt line:

   Location: 1 Continuous; 2 Bin Number; 3 Manual: 0

8. Select the option corresponding to the paper source. If you select Bin Number, you'll see the prompt

   Bin number:

   Enter the letter or number of the paper tray or bin containing the paper you'll be using.

9. Now look at the Prompt to Load option. No at this option means that the form is available for use and WordPerfect will not stop and prompt you to insert the proper size paper. If you want to change this option, press **4** or **r**, then **Y**. The other options on this menu are used as follows:

   ■ *Font Type*—used for laser printers to select *Portrait* or *Landscape* orientation. If your laser printer requires separate portrait and landscape fonts, then set this option to Landscape when selecting a landscape form size.

   ■ *Double Sided Printing*—used for laser printers that print on both sides of the page. Select Yes or No.

- *Binding Edge*—used to leave extra space at the edge where pages are to be bound. The options are Top and Left.

- *Labels*—used for creating forms to print labels.

- *Text Adjustment*—sets any additional margin space at the top or left of the form. For example, multipart 8 1/2" by 11" forms often have a narrow area before the perforation at the top margin. The total form length is actually 8 1/2 by 11 1/2 inches. A top page offset of 1/2 inch and a top margin of 1 inch would advance the form 1 1/2 inches before printing. Left offsets can be used with continuous form paper to accommodate the tractor holes.

10. Press F7 three times to return to the typing window.

This form definition is now added to those available and can be selected as described previously.

Creating Custom Sizes   To use a page size not shown in the Paper Size menu, such as 3-inch by 5-inch index cards, follow these steps:

1. Press Shift-F8 2 7 2 or select **L**ayout **P**age **P**aper **S**ize **A**dd to display the Paper Type menu.

2. Press **9** or **O** to see the prompt:

   Other form type:

3. Type a form type, such as Index, then press Return. The Edit Paper Definition menu appears.

4. Press **1** or **s** to display the Size options.

5. Press **o** for the prompt:

   Width: 0"   Height:

6. Type the width, such as **5**, then press Return.

7. Type the length, such as **3**, then press Return.

8. Set the Location and Prompt to Load options to match your hardware.

9. Press F7. The Paper Size/Type list appears with the newly created form highlighted.

10. Press Return to select the form, then F7 to return to the typing window.

MOUSE AND MENU EQUIVALENTS

Function	Keyboard	Pull-Down Menus
Base Font	Ctrl-F8 4	Font Base Font
Block Protect	Alt-F4	Edit Protect Block
Boldface	F6	Font Appearance Bold
Center Text	Shift-F6	Layout Align Center
Color	Ctrl-F8 5	Font Print Color
Conditional End of Page	Shift-F8 4 2	Layout Other Conditional End of Page
Convert Case	Shift-F3	Edit Convert Case
Font Sizes	Ctrl-F8 1	Font (size)
Font Appearance	Ctrl-F8	Font Appearance (type)
Hyphenation	Shift-F8 1 1	Layout Line Hyphenation
Indent ->	F4	Layout Align Indent ->
Indent -><-	Shift-F4	Layout Align Indent -><-
Justification	Shift-F8 1 3	Layout Justify
Line Numbering	Shift-F8 1 5	Layout Line Line Numbering
Line Height	Shift-F8 1 4	Layout Line Line Height
Line Spacing	Shift-F8 1 6	Layout Line Line Spacing
Margins, Top and Bottom	Shift-F8 2 5	Layout Page Margins
Margins, Left and Right	Shift-F8 1 7	Layout Line Margins
Overstrike	Shift-F8 4 5	Layout Other Overstrike
Paper Size	Shift-F8 2 7	Layout Page Paper Size
Remove Redline	Alt-F5 6 1	Mark Generate Remove
Right Align	Alt-F6	Layout Align Flush Right

Function	Keyboard	Pull-Down Menus
Set Tabs	Shift-F8 1 8	Layout Line Tab Set
Subscript	Ctrl-F8 1 2	Font Subscript
Superscript	Ctrl-F8 1 1	Font Superscript
Underline	F8	Font Appearance Underline

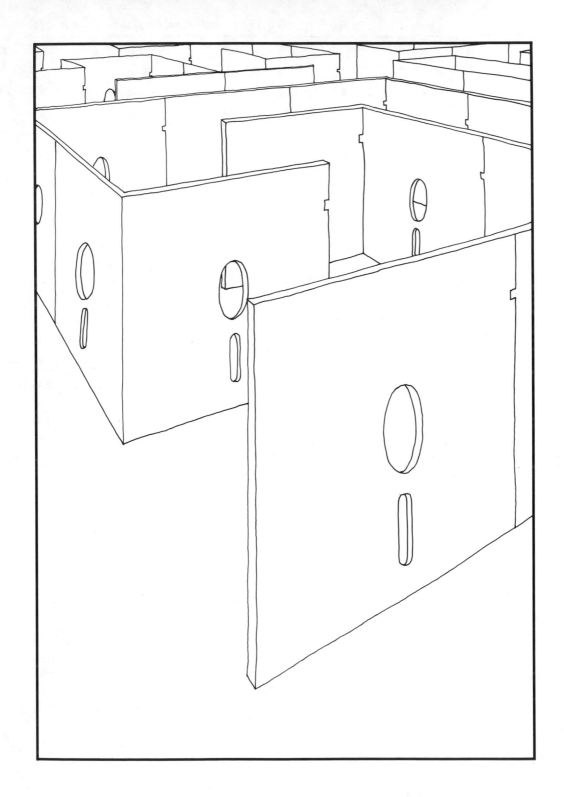

4

CONTROLLING THE PRINTING PROCESS

New Feature
Additional related features in version 5.1 are discussed under "Print Options," page 94.

The printing process can be as simple or as complex as you want to make it, depending on how you want to print your documents. If you have already selected the proper printer, you can print either the document currently on the screen or one on the disk; you can print just selected pages, and you can even print one document while you work on another.

WordPerfect uses a *print queue* to control your printing. The queue is a waiting line where WordPerfect stores the names of documents that you've sent to the printer. Because of this, you can give the command to print a document even while another document is still being printed. Each document will be stored in the queue until the previous one is completed.

You learned how to select printers in Appendix A and you already know that you press Shift-F7 1 to print the entire document or Shift-F7 2 to print just one page.

Now let's look at the other printing options in WordPerfect. Because these options control the printing process and operation of the print queue, they contribute to your overall capability to manage a large number of documents.

PRINTING DOCUMENTS ON DISK

Note
Version 5.1 can print Fast Saved documents.

You can print a document that's stored on the disk without first displaying it on the screen. The document must have been saved formatted; that is, with the Fast Save option on the Setup menu turned off, the default. If you changed this setting, which is discussed in Chapter 5, then your documents have been saved unformatted, and you won't be able to print them from the disk as shown here.

To print a document from the disk, press Shift-F7 to display the Print menu then *3* or *d* to select Document on Disk. The status line changes to

Document Name:

Type the name of the document you'd like to print, then press Return. You'll see the prompt

Page(s): (All)

Press Return to print the entire document, or type the page or range of pages you want to print, then press Return. Press F7 to return to the current document.

PRINTING SELECTED PAGES

If your document is numbered consecutively, without a new page number set, print a range of pages according to these rules:

- For a single page, type the number and press Return.

- For a range of pages, type the starting page, a hyphen, the ending page, and Return. For example, to print pages 2 through 6, type *2–6* and press Return.

- From a given page to the end of the document, type the starting page number, a hyphen, and Return. The command 8– Return will print from page 8 to the end of the document.

- From the first page of a document through a specific page, type a hyphen, enter the last page you want printed, and press Return. Type –6 Return to print pages 1 through 6.

- Use a comma to separate sections that you want to print. For example, the command *1–5,10–15* prints pages 1 through 5 and 10 through 15.

No spaces are allowed in any of these entries. Use lowercase Roman numerals if you set that type of page numbering.

If your document is divided into sections because you used the New Page Number command from the Page Format menu, then you must specify what sections contain the pages to be printed. Type the section number and a colon before entering the page number.

Here are some examples:

Range	Will Print
i–iv	The first five pages numbered with Roman numerals.
–10	From the start of the document through page 10.
2:1–2:8	The second set of pages numbered 1 through 8.
1:1–3:1	The first page numbered 1 through the third page numbered 1.
2:8–	From the second page numbered 8 to the end of the document.
–3:1	From the start of the document through the third page numbered 1.

PRINTING FROM THE DIRECTORY LISTING

You can also print a document from the directory listing displayed by pressing F5 Return. Highlight the name of a document not saved with Fast Save then press *4* or *p* for the Print option. The Pages prompt line will appear. Enter the range of pages you want to print then press Return.

If you saved the document under the Fast Save option, you'll see the prompt

Error: This document was Fast Saved. Must be retrieved to print.

Recall the document first and print it from the screen.

Note
Version 5.1 can print Fast Saved documents from the List Files directory, so the error message will not appear.

■ CONTROL PRINTER

The Control Printer option on the Print menu lets you manipulate the queue and the order of documents in it from the Control Printer menu (Figure 4.1). You can also use this menu to check on the progress of a document, to see which page is currently being printed.

To display this menu, press Shift-F7 to reveal the Print menu, then *4* or *c*.

The top of the menu reports on the status of the queue and the current print job. The page being printed, and the copy number if you're printing more than one, are shown on the right. On the left is the job number, the paper size and type, the location of the feed, and a report of any problems encountered.

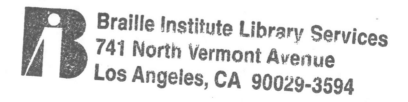

```
Print: Control Printer

Current Job

Job Number: n/a                              Page Number:  n/a
Job Status: n/a                              Current Copy: n/a
Paper:      n/a
Location:   n/a
Message:    No print jobs


Job List

Job  Document                  Destination           Print Options




Additional Jobs Not Shown: Ø



1 Cancel Job(s); 2 Rush Job; 3 Display Jobs; 4 Go (start printer); 5 Stop: Ø
```

■**FIGURE 4.1:**   *Control Printer menu*

A numbered list of documents in the queue will be displayed in the job list section. If you're printing a document from the disk, its name will appear. Documents printing from the display are shown as *(screen)*.

If you have more documents than can be displayed on the job list, you'll see the number in the Additional Jobs prompt. You're queue control panel is the prompt line at the bottom of the screen. Here are the options:

1 Cancel job(s)	Cancels one or more print jobs. Press *1* or *c,* type the number of the document shown in the job list, then press Return. Cancel everything in the queue by entering an asterisk (*) in place of a number. Some printers have a built-in queue, called a *print buffer.* Any text in the buffer will still be printed even if you cancel the job. Turn your printer off then on again to stop printing what's in the buffer.
2 Rush job	Places a document first in line in the queue. Press *2* or *r.* You'll be prompted to enter the number of the job you want to print next.

		This does not cancel the job currently being printed.
	3 Display jobs	Lists the names of the documents in the print queue, if they cannot all be listed at the bottom of the menu.
	4 Go	Resumes printing after a Stop Print command or when you're using individual sheets of paper.
	5 Stop	Halts the printing process. Restart the current job with the Go (G) command. Any text in your printer's buffer will continue to be printed.

Note
The appearance of the version 5.1 screen is slightly different, but the steps listed here still apply.

If you try to exit WordPerfect while jobs are in the print queue, you'll see the warning

> Cancel all print jobs (Y/N)? No

Press *N* to remain in WordPerfect and let the documents be printed. Press *Y* to leave WordPerfect, canceling any jobs in the queue including the one currently being printed.

■ TYPE THROUGH

Another way to print documents is as you type them, just like a typewriter. You'll lose the editing powers of WordPerfect, but it is a convenient method of filling out complicated preprinted forms. Each character or line (depending on what option you select and how your printer works) will be printed as soon as you type it.

Warning
Type Through is not available in version 5.1 and is optional in later releases of version 5.0.

Press Shift-F7 5 to select Type Through printing. If you see the prompt *Feature not available on this printer* then your printer is not set up for this mode. Otherwise, you'll see

> Type Through by: 1 Line; 2 Character:0

If you press *1*, you will see the screen shown in Figure 4.2. Type a line of text, and when you press Return, the line will be sent to the printer.

```
 _


Line Type Through printing

Function Key       Action

Move               Retrieve the previous line for editing
Format             Do a printer command
Enter              Print the line
Exit/Cancel        Exit without printing




                                                    Pos 1
```

■**FIGURE 4.2:**   *The Line Type Through Printing screen*

If you press *2* from the Type Through prompt, you'll see the Character Type Through Printing screen. Now each character is sent to the printer immediately after it is typed.

What occurs when text is sent to the printer depends on your hardware. With some printers, like many that use daisy wheels, the line or character will actually be printed. With other printers, however, it may seem like nothing has happened! Laser printers, for example, are page printers. Nothing will be ejected from the printer until a page is completed or an end-of-page command is received. In this case, you'll have to manually eject the page from the printer.

Other printers, such as many dot matrix devices, will not print individual characters until you press Return. Although the individual characters are actually in the printer, it will not print them until a line has ended.

VIEWING DOCUMENTS

With the few exceptions already noted, documents will be printed as they appear on the screen. However, you may want to see exactly how format settings such as justification will affect the final appearance by using View mode.

Press Shift-F7 6 for the View option. The page where the cursor is located will be displayed (Figure 4.3).

By default, the entire page is shown. While you won't be able to read the text in this mode, you can get an idea of how the page will appear when printed. Use the PgUp and PgDn keys to view other pages of the document.

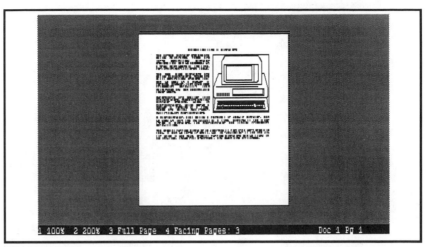

■**FIGURE 4.3:**   *Page in View mode*

To see the page in more detail, select either option 1 (100%) or option 2 (200%) from the prompt line. With each enlargement you'll be able to see the text in more detail, but you can't see all of the page (Figure 4.4). Use the cursor movement keys to scroll more of the document into view.

In the View mode, you cannot insert or delete any text. The Facing Page option will show two pages on the screen at one time. This will be one even-numbered and one odd-numbered page. The first page of the document has no facing page.

Press F7 to cancel the preview. You'll be returned to the page last seen in View mode.

INITIALIZE PRINTER

Some printers have a special series of codes that are sent to it when you start WordPerfect or whenever a new document begins printing. Sending these codes is called *initializing* the printer since the codes prepare it for producing your document.

Often, the initialization codes place the printer in its default state, canceling any special codes that it may have received with the last document. If you are using downloaded fonts, initialize printer will download the fonts from the disk into your printer.

To initialize your printer, press Shift-F7 7.

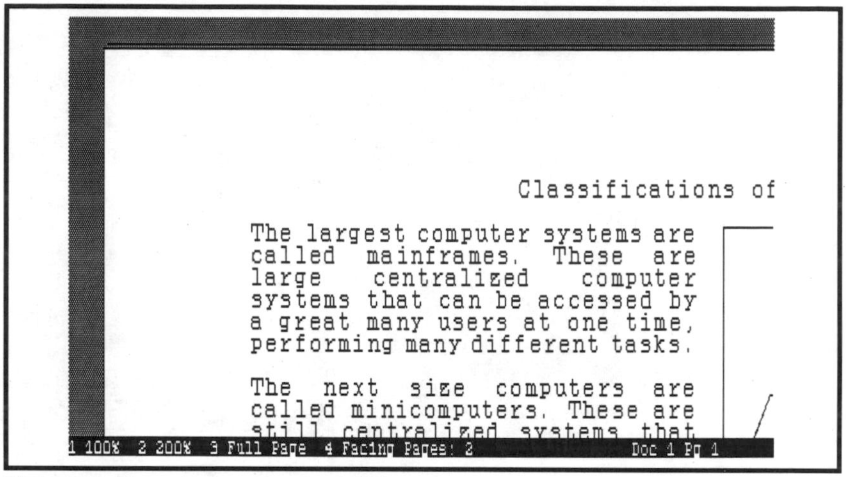

```
                                        Classifications of

          The largest computer systems are
          called  mainframes.  These  are
          large   centralized   computer
          systems that can be accessed by
          a great many users at one time,
          performing many different tasks.

          The  next  size  computers  are
          called minicomputers. These are
          still centralized systems that

 1 100%  2 200%  3 Full Page  4 Facing Pages: 2            Doc 1 Pg 1
```

■**FIGURE 4.4:**   *Page viewed at 200%*

BINDING

Note
This option is
called Binding
Offset in ver-
sion 5.1.

Documents normally start printing at the left margin. If you plan to bind the pages into a book, you'll need some extra margin space or *binding width*. For instance, with a three-ring binder you should insert extra space or else the holes might be punched too close to the text, if not directly on it. With the Binding option, you can add extra space to the left margin of odd-numbered pages and to the right margin of even-numbered pages.

From the Print menu, press *B* to select Binding. Type the amount of extra space you want to add to the left margin, then press Return.

The value you enter stays in effect until you exit WordPerfect.

NUMBER OF COPIES

Change this option to print more than one copy of the text. With the Print menu displayed, press *N,* type the number of copies desired, then press Return. Like binding, this option stays in effect until you exit WordPerfect. So change it back to 1 if you want to print a single copy later on.

■ GRAPHICS QUALITY

As you'll learn in Chapters 24 and 25, you can add graphics to your documents for maximum impact. This option determines whether you want to print the graphics, and, if so, the quality of the final printout.

Press *G* from the Print menu to display the prompt

Graphics Quality: 1 Do Not Print; 2 Draft; 3 Medium; 4 High: 3

Press the number or letter of your choice, then print the document.

When would you not want to print graphics that you've added to your document? Well, graphics take a long time to print, particularly on dot matrix printers. So for a quick rough copy, turn graphics off and print the document. If you're using a laser printer, it might not have enough memory to print an entire page of text and graphics. So select option 1 to print just the text of the document. Reinsert the same piece of paper, turn off text printing (you'll see how soon), and turn graphics printing back on by selecting option 2, 3, or 4. Print the document a second time. Now the graphics will be printed.

Options 2, 3, and 4 set the resolution of the graphics, low (2), medium (3), or high (4). While high resolution looks the best, it takes the longest time to print.

■ TEXT QUALITY

Press *T* from the Print menu to display the prompt

Text Quality: 1 Do Not Print; 2 Draft; 3 Medium; 4 High: 3

These options work just the same as those described above for graphics, but they only affect the text. So to print only the graphic images, select *1* from this prompt. Selecting option 2, 3, or 4 turns text printing back on and sets the quality.

■ PRINTING BLOCKS

Note
The appearance of the version 5.1 screen is slightly different, but the steps listed here still apply.

This option isn't part of the Print menu, but it comes in handy when you want to print small amounts of text. Press Alt-F4 to highlight the text, then press Shift-F7. This displays the prompt

Print block? (Y/N) N

Press *Y* to print just the highlighted text.

■ # VERSION 5.1 FEATURES

PRINT OPTIONS

Two additional Print options are available:

Multiple Pages   This option lets you print selected pages from the document shown on the screen. From the Print menu, press *5* or *m* to see the prompt

> Page(s):

Enter the pages you want to print using the techniques described earlier in this chapter under "Printing Selected Pages."

Multiple Copies Generated By   Press *u* to see the prompt:

> Multiple Copies Generated By: 1 WordPerfect; 2 Printer: 1

Using the default setting, WordPerfect transmits the document to the printer once for each copy being printed. Some printers, such as Hewlett-Packard LaserJets, have their own built-in function for printing multiple copies. When you select Printer, WordPerfect transmits a code to the printer for multiple copies, then the document itself only one time. This can greatly increase printer speed, especially for complex documents combining fonts and graphics.

MOUSE AND MENU EQUIVALENTS

Function	Keyboard	Pull-Down Menus
Print	Shift-F7	File Print

PART 2

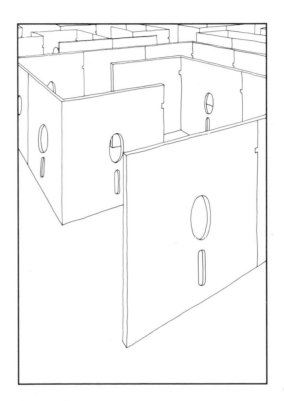

ADVANCED FEATURES FOR SPECIALIZED DOCUMENTS

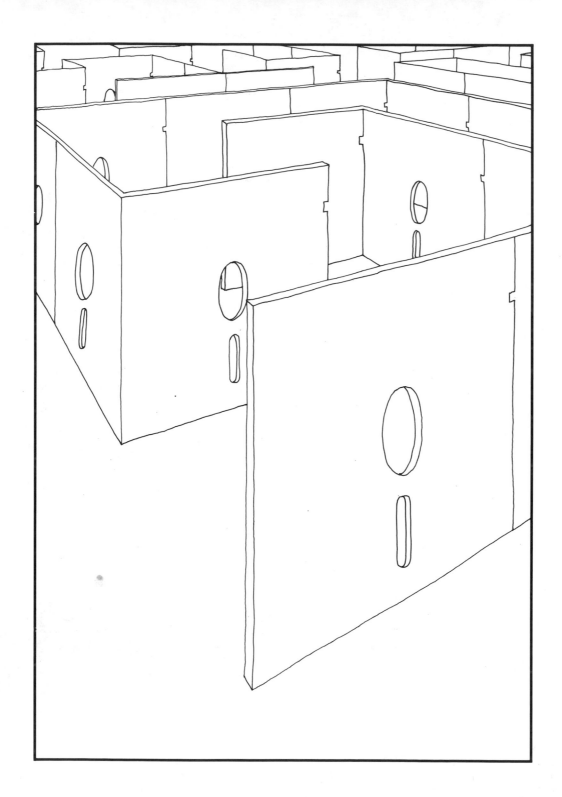

5

CUSTOMIZING WORDPERFECT FOR THE WAY YOU WORK

If you prefer the default settings and printer fonts provided with WordPerfect, you can simply start the program and begin typing.

But you just can't please everybody. Some people prefer different line lengths. Others use 8 1/2 by 14-inch legal paper or want every document to have page numbers. And there are users who want to take advantage of the special printer fonts that are available with many dot-matrix and laser printers.

You can always change WordPerfect's default settings temporarily for a specific document by using the formatting methods described in Chapter 3. But this becomes tedious if you use the different settings often.

This chapter describes how to change the default settings to suit your own needs. You'll also learn how to make backup copies automatically and how to create style sheets to quickly format documents even when you don't want to change the default settings.

Style sheets are useful to ensure consistent formats in similar documents. This is particularly important in a busy office, where several standard types of documents are produced regularly.

We will only be discussing in detail a few of the default settings that you can change using the Setup menus. When you have time, however, review all of the menu options to see which provide a custom feature that may streamline your own work.

First, however, let's see how to adjust the way WordPerfect appears on your screen.

Warning
The Setup menus have been changed in Version 5.1. While alternate keystrokes are shown in margin notes, refer to the section "Setting Up WordPerfect 5.1" on page 120 for an overall review.

■ ADJUSTING THE SCREEN DISPLAY

You can adjust the way boldfacing, underlining, and characters of all sizes and appearances are displayed on your screen. Through the Setup menu, you can customize the "look" of WordPerfect, especially if you have a color or composite monitor.

1. Start WordPerfect.

2. Press Shift-F1 to display the Setup menu (Figure 5.1).

   This menu contains a number of standard WordPerfect settings that you can modify; the options are summarized in Figure 5.2.

3. Press **3** or **d** for the Display option. You'll see the Setup Display menu (Figure 5.3). There are quite a few options on this menu. While all of them are summarized in Figure 5.4, let's concentrate on setting colors, fonts, and attributes.

4. Press **2** to select the Colors/Fonts/Attributes option. The exact menu you see next depends on your graphics card.

5. Press **1** for the Color option to display the Colors menu (Figure 5.5).
   Use this menu to set the foreground and background colors of all attributes (such as boldfacing and underlining), sizes (fine to extra large), and appearances (such as italics). The four columns list the type of character, the foreground and background colors, and a sample of how your

Warning

Steps 2 to 5:
With version
5.1, press Shift-
F1 2 1 1.

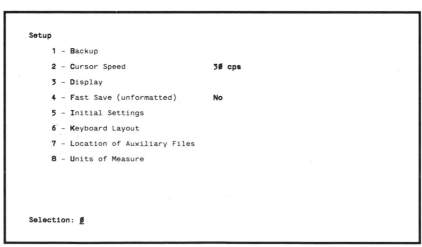

```
Setup

    1 - Backup

    2 - Cursor Speed                30 cps

    3 - Display

    4 - Fast Save (unformatted)     No

    5 - Initial Settings

    6 - Keyboard Layout

    7 - Location of Auxiliary Files

    8 - Units of Measure




Selection: 0
```

■**FIGURE 5.1:**   *Setup menu*

current selections appear. The possible colors are shown on top of the menu.

6. Press the directional arrows to reach the attribute you want to change, then type the letter representing the color.

- **Backup**

  Allows you to make automatic backup copies of the document you're editing.

- **Cursor Speed**

  Determines the speed at which the cursor moves if you hold down a directional or character key.

- **Display**

  Sets the monitor and graphic board type, colors displayed on the screen, and other aspects of the way text is displayed.

- **Fast Save (unformatted)**

  Allows you to save text formatted or unformatted. Formatted text takes longer to save but can be printed from the disk as explained in the chapter.

- **Initial Settings**

  Determines what default settings are used for the format of the date and table of authorities, when warning beeps occur, whether codes are automatically displayed, how many repeats are used for the ESC key, and whether summaries are automatically created when the document is saved.

- **Keyboard Layout**

  Lets you redefine the purpose of function keys.

- **Location of Auxiliary Files**

  Determines where WordPerfect expects to find the dictionary and thesaurus, keyboard and macro files, backups, printer files, and hyphenation modules.

- **Units of Measure**

  Determines how certain measurements are entered—either as the default inches or centimeters, as points, or as lines and columns.

■**FIGURE 5.2:** *Summary of Setup options*

```
Setup: Display

    1 - Automatically Format and Rewrite      Yes

    2 - Colors/Fonts/Attributes

    3 - Display Document Comments              Yes

    4 - Filename on the Status Line            Yes

    5 - Graphics Screen Type                   IBM CGA 640x200 mono

    6 - Hard Return Display Character

    7 - Menu Letter Display                    BOLD

    8 - Side-by-side Columns Display           Yes




Selection: 0
```

■**FIGURE 5.3:**   *Setup Display menu*

- **Automatically Format and Rewrite**
  When this option is set to NO, WordPerfect will not format your text as you edit it, so you must rewrite the screen or scroll through it. Select YES for this option to have WordPerfect automatically adjust the text as you add or delete characters.

- **Colors/Fonts/Attributes**
  Allows you to set the colors used to display the various size and appearance selections.

- **Filename on the Status Line**
  Select NO for this option if you don't want the name of your document to appear on the status line.

- **Graphics Screen Type**
  WordPerfect automatically senses what type of graphics card you're using. However, you can select another mode through this menu, as long as it's compatible with your hardware.

- **Hard Return Display Character**
  When you press Return, only an invisible [HRt] code is inserted into the text. Through this option, you can select to have some graphics symbol or character appear on the screen at each location where you pressed Return.

■**FIGURE 5.4:**   *Summary of display options*

- **Menu Letter Display**
  Each numbered option on a selection line or menu has one character in boldface. Through this option, you can select to have the character appear in any of the colors or attributes used to display font sizes and appearances.

- **Side-by-Side Columns Display**
  When you create multicolumn documents with WordPerfect, the columns will appear next to each other on the screen, just as they will when printed. Some typists find it easier to edit columns, however, if they are under each other. Select NO to display columns under each other, but still print them side by side.

■**FIGURE 5.4:** *Summary of display options (continued)*

The two options on the prompt line are:

Switch   Press Shift-F3 to set the colors on the other document (for example, on Doc 2 if you've been working on Doc 1).

Move   Press Ctrl-F3 to copy the settings from the other document to the Colors menu displayed.

7. Press F7 twice to save the changes and return to the document.

■ CHANGING COMMON DEFAULT SETTINGS

Aside from the screen display, the most common changes that users make include adding automatic page numbering and selecting another page size and top margin. Many users also like to have WordPerfect make backup copies of each document after it has been edited so that the unedited version is still available. As an example, let's see how to change the Fast Save option. We'll also change the default values so WordPerfect makes backup copies and prints the page number in the bottom center of every page.

```
Setup: Colors          A B C D E F G H I J K L M N O P
                       A B C D E F G H I J K L M N O P
     Attribute         Foreground  Background  Sample
     Normal                H            A       Sample
     Blocked               A            H       Sample
     Underline             A            H       Sample
     Strikeout             C            B       Sample
     Bold                  P            A       Sample
     Double Underline      F            B       Sample
     Redline               E            B       Sample
     Shadow                B            D       Sample
     Italics               G            B       Sample
     Small Caps            I            B       Sample
     Outline               G            B       Sample
     Subscript             E            D       Sample
     Superscript           M            D       Sample
     Fine Print            K            B       Sample
     Small Print           L            B       Sample
     Large Print           M            B       Sample
     Very Large Print      N            B       Sample
     Extra Large Print     O            B       Sample
     Bold & Underline      P            A       Sample
     Other Combinations    A            G       Sample

     Switch to switch;  Move to copy settings      Doc 1
```

■**FIGURE 5.5:** *Colors menu*

FAST SAVE

Warning

Fast Save is the default value with version 5.1. To turn it off, press Shift-F1 3 5 N F7.

First let's turn on and off the Fast Save option. Remember, turning it on will speed up the saving process, but you won't be able to print specific pages or *batch-print* several documents directly from the disk.

1. Press Shift-F1 to display the Setup menu.

2. Press **4** to select the Fast Save option.

3. Press **Y** for Yes, then press **N** if you want to turn it back off.

Fast Save does not affect the appearance of a document on the screen or in View mode.

Leave the Setup menu on the screen for now. If you wanted to return to the document, you would press F7.

BACKUP COPIES

Now let's set the system to make backup copies. Actually, there are two types of backup copies that you can make—*timed* backups and *original document* backups.

■ With timed backups, WordPerfect automatically saves a special copy of your document at regular intervals. So if someone accidentally turns off your computer you'll only lose what you've typed since the last timed backup or since you last saved with F10.

■ With original document backups, when you save a document that's already on the disk, WordPerfect first makes a copy of the original version. So you can always go back to the unedited document.

You can use either or both of these backups. If you only want one and you type long documents, I suggest timed backups. After all, the longer your computer is on the more chance there is of something going haywire or of accidents happening. The timed backup saves you the trouble of manually saving your text periodically. But for this exercise, let's get the most insurance we can and have both types of backup copies made.

The Setup menu should still be displayed. If not, press Shift-F1.

Warning
Step 1: With Version 5.1, press 3 1. Timed backups every 30 minutes is the default setting.

1. Press **1** or **b** for the Backup option. The screen displays the Setup Backup menu (Figure 5.6).

2. Press **1** or **t** to select Timed Document Backup.

3. Press **Y** (you'd press **N** to turn off the feature). The cursor moves to the Minutes Between Backups option.

4. Type the number of minutes you'd like between backups. I set mine for 15 minutes.

5. Press Return.

```
Setup: Backup

     Timed backup files are deleted when you exit WP normally.  If you
     have a power or machine failure, you will find the backup file in the
     backup directory indicated in Setup: Location of Files.

        Backup Directory

     1 - Timed Document Backup               No
         Minutes Between Backups             15


     Original backup will save the original document with a .BK! extension
     whenever you replace it during a Save or Exit.

     2 - Original Document Backup            No




Selection: 0
```

■**FIGURE 5.6:** *Setup Backup menu*

At the intervals you entered, a backup copy of your document will be saved on the WordPerfect disk. The backups are stored as WP{WP}BK.1 (document 1) and WP{WP}BK.2 (document 2). Soon I'll show you how to change the disk and directory where the backup copies are stored.

These files will be erased when you properly exit WordPerfect, but not if some machine failure or power problem occurs. In that case, you would start your computer again and use your operating system's Rename command to change the name of the backup file to a document name. Then start WordPerfect. Before it starts you might see the prompt

Are other copies of WordPerfect currently running? (Y/N)

Press *N*. If you don't rename the backup file, then when WordPerfect is ready to make the first timed backup after the failure, you'll hear a beep and see

Old backup file exists. 1 Rename; 2 Delete:

Press *R* and enter a name for the backup file or press *2*. The old backup file will be deleted.

Now let's set the system for original document backups. The Setup Backup menu should still be displayed.

6. Press **2** for the Original Document Backup option.

7. Press **Y** (you'd press **N** to later turn off this feature).

8. Press Return to accept the changes and redisplay the Setup menu.

Now when you save a document that's already on the disk, WordPerfect will first add the extension BK! to the original version. So suppose you save a document called LETTER. The original version will be stored as LETTER.BK!, the new version as LETTER. You now have a copy of the document that was on disk before you made any changes.

Warning
With version
5.1, press **6** or **l**
for the Location
of Files menu.

If you want to change the disk or directory where backups and other files are stored, press *7* or *l* for the Location of Auxiliary Files menu (Figure 5.7).

Press *1* or *b* for the Backup Directory option, type the drive where you want to store backup files, followed by a colon, then press Return. Change any of the other file locations in the same way, then press Return to return to the Setup menu. In later chapters you'll see why some of the other file locations might need changing.

```
Setup: Location of Auxiliary Files
      1 - Backup Directory
      2 - Hyphenation Module(s)
      3 - Keyboard/Macro Files
      4 - Main Dictionary(s)
      5 - Printer Files              C:\WP5
      6 - Style Library Filename
      7 - Supplementary Dictionary(s)
      8 - Thesaurus



   Selection: 0
```

■**FIGURE 5.7:** *Location of Auxiliary Files menu*

PAGE NUMBERS

Now let's make one last default change—adding page numbers to the bottom center of each page. The details of page numbering will be covered in Chapter 14.

The Setup menu should still be displayed on the screen. If not, press Shift-F1.

Warning
Steps 1 to 8: With version 5.1, press Shift-F1 4 5 Shift-F8 2 6 4 6 F7 F7 Return Return. Refer to the section "Page Numbers" in Chapter 14 for more information.

1. Press **5** or **i** to select the Initial Settings option. You'll see the Initial Settings menu (Figure 5.8).

   The options on this menu are summarized in Figure 5.9. For now, let's concentrate on option 4—Initial Codes.

2. Press **4** or **i** for the Initial Codes option. The screen divides into two just as if you've revealed the codes.

   With this screen displayed, you change any of the default values using the formatting techniques discussed in Chapter 3. Instead of setting the format of a particular document, however, the codes you enter will be loaded whenever you start WordPerfect. For example, if you wanted to change the default top margin to 2 inches, you'd just change the margin as described in Chapter 3, but from the Initial Code screen.

   Let's add default page numbering to the system.

3. Press Shift-F8 2 to display the Format Page menu.

4. Press **7** or **p** for the Page Numbering option. The Page Number Position menu appears (Figure 5.10).

Each of the options on the menu represents the position of page numbers and whether they should appear on every page or on alternating odd and even pages. Option 9 cancels page numbering.

5. Press **6** for a page number at the bottom center of the page. The Format Page menu appears.

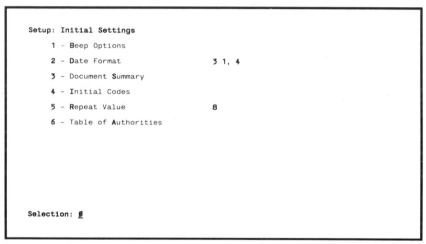

```
Setup: Initial Settings
      1 - Beep Options
      2 - Date Format                    3 1, 4
      3 - Document Summary
      4 - Initial Codes
      5 - Repeat Value                   8
      6 - Table of Authorities




      Selection: 0
```

■**FIGURE 5.8:**   *Initial Settings menu*

■ **Beep Options**
WordPerfect sounds a small beep when it suggests a hyphenation location. With this option, you can turn this beep off, and turn on a beep when you make an error or when a search fails to locate a match.

■ **Date Format**
You can have WordPerfect insert the date and time for you. This options controls the format of the date.

■ **Summary**
Select this option to display the summary screen whenever you save a document. Use this when you want every document to have a summary.

■**FIGURE 5.9:**   *Summary of Initial Setting options*

- **Initial Codes**
  This option lets you change the default format settings.

- **Repeat Value**
  Lets you change from the default 8 the number of repetitions performed when you press ESC.

- **Table of Authorities**
  Controls certain formats for tables of authorities, discussed in Chapter 13.

■**Figure 5.9:** *Summary of Initial Setting options (continued)*

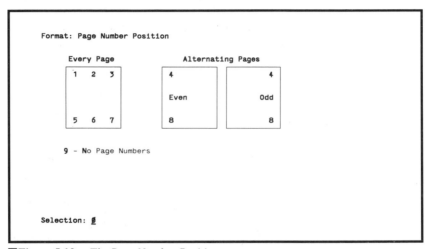

■**Figure 5.10:** *The Page Number Position menu*

6. Press F7. The screen again shows the scale line in the center. But now the code [Pg Numbering:Bottom Center] is displayed. If you made any other format changes, their codes would also appear.

7. Press F7 then wait until the Initial Settings menu appears.

8. Press Return once to return to the Setup menu, and again to display the typing screen.

9. Press F7 N Y to exit WordPerfect.

Whenever you start WordPerfect, the Fast Save option will be turned off and backup copies—both timed and original document—will be made. Your documents will have page numbers printed at the bottom center of each page.

CHANGING NEW DEFAULTS

Warning

With version 5.1, press Shift-F1 4 5 to change new defaults.

If you want to change or remove your new default values, press Shift-F1 to display the Setup menu, press *5* for Initial Settings, then press *4* for Initial Codes. The screen will show the scale line with your codes in the bottom window. Delete the codes you want to remove or change, then set any new formats desired, just as you did above. To return to the original WordPerfect default values, delete all of the displayed codes then press F7 twice.

■   STYLE SHEETS

There's only one problem with changing default values—you must want to use them with every document you type. That's fine as far as backup copies are concerned. But what if, for example, you don't want page numbers on every document, or you use special margins for only half of the documents you type?

This is where *style sheets* come in. A style sheet is a special file that contains only formatting codes. Each style sheet can contain any number of styles—collections of codes for a specific format. For instance, say you sometimes type documents on legal paper, but using a variety of top and bottom margins—one set for leases and contracts, another for premarital agreements, etc.

You don't want to make legal size the default since you often use standard 8 1/2 by 11-inch paper. And you can't set any of the margins as defaults because they vary with the type of document.

You might also switch between plain paper and stationery with a preprinted letterhead. So you have to change the top margin for the first page and reset to the default for remaining pages.

Instead of changing to these formats every time you need them, you might create a style sheet containing four styles. One style will contain the codes for changing to legal-sized paper, two others for different top and bottom margins, and another for letterhead paper. You'd give names to both the style sheet and the styles themselves. Then, when you want to format a document, you call up the style sheet and use the Style command to activate the styles you need.

You can also have a default style sheet, called the *style library,* containing codes that you use often—but that you don't want to make default values.

We'll be using styles and style sheets a great deal in later chapters to really streamline your work. But in this section, let's try style sheets for some fundamental uses.

CREATING A STYLE SHEET

Let's create a style sheet similar to the one described in the example above. It will include a style to change to legal paper, one to accommodate stationery with a printed letterhead, and one for large boldfaced characters. For those of you without letterhead paper, we'll include a style that contains the text of a letterhead as well.

Note

Refer to "Changing the Style Library," page 123.

1. Start WordPerfect.

2. Press Alt-F8. You'll see the Style menu (Figure 5.11). There are no style names and descriptions listed on the menu because you haven't defined any yet. So let's create a style to use legal-sized paper.

3. Press **3** or **c** to create a style. The Style Edit menu appears (Figure 5.12). You use this menu to create a style format that you want to add to the style sheet. The format includes the following:

   ■ The style *name* (no more then eleven characters) is used to retrieve the styles from the style sheet. Make it something that clearly identifies the purpose of the style, such as *legal* for legal-sized paper or *boldund* for bold underlined characters.

   ■ Two *types* are allowed, paired and open. A paired style includes codes to turn on and turn off the style. Use these for formats that will not be used for an entire document, much like the [BOLD] and [bold] codes to turn on and off boldfacing. Open styles are used for the entire document.

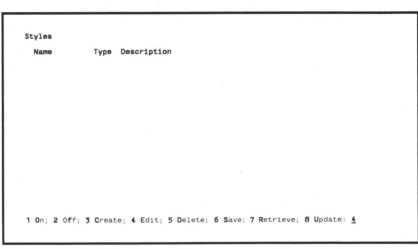

```
    Styles

      Name          Type  Description






















    1 On; 2 Off; 3 Create; 4 Edit; 5 Delete; 6 Save; 7 Retrieve; 8 Update: 4
```

■**FIGURE 5.11:** *Style menu*

- The *description* is used to explain the purpose of the style. It can be up to 54 characters.

- When you select *codes*, you will be able to use the formatting commands to create the style, much like you did when you changed defaults using the Initial Codes options.

- The *enter* option is only available with paired styles. You use it to determine the function of the Return key, whether it performs a carriage return and line feed as normal, or turns off the style.

Note
The appearance of the version 5.1 screen is slightly different, but the steps listed here still apply.

4. Press **1** or **n** to select the Name option.

5. Type **Legal** then press Return. The Legal style will select legal-sized paper. Since this style applies to the entire document, select the open type.

6. Press **2** or **t** for the Type option. The prompt line will change to

   Type: 1 Paired; 2 Open: 0

7. Press **2** or **o** for Open. The word Open appears at the Type item on the menu and the Enter option disappears.

8. Press **3** or **d** to enter a description.

9. Type the following then press Return:

   Changes paper size to legal

```
Styles: Edit
     1 - Name
     2 - Type          Paired
     3 - Description
     4 - Codes
     5 - Enter          HRt




     Selection: 0
```

■**FIGURE 5.12:**   *Style Edit menu*

Now let's enter the actual codes for legal-sized paper. This assumes that a legal size form has been defined for your printer.

10. Press **4** or **c** for the Codes option. The screen will clear, displaying just the scale line in the center.

Warning
Users of version 5.1 should follow the special instructions under "Legal-Sized Forms," page 126.

11. Select legal-sized paper.

    a. Press Shift-F8 2 to display the Format Page menu.

    b. Press **8** or **s** to select Paper Size and display the Paper Size options.

    c. Press **3** for legal size. You'll then see the paper types listed.

    d. Press **1** to select Standard.

    e. Press Return twice.

    The code [Paper Sz/Typ:8.5" x 14",Standard] appears below the scale line.

12. Press F7 twice to return to the Style menu. The name, type, and description appear on the menu.
    Now let's select a style to accommodate preprinted letterheads.

13. Press **3** or **c** to create a style and display the Style Edit menu.

14. Press **1** or **n** to select the Name option.

15. Type **Lethead** then press Return.
    At first glance it seems that you want a paired type—you'd turn it on for the first page and off for the remaining ones. But this means turning the style on at the start of the first page and off at the start of the second, so if you later edit the document, the Off code might not appear at the page break. Instead, use an open style that merely adds six extra returns at the start of the document.

16. Press **2** or **t** for the Type option.

17. Press **2** or **o** for Open.

18. Press **3** or **d** to enter a description.

19. Type the following then press Return:

    Extra margin for letterhead stationery

    Now let's enter the actual codes for standard 8 1/2 by 11-inch paper with a preprinted letterhead and with page numbers on the bottom of every page.

20. Press **4** or **c** for the Codes option.
    If we just add the codes for the extra margin, then it might be possible

to mistakenly use this style after you've selected the legal size form.

Since we want this style to specifically handle standard-sized letterhead paper, let's start this style with the codes to select 8 1/2 by 11-inch paper, making sure the correct form is used.

Warning

Users of version 5.1 should follow the special instructions under "Selecting Standard Paper," page 126.

21. Select standard-sized paper.

    a. Press Shift-F8 2 to display the Page Format menu.

    b. Press **8** or **s** to select the Paper Size option.

    c. Press **1** to select the Standard size.

    d. Press **1** to select the Standard type.

    e. Press Return twice.

The [Paper Sz/Typ:8.5" x 11",Standard] code is on the screen.

Warning

Step 22: With version 5.1, press Shift-F8 2 6 4 6 F7.

22. Now turn on page numbering.

    a. Press Shift-F8 2 to display the Format Page menu.

    b. Press **7** or **p** for the Page Numbering option.

    c. Press **6** for a page number at the bottom center of the page.

    d. Press F7.

The last part of this style should add the codes for an extra 2-inch margin.

23. Press Return twelve times.

Why didn't we change the actual top margin setting to 3 inches here? If we did, then every page in the document would have a 3-inch margin, even though letterhead is usually used only for the first page.

By using returns instead, we kept the extra margin on the first page only.

24. Press F7 twice to display the Style menu. Now both styles are included. Notice that the Lethead style contains a number of formatting codes. You can have as many formatting codes in a style as you want. Just keep in mind that they all will be inserted into the document as a group and can only be deleted as a group, not separately.

The next style will easily create large boldfaced characters for use as titles.

25. Press **3** or **c** to create a style and display the Style Edit menu.

26. Press **1** or **n** to select the Name option.

27. Type **Bigbold** then press Return.

    You can accept the default type (paired) since you want to turn this style on to type the characters then off at the end of the line.

28. Press **3** or **d** to enter a description.

29. Type the following then press Return:

    ### Large boldfaced characters

30. Press **4** or **c** for the Codes option. The screen will clear, displaying just the scale line but with a comment (Figure 5.13). You enter the codes that turn on the function to the left of the comment, the codes that turn it off to the right.

31. Enter the codes to turn the function on.

    a. Press Ctrl-F8 1 for the Size selection line.

    b. Press **5** for large printing.

    c. Press F6 for boldface.

32. Press the → key to move the cursor to the right of the comment.

33. Press Ctrl-F8 3 for Normal. The End Bold code [bold] will appear along with the End Large code [large].

    When you use this style, you want to turn it on, enter the characters, then turn it off as easily as possible. For this, let's use the Enter option.

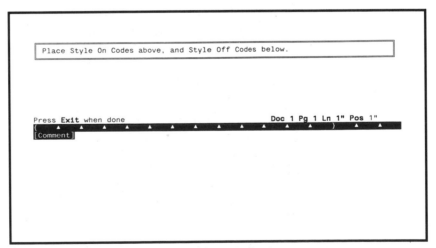

■**FIGURE 5.13:** *Code Entry screen for a paired style*

34. Press F7 then **5** or **e** for the Enter option. The prompt line changes to

    Enter: 1 Hrt; 2 Off; 3 Off/On:0

    With the default option 1, the Return key works as usual, adding a carriage return and line feed into the text. With option 2, pressing Return when a style is on issues the Style Off code. The last option, 3, turns the code on.

35. Press **2** or **f** to select Off.

36. Press F7 to display the Style menu.
    Finally, let's create a style that includes both text and codes. This style will display your personal letterhead on the top of the page.

37. Press **3** or **c** to create a style and display the Style Edit menu.

38. Press **1** or **n** to select the Name option.

39. Type **Address** then press Return.

40. Press **2** or **t** for the Type option.

41. Press **2** or **o** for Open.

42. Press **3** or **d** to enter a description.

43. Type the following then press Return:

    Inside address for letterhead

44. Press **4** or **c** for the Codes option.

45. Press Shift-F6 to center the cursor, type your name, then press Return.

46. Press Shift-F6, type your address, then press Return.

47. Press Shift-F6, type your city, state, and zip code, then press Return.

48. Press Return to double-space after the address. Figure 5.14 shows the codes for this style.

49. Press F7 twice to display the Style menu (Figure 5.15).
    You could return to the document now but your style sheet wouldn't be saved on the disk. Let's save it so you can recall it and use the styles at any time.

50. Press **6** or **s** for the Save option. The prompt changes to

    Filename:

Warning
Users of version 5.1 should follow the special instructions under "Deleting Styles," page 125.

51. Type the name for the style sheet, **STYLES**, then press Return.

You now have four styles defined and collected in one style sheet saved on the disk. If you want to delete a style, use the arrow keys to highlight its name on the Style menu, press *5* or *d* (for Delete), then press *Y* to the prompt

Delete Style? (Y/N) No

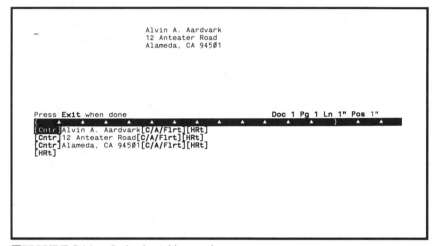

■**FIGURE 5.14:** *Codes for Address style*

```
Styles

     Name         Type   Description

     Address      Open   Inside address for letterhead
     Bigbold      Paired Large boldfaced characters
     Legal        Open   Changes paper size to legal
     Lethead      Open   Extra margin for letterhead stationary



















 1 On; 2 Off; 3 Create; 4 Edit; 5 Delete; 6 Save; 7 Retrieve; 8 Update: 4
```

■**FIGURE 5.15:** *Completed style sheet*

To edit a style, highlight its name then press *4* or *e* (for Edit) to display the Styles Edit menu. Make any changes desired then press F7.

52. Press F7 to exit the Style menu and return to the document window.

USING STYLES

Now that you've defined the styles, you can use them whenever you want. If you're just starting WordPerfect, however, you have to retrieve the style sheet from the disk. To do this, press Alt-F8 to display the Style menu, then *7* or *r* to retrieve the file. Type the name of the style sheet at the Filename prompt then press Return.

You can retrieve more than one style sheet and merge them together, just like you could retrieve more than one document to the screen. However, if you try to load a style sheet with styles having the same names as ones already loaded, you'll see the prompt

Note
The appearance of the version 5.1 screen is slightly different, but the steps listed here still apply.

Style(s) already exist. Replace? (Y/N) No

Press *N* to load only those styles without matching names, or *Y* to replace the existing ones with those from the disk.

Now let's see how to use the styles. Suppose you want to write a letter on legal-sized paper. You want to add your own inside address then print the title *Commercial Lease* in large boldfaced characters.

Follow these steps. If you quit WordPerfect after creating the style sheet above, retrieve it as just explained.

1. Press Alt-F8 to display the style sheet.

2. Highlight the Legal style.

3. Press **1** or **o** for On. The document screen returns but the code [Style On:Legal] has been inserted to select the legal-sized form.

4. Now select the style to insert your address.

   a. Press Alt-F8 to display the style sheet.

   b. Highlight the style named Address.

   c. Press **1** or **o** for On.

The document appears with your address centered. Both of these styles were open type, so you just turn them on without worrying about turning them off afterward. Now try the paired style for large boldfaced printing.

5. Turn on large boldfaced printing.

   a. Press Alt-F8 to display the style sheet.

   b. Highlight the style named Bigbold.

   c. Press **1** or **o** for On.

6. Type

   Commercial Lease

7. Press Return. The cursor did not go to the next line. Instead, it turned off the large boldfaced style because of how you defined the purpose of the Return key for this paired style.

8. Press Return again. With the style off, Return performed as normal.

9. Press F7 N N to clear the screen.

When a style is inserted, it includes all of the codes used to create it. They are treated as a unit, no matter how many individual formatting codes are included. To delete the format from the document, just delete the [Style On:] code from the text.

If you have a variety of codes that you use often, think about whether you sometimes use them together and sometimes alone. If you ever use them individually, enter each code in its own style. Then you can use them separately, or use several styles in the same document in combinations.

STYLE LIBRARY

If you use certain styles often, add them to the style library. This is a default style sheet that WordPerfect will load automatically the first time you press Alt-F8.

Warning
Users of version 5.1 should follow the special instructions under "Changing the Style Library," page 123.

Start by creating the styles and saving the style sheet. Then press Shift-F1 for the Setup menu and select *7* for the Location of Auxiliary Files option. Press *6* for the Style Library File option and enter the name of the style sheet that you want to use. Press Return three times to return to the document.

When you press Alt-F8 for the first time after starting WordPerfect, that style sheet will be loaded and the style names will be available on the menu.

To use a different style sheet as the library, just enter its name as the style library file. If you no longer want a library, delete the name at the prompt.

Finally, the Update option on the Style menu prompt line will reload the style library. Use this if you accidentally delete or edit styles in the library and you want to retrieve the original. If you really want to edit styles in the library, you must save the file again when you're done.

WordPerfect supplies a sample style library called LIBRARY.STY. It contains a number of useful formats. To use it, enter **LIBRARY.STY** at the Style Library File prompt.

SUMMARY

The style sheets and the style library can be powerful editing and formatting tools. They provide a means of creating and saving formatting styles and text that you use often. Once they are created, you can quickly format documents without repeating all of the keystrokes needed to reenter the codes—just turn on the style.

Remember, use the Style Library for those styles that you use often. Create and save other style sheets for styles and text that you use periodically but not every day. Then retrieve the appropriate style sheet when you have to enter a document that uses those formats.

Styles are very similar to another WordPerfect feature called *macros*. A macro is also a way to save and quickly recall codes and text. However, macros actually repeat the keystrokes, displaying any menus or selection lines on the screen as they are repeated. Styles are much faster because they are simply small sections of text (or codes) that are inserted.

■ DOCUMENT STYLES

There's still one other alternative to actually changing the default values: creating a *document style* with the Initial Codes option. This is a collection of formats just like a style in a style sheet except it's linked to one document. It holds the default values for that document without inserting any codes into the document, not even the [Style On] code that appears when you use style sheets.

Document styles, however, are only useful for line, page, and document formats, not for character formats such as boldface or underlining.

You can use a document style to store a collection of formats that you use quite often. Because they load automatically with the document, you don't have to load a style sheet or turn any codes on and off. And because you're not changing the default values, they don't interfere with documents you want formatted in other ways.

The best use of the document style is as a *template*—a document containing nothing but codes. When you want text formatted by those codes, start by recalling the template. Type the text but save it under a different name when you're done. This leaves the original template unchanged for use later on.

Follow these steps to create a document style for use with 3" by 5" index cards:

Warning

Users of version 5.1 should follow the special instructions under "Formatting Index Cards," page 126.

1. Press Shift-F8 3 to display the Format Document menu.

2. Press **2** or **c** for the Initial Codes option. The screen clears except for the scale line, just as it did when you entered codes to change the default values.

3. Enter the codes for a 3" by 5" form.

   a. Press Shift-F8 2 for the Format Page menu.

   b. Press **8** or **s** for the Paper Size option. The list of sizes appears.

   c. Press **O** to select Other and show the Width prompt.

   d. Type **5**, then press Return to reveal the Height prompt.

   e. Type **3**, then press Return. The list of types appears.

   f. Press **1** for the standard type.

   g. Press F7 three times to return to the document.

4. Save the template under the name INDEX.

   a. Press F7.

   b. Type *Index,* then press Return.

   c. Press **N** to clear the screen and remain in WordPerfect.

The Paper Size code is now attached to the document on the screen. You won't see anything if you reveal the codes, but the document now uses a 3" by 5" form.

The only way to change the initial settings is to repeat steps 1 and 2 above, then delete the codes displayed on the screen.

Whenever you want to use 3" by 5" index cards, recall the document INDEX. It will automatically be formatted by the initial settings selected.

You can also use the Format Document menu to change the default base font for the document. Press Shift-F8 3 3 to select the Initial Font option. The list of possible base fonts will be displayed. Highlight the font desired then press Return three times. No codes will be inserted in the text, but the selected base font will be used.

Style sheets and document styles with initial settings are useful in almost any application. However, they are ideal in offices where a number of specific formats are used. Style sheets and document styles save the typist from repeating the keystrokes necessary to format individual documents.

In several upcoming chapters, you'll see how handy these features can be.

VERSION 5.1 FEATURES

SETTING UP WORDPERFECT 5.1

Version 5.1 has several additional menus and options for changing default values. The main Setup menu, shown in Figure 5.16, contains these options:

Mouse	Determines the mouse type and port, double-click interval rate, submenu delay time, acceleration factor, whether you're using your mouse with the left or right hand, and the position of the mouse pointer after clicking with the right button.
Display	Sets the monitor and graphics board type, text screen type, the way text and menus are displayed on the screen, and options for the View Document display.
Environment	Sets default values for various WordPerfect operations.
Initial Settings	Determines the default settings for the format of the date, equations, and tables of authorities; the number of repeats used for the Esc key; merge code delimiters; codes to be used as the default document format; and print options normally set from the Print menu.
Keyboard Layout	Lets you redefine the function of almost any key and key combination.
Location of Files	Determines where WordPerfect expects to find files: the dictionary and thesaurus, style sheets, keyboard and macro files, document backups, and printer, document, and graphic files.

Adjusting the Screen Display   Press Shift-F1 or select File Setup to display the main Setup menu, then press *2* or *d* for the Display option. You'll see the Display menu (Figure 5.17). Press *1* for the Colors/Fonts/Attributes option, then press *1* for the Screen Colors option. Select attributes as discussed for version 5.0.

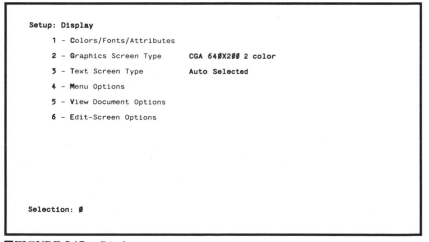

```
Setup

    1 - Mouse

    2 - Display

    3 - Environment

    4 - Initial Settings

    5 - Keyboard Layout

    6 - Location of Files




Selection: 0
```

■**FIGURE 5.16:** *Main Setup menu for version 5.1*

```
Setup: Display

    1 - Colors/Fonts/Attributes

    2 - Graphics Screen Type        CGA 640X200 2 color

    3 - Text Screen Type            Auto Selected

    4 - Menu Options

    5 - View Document Options

    6 - Edit-Screen Options




Selection: 0
```

■**FIGURE 5.17:** *Display menu*

Environment Options   You display the Environment menu (Figure 5.18) by pressing *3* or *e* from the main Setup menu. Environment options include:

Backup   Allows you to make automatic backup
                           copies of the document you're editing.

Beep Options	Determines when WordPerfect sounds a warning beep: on errors, hyphenation prompts, and search failure.
Cursor Speed	Sets the speed at which the cursor moves if you hold down a directional or character key.
Document Management/Summary	Sets whether summaries are to be automatically created when the document is saved, the subject search phrase, whether long document names should appear in the List Files directory, and the default document type.
Fast Save	Allows you to save text formatted or unformatted. Formatted text takes longer to save but will be printed faster from List Files.
Hyphenation	Chooses between use of the external dictionary or internal rules for automatic hyphenation. With the external dictionary, WordPerfect looks up the exact hyphenation point rather than using the general grammatical guidelines in the internal rules. Using the dictionary is slower but more exact.
Prompt for Hyphenation	Sets how frequently automatic hyphenation prompts you for input: Never, When Required, or Always. Select When Required as a compromise between totally automatic hyphenation (Never) and prompted (Always).
Units of Measure	Determines how certain measurements are entered: in inches (the default), or in centimeters, points, or lines and columns.

Changing File Location   When you want to change the storage of certain categories of files, press Shift-F1 or select File Setup to display the Setup menu, then press *6* or *l* for the Location of Files menu (Figure 5.19).

Select the category of files you want to specify, enter the complete path, then press Return. Press F7 to save the changes and return to the document.

Changing the Style Library   WordPerfect automatically tries to recall the file LIBRARY.STY when you first press the Style key, Alt-F8. If you want to use a set of files often, save it as a file and name the file LIBRARY.STY. Alternatively, you can make another style file the default style library and have it recalled whenever you press Alt-F8.

```
Setup: Environment

     1 - Backup Options

     2 - Beep Options

     3 - Cursor Speed                 50 cps

     4 - Document Management/Summary

     5 - Fast Save (unformatted)      Yes

     6 - Hyphenation                  External Dictionary/Rules

     7 - Prompt for Hyphenation       When Required

     8 - Units of Measure




Selection: 0
```

■**FIGURE 5.18:**   *Environment menu*

```
Setup: Location of Files

     1 - Backup Files

     2 - Keyboard/Macro Files          C:\WP51

     3 - Thesaurus/Spell/Hyphenation
                          Main         C:\WP51
                          Supplementary C:\WP51

     4 - Printer Files                 C:\WP51

     5 - Style Files                   C:\WP51
             Library Filename          C:\WP51\LIBRARY.STY

     6 - Graphic Files                 C:\WP51

     7 - Documents




Selection: 0
```

■**FIGURE 5.19:**   *Location of Files menu for version 5.1*

To change the default style library, press Shift-F1 6 (or File Setup Location of Files) and press 5 or *s* to select Style Files. Then press Return to reach the Library Filename prompt (or first enter a new location for style files if you wish), type a new file name, and press Return three times to return to the typing area.

Changing Mouse Defaults   You can adjust some features of the mouse through the Setup menu. Press Shift-F1 1 or select File Setup Mouse. You'll see options for changing:

Mouse Type	Designates the manufacturer of your mouse and its type.
Port	Designates the port to which the mouse is attached.
Double-Click Interval	Sets the amount of time you have between clicks when double-clicking. Setting the rate too fast might make it difficult to double-click within the interval; setting it too slow might result in two separate clicks being interpreted as a double-click.
Sub-Menu Delay Time	When you select a menu item, WordPerfect waits this amount of time before displaying any associated submenu. This also sets the amount of time the submenu is displayed before you can select an item on the menu.
Acceleration Factor	Determines how responsive the mouse pointer is to movement of the mouse. A higher acceleration factor makes the mouse pointer more responsive to movement. A factor too high, however, might make it difficult to make small and concise pointer movements.
Left-Handed Mouse	Lets WordPerfect know if you're using your left hand for mouse movements. If you set this option to Yes, then all button functions are the reverse of those listed previously. For example, clicking the left button displays the menu bar.

| Assisted Mouse Pointer Movement | When you display the menu bar or other menu with the mouse, the pointer usually remains at its current position. With this option set to Yes, the pointer jumps to the menu automatically when it appears on the screen. |

STYLES

The Style feature is basically the same as in version 5.0, with two exceptions. There is now an outline style type and several options for deleting styles:

Outline Styles   When you select Type from the Styles Edit menu you'll see the prompt

Type: 1 Paired; 2 Open; 3 Outline: 0

The Outline option is used to create a custom outline format. This will be discussed in Chapter 16.

Deleting Styles   When you delete a style, you'll see the prompt:

Delete Styles: 1 Leaving Codes; 2 Including Codes; 3 Definition Only: 0

Leaving Codes	Deletes the style, and replaces the Style codes in the document with the formatting codes of the style. Even though the style is deleted, the text remains formatted.
Including Codes	Deletes the styles, the Style codes, and the formatting codes. The text previously formatted by the style returns to the default format.
Definition Only	Temporarily deletes the style definition from the list of styles but leaves the Style codes and formats in the document. If you do not remove the Style code itself from the document and later return to the Style menu, the definition will again be listed. Use this option to delete styles that you are not actually using in the document.

SELECTING FORMS

Remember that forms are handled in a new way in version 5.1. Unless the form is predefined, or you've already defined it yourself, you must create the form before selecting it as a style.

Legal-Sized Forms   If you already have a legal-sized form for your printer, press Shift-F8 2 7 or select **L**ayout **P**age Paper **S**ize, highlight the form, then press Return three times.

 Otherwise, follow these steps in place of steps 11 and 12 under "Creating a Style Sheet":

11. Create and select a legal-sized form.

 a. Press Shift-F8 2 7 2 or select **L**ayout **P**age Paper **S**ize **A**dd to display the Paper Type menu.

 b. Press **1** to select Standard and display the Edit Paper Definition menu.

 c. Press **1** for the Size option, then press **3** for Legal size.

12. Press Return four times to select and enter the style codes.

Selecting Standard Paper   Follow these steps in place of step 21:

21. Select the standard form.

 a. Press Shift-F8 2 7 or select **L**ayout **P**age Paper **S**ize.

 b. Highlight the standard form.

 c. Press Return three times.

Formatting Index Cards   Follow these steps in place of step 3 under "Document Styles":

3. Create and select a 3-inch by 5-inch index card style using these steps:

 a. Press Shift-F8 2 7 2 or select **L**ayout **P**age Paper **S**ize **A**dd to display the Paper Type menu.

 b. Press **9** or **O** to select Other, displaying the prompt:

 Other form type:

 c. Type Index, then press Return. The Edit Paper Definition menu appears.

    d. Press **1** to display the Size options.

    e. Press **O** to display the prompt:

       Width: 0"   Height:

    f. Type **5**, then press Return.

    g. Type **3**, then press Return.

    h. Press Return four times to return to the typing window.

MOUSE AND MENU EQUIVALENTS

Function	Keyboard	Pull-Down Menus
Setup	Shift-F1	File Setup
Styles	Alt-F8	Layout Styles

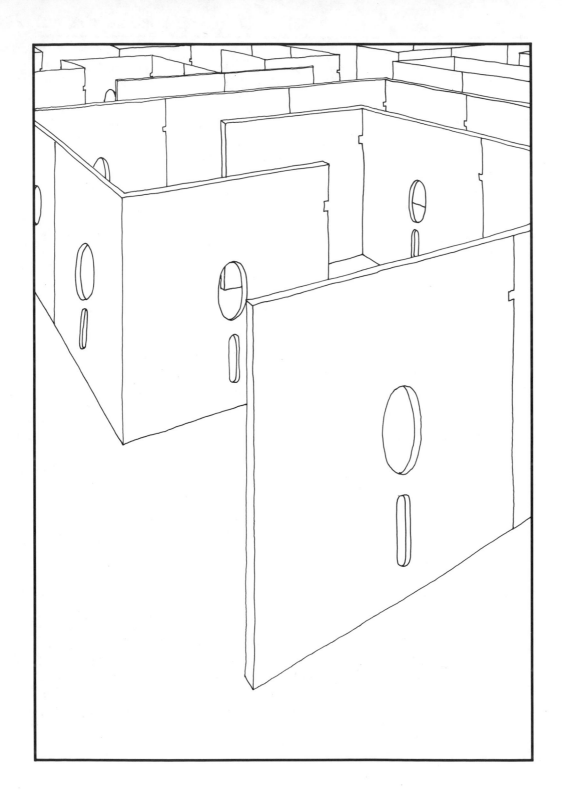

6

FORM LETTERS MADE EASY

Mr. Wilson, YOU can win $50 billion by just. . . .

Form Letters—Junk Mail—Mass Mailings.

Over the years, form letters have earned a bad reputation. They were pretty obvious in the old days. Some advertisement or letter was mass-produced, and then your name was just inserted in a few places.

Businesses had the same problem. When an office manager needed to send letters to every member of the board of directors, for example, there were two choices. The basic letter could be duplicated, then just the names and addresses typed in, or a secretary could spend the day typing individual copies.

Programs like WordPerfect have changed all that. Form documents, whether letters, legal contracts, or any other type of communication, can be produced quickly, with each copy looking like it was individually typed. In this chapter, you will learn some methods for producing such documents.

USING TEMPLATES

Most people think of using form documents only when they must produce a large volume of letters. But form documents can be used in a variety of situations. You might be sending an announcement to only 25 customers, requesting information from 10 different companies, or preparing a new lease for 12 tenants. You might produce one or two copies of a standard contract, agreement, or letter periodically throughout the year. Like the mass-produced letter, these documents generally remain the same; only a few words or phrases vary with each copy. In all of these cases, form documents can save you the trouble of typing the same document many times.

Form documents consist of two parts: shell text and variable information. *Shell text* is the part of the document that does not change. *Variable information,* on the other hand, must be personalized for each copy of the document. This might be a name and address, an amount due, or a quantity ordered. With WordPerfect, once the shell text is created, only the variable information must be typed for each document.

There are several methods of creating form documents with WordPerfect. The most efficient way to produce a small number of form documents, like those mentioned above, is to create a template. For larger productions, it's more efficient to use WordPerfect's Merge features, which are described in Chapter 20.

A *template* is a document that contains all of the shell text and formatting for the final copies. You add the variable information just before printing each copy.

CREATING THE ENVELOPE STYLE

You can streamline templates even more by using style sheets. So to get ready for creating form letters and envelopes in this chapter, you'll create a style that contains the codes for selecting and formatting the envelope form. Having these codes collected in a style will save you many keystrokes in your subsequent work.

Warning
Users of version 5.1 should follow the special instructions under "Creating the Envelope Form," page 145.

First, make sure you have an envelope form defined for your printer, and that Initially Present has been set to No.

If you don't have a laser printer, the form should use the envelope type (5) and size (5).

If you have a laser printer, things are a little more complicated. Not every laser printer feeds envelopes in the same way. The instructions here have been tested on a Hewlett Packard LaserJet printer. There are other possible combinations that may work—changing the page offsets, for example—depending on your own printer.

The method recommended is to create a form using the envelope type but a size of Standard Wide (11" by 8 1/2") in landscape orientation. Because of the envelope size and the way it feeds into the printer, a top margin of 6 inches places the address at the proper position.

In all cases, make sure Initially Present is set to No. This way, the printer will pause so you can insert an envelope after the letter is printed.

Press Shift-F7 S 3 4 to list the defined forms. If you don't see the correct envelope form, create it using the techniques explained in Chapter 3 and the specifications given above for your type of printer. Once the form is defined, follow these steps to use it in an envelope style:

1. Press Alt-F8 for the Style menu.

2. Press **3** or **c** to create a style.

3. Press **1** to select the Name option, type **Envelope**, then press Return.

4. Press **2 2** to set an open style type.

5. Press **4** or **c** to display the Codes screen.

6. If you do not have a laser printer, follow these steps to set the form and margins. We'll assume you defined an envelope form with manual feed, not initially present.

   a. Press Shift-F8 2 to display the Format Page menu.

   b. Press **8** or **s** to select Paper Size and display the Paper Size options.

   c. Press **5** or **e** for the envelope size.

   d. Press **5** or **e** for the envelope type. The Format Page menu should still be on the screen.

   e. Press **5** or **m** for the Margins option.

   f. Type **0** then press Return three times to eliminate the top margin. The Format menu will reappear.

   g. Press **1** for the Format Line menu.

   h. Press **7** or **m** to select the Margin option.

   i. Type **4**, press Return, then type **.5**.

   j. Press Return three times to accept the codes. Figure 6.1 shows the codes for this style sheet.

7. If you have a laser printer, follow these steps. We'll assume you defined the form as explained above—envelope type, Standard Wide, landscape orientation, not initially present.

   a. Press Shift-F8 2 to display the Format Page menu.

   b. Press **8** or **s** to select Paper Size and display the Paper Size options.

   c. Press **2** or **t** for the standard landscape size (the same as Standard Wide when defining the form).

   d. Press **5** or **e** for the envelope type. The Format Page menu should still be on the screen.

   e. Press **5** or **m** for the Margins option.

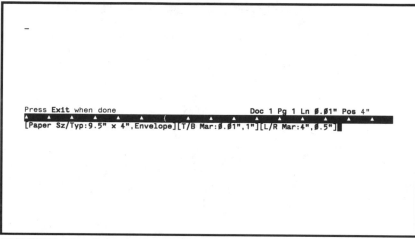

■**FIGURE 6.1:**   *Completed codes*

    f. Type **6** then press Return three times for a 6-inch top margin. The Format menu will reappear.

    g. Press **1** for the Format Line menu.

    h. Press **7** or **m** to select the Margins option.

    i. Type **5** then press Return four times. The codes are entered.

8. Press F7 twice to return to the Style menu.

9. Press **6** or **s** to save the style sheet.

10. Type **FORMS** then press Return.

11. Press F7 to return to the document.

CREATING A FORM DOCUMENT TEMPLATE

We will now create a model form document—a template. It will include the shell text that is needed for every copy of the document. At each place where some variable information is needed, we will insert a variable name. Next, we will personalize each letter by replacing the variable names with the appropriate information.

This example uses the envelope style you just created.

Follow the procedure below to create the form document template:

1. Start WordPerfect.

2. Press Shift-F6 to center the cursor on the page.

3. Press Shift-F5. This displays the prompt line

   1 Date Text; 2 Date Code; 3 Date Format; 4 Outline;
   5 Para Num; 6 Define:0

4. Press **2**. This inserts a Date Function code into the text. Although the current date is displayed on the screen, the date when the document is actually printed will appear on the finished copy. If you do not have an automatic clock circuit in your computer, the date printed will be the one that you entered when you started your computer. If you want all of the letters dated with the current date, select option 1 from the prompt line to insert the current system date as text, rather than as a code function. This date will appear on the finished copy, no matter when the letter is printed. In either case, the date will appear as the full month, day, and year (such as *May 2, 1991*). At the end of this chapter is a summary of how to change the date format.

5. Press Return.

6. Type the body of the letter, exactly as shown below.

   ADDRESS

   Dear SALUTATION:

   I want to welcome you to the growing family of companies entrusting their computer service to Emlen Electronics.

   Let me assure you, however, that FIRM will not become just another "client." Our goal is to do more than just respond to service calls. We want to maintain the total integrity of your computer system, preventing downtime and costly repairs. Toward this goal, I have asked REP to serve as your personal liaison with Emlen Electronics. FIRST will be calling you soon.

   Sincerely,

   John Emlen

   President

7. Press Ctrl-Return. This inserts a page break between the cover letter and the envelope template, as shown in Figure 6.2.

```
                              March 8, 1991

         ADDRESS

         Dear SALUTATION:

         I want to welcome you to the growing family of companies entrusting
         their computer service to Emlen Electronics.

         Let me assure you, however, that FIRM will not become just another
         "client." Our goal is to do more than just respond to service
         calls. We want to maintain the total integrity of your computer
         system, preventing downtime and costly repairs. Toward this goal,
         I have asked REP to serve as your personal liaison with Emlen
         Electronics. FIRST will be calling you soon.

         Sincerely,

         John Emlen
         President
         ==============================================================================


                                                    Doc 1 Pg 2 Ln 1" Pos 1"
```

■**FIGURE 6.2:** *A page break between the cover letter and the envelope template*

8. Insert the envelope style here so the second page is formatted correctly. (The style should still be available. If you left WordPerfect after creating the style sheet, however, recall the FORMS style sheet from the disk.)

   a. Press Alt-F8 to display the Style menu. The envelope style should be highlighted.

   b. Press **1** or **o** to turn the style on.

9. Press F7 Y to save the template.

10. Type **SERVICE** and press Return.

11. Press **Y** to exit WordPerfect.

This letter contains variable names in five places. Specific information for ADDRESS, SALUTATION, FIRM, REP, and FIRST must be added when each copy of the form letter is printed. The template also includes the formatting codes to print the envelope and a Date Function code to print the system date when each letter is printed.

PERSONALIZING FORM DOCUMENTS

Now that you've created the template for a form letter, you can easily personalize each one by inserting the appropriate variable information. To see how this works, we will recall the SERVICE template from the disk and replace each variable with specific information. The finished letter will look like Figure 6.3.

```
                          March 8, 1991

        Miss Nancy Harriet Chesin
        1Ø2 Adam Road
        Dallas, TX  976Ø1

        Dear Miss Chesin:

        I want to welcome you to the growing family of companies entrusting
        their computer service to Emlen Electronics.

        Let me assure you, however, that Reynolds Data Services will not
        become just another "client." Our goal is to do more than just
        respond to service calls. We want to maintain the total integrity
        of your computer system, preventing downtime and costly repairs.
        Toward this goal, I have asked Sigmund Delvany to serve as your
        personal liaison with Emlen Electronics. Sig will be calling you
        soon.

        Sincerely,

        John Emlen
        President
================================================================================
C:\WP5Ø\SERVICE                              Doc 1 Pg 1 Ln 1" Pos 4.9"
```

■**FIGURE 6.3:** *The sample form letter*

1. Start WordPerfect.

2. Press Shift-F10 to recall the template.

3. Type **SERVICE** and press Return. The SERVICE template appears on the screen.

4. Position the cursor on the variable name ADDRESS.

5. Press Ctrl-Backspace to delete the variable name from the text.

6. Type the following address:

   > Miss Nancy Harriet Chesin
   > 102 Adam Road
   > Dallas, TX 97601

7. Position the cursor on the word SALUTATION.

8. Press Ctrl-Backspace.

9. Type **Miss Chesin:**

10. In the same manner, replace FIRM with **Reynolds Data Services**, REP with **Sigmund Delvany**, and FIRST with **Sig**.

11. Place the cursor at the beginning of the first line of the address, press Alt-F4, and press ↓ until the entire address is highlighted.

12. Press Ctrl-F4 1 2 to copy the address.

13. Press PgDn to get to the top of the next page.

14. Press → to place the cursor at the proper indented position for printing the envelope. This moves the cursor past the [Style On] code.

15. Press Return to insert the address into the envelope template.

Do not save the personalized template on the disk with the same name as the original template. If you are not ready to print the form letter, save it under a different name. This way, the original template is available for producing more copies of the form letter to send to other clients.

PRINTING FORM LETTERS AND ENVELOPES

We will now print a copy of the form letter and its envelope. Because of the change of form, WordPerfect will pause so you can insert the envelope. Insert a piece of paper in your printer, then follow these steps:

1. Press Shift-F7 1 to print the first copy of the letter.
   The letter on the first page will print on the default standard type and size paper. After that page is ejected from the printer, the code for changing to an envelope form will take effect. Because the envelope form was set for manual feed and not initially present, WordPerfect will beep when it is ready to print.

2. Insert the envelope into the printer.
   If you have a laser printer, insert the envelope into the manual feed tray in the back of the machine. Insert it so the side to be printed on is facing up and the top of the envelope is facing toward the center of the tray, away from the alignment edge. Gently push the envelope in until it stops.

3. Press Shift-F7 4 G to print the envelope.

Remember, do not save this copy of the document.

To print the other letters, first press F7 N N. This clears the first personalized form letter from the screen. Then retrieve the original template and repeat the steps for inserting the variables and printing the letter and envelope.

Producing form letters in larger volumes is discussed in Chapters 20 and 21.

■ USING WINDOWS TO CREATE FORM LETTERS

If you need to produce form letters that are exactly the same except for the inside addresses and salutations, you can copy that information from one documentto another instead of typing it in. This technique is particularly useful if you will be using the same personal information for another group of letters or other documents.

CREATING A FORM LETTER TEMPLATE

Now we will create the form letter template into which we will later copy variable information from another document. Since only the address and salutation differ for each letter, we will not insert variable names. Follow these steps:

1. Start WordPerfect.

2. Type the following template, inserting three blank lines between the date and the body of the letter. You can press Shift-F5 1 to enter the date as text, or Shift-F5 2 to enter a Date code instead of typing the date itself.

   October 22, 1991

   The official registration period is now past, and our records indicate that you have not yet seen your departmental advisor. Your advisor must approve your course selection before you can register.

   If you plan to attend classes next semester, please make an appointment with Mrs. Wilson at 555-9869 by the end of this week.

   Dr. In Ho Kim
   Chairperson

3. Press F7 Y to save the template.

4. Type **NOTICE** and press Return.

5. Press **N** to clear the screen and remain in WordPerfect.

CREATING THE VARIABLE LIST DOCUMENT

In the previous example, you created form letters by typing the information directly into the template. After printing each letter, however, you did not save the personalized version, but instead reloaded the original template. This technique is fine as long as you will not need to use that personal information again. However, you might have a list of persons to whom you will be sending letters periodically. Rather than retyping the names and addresses each time, you can create a *variable list document* to be used with each group of form letters.

Follow the procedure below to create the variable list document.

1. The screen should already be empty. If not, press F7 N N.

2. Type the following addresses and salutations:

   Jeff Pague
   875 Fifth Street
   Philadelphia, PA 19114

   Dear Jeff:

   Kathi Siravo
   652B Holmes Avenue
   Philadelphia, PA 19116

   Dear Kathi:

   Victor Rossi
   54th and Woodland Avenues
   Philadelphia, PA 19115

   Dear Victor:

3. Press F7 Y to save the document and exit the program.

4. Type **LIST** and press Return.

5. Press **Y** to exit WordPerfect.

DISPLAYING THE TEMPLATE AND VARIABLE LIST

We now have two documents: a template of the shell text and a variable list. To insert the variable information into the template, we will first divide the screen into two windows. One window will contain the template; the other will display the variable list. Then we will copy the variable information into the template for each copy of the letter. Follow these steps:

1. Start WordPerfect.

2. Press Ctrl-F3 1 12 Return. The screen divides in half to display two windows.

3. Press Shift-F10.

4. Type **NOTICE** and press Return.

5. Press Shift-F3 to move the cursor to the second document window.

6. Press Shift-F10.

7. Type **LIST** and press Return. The variable list document appears in the bottom window, as shown in Figure 6.4.

```
    October 22, 1991


    The official registration period is now past, and our records
    indicate that you have not yet seen your departmental advisor. Your
    advisor must approve your course selection before you can register.

    If you plan to attend classes next semester, please make an
    appointment with Mrs. Wilson at 555-9869 by the end of this week.

  C:\WP5Ø\NOTICE                              Doc 1 Pg 1 Ln 2.5" Pos 7.5"
  (   ▼    ▼     ▼     ▼   · ▼     ▼     ▼     ▼    ▼     ▼   )   ▼     ▼
  Jeff Pague
  875 Fifth Street
  Philadelphia, PA  19114

  Dear Jeff:

  Kathi Siravo
  6528 Holmes Avenue
  Philadelphia, PA 19116

  C:\WP5Ø\LIST                                Doc 2 Pg 1 Ln 1" Pos 1"
```

■**FIGURE 6.4:** *The letter and variable list documents displayed for merging*

COPYING THE VARIABLE INFORMATION INTO THE TEMPLATE

Both the template and the variable information now appear on the screen. We will copy an inside address and salutation from document 2 to document 1 and print the first letter. Here is the procedure:

1. The cursor should already be in document 2. If not, press Shift-F3 to switch documents.

2. Place the cursor at the beginning of the first address and salutation.

3. Press Alt-F4, then press ↓ until the address and its corresponding salutation are highlighted.

4. Press Ctrl-F4 1 2 to copy the highlighted block.

5. Press Shift-F3 to switch to the top document.

6. Place the cursor at the left margin, two lines below the date in document 1.

7. Press Return to insert the address and salutation into the template.

8. Press Shift-F7 1 to print the form letter.

To print the next letter, delete the address and salutation from the template, then repeat the procedure above. Press F7 N Y when you are finished printing all the letters.

PRINTING ENVELOPES FROM THE VARIABLE LIST

You can print envelopes to accompany the form letters that we just printed. To do this, you will create a file of addresses using the same variable list document. The file will be formatted to print envelopes using a friction feed printer. Follow these steps:

1. Start WordPerfect.

2. Press Shift-F10.

3. Type **LIST** to recall the variable list document.

4. Press Home Home ↑ to make sure that the cursor is at the start of the document.

5. Recall the style sheet FORMS and insert the Envelope style into the document.

    a. Press Alt-F8 to display the Style menu.

    b. Press **7** or **r** for the Retrieve option.

    c. Type **FORMS** then press Return. The style sheet is retrieved and the envelope style is highlighted.

    d. Press **1** or **o** to turn on the style.

    e. Press F7 to return to the document.

6. Press F2 to start the search procedure.

7. Type **Dear** and press F2. The first salutation is displayed.

8. Press Ctrl-F4 2 3 to delete the salutation line.

9. Press Ctrl-Return to enter a page break.

10. Press F2 twice to locate the next salutation line.

11. Repeat steps 9, 10, and 11 until only the addresses remain.

12. Press F10.

13. Type **ENV** to save the document under a new name.

14. Position an envelope in the printer so that the printhead is where you want the first line of the address to appear.

15. Press Shift-F7 1 to print the document. You'll hear a beep, since Word-Perfect is waiting for the envelope to be inserted and the Go command to be given.

16. Press Shift-F8 4 G. The envelope will be printed.

17. Repeat steps 14 through 16 until all of the envelopes have been printed.

18. Press F7 N Y to exit WordPerfect.

■ USING THE REPLACE COMMAND WITH FORM DOCUMENTS

In the form letter in the first example, each variable name was used one time. It was a short document—short enough for you to find each variable by scrolling through the text with the ↓ key. Most mass-mailing form letters are like this.

But other form documents, such as contracts and proposals, may have the same variables repeated throughout. The name of the client, the company name, or specific terms might appear in several places. In these instances, the Replace command can be used to streamline the process of inserting variable information.

CREATING A CONTRACT WITH REPEATED VARIABLES

To see how the Replace command can be used to insert variable information, we will create a form document in which the same variable information is used several times. Follow this procedure:

1. Start WordPerfect.

2. Type the following text. Be sure to type all uppercase characters for the variable names.

   Agreement, dated DATE, between Emlen Electronics, a Pennsylvania Corporation, and CLIENT.

   CLIENT agrees to pay Emlen Electronics the sum of $AMOUNT within 30 days of DATE. In consideration for said payment, Emlen Electronics will provide repair services, including all parts and labor, for the following equipment maintained and operated at the offices of CLIENT:

ITEM   SERIAL   QUANTITY

CLIENT will contact Emlen Electronics when repair services are needed. Emlen Electronics will report on-site at the offices of CLIENT within 24 hours of contact.

If repair parts for equipment covered under this contract become unavailable, Emlen Electronics will notify CLIENT in writing. Thirty (30) days from said notice, Emlen Electronics will reimburse CLIENT a prorated share of the contracted service price. Said equipment will no longer be covered by the terms of this agreement.

Emlen Electronics

CLIENT

3. Press F7 Y.

4. Type **CONTRACT** and press Return.

5. Press **Y** to exit WordPerfect.

INSERTING INFORMATION WITH
THE REPLACE COMMAND

Now we will load the contract and use the Replace command to insert the variable information. Follow these steps:

1. Start WordPerfect.

2. Press Shift-F10.

3. Type **CONTRACT** and press Return.

4. Press Home Home ↑ to place the cursor at the beginning of the document.

5. Press Alt-F2 to begin the search and replace procedure. The status line changes to

w/Confirm? (Y/N) No

Note

The appearance of the version 5.1 screen is slightly different, but the steps listed here still apply.

6. Press Return to have each occurrence of the variable name replaced without confirmation.

7. Type **DATE**.

8. Press F2 and type **October 22, 1991**.

9. Press F2. Each occurrence of the word DATE will be replaced with *October 22, 1991*.

10. Press Home Home ↑. You will do this before inserting each variable to start the replacement procedure at the beginning of the document.

11. Press Alt-F2 Return.

12. Type **CLIENT**, press F2, type **Reynolds Data Services**, and press F2.

13. Press Home Home ↑.

14. Press Alt-F2 Return.

15. Type **AMOUNT**, press F2, type **2500**, and press F2.

16. Position the cursor under the column heading ITEM. Enter the following columns for ITEM, SERIAL, and QUANTITY:

IBM	PC3581	2
IBM	PC6409	50
IBM	PC4297	57
IBM	PC6542	87

Our sample contract is completed and ready to print. Although unconfirmed replacement is often risky, we could use it with the contract template because we took some precautions, such as typing each variable name in all uppercase letters. We also entered the search words in uppercase letters. If we had used lowercase letters in both places, the word *dated* in the first line would have been changed to *October 22, 1991d*.

PRINTING THE CONTRACT

Print this form document as you would any other. The next time you need to produce the same type of contract, simply recall the original template (by pressing Shift-F10 and typing *CONTRACT*) and repeat the replacement procedure.

After printing the form document, exit WordPerfect without saving the edited copy. This leaves the original template on the disk, ready for the next session.

■
THE DATE FORMAT

By default, the Shift-F5 options display the date as the complete month, day, and year, as in *May 2, 1991*. You can change the format to include all numerals (5/2/91), partial dates (5/1991), the exact time (May 2, 1991 10:35 am), the day of the week (May 2, 1991 Saturday), or even abbreviated months and days (Jan 1, 1991).

Follow these steps to change the date format:

Note

The appearance of the version 5.1 screen is slightly different, but the steps listed here still apply.

1. Start WordPerfect.

2. Press Shift-F5 3 to display the Date Format menu, shown in Figure 6.5.

3. Type the numbers corresponding to the elements that you want printed when the date or the Date code is entered. Enter them in the same order that you want them to appear, and add any text or punctuation to be included.

   You can insert leading zeros in front of date and time numbers that are less than ten, and abbreviate month and day names, by placing a percent sign (%) in front of the number.

New Feature

Additional related features in version 5.1 are discussed under "Date Formats," page 146.

   Here are some additional examples:

6, 3 1, 4	Tuesday, December 25, 1990
7:9 (0)	23:30 (pm)
(6) 2/1/5	(Friday) 3/19/91

```
Date Format

      Character    Meaning
         1         Day of the Month
         2         Month (number)
         3         Month (word)
         4         Year (all four digits)
         5         Year (last two digits)
         6         Day of the Week (word)
         7         Hour (24-hour clock)
         8         Hour (12-hour clock)
         9         Minute
         Ø         am / pm
         %         Used before a number, will:
                       Pad numbers less than 1Ø with a leading zero
                       Output only 3 letters for the month or day of the week


      Examples:  3 1, 4      = December 25, 1984
                 %6 %3 1, 4  = Tue Dec 25, 1984
                 %2/%1/5 (6) = Ø1/Ø1/85 (Tuesday)
                 8:9Ø        = 1Ø:55am


Date format: 3 1, 4
```

■FIGURE 6.5:   *The Date Format menu*

%2/%1/5   03/19/91

%3 1, 4   Dec 25, 1991

4. Press Return.

VERSION 5.1 FEATURES

CREATING THE ENVELOPE FORM

Check to see if you already have an envelope form defined for your printer. Press Shift-F8 2 7 to list the defined forms. Make sure the Prompt option is set at Yes, so the printer will pause for you to insert an envelope after the letter is printed.

If you don't have the form already defined, you can create it using the techniques explained in Chapter 3. The form should use the envelope type (5) and size (5).

There is already an envelope size predefined when you're using a laser printer. However, because of the way different laser printers handle manually fed envelopes, follow these suggestions:

■ Use or create a *standard wide* form—11 by 8 1/2 inches with a landscape font type.

■ Either set the location as manual, or use the printer's control panel to select manual feed.

CREATING THE ENVELOPE STYLE

We'll assume you have already created an envelope form with manual feed, and the Prompt option is set at Yes. Follow steps 1 to 5 in this chapter under "Creating the Envelope Style," and then continue here.

6. If you don't have a laser printer, follow these steps to create the envelope style:

   a. Press Shift-F8 2 7, highlight the Envelope form, then press Return to display the Format Page menu.

   b. Press **5** or **m** for the Margins option.

   c. Type **0** then press Return three times to eliminate the top margin. The main Format menu appears.

d. Press **1** or **L** for the Format Line menu.

e. Press **7** or **m** to select the Margin option.

f. Type **4**, press Return, then type **.5**

g. Press Return three times to accept the codes.

ENVELOPE STYLE FOR LASER PRINTERS

We'll assume that you defined the form as explained previously—as a standard wide form.

7. If you have a laser printer, follow these steps to create the envelope style:

a. Press Shift-F8 2 7, highlight the Envelope form, then press Return to display the Format Page menu.

b. Press **5** or **m** for the Margins option.

c. With printers such as the LaserJet II, IID, and IIP, type **4.5**. With older-model LaserJet printers, type **6.5**. These settings are for printing the address. You might have to adjust these settings to suit your own envelopes and spacing requirements.

d. Press Return three times to display the main Format menu.

e. Press **1** or **L** for the Format Line menu.

f. Press **7** or **m** to select the Margins option.

g. Type **4.5** and press Return four times to accept the codes.

DATE FORMATS

In addition to the percent sign (%) for padding numbers with zeroes, version 5.1 offers the dollar sign ($) for padding with spaces. Compare these formats:

2/1/5   1/1/91

%2/%1/5   01/01/91

$2/$1/5   1/ 1/91

Like the percent sign, the dollar sign also abbreviates the month and the day of the week.

MOUSE AND MENU EQUIVALENTS

Function	Keyboard	Keyboard
Date Code	Shift-F5 C	Tools Date Code
Date Format	Shift-F5 F	Tools Date Format

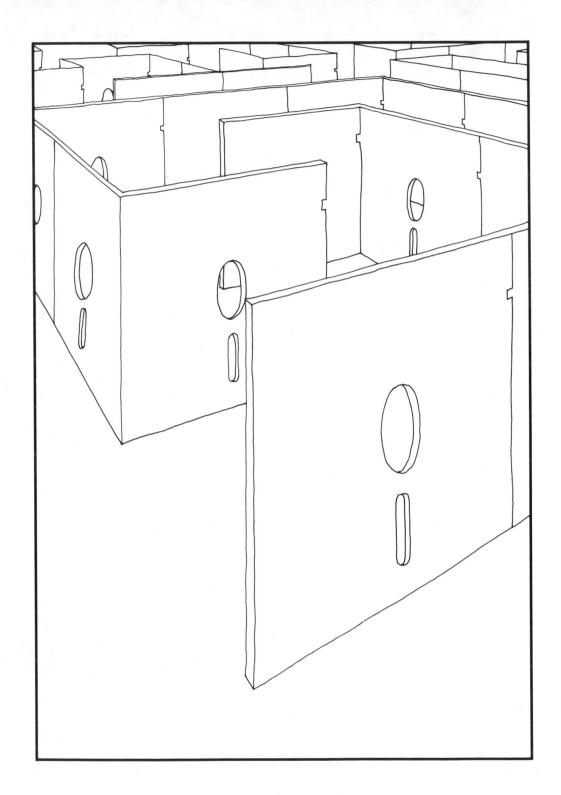

7

AUTOMATING YOUR WORK WITH MACROS AND BOILERPLATE TEXT

In the last chapter, you learned how to create form documents. We used a template and inserted or copied text wherever variable information was needed. In all of the examples, the variable text was only a word or two.

In this chapter, you will learn how to create documents using larger blocks of text, which are called *boilerplate* text. You already used boilerplate text in Chapter 5 when you created a style that contained the text of your address. That was boilerplate text because it contained text that you could quickly and easily insert into your document without typing it.

In this chapter, you will learn more about boilerplate text and something about WordPerfect's macros.

Boilerplate text and macros can be powerful tools for streamlining document creation. You can use macros as well as style sheets to enter often-used names, phrases, and complex format changes. We'll continue to explore the full potential of macros in later chapters.

USING BOILERPLATE MACROS

Boilerplate text is a sentence, paragraph, or entire section of text that is used in many different documents. It may be some special legal wording, a signature block, an advertising message, or a contractual term that is used repeatedly. Boilerplate text can be inserted into a document with a few keystrokes. In fact, some documents may be composed almost entirely of boilerplate paragraphs, with only a few words or lines typed individually.

A *macro* is a special command that activates a series of keystrokes automatically. You define the macro by deciding which keystrokes are activated and which keys are used to give the command. For example, you could define the keystrokes Alt-C to represent your standard letter closing. When you wanted to close a letter, you would just press Alt-C instead of typing the text.

Macros can be temporary—remembered by WordPerfect just during the current word processing session—or stored on disk. Temporary macros are handy when you will use a word or phrase frequently in a specific document. Macros stored on disk are useful when you will use a series of keystrokes in many different documents. First we'll explore the applications of stored macros. Temporary macros are discussed at the end of the chapter.

The most serious limitation of stored macros is disk space. You must have enough space on your disk to store your documents as well as the macro instructions. And, of course, to activate a macro you must use the disk containing it.

Depending on their type, macros are defined using the Ctrl-F10 or Ctrl-PgUp key combinations. You define a stored macro using Ctrl-F10 in one of two ways: give it a name up to eight characters long, or give it an Alt-letter combination. Alt-number macros, defined using Ctrl-PgUp, are temporary, not stored on disk. These are discussed later in the chapter. You can have a maximum of 26 Alt-letter macros on one disk (Alt-A to Alt-Z) and up to 10 Alt-number macros (Alt-0 to Alt-9) in the computer's memory. It's a good idea to use Alt-letter combinations to define macros that you will use often.

CREATING MACROS

As an example of how to define both named and Alt-letter macros, we'll create a series of macros for preparing project bids. Follow these steps:

1. Start WordPerfect.

2. Press Ctrl-F10. The status line displays

    Define Macro:

3. Press Alt-A. The prompt line changes to

    Description:

    This is your chance to briefly describe the function of the macro. It is only optional.

4. Type the following then press Return:

    Company name

    The words

    Define macro:

appear on the status line.

5. Type the following. (Do not press Return after typing boilerplate text to be stored as a macro, unless you want the return included in the text.)

    Fox and Associates, Inc.,

6. Press Ctrl-F10. This stores the text on disk under the name ALTA.WPM. The Alt-B macro would be stored as ALTB.WPM, etc.

7. Press Ctrl-F10 to define the next macro.

8. Type **NYLAW** and press Return twice to skip entering a description for the macro.

9. Type the following then press Return:

    This bid is submitted pursuant to the laws of New York State and, if accepted, its terms shall be binding on both parties.

10. Press Ctrl-F10 to save the keystrokes.

11. Press Ctrl-F10 to define a third macro.

12. Type **AMOUNT** and press Return twice.

13. Type the following then press Return Ctrl-F10:

    In consideration for the amount of $, Fox and Associates will perform the following services:

14. Using the same procedure, define and save a macro for the following paragraph. Name it ESTIMATE.

    This proposal represents an estimate of the cost of materials and labor. While every effort has been made to accurately compute all costs involved, the actual price of services, binding on both parties, will be stated in the final contract.

15. Define and save a macro for the following paragraph. Name it SIXTY.

    Fox and Associates will guarantee this price only for the next 60 days. We maintain the authority to adjust the bid if contracts are not formalized in that period.

16. Define and save a macro for the following paragraph. Name it THANKS.

    Fox and Associates greatly appreciates the opportunity to bid on this project.

17. Press F7 N Y to exit WordPerfect.

USING BOILERPLATE MACROS

An Alt-letter macro is retrieved by pressing its Alt-key combination. To retrieve a named macro, press Alt-F10 and enter the macro name.

Now we'll use the macros that we just created to prepare the bid shown in Figure 7.1. Follow this procedure:

1. Start WordPerfect.

2. Press Tab to indent the first paragraph.

3. Press Alt-A. The company name macro is recalled from disk, and the words *Fox and Associates, Inc.*, are inserted into the text.

4. Type the following, including two spaces after the last period:

    is happy to bid on your proposal for data processing training.
    We have been professional trainers for over 15 years.

5. Press Alt-A to insert the company name again.

```
        Fox and Associates, Inc. is happy to bid on your proposal
for data processing training. We have been professional trainers
for over 15 years. Fox and Associates, Inc. has earned an
outstanding reputation and we will be pleased to provide
references upon request.

        In consideration for the amount of $800.00,  Fox and
Associates will perform the following services:

        Provide two days of training on DBaseIII+ for two operators
at 6543 Fifth Avenue, Boston.

        Fox and Associates will guarantee this price only for the
next 60 days. We maintain the authority to adjust the bid if
contracts are not formalized in that period.

        This bid is submitted pursuant to the laws of New York State
and, if accepted, its terms shall be binding on both parties.

        Fox and Associates greatly appreciates the opportunity to
bid on this project.

        This proposal represents an estimate of the cost of
materials and labor.  While  every effort has been made to
accurately compute all costs involved, the actual price of
services, binding on both parties,  will be stated in the final
contract.
```

■**FIGURE 7.1:** *Sample bid document*

6. Type the rest of the sentence.

   has earned an outstanding reputation, and we will be pleased to provide references upon request.

7. Press Return.

8. Press Alt-F10. The prompt reads

   Macro:

9. Type **AMOUNT**, then press Return. The boilerplate text is recalled from the disk and inserted into the text.

10. Place the cursor following the dollar sign in that paragraph and type **800.00**. Delete any extra spaces between the number and the comma.

11. Place the cursor after the sentence, then press Return.

12. Type the following:

    Provide two days of training on dBASE III+ for two operators at 6543 Fifth Avenue, Boston, Massachusetts.

13. Press Return.

14. Press Alt-F10, type **SIXTY**, and press Return twice.

15. Press Alt-F10, type **NYLAW**, and press Return twice.

16. Press Alt-F10, type **THANKS**, and press Return twice.

17. Press Alt-F10, type **ESTIMATE**, and press Return. The document is now complete.

18. Press F7 N Y to exit WordPerfect.

PRINTING A MACRO CATALOG

Even the best word processor may forget what text is stored in each boilerplate macro. A list of macro names and the text that they include can be used for quick reference. In the following exercise, we will view and print a catalog of the macros that we just created. Here's the procedure:

1. Start WordPerfect.

2. Press F5.

3. Type ***.WPM**, then press Return. The screen displays a list of the macros stored on your default disk drive. To display macros on another disk,

precede this with the drive or subdirectory designator (e.g., C:\macs*.WPM).

4. Make a note of the macros, then press F7.

5. Type **ALT-A**, then press Return.

6. Press Alt-A, then press Return twice.

7. Type **AMOUNT**, then press Return.

8. Press Alt-F10, type **AMOUNT**, and press Return twice.

9. Type **SIXTY**, then press Return.

10. Press Alt-F10, type **SIXTY**, and press Return twice.

11. Type **NYLAW**, then press Return.

12. Press Alt-F10, type **NYLAW**, and press Return twice.

13. Type **THANKS**, then press Return.

14. Press Alt-F10, type **THANKS**, and press Return twice.

15. Type **ESTIMATE**, then press Return.

16. Press Alt-F10, type **ESTIMATE**, and press Return.

17. Press Shift-F7 1 to print the document. It shows each macro name, followed by the text it represents. You could also save this document on the disk under a name like WPM.CAT and recall it whenever you needed to refer to it.

18. Press F7 N Y to exit WordPerfect.

■ CREATING MACROS FOR FORMATTING AND PRINTING

So far, we have discussed boilerplate macros in terms of text. But boilerplate actually refers to any frequently repeated sequence of keystrokes. Thus, you can use boilerplate macros for such procedures as changing formats, printing documents, and moving blocks of text.

As an example of how these types of macros work, we will create several of them to be used with everyday correspondence.

A LETTERHEAD MACRO

This first macro is just like the ADDRESS style you created in Chapter 3. That is, it will print a letterhead name and address, centered on the page. Follow these steps to create it:

1. Start WordPerfect.

2. Press Ctrl-F10, type **HEAD**, and press Return.

3. Type **My letterhead** then press Return for the description.

4. Press Shift-F6, type **Chesin College**, and press Return.

5. Press Shift-F6, type **43rd and Walnut Streets**, and press Return.

6. Press Shift-F6, type **New York, NY 10012**, and press Return.

7. Press Return twice.

8. Press Ctrl-F10.

INDENTED PARAGRAPH MACROS

Our next macros will create a double spaced paragraph, indented 1 inch from both margins, and then return the settings to normal. Follow these steps:

1. Press Ctrl-F10 Alt-Z then Return to bypass the description.

2. Select double spacing.

    a. Press Shift-F8 1 to display the Format Line menu.

    b. Press **6** or **s** for the Line Spacing option.

    c. Press **2**.

    d. Press Return three times.

3. Press Shift-F4 Shift-F4 to indent two tab stops.

4. Press Ctrl-F10 to stop the macro definition, then press Return twice.

5. Press Ctrl-F10 Alt-X Return to create the macro that returns the settings to normal.

6. Enter the keystrokes for that macro.

    a. Press Shift-F8 1 to display the Format Line menu.

    b. Press **6** or **s** for the Line Spacing option.

    c. Press **1**.

    d. Press Return three times.

7. Press Ctrl-F10. This returns the text to single spacing. (We do not have to cancel the margin indentations because pressing Return after the end of the indented paragraph returns the margins to normal.)

CREATING MACROS FOR PRINTING

Our final macro will print the document in Draft mode. You would use this for quick copies of documents with graphics.

1. Make sure your printer is turned on. This is necessary because when you create a macro in this way, the keystrokes or commands are actually followed.

2. Press Ctrl-F10 Alt-C Return.

3. Press Shift-F7 to display the Print menu.

4. Press **T** for Text Quality, **2** for Draft mode, then Return.

5. Press Shift-F7 1 for the Print command.

6. Press Ctrl-F10 to end the macro definition.

USING MACROS FOR FORMATTING AND PRINTING

Formatting and printing macros are used in much the same way as boilerplate text macros. You'll see how handy they are in the following example, in which we'll create the letter shown in Figure 7.2 and print it in Draft mode.

1. Start WordPerfect.

2. Press Alt-F10, type **HEAD**, and press Return. Our letterhead appears.

3. Type the beginning of the letter.

    January 12, 1991

    Mr. Robert Williams
    53 Kinder Lane
    Willow Grove, PA 18985

Dear Mr. Williams:

The admissions committee has reviewed your application and is pleased to offer you a place in our September class.

4. Press Alt-Z to activate the macro for double spaced indented paragraphs.

5. Type the following:

However, it is imperative that you notify this office within ten days to hold your position. If we do not hear from you in that time, we will offer the seat to another student.

6. Press Alt-X to return to the normal format.

7. Type the following:

We are looking forward to hearing from you. We are confident the next year will be an exciting one for you.

Sincerely,

```
                        Chesin College
                    43rd and Walnut Streets
                      New York, NY 10012


January 12, 1991

Mr. Robert Williams
53 Kinder Lane
Willow Grove, PA  18985

Dear Mr. Williams:

     The admissions committee has reviewed your application and is
pleased to offer you a place in our September class.

                 However, it is imperative that you notify this

                 office within ten days to hold your position.

                 If we do not hear from you in that time, we

                 will offer the seat to another student.


     We are looking forward to hearing from you. We are confident
the next year will be an exciting one for you.

                              Sincerely,

                              Wilfred Magatel
                              Admissions Director
```

■FIGURE 7.2: *Sample letter*

Wilfred Magatel
Admissions Director

8. Press Alt-C to print a draft copy of the document.

As you can see, these types of macros are extremely useful tools. You can create similar macros to accomplish any task performed by a sequence of keystrokes.

■ EDITING MACROS

Macros are stored on the disk, but not like regular documents. The codes and characters that make up the macro cannot be printed from the disk, nor can they be recalled like a document and edited.

If you want to edit the text in a macro, or change any of the codes, you have to do so through a special Macro Edit function.

Let's see how to edit a macro. Suppose you just moved and you want to change your address in the HEAD macro that you created earlier. Follow these steps:

1. Press Ctrl-F10.

Note
The appearance of the version 5.1 screen is slightly different, but the steps listed here still apply.

2. Type **HEAD** and press Return. Instead of the Description prompt, you'll see

   HEAD.WPM is Already Defined. 1 Replace; 2 Edit:0

   You'll see this prompt when you try to create a macro with the same name as an existing one. If you want to create an entirely new macro, or rewrite a simple one instead of editing it, press **1** or **r**.

Note
The appearance of the version 5.1 screen is slightly different, but the steps listed here still apply.

3. Press **2** or **e** to edit the HEAD macro. The Macro Edit screen appears (Figure 7.3). The name and description you gave the macro appear on the top of the menu, and the text of the macro itself is in the box. Notice that formatting and other codes are shown by their function name within curly braces; these are not the codes you see displayed when you press Alt-F3. Also note that the macro is not shown fully formatted, so text isn't centered at the {Center} codes. That's because WordPerfect only formats the text according to the codes in the document.

   If you used any of the arrow or editing keys to correct mistakes while creating your macro, these keystrokes will also appear. For example, if you pressed Backspace to correct a mistake, the {Backspace} code will appear. This is your chance to delete these extra codes and characters.

The code {DISPLAY OFF} at the start of the macro is a special command inserted by WordPerfect. It causes the macro to be repeated without showing any menus or prompt lines that would appear if you were actually entering the keystrokes yourself. This way, the keystrokes don't appear one by one on the screen; instead, the entire macro is performed, then any codes or text inserted by it appear all at once.

If you want the keystrokes, menus, or prompt lines to appear, delete the {DISPLAY OFF} code as explained in step 4 below. However, macros without the code will take longer to execute.

To change the description, you would press *1* or *d*, enter the new description, then press Return. To change the macro itself, you press *2* or *a*. Let's do this now.

Warning
Users of version 5.1 should follow the special instructions under "Changing a Macro Description."

Warning
In version 5.1, the cursor automatically appears in the editing box.

4. Press **2** or **a** for Action. The cursor moves into the box.

    Inside the box, you insert and delete text, or delete codes, as you would in any document. To enter codes, however, you have to be in Macro Define mode.

    For example, say you want to change your address and add three blank lines at the end of the macro.

5. Using regular editing techniques, change the address to

    43rd and Chestnut Streets

6. Press Home Home ↓ to place the cursor at the end of the macro.

    If you press Return, the cursor will go to the next line but no {Enter}

```
    Macro: Edit

            File          HEAD.WPM

        1 - Description   My letterhead

        2 - Action

           ┌────────────────────────────────────────────────┐
           │{DISPLAY OFF}{Center}Chesin·Pharmaceuticals{Enter}│
           │{Center}43rd·and·Walnut·Streets{Enter}           │
           │{Center}New·York,·NY·10012{Enter}                │
           │{Enter}                                          │
           │{Enter}                                          │
           │                                                 │
           └────────────────────────────────────────────────┘

        Selection: 0
```

■**FIGURE 7.3:** *Macro Edit screen*

or [HRt] codes will be inserted and the returns will not be performed when you recall the macro later. To enter codes, you must be in Macro Define mode.

7. Press Ctrl-F10. The prompt

Press Macro Define to enable editing

appears under the box. In Macro Define mode you can enter codes and characters but you cannot edit. If you press the ← key to move the cursor you'll insert the {Left} command, and if you press the Backspace key you'll see {Backspace}.

8. Press Return twice to insert the extra lines. Two {Enter} codes appear next to each other at the end of the macro.

9. Press Ctrl-F10 to return to Edit mode.

10. Press F7 to leave Edit mode. The macro has now been changed.

11. Press F7 to return to the document.

Note
Step 10: version 5.1 users do not have to press F7 to exit the Edit mode.

When you use the HEAD macro, the new address and extra blank lines will be displayed.

■
SPECIAL MACROS

There are two alternatives to named and Alt-key macros that offer special advantages and reduce disk space usage.

UNNAMED MACROS

An unnamed macro is stored on disk under the default name WP{WP}.WPM. You can have only one unnamed macro, so when you define another later on, it replaces the original without giving you any warning or prompt. This makes it easy to rcplacc and useful for keystrokes that you only need to remember for a particular document.

To define an unnamed macro, just don't give it a name when you see the Macro Define prompt. Simply press Return. Enter the macro keystrokes then press Ctrl-F10 to end the definition.

To activate the macro, just press Alt-F10 Return.

ALT-NUMBER MACROS

An Alt-number macro (sometimes called an *assigned* macro) isn't saved on disk at all. It is linked with a combination from Alt-0 to Alt-9 and is recalled just by pressing the key combination. However, you don't create these using Ctrl-F10 but rather with Ctrl-PgUp. Here's how:

1. Press Ctrl-PgUp to see the prompt

   Variable:

2. Enter a number from 0 to 9. If you had text highlighted as a block when you pressed Ctrl-PgUp, that text will now be assigned to the Alt-number macro, so you would skip the rest of these steps.

   Otherwise, you'll see the prompt

   Value:

3. Type the text of the macro. Alt-number macros cannot include codes and can be up to 119 characters long.

4. Press Return.

To repeat the characters, press the Alt-number combination.

Using Alt-number Macros for Math   Alt-number macros can also be used to perform simple math operations such as addition (+), subtraction (−), multiplication (*), and division (/). Each macro can perform only one operation.

When you see the Value prompt, type a simple math operation, such as *34*65*, then press Return. To see the results of the operation, press the Alt-number combination.

You can't use any decimal or negative numbers in the operation. All results will be shown as positive whole numbers.

It certainly isn't a very useful or powerful way of doing math. But don't worry. In Chapter 19 you'll learn how WordPerfect can perform complex math operations. And in Chapter 20, you'll learn the real power behind these macros.

■ RUNNING A MACRO ON STARTUP

You can start WordPerfect and run one of your macros automatically by typing

   WP/M-(macroname)

The macro named on the command line will be executed as soon as the program is loaded. Let's say you have a macro called LEGAL that changes the form to legal-sized paper. To start WordPerfect and use that form immediately, enter

    WP/M-LEGAL

■ MACROS VERSUS STYLES

You now know two ways to store commonly used sections of text and codes—macros and styles. Each method has certain advantages that make it useful in specific applications.

For example, Alt-letter and Alt-number macros can be recalled instantly—Alt-letter from disk and Alt-number from the computer's memory. You don't have to go through any style menus or select from any prompt lines. Of course you are limited to 26 Alt-letter macros on one disk and 10 Alt-number macros in memory at any time.

Styles, on the other hand, can be linked with specific documents or stored in style sheets for collections of complex formatting instructions. You can have as many styles as will fit on your disk, including paired styles that turn on and off formatting functions. When in a style sheet, you can list the styles on the screen, read their descriptions, and edit their codes without worrying about switching between the Edit and Macro Define modes.

Both macros and styles are extremely useful when you need to repeat frequently used keystrokes, whether text or codes.

■ A USEFUL LIBRARY OF MACROS

Macros are so useful that you should build libraries of them and store them on disk. Floppy disk users must be prudent in the number of macros on their disks since macros take up room that may be needed for documents. If you have a floppy disk system, you can avoid the problem of filling up a disk with macros by creating several macro libraries and storing each on a different working copy of your system disk. Then, while you're working, use the disk containing the macros needed for that particular job. Hard disk users are fortunate; they can store an almost unlimited number of useful macros.

Here is a set of macros that most WordPerfect users find practical. Some of these can be used in place of the sample macros created earlier in this chapter.

GO—ALT-G

Issues the Go command when printing individual sheets of paper or envelopes.

Ctrl-F10 Alt-G Return Shift-F7 4 G Return Return Ctrl-F10

FORMAT RESET—ALT-F

Resets margins, tabs, fonts, and line spacing to normal.

Ctrl-F10 Alt-F Return Shift-F8 1 6 1 Return 7 1 Return 1 Return 8
Home Home ← Ctrl-End 0.0,.5 Return F7 F7 Ctrl-F8 3 Ctrl-F10

Warning
Users of version 5.1 should follow the special instructions under "Macro Library."

TITLE PAGE—ALT-P

Centers text between the top and bottom margins.

Ctrl-F10 Alt-P Return Shift-F8 2 1 F7 Ctrl-F10

DOUBLE SPACE—ALT-D

Changes to double spacing. Earlier in this book we defined an Alt-D macro. So the *1* after the first Return is used to select Replace. If you didn't define the macro earlier, or did so on another directory, don't enter the first *1* when creating the macro here.

Ctrl-F10 Alt-D Return 1 Shift-F8 1 6 2 Return Return Return
Ctrl-F10

Warning
Users of version 5.1 should follow the special instructions under "Macro Library."

PAGE NUMBER—ALT-N

Turns on page numbering at the bottom center of each page.

Ctrl-F10 Alt-N Return Shift-F8 2 7 6 Return Return Ctrl-F10

LEGAL FORM—ALT-L

Selects the legal-sized form.

Ctrl-F10 Alt-L Return Shift-F8 2 8 3 1 Return Return Ctrl-F10

FONT CHANGE MACROS

Use these macros for a quick change to a new printing font. The letters used are on the top row of the keyboard running left to right from fine to extra large. For example, Alt-Q changes to the fine font, the smallest, while Alt-Y is used for extra large. Each macro first resets the font to normal to avoid conflicting formats. Alt-E selects the normal font alone.

FINE FONT—ALT-Q

Ctrl-F10 Alt-Q Return Ctrl-F8 3 Ctrl-F8 1 3 Ctrl-F10

SMALL FONT—ALT-W

Ctrl-F10 Alt-W Return Ctrl-F8 3 Ctrl-F8 1 4 Ctrl-F10

NORMAL FONT—ALT-E

Ctrl-F10 Alt-E Return Ctrl-F8 3 Ctrl-F10

LARGE FONT—ALT-R

Ctrl-F10 Alt-R Return Ctrl-F8 3 Ctrl-F8 1 5 Ctrl-F10

VERY LARGE FONT—ALT-T

Ctrl-F10 Alt-T Return Ctrl-F8 3 Ctrl-F8 1 6 Ctrl-F10

EXTRA LARGE FONT—ALT-Y

Ctrl-F10 Alt-Y Return Ctrl-F8 3 Ctrl-F8 1 7 Ctrl-F10

■

VERSION 5.1 FEATURES

CHANGING A MACRO DESCRIPTION

When you enter the name of an existing macro at the Define Macro prompt, you'll see the prompt

Macro-name.WPM is Already Defined. 1 Replace; 2 Edit; 3 Description: 0

To change the description, press *3*, type the new description, then press Return. The Macro editing screen appears. If you don't want to edit the macro itself, press F7 to return to the document. Otherwise, edit the macro as explained under "Editing Macros," then press F7.

MACRO LIBRARY

Because of changes in the format menus, the keystrokes for creating several macros in version 5.1 are different from those given earlier. Uses these keystrokes instead:

Title Page Macro	Ctrl-F10 Alt-P Return Shift-F8 2 1 Y F7 Ctrl-F10
Page Number Macro	Ctrl-F10 Alt-N Return Shift-F8 2 6 4 6 Return Return Return Ctrl-F10

MOUSE AND MENU EQUIVALENTS

Function	Keyboard	Pull-Down Menus
Create Macro	Ctrl-F10	Tools Macro Define
Execute Macro	Alt-F10	Tools Macro Execute

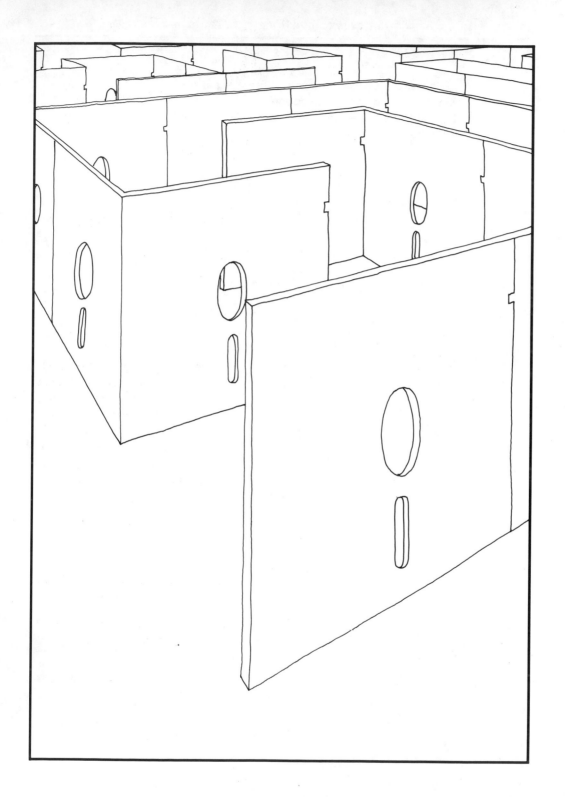

8

PARAGRAPH INDENTATIONS FOR ADDED EMPHASIS AND FLEXIBILITY

The default paragraph format used by WordPerfect is *block style*. Every line, including the first one in each paragraph, starts at the left margin, and sentences wrap around when they reach the right margin.

When you want to use an indented paragraph format, you have several options. As with all of WordPerfect's settings, you can change the default paragraph style, or you can use the Tab key to indent paragraphs or type columns of numbers. Another alternative is to change the left or right margin, or both.

But in some documents, none of those methods are efficient because more frequent paragraph format changes are required. Some paragraphs should be wide, some narrow. Long quotations, for example, should be indented from both the left and right margins. Sections of legal contracts might be indented at several levels, with each level representing a refinement of the point before it.

In this chapter, you will learn how to create various indented paragraph formats that you can switch in and out of quickly.

INDENTING ENTIRE PARAGRAPHS

You might want to indent a whole paragraph, like this one, to make a specific point stand out. Because all of the lines are indented, the paragraph catches the reader's eye and adds impact to the text.

Or, you might need several indented levels to stress relationships among the subjects discussed at each level.

You might also want to indent a paragraph on both the right and left margins. This is the format for long quotations.

The first two examples have a new left margin. Word wrap returned the cursor to the new setting, not to the original margin position. The last example has new right and left margins.

These paragraphs could be created by actually resetting the margins, but this is cumbersome if you want to switch back and forth among several paragraph styles in one document. Instead, you can change the margin temporarily. When you use WordPerfect's Indentation function, the new margins stay in effect until you press the Return key, which means that you can format individual paragraphs quickly.

LEFT INDENTATIONS

Pressing the F4 key creates a temporarily indented left margin. Each time you press the key, the left margin moves to the next tab stop on the right. Press F4 once to indent a paragraph 1/2 inch, twice for a 1-inch indentation, and so on.

To see how this works, we will create a document with several levels of indented paragraphs. Follow the steps below:

1. Start WordPerfect.

2. Press Shift-F6 to center the cursor.

3. Type the following heading:

   Classifications of Living Things

4. Press Return.

5. Type the following paragraphs using the default paragraph format. Remember to press Return between paragraphs.

   Living things are classified to identify the groups to which they belong. The several levels of classification refine the group from general to specific.

   The first level is Kingdom. This group is divided into plants and animals. It is the largest division of living things. Because it is so large, knowing the Kingdom of a living thing does not tell us much about the organism. The Kingdom of the anteater is Animalia.

6. Press Return, press F4 to indent the next paragraph 1/2 inch, and type the following text:

> The second level is Phylum. Phylum is the largest division of a Kingdom. It is based on specific traits from the appearance of the living thing. The Phylum of the anteater is Chordata.

7. Press Return, press F4 twice to indent the next paragraph 1 inch, and type the following text:

> The third level is Class. Class is the largest division of a Phylum. The Class of the anteater is Mammalia.

8. Press Return, press F4 three times, and type the following text:

> The fourth level is Order. The members of this division possess body parts and structures that are very much alike. The Order of the anteater is Edentata.

9. Press Return, press F4 four times, and type the following text:

> The fifth level is Family. This is a division within an Order. The Family of the anteater is Myrmecophagidae.

10. Press Return, press F4 five times, and type the following text:

> The sixth level is Genus. These living things share closely related features. The Genus of the anteater is Myrmecophaga.

11. Press Return, press F4 six times, and type the following text. You'll have to press F4 six times again to enter the second paragraph since you'll cancel the indentation when you press Return.

> The seventh level is Species. This is normally the lowest unit. It includes all organisms of similar kind. The Species of the anteater is Tridactyla.
>
> The Species of the octopus is Vulgaris.

12. Press Return, press F4 five times, and type the following text:

> The Genus of the octopus is Octopus.

13. Press Return, press F4 four times, and type the following text:

> The Family of the octopus is Octopodidae.

14. Press Return, press F4 three times, and type the following text:

> The Order of the octopus is Octopoda.

15. Press Return, press F4 twice, and type the following text:

The Class of the octopus is Cephalopoda.

16. Press Return, press F4 once, and type the following text:

The Phylum of the octopus is Mollusca.

17. Press Return, then type the following text:

The Kingdom of the octopus is Animalia.

18. Press Shift-F7 1 to print the document.

19. Press F7 N Y to exit WordPerfect without saving the text.

As this example demonstrates, the F4 key gives you the flexibility to vary the paragraph format quickly.

■   ADJUSTING INDENTATION LEVELS

Since the levels of indentation created by the F4 key are always at the tab stop positions, 1/2 inch apart, you can actually have eleven levels across the page. However, this becomes impractical after about six indentations because the resulting paragraphs are very narrow. Using the default tab stops, for example, the ninth level paragraph would be only about 20 characters wide.

Paragraph 1

Paragraph 2

Paragraph 3

Paragraph 4

Paragraph 5

Paragraph 6

Paragraph 7

Paragraph 8

Paragraph 9

Notice how narrow
this paragraph is!

You can increase the number of practical levels by setting the tab stops closer together.

To change the tab stops for smaller indentation levels, press Shift-F8 1 8 to display the Tab Set form. Press Ctrl-End to delete all tab stops, then reset them. For example, you could set tab stops every two spaces across the page by pressing 1,.2 Return F7.

The indentation levels would appear like this:

Paragraph 1

   Paragraph 2

      Paragraph 3

         Paragraph 4

            Paragraph 5

               Paragraph 6

                  Paragraph 7

                     Paragraph 8

                        Paragraph 9

CENTERING PARAGRAPHS—INDENTING BOTH MARGINS

The F4 key can only be used to indent the left margin of paragraphs. If you want both the left and right margins indented, such as for a long quotation, use the Shift-F4 key combination. Each time you press Shift-F4, the left margin moves 1/2 inch to the right, and the right margin moves 1/2 inch to the left. When text is justified, Shift-F4 has the effect of centering the paragraph as a block on the page. (Shift-F6 centers only individual lines.) Unjustified lines will not appear centered because the right margin will not be aligned at the indentation position.

If you want the normal right and left margins indented for an entire document, then you should reset the margins using the Format Line menu. When you want to center only one or a few paragraphs, use Shift-F4 instead.

Let's use the Shift-F4 key combination to produce the document shown in Figure 8.1. Follow these steps:

1. Start WordPerfect.

```
The organizational structure of the College clearly reflects its
emphasis on administrative excellence, academic research, and
integrity. This emphasis is expressed in the Statement of College
Goals.

     "The President directs the overall effort of the College
     to meet its goals and commitments. He serves on the Board
     of Trustees."

          "The Academic Vice President guides the various
          academic departments. The Vice President is
          responsible for maintaining the cohesiveness
          which supports a progressive educational
          program."

               "The Academic Dean maintains high
               quality   education   and   support
               programs."
```

■**FIGURE 8.1:**   *Master document containing Subdoc codes*

2. Type the first paragraph using the default paragraph format.

   The organizational structure of the College clearly reflects its emphasis on administrative excellence, academic research, and integrity. This emphasis is expressed in the Statement of College Goals.

3. Press Return, press Shift-F4, and type the following text:

   "The President directs the overall effort of the College to meet its goals and commitments. He serves on the Board of Trustees."

4. Press Return, press Shift-F4 twice, and type the next paragraph. You do not have to release the Shift key each time—hold the Shift key down while you press F4 twice.

   "The Academic Vice President guides the various academic departments. The Vice President is responsible for maintaining the cohesiveness which supports a progressive educational program."

5. Press Return, press Shift-F4 three times, and type the final paragraph.

   "The Academic Dean maintains high quality education and support programs."

6. Press Shift-F7 1 to print the document. If WordPerfect is set for justified printing, each paragraph will appear neatly centered below the one above.

7. Press F7 N Y to exit WordPerfect.

Make sure that you understand the difference between left and right indentations and left and right margins. Indentations are temporary margins set by pressing F4 or Shift-F4. The effects of these keys are canceled when you press Return. To indent more than one paragraph, you must press F4 or Shift-F4 before you type each one. Margins, on the other hand, stay in effect for the entire document or until you change them.

■ INDENTING EXISTING PARAGRAPHS

If you've already typed the text using the default margins or another paragraph style, you can still indent it. First delete any tab stop spaces in the first line. Then, with the cursor on the first character of the paragraph, press F4 or Shift-F4 to reach the desired level. When you move the cursor, the entire paragraph will adjust to that indentation.

■ HANGING INDENTATIONS

A common paragraph format is to have the first line indented, with the remaining text flush on the left. *Hanging indentations* are just the opposite. Subsequent lines are indented to the right of the first line, which "hangs" out to the left.

1. These lines are an example of a paragraph with hanging indentation. The text is indented to the right of the level number. In this case, the level number *1.* is at the left margin.

To create a paragraph with an indented first line, you press Tab to indent the first line at the tab stop, and word wrap aligns the continuing text lines at the left margin. For hanging indentations, the two actions are reversed. The first line starts at the left margin, and word wrap continues long lines at the indented margin (the tab stop).

By moving the left margin and indentation positions, you can create several levels of hanging indentations.

NUMBERED PARAGRAPHS AND QUICK OUTLINES

Hanging indentations are commonly used to create numbered paragraphs and outlines. WordPerfect provides an outline feature (discussed in Chapter 16) that will automatically add the appropriate outline numbers for the level of indentation. But if you're entering a short outline, you can enter the numbers yourself and create the indentation levels using the F4 and Tab keys.

As an example, we'll create the portion of a topical outline shown in Figure 8.2. Follow these steps:

1. Start WordPerfect.

2. Press Shift-F6 then type **The Mexican War of 1846.**

3. Press Return twice.

4. Type **1.** then press F4.

5. Type **Basic Causes** then press Return.

6. Press Tab to reach the second outline level.

7. Type **a.** then press F4.

8. Type **Texas** then press Return.

9. Press Tab twice to reach the third outline level.

10. Type **(1)** then press F4.

```
                    The Mexican War of 1846.

1.      Basic Causes
        a.      Texas
                (1)     Government claim that Texas bordered on the Rio
                        Grande
                (2)     Mexican resentment over Texan War for Independence
                        1836
        b.      Other Policies
                (1)     Policy of manifest destiny
                (2)     Previous failure to purchase New Mexican Territory.


2.      Precipitative Causes
        a.      President Polk ordered General Taylor to the dispute area
        b.      General Taylor's troops encountered Mexican troops
        c.      Hostilities erupted, and lives were lost on both sides
        d.      President Polk asked Congress to declare war
```

■**FIGURE 8.2:** *Sample outline*

11. Type **Government claim that Texas bordered on the Rio Grande** then press Return.

12. Press Tab twice.

13. Type **(2)** then press F4.

14. Type **Mexican resentment over Texan War for Independence 1836**, then press Return.

15. Press Tab once.

16. Type **b.** then press F4.

17. Type **Other Policies** then press Return.

18. Press Tab twice.

19. Type **(1)** then press F4.

20. Type **Policy of manifest destiny** then press Return.

21. Press Tab twice.

22. Type **(2)** then press F4.

23. Type **Previous failure to purchase New Mexican Territory**.

24. Press Return twice. The first section is completed.

25. Enter the second paragraph. Type the first-level number, **2.**, at the left margin, then press F4 to indent the text. Use the Tab key to indent to the additional levels, type the number, then press F4 to indent the text.

> 2. Precipitative Causes
>   a. President Polk ordered General Taylor to the dispute area
>   b. General Taylor's troops encountered Mexican troops
>   c. Hostilities erupted, and lives were lost on both sides
>   d. President Polk asked Congress to declare war

26. Press Shift-F7 1 to print a copy of the outline.

27. Press F7 N Y to exit WordPerfect.

As our example shows, pressing F4 sets a temporary left margin at the tab stop to the right of the cursor. If you are typing hanging indentations for numbered paragraphs, use the Tab key to reach the position where you want the hanging number to appear. Type the number, then press F4. Subsequent lines will be indented to the right of the number.

For large projects, this technique is not as efficient as WordPerfect's automatic outlining feature, but for smaller documents, it actually saves a few keystrokes.

HANGING TEXT

This is also an example of a hanging indentation. The first line "hangs" to the
    left of the remaining text in the paragraph.

Hanging paragraphs, just like indented ones, can have various levels. This kind of hanging indentation cannot be created with the Tab key. Here, there is no tab space between the hanging characters and the remaining text on the first line. You create this style using Shift-Tab to release the left margin. The process is just the reverse of that used for numbered paragraphs. For this style, press F4 until you reach the tab stop where you want word wrap to continue long lines, then press Shift-Tab to back up until the cursor is positioned where the first line should start.

Let's create the document shown in Figure 8.3. Follow these steps:

1. Start WordPerfect.

2. Press Shift-F6 to center the cursor, then type **Work Rule Notification**.

3. Press Return twice. Notice that the first paragraph contains hanging text. Only the first line starts at the left margin; the remaining lines are indented 1/2 inch.

```
                    Work Rule Notification

All supervisors must notify their shift workers that the new work
    rules go into effect at 9 a.m. this Monday. Make sure they
    understand the following major points:

    Lunch must now be taken between noon and 1 p.m. Floating lunch
        periods are no longer allowed.

    Breaks must be taken as posted on the duty roster at the plant
        entrance.  Scheduling breaks  in  this  way  ensures  no
        downtime.

        Penalties will be applied if break times are changed or
            breaks exceed the allotted period.

        Employees  wishing  to  change  their  break  times  due  to
            health   or   other   reasons   must   first   receive
            permission from their shift supervisor.
```

■**FIGURE 8.3:** *The menu for adding a new student to the address list*

4. Press F4 to place the cursor on the indented position.

5. Press Shift-Tab. This moves the cursor back one tab stop.

6. Type the first paragraph. Word wrap will indent the second and third lines.

> All supervisors must notify their shift workers that the new work rules go into effect at 9 a.m. this Monday. Make sure they understand the following major points: ·

7. Press Return to end the paragraph and cancel the indentations, then press Return again.

8. Press F4 twice, then press Shift-Tab.

9. Type the next paragraph, which will be indented 1/2 inch from the first paragraph.

> Lunch must now be taken between noon and 1 p.m. Floating lunch periods are no longer allowed.

10. Press F4 twice, then press Shift-Tab.

11. Type the next paragraph.

> Breaks must be taken as posted on the duty roster at the plant entrance. Scheduling breaks in this way ensures no downtime.

12. Press Return twice. The final two paragraphs will be indented one additional level.

13. Press F4 three times, then press Shift-Tab.

14. Type the next paragraph.

> Penalties will be applied if break times are changed or breaks exceed the allotted period.

15. Press Return twice.

16. Press F4 three times, then press Shift-Tab.

17. Type the last paragraph.

> Employees wishing to change their break times due to health or other reasons must first receive permission from their shift supervisor.

18. Press Shift-F7 1 to print a copy of the text.

19. Press F7 N Y to exit WordPerfect.

As with regular indented paragraphs, hanging indentations become impractical after the seventh or eighth level. Using the default tab stops, for example, the ninth text paragraph would have a twenty-character first line and fifteen-character lines following.

■ OTHER INDENTED FORMATS

With WordPerfect, you can create a variety of indented formats. For example, take a look at the text below:

Speakers for each session are:

Morning

Mrs. Barbara Neibauer
Philadelphia College of Pharmacy and Science

Sister Loretta
Holy Family College, Philadelphia

Mr. John B. Smiler
Philadelphia College of Textiles and Science

Afternoon

Dr. Vince Gorman
Princeton University

Dr. Averil H. Boxiter
Williamsport College

This format can be created in a number of ways. The easiest method is to use Alt-F6, which moves the cursor to the right margin. As you type, the characters will move toward the left. Like Shift-F6, Alt-F6 only works on the current line, so press Return when the text extends as far left as you want it. In two of the lines above, Alt-F6 was pressed after typing a word on the line (*Morning* and *Afternoon*).

Many other combinations of paragraph styles are possible. The example below was created using Shift-F4 to indent both margins and Alt-F6 to right-align the dollar amount.

For three hours of word processing
training at your offices: $180.00

For monthly maintenance as per our
service agreement: $225.00

■ DELETING INDENTATIONS

You can remove or change paragraph indentations without revealing the codes, but it is much easier with the codes displayed (by pressing Alt-F3). Then you can remove indentations by simply placing the cursor on the Indentation code and pressing Del. Keep pressing Del until the paragraph appears as desired.

If the codes aren't revealed, place the cursor in the blank space to the left of the first line of the indented text, then press Del.

This information should give you the courage to experiment with indented paragraph formats. If you don't like a format, just delete the codes and start over.

■ INDENTATIONS AND PITCH CHANGES

WordPerfect automatically adjusts the spacing when you select a font other than normal size. You don't have to make any special adjustments to the margins.

■ VERSION 5.1 FEATURES

MOUSE AND MENU EQUIVALENTS

Function	Keyboard	Pull-Down Menus
Flush Right	Alt-F6	Layout Align **F**lush Right
Indent	F4	Layout Align **I**ndent ->
Indent	Shift-F4	Layout Align In**d**ent -><-
Margin Release	Shift-Tab	Layout Align **M**argin Rel <-

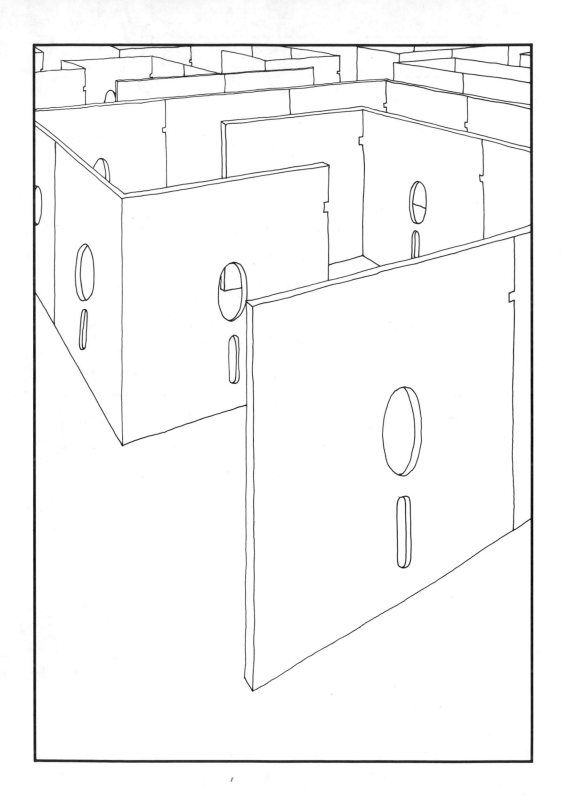

9

MULTICOLUMN DOCUMENTS: THE FIRST STEPS IN DESKTOP PUBLISHING

In all of the exercises up to this point, you've typed single-column text—each line stretches across the entire page. In fact, most business documents are typed as a single column. No matter what the margins are, there is just one line of text on each line of the page.

Newsletters, journals, and some other types of documents appear in more than one column. The text is printed in several lines across the page. Short columns like this are often easier to read.

There are several key factors in creating multicolumn pages. You must consider the width of the page, the number of columns desired, and the amount of space between each column.

This chapter presents techniques for creating multicolumn documents, including those with single-column and multicolumn text on the same page—a common newsletter format. You will learn how to create documents containing both newspaper-type and parallel columns. *Newspaper* columns are those in which the text automatically runs from one column to the next, as shown in Figure 9.1. With this style, the writer does not care which text falls in which column. *Parallel* columns contain text that must remain side by side, as in Figure 9.2. Usually, the text in one column refers directly to the text in the column next to it.

■ COLUMNS AND PAGE LAYOUTS

You should not create columns of text haphazardly. Columns that are too narrow are unattractive and difficult to read.

This para-
graph, for
example, is
just 1 inch
wide. It's
not the type
of thing
you could
read all
day.

Columns that are too close together are also difficult to read. The text appears as one large block.

These three There is not enough room should have left more
columns, for between the columns to "white space" around
example, are too make them pleasant to read. each of the columns.
close together. The word processor

As a rule, don't try to fit columns that are too wide into too little space. The white space on a page contributes greatly to its overall appearance and readability. Leave enough room for adequate right and left margins. Fortunately, WordPerfect does most of the page layout work for you—it calculates the appropriate sizes of columns and margins. You only need to specify how much distance you want between columns.

The real power of WordPerfect lies in the fact that the columns will appear on the screen exactly as they will when the document is printed. You don't have to enter the text in one long column and imagine how it will appear when printed, as with some other word processing programs. You can have up to 24 columns on a page.

If you have version 5.1, you can also create multicolumn documents using the Tables feature. Parallel columns can be quickly formatted, complete with optional surrounding lines. Tables in version 5.1 are discussed in Chapter 10.

CREATING A NEWSLETTER

A typical newsletter may mix single-column and multicolumn text. On the first page, for example, a single-column introductory paragraph may appear at the top of the page, followed by two-column text. Subsequent pages may have a header containing the name and date of the publication. Such newsletters are easy to lay out with WordPerfect.

Now we'll create a newsletter with the format shown in Figure 9.3 using WordPerfect's Column and Header features. We will first design the header that

■**FIGURE 9.1:**   *Text layout in newspaper columns*

will appear at the top of the second and subsequent pages. Then we will enter the single-column text that appears on the first page before the columns. We will define the columns and turn on the Column feature. Finally, we will enter the text for the columns.

■**FIGURE 9.2:**   *Text layout in parallel columns*

THE PAGE HEADER

The header contains the date of the newsletter and the page number. It will be printed on every page starting with the second one. For odd-numbered pages, we want the date and page number to appear on the right side of the page, with a line across the top, like this:

January 1991   Page 3

The header for even-numbered pages is just the opposite:

Page 2   January 1991

Follow these steps to create the header:

1. Start WordPerfect.

2. Press Shift-F8 2 to display the Page Format menu.

3. Select **3** or **h**, Headers, to display

    1 Header A; 2 Header B: 0

4. Press **1** to select header A. The prompt line changes to

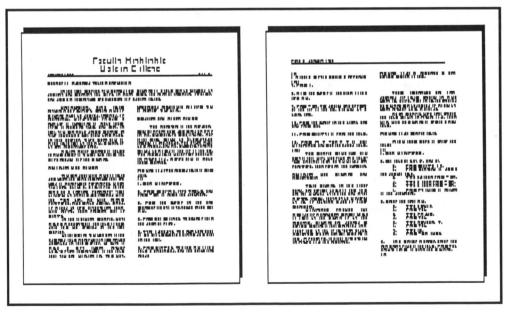

■**FIGURE 9.3:** *The layout of the sample newsletter*

> 1 Discontinue; 2 Every page; 3 Odd pages;
> 4 Even pages; 5 Edit:0

Note
The appearance
of the version
5.1 screen is
slightly dif-
ferent, but the
steps listed here
still apply.

5. Press **3** or **o** for odd-numbered pages. The screen clears, and the message

    Press EXIT when done   Ln 1" Pos 1"

    appears on the status line. This is the typing area where you enter the header information.

6. Later, we will use an enlarged font for the newsletter's masthead. To ensure that the headers print in normal type, we must enter a font change before typing the header text. Press Ctrl-F8 3 to select normal characters.

7. Press F8 to turn on underlining.

8. Press Alt-F6 to align the text flush right.

9. Press the space bar 49 times.

10. Type **January 1991 Page**.

11. Press the space bar after the word Page, then press Ctrl-B. The page number of the document will appear where the ^B code is in the header text.

12. Press Return, then press F7 to return to the Format Page menu.

13. Press **3 2 4** to select header B for even pages.

14. Press Ctrl-F8 3 to select normal characters.

15. Press F8 to underline, then type **Page**.

16. Press Ctrl-B, then type **January 1991**.

17. Press the space bar 49 times.

18. Press Return, then press F7 to return to the Format Page menu.

Warning
Step 19: With
version 5.1,
press **8 1**.

19. Press **9 1** then press Return three times. This keeps page numbers and headers and footers from printing on the first page.

THE MASTHEAD AND INTRODUCTORY PARAGRAPH

The first page of the newsletter will contain a masthead in enlarged characters and a short paragraph introducing the journal. If you have a laser printer or another type of printer with a variety of type styles and sizes, you can use them to design an attractive masthead.

Follow this procedure to begin the newsletter:

1. Press Ctrl-F8 1 7 to switch to extra large printing.

2. Press Shift-F6 to center the cursor.

3. Type **Faculty Highlights** then press Return.

4. Press Ctrl-F8 3 Ctrl-F8 1 5 to select large printing.

5. Press Shift-F6, then type **Watson College**.

6. Press Ctrl-F8 3 to revert to normal printing, then press Return to add several blank lines.

7. Type **January 1988**.

8. Press Alt-F6 to right-align the remaining text.

9. Type **Vol. 5 No. 6**. If you have a laser printer and you're using a downloadable or proportional spacing font, make a note of the position indicator at the end of that line.

10. Press Return.

11. Press the underline character until it reaches the left margin. Your screen should look like this:

January 1991   Vol. 5 No. 6

If you have a laser printer, make sure the line ends at the same position you noted in step 9. It's possible for the line to appear aligned with the end of the line above but really print shorter. Press the underline character until the position indicator shows the same number as the end of the line that you entered in step 9—it may appear longer on the screen but it will print correctly.

12. Press Return twice.

13. Type the introductory paragraph.

> This issue focuses on several of the faculty research projects that involved use of computers within various humanities areas. The next edition will treat technical and professional applications.

14. Press Return twice.

DEFINING THE COLUMNS

We've entered the headers, masthead, and first paragraph. Before typing the text for the two-column newsletter, however, we must first define how we want the columns laid out on the page and turn on the Column feature.

When you define columns, you must specify the type (newspaper or parallel), the number, and their spacing on the page. The spacing procedure includes setting column margins to determine their width and determining the amount of space between each column.

Follow these steps to define our newsletter columns:

Warning

Steps 1 to 4: With version 5.1, press Alt-F7 1 3 Return 1. The differences in keystrokes are explained in "Defining and Turning On Columns," page 200.

1. Press Alt-F7. You see the prompt

    1 Math On; 2 Math Def; 3 Column On/Off; 4 Column Def: 0

2. Press **4** to display the Text Column Definition menu, shown in Figure 9.4.

    The default column definition is two newspaper columns, each 3 inches wide. The first column has margins at 1 and 4 inches, the second at 4 1/2 and 7 1/2.

    If you wanted to change the number of columns or their spacing, you would select the appropriate option. For instance, for three columns, you'd press *2*—Number of Columns—then enter *3*. The measurements for three equally wide columns would automatically appear. Change intercolumn spacing by entering the measurement at option *3*—Distance Between Columns—or customize column width through option *4*—Margins.

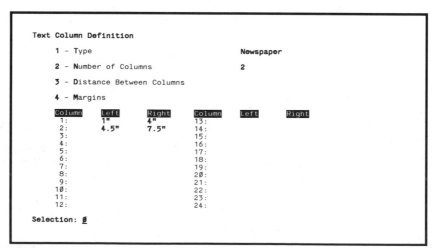

■**FIGURE 9.4:** *The Text Column Definition menu*

3. Press Return to accept the default definition and redisplay the Column selection line.

4. Press **3** to turn on the Column feature. The indicator Col 1 has been added to the status line to let you know which column you're working in. Now the text that you enter will conform to your column definition.

You must define your column format (by pressing Alt-F7 4) before you turn on the Column feature. If no definition has been made, a warning message will appear on the status line. However, once you have defined the column format, it will stay in effect for the entire document, or until you enter a new column definition. You can switch back and forth between multicolumn and single-column text by simply turning the Column feature on or off. You do not have to define the columns each time—only if you want to change the format.

ENTERING COLUMNS

Entering columns is now as simple as standard typing. As you type, word wrap will take effect at 4 inches, the right margin of the first column. When that column reaches the bottom of the page, the cursor will move to the top of the second column and the Col indicator on the status line will change to 2. When that column reaches the bottom of the page, the page division line will appear, and the cursor will move back to the left column of the next page. Soon, you'll learn how you can end a column, or the page, at any time.

Now let's enter some text into our sample newsletter columns.

1. Type the following paragraphs. You'll notice that the text appears on the screen in its column width. When you reach the bottom of the page, the cursor moves to the top of the next column, and text continues from there.

Factors Involved in French Language Word Processing Utilizing the Standard English Language Keyboard, Dr. Renee Voltaire, French Department.
Dr. Voltaire analyzed several popular word-processing programs for their capability to display and print French language characters. Dr. Voltaire then studied the difficulties encountered in typing French documents using the standard QWERTY keyboard.

The Possible Contributions of Computers to the Creative Writing Process, Dr. Leslie Van Mot, English Department.
Dr. Van Mot tested the effects of using word-processing

programs on the creative output of students. The writing of student volunteers was evaluated using several measurements. These included sentence complexity, character development, and grammatical accuracy. The students were divided into two groups: a test group and a control group. The test group was trained in using a word-processing program; the control group was given standard writing practice exercises. The report studies the effects of the word-processing training on the students' writing.

The Economic Impact of Computer Technology on the Gross National Product, Dr. William Duke, Economics Department. Dr. Duke abstracted data from the past 10 years supplied by the National Economics Institute. He concludes that, starting in 1984, there has been a direct relationship between the GNP and the fortunes of the computer industry.

Art Education and the Computer, Dr. Wilma Stephens, Art Department.
Dr. Stephens has been researching the use of computer technology in the art design process. Her primary interest is in the use of simulated graphics to project light patterns on angular objects and their effects on color density as observed by the human eye.

Warning
Step 2: With version 5.1, press Alt-F7 1 2.

2. Press Alt-F7 3 to turn off Column mode and place the cursor at the left margin under the leftmost column. (At this point, you could enter more single-column text.)

3. Press Shift-F7 1 to print the newsletter.

4. Press F7 N Y to exit WordPerfect.

ENDING COLUMNS

The advantage of the newspaper column style is that you don't have to take any action to divide text between columns or pages as you type or edit. However, WordPerfect also allows you to end a column anywhere and go on to the next one. Thus, for example, you could end a column at the end of a newsletter article and begin the next article on the next column or the following page.

Press Ctrl-Return to end a column. If you are entering any column but the rightmost one on the page, the cursor will move to the beginning of the next column. If you press Ctrl-Return while in the rightmost column, WordPerfect will insert a page break and begin the left column on the next page.

This column or page end is different from the soft column/page end that Word-Perfect enters at the end of each page or column. In columns where WordPerfect has entered a Soft Column/Page End code, you can delete or insert text and the columns will automatically adjust to accommodate the changes. If necessary, WordPerfect will move the text from column to column or page to page.

On the other hand, the Hard Column/Page End code that you insert with Ctrl-Return isolates that column from the others. Adding text to such a column will not affect the others.

When you are concerned about where columns end and in which column text appears, you should use the other type of columns provided by WordPerfect—parallel columns.

■ PARALLEL COLUMNS

In many cases, you don't want the text to flow freely from column to column, page to page. Material in a paragraph on the right, for example, may relate direct-ly to text on the left. You want to keep the two columns next to each other, no matter how much text is added or deleted. These are called parallel columns. Figure 9.5 shows an example of a document with two columns of text that must appear side by side.

Parallel columns can be regular or block-protected. *Block-protected* parallel columns are kept next to each other even if it means moving them both to a new page. Regular parallel columns, on the other hand, will span a page break.

When you are entering text in parallel columns, you control the movement of the cursor from one column to another by pressing Ctrl-Return (unlike in newspaper style, this key combination does not insert a page break when you press it from the rightmost column).

With regular parallel columns, WordPerfect uses the Ctrl-Return codes to move from column to column. However, with block-protected columns, special codes—[Block Pro:On] and [Block Pro:Off]—surround each column. Word-Perfect uses these to determine which blocks will be kept on the same page. If text in one column extends into the new page, both blocks will be carried over so they start on that page. If you select regular parallel columns, the longer column will span the page break.

CREATING A SAMPLE DOCUMENT

As an example, let's enter the document shown in Figure 9.6. This document has two sets of double-column text surrounded by single-column paragraphs.

Since we want the left and right columns kept side by side, we will use parallel columns, and since the document is short we can select regular parallel columns. However, the columns are not of the same width. The left column is 2 inches wide, while the right column is about 4 inches wide.

1. Start WordPerfect.

2. Type the following paragraph:

    The research staff will be divided into two major project teams. Team one is responsible for the collection and analysis

---

Types of Software

Word processing, *database management,* spreadsheet, graphics, project planning	These are *applications software packages.* They are designed to perform a specific useful function. For most users in business and academic areas, applications software is the most important to master.
BASIC, COBOL, Pascal, C, Forth, PL/1, FORTRAN, Assembly	These are *programming languages.* They are used to write specific applications for which appropriate or adequate application software is not available. Most programming is performed by professionals. For the average computer user, it is usually more efficient to purchase a completed application.
PC/DOS, MS/DOS, TRS/DOS, UNIX	These are *disk operating systems.* The operating system is a very sophisticated software package that handles the interface between the computer, devices that are attached to it, and the user.

■**FIGURE 9.5:** *A document with two columns of text that must appear side by side* of raw data received from the volunteer force. This team and its tasks are defined below.

3. Press Return twice.

Warning

Step 4: With version 5.1, press Alt-F7 1 3.

4. Press Alt-F7 4 to display the Text Column Definition menu.

5. Press **1** or **t** to select Column Type. The prompt line changes to

   Column Type: 1 Newspaper; 2 Parallel; 3 Parallel with Block Protect:0

6. Press **2** for regular parallel columns. The number of columns and the column spacing remain at the default two. So let's change the width of the columns using the Margin option.

```
        The research staff will be divided into two major project
    teams. Team one is responsible for the collection and analysis of
    raw data received from the volunteer force. This team and its
    tasks are defined below.


    William Watson, team        This team will design the
    leader; Rose Savage,        questionnaire, organize and coordinate
    Ray Brown, Lynn Kuder       the student volunteer force, collect
                                and control the completed
                                questionnaires, and analyze the results
                                according to the project proposal using
                                a standard statistical package.

        The second team has broad responsibility for the design and
    development of the on-site testing facilities. Because of the
    extensive nature of this task, the team has two project leaders.


    Joseph Viola, team          The two team leaders will decide on how
    leader; Rita                the specific tasks will be divided
    Witowski, Steve             between the two subgroups. The teams
    Cieka, John Barclay         must complete the following objectives:
                                locate and obtain a suitable field
    Jackie Betoff, team         site, design and implement facility
    leader; Mike Short,         development, and install and prepare
    Danielle Papantonis,        required equipment.
    Debra Mullen

        The teams were selected on the basis of the experience and
    expertise of their members. Personnel wishing to discuss team
    placement should first consult their team leader. If a problem
    still exists, consult the Vice President for Research and
    Development. However, once the project is under way, no
    personnel changes will be allowed.
```

■**FIGURE 9.6:** *Sample document with parallel columns*

7. Press **4** or **m** for Margins. The cursor moves to the left margin setting for the first column.

8. Press Return to accept the default 1-inch setting. The cursor moves to the right margin for that column.

9. Type **3** for its right margin, then press Return. The cursor moves to the left margin setting for the second column.

10. Type **3.6** for its left margin, then press Return.

11. Press Return to accept the default right margin of 7 1/2 inches.

12. Press Return to return to the typing area. The Column selection line is still displayed.

13. Press **3** to turn on the Column feature.

14. Type the first column.

> William Watson, team leader; Rose Savage, Ray Brown, Lynn Kuder

15. Press Ctrl-Return. The cursor moves to the top of the rightmost column.

16. Type the second column.

> This team will design the questionnaire, organize and coordinate the student volunteer force, collect and control the completed questionnaires, and analyze the results according to the project proposal using a standard statistical package.

17. Press Ctrl-Return to end that column.

Warning
Step 18: With version 5.1, press Alt-F7 1 2.

18. Press Alt-F7 3 to turn off the Column feature since you now want to enter single-column text.

19. Type the following paragraph:

> The second team has broad responsibility for the design and development of the on-site testing facilities. Because of the extensive nature of this task, the team has two project leaders.

20. Press Return twice.

Warning
Step 21: With version 5.1, press Alt-F7 1 1.

21. Press Alt-F7 3 to turn Columns on. Since the columns are already defined, you only need to turn the Column feature on, and the new columns will be formatted in the same way as the columns above.

22. Type the first column. It contains two paragraphs.

Joseph Viola, team leader; Rita Witowski, Steve Cieka, John Barclay

Jackie Betoff, team leader; Mike Short, Danielle Papantonis, Debra Mullen

23. Press Ctrl-Return.

24. Type the second column.

The two team leaders will decide on how the specific tasks will be divided between the two subgroups. The teams must complete the following objectives: locate and obtain a suitable field site, design and implement facility development, and install and prepare required equipment.

Warning
Step 25: With version 5.1, press Alt-F7 1 2.

25. Press Ctrl-Return, then press Alt-F7 3 to turn off the Column feature.

26. Press Return twice.

27. Type the last single-column paragraph.

The teams were selected on the basis of the experience and expertise of their members. Personnel wishing to discuss team placement should first consult their team leader. If a problem still exists, consult the Vice President for Research and Development. However, once the project is under way, no personnel changes will be allowed.

28. Press Shift-F7 1 to print the document.

29. Press F7 N Y to exit WordPerfect.

■ CHANGING COLUMN FORMATS

Sometimes a column format just doesn't work. This happens often when you create a document with uneven columns. For example, the column below has a left margin at 1 inch and a right margin at 2 inches.

Joseph
Viola, team
leader;
Rita
Witowski,

Steve
Cieka, John
Barclay

It is obvious that the column is too narrow. At the very least, the full name of the first individual should fit on the first line.

Two codes are required to enter columns: the Column Definition code, [Col Def], and the Column On code, [Col on]. Both codes precede the column text. To change column widths, first delete the Column Definition code, then redefine the column format. When you define a new format, the text will automatically adjust, since the Column On code is still in the text.

To change from multiple columns to a single column, simply delete the [Col on] code. The [Col Def] code will remain in the text, but it will have no effect until you turn on the Column feature again and insert another [Col on] code.

USING THE BINDING WIDTH OPTION

Note
In version 5.1, this option is called Binding Offset.

When you are planning the layout of a folded newsletter, consider the need for some additional binding area. If you plan to punch holes for a three-ring binder, as shown in Figure 9.7, the document will need a wider margin on the binding side. On odd-numbered pages, this extra margin must be on the left side of the page; on even-numbered pages, it will be on the right side. Since the requirements differ from page to page, the regular margin control won't work.

To adjust the margins for bound documents, press Shift-F7 to display the Print menu, then press *B* to select the Binding Width option.

Enter the amount of extra binding width. For example, to leave an extra 1/2-inch margin, enter *.5* and press Return twice to return to the document.

PLACEMENT OF HEADERS AND FOOTERS

Our sample newsletter used a *header* as the date line. If you plan on using headers and footers in other documents, consider how their placement affects the amount of text per page.

Headers start at the first text line of the document, rather than within the top margin. Footers start printing on the last text line, with additional footer lines running into the bottom margin. WordPerfect leaves an extra blank line between the text and the header or footer. If you have a two-line header and a one-line footer, you are actually giving up five lines of text on each page.

If you want headers to be printed in the top margin, you must reset the top margin so that the first text line is where you want the header to begin printing. Then add extra blank header lines to begin the first line of text at an appropriate number of line spaces below the header.

Suppose that you have a two-line header and you want the text to begin after the normal 1-inch top margin. You would set the top margin at .5 inch and enter the two-line header with a third blank line. The header will print on lines 3, 4, and 5. WordPerfect will leave its extra blank line following the header and start the text on line 7, and you will have a 1-inch top margin.

■ WORKING WITH MAILING LISTS

At times you might find it easier to type text in one long column and then convert the single column into several columns. Take the typical name and address list. Some are printed two columns across, some three—it usually depends on the number of names in the list. It may be more convenient to type the names in

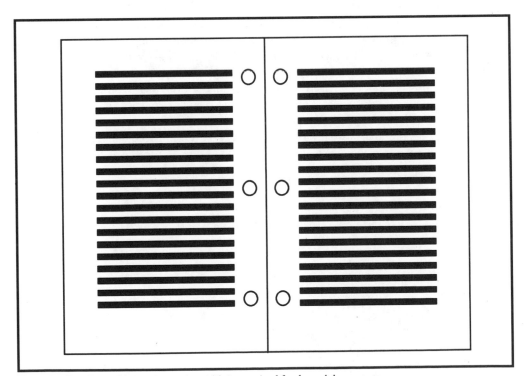

■**FIGURE 9.7:** *Additional margin width is required for bound documents*

one column, then reformat the document to be printed as several columns across the page.

You can do this two ways—by turning off side-by-side display or by later reformatting single-column text into multicolumn.

SIDE-BY-SIDE DISPLAY

Warning
Users of version 5.1 should follow the special instructions under "Side-by-Side Display," page 201.

You can turn off the side-by-side display of columns, so that WordPerfect displays each column on a separate page but at its proper position, either on the left or right, for example. The columns will still be printed side by side no matter how they appear on the screen. To have the columns appear under each other, press Shift-F1 3 to show the Setup Display menu. Select *8* for the Side-by-Side option, press *N,* then press Return twice.

CONVERTING SINGLE COLUMNS TO MULTIPLE

You can also type the names without defining columns, then reformat the document to print several columns across the page. This is a simple process as long as the columns are at least as wide as the longest line in the list.

To convert a single-column address list to two columns, place the cursor at the beginning of the list and define a two-column, evenly spaced format. When you turn on the Column feature, the document will be reformatted, placing two columns of addresses side by side. Using newspaper style, however, some addresses may be divided between columns or even pages. After you've reformatted the document, scan the list and insert column and page breaks (both using Ctrl-Return) at the appropriate locations.

A problem with this method is that two evenly spaced columns, five spaces apart and using the default margin settings, are only 2.9" (29 characters) long. So, after you've formatted the document into columns, the entry

Dr. Stan M. Tobler
Academic Dean
Philadelphia College of Pharmacy and Science
43rd and Kingsessing Mall
Philadelphia, PA 19104

will appear as

Dr. Stan M. Tobler
Academic Dean
Philadelphia College of
Pharmacy and Science

43rd and Kingsessing Mall
Philadelphia, PA 19104

As part of a three-column list, the entry would be reformatted to

Dr. Stan M. Tobler
Academic Dean
Philadelphia
College of Pharmacy
and Science
43rd and
Kingsessing Mall
Philadelphia, PA 19104

You could prevent the addresses from being split this way by counting the length of the longest line in the list. Just place the cursor on the end of that line and subtract 1" (the left margin) from the number next to the Pos indicator. Then adjust the margins and column settings so that the columns are at least that wide.

■ COLUMN MACROS

Warning
Users of version 5.1 should follow the special instructions under "Column Macros," page 201.

Here are two macros that you can use to create multicolumn documents:

Function	Alt-Letter	Macro
Sets and turns on the column definition for two-column newspaper style text	Alt-J	Ctrl-F10 Alt-J Return Alt-F7 4 Return 3 Ctrl-F10
Sets and turns on the column definition for two-column parallel text.	Alt-K	Ctrl-F10 Alt-K Return Alt-F7 4 1 2 Return 3 Ctrl-F10

■ COLUMNS AND STYLES

If you use columns often, consider creating styles to hold the definitions.

Using the techniques covered in Chapter 3, for example, you could create a style sheet with all of the formats needed for a standard monthly newsletter. For instance, create one style that contains all of the text and formatting codes for your masthead. Create another style for large column headings—such as a paired style that turns on extra large printing and centers the cursor. Add a third style that defines and turns on the number of columns that you use.

Plan your newsletter and identify standard elements that you use often. Then create a separate style for each element on a style sheet called MONTHLY.

When you want to produce a newsletter, start WordPerfect and recall the style sheet. Turn on the masthead style to insert the masthead into the document as a single unit, use the heading style to format your main headline, then turn on the column style and type your lead story.

This way, the look of your newsletter will be consistent from month to month, and once you've designed your format you won't have to do it again.

In later chapters you'll learn how to add some advanced features to your newsletters—including graphics, text boxes, and borders.

■ VERSION 5.1 FEATURES

Parallel columns can also be created using the Tables feature discussed in Chapter 10. With the Table Editor, you can easily expand or contract the size of columns until the spacing is correct, and even enclose paragraphs within boxes or separate them with lines.

DEFINING AND TURNING ON COLUMNS

While the Text Column Definition menu is the same as in earlier versions, the keystrokes to display the menu and turn columns off and on differ.

Defining Columns   To define columns, press Alt-F7 to see the prompt

    1 Columns; 2 Tables; 3 Math: 0

Press *1* or *c* to select Columns and display the prompt line

    Columns: 1 On; 2 Off; 3 Define: 0

Press **3** to display the Text Column Definition menu. After defining the columns, as explained earlier in this chapter, press Return to exit the menu. You'll see the Columns prompt line again.

If you want to turn columns on immediately, press *1*. Otherwise, press Return to accept the default value and return to the document.

Turning Columns On and Off   Once columns are defined, turn them on by pressing Alt-F7 1 1. Press Alt-F7 1 2 to turn them off.

SIDE-BY-SIDE DISPLAY

To turn side-by-side display off, press Shift-F1 2 to reach the Setup Display menu, then press *6* or *e* for the Edit-Screen Options menu (Figure 9.8). Press *7* or *S* for the Side-by-side Columns Display option, press *n*, then press Return three times.

COLUMN MACROS

Because of changes in the keystrokes for defining columns, the macros in version 5.1 are different from those given earlier. Use these keystrokes instead:

Function	Alt-Letter	Macro
Two-column newspapers-style	Alt-J	Ctrl-F10 Alt-J Return Alt-F7 1 3 Return 1 Ctrl-F10

```
Setup: Edit-Screen Options

    1 - Automatically Format and Rewrite    Yes

    2 - Comments Display                     Yes

    3 - Filename on the Status Line          Yes

    4 - Hard Return Display Character

    5 - Merge Codes Display                  Yes

    6 - Reveal Codes Window Size             10

    7 - Side-by-side Columns Display         Yes




    Selection: 0
```

■**FIGURE 9.8:** *Edit-Screen Options menu*

Two-column parallel-style	Alt-K	Ctrl-F10 Alt-K Return Alt-F7 1 3 1 2 Return 1 Ctrl-F10

MOUSE AND MENU EQUIVALENTS

Function	Keyboard	Pull-Down Menus
Columns Off	Alt-F7 1 2	**Layout Columns Off**
Columns On	Alt-F7 1 1	**Layout Columns On**
Define Columns	Alt-F7 1 3	**Layout Columns Define**
Footers	Shift-F8 2 4	**Layout Page Footers**
Headers	Shift-F8 2 3	**Layout Page Headers**

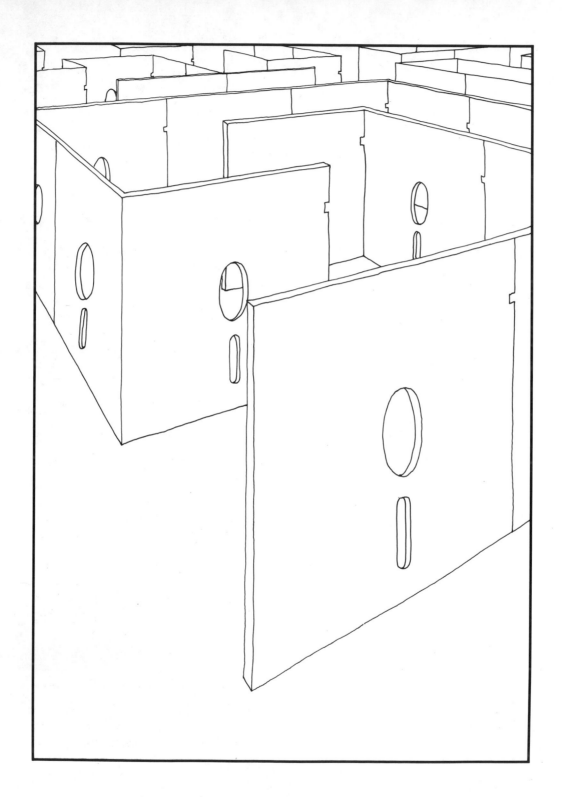

10

CREATING AND EDITING TABLES

Tables contain columns of words or numbers. They are easy to create and are an excellent means of presenting detailed information. In fact, even the simplest table can convey information that would require several paragraphs of text. Look at the table below:

	First Quarter	Second Quarter	Third Quarter	Fourth Quarter
Sales	40,000	20,000	35,000	37,500
Costs	25,000	22,000	24,000	26,000
Profits	15,000	-2,000	11,000	11,500

You can tell at a glance how this company is doing. It is clear that the second quarter was the company's weakest period and that the first was its strongest.

In this chapter, you will learn how to create typical tables, such as the one above, by setting and using tab stops and WordPerfect's other formatting features. We will also review some basic techniques for editing tables. The more advanced editing techniques are discussed in Chapter 11, which explains how to manipulate rows and columns, and Chapter 12, which describes how to use WordPerfect's powerful sorting feature.

New Feature
Additional related features in version 5.1 are discussed under "Automatic Tables," page 224.

PLANNING TABLES

Before you start typing a table, you should have some idea of how you want the completed table to look. You should know the number of columns, the way each column is to be aligned, and the total width of the table. Although you can see only 80 characters on the screen at one time, WordPerfect can handle tables up to 54 inches wide. Using a 10-pitch typeface, that's 540 characters per line!

But even though WordPerfect can print such wide documents, it is easiest to create tables no wider than 7 1/2 inches. This way, you can view the entire table at once. When you're working with wider tables, you must scroll the screen horizontally to view the columns.

COLUMN ALIGNMENT

Your tables can have columns that are left-, center-, right-, or character-aligned; you can have more than one type of column alignment in a single table. You create these alignments using special tabs or function keys.

A left-aligned column like this:

Sales
Costs
Rent
Profits

is created by setting a tab stop (or using the default one) and using the Tab key.

A center-aligned column like this:

William Morris
Sam Spady
Jane Pascalli

is created either by setting a center tab or by using the Shift-F6 key combination.

A right-aligned column like this:

Internal Rate of Return
Net Present Value
Per Share Income

is created using a right tab stop or the Ctrl-F6 key combination.

Ctrl-F6 is also used to format decimal-aligned columns. Notice that numbers aligned on the decimal point are easier to read than left-aligned numeric columns:

```
   345.34    345.34
23,456.00    23,456.00
     1.12    1.12
```

And all tabs stop can include dot leaders such as:

President . . . . Wilma Wintchell
Vice President . . . . .Dan Druther

■ ## TAB STOPS VERSUS FUNCTION KEYS

There are often two ways to create the same format. In these cases you can either set a formatted tab (left, center, right, or decimal), as you learned how to do in Chapter 2, or use the function key combinations.

Each method has its advantages. Setting formatted tab stops allows you to reach and align every type of column simply by pressing the Tab key. You don't have to remember which key combination performs which alignment. You can also add dot leaders to your tabs.

The function key method, however, saves you from using the Tab Set form every time you want to create an alignment other than left. So a tab can serve as a regular tab on one line, then as a centered or decimal-aligned tab on the next line without any menu commands. (Of course, if you plan to type a similar table often, create a style containing the tab stops, then just recall the style when needed.)

If you have a large table to type, you're better off setting the correctly formatted tabs at one time, then only using the Tab key to type entries. You should also set specific tabs if you plan to sort or rearrange the table, as you'll learn in Chapter 12.

If you have a short table to type, then use the function key combinations.

■ ## BEWARE OF COLLIDING TABS

When you use the regular Tab key, the characters that you enter move to the right. If you press Tab again, the cursor moves to the next tab stop to the right, and new text will not interfere with that already entered. When you use Ctrl-F6, however, text moves to the left until you enter the alignment character. Thus, it is possible to type a long number or word that "collides" with text already on that line.

WordPerfect has a unique way of handling (or, more accurately, *not* handling) this problem. Look at the following line:

Net Profit   _.

Ctrl-F6 placed the cursor in position 3" in preparation for decimal alignment of a number. Unfortunately, there are only five character positions (1/2") between the tab stop and the end of the text. Let's see what happens if the number 109,087.00 is entered:

Net Profi109,087.00.

The number shifted to the left, apparently typing over the text already on the line. But if you pressed Alt-F3 to reveal the codes, you would see

[Tab]Net Profit[Align]109,087.00[C/A/Flrt].

Note
With version 5.1, Ctrl-F6 inserts the [DEC TAB] code.

The characters have been erased from the screen, but they are still in the document. When you print this table, WordPerfect will print the words Net Profit, then back up and print the number in the same position, so that the characters *t* and *1* overlap.

Make sure that you set tab stops far enough apart to prevent collisions of this type. Set them at distances that would accommodate the largest possible entry in that column.

TABLE TECHNIQUES

You can speed up the process of creating tables and ensure that they are printed properly by applying two simple rules:

■ Set only the necessary tab stops.

■ Protect tables from being split between pages.

If your columns are spread out over the page, you'll have to press Tab or Ctrl-F6 several times to reach the correct position. For long tables, this can amount to many extra keystrokes. It also makes it difficult to rearrange the columns later.

You can avoid extra tab stops by carefully planning the spacing of your columns. Practice with one row, making a note of the positions of the tab stops used. Then delete all of the tab stops and reset only those required for the table. When you have entered the table, reset all of the original tab stops.

Unless the table itself is longer than one page, the entire table should be printed on the same page. While it may appear this way when created, adding or deleting lines elsewhere in the document may cause the printed table to be divided between pages. Divided tables are difficult to read and lose some of their impact. Use the block protection or conditional end of page techniques discussed in Chapter 3 to avoid this situation.

■ THE CHOICE: BY ROW OR BY COLUMN

Tables can be viewed either as a series of individual rows or as a series of columns. How you create your table depends on how you prefer to enter the data—by row or by column.

Suppose that the table you are creating will contain the amounts of regional and national sales for four salespersons, as shown in Figure 10.1. The information is stored on index cards, with each card listing the totals for each individual salesperson. Since you have the information in that order, it is easiest to enter all the data for each salesperson row by row.

On the other hand, suppose you are entering your company's budget summary for the past four years. The first column will list the budget items, and the other columns will contain the figures for each year, as shown in Figure 10.2. The data are on individual budget sheets that list the figures for all the budget areas for each year. Using the 1990 budget sheet as a guide, you'll type in the entire second column, using the 1989 annual report you'll type in the third column, and so on. You would enter this type of table column by column.

First we'll see how to enter a table row by row, which is the most common method. We'll discuss tables entered by columns later in this chapter.

```
                    Aardvark Seed Company
              Outstanding Salesperson Competition

                           Regional Total National Total

        James P. Armitage      1,004,765.00   1,043,876.00
     Wilson C. Landsmokker        98,654.00      99,864.00
            June Meyers           92,765.00      96,764.00
        Rosalie Butchalski       91,765.00      93,762.00
```

■**FIGURE 10.1:**   *Table of sales data entered row by row*

ENTERING TABLES BY ROWS

Tables entered as rows are very flexible. You can sort these tables and even perform mathematical operations on them. The number of columns is limited only by the width of the page.

As an example, we'll create the table shown in Figure 10.1. It has both centered and decimal-aligned columns. For this example, we'll set regular left-aligned tabs but use the function keys to align the columns. In a later example we'll set and use formatted tabs.

Follow this procedure to enter the table:

1. Start WordPerfect.

2. Press Shift-F6 to center the first line of the title.

3. Type **Aardvark Seed Company**.

4. Press Return, then press Shift-F6 to center the second line of the title.

5. Type **Outstanding Salesperson Competition**.

6. Press Return twice.

7. Press Tab five times to reach the position for the Regional Total heading.

8. Type **Regional Total**.

9. Press Tab.

10. Type **National Total**.

11. Press Return twice.

12. Now set tab stops at 2.1", 4.5", and 6". To show how the functions keys

Warning

Users of version 5.1 should refer to the section "Setting Absolute Tabs" on page 223 before completing this chapter.

Comparative Budget Summary (in thousands)				
Budget Area	1991	1990	1989	1988
Sales Income$	87,000	85,000	81,000	76,000
Interest Income$	856	865	856	856
Rental Income$	500	500	500	500
Wages and Salaries$	9,000	9,000	8,500	7,900
Commissions$	900	878	756	687
Office Expenses$	58	65	89	34
Misc. Expenses$	32	24	12	9

■**FIGURE 10.2:** *Budget summary table entered column by column* are used, you'll set regular left-aligned tabs.

    a. Press Shift-F8 1 8 to display the Tab Set form.

    b. Press Ctrl-End to delete the default tab stops.

    c. Type **2.1** and press Return.

    d. Type **4.5** and press Return.

    e. Type **6** and press Return.

    f. Press F7 twice to return to the document.

13. Press Tab to reach position 21. Check the position indicator on the status line, as shown in Figure 10.3.

14. Press Shift-F6 to center the first name in the first column.

15. Type **James P. Armitage**. Notice that the characters are centered around position 2.1". If you press Shift-F6 when the cursor is at the left margin, text will be centered on the page. If you press Shift-F6 at any other position on the line, as you did here, that position becomes the centering point.

16. Press Ctrl-F6. The cursor shifts to the next tab stop and the status line reads

    Align Char = .

17. Type **1,004,765.00**. Notice that as you type the number, the characters shift to the left, instead of to the right as normal. The decimal point (the period) stays at the tab stop position (position 4.5" in this case), and the

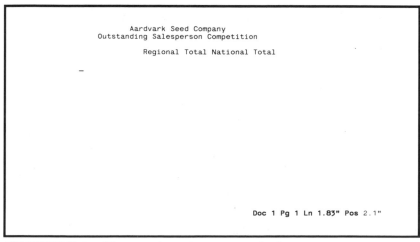

■**FIGURE 10.3:**   *The cursor in position to enter the first name*

subsequent characters move to the right. Ctrl-F6 performs what is called the *tab-align* function. It aligns columns along a specific character. When you press Ctrl-F6, the cursor moves to the next tab stop on the line, and the current alignment character (by default, the decimal point) appears on the status line.

18. Press Ctrl-F6 to reach position 6".

19. Type **1,043,876.00**.

20. Press Return.

21. Enter the second row.

  a. Press Tab.

  b. Press Shift-F6.

  c. Type **Wilson C. Landsmokker**.

  d. Press Ctrl-F6.

  e. Type **98,654.00**.

  f. Press Ctrl-F6.

  g. Type **99,864.00**.

  h. Press Return.

22. Enter the third row.

  a. Press Tab.

  b. Press Shift-F6.

  c. Type **June Meyers**.

  d. Press Ctrl-F6.

  e. Type **92,765.00**.

  f. Press Ctrl-F6.

  g. Type **96,764.00**.

  h. Press Return.

23. Enter the final row.

  a. Press Tab.

  b. Press Shift-F6.

    c. Type **Rosalie Butchalski**.

    d. Press Ctrl-F6.

    e. Type **91,765.00**.

    f. Press Ctrl-F6.

    g. Type **93,762.00**.

    h. Press Return.

24. Press F10, type **TABLE**, then press Return to save the table.

25. Press Shift-F7 1 to print the table.

■ EDITING AND REFORMATTING TABLES

Editing tables differs from editing other text only in that tables contain Tab and Tab-Align codes. Deleting and inserting tab stops and tab-alignment characters in an existing table will change the placement of the columns.

CHANGING TAB STOPS

Take a look at the two numbers below. They were entered using the regular Tab key at the tab stops at positions 20 and 40.

    123.45   1234.56.

If all of the tab stops were deleted (Shift-F8 1 8 Ctrl-End F7 F7), the text would appear like this:

    123.451234.56.

However, with codes revealed, the same text appears as

    [TAB][TAB]123.45[TAB][TAB][TAB]1234.56.

The Tab codes are still in the text, even though no tab stops are set and no tab spaces appear on the screen.

What do the Tab codes really mean? Each press of the Tab key instructs Word-Perfect to move to the next tab stop. Removing the tab stops does not remove the instruction; there are just no tab stops for the text to move to. If you set new tab stops, the table text will adjust accordingly. For example, suppose that you deleted all the tab stops in a two-column table, then set two new ones at 3" (character position 30) and 6" (position 60). Since the Tab codes are still in the text, the columns will automatically shift to the new tab stop positions.

Tab-Align codes ([Align]), like Tab codes, remain in the document even if you delete the tab stop.

Note

With version 5.1, Tab-Align codes are [DEC TAB].

However, when you delete all of the tab stops on the line, WordPerfect may use the [Tab] or [Align] codes to shift text to the next line on the screen, adding [HRt] codes. So it's best to delete the old tabs and set the new ones at one time, then exit the Tab Set screen. Text will conform nicely.

Text centered in columns also behaves quite strangely at times. If you move the cursor from left to right over centered columns, some of the characters disappear from the screen. When you reach the center point, however, they pop back into view, and the cursor jumps back to the start of the text. This makes it tricky to change text in centered columns. Your changes will take effect, but you might have to move the cursor off of the line to see how the finished column will appear.

TECHNIQUES FOR REFORMATTING

After you have entered a table, you may want to reformat it to improve its appearance. You can change the format of a table by deleting and inserting tab stops.

As an example, we will now reformat our sample table to appear as shown in Figure 10.4. We will shift the two decimal-aligned columns one tab stop to the right and then realign the column headings.

1. Place the cursor at the left margin of the first line of names (James P. Armitage). If you display codes, you'll see that the cursor is just to the right of the [Tab Set] code.

2. Delete the tab stops at 4.5" and 6".

   a. Press Shift-F8 1 8.

```
                        Aardvark Seed Company
                   Outstanding Salesperson Competition

                            Regional Total        National Total

        James P. Armitage       1,004,765.00        1,043,876.00
     Wilson C. Landsmokker          98,654.00           99,864.00
          June Meyers               92,765.00           96,764.00
        Rosalie Butchalski          91,765.00           93,762.00
```

■**FIGURE 10.4:** *The reformatted table*

    b. Type **4.5** then press Return Del.

    c. Type **6** then press Return Del.

3. Set the new tabs at 5" and 7".

    a. Type **5** then press Return.

    b. Type **7** then press Return.

    c. Press F7 twice to return to the document.

The columns automatically aligned to the new tab stops because the [Align] codes are still in place. But now the column headings are out of line.

4. Place the cursor on the line just above the column headings.

5. Delete the tabs at 3.5", 5", and 5.5".

    a. Press Shift-F8 1 8.

    b. Type **3.5** then press Return Del.

    c. Type **5** then press Return Del.

    d. Type **5.5** then press Return Del.

    e. Press F7 twice.

With the tab stops at 3.5", 5", and 5.5" deleted, the headings shift to more appropriate locations.

6. Press F7 Y Return Y Y to save the table and exit WordPerfect.

OTHER ALIGNMENT CHARACTERS

WordPerfect's Tab-Alignment feature can be used to create a number of effects other than decimal-aligned columns. Any character can be used for alignment, or even none at all (for right-aligned columns). Here are some examples:

Stephen Chesin
Nancy Chesin
Jean Kohl
Raymond Kohl

TO:
FROM:

```
                   SUBJECT:
                   DATE:

               Total Sales $
            Total Expenses $
               Net Profit $
         Retained Earnings $
```

In the second and third examples above, a different alignment character is used. One column uses a colon, the other a dollar sign. You could use a right-aligned tab for all of these formats or even Ctrl-F6 as long as you want to press Return, Tab, or Ctrl-F6 at the end of the alignment. These keystrokes act just like the period in ending the leftward movement of characters.

But if the text in the column includes a period, it will act as the alignment character first. So, to right-align text that contains periods (such as *William P. Watson*), first change the alignment character to something you know will not occur in the text.

To do this, press Shift-F8 4 for the Format Other menu, then *3* or *d* to reach the prompt

```
3 - Decimal/Align Character    ..
Thousands' Separator        ,.
```

Enter the character you want to use for column alignment in place of the period, then press Return three times. (The Thousand's Separator character is used for math, as discussed in Chapter 18.)

Now when you press Ctrl-F6, the cursor will move to the next tab stop, and the prompt line will show that alignment character.

■
WORKING WITH WIDE DOCUMENTS

Most letters and other business documents are printed on paper 8 1/2 inches wide. But statistical data, financial reports, and tables are often printed across wider paper. Printers using 14-inch wide paper are not uncommon, and most 8 1/2-inch-wide dot matrix printers are able to print in fine or small type.

If you have a wide-carriage printer, just select a form size that matches the paper you're using. If your printer has a fine or small typeface, just select that size. With a smaller type font you'll be able to fit more characters on the line to accommodate a wider table on standard 8 1/2 by 11-inch paper. For example, with some smaller fonts you can print up to 130 characters across. You don't have to worry about adjusting the margins (unless you want them smaller) because WordPerfect takes care of this automatically.

With earlier versions of WordPerfect you had to adjust the margins yourself when changing type sizes because margins were set in character positions, not inches. Using a standard 10-pitch font, for instance, the 10-character left and right margins were 1 inch wide. If you changed to a 16-pitch font, however, you'd still have 10-character margins—but now they'd be about two thirds of an inch wide.

WordPerfect uses inches, not character positions, for setting margins. So when you change font sizes, WordPerfect makes the necessary adjustments to maintain the margins. With a 10-pitch font, 1-inch margins will be 10 characters wide; with a 16-pitch font, they will be 16 characters wide.

In some cases, however, a printer that does not respond to the font size change may still have a built-in Condensed Printing mode. This may occur if you couldn't find your printer's name on the list when you selected printers in Appendix A. Check your printer's manual for some command or "escape" code that shifts it into small printing. To issue such a command to the printer, press Shift-F8 4 for the Format Other menu, then press 6 or *p* for Printer Functions. You'll see the Format Printer Functions menu (Figure 10.5).

Options 1, 3, and 4 are used to make minor adjustments to the spacing of characters on the line. Use option 2 to send commands directly to your printer.

Press *2* or *p* to display the prompt

1 Command; 2 Filename:0.

Option 2 is used to transfer a series of commands from a disk file to the printer,

Note
The appearance of the version 5.1 screen is slightly different, but the steps listed here still apply.

New Feature
Related features in version 5.1 are discussed under "Additional Printer Functions," page 223.

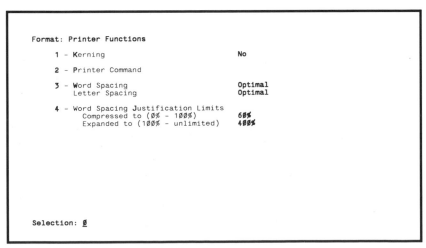

```
Format: Printer Functions

    1 - Kerning                              No

    2 - Printer Command

    3 - Word Spacing                         Optimal
        Letter Spacing                       Optimal

    4 - Word Spacing Justification Limits
        Compressed to (0% - 100%)            60%
        Expanded to (100% - unlimited)       400%




    Selection: 0
```

■**FIGURE 10.5:** *Format Printer Functions menu*

such as in downloading fonts. We're interested in option 1.

Press *1* or *c* for the prompt

Command:.

Type your printer's command for condensed print. If your printer uses an Escape command, type <27> then the code. Then press Return four times.

■ CREATING TABLES AS COLUMNS

As mentioned earlier, it's often easier to enter data downward in columns rather than across in rows. Unfortunately, there are several limitations to this method. Tables entered this way are difficult to sort, and mathematical operations, which can be used to compute the total of the columns, cannot be used for any computations across rows. (You'll see how serious these two limitations may be in Chapters 12 and 18.)

Refer back to Figure 10.2. This table has five columns. The first column contains text aligned on the dollar sign, while the remaining columns have numbers aligned on the right.

Now we'll recreate this table as multicolumn text. Follow these steps:

1. Start WordPerfect.

2. Press Shift-F6 to center the first line of the title.

3. Type **Comparative Budget Summary**.

4. Press Return.

5. Press Shift-F6 to center the second line of the title.

6. Type **(in thousands)**.

7. Press Return twice.

8. Press Alt-F7 4 to display the Text Column Definition menu.

9. Press **1 3** to select parallel columns with block protection.

10. Press **2 5** then Return for five columns.

11. Press **4** or **m** to select Margins.

12. Change the size of the columns. The first column will be 2" wide, and the remaining ones will be 0.7" wide, with four spaces between each of them.

Warning
Step 8: With version 5.1, press Alt-F7 1 3.

a. Type **1** for the left margin of column 1, press Return, type **2.9** for the right margin, and press Return.

b. Type **3.4** for the left margin of column 2, press Return, type **4** for the right margin, and press Return.

c. Type **4.5** for the left margin of column 3, press Return, type **5.1** for the right margin, and press Return.

d. Type **5.6** for the left margin of column 4, press Return, type **6.2** for the right margin, and press Return.

e. Type **6.7** for the left margin of column 5, press Return, type **7.3** for the right margin, and press Return. The completed column definition appears in Figure 10.6.

f. Press F7 to return to the document.

13. Press **3** to turn on the Column feature.

Warning
Step 13: With version 5.1, press **1**.

14. Set right tab stops.

a. Press Shift-F8 1 8.

b. Press Ctrl-End to delete all of the tab stops.

c. Type **2.9** then press Return R.

d. Type **4** then press Return R.

e. Type **5.1** then press Return R.

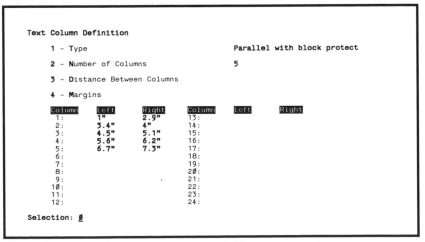

■FIGURE 10.6: *The completed column definition for the sample table*

f. Type **6.2** then press Return R.

g. Type **7.3** then press Return R.

h. Press F7 twice.

15. Enter the first column.

a. Press Tab and type **Budget Area**.

b. Press Return twice.

c. Enter the remainder of the first column. Press Tab before each entry, type the text, then press Return.

> Sales Income$
> Interest Income$
> Rental Income$
> Wages and Salaries$
> Commissions$
> Office Expenses$
> Misc. Expenses$

Because you pressed Return after each entry, the column aligns on the last character ($).

16. Press Ctrl-Return to move to the next column.

17. Enter the second column.

a. Press Tab.

b. Type **1991**.

c. Press Return twice.

d. Enter the remainder of the column. As before, press Tab before each entry, type the text, then press Return.

> 87,000
> 856
> 500
> 9,000
> 900
> 58
> 32

18. Press Ctrl-Return to move to the next column.

19. Enter the third column.

    a. Press Tab.

    b. Type **1990**.

    c. Press Return twice.

    d. Enter the rest of the column.

```
85,000
   865
   500
 9,000
   878
    65
    24
```

20. Press Ctrl-Return to move to the next column.

21. Enter the third column in the same manner.

    a. Press Tab.

    b. Type **1989**.

    c. Press Return twice.

    d. Enter the rest of the column.

```
81,000
   856
   500
 8,500
   756
    89.
    12.
```

22. Press Ctrl-Return to move to the last column.

23. Enter the final column.

    a. Press Tab.

    b. Type **1988**.

    c. Press Return twice.

    d. Enter the rest of the column.

```
76,000
   856
   500
```

7,900

687

34

9

24. Press Ctrl-Return.

25. Press Shift-F7 1 to print the table.

26. Press F7 N Y to exit WordPerfect.

As you can see from this example, there is definitely more work to creating a table as multicolumn text. However, if your data are available on a column-by-column basis, this extra effort will actually save you time at the keyboard.

TABLE MACROS

Here are several macros that can help you to create tables. Note that an Alt-A macro has already been defined. When you try to redefine it, the prompt changes to

ALTA.WPM is Already Defined. 1 Replace; 2 Edit:0.

Press *1* or *r* to continue with the definition.

Note

The appearance of the version 5.1 screen is slightly different, but the steps listed here still apply.

Function	Alt-Letter	Macro
Deletes all tab stops	Alt-A	Ctrl-F10 Alt-A Return Shift-F8 1 8 Ctrl-End F7 F7 Ctrl-F10
Changes the alignment character to $	Alt-F	Ctrl-F10 Alt-F Return Shift-F8 4 3 $ Return Return Return Ctrl-F10
Resets default tab stops	Alt-H	Ctrl-F10 Alt-H Return Shift-F8 1 8 1,.5 Return F7 F7 Ctrl-F10

You can use these macros and the other procedures described in this chapter to create and edit simple or complex tables. Just take the time to plan the table before you actually begin typing entries.

VERSION 5.1 FEATURES

SETTING ABSOLUTE TABS

Using the default relative tab type of version 5.1, all of the tab settings discussed in this chapter will be off 1 inch. In order to perform the keystrokes as given, change the tab type to absolute before setting the first tab.

Do this by pressing Shift-F7 1 8 to display the Tab Selection menu, then press T 1 F7.

If you prefer to use relative tabs, subtract 1 inch from each of the tab stop settings.

ADDITIONAL PRINTER FUNCTIONS

Two additional (and relatively technical) options are available in the version 5.1 Printer Functions menu:

```
5 - Baseline Placement for Typesetters        No
      (First baseline at top margin)
6 - Leading --  Primary -    [SRt]            Optimal
                Secondary -  [HRt]            Optional
```

When outputting to typesetting hardware using a fixed line height, Baseline Placement for Typesetters determines the position of the first baseline. The default setting places the baseline one line below the top margin. Change the setting to Yes to place the baseline directly on the top margin.

Leading is extra white space between lines. Using fixed width fonts, WordPerfect adds no extra leading. But with proportionally spaced fonts it adds 2 extra points between lines.

Primary leading is extra space between lines within a paragraph—those ending with the soft returns entered by word wrap. Secondary leading is inserted when you press Return. Use this, for example, to automatically double-space between paragraphs.

To change the leading, select the Leading option, and enter the leading in points, such as *3p* for 3 points.

AUTOMATIC TABLES

WordPerfect 5.1 has a powerful Table Editor that lets you create spreadsheet-like tables almost effortlessly. You can still use tabs to create tables, as explained earlier in this chapter. But the Table Editor will handle all of the spacing details for you automatically, even draw lines between rows and columns, and adjust row height dynamically as you type.

We'll discuss Table Editor features in several chapters. In this chapter you'll learn how to create tables and perform some basic formatting. You'll learn advanced table formatting in Chapter 11 and sorting tables in Chapter 12. In Chapter 17 you'll learn how to use tables to create ruled forms. Chapter 20 focuses on using the Table Editor for preparing spreadsheets—complete with mathematical formulas for "what-if" calculations.

CREATING TABLES

Follow these steps to create and format the table shown in Figure 10.7, an enhanced version of the table created with tabs earlier in this chapter.

Aardvark Seed Company Outstanding Salesperson Competition		
	Regional	National
Rosalie Butchalski	91,765.00	1,056,090.00
James P. Armitage	1,004,765.00	1,043,876.00
Wilson C. Landsmokker	98,654.00	99,864.00
June Meyers	92,765.00	96,764.00

■**FIGURE 10.7:**   *Enhanced table*

1. Press Alt-F7 2 1 or select **L**ayout **T**ables Create to see the prompt

   Number of Columns: 3

2. Press Return to accept the default *3*. If you wanted a different number of columns, type the number then press Return. You can always add or delete rows later on.

The prompt changes to

Number of Rows: 1

3. Type **6**, the number of rows needed to include the table title and column headings along with the data, then press Return. Pressing Return by itself accepts the default *1*. As with rows, you'll be able to add or delete columns later.

The Table Editor appears with the blank outline of the table on the screen using the default line style: double lines along the perimeter, single lines inside (Figure 10.8).

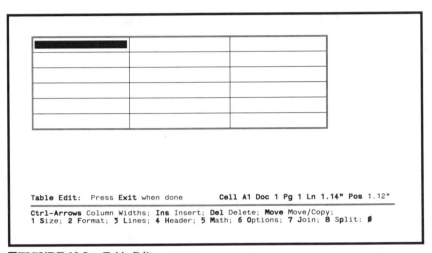

```
Table Edit:  Press Exit when done        Cell A1 Doc 1 Pg 1 Ln 1.14" Pos 1.12"

Ctrl-Arrows Column Widths; Ins Insert; Del Delete; Move Move/Copy;
1 Size; 2 Format; 3 Lines; 4 Header; 5 Math; 6 Options; 7 Join; 8 Split: 0
```

■**FIGURE 10.8:** *Table Editor screen*

You use the Table Editor only to format the table. To enter text into the table, you must exit the Editor by pressing F7.

The commands available while in the Table Editor are shown across the bottom of the screen:

Size	Changes the number of rows or columns.
Format	Changes characteristics of cells and columns, and the height of rows.
Line	Changes the type of lines used to draw the boxes around the cells. You can even remove the line completely.
Header	Designates a row or rows that will appear at the top of every page.

Math	Performs calculations on row, column, and cell contents.
Options	Adjusts spacing between text and lines, determines how negative numbers are displayed, sets the position of the table on the page, and sets a gray shading for the table background.
Join	Combines several cells into one.
Split	Splits a cell into more than one.

Above the prompt line are special keys that can be used to adjust the appearance of the table:

- Press Ctrl and a left or right arrow key to adjust the width of columns.

- Press Insert to insert additional rows or columns.

- Press Del to delete rows or columns.

- Press Move—Ctrl-F4—to move or copy cells, rows, or columns.

While the pull-down menus are not available in the Editor, you can use the mouse to select commands.

Notice that the *cell number* is added to the status line. Each block in the table is called a cell. Columns are referenced by letters, rows by numbers. So the top left-hand cell is A1, the one to the right B1, the one underneath A2, and so on.

In the Table Editor, the cursor highlights, or selects, the entire cell. To move from cell to cell, use the arrow keys or these keystrokes:

To Move to	Press
First cell in row	Home ←
Last cell in row	Home →
First cell in column	Home ↑
Last cell in column	Home ↓

The most obvious problem with the table is the first row—it is divided into three columns instead of one. Let's take care of that now by joining the three cells together. When you join cells together, you remove the lines between them, creating a single larger cell.

4. Press Alt-F4 to turn on the Block function.

5. Press → twice to select the top three cells.

6. Press **7** or **j** for the Join command. The prompt line changes to

   Join cells? **No (Yes)**

7. Press **Y**. The lines between cells disappear.

Other uses for joining and splitting will be discussed in Chapter 17. Now let's leave the Table Editor to enter the rows and columns.

8. Press F7. The table appears on the screen. The cursor is in cell A1, the cell number indicated in the status line.

When working in a table, always use the arrow keys to move from cell to cell. If there is no text in the cell, pressing an arrow key moves the cursor to the adjacent cell. With text, the arrow keys move through the text first, character by character or line by line.

You can quickly move from cell to cell using these keystrokes:

To Move To	Press
Next cell to the right	Tab
Next cell to the left	Shift-Tab
First cell in row	Ctrl-Home Home ←
Last cell in row	Ctrl-Home Home →
First cell in column	Ctrl-Home Home ↑
Last cell in column	Ctrl-Home Home ↓
First cell in table	Ctrl-Home Home Home ↑
Last cell in table	Ctrl-Home Home Home ↓

Do not press Return unless you want to make the cell larger. You'll see how this works in a moment.

9. Enter the first title.

   a. Press Shift-F6.

   b. Type **Aardvark Seed Company**

   c. Press Return.

When you pressed Return the box automatically grew to two lines deep. If you press Return by accident, press Backspace. The box will become smaller.

10. Enter the next title line but do not press Return when done.

   a. Press Shift-F6.

   b. Type **Outstanding Salesperson Competition**

11. Press the ↓ to move to the first cell in the next row, then the → to move to the second column.

12. Enter the two column headings.

   a. Press Shift-F6.

   b. Type **Regional**

   c. Press →

   d. Press Shift-F6.

   e. Type **National**

In entering the names and numbers into the rest of the table, ignore the format for now. We'll take care of this later.

13. Enter the first row.

   a. Press → to reach the first cell in the next row.

   b. Press Shift-F6.

   c. Type **James P. Armitage**

   d. Press →

   e. Type **1,004,765.00**

   f. Press →

   g. Type **1,043,876.00**

14. Enter the next row.

   a. Press → to reach the first cell in the next row.

   b. Press Shift-F6.

    c. Type **Wilson C. Landsmokker**. Since the name is too long to fit in the cell, it is automatically wrapped to the next line, expanding the cell height (Figure 10.9). Don't worry about this now.

    d. Press →

    e. Type **98,654.00**

    f. Press →

    g. Type **99,864.00**

15. In the same way, enter the next two rows, leaving the cursor at the end of the last cell.

Aardvark Seed Company Outstanding Salesperson Competition		
	Regional	National
James P. Armitage	1,004,765.00	1,043,876.00
Wilson C. Landsmokker		

Cell A4 Doc 1 Pg 1 Ln 2.31" Pos 2.22"

■**FIGURE 10.9:**   *Word wrap increases cell height*

FORMATTING TABLES

Now that the basic table is created, we can format the cells in the Table Editor. Follow these steps:

1. Press Alt-F7 or select **L**ayout **T**able **E**dit. If the cursor is in a table, pressing Alt-F7 automatically displays the Table Editor.

First, let's widen column 1 so the names fit on one line.

2. Move the cursor to any cell in the first column except A1.

3. Press Ctrl-→ twice. The Ctrl-arrow keys adjust the width of columns—Ctrl-→ widens columns, Ctrl-← makes them narrower. When the column is wide enough, the long name in cell A4 adjusts and the row shrinks to one line high (Figure 10.10).

Now let's format the next columns so the numbers align on the decimal point.

4. Press → key to reach the next column.

5. Press **2** or **f** to display the Format prompt line:

   Format: 1 Cell; 2 Column, 3 Row Height: 0

6. Press **2** or **l** to select Column, displaying:

   Column: 1 Width; 2 Attribute; 3 Justify; 4 # Digits: 0

7. Press **3** or **j** to show Justification options:

   Justification: 1 Left; 2 Center; 3 Right; 4 Full; 5 Decimal Align: 0

8. Press **5** or **d** to align the column on the decimal point. All of the entries in the column—including the heading—now align on the decimal point, and the word *align* appears on the status line.

9. Center the heading in the second column.

   a. Move the cursor to cell C2.

   b. Press 2 1 3 2 (**F**ormat **C**ell **J**ustify Center).

```
                    Aardvark Seed Company
                Outstanding Salesperson Competition

                          │  Regional   │   National
        ──────────────────┼─────────────┼──────────────
        James P. Armitage │ 1,004,765.00│ 1,043,876.00
        ──────────────────┼─────────────┼──────────────
   Wilson C. Landsmokker  │ 98,654.00   │ 99,864.00
        ──────────────────┼─────────────┼──────────────
        June Meyers       │ 92,765.00   │ 96,764.00
        ──────────────────┼─────────────┼──────────────
     Rosalie Butchalski   │ 91,765.00   │ 93,762.00
```

Table Edit: Press **Exit** when done   **Cell A3 Doc 1 Pg 1 Ln 1.87" Pos** 1.12"

Ctrl-Arrows Column Widths; **Ins** Insert; **Del** Delete; **Move** Move/Copy;
1 Size; **2** Format; **3** Lines; **4** Header; **5** Math; **6** Options; **7** Join; **8** Split: **0**

■**FIGURE 10.10:**   *Use Ctrl-→ to widen columns*

10. Format the next column as a block, without changing the position of its heading.

   a. Move the cursor to cell C3.

   b. Press Alt-F4 to turn on the Block mode.

   c. Press ↓ three times to select the four cells.

   d. Press 2 1 3 5 (**F**ormat **C**ell **J**ustify **D**ecimal Align).

Select *cell* from the Format prompt line when adjusting blocked cells. The numbers in that column now align properly, with the column heading still centered.

11. Press F7 to return to the document.

12. Press F10 or select **F**ile **S**ave, type **TABLE**, then press Return to save the table. You'll be formatting it further in Chapter 11.

13. Press Shift-F7 1 or select **F**ile **P**rint **F**ull Document to print the table.

OTHER FORMATS

The Format option can be used for more than justifying the characters within cells. Other Column Format options are:

Width	Sets column width to a specific measurement.
Attribute	Sets the size and appearance of characters in the cell.
# Digits	Determines the number of decimal places to be displayed.
Type	Designates cell as either numeric (the default) or text.
Vertical Alignment	Determines if text is aligned at the top, bottom, or center of the cell.
Lock	Protects the cell from being edited.

MOUSE AND MENU EQUIVALENTS

Function	Keyboard	Pull-Down Menus
Create Table	Alt-F7 2	Layout Tables Create
Decimal Tab	Ctrl-F6	Layout Align Tab Align
Edit Table	Alt-F7	Layout Tables Edit
Printer Functions	Shift-F8 4 6	Layout Other Printer
Set Tab	Shift-F8 1 8	Layout Line Tab Set

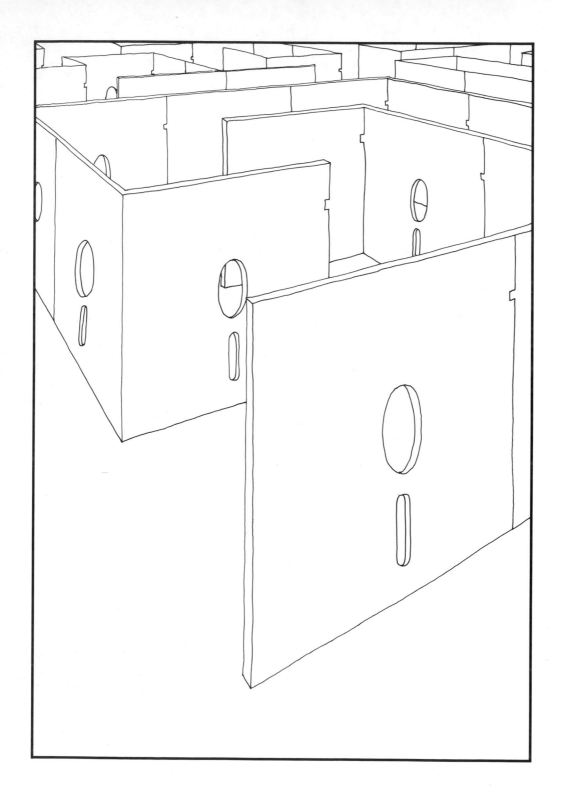

11

ADVANCED TABLE MANIPULATION

In the last chapter, you learned that you can adjust columns of a table by deleting and changing tab stops. In many cases, the usual techniques of insertion, typeover, and deletion are sufficient for editing tables.

Unfortunately, some tables require major surgery. Entire rows or columns must be inserted, deleted, or rearranged. WordPerfect provides a number of functions to make these types of revisions quick and easy. In fact, you can make drastic changes in your tables with just a few keystrokes. In this chapter, you'll learn how to move tabular text by row, by column, or by any rectangular area.

Making major changes to tables is much easier if you set just those tab stops needed for the columns.

■ WORKING WITH ROWS

You can deal with rows of tabular data using the same techniques that are used to manipulate paragraphs. When you think about it, a row of a table is the same as a one-line paragraph—text bordered by [HRt] codes that are inserted with the Return key. As with normal paragraphs, rows can be deleted, copied, or moved by first highlighting them with Alt-F4, then pressing Del or Ctrl-F4.

In the upcoming example, we'll make some changes to the table of sales data that we created in the last chapter.

Note: Before you use any of the advanced table manipulation techniques described in this chapter, be sure to make a copy (using regular block-copying techniques) of the table that you are working on. This way, unexpected results will not force you to reenter your work.

EDITING AND MOVING ROWS

The managers of the Aardvark Seed Company have discovered an error in Ms. Butchalski's sales figures. Her total sales should be $1,056,090.00 instead of $93,762.00. The figure must be corrected, and Ms. Butchalski's name should be moved to the top of the list. The revised table will appear as shown in Figure 11.1. Here's how to make these changes:

1. Start WordPerfect.

2. Press Shift-F10, type **TABLE**, and press Return to recall the document.

3. Place the cursor on the first character (the *9*) of *93,762.00* in the last row.

4. Press Del six times. The cursor is on the decimal point.

5. Type *1,056,090*. The numbers shift to the left because the Align code is still in the text.

6. Press Ctrl-F4 2. The last row of the table is highlighted, and the status line reads

   1 Move; 2 Copy; 3 Delete; 4 Append:0

7. Press **1**.

8. Move the cursor to the start of the first row.

9. Press Return. The deleted line appears at the top of the list, followed by a blank line.

10. Place the cursor on the blank line and press Del.

11. Press Shift-F7 1 to print the table.

12. Press F7 Y Return Y Y to exit WordPerfect and save the edited table.

```
                          Aardvark Seed Company
                     Outstanding Salesperson Competition

                              Regional Total       National Total

        Rosalie Butchalski        91,765.00         1,056,090.00
        James P. Armitage      1,004,765.00         1,043,876.00
     Wilson C. Landsmokker        98,654.00            99,864.00
             June Meyers          92,765.00            96,764.00
```

■**FIGURE 11.1:** *The revised table of sales data*

This example shows just how easy it is to work with rows in a table—just highlight them as you would any paragraph, then perform the function.

■ WORKING WITH COLUMNS AND RECTANGLES

Table columns, on the other hand, are vertical blocks of text that are not bounded by the left and right margins. Instead, they may be bordered by Tab or Tab-Align codes or other characters.

WordPerfect provides two methods for manipulating vertical blocks of text: by the column or by the rectangle. Columns are defined as vertical sections of text separated from other text by Tab or Tab-Align codes. Rectangles are any vertical sections of text. For example, the text highlighted in Figure 11.2 is a rectangle.

These techniques are only designed for tables created in rows using tab stops. Text in tables created as columns can be deleted or moved by using regular block methods.

As an example, we'll first create the table shown in Figure 11.3, then work with its columns to create a new table.

Follow these steps to enter the table:

1. Start WordPerfect.

Warning

With version 5.1, set tabs to absolute or subtract 1 inch from each of the tab stops set in this chapter.

```
Early Toys

    The toy consisted of two disks mounted parallel on a rod. The
front disk contained small slits; the rear disk a series of
pictures. When the child pulled a string, the disks rotated giving
the illusion of a moving object.

Other Claims

    The inventor of a more sophisticated moving picture is a
question of some doubt. In addition to Edison, both W. K. L.
Dickson and William Friese-Greene claim the honors.2 Dickson, for
example, claims to have originated the idea while working as
Edison's assistant.3

Dickson's Claim

    Both Dickson and Friese-Greene worked as Edison's assistants.
Dickson, however, played a direct role in Edison's initial
experimentation with the motion picture camera and film. According
to Dickson, he had the idea for the motion picture when Edison was
in France on other business.4 (see page 3)

1 Move; 2 Copy; 3 Delete; 4 Append: 0
```

■**FIGURE 11.2:** *A rectangle is any vertical section of text*

```
Vendor          Product         Aardvark #       ID

Burack          Manual          AR-65411         101
Paller          Wire            AR-76544         102
Slerppy         Hardware        AR-76541         103
Stanwick        Tape            AR-87614         104
Digital         Chips           AR-97165         105
Capital         Solder          AR-11001         106
Sims Bros.      Diodes          AR-65412         107
```

■**FIGURE 11.3:**   *Sample table*

2. Set tabs at 2.5", 4", and 6".

    a. Press Shift-F8 1 8.

    b. Press Ctrl-End to delete the default tabs.

    c. Type **2.5**, then press Return.

    d. Type **4.**, then press Return

    e. Type **6**, then press Return.

    f. Press F7 twice to return to the document.

3. Enter the first row.

    a. Type **Vendor**.

    b. Press Tab.

    c. Type **Product**.

    d. Press Tab.

    e. Type **Aardvark #**.

    f. Press Tab.

    g. Type **ID**.

    h. Press Return twice.

4. In a similar manner, enter the remaining rows of the table. Use Tab to align the columns.

```
Burack          Manual          AR-65411    101
Paller          Wire            AR-76544    102
Slerppy         Hardware        AR-76541    103
Stanwick        Tape            AR-87614    104
Digital         Chips           AR-97165    105
```

Capital	Solder	AR-11001	106
Sims Bros.	Diodes	AR-65412	107

5. Press Return three times.

6. Press F10, type **COLUMNS**, and press Return to save the table.

COPYING AND MOVING COLUMNS

The Aardvark Seed Company managers want to make a new table from the one shown in Figure 11.3. First, they only want two columns, one for the vendors' names and the other for the Aardvark stock numbers of the items. They also want to delete *AR-* from each of the stock numbers. All of these changes can be made without retyping.

Follow these steps to copy the two columns:

1. You should still be in WordPerfect with the table displayed. If not, recall the document COLUMNS from the disk.

2. Place the cursor on the first character of the first heading in the table (on the *V* in *Vendor*).

3. Press Alt-F4 to turn on the highlighting.

4. Move the cursor so that it is right after the period in *Sims Bros.,* as shown in Figure 11.4.

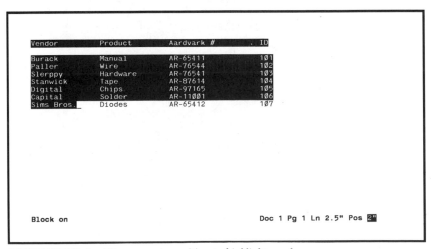

■**FIGURE 11.4:** *The cursor in position to highlight a column*

5. Press Ctrl-F4 to display the prompt line

   Move: 1 Block; 2 Tabular Column; 3 Rectangle:0

6. Press **2** or **c**. The highlighting changes to include only that column, as shown in Figure 11.5, and the prompt line reads

   1 Move; 2 Copy; 3 Delete; 4 Append:0

7. Press **2** to copy the block.

8. Move the cursor to the blank line following the table.

9. Press Return to insert the copied column.

10. Place the cursor on the first character of the third column's heading (the *A* in *Aardvark*).

11. Press Alt-F4 to turn on the highlighting.

12. Move the cursor to the last row, just following *AR-65412,* as shown in Figure 11.6.

13. Press Ctrl-F4 2 to highlight the column and the tab spaces before it.

14. Press **2** to copy the column.

15. Move the cursor to the *V* in the heading *Vendor* in the column that you just moved under the table.

16. Press End to place the cursor at the end of the line.

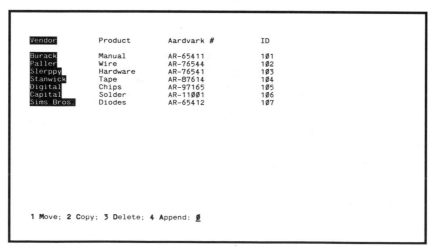

■**FIGURE 11.5:** *The first column highlighted for moving*

17. Press Return to retrieve the stock number column. Because the preceding Tab code was included in the highlighted column, the proper spacing is maintained after the move.

We copied two complete columns to another table. These are defined as columns because they were separated from each other with Tab codes. The next job is to delete *AR-* from the table. In this case, the text cannot be handled as a column because there are no Tab codes after these characters. We will treat this vertical section as a rectangle.

WORKING WITH RECTANGLES

The start of a rectangle is the location of the cursor when you press Alt-F4. The opposite end of the rectangle is the cursor position when you press Ctrl-F4.

Follow these steps to delete the *AR-* characters from our new table:

1. Place the cursor on the *A* in *AR-65411*, the first number of the column.

2. Press Alt-F4 to turn on the highlighting. This position will mark the upper left corner of the rectangle.

3. Move the cursor to the *6* in *AR-65412*, the last number of the column, as shown in Figure 11.7.

4. Press Ctrl-F4 3 to select the rectangle. The highlighting will appear only around the text to be moved—the characters *AR-*.

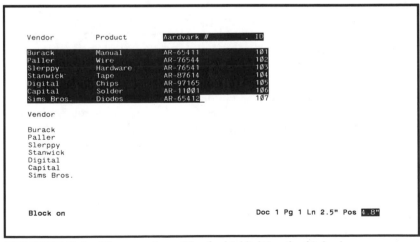

■FIGURE 11.6:   *The cursor in position for highlighting the third column*

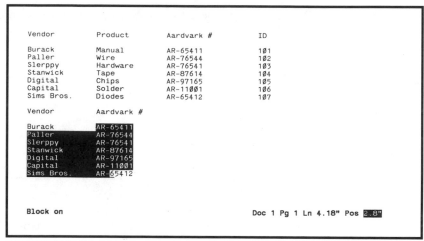

```
Vendor         Product         Aardvark #      ID

Burack         Manual          AR-65411        101
Paller         Wire            AR-76544        102
Slerppy        Hardware        AR-76541        103
Stanwick       Tape            AR-87614        104
Digital        Chips           AR-97165        105
Capital        Solder          AR-11001        106
Sims Bros.     Diodes          AR-65412        107

Vendor         Aardvark #

Burack         AR-65411
Paller         AR-76544
Slerppy        AR-76541
Stanwick       AR-87614
Digital        AR-97165
Capital        AR-11001
Sims Bros.     AR-65412



Block on                                        Doc 1 Pg 1 Ln 4.18" Pos 2.8"
```

■**FIGURE 11.7:**   *The cursor in position to highlight the rectangle*

5. Press *3* to delete the rectangle. The *AR-* prefixes are deleted from each number in the column.

6. Press Shift-F7 1 to print both tables.

7. Press F7 N Y to exit WordPerfect.

Notice that the entire second column was not highlighted during this procedure. Instead, the Rectangle command used the exact position of the cursor to define the vertical section of text.

■
SIDE EFFECTS OF MOVING COLUMNS AND RECTANGLES

When you move a normal block of text, you move the hard and soft carriage returns with it. Thus, when you insert the block into other text, existing characters move to the right and down to make room. Columns and rectangles do not behave so nicely. When you move a column, the Tab codes on the left side come with it. When you move a rectangle, only the text moves. Inserting these vertical blocks into existing text will not move existing text down.

For example, suppose that you want to move the Vendor column from our sample table to a point between the two sentences below:

The company obtains raw materials from a variety of vendors.
Each vendor has been selected based on an exhaustive
evaluation of its product quality and delivery record.

You would highlight the column as a block and select Cut/Copy Column from the prompt line. But if you placed the cursor between the two sentences and retrieved the column, the result would look like this:

The company obtains raw materials from a variety of vendors.
Vendor
Each vendor has been selected based on an exhaustive
evaluation of
Burack its product quality and delivery record.
Paller
Slerppy
Stanwick
Digital
Capital
Sims Bros.

The text of the column is intermixed within the paragraph itself. This is because column lines, unlike lines of regular text, do not end in carriage returns.

To insert columns or rectangles in other text, you must first press Return at the point of insertion enough times to add the correct number of blank lines to accommodate the insertion.

■ MOVING COLUMNS WITHIN TABLES

The side effects mentioned above must also be considered when you're moving columns within tables. You must be particularly careful when you are working with the first column and when there are different numbers of Tab codes between columns.

When you move a column, you also move the Tab code that came before it. If you move the first column, however, there is no Tab code, so the column will not automatically align at another position. And if you move another column to that position, the Tab code that is before it shifts the text over from the left margin.

Let's see what happens when we try to rearrange the columns of the table shown in Figure 11.3. We want to change the order of the columns to Aardvark #, Product, ID, and Vendor.

Follow these steps:

1. Start WordPerfect.

2. Press Shift-F10, type **COLUMNS**, and press Return to recall the table.

3. Place the cursor on the first letter of the third column's heading (the *A* in *Aardvark*).

4. Press Alt-F4 to turn on the highlighting.

    Rather than move the Aardvark column as a column, let's move it as a rectangle, including the tab after it, so the text aligns with the left margin and the second column shifts over accordingly.

5. Place the cursor on the last character of that column (the *2* in *AR-65412*), then press → twice to highlight both the text and the tab following it (Figure 11.8). Without this code, the columns would not align correctly when rearranged.

6. Press Ctrl-F4 3 1 to move the rectangle.

7. Place the cursor on the *V* in *Vendor*.

8. Press Return to retrieve the column. Figure 11.9 shows the table with these changes. Even though the cursor was on the word Vendor when you inserted the column, the tab spacing was maintained because you moved the Tab codes along with the Aardvark # column.

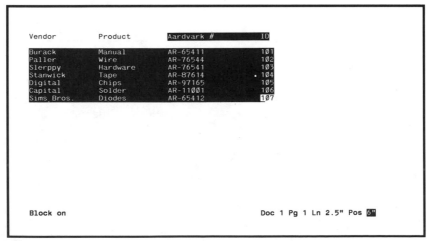

■**FIGURE 11.8:** *Highlighting the column to be moved*

Figure 11.10 illustrates how the same table would appear if you moved it as a column with the tab before it.

9. Place the cursor on the *V* in *Vendor*. We will now move the Vendor column to the end of the table.

10. Press Alt-F4 to turn on the highlighting.

```
Aardvark #       Vendor          Product         ID

AR-65411         Burack          Manual          101
AR-76544         Paller          Wire            102
AR-76541         Slerppy         Hardware        103
AR-87614         Stanwick        Tape            104
AR-97165         Digital         Chips           105
AR-11001         Capital         Solder          106
AR-65412         Sims Bros.      Diodes          107




C:\WP5\COLUMNS                              Doc 1 Pg 1 Ln 1.16" Pos 1"
```

■FIGURE 11.9:   *The Aardvark # and Product columns rearranged correctly*

```
    _            Aardvark #Vendor            ProductID

                 AR-65411Burack Manual       101
                 AR-76544Paller Wire         102
                 AR-76541Slerppy             Hardware103
                 AR-87614Stanwick            Tape104
                 AR-97165Digital             Chips105
                 AR-11001Capital             Solder106
                 AR-65412Sims Bros.          Diodes107




C:\WP5\COLUMNS                              Doc 1 Pg 1 Ln 1.16" Pos 1"
```

■FIGURE 11.10:   *The Aardvark # and Product columns spaced incorrectly when moved as a column*

11. Move the cursor past *Bros.* at the end of the first column.

12. Press Ctrl-F4 2 1 to move the column.

13. Position the cursor after the ID column heading, then press Return.

Editing tables requires some planning and careful action. But working with blocks, either horizontal or vertical, allows you to perform even major revisions without retyping. If you had not set only the tab stops needed for the table, the column and rectangle moves would not have gone so smoothly.

VERSION 5.1 FEATURES

While all of the column and rectangular block functions described in the chapter can still be applied to version 5.1, rows and columns can be manipulated much easier using the Table Editor.

In this section, you'll learn how to move and copy cells, rows, and columns, and how to adjust the type of lines. You'll also learn how to insert and delete rows and columns, change table size, and add shadings.

All formatting is performed in the Table Editor. So always place the cursor in the table then press Alt-F7, or select **L**ayout **T**able **E**dit. When you recall a table that starts a document, the cursor will be placed at the upper left corner of the table border; press the ↓ key to enter cell A1.

TABLE OPTIONS

When you first create a table, WordPerfect divides the full width of the page evenly between the columns. So by default, the table is as wide as your page.

If you reduce a column's width using Ctrl-←, the table will no longer be the full width of the page and will align with the left margin.

You can change the position of tables, and several other features, by selecting *Options* from the Table Editor prompt line. The Table Options menu appears (Figure 11.11).

Spacing Between Text and Line determines how much space appears between the text and the left, right, top, and bottom lines of the cell. *Display Negative Results* determines how the automatic math function shows negative numbers. (Math is explained in Chapter 19.)

To change the position of the table, press *3* or *P* for the prompt line:

Table Position: 1 Left; 2 Right; 3 Center; 4 Full; 5 Set Position:0

Full returns the table to the full page width; *Set Position* prompts you to enter a specific position from the left edge of the page.

Gray Shading determines the degree of shading that can print in the background. The default is 10%. This option only sets the degree of shading. You turn it on and off for specific cells using the Lines commands, as you'll soon learn.

TABLE SIZE

To change the number of rows or columns, press **l** or **s** from the Table Editor prompt line to reveal

Table Size: 1 Rows; 2 Columns: 0

Select either Rows or Columns, enter the number desired, then press Return. New columns are added to the right side of the table, new rows to the end.

INSERTING AND DELETING ROWS AND COLUMNS

When you insert a row, it appears above the one in which the cursor is placed. Inserted columns appear to the left of the current position. So place the cursor in the appropriate location then press Ins to see the prompt

Insert: 1 Rows; 2 Columns:0

Select Rows or Columns to see the prompt

Number of rows (columns): 1

```
Table Options

    1 - Spacing Between Text and Lines
            Left                     Ø.Ø83"
            Right                    Ø.Ø83"
            Top                      Ø.1"
            Bottom                   Ø"

    2 - Display Negative Results         1
            1 = with minus signs
            2 = with parentheses

    3 - Position of Table            Left

    4 - Gray Shading (% of black)    1Ø%




    Selection: Ø
```

■**FIGURE 11.11:**   *Table Options menu*

Type the number of rows or columns you want to insert, then press Return.

To delete rows or columns, position the cursor, in the first row or column you want to delete, then press Del for the prompt

Delete: 1 Rows; 2 Columns:0

Select Rows or Columns to see the prompt

Number of rows: 1

or

Number of columns: 1

Type the number of rows or columns you want to delete, then press Return.

WordPerfect deletes multiple rows downward. For example, with the cursor in row 2, deleting three rows removes rows 2, 3, and 4 from the table. Multiple columns are deleted toward the right.

MOVING AND COPYING CELLS

The procedure to move parts of tables is similar to moving text within the document.

Within the Table Editor press Ctrl-F4 to see the prompt line

Move: 1 Block; 2 Row; 3 Column; 4 Retrieve; 0

Select either of the first three options (use Block for selected cells) to see the prompt line:

1 Move; 2 Copy; 3 Delete:0

Select your option. If you choose Move or Copy, place the cursor where you want to insert the cells, then press Return. To place the cells at a later time, press F1. When you want to insert the cells from within the Table Editor, press Ctrl-F4 4.

REFORMATTING TABLES

Unfortunately, moving and copying rows or columns may have unexpected results. As an example, let's make the changes and format the table as shown in Figure 11.12.

1. Press Shift-F10 or select **File Retrieve**, type **Table**, and press Return to recall the table you created and saved in Chapter 10.

2. Place the cursor on the first character (*9*) of $93,762.00 in the last row.

3. Press Del six times.

4. Type **1,056,090**. You now have to move the row to the first position.

5. Press Alt-F7 or select **L**ayout **T**able Edit. The cursor is already in the row you want to move.

6. Press Ctrl-F4 2 1 to move the row.

7. Press ↑ twice, then press Return. The row is inserted but along with the double-lines that it had when at the end of the table (Figure 11.13).

When you move or copy a cell, its lines move along with it. Since we only want double-lines around the perimeter, we have to adjust the lines for that row.

```
        Aardvark Seed Company
     Outstanding Salesperson Competition
                      Regional          National
 Rosalie Butchalski      91,765.00      1,056,090.00
 James P. Armitage     1,004,765.00     1,043,876.00
 Wilson C. Landsmokker    98,654.00        99,864.00
     June Meyers          92,765.00        96,764.00
```

■**FIGURE 11.12:** *Revised table*

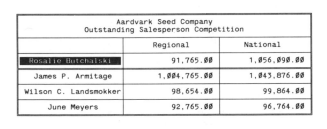

■**FIGURE 11.13:** *The double-lines moved with the row*

8. Press Alt-F4 to turn on the Block function, and then press → twice to select the row.

9. Press **3** or **l** to see the prompt line

> Lines: 1 Left; 2 Right; 3 Top; 4 Bottom; 5 Inside; 6 Outside;
> 7 All; 8: Shade:0

These options determine the lines you wish to format. *Inside* refers to all of the line inside the highlighted block; *Outside* to all lines immediately outside of the block. *All* means all of the lines in the table.

Above the prompt line is a description of the lines for that cell, such as

> Top=Single; Left=Double; Bottom=Double; Right=None

Notice that the Right option is set at None—meaning no line on the right side of the cell. The line separating cells in a row is determined by the line definition of the cell on the right. So the line between cells A1 and A2 is determined by the Left setting of cell A2, not the Right setting of cell A1.

Normally, a common line between cells—in rows or columns—is defined as None in one cell. Later we'll discuss the effects of both cells defining a common line other than None.

10. Press **4** or **b** to select *Bottom*. The prompt line changes to:

> 1 None; 2 Single; 3 Double; 4 Dashed; 5 Dotted; 6 Thick;
> 7 Extra Thick: 0

11. Press **1** or **n**. The single top line format of row 4 now takes effect.

Now for final emphasis, let's add shading to the table title and the highest sales figures, and adjust the lines.

12. Place the cursor in cell A1.

13. Press **3 8** (Lines Shade) to see the prompt line

> Shading: 1 On; 2 Off: 0

14. Press **1** or **o** to turn on shading (or **2** or **f** to later turn it off). The shading will not appear unless you preview or print the table.

15. Remove the lines that surround the title.

a. Press **3** or **l** for the lines option.

b. Press **6** or **o** for Outside.

c. Press **1** or **n** for None.

Even though there are no longer lines surrounding the title, it is still part of the table and still cell A1. In fact, removing all of the lines from the table does not change how you can work with it as a table.

16. Change the single line now on top of the "box" to double lines.

    a. Place the cursor in cell A2.

    b. Press Alt-F4, then the → twice.

    c. Press **3 3 3** (**L**ines **T**op **D**ouble) for double lines.

17. Shade the highest sales figure.

    a. Place the cursor in cell C3.

    b. Press **3 8 1** (**L**ines **S**hade **O**n).

18. Press F7 to return to the document.

19. Press Shift-F7 1 or **F**ile **P**rint **F**ull to print the table.

20. Press F7 N Y or select **F**ile **E**xit **N**o **Y**es to exit WordPerfect.

LINE PRIORITIES

Adjacent cells have one line in common—the bottom of cell A1, for example, is the top of cell A2.

In the Table Editor display, when the formats of common lines conflict, the line format number has priority.

For example, consider these possible line definitions:

Cell A1
Top=Single; Left=Double; Bottom=Double; Right=None

Cell A2
Top=Dotted; Left=Double; Bottom=Double; Right=None

In the list of line types, the dotted format (5) has a higher number than double (3), so the line will appear dotted on your screen.

If changes to a line format seem to have no effect, or result in a different format than selected, then check the format of the adjacent cell. Using the lines shown above, for instance, what would occur if you changed A2 to a single top line? It would become double since the format in cell A1 would now have priority.

But while the line type has priority over what's displayed in the Table Editor, the table will be printed exactly as formatted. If a common line is formatted as a line type other than None by both adjacent cells, both lines will be printed. While this can be used to create special effects, as shown in Figure 11.14, it might not result in the format you had intended. So no matter how the line appears in the Table Editor, check the format of common lines carefully before printing.

The Table Editor is a powerful feature, and you'll learn other uses for it in later chapters.

```
Top line = Double          Bottom line = Single
Top line = Single          Bottom line = Single
Top line = Dotted          Bottom line = Single
Top line = Double          Bottom line = Extra Thick
Top line = Dashed          Bottom line = Double
Top line = Double          Bottom line = Double
```

■**FIGURE 11.14:**   *Common line format conflict*

MOUSE AND MENU EQUIVALENTS

Function	Keyboard	Pull-Down Menus
Copy	Ctrl-F4 1 2	**E**dit **C**opy
Move	Ctrl-F4 1 1	**E**dit **M**ove
Rectangle	Ctrl-F4 3	**E**dit **S**elect **R**ectangle
Tabular Column	Ctrl-F4 2	**E**dit **S**elect Tabular Column

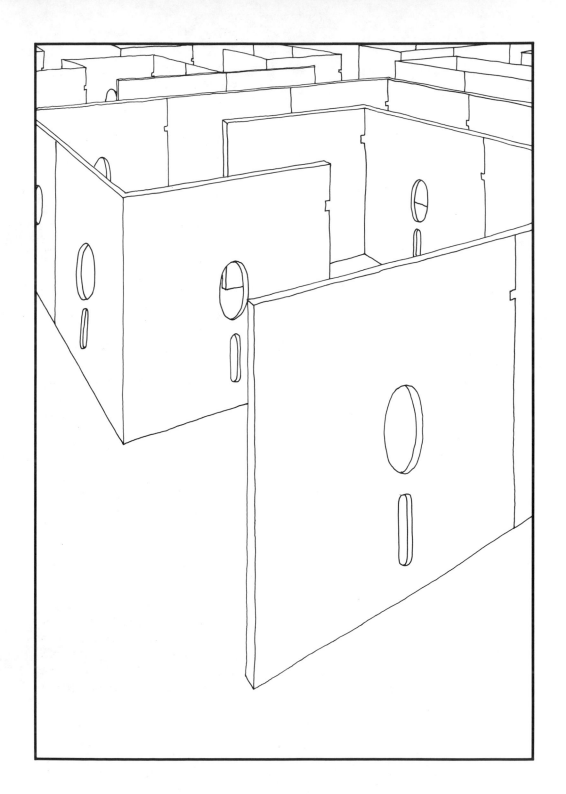

12

SORTING TABLES AND LISTS: EASY ACCESS TO YOUR DATA

Although you can rearrange rows in tables by moving them as blocks, the usefulness of this technique is limited. In the last chapter, we moved a row as a block in a table listing four salespeople and their sales amounts. Imagine trying to rearrange a table consisting of 100 salespeople into alphabetical order by name or into numerical order by sales amount. You would have to manually sort your input cards (if you had them), then rearrange the names in the correct order. Switching 100 individual rows to put them in order just doesn't seem to meet the promise of the computer age.

WordPerfect offers a solution. In this chapter, you will learn how to use the Sort feature to manipulate the data in tables and lists. You can enter the rows of a table in any order, then sort them in a number of ways. You'll also get an introduction to the powerful features that can turn WordPerfect into a database-management system, a subject dealt with in some detail later on.

PREPARING TABLES FOR SORTING

WordPerfect's Sort feature automatically arranges your table in numerical or alphabetical order. You can change the order of a table as many times as necessary. For example, you could arrange a client list alphabetically to locate customers by name, rearrange it to find the client that owes you the most money, then change it again to see who purchased a certain product. However, a little thought in preparing your tables is necessary to make the sorting process go smoothly.

Remember, tables created as multicolumn text cannot be sorted properly. If you think that you'll want to rearrange a table after it is typed, be sure to enter it row by row.

SETTING TAB STOPS

Here's the most important rule to follow in setting up a table: Set only the tab stops that are necessary. Before entering the table, clear all the tab stops by pressing Shift-F8 1 8 Ctrl-End and then set only those tabs needed for the table. This is particularly important when a column has entries of different lengths. Look at this example:

Name	Amount
John Doe	$16,000.00
William P. Smythe	$15,000.00

Although the columns appear even, WordPerfect would have difficulty sorting this table according to the dollar figure in the second column because there are different numbers of Tab codes between the entries in the first and second rows. With the codes revealed, the table appears on screen like this:

```
Name[TAB][TAB][TAB][TAB]Amount[HRt]
[HRt]
John Doe[TAB][TAB][TAB]$16,000.00[HRt]
William P. Smythe[TAB]$15,000.00[HRt]
```

The Tab key was pressed three times between the name and the amount on the first row, but only once on the second row.

To sort tables successfully, you should have the same number of Tab codes between all entries. If you had cleared all of the tab stops and then set one for the second column, the table would appear the same on screen, but it would look like this with the codes revealed:

```
Name[TAB]Amount[HRt]
[HRt]
John Doe[TAB]$16,000.00[HRt]
William P. Smythe[TAB]$15,000.00[HRt]
```

It doesn't matter whether you use the Tab key or Ctrl-F6 to create your table. There should be the same number of codes between each column.

Before you begin typing your table, make a note of the items that you want to include in each column—full names, just last names, dollar amounts, etc.

Then count the characters in what you think will be the longest entry in each column. If a column is to be aligned on the decimal point, count the characters in the largest number that will be entered. Then set the tab stop so that the number will not collide with the longest entry in the column before. Remember to set the tab stop where you want the decimal point to appear, not at the leftmost position in the column.

■ ENTERING TABLES TO BE SORTED

Let's create a table to sort. For sorting purposes, each column is called a *field,* and each row is called a *record.* Our table will have three fields: one for the client's name (first then last name), one for the amount due, and one for the total credit.

In this table, the longest name in the first column will be 16 characters wide. The longest number in the second column will be six characters to the left of the decimal point. To allow some space in case the longest name is in the same row as the longest number, the first tab stop will be set at position 3.5". The largest number, aligned on the decimal, will shift to position 2.9", while the longest name on the table will go as far as position 2.5" (16 characters from margin position 1"). Even in the worst case, there will still be four blank spaces between columns. The second tab stop, for the third column, will be set 5.5". Remember, three columns require only two tab stops; the first column starts at the left margin.

Follow these steps to enter the table:

Warning
With version 5.1, set tabs to absolute or subtract 1 inch from each of the tab stops set in this chapter.

1. Start WordPerfect.

2. Press Shift-F8 1 8 Ctrl-End to delete all of the tab stops.

3. Type **3.5** then press Return D.

4. Type **5.5** then press Return D. This sets tab stops at 3.5" and 5.5" for decimal-aligned columns.

5. Press F7 twice to return to the document.

6. Type the following table. Because you set decimal tabs, just press the Tab key, not Ctrl-F6, to align the second and third columns.

Name	Amount	Credit
Adam M. Chesin	654.19	15,000.00
Pam McQuen	2.49	15,000.00

Nancy Caulder	142.98	10,000.00
Diane Bayzik	2,000.00	5,000.00
Victor Rossi	542.86	12,000.00
Allen Misher	876.87	5,000.00
Nam Paek	1,609.12	12,000.00
William Watson	32.09	10,000.00
Barbara Ward	38,761.00	5,000.00
Richard Channing	541.09	12,000.00
Herb Fried	12.09	500.00
Tina Roberts	599.00	7,000.00

Because we set only two tab stops, the second and third fields have only one Tab code between them, no matter how long the first field is. Also note that the numeric entries can include commas and—though not in this case—dollar signs.

7. Press F10, type **SORT**, and press Return to save the table.

■ SINGLE-KEY SORTING

The field that is the basis for the sort is called the *key*. For example, if we wanted to print our sample table in the order of amount due, the key would be the second field.

Each time you sort a table, you must define the key that will be used. The key definition includes three elements: whether the field is alphanumeric or numeric, the location of the field in the table, and the location of the key word within that field.

NUMERIC AND ALPHANUMERIC FIELDS

Numeric fields, which can be of any length, consist only of numbers, dollar signs, commas, and periods. Alphanumeric fields consist of letters, numbers, or both. If the field does not contain all numbers, consider it alphanumeric. For example, if you entered this column of telephone numbers:

```
676-9851
WA7-1111
555-9861
555-5412
NE7-7700
```

and then sorted it as an alphanumeric field, the result would be:

```
555-5412
555-9861
676-9851
NE7-7700
WA7-1111
```

Notice that WordPerfect places telephone numbers starting with numbers before those starting with letters. This is because WordPerfect uses the American Standard Code for Information Interchange system (ASCII) to determine the sequence for placing letters and numbers in order. Using the ASCII system, numbers come first, then uppercase letters, and finally lowercase letters.

If you sorted this same column as a numeric field, it would appear as:

```
WA7-1111
NE7-7700
555-5412
555-9861
676-9851
```

Numeric sorts use the value of characters, not their place in the ASCII sequence. Alphabetic characters come first because they are evaluated as having no value—zero.

■ SORTING ON A NUMERIC FIELD IN ASCENDING OR DESCENDING ORDER

As an example of single-key sorting, we'll sort our sample table by the Amount field. Follow these steps:

1. Place the cursor at the start of the first row, on the *A* in *Adam M. Chesin.*

2. Press Alt-F4 to highlight the table.

3. Move the cursor to the end of the table. The entire table will be highlighted, as shown in Figure 12.1.

4. Press Ctrl-F9. The bottom of the screen will display the Sort by Line menu, shown in Figure 12.2. The line above the prompt line gives the current status of the sort—ascending order by line.

   Notice the default entry for the first key. It is set to sort alphabetically (type a), on the first column (field 1), and on the first word in that column

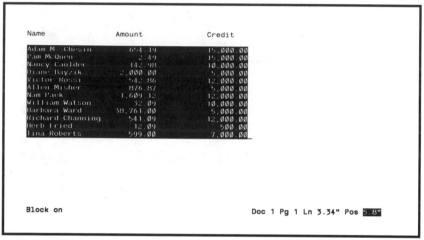

■FIGURE 12.1: *Highlighting the entire table for sorting*

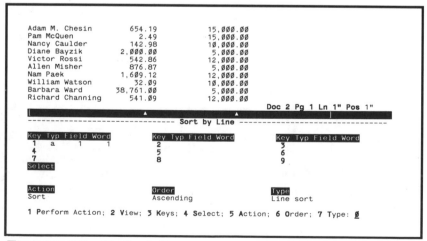

■FIGURE 12.2: *The Sort by Line menu*

(word 1). Since we want to sort this table numerically on the second field, we must change the default entries for the key.

5. Press **3** to change the keys. The cursor appears next to key 1.

6. Press **N** for numeric sort. The cursor automatically moves to the field number.

7. Press **2** to select the second field.

8. Press F7 to return to the bottom prompt line. We don't need to change the word for sorting because it is already set to 1, and there is only one word in the column that we are using as the key. In some other cases, however, you might not use the first word in the column as a key. If you wanted to sort the table by the person's last name, for example, you would not select the first word, since that contains the first name. You'll see how tables are sorted this way in a moment. Your screen should now look like Figure 12.3.

9. Press **1** to select Perform Action.

WordPerfect will sort the entire table, placing the field with the lowest amount at the top of the list, as shown in Figure 12.4. This is an ascending sort, the default setting.

Let's sort the table again so that the field with the highest amount is on top—a descending sort. Since we will sort on the same elements, we do not need to change the key definition. It will remain the same until you change it for another

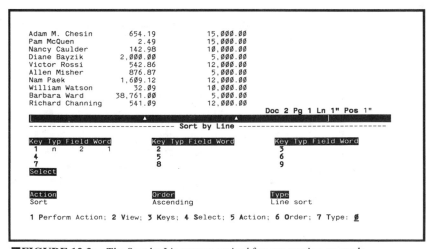

■FIGURE 12.3:   *The Sort by Line menu revised for our sorting example*

```
Name                   Amount            Credit

Pam McQuen               2.49          15,000.00
Herb Fried              12.09             500.00
William Watson          32.09          10,000.00
Nancy Caulder          142.98          10,000.00
Richard Channing       541.09          12,000.00
Victor Rossi           542.86          12,000.00
Tina Roberts           599.00           7,000.00
Adam M. Chesin         654.19          15,000.00
Allen Misher           876.87           5,000.00
Nam Paek             1,609.12          12,000.00
Diane Bayzik         2,000.00           5,000.00
Barbara Ward        38,761.00           5,000.00
```

■**FIGURE 12.4:**   *Sample table sorted by the second field in ascending order*

sort or exit WordPerfect.

Follow these steps to sort our table in descending order:

1. Place the cursor at the start of the first row, on the *P* in *Pam McQuen*.

2. Press Alt-F4.

3. Move the cursor to the end of the table.

4. Press Ctrl-F9 to display the Sort by Line menu.

5. Press **6** to select Order. The prompt line displays

   Direction: 1 Ascending; 2 Descending: 0

6. Press **2** or **d** for a descending sort. The regular Sort prompt reappears.

7. Press **1** to select Perform Action. The table is now sorted in descending order according to the Amount field, as shown in Figure 12.5.

Note
The appearance of the version 5.1 screen is slightly different, but the steps listed here still apply.

■ MULTIKEY SORTING

WordPerfect will sort on up to nine keys (or fields). As with single-field sorting, the fields in multikey sorting can be either numeric or alphanumeric. You can use multikey sorts to group records (rows) together as well as to sort them. For example, suppose that we want our sample table sorted by the Credit field. Notice that several clients have the same credit. We can have all of the clients with the same credit next to each other in the table, then sort them within the group by the Amount field.

```
Name                 Amount              Credit

Barbara Ward        38,761.00           5,000.00
Diane Bayzik         2,000.00           5,000.00
Nam Paek             1,609.12          12,000.00
Allen Misher           876.87           5,000.00
Adam M. Chesin         654.19          15,000.00
Tina Roberts           599.00           7,000.00
Victor Rossi           542.86          12,000.00
Richard Channing       541.09          12,000.00
Nancy Caulder          142.98          10,000.00
William Watson          32.09          10,000.00
Herb Fried              12.09             500.00
Pam McQuen               2.49          15,000.00
```

■**FIGURE 12.5:** *Sample table sorted by the second field in descending order*

This sort will require two keys, and each element (type, field, and word) must be defined for each key.

Follow these steps:

1. You should still have the table on the screen. If not, start WordPerfect and recall the document named SORT.

2. Place the cursor at the start of the first row, on the *B* in *Barbara Ward*.

3. Press Alt-F4.

4. Move the cursor to the end of the table.

5. Press Ctrl-F9. The bottom of the screen displays the Sort by Line menu with the descending sort still selected. We must first change key 1 to the third field.

6. Press **3** to change the keys. The cursor appears next to key 1.

7. Press **N** to specify a numeric key and move to the Field option.

8. Press **3** to select the third field.

9. Press Return twice to reach the second key.

10. Press **N** to select a numeric field.

11. Press **2** to use the second field as key 2.

12. Press F7.

13. Press **6** then **1** to select an ascending sort. The revised Sort by Line menu should look like Figure 12.6.

14. Press **1** to sort the table.

WordPerfect sorts the table so that the clients are grouped by their credit rating; within groups of identical credit rating, they are sorted by amount due, as shown in Figure 12.7.

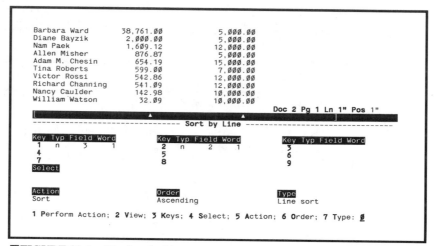

```
Barbara Ward        38,761.00          5,000.00
Diane Bayzik         2,000.00          5,000.00
Nam Paek             1,609.12         12,000.00
Allen Misher           876.87          5,000.00
Adam M. Chesin         654.19         15,000.00
Tina Roberts           599.00          7,000.00
Victor Rossi           542.86         12,000.00
Richard Channing       541.09         12,000.00
Nancy Caulder          142.98         10,000.00
William Watson          32.09         10,000.00
                                                    Doc 2 Pg 1 Ln 1" Pos 1"

                 ▲                        ▲
------------------------------ Sort by Line ------------------------------

Key Typ Field Word      Key Typ Field Word      Key Typ Field Word
 1   n    3    1          2   n    2    1         3
 4                        5                       6
 7                        8                       9
Select

Action                  Order                   Type
Sort                    Ascending               Line sort

 1 Perform Action; 2 View; 3 Keys; 4 Select; 5 Action; 6 Order; 7 Type: 0
```

■**FIGURE 12.6:** *The Sort by Line menu revised for our multikey sorting example*

Name	Amount	Credit
Herb Fried	12.09	500.00
Allen Misher	876.87	5,000.00
Diane Bayzik	2,000.00	5,000.00
Barbara Ward	38,761.00	5,000.00
Tina Roberts	599.00	7,000.00
William Watson	32.09	10,000.00
Nancy Caulder	142.98	10,000.00
Richard Channing	541.09	12,000.00
Victor Rossi	542.86	12,000.00
Nam Paek	1,609.12	12,000.00
Pam McQuen	2.49	15,000.00
Adam M. Chesin	654.19	15,000.00

■**FIGURE 12.7:** *Sample table sorted by the Credit field as the first key and the Amount field as the second key*

REVERSE FIELD SORTING

It would seem that our sample table could easily be sorted by the clients' names. However, there is one small problem: we've entered first names first and last names second. If we select the first field as the key, the list will actually be sorted alphabetically by first name, as shown in Figure 12.8.

Remember that by default WordPerfect sorts on the first word of the first field, which, in this case, is the client's first name. We could try using the second word as the sort key; however, in one case the middle initial would be used in the sort. The result would be:

Diane Bayzik
Nancy Caulder
Richard Channing
Herb Fried
Adam M. Chesin
Pam McQuen
Allen Misher
Nam Paek
Tina Roberts
Victor Rossi
Barbara Ward
William Watson

Adam M. Chesin is in the wrong position in the list because his middle initial, not his last name, was used for the sort.

```
Name                Amount          Credit

Adam M. Chesin        654.19        15,000.00
Allen Misher          876.87         5,000.00
Barbara Ward       38,761.00         5,000.00
Diane Bayzik        2,000.00         5,000.00
Herb Fried             12.09           500.00
Nam Paek            1,609.12        12,000.00
Nancy Caulder         142.98        10,000.00
Pam McQuen              2.49        15,000.00
Richard Channing      541.09        12,000.00
Tina Roberts          599.00         7,000.00
Victor Rossi          542.86        12,000.00
William Watson         32.09        10,000.00
```

■**FIGURE 12.8:** *Sample table sorted alphabetically by the first word of the field*

The solution is to use the last word in the field, which, in this case, will always be the last name. Since the names have different numbers of words, you cannot count forward to arrive at the word number. Instead, work backwards from the end of the field and use a minus sign to enter your choice. Although this technique will work with our sample table, it cannot be used if some of the names have special endings, such as Jr., Sr., or III. If the names in a column include these endings and different numbers of words, use a hard space (Home-space bar) to separate the ending from the last name.

Since the names in our table contain no such endings, follow these steps to sort them alphabetically:

1. Place the cursor at the start of the first row.

2. Press Alt-F4.

3. Move the cursor to the end of the table.

4. Press Ctrl-F9.

5. Press **3** to change the key.

6. Press **A** for an alphanumeric sort.

7. Press **1** to select the first field.

8. Press Return to reach the Word option.

9. Type **−1**. This tells WordPerfect to use the first word to the left of the end of the column.

10. If you still have a second key defined, press Return to reach that key, then press Del to erase the Field and Word entries for key 2.

11. Press F7 to return to the Sort prompt line.

12. Press **1** to select Perform Action. The table will be sorted alphabetically by last name.

SELECTING RECORDS

You can remove portions of tables by deleting them as blocks, columns, or rectangles, but in long tables this can be a time-consuming task. For this type of table manipulation, WordPerfect provides the Select feature. You can select specific records to either remain in the table or be deleted from it. By using Select, you can create a list of clients who owe a certain amount or live in a particular zip code area. A class list can be turned into a dean's list by selecting students with certain averages, or into a warning list of those who need special help. Any of the sorting key elements can be used for the selection process.

CRITERIA FOR SELECTION

Selection can be simple, based on the value of one key, or complex, based on a number of keys.

A simple selection is based on comparing a key with a specific value, either alphanumeric or numeric. The comparisons can include the following:

Comparison	Symbol	Example
Equals	=	key1 = $500.00
Does not equal	< >	key1 < > NJ
Greater than	>	key2 > 200
Less than	<	key3 < 1000.00
Greater than or equal to	>=	key1 >= 500.00
Less than or equal to	<=	key1 <= 500.00

Note the difference between < and >, and <= and >=. If you want to include records with the value you're specifying, make sure that you include the equal sign in the selection criteria.

Complex selections compare the values of more than one key using the + (OR) and * (AND) operators. For example, if you want to list clients who owe you more than $5,000.00 and live in Pennsylvania, the selection criteria might be:

key1=PA * key2>$5,000.00

As with sorting, you can use dollar signs, commas, and periods in the numeric values for selection. Alphanumeric values, such as PA in the example above, do not have to be enclosed in quotation marks as they would in comparisons performed by most computer languages.

To find the clients who either owe you more than $5,000.00 or live in Pennsylvania (no matter how much they owe), the selection criteria might be:

key1=PA + key2>$5,000.00

PERFORMING A SELECTION

Let's use our sample table to see how selection works.

We want to transform this table into one that contains only those clients who have a credit of $10,000 or more but who owe more than $500.00. We also want this table sorted by the amount that the clients owe, in descending order. Follow these steps:

1. You should still have the table on the screen. If not, start WordPerfect and recall the document named SORT.

2. Place the cursor at the start of the first row.

3. Press Alt-F4.

4. Move the cursor to the end of the table.

5. Press Ctrl-F9.

6. Press **3** to change the keys. The cursor appears next to key 1.

7. Press **N** for a numeric field.

8. Press **2** to select the second field as the first key.

9. Press Return.

10. Press **1** to select the first word in the field.

11. Press Return to reach the second key.

12. Press **N** to select a numeric field.

13. Press **3** to use the third column as key 2.

14. Press F7.

15. Press **4** for Select. The cursor moves up, and the prompt line changes to

    +(OR), *(AND), =, <>, >, <, >=, <=;
    Press EXIT when done

    You can now enter the conditions that the record must meet to be selected.

16. Type **key2>=10,000 * key1>500**. This selects all records where key 2 (Credit) is greater than or equal to $10,000 and key 1 (Amount) is greater than $500. Figure 12.9 shows how your menu should look at this point.

17. Press F7.

18. Press **6** to select Order.

19. Press **2** for a descending sort.

20. Press **1** to sort the table. The resulting table appears in Figure 12.10.

21. Press F7 N Y if you want to exit WordPerfect.

Where have the other rows gone? If you pressed F1 to undelete the selection, the entire table would reappear on the screen, highlighted and ready to be undeleted.

Before sorting or selecting, WordPerfect actually makes a copy of the original table and stores it temporarily. During the selection process, it is this table that is used. In fact, if the table is long enough, say 50 entries, you might see words like

50 Records Examined

on the screen as the action is taking place and

n Records Transferred

as the new table is created (the *n* represents the number of records in the new table). For small tables, the process is so fast you might not see these prompts.

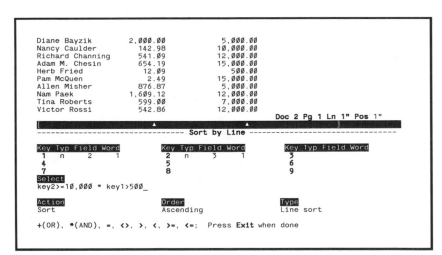

■**FIGURE 12.9:** *The Sort by Line menu with the selection line completed*

Name	Amount	Credit
Richard Channing	541.09	12,000.00
Victor Rossi	542.86	12,000.00
Adam M. Chesin	654.19	15,000.00
Nam Paek	1,609.12	12,000.00

■**FIGURE 12.10:** *The table produced by the selection process*

When the selection process is completed, check the results carefully before you go on to something else. If you delete other text, you will not be able to retrieve the deleted records of the original table using F1.

Selection Without Sorting   In the last example, we selected and sorted records of the table. You can also perform the selection by itself.

To select without sorting, first define the selection condition, then press **5** to select the Action option. The prompt line displays

Action: 1 Select and Sort; 2 Select Only

Press *2,* and the selected records will not be sorted.

■ COMPLEX SELECTIONS

You can define more complex selection conditions by combining the AND (*) and OR (+) operators. For example, the following selection line creates a table that lists clients who have a credit rating under $10,000 and who owe more than $500.00, but the table also includes any clients named Chesin (key 1 uses the −1 word) no matter what they owe or what their credit is:

key1 = Chesin + (key2>500 * key3<10,000)

Since the conditions would normally be tested from left to right, the parentheses are needed to select the proper records. Without the parentheses, Word-Perfect would create a table that included clients who either are named Chesin or owe more than $500, and all clients with credit less than $10,000.

In tables made up of only alphanumeric fields, you can also use the global key *keyg*. For example, the following table lists salespeople and the states that make up their territory:

Salesperson	State 1	State 2	State 3	State 4
Chesin	PA	NJ	NY	CT
Reynolds	DC	DE	MD	PA
Cooper	MI	PA	OH	WV

The following condition would select only those salespersons assigned to Ohio or New Jersey:

keyg=OH + keyg=NJ

Keyg refers to any alphanumeric column in the table. You do not have to define individual keys.

■ WORKING WITH MAILING LISTS

The Sort and Select features can also help you handle documents like mailing lists.

What do mailing lists have in common with tables? Well, the typical mailing list also contains a series of records divided into fields. However, rather than being entered across the page, like a table, they are typed in one column. In the upcoming example, each record includes three lines or fields: name, street address, and city, state, and zip code. Each record is separated from the next one by a blank line.

You can use techniques similar to those used for tables to select specific records, or you can sort the list by name, zip code, or any other item.

First, let's create a sample mailing list:

1. If necessary, start WordPerfect.

2. Type the following list in a single column. Place only one blank line between each record.

   Adam M. Chesin
   412 Lockhard Street
   Philadelphia, PA 19116

   Jean Gilardi
   765 Northeast Ave.
   Philadelphia, PA 19114

   Betty Teller
   654 Pine Road
   Huntingdon Valley, PA 19087

   Lynn Lester
   65 Forrest Ave.
   Broomall, PA 19008

   Mike Royko
   1901 Grant Ave.
   Cherry Hill, NJ 18098

Joe Cetellei
121 Lincoln Highway
Pennsauken, NJ 18096

3. Press Return after typing the last line.

4. Press F7 Y, type **LIST**, press Return, then press **Y** to exit WordPerfect.

SORTING MAILING LISTS

While the two most common sorts for mailing lists are by name and zip code, any field can be used.

Let's sort the mailing list by last name, and then by zip code.

1. Start WordPerfect.

New Feature
Additional re-
lated features in
version 5.1 are
discussed under
"Converting
Older Merge
Files," page 276.

2. Press Ctrl-F9. Since no text is highlighted, you'll see this prompt line

   1 Merge; 2 Sort; 3 Sort Order: 0

   instead of the Sort menu.

3. Press **2** or **s** to sort. The prompt line displays

   Input file to sort: (screen)

4. Type **LIST**, then press Return. The prompt line displays

   Output file for sort: (screen)

5. Press Return to display the sorted mailing list on the screen when the process is completed. If you enter a document name, the sorted list will be saved on the disk under that name. The Sort by Line menu appears on the screen.

6. Press **7**. The prompt line shows the three types of sorts available:

   Type 1 Merge; 2 Line; 3 Paragraph: 0

7. Press **3** for a paragraph sort. The Sort by Paragraph menu, shown in Figure 12.11, appears. Notice that the key now includes a new element, *line*, in addition to type, field, and word. The first sort will be according to last name, the last word in the first line of every record. The name is in the first field because it is in the first line.

8. Press **3** to change the key.

9. Press **A** for an alphanumeric sort. (If the default *a* is already there, just press Return.)

10. Press **1** to select the first line, then press Return.

11. Press **1** to select the first field, then press Return.

12. Type **−1** to select the first word on the right side of the field.

13. Press F7.

14. Press **1** to sort the list.

WordPerfect will read the file LIST, sort it according to the key, and display the resulting list on the screen.

Now let's sort the mailing list that's on the screen by zip code:

1. Press Ctrl-F9 2 to select the Sort option. The prompt reads

    Input file to sort: (screen)

2. Press Return to sort the document on the screen. The prompt displays

    Output file for sort: (screen)

3. Press Return to display the sorted mailing list on the screen when the process is completed.

4. Press **7 3** to select a paragraph sort.

5. Press **3** to change the key.

6. Press **N** for a numeric sort.

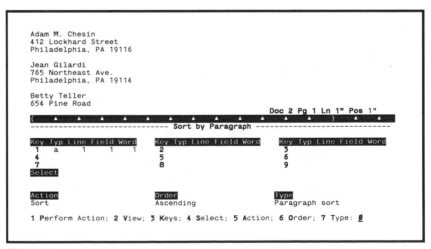

■**FIGURE 12.11:** *The Sort by Paragraph menu*

7. Press **3** to select the third line, then press Return.

8. Press **1** to select the first field, then press Return.

9. Type **−1** to select the first word on the right side of the field.

10. Press F7.

11. Press **1** to sort the list. The records will be sorted by zip code and displayed on the screen.

SELECTING MAILING LIST RECORDS

You can select certain records from mailing lists just as you select them from tables. For example, to select a list of persons from New Jersey in our sample mailing list, set the key as line 3, field 1, word −2. Then enter key1 = NJ as the selection condition.

You can also perform multikey sorts and complex selections with mailing lists, or with any list that consists of a series of records divided into lines.

A NOTE TO TEACHERS

Teachers can use the Sort feature very practically during examination time. After you type and print a test of numbered questions, change the numbers, then do a paragraph sort. Print a copy of the test in that new order.

Duplicate both versions of the test, then distribute them alternately. Now students who attempt to read their neighbors' answers will be in for a shock!

A SORTING MACRO

This macro selects paragraph sorting with the last word of the first line as the key:

Ctrl-F10 Alt-L Return Ctrl-F9 2 Return Return 7 3 3 A 1 Return 1 Return −1 F7 1 Ctrl-F10

WordPerfect's Sort and Select functions can be used for tasks that are far more complex than sorting mailing lists. In Chapters 20 and 21, you'll learn how to use these functions to manage databases and produce form letters in volume.

VERSION 5.1 FEATURES

SORTING TABLES

You can sort tables created with the Table Editor, but it is important how you initiate the action.

If the table contains no column headings or titles, place the cursor anywhere in the table and press Ctrl-F9 2 or **T**ools **S**ort. The Sort menu will be table-oriented, with the keys now including a cell number (Figure 12.12). The cell number refers to the column you want to use for the sort. Select the keys and other options as discussed earlier in this chapter, and then press *1* or *p* to begin the sort.

If the table includes column headings, this technique will sort the headings along with the data. To avoid this, start by blocking the rows that you want to sort, and then press Ctrl-F9 or **T**ools **S**ort.

Unfortunately, the lines linked with the cells move along with the rows, so you can get some undesirable side effects (Figure 12.13). If this happens to your table, press Alt-F7 and use the Lines command to correct the appearance of the sorted table.

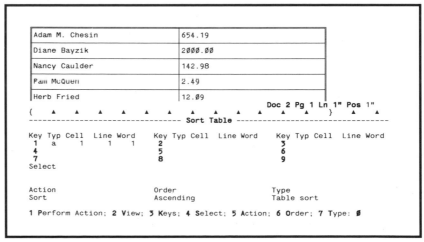

■**FIGURE 12.12:** *Table Sort menu*

```
┌─────────────────────────────────────────────────────┐
│  ┌──────────────────────┬──────────────────────┐     │
│  │ Diane Bayzik         │ 2000.00              │     │
│  ├──────────────────────┼──────────────────────┤     │
│  │ Nancy Caulder        │ 142.98               │     │
│  ├──────────────────────┼──────────────────────┤     │
│  │ Adam M. Chesin       │ 654.19               │     │
│  ├──────────────────────┼──────────────────────┤     │
│  │ Herb Fried           │ 12.09                │     │
│  ├──────────────────────┼──────────────────────┤     │
│  │ Pam McQuen           │ 2.49                 │     │
│  └──────────────────────┴──────────────────────┘     │
│                                                       │
│                                                       │
│                                                       │
│                        Doc 1 Pg 1 Ln 1" Pos 1"        │
└─────────────────────────────────────────────────────┘
```

■**FIGURE 12.13:**   *Sorting tables affects lines*

CONVERTING OLDER MERGE FILES

The Merge/Sort prompt line in version 5.1 contains the following options:

> 1 Merge; 2 Sort; 3 Convert Old Merge Codes: 0

Option 3 is used to automatically convert merge codes from version 5.0 to 5.1 format. This is discussed in Chapter 20.

MOUSE AND MENU EQUIVALENTS

Function	Keyboard	Pull-Down Menus
Sort	Ctrl-F9 2	**T**ools **S**ort

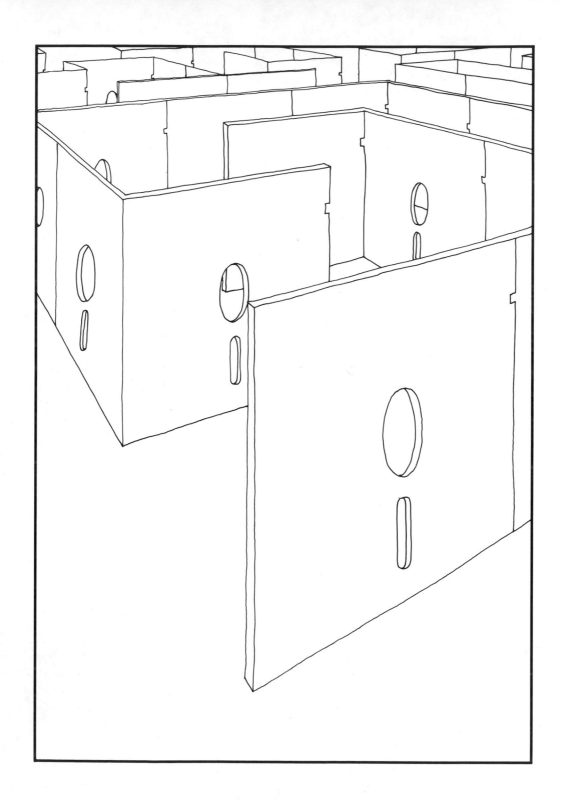

13

WORDPERFECT'S
REFERENCE TOOLS

Lengthy documents, such as academic and professional papers and business reports, should include a table of contents and an index to aid the reader. If your document incorporates illustrations, graphs, or tables of data, a reference list showing the page number where these items can be found is also very useful.

WordPerfect lets you create these reference sections, or any other list citing the specific page numbers of certain items in a document, automatically. This same feature also can be used to prepare an abstract of your document after it is typed or to produce a list of key words. And if you're in the legal profession, you can create tables of authorities using many of the same methods.

You can create an index quickly using a *concordance file*—a special document containing a list of words that you want to include in the index.

In this chapter you'll learn how to create such reference lists. The next chapter explains how to combine reference sections with the rest of your document.

GENERAL PROCEDURE

You use the same basic procedure to create any type of reference list for a WordPerfect document.

First, mark the text that you want to include in a reference section. In some cases you mark the text first by pressing Alt-F4 to highlight it, then press Alt-F5. You can mark the entries for inclusion either as you type or after you've completed the document. Some writers feel that marking text during the writing process is distracting and cumbersome. Instead, they mark citations as they are proofreading their text. Others prefer to mark citations as they type. This way, they can generate a partial index or table of contents at any time.

After you have marked all the text for the reference section, you must define its style and location in the completed document. An index must be defined at the end of the document, but other reference lists can be placed anywhere. Move the cursor to where you want the section to appear in the document (insert a page break if you want it to appear on a separate page), then press Alt-F5. Select the appropriate option to define the style and format of the reference section.

Once the words in the document are marked and the reference section is defined, you can generate it by pressing Alt-F5 6.

CREATING TABLES OF CONTENTS AND INDEXES

WordPerfect offers five different formats for tables of contents and indexes:

- No page numbers (essentially just a list of the entries)
- Page numbers following the entries
- Page numbers in parentheses following the entries
- Flush-right page numbers
- Flush-right page numbers with dot leaders

Tables of contents can include up to five levels, and you can use a different format for each one. On the printed copy, each level is indented 1/2 inch from the one before. Indexes can have two levels: one for headings and one for subheadings.

MARKING TEXT

Let's use the text shown in Figure 13.1 to create a sample index and table of contents. In this example, we'll enter the text first, then mark it for the table of contents. To really demonstrate the power of marking text, press Ctrl-Return to insert a page break after each paragraph. This way you'll see how WordPerfect automatically picks up the page numbers for the reference sections.

Follow these steps:

1. Start WordPerfect.

2. Type the text shown in Figure 13.1. Press Ctrl-Return after each paragraph.

3. Press Home Home ↑ to reach the start of the text.

4. Place the cursor on the first character of the word *Introduction*.

5. Press Alt-F4 End to highlight the title.

6. Press Alt-F5 to display the prompt line

   Mark for: 1 ToC; 2 List; 3 Index; 4 ToA:0

7. Press **1** to display the prompt

   ToC Level:

Warning
With version 5.1, always press Return after entering the level number.

8. Press **1**. The word *Introduction* is now marked for level one of the table of contents. With the codes revealed, it appears as

   [Mark:ToC,1]Introduction[End Mark:ToC,1]

```
                        Introduction

A Question of Origin

     The exact origin of the motion picture is not known. While
credit is usually given to Thomas Edison, animated pictures in the
form of toys appeared in Europe long before Edison's experiments
began.

Early Toys

     The toy consisted of two disks mounted parallel on a rod. The
front disk contained small slits; the rear disk, a series of
pictures. When the child pulled a string, the disks rotated, giving
the illusion of a moving object.

Other Claims

     The inventor of a more sophisticated moving picture is a
question of some doubt. In addition to Edison, both W. K. L.
Dickson and William Friese-Greene claim the honors. Dickson, for
example, claims to have originated the idea while working as
Edison's assistant.

Dickson's Claim

     Both Dickson and Friese-Greene worked as Edison's assistants.
Dickson, however, played a direct role in Edison's initial
experimentation with the motion picture camera and film. According
to Dickson, he had the idea for the motion picture when Edison was
in France on other business.
```

■**FIGURE 13.1:** *Sample text for table of contents and index*

9. Move the cursor to the subtitle *A Question of Origin*.

10. Press Alt-F4 End to highlight it.

11. Press Alt-F5 1 2. This subtitle is now marked as a second-level heading.

12. In the same manner, mark the next subtitle.

    a. Place the cursor on the start of *Early Toys*.

    b. Press Alt-F4 End.

    c. Press Alt-F5 1 2.

13. Mark the next level-one heading.

    a. Place the cursor at the start of *Other Claims*.

    b. Press Alt-F4 End.

    c. Press Alt-F5 1 1.

14. Mark the last subtitle.

    a. Place the cursor on the start of *Dickson's Claim*.

    b. Press Alt-F4 End.

    c. Press Alt-F5 1 2.

Marking Index Entries   All of the titles and subtitles have been marked for the table of contents. Now let's return to the start of the document and mark the words for the index.

1. Press Home Home ↑.

2. Place the cursor anywhere in the word *origin* in the first paragraph, then press Alt-F5 to see the prompt

Note
The appearance of the version 5.1 screen is slightly different, but the steps listed here still apply.

1 Auto Ref; 2 Subdoc; 3 Index; 4 ToA Short Form; 5 Define; 6 Generate: 0

3. Press **3** to select the Index option. The prompt changes to

Index heading: Origin

Notice that WordPerfect capitalizes the first letter of the word.

4. Press Return to accept the word shown in the prompt as the index heading. The prompt changes to

Subheading:

5. Press Return. There will be no subheading under this heading.

6. Move the cursor to *Edison* and press Alt-F5 3 Return to mark the word as a heading. The subheading prompt reappears.

7. Type **early credit** then press Return. This will be a subheading under Edison.

8. Place the cursor on the first letter of *animated* and press Alt-F4.

9. Press → to highlight *animated pictures*. To mark more than one word for an index, they must be highlighted as a block, as with table of contents entries.

10. Press Alt-F5 3 Return to mark the words as a heading.

11. Type **toys** at the subheading prompt, then press Return.

12. Place the cursor on *toys* and press Alt-F5 3 Return Return.

13. Place the cursor on *experiments* and press Alt-F5 3. We want this to be a subheading under the heading Edison. The prompt now says

    Index heading: Experiments

14. Type **Edison** then press Return. The prompt shows

    Subheading: experiments

    When you enter a new word for the heading, the original word appears in the

    Subheading

    prompt. You can press Return to accept that word as the subheading, type in another choice, or press Del if you don't want a subheading.

15. Press Return.

16. Place the cursor on *Toys* in the next subtitle and press Alt-F5 3 Return Return.

17. Move the cursor to the paragraph under *Other Claims* and mark *Edison, Dickson,* and *Friese-Greene* by placing the cursor on the word and pressing Alt-F5 3 Return Return.

18. Move the cursor to the final paragraph and mark *Dickson* and *Friese-Greene* in the same manner.

19. Place the cursor on the word *Edison's* in the last paragraph and then press Alt-F5 3.

20. Type **Edison** then press Return.

21. Press Ctrl-End to erase the subheading, then press Return.

22. Place the cursor on the word *France* and then press Alt-F5 3 Return Return.

23. Press F10, type **EDISON** then press Return to save the document.

If you did not add page breaks between the paragraphs, all of the citations in the index will be listed with the same page number. Certainly, if your document is completed and paginated correctly, you can save time by not marking the same word more than once on a page, except if there is a different heading or subheading related to it.

If you are indexing as you type, then you should mark each occurrence of the word. You may later add or delete text that changes the page on which the citation appears.

DEFINING THE TABLE OF CONTENTS AND INDEX

Now that our sample document has been marked, we'll define the location and format of the table of contents and the index. We must also adjust the pagination so that the first page of the text, not the table of contents, is number one.

Before beginning the definition procedure, always place the cursor where you want the reference section to appear. Always define the index at the end of the document.

Follow these steps to place the table of contents on a separate page at the beginning of our document and to select its format:

1. Press Home Home ↑ to reach the start of the text.

2. Press Ctrl-Return to insert a page break so that the table of contents is printed on a separate page.

Warning
Step 3: With version 5.1, press Shift-F8 2 6 1 1, then Return four times.

3. Press Shift-F8 2 6 1 Return Return Return. The page indicator on the status line changes to 1, even though this is actually the second page in the document. Later you'll turn on page numbering so the numbers are printed with the final document.

4. Press ↑ to move the cursor above the page break line.

5. Press Shift-F6 to center the cursor.

6. Type **Table of Contents** then press Return twice.

7. Press Alt-F5 5 to select the Define option from the prompt line. You'll see the Mark Text Define menu (Figure 13.2).

8. Press **1** or **C** to display the Table of Contents Definition menu as seen in Figure 13.3.

9. Press **1** or **n** for the Number of Levels option.

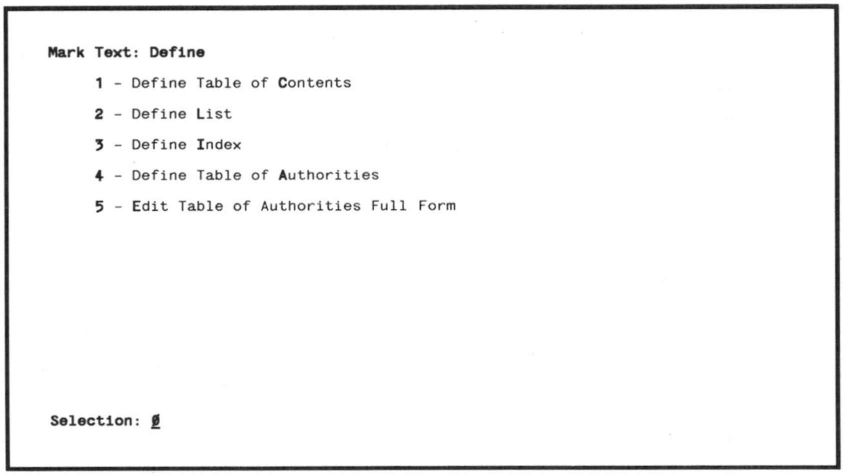

```
Mark Text: Define
        1 - Define Table of Contents
        2 - Define List
        3 - Define Index
        4 - Define Table of Authorities
        5 - Edit Table of Authorities Full Form




    Selection: 0
```

■FIGURE 13.2: *Mark Text Define menu*

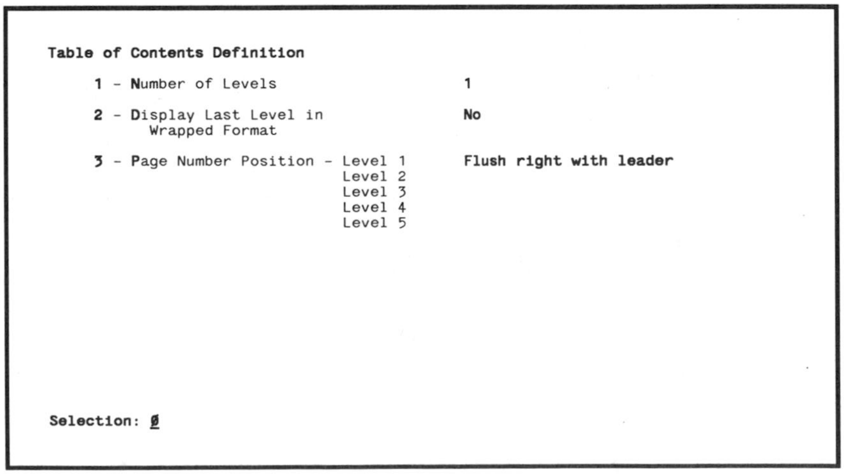

```
Table of Contents Definition
        1 - Number of Levels                    1

        2 - Display Last Level in               No
            Wrapped Format

        3 - Page Number Position - Level 1      Flush right with leader
                                   Level 2
                                   Level 3
                                   Level 4
                                   Level 5




    Selection: 0
```

■FIGURE 13.3: *Table of Contents Definition menu*

10. Press **2** to define two levels. The Page Number Position option displays the default *Flush right with leader* next to both levels.

    Option 2 allows you to set up the table of contents in *wrapped* format, where subheadings appear as in a paragraph under the heading. Figure 13.4 shows a table of contents in wrapped format.

11. Change the format of the second level to have the page numbers follow the entries without parentheses.

    a. Press **3** to select the Page Number Position option. The cursor moves to the first level and the prompt line changes to

       1 None; 2 Pg # Follows; 3 (Pg # Follows); 4 Flush Rt; 5 Flush Rt with Leader

    b. Press ↓ to reach the second level.

    c. Press **2** for the Pg # Follows style.

    d. Press F7 twice to return to the document.

The menu disappears, and the document returns to the screen. Now we'll select the format and location of the index.

1. Press Home Home ↓ to reach the end of the document.

2. Press Ctrl-Return to insert a page break so that the index is printed on a separate page.

3. Press Shift-F6.

4. Type **Index** then press Return twice.

5. Press Alt-F5 5 3 to display the prompt

   Concordance Filename (Enter=none):

```
Period of Exploration . . . . . . . . . . . . . . . . . . .  1
        Portuguese (1); Spanish (5); French (10); English (15)

Colonization  . . . . . . . . . . . . . . . . . . . . . . . 20
        Portuguese (20); Spanish (25); French (31) English
        (34); Dutch (38)

Conflict with England . . . . . . . . . . . . . . . . . . . 41
        Navagation and Trade Laws (41); The Stamp Act (46)
```

■**FIGURE 13.4:** *A table of contents with its last level in wrapped format*

Press Return to ignore the prompt for now and to display the Index Definition menu (Figure 13.5) with the list of page number position options.

6. Press **2** to have page numbers follow the entries.

Now that the table of contents and index have been defined, these reference sections can be generated at any time.

GENERATING THE TABLE OF CONTENTS AND INDEX

WordPerfect can generate our table of contents and index (or any marked and defined reference section) with the cursor anywhere in the document. Follow these steps:

1. Press Alt-F5 6 5. The prompt changes to

   Existing tables, lists, and indexes will be replaced. Continue? (Y/N) Yes

Note
The appearance of the version 5.1 screen is slightly different, but the steps listed here still apply.

2. Press **Y** to generate the index and table, or **N** to return to the document.

   If you press *Y*, any existing tables and indexes will be erased. If you have already generated a reference section and are about to regenerate it, you should press *N*. WordPerfect will locate the section and ask you to confirm deleting it. For our table of contents and index example, press *Y* because this is the first time that we have generated the sections.

   When you press *Y*, WordPerfect begins scanning the document for

```
Index Definition

     1 - No Page Numbers

     2 - Page Numbers Follow Entries

     3 - (Page Numbers) Follow Entries

     4 - Flush Right Page Numbers

     5 - Flush Right Page Numbers with Leaders



Selection: 0
```

■**FIGURE 13.5:** *Index Definition menu*

marked text codes. When it finds a code, it adds the citation to the table of contents or index. The status line shows

Generation in progress. Pass: 1 Page: 2

When you use the Generate command, WordPerfect scans the document to create any reference sections that have been defined. Each reference is created in one *pass,* or search through the text for marked entries. The pass being made, and the page being scanned for marked words, appear in the status line.

Our table of contents and index appear as shown in Figures 13.6 and 13.7 respectively. Just as we selected, the first level of the table of contents has flush-right page numbers with leading periods, and the page numbers follow the level-two entries.

The index is sorted alphanumerically, with the page numbers directly following the entries. However, there is no page number listed for *Animated pictures.* This is because it was marked with an associated heading and not by itself. When a heading always has an associated subheading, no page number is included.

```
                         Table of Contents

Introduction  . . . . . . . . . . . . . . . . . . . . . . . . .  1
      A Question of Origin  1
      Early Toys  2

Other Claims  . . . . . . . . . . . . . . . . . . . . . . . . .  3
      Dickson's Claim  4
```

■**FIGURE 13.6:**   *Sample table of contents*

```
                              Index

Animated pictures
      Toys  1
Dickson  3, 4
Edison  3, 4
      Early Credit  1
      experiments  1
France  4
Friese-Greene  3, 4
Origin  1
Toys  1, 2
```

■**FIGURE 13.7:**   *Sample index*

Remember that you can enter a heading or subheading manually. If you type in a heading, WordPerfect will use the word at the cursor location as the subheading unless you tell it otherwise.

■ CONCORDANCE FILES

In most documents, a word to be indexed will probably appear in more than one location. For an accurate index, this means that each occurrence of the word must be marked—a time-consuming task.

Instead of marking individual entries, you should use a *concordance file*—a special document that contains a list of the headings and subheadings to be indexed. You just mark each of these words once, then WordPerfect scans the document for each occurrence of the marked words, creating an index for you.

If you use a concordance file, do not mark the words in the text. Also, you must name the concordance file when defining the index format.

Here are the steps to create an index for the sample document:

1. Save the current document, then clear the screen.

2. Type the following:

   Toys
   Dickson
   Edison
   Experiments
   France
   Friese-Greene
   Origin

   Make sure you press Return after the last word.

3. Since these are the words you want indexed, each must be marked as a heading or subheading. First, mark them all to be included as headings.

   a. Place the cursor on *Toys*.

   b. Press Alt-F5 3.

   c. Press Return twice.

   d. Repeat steps a through c for each word.

4. Now mark *Toys* as a subheading under *Animation*.

   a. Place the cursor on *Toys*.

     b. Press Alt-F5 3 to display the prompt

       Index Heading: Toys

     c. Type **Animation**.

     d. Press Return twice.

5. Now mark *Experiments* as a subheading under *Edison*.

     a. Place the cursor on *Experiments*.

     b. Press Alt-F5 3.

     c. Type **Edison**.

     d. Press Return twice.

6. Press F7 Y, type **CONCORD**, and press Return N to save the concordance file and clear the screen.

REMOVING INDIVIDUAL MARKINGS

When using a concordance file, you do not mark words in the document, and you define the index format as explained in the next section, not as you learned earlier for a marked document. However, the document EDISON now contains markings and definitions that will interfere with the operation of the concordance file. So if you want to use a concordance file with the document EDISON, delete each of the index marks and the index definition.

Remember, this step is not necessary if you use the concordance file method from the beginning.

1. Press Shift-F10, type **EDISON**, then press Return.

2. Press Alt-F2 Return to choose unconfirmed replacement and to display the -> Srch prompt.

3. Press Alt-F5 to display the prompt

     1 ToC/List; 2 EndMark; 3 Index; 4 ToA; 5 Defs and Refs; 6 Subdocs:0

4. Press **3** then F2 to search for the index marking and display the *Replace with* prompt.

5. Press F2 to delete all Index Mark codes.

     You also have to delete the current index definition. Leave the cursor where it is.

6. Press Alt-F2 Return.

7. Press Alt-F5 5 to see the prompt

   1 DefMark; 2 EndDef; 3 Ref; 4 Target:0

8. Press **1** or **d** to select DefMark.

9. Press F2 twice. Because the cursor was not at the beginning of the document, only the index definition—not the table of contents definition—was deleted.

DEFINING THE INDEX TO USE
A CONCORDANCE FILE

With the original Index Definition codes deleted, you must now insert a code specifying the concordance file that you want to use for creating the index.

1. Place the cursor just before the index already in your document.

2. Press Alt-F5 5 3 to display the prompt

   Concordance Filename (Enter=none):

3. Type **CONCORD**, which is the name of the concordance file, then press Return to display the Index Format menu.

4. Select the desired style.

When you generate the index as explained earlier, WordPerfect will search the document for the words listed in the concordance file. They will be treated as headings or subheadings based on the index marks entered in the concordance document.

Using a concordance file can save you a great deal of time. You do not have to mark every occurrence of a word to produce a complete index. In fact, the index produced with the concordance file is even more complete because it found every occurrence of the index words, not just those you marked manually. Your new index looks like this:

Animation
   Toys 1, 2
Dickson 3, 4
Edison 1, 3, 4
   Experiments 1
Experiments 1
France 4

Friese-Greene 3, 4
Origin 1
Toys 1, 2

CREATING A VOCABULARY LIST
OF KEY WORDS

A common teaching tool is a vocabulary list that accompanies the students' lessons or other materials distributed to the class. To create such a list, mark each vocabulary word as an index heading without a subheading. Then define the index with no page numbers. The generated "index" will contain those words in alphanumeric order. For example, the following might be a vocabulary list for our sample document:

Animated

Experiments

Illusion

Initial

Originated

Parallel

Rotated

Sophisticated

OTHER LISTS

Note
Version 5.1 allows up to 10 lists.

You can also use Alt-F5 to mark text for inclusion in up to nine lists. Lists have the same format definition choices as an index, but instead of sorting them alphanumerically, WordPerfect lists them in the order that they appear in the text. This is why you create a vocabulary list, or any other list that you want sorted, as an index rather than as a list.

Common applications for lists include catalogs of figures or charts in a document. These are often added after the table of contents or as an appendix, to help the reader locate specific material.

If any of the list entries is longer than one line, WordPerfect formats it as a hanging indentation. If you prefer another format, reveal and delete the codes in the generated list, then reformat the list.

CREATING AN ABSTRACT

The List feature can be used to prepare an *abstract*—a condensation of a lengthy report or paper. As an example, let's create a condensed version of our sample document about Thomas Edison.

Marking Sentences for the Abstract   Follow these steps to mark the sentences to be used in the abstract:

1. If the document is not still on the screen, start WordPerfect and recall EDISON.

2. Place the cursor on the first sentence of the paper, starting with *The exact origin,* and press Alt-F4 to turn on the highlighting.

3. Press → until just that sentence is highlighted.

4. Press Alt-F5 2 to select the List option from the Text Marking prompt line. The prompt changes to

   List Number:

Warning
With version 5.1, always press Return after entering the list number.

5. Press **1**.

6. In the same manner, highlight and mark the sentence *In addition to Edison, both W. K. L. Dickson and William Friese-Greene claim the honors.* Place the cursor at the start of the sentence and press Alt-F4, then move the cursor to the end of the sentence and press Alt-F5 2 1.

7. Highlight and mark the sentence *According to Dickson, he had the idea for the motion picture when Edison was in France on other business.*

Defining the Abstract   Now we will define the location and style of the abstract.

1. Place the cursor after the table of contents.

2. Press Alt-F3 to confirm that the cursor is to the right of the [End Def] code. If it is not, press the ← key.

3. Press Alt-F3 to turn off the codes.

4. Press Ctrl-Return to insert a page break so that the abstract will appear on a separate page.

5. Press Shift-F6 to center the abstract's heading.

6. Type **Abstract**.

7. Press Return twice.

8. Press Alt-F5 5 2 to select the Define List option from the Mark Text Define menu. The prompt changes to

    List Number (1 - 9):

Note

The appearance
of the version
5.1 screen is
slightly dif-
ferent, but the
steps listed here
still apply.

9. Type **1**, which is the number of the list you want to define. The List 1 Definition menu appears with the same page number options available for an index. Select the format desired.

10. Press **1** for no page numbers.

Generating the Abstract   Now generate the abstract just as you did for the table of contents and index. The list (our abstract) and new copies of the index and table of contents are generated and placed in the document. However, WordPerfect formatted the individual sentences as hanging indentations, the default format for lists. Our next task is to reformat it into a normal paragraph.

1. Move the cursor to the top of the abstract and press Alt-F3 to reveal the codes.

2. Delete the Indentation and Margin Release codes on that page.

3. Delete the Hard Carriage Return codes, [HRt], at the end of the first and second sentences.

4. Press Alt-F3 to hide the codes.

5. Place the cursor on the first line and press Tab to indent the first sentence. The abstract is now formatted as a standard paragraph (Figure 13.8).

6. Press F7 Y Return Y Y to save the completed document.

In the next chapter, we'll add some final touches to this sample paper.

```
Other Claims . . . . . . . . . . . . . . . . . . . . . . . . 3
        Dickson's Claim  4

===========================================================================
                              Abstract
       The exact origin of the motion picture is not known. In
addition to Edison, both W. K. L. Dickson and William Friese-Greene
claim the honors. According to Dickson, he had the idea for the
motion picture when Edison was in France on other business.

===========================================================================
Introduction

A Question of Origin

       The exact origin of the motion picture is not known. While
credit is usually given to Thomas Edison, animated pictures in the
forms of toys appeared in Europe long before Edison's experiments
began.

===========================================================================
C:\WP5\EDISON                                   Doc 1 Pg 2 Ln 1.33" Pos 1.5"
```

■**FIGURE 13.8:** *Sample abstract formatted as regular text*

■ TABLES OF AUTHORITIES

One reference feature particularly useful to those in the legal profession is the automatic creation of a *table of authorities*. This table lists all citations in the document and the pages that refer to the citation. It is very similar to an index except that the table can be divided into sixteen sections, each representing citations such as cases, regulations, or statutes. Entries are sorted alphabetically within each section.

The first time you mark a reference to an authority, you enter what is called the *long form,* the detailed bibliographic citation and the section number in the table. You also give the citation a nickname, or *short form* name. When you next have to cite that same authority, you just position the cursor and enter the short form name. You do not have to highlight any text or retype the entire entry.

Once all the references are marked, you must define the location of the table and the format of each section before generating the table. If a citation is referenced on more than two consecutive pages, the page numbers are displayed as a range, such as 3–7.

PREPARING THE TABLE OF AUTHORITIES

When you mark text for a table of authorities, you must designate the section in which the citation should appear. So first you should plan which sections will contain which types of references.

Your firm may have an established order for sections, such as:

- Cases

- Statutes

- Regulations

- Legislation

- Treaties

Make a note of what type of citation each section will contain, and try to be consistent among documents.

MARKING THE LONG FORM

Follow these steps the first time you mark a citation reference in the text:

1. Highlight the text that you want listed in the table. If you do not want any of the current text to appear in the table, but you still want to mark a citation and manually type in the full form entry, just highlight the first word of the reference.

2. Press Alt-F5 4 to select the Table of Authorities option (ToA) from the prompt line. The prompt will change to:

   ToA Section Number (Press Enter for Short Form Only):

3. Type the section number and press Return. The screen will clear and the highlighted text will appear by itself in a special typing area, much like the one used for entering headers and footers.

4. Format or edit the text so it appears exactly as you want it to be printed in the table. You can insert and delete characters, indent, boldface, underline, or change fonts. Long form text can be up to 30 lines long.

   If you highlighted some text just to display the Full Form screen, press Ctrl-End to delete it, then type your own full form entry.

5. Press F7. The prompt changes to

   Short Form:

followed by up to 40 characters of the long form.

6. Type a nickname for the form, or edit the characters displayed at the prompt, then press Return. This is the short form name that you would use later to reference the same citation. If you enter a short form that has already been used, a warning message will appear when you later generate the table. WordPerfect will complete the generation but place asterisks after the name, instead of a page number. This alerts you that WordPerfect is unsure which short form you are referring to.

   With codes revealed, a marking for section 1 would appear as

   [ToA:1;Short-form name;Full Form]

MARKING LATER REFERENCES—THE SHORT FORM

When you want to mark a subsequent reference to a citation, follow these steps:

1. Place the cursor on the page containing the reference.

2. Press Alt-F5 4 to select the Short Form option. The prompt changes to

   Short Form:

   followed by the name of the last short form entered.

3. Type the short form name that refers to that citation, then press Return. With codes revealed, the short form reference appears as

   [ToA:;(short-form name);]

If you enter a short form that is not associated with a long form, asterisks will appear at the beginning of the table when it is generated.

PREPARING FOR TABLE DEFINITION

The location and format of each section must be defined separately. Each section can be formatted differently and may appear anywhere in the document. However, for accuracy, the table of authorities should be defined before the first Mark Text code in the text. There should be a page break after the definition, and a new page number should be inserted.

So before defining the table, follow these steps:

1. Press Home Home ↑.

2. Press Ctrl-Return to insert a page break.

Warning
With version 5.1,
press Shift-F8 2
6 1 in step 3. In
step 4, press
Return four
times after enter-
ing the number.

3. Press Shift-F8 2 6 for the New Page Number prompt.

4. Type the number that you want to appear on that page, then press Return three times.

5. Press Home Home ↑.

DEFINING THE TABLE

Now follow these steps for each section of the table:

1. Place the cursor at the start of the document.

2. Press Alt-F5 5 4 to display the prompt

    Section Number (1-16):

3. Type the section number you want to define, then press Return. The Definition for Table of Authorities menu will appear for that section (Figure 13.9).

    There are three options available on this menu:

Dot Leaders	The default (Yes) will print dot leaders between the end of the citation and the page number. Press *1 N* to change the default.
Underlining Allowed	The default (No) will ignore any Underline codes when the table is generated. Press *2 Y* to have underlines appear.
Blank Lines Between Authorities	The default (Yes) will insert a blank line between all entries in the generated table. For single spacing, press *3 N.*

4. Make your selections from the menu, then press Return.

GENERATING THE TABLE OF AUTHORITIES

Once all of the sections with references have been defined, just follow the same steps given for generating a table of contents or index. Press Alt-F5 6 5.

```
    Definition for Table of Authorities 1

        1 - Dot Leaders                      Yes

        2 - Underlining Allowed              No

        3 - Blank Line Between Authorities   Yes
```

```
    Selection: 0
```

■**FIGURE 13.9:** *Definition for Table of Authorities menu*

EDITING AUTHORITIES

You can edit the text of the full form and change its section number if you made a mistake or later want to rearrange the table. To edit a full form:

1. Press Alt-F3 to reveal the codes.

2. Place the cursor immediately following the Mark Text code.

3. Press Alt-F3 to turn off the codes.

4. Press Alt-F5 5 5 for the Edit Table of Authorities Full Form option. The full form will appear on the screen.

5. Make any changes desired on the form, then press F7. The prompt changes to:

    Enter section number (1-16):

6. Type the section number desired, then press Return. The document will again be displayed.

While the table of authorities is designed for attorneys, it can be used by any writer. In many ways, the table is merely a special type of index that can be divided into sections. It can be used to refer to bibliographic entries, to list credit lines, or to index concepts, rather than words.

■   AUTOMATIC REFERENCES

Sometimes you want to refer to another page in your document, using a reference like *(see page 3)*. But just as with footnote references, editing the document may change the location of the text you want to reference.

An *automatic reference* is a system of two codes that keeps track of these references for you and adjusts the page numbers during printing. When you want to refer to the page in your document, you add a Reference code instead of the page number itself. At the text you're referring to, you enter a Target code. During printing, WordPerfect matches each Reference code to a Target code elsewhere in the document.

You can have a reference refer to several targets, as in *(see pages 15, 21, 24)*, and a target can be referred to in several references.

For academic papers, you can use automatic references to cite the same footnote or bibliographic reference more than once. If you add or delete footnotes, the references will automatically adjust.

When you add a reference, you can mark the target and reference at the same time or individually.

Let's add an automatic reference to the document EDISON. In Chapter 14 you'll use this feature to add multiple footnote citations. Recall the document then follow these steps:

1. Place the cursor at the end of the last paragraph in the document.

2. Type (**see page** then press the space bar.

3. Press Alt-F5 1 to select the Auto Ref option and display the Mark Text Automatic Reference menu (Figure 13.10).

4. Press **3** or **b** to mark both the reference and the target at the same time. The screen changes to the Tie Reference To menu (Figure 13.11).

    This menu determines the type of target you want to refer to—a page number, paragraph or outline number, footnote, endnote, or graphic box.

5. Press **1** or **p** to tie this reference to a page number. The document will reappear with the prompt line

    Press Enter to select page

6. Move the cursor to the end of the paragraph on the preceding page, the sentence ending with *Edison's assistant*.

7. Press Return. The status line changes to

    Target Name:

The name of the last target defined, if any, will appear at the prompt. Since this is the first automatic reference, you have to enter a name that ties the target and reference together.

8. Type **Dickson** then press Return. The cursor will appear at the reference location, which now appears as

(see page 3

```
Mark Text: Automatic Reference
        1 - Mark Reference
        2 - Mark Target
        3 - Mark Both Reference and Target




        Selection: 0
```

■**FIGURE 13.10:** *Mark Text Automatic Reference menu*

```
Tie Reference to:
        1 - Page Number
        2 - Paragraph/Outline Number
        3 - Footnote Number
        4 - Endnote Number
        5 - Graphics Box Number
After selecting a reference type, go to the location of the item you want to
reference in your document and press Enter to mark it as the "target".




        Selection: 0
```

■**FIGURE 13.11:** *Tie Reference To menu*

9. Press) to close off the citation.

    While the page number appears on the screen, the code [Ref (Dickson): Pg 3] is inserted at the reference and [Target (Dickson)] appears at the target. If the page number of the target changes due to editing, the number at the reference will adjust accordingly.

10. Press F7 Y Return Y Y to save the document and exit WordPerfect. You'll be adding some finishing touches to this document in Chapter 14.

MARKING REFERENCES OR TARGETS ONLY

If you want to refer to an already marked target, or create a reference for a target you'll define later, then mark the target or reference individually.

To mark a reference by itself, place the cursor at the reference location and press Alt-F5 1 1 for the Tie Reference To menu. Select the type of target, then at the Target Name prompt type the name of an existing target, or one you plan to define later, then press Return.

If the target has not yet been defined, a question mark instead of a page or other number will appear in the document and in the code, such as

[Ref (Dickson): Pg ?]

But when you later define the target and generate the references, the proper page or other citation number will be inserted at the reference.

To mark the target, place the cursor at the target location and press Alt-F5 1 2 to select Mark Target and see the Target Name prompt. Type the name of the target you've already referenced or plan to reference, then press Return.

MULTIPLE REFERENCES

If you want to refer to more than one target, just place the cursor at the end of the reference and follow the procedures above.

When citing a target in multiple references, mark only the reference. You name the target just once, then refer to it as often as you wish. Of course, after the target has been named the first time, select Mark Reference from the Mark Text Automatic Reference menu.

GENERATING REFERENCES

You should generate the references just before printing to update any page, footnote, or other citation numbers that have changed due to editing. Generate references by pressing Alt-F5 6 5 Y.

■ REFERENCE SECTION MACROS

Use these macros to mark text for tables of contents and indices.

MARK INDEX MACRO—ALT-Z

This macro marks words for an index. To use it, place the cursor on the word to be indexed and press the Alt-letter combination.

Ctrl-F10 Alt-Z Return Alt-F5 3 Return Return Ctrl-F10

MARK TABLE OF CONTENTS MACRO—ALT-X

This macro marks words for a table of contents. To use it, place the cursor on the first character of the title or subtitle and press the Alt-letter combination. The entire line will be highlighted. When the prompt appears, press the level number of the entry.

Ctrl-F10 Alt-X Return Alt-F4 End Alt-F5 1 Ctrl-F10

■ VERSION 5.1 FEATURES

MOUSE AND MENU EQUIVALENTS

Function	Keyboard	Pull-Down Menus
Cross-Reference	Alt-F5 1	Mark Cross Reference
Define Index	Alt-F5 5 3	Mark Define Index
Define List	Alt-F5 5 2	Mark Define List
Define Table of Authorities	Alt-F5 5 4	Mark Define Table of Authorities
Define Table of Contents	Alt-F5 5 1	Mark Define Table of Contents
Generate	Alt-F5 6	Mark Generate
Index	Alt-F5 3	Mark Index

Function	Keyboard	Pull-Down Menus
List	Alt-F5 2	**M**ark **L**ist
Table of Authority	Alt-F5 4	**M**ark Table of **A**uthorities
Table of Contents	Alt-F5 1 (with text highlighted)	**M**ark Table of **C**ontents

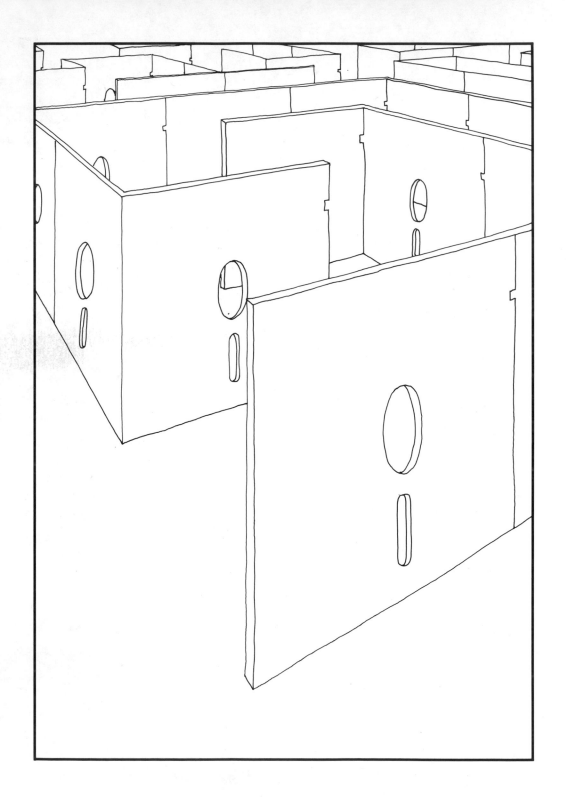

14

FINISHING TOUCHES FOR MAJOR DOCUMENTS

You have already mastered most of the skills needed to create major documents, such as business reports and academic papers. A table of contents, headers and footers, page numbers, and an index—all of these elements enhance the readability and impact of a long manuscript. A title page, footnotes, and endnotes can also add a professional look to an important document.

This chapter describes how to put together all of your skills for those polishing touches. As an example, we'll use the sample paper about Thomas Edison that we created in the last chapter.

That multipage document already contains an abstract, table of contents, index, and automatic reference. In this chapter you'll add a title page, footnotes, and endnotes, and you'll learn how to add multiple references to a footnote or endnote.

■ TITLE PAGES

A title page usually contains the name and date of the report, along with the name of the author and maybe some other brief, identifying data. Most writers center the title on the page, but there is no definitive style.

The title page should be unnumbered and should not even count in the numbering scheme. It's easy to avoid printing a number on the page—in fact, that's the default setting—but it's more difficult to make sure that WordPerfect doesn't count it as a page.

Let's retrieve the sample report about Thomas Edison and add a title page. Follow these steps:

1. Start WordPerfect.

2. Press Shift-F10, type EDISON, and press Return. The first page of the document, the table of contents, appears.

3. Press Ctrl-Return to insert a new page, then press ↑.

Warning
Step 4: With version 5.1, press Shift-F8 2 1 Y Return Return.

4. Press Shift-F8 2 1 Return Return. The Center Page code is inserted into the text. With this code on the first line of the page, the text will be centered between the top and bottom margins.

5. Press Shift-F6 to center the title.

6. Type **The Edison Motion Picture Myth**.

7. Press Return twice.

8. Press Shift-F6.

9. Type **by**.

10. Press Return twice.

11. Press Shift-F6.

12. Type **Alvin A. Aardvark**. Figure 14.1 shows how the title page looks so far with the codes revealed.

13. Press Return four times.

14. Press Shift-F6.

15. Type **English 101**.

16. Press Return twice.

17. Press Shift-F6.

18. Type **Fall 1990**. The completed title page in View mode appears in Figure 14.2. As this figure shows, these eleven lines are centered on the printed page both vertically and horizontally.

Leave the document on the screen; we will continue to work with it throughout this chapter.

```
                     The Edison Motion Picture Myth
                                 by_
                          Alvin A. Aardvark
==============================================================================
                          Table of Contents
Introduction . . . . . . . . . . . . . . . . . . . . . . . . 1
         A Question of Origin  1
         Early Toys  2
C:\WP5\EDISON                              Doc 1 Pg 1 Ln 1.33" Pos 4.35"
(       ▲     ▲    ▲    ▲'   ▲    ▲    ▲    ▲   ▲    )   ▲    ▲
[Center Pg][Cntr]The Edison Motion Picture Myth[C/A/Flrt][HRt]
[HRt]
[Cntr]by[C/A/Flrt][HRt]
[HRt]
[Cntr]Alvin A. Aardvark[C/A/Flrt][HPg]
[Cntr]Table of Contents[C/A/Flrt][HRt]
[Def Mark:ToC,2:5,2][HRt]
[:Indent;][;Mar Rel]Introduction[Flsh Rt]  1[C/A/Flrt][HRt]
[:Indent;][:Indent][;Mar Rel]A Question of Origin  1[HRt]
[:Indent;][:Indent][;Mar Rel]Early Toys  2[HRt]

Press Reveal Codes to restore screen
```

■**FIGURE 14.1:** *The codes revealed for the title page with the title and author*

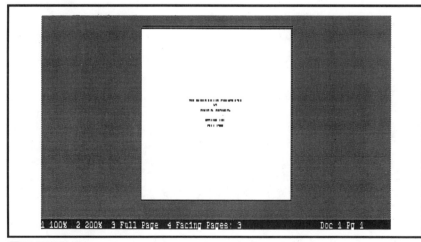

■**FIGURE 14.2:** *The completed title page in View mode*

■ PAGE NUMBERS

The type and placement of page numbers depends upon the style of the individual writer, the company, or the academic institution. Most schools have adopted one of the standard writing styles, and your own profession, business, or trade may use some specific format.

PAGE NUMBER FORMATS

Numbers can appear at the top or bottom of the page, on one side, or on alternate sides of odd and even pages. Page numbers in the text normally have Arabic numerals, and front matter pages, such as the table of contents and abstract, usually have lowercase Roman numerals.

The numbering scheme can be consecutive throughout the entire document or section by section. A number such as 2.3, for example, would represent the third page of section 2, even though it is the fortieth page of the document. Many writers number pages in the appendices consecutively, as Appendix 1, Appendix 2, etc., or with designations such as A1 or A-2.

The number itself can appear alone or with other text. Some styles include the following:

Page 2

- 3 -

Section 1 Page 4

Introduction iv

Appendix A Page iii

Page 3 of 10

Note
With version 5.1, text can be included in page numbers. Refer to "Page Numbering," page 322.

Page numbers with text must be created as headers or footers. Those without any text can be created by pressing Shift-F8 2 7 to select Page Numbering and display the Page Number Position menu (Figure 5.10). There are several choices available from the menu. Each will place the page number at the selected position. Use option 9, *No page numbers,* to turn off page numbering, and use option 4 or 8 to place the numbers on alternating sides of the page.

If you are not required to use any specific pagination style, select a format that clearly identifies pages but that does not distract from the document.

NUMBERING FRONT MATTER

Our sample document has two pieces of front matter, an abstract and a table of contents. Let's number them with lowercase Roman numerals in the bottom center of each page. Follow these steps:

1. Place the cursor on the same line as the heading *Table of Contents,* just under the page break line.

2. Press Shift-F8 2 6 to select the New Page Number option from the For-mat Page menu.

3. Press **i** as the starting number. The table of contents will now be considered page 1 but numbered *i* when printed.

4. Press Return.

5. Press **7** to select Page Numbering and display the Page Number Position menu.

6. Press **6** to have the numbers printed in the bottom center of every page.

7. Press Return twice to return to the document.

The table of contents is now page i, and the abstract is page ii. The Pg in-dicator on the status line, however, will still show them as 1 and 2. In fact, as you scroll through the document, the title page, table of contents, and first page of the text will all appear as page 1 on the status line.

NUMBERING THE TEXT

Now that the front matter is numbered, we can concentrate on the text itself. In the last chapter, we used the New Page Number option to number the beginning of the text as page 1. This was necessary so that the table of contents did not count as a page. However, even though we adjusted the pagination, the page numbers still will not automatically be printed with the document.

Let's create a simple footer to number the pages in the format

   - 2 -

at the bottom center of every page except the first one.

Follow these steps to number the text pages:

1. Place the cursor at the start of the first page of text, following the abstract.

2. Press Shift-F8 2 4 to select the Footer option.

3. Press **1 2** to place footer 1 on every page. The Footer Edit screen appears.

4. Press Shift-F6 to center the cursor.

5. Type the footer.

   a. Press – (the hyphen character).

   b. Press the space bar.

       c. Press Ctrl-B.

       d. Press the space bar.

       e. Press –. The footer is displayed as

          - ^B -

6. Press F7 to return to the Page Format menu.

Warning

Users of version 5.1: In step 7, press *8* or *u*. In step 9, press Return three times.

7. Press **9** or **u** to display the *Suppress (this page only)* menu (Figure 14.3).

8. Press **1** or **a** to select Suppress All Page Numbering, Headers and Footers.

9. Press F7 twice to return to the document. The page number will not appear on the first page of the text.

As our page numbering exercises have demonstrated, there are two methods for printing page numbers automatically on every page. One method is to set the page number position through the Page Format menu; the other is to enter Ctrl-N in a header or footer. You can mix the methods in the same document, but don't use both on the same page. If you do, WordPerfect will print two numbers on that page.

Numbering Single Pages   There is yet a third way to number pages: press Ctrl-B in the text itself. The symbol ^B appears on the screen with the document; it is not an invisible code. During printing, the current page number will replace the ^B on that page.

Placing ^B on one page, however, only inserts the number at that location on

```
Format: Suppress (this page only)

    1 - Suppress All Page Numbering, Headers and Footers

    2 - Suppress Headers and Footers

    3 - Print Page Number at Bottom Center   No

    4 - Suppress Page Numbering              No

    5 - Suppress Header A                    No

    6 - Suppress Header B                    No

    7 - Suppress Footer A                    No

    8 - Suppress Footer B                    No



Selection: 0
```

■**FIGURE 14.3:** *The Suppress (this page only) menu*

that specific page. Ctrl-B is limited to some special applications in which you want the page number included in the text. To print the page number on each page with this technique, you would have to press Ctrl-B on every page.

■ HEADERS AND FOOTERS

You've already learned how to enter headers and footers into a document for page numbering, but there are various other uses for them. A header or footer could include the name of the report, the author, or the company presenting or receiving it. Typical headers include such lines as:

> (Continued)
> Prepared for Harrison Widget Company
> Confidential

Typical footers include:

> (Continued)
> Please Turn The Page

Even some advertising or public relations message could be used, such as:

> Thank you for your business
> Harrison Widgets are Number 1!

As with page numbers, simplicity is often the wisest goal. If you do include headers or footers, make them relevant and purposeful. Avoid using both headers and footers on the same page unless one of them contains just a simple page number.

■ FOOTNOTES AND ENDNOTES

Footnotes appear at the bottom of the page on which they are referenced; endnotes appear in a group at the end of the document. Some documents have footnotes as well as endnotes. In these cases, usually the footnotes are used for expository material, and the endnotes contain formal references.

You won't see footnotes or endnotes in the document on the screen, except in View mode. But, as with headers and footers, you can display them in special typing areas, and they'll be printed along with the document.

FOOTNOTE AND ENDNOTE STYLES

WordPerfect provides a number of options for formatting footnotes and endnotes.

- The line spacing within and between notes can be set, as can the number of lines to keep together. The default is single spacing.

- You can number footnotes consecutively throughout the document or start each page with footnote number 1. You also have a choice of using numbers, lowercase letters, or special characters as the reference numbering system. The default numbering system is consecutive numbers. Endnotes have the same numbering options. If you are using both endnotes and footnotes, select a different numbering scheme for each.

- WordPerfect will insert a line to separate footnotes from the text. The default setting will print a 2-inch line between the end of the text and the footnotes. You can change this to a line across the page or no line at all.

- By default, footnotes appear at the bottom of each page. You can change this to have them printed immediately after the last line of text on the page. This option is usually selected for a concluding page with a small amount of text. The footnote will appear after the text, not at the bottom of the page.

- The footnote and endnote numbers printed in the text will be superscripted if your printer is capable of printing in this style. In the footnotes themselves, they appear as superscripts, indented 1/2 inch. Endnote citation numbers at the end of the document are not superscripts. As with the other default settings, you can change the way that the numbers (or characters) appear.

CREATING FOOTNOTES AND ENDNOTES

WordPerfect provides what are known as *floating* footnotes. The program keeps track of the footnotes, numbers them automatically, and makes sure that they are printed at the bottom of the appropriate page. If you delete or insert a footnote, the others will be renumbered automatically.

As you enter a footnote or endnote, WordPerfect displays the number that corresponds to the current order, but these numbers are just for your reference. It actually stores them with the code [Note #]. This way, the numbers will adjust if you add or delete notes. WordPerfect handles endnotes in the same manner, except that they are printed as a group at the end of the document.

Now we'll add some footnotes and endnotes to our sample paper.

1. Place the cursor at the end of the first paragraph and press Ctrl-F7 to display the prompt line

   1 Footnote; 2 Endnote; 3 Endnote Placement:0

2. Press **1** or **f** to select Footnote and display the prompt line

   Footnote: 1 Create; 2 Edit; 3 New Number; 4 Options: 0

   (Option 3 on the prompt line is used to restart numbering at some specific number. By default, WordPerfect will start with 1 and number your notes consecutively throughout the document. But perhaps you're typing a document in sections, and you've already entered some notes in a previous file. Before creating the first note in the new section, select option 3 and enter the next note number—one higher than the last note already used. Notes in this section will be numbered consecutively starting at the new number entered. You can easily create a document in sections using the Master Document feature discussed in Chapter 23.)

3. Press **1** to create a footnote and display the Footnote screen (Figure 14.4).

4. Type the first footnote.

   Scientific American, November 16, 1889, *The Electric Tachyscope,* Vol 3 No 6, page 23.

5. Press F7. The document reappears, and the number 1 is next to the text.

Note
The appearance of the version 5.1 screen is slightly different, but the steps listed here still apply.

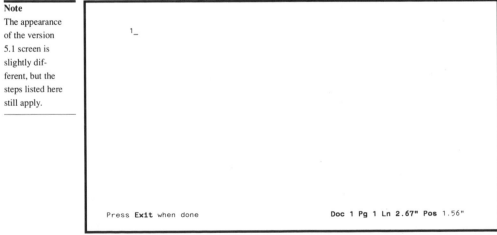

■**FIGURE 14.4:** *The Footnote screen*

With the codes revealed, the footnote looks like this:

[Note: Footnote,1;[Note Num]Scientific American,
November 16, 1889, [Und] The Elec. . . .]

6. Place the cursor past the end of the paragraph subtitled *Early Toys.* We will enter an endnote. But first, to avoid confusion between the footnotes and endnotes, we must change the default citation numbers to letters.

7. Press Ctrl-F7 2 4 to select Endnote Options and display the Endnote Options menu (Figure 14.5).

   Notice that option 5, Endnote Numbering Method, is set for numbers. The other options control the spacing of endnotes and the style used to print the citation numbers in the text and in the note itself.

8. Press **5** to change the numbering mode and display the prompt

   1 Numbers; 2 Letters; 3 Characters:0

   Characters would be used to "number" endnotes with some symbol. For example, if you select an asterisk, the first endnote will be marked *, the second **, etc.

9. Press **2** to select Letters.

10. Press Return to return to the document. The cursor is already in position for the endnote.

11. Press Ctrl-F7 2 1 to create an endnote. The endnote screen appears with the letter *a* in place.

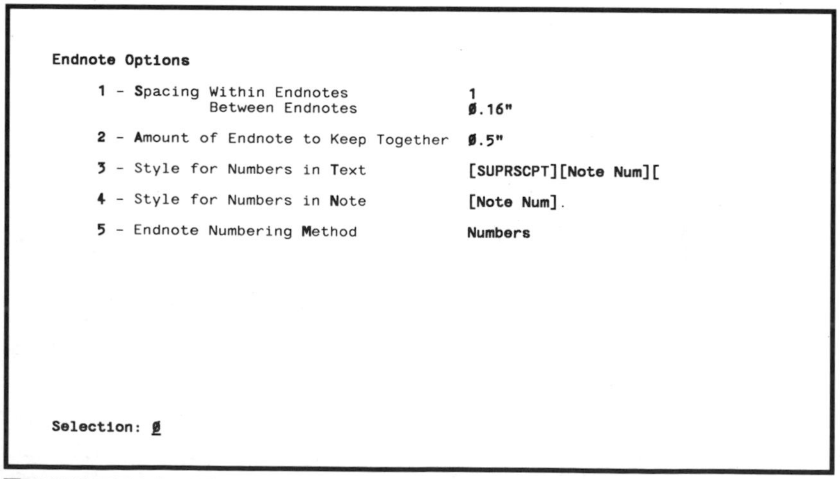

```
Endnote Options

    1 - Spacing Within Endnotes              1
                Between Endnotes             Ø.16"

    2 - Amount of Endnote to Keep Together   Ø.5"

    3 - Style for Numbers in Text            [SUPRSCPT][Note Num][

    4 - Style for Numbers in Note            [Note Num].

    5 - Endnote Numbering Method             Numbers




    Selection: Ø
```

■**FIGURE 14.5:**   *The Endnote Options menu*

12. Press Tab.

13. Type the first endnote.

> A working model of this toy can be seen at Edison's studio in East Orange, New Jersey.

14. Press F7. The letter is now in the text.

15. Move the cursor to the end of the paragraph entitled *Other Claims.*

16. Press Ctrl-F7 1 1. The Footnote screen displays the number 2.

17. Type the second footnote.

> Gordon Hendricks, The Edison Motion Picture Myth, Williams, California, 1961, page 45.

18. Press F7. The number 2 appears in the text.

19. Place the cursor after the sentence *Both Dickson and Friese-Greene worked as Edison's assistants.*

20. Press Ctrl-F7 2 1 to create another endnote.

21. Press Tab.

22. Type the second endnote.

> Both worked for Edison at different times along with at least fifteen other assistants.

23. Press F7. The letter *b* is inserted in the text.

24. Move the cursor past the last paragraph in the document but before the automatic reference to page 3.

25. Press Ctrl-F7 1 1.

26. Type the third footnote.

> Century Magazine, June 1894, page 6.

27. Press F7. The number 3 appears at the end of the text.

Leave the document on the screen, and we'll see what happens when we change these notes.

ADDING, DELETING, AND EDITING NOTES

As you edit a document, you may find that footnotes and endnotes must be added, deleted, or changed in some way. The process is a simple one with WordPerfect.

We will now insert a new footnote, delete an endnote, and edit the remaining endnote. Since there will be only one endnote in the document, we will change the numbering mode to use an asterisk instead of letters. Follow these steps:

1. Place the cursor after the sentence *In addition to Edison, both W. K. L. Dickson and William Friese-Greene claim the honors.*

2. Press Ctrl-F7 1 1 to insert a new footnote. The Footnote screen displays the number 2, even though there is already a footnote with that number. WordPerfect checks the number of the footnote, if any, immediately preceding the position of the cursor. Since the last footnote was number 1, it assigns the next number—2—to the note you're now creating. That's okay because following notes will be renumbered automatically.

3. Type the new footnote.

   New York World, Edison's Talking Baby, June 3, 1888.

4. Press F7. The number 2 is inserted in the text. If you scroll through the text with the arrow keys, you'll see that the existing footnotes have been renumbered.

5. Place the cursor on the endnote citation *a* at the end of the second paragraph.

6. Press Del. The prompt changes to

   Delete [Endnote:a]? (Y/N) No

Note
The appearance of the version 5.1 screen is slightly different, but the steps listed here still apply.

7. Press **Y**. The reference is deleted, and the second endnote's designator is changed to *a*. Let's edit that endnote.

8. Press Ctrl-F7 2 2 to select Edit Endnote. The prompt changes to

   Endnote number? [a:]

9. Press Return. The Endnote screen contains the text of the endnote.

10. Place the cursor at the end of the note and type the following sentence:

    It is unclear what responsibilities each had in the development of the motion picture during his work with Edison.

11. Press F7. The cursor moves to the endnote citation just edited.

12. Press ← twice to move the cursor to the left of the Endnote code. This way, the change in note format that you're about to make will affect the endnote in the text.

13. Press Ctrl-F7 2 4 to display the Footnote Options menu.

14. Press **5 3** to select Characters and place the cursor at the end of the Endnote Numbering Method option.

15. Press * followed by Return. The selection changes to

    Characters, *

    If you returned to the document now, the asterisk in the endnote would be followed by a period, the default style. Let's delete this period.

16. Press **4** or **n** to select Style for Numbers in Note. The prompt changes to

    Replace with: [Note Num].

17. Press End then Backspace to delete the period after the code.

18. Press Return to accept the change.

19. Press Return to return to the document.

Leave the document on the screen. We still have a little more work to do.

■ FINAL TOUCHES

The document is almost ready to be printed except for some final touches. We must create a separate Notes page at the end of the document and regenerate the reference sections. Follow these steps:

1. Press Home Home ↓ to place the cursor at the bottom of the page containing the index and press Ctrl-Return to insert a page break. The endnote will now appear on a separate page.

2. Press Shift-F6.

3. Type **Notes**.

4. Press Return twice.

5. Press Alt-F5 6 5 Y to generate a new table of contents and index for the document.

6. Press Shift-F7 1 to print the document.

Note that the endnotes were printed as the last page, following the index. If you want the index to appear at the end and to include the Notes page in the table of contents and index, you'll have to perform a little WordPerfect trickery.

NOTE PLACEMENT AND FORMAT

WordPerfect normally prints footnotes at the bottom of the appropriate pages, adding blank lines if necessary following the last line of text. But you can choose to have them printed immediately following the last line of text, as well as control their format and spacing, through the Footnote Options menu (Figure 14.6).

The options on this menu let you adjust the appearance and placement of footnotes, or include a continuation message if the note extends onto the next page. To print the footnotes right after the text on the page, for example, press Ctrl-F7 1 4 to display the menu, then press *9* or *b* to select Footnotes at Bottom of Page, *N* for No, then Return to return to the document.

Endnotes are normally printed as the last page of the text, after the index. If you want to have the endnotes appear before the index, or at any other place except the end, you must insert an Endnote Placement code in the text at that location.

Note
The appearance of the version 5.1 screen is slightly different, but the steps listed here still apply.

```
Footnote Options

    1 - Spacing Within Footnotes          1
              Between Footnotes           0.16"

    2 - Amount of Note to Keep Together   0.5"

    3 - Style for Number in Text          [SUPRSCPT][Note Num]

    4 - Style for Number in Note                    [SUPRSCPT][Note

    5 - Footnote Numbering Method         Numbers

    6 - Start Footnote Numbers each Page  No

    7 - Line Separating Text and Footnotes  2-inch Line

    8 - Print Continued Message           No

    9 - Footnotes at Bottom of Page       Yes


Selection: 0
```

■**FIGURE 14.6:** *Footnote Options menu*

When WordPerfect encounters an Endnote Placement code, it inserts any endnotes that occur between it and the previous Endnote Placement code (or the start of the document if there were none).

To insert the code, place the cursor where you want the endnotes to appear, then press Ctrl-F7 3 or p to select Endnote Placement. You'll see the prompt

Restart endnote numbering? (Y/N) Yes

Press Return to accept the default if you want the endnotes to start numbering from 1 (or i or * if that's what you chose) in this section. Press *N* to number them consecutively throughout the document.

You'll see an Endnote Placement message inserted in the text, followed by a hard page break (Figure 14.7). This message means that WordPerfect doesn't know at this point how many lines of text to actually reserve for the endnotes.

Press Alt-F5 6 5 Y to generate all the reference sections. During this process, WordPerfect computes the size of the endnotes and inserts an Endnote message reserving that space.

■   MULTIPLE NOTE REFERENCES

When you use the Footnote and/or Endnote functions, each citation number (or letter or character) refers to one note. But in many instances, particularly in academic papers, the same footnote or endnote needs to be referenced at several

```
question of some doubt. In addition to Edison, both W. K. L.
Dickson and William Friese-Greene claim the honors.2 Dickson, for
example, claims to have originated the idea while working as
Edison's assistant.3

===========================================================================

Dickson's Claim

     Both Dickson and Friese-Greene worked as Edison's assistants.*
Dickson, however, played a direct role in Edison's initial
experimentation with the motion picture camera and film. According
to Dickson, he had the idea for the motion picture when Edison was
in France on other business.4 (see page 3)


  ┌─────────────────────────────────────────────────────────────────┐
  │ Endnote Placement                                                 │
  │ It is not known how much space endnotes will occupy here.         │
  │ Generate to determine.                                            │
  └─────────────────────────────────────────────────────────────────┘


===========================================================================

C:\WP5\EDISON                                  Doc 1 Pg 5 Ln 1" Pos 1"
```

■**FIGURE 14.7:** *Endnote Placement message*

locations in the document. To maintain the Automatic Renumbering feature of WordPerfect, however, any second or subsequent reference to a note must be performed using the Automatic Reference feature (or Cross-reference feature in version 5.1). This is not a feature in earlier versions.

Let's say that you've already entered the first citation for a note using the regular footnote or endnote procedures as explained in this chapter. The next time you want to reference that note, consider the note as the target and the text relating to it as the reference. With the cursor at the reference, press Alt-F5 1, then *3* to mark both the reference and the target. Select *3* or *f* for a footnote reference (or *4* or *e* for an endnote). Without moving the cursor, press Ctrl-F7, then *1* for a footnote (or *2* for an endnote), then *2* for Edit. Type the number of the note you want to reference. The note will be displayed in its editing area. Press Return for the Target Name prompt, type the name of the target (something like *Note 1* would be appropriate), then press Return.

Now that the note has a target name, refer to it again when needed by defining just a reference.

If you know in advance that you're going to use a note in more than one reference, mark it as a target as explained in Chapter 13. Then just enter that target name when defining the reference later on.

When you add or delete notes, however, only the citation numbers entered as regular footnotes or endnotes will adjust automatically. To update the automatic references, press Alt-F5 6 5 Y.

■ VERSION 5.1 FEATURES

PAGE NUMBERING

The menus used to select page numbers have been modified in version 5.1. To insert or change page numbers, press Shift-F8 2 6 or select **L**ayout **P**age Page Numbering to display the Page Numbering menu (Figure 14.8).

New Page Number   To start numbering on the current page with a new page number, press *1* or *n*, enter the page number, and press Return. Press F7 to return to the document. To use lowercase or uppercase roman numerals, enter *i* or *I*.

```
Format: Page Numbering
    1 - New Page Number        1
    2 - Page Number Style      ^B
    3 - Insert Page Number
    4 - Page Number Position  No page numbering




    Selection: 0
```

■**Figure 14.8:** *Page Numbering menu for version 5.1*

Page Number Style   The code ^B means that by default, only the number itself will be printed when you select a page number position using options 3 and 4 on this menu. If you want text with the number, such as

Page 1

press *2* or *s*, type the text (pressing Ctrl-B where you want the number itself to appear), and press Return. For example, enter - *Page ^B* - to have the number appear as - *Page 1* -.

If you don't enter B, WordPerfect will insert it for you at the end of the text. If you enter *PAGE* and then press Return, for example, the option will appear as *PAGE ^B*.

INSERT PAGE NUMBER

This option places the page number, including any text entered at the Page Number Style option, at the position of the cursor in the text. You can also enter a page number alone anywhere in the document by pressing Ctrl-B.

Page Number Position   This option determines the placement of a page number as explained in Chapter 5 (Figure 5.10).

MOUSE AND MENU EQUIVALENTS:

Function	Keyboard	Pull-Down Menus
Center Page	Shift-F8 2 1	Layout Page Center Page
Endnote	Ctrl-F7 2	Layout Endnote
Footnote	Ctrl-F7 1	Layout Footnote
Page Numbering	Shift-F8 2 6	Layout Page Page Numbering

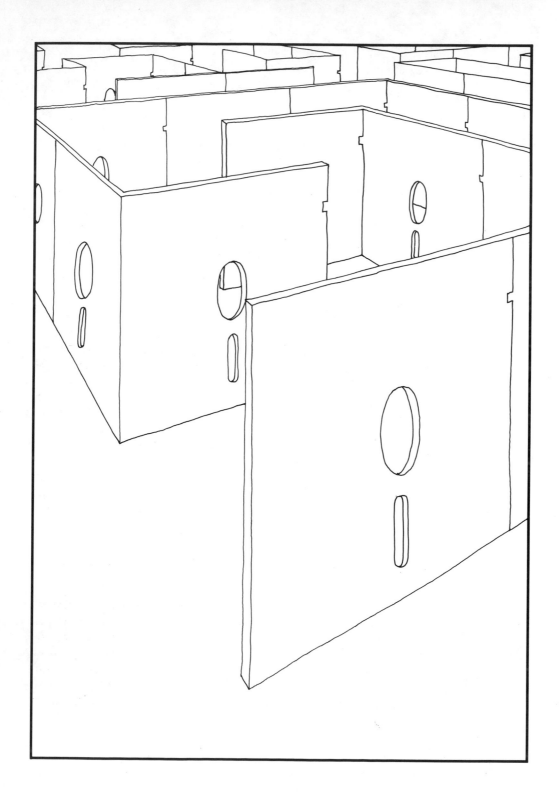

15

SPECIAL CHARACTERS FOR TECHNICAL AND FOREIGN-LANGUAGE DOCUMENTS

The increase in technical and international trade affects not only the economy, but the academic and business worlds as well. Foreign correspondence and multilingual documents are no longer rare, and it is not uncommon to find foreign-language characters in contracts, proposals, and letters. The growing technology and our increasing dependence on computers and automation also affect the printed word. Mathematical symbols and formulas are finding their way into our written work. Luckily, modern computers are capable of handling these types of documents.

There are three special typing problems associated with technical and foreign-language documents. First, is your printer even capable of printing special symbols and foreign-language characters? Second, how do you access all of the unique characters available in your computer? Finally, how do you format them to print correctly? In this chapter, you'll learn how to deal with these problems.

■ SPECIAL CHARACTERS AND YOUR HARDWARE

New Feature
Version 5.1 can print all special characters on most printers. See "Word-Perfect Characters," page 342.

Before going on, let's consider the problem of printing these special characters. Graphic dot-matrix printers can print most of them. Letter-quality and laser printers can print many of the characters, but the printer must have the appropriate font element or cartridge. Almost all printers, including graphic dot-matrix, *cannot* print a special series of characters that can be displayed on the screen. These include the small smiling face, card suits, and other characters that fall within the ASCII sequence below the space, the first printable character. (These are the ASCII codes 1 to 31.)

If your printer was listed specifically as a choice during the printer selection process, WordPerfect will print as many of the special characters as possible, even if it means combining several characters at the same position.

Which characters you can see on the screen depends on your monitor and graphics card. If you try to produce a character that your screen can't display, it will appear as a small box.

ACCESSING SPECIAL CHARACTERS

As you'll soon see, there are two ways to access special characters—Overstrike and Compose. Compose is more powerful because of the large number of characters it can create. However, refer to the WordPerfect manual for a complete list of characters that can be created using Compose. If the character you want is not shown, then determine if it can be created by combining two standard keyboard characters.

Some special characters can be created by striking one character over another, such as creating Ø by overstriking 0 and /. Using this method, you can combine any of the regular characters that your printer is able to produce. Just press Shift-F8 4 5 1 for the Create Overstrike option on the Format Other menu. Type the characters you want to print at the same position, then press Return three times.

But you can also create special characters using Ctrl-2, the Compose command. With Ctrl-2, you can create a number of standard digraphs and accented characters, as shown in Figure 15.1. You can also display a larger number of

To create this:	Press Ctrl-2 then this:
Æ	AE
æ	ae
Œ	OE
œ	oe
§	ss
£	-L
á	'a
É	'E
ö	"o
ç	,c
ñ	~n
û	^u
â	^a
Ø	/0

■**FIGURE 15.1:** *Digraphs and diacriticals using Ctrl-2*

characters from WordPerfect's thirteen character sets. Figure 15.2 summarizes the sets available.

Just keep in mind that many printers will be unable to produce most of these characters unless they are equipped with daisy wheels, special cartridges, or downloaded fonts.

USING COMPOSE

To create one of the characters shown in Figure 15.1, press Ctrl-2 followed by the two characters illustrated that create it. Nothing will appear until you press the second character. For example, to create Æ, press Ctrl-2 A E.

More characters are available in the character sets illustrated in the Word-Perfect manual. Each set has a number of characters in it, so each character must be represented by both its set number and its character number. To display one of these characters, press Ctrl-2, the set number, a comma, the character number, then the space bar or any cursor movement key. Nothing will appear until you press the space bar, or any other key to move the cursor.

For example, the character → is in set 6, number 21. So to display it, type Ctrl-2 6,21 space bar.

■ PRINTING A CHARACTER DIRECTORY

If you don't use special characters often, you'll have to refer to your manual or the figures in this book. But it is even more convenient to have a printed directory of these symbols to keep handy by the computer.

This printout serves as a quick reminder of the key combinations and a good test of your printer's ability to print the characters. Follow these steps:

1. Starting with a blank screen, type **Character**, press Tab twice, then type **Set and Number**.

2. Press Return twice.

3. Press Ctrl-2 1,27.

4. Press Tab five times, once to display the character (á), then four more times to reach the next column.

5. Type **1,27** followed by Return.

6. In the same manner, type each of the following characters using the appropriate key combination.

¿	4,8
Ñ	1,56
ç	1,39
Ç	1,38
ñ	1,57
é	1,41
í	1,49
ó	1,59
ú	1,67
¡	4,7
1/2	4,17
1/4	4,18
√	5,14
⌠	7,0
⌡	7,1
π	8,33

7. Press Shift-F7 1 to print the character directory.

Your screen and printout should resemble Figure 15.3. If your printout is not correct, make sure that you are using the correct printer definition. If your printer definition is not the problem, then your printer may not be able to produce these characters.

FOREIGN-LANGUAGE TYPING

You can refer to your character directory to see which keys to press when typing foreign-language documents. Practice typing in a foreign language by entering these sentences in Spanish:

Cuando llegó Cortés a México, hace más de cuatrocientos años, encontró allí a los indios, que ya tenían sus artes indígenas. ¿Cómo está usted?

Press Shift-F7 1 if you want to print a copy of the document, then press F7 N Y if you want to exit WordPerfect.

Set	Characters	Name	Purpose
0	32-126	ASCII	The same characters available from the regular keyboard keys
1	0-233	Multinational 1	Common international characters
2	0-27	Multinational 2	Rarely used international characters
3	0-87	Box Drawing	Graphics, single and double lines
4	0-78	Typographical	Typographical symbols
5	0-34	Icons	Picture symbols
6	0-218	Math/Scientific	Regular size math and scientific characters
7	0-222	Math/Scietific Extension	Extensible and oversized math and scientific characters
8	0-199	Greek	Greek characters, both ancient and modern
9	0-43	Hebrew	Hebrew characters, vowel signs and punctuation
10	0-101	Cyrillic	Cyrillic characters, both ancient and modern
11	0-99	Japanese Kana	Hiragana or Katakana characters
12	0-254	User-defined	

■**FIGURE 15.2:** *WordPerfect character sets*

■ MATHEMATICAL TYPING

New Feature
Additional related features in version 5.1 are discussed under "The Equation Editor," page 342.

Typing statistical and mathematical formulas presents some real challenges. In many instances, both regular and special characters are used, just as in typing foreign-language documents. But what makes these characters especially difficult to enter is that not all of them are on the same line, as in these examples:

$$\int_1^5 2x \ dx = 24 \qquad (S_6 = \frac{1[-(1/2)^6]}{(1-r)} \quad)$$

In the first example, the characters with codes 7,0 and 7,1 were combined to form the integral sign, and the characters that follow are above and below the line. The other example uses four levels of characters, along with the 1/2 symbol.

Before we enter these formulas, let's consider how your printer handles subscripts and superscripts. On daisy wheel printers, and on some dot-matrix and laser printers, every character is the same size, so subscripts and superscripts are regular characters 1/2 line above or below the base line.

Other printers, such as laser printers with multiple fonts and dot-matrix printers with graphics, can print very small characters. Figure 15.4 shows these two styles.

The instructions below are for printers that have no small font to use for superscripts and subscripts. Separate instructions will follow for other printers.

With certain display cards, superscripts and subscripts appear on the screen as small characters. Even with these systems, however, use the method that works with your printer.

```
         Character              Set and Number

         á                           1,27
         ¿                           4,8
         Ñ                           1,56
         ç                           1,39
         Ç                           1,38
         ñ                           1,57
         é                           1,41
         í                           1,49
         ó                           1,59
         ú                           1,67
         ¡                           4,7
         ½                           4,17
         ¼                           4,18
         √                           5,14
         ∫                           7,0
         ∫                           7,1
         π                           8,33_



                                                    Doc 1 Pg 1 Ln 4" Pos 3.33"
```

■**FIGURE 15.3:**   *The sample character directory*

Superscripts and Subscripts are regular characters

$$(S_6 = \frac{1 \ [\ -(\frac{1}{2})^6]}{(1-r)})$$

Superscripts and Subscripts are small characters

$$(S_6 = \frac{1 \ [\ -(\frac{1}{2})^6]}{(1-r)} \ )$$

■**FIGURE 15.4:**   *Different printer styles for subscripts and superscripts*

Now we'll enter the two formulas. Follow these steps to enter the first one:

1. If necessary, start WordPerfect.

2. Press Ctrl-2 7,0 space bar. This displays one half of the integral sign on the screen.

3. Press Ctrl-F8 1 1 for a superscript.

4. Press **5** then → Return to return to normal characters and move to the next line.

5. Press Ctrl-2 7,1 space bar. The bottom half of the integral sign appears. Since it is directly under its upper counterpart, together they appear as one character.

6. Press Ctrl-F8 1 2 for a subscript.

7. Press **1** followed by →.

8. Press Ctrl-F8 1 1 for a superscript again. The characters you enter now will be printed directly between the superscripted 5 and the subscripted 1, right in the middle of the integral sign.

9. Type **2x dx = 24** on that same line.

10. Press →.

11. Press Return three times.

We've completed the first formula. The subscripts and superscripts are displayed on the same line as the other text, but they will be printed correctly.

CHANGING THE DEFAULT STATUS LINE

The status line shows the line and position of the cursor in inches. This is convenient because you can quickly tell where the cursor is on the page, particularly when using several type sizes in the same document.

When entering multiple-level formulas, however, you will be changing to half-line spacing. If you used the default status line, the Ln indicator would change in small decimal amounts—making it difficult to really locate the cursor in relation to the original line position.

So instead of using inches, let's change the status line so it reports the line and character position numbers—the method used in WordPerfect 4.2.

1. Press Shift-F1 for the Setup menu.

Warning

Step 2: With version 5.1, press *3* and then *8* to display the Units of Measure menu.

2. Press **8** or **u** to display the Units of Measure menu.

3. Press **2** or **s** to change the status line display. The options available are

   - ■ **"** to use inch measurements, the default display

   - ■ **i** for inches displayed as *2i* rather than *2"*

   - ■ **c** for centimeters

   - ■ **p** for points

   - ■ **w** for 1200ths of an inch

   - ■ **u** for line and character positions, or "Version 4.2 Units"

4. Press **u** then press Return twice.

MULTIPLE-LEVEL FORMULAS

The next formula requires special line spacing. You will first change the line spacing to .5, then create a blank area in which to work. Follow these steps:

1. Press Shift-F8 1 6 to reach the Line Spacing prompt.

2. Type **.5** then press Return three times.

3. Press Esc, type **60**, then press the space bar. This inserts 60 blank spaces into the line.

4. Press Ctrl-F3 2 6 to select the Move option on the Line Draw prompt line. (Line drawing is discussed in detail in Chapter 17.)

5. Press Esc, type **15**, and press ↓. The cursor moves down fifteen lines, in 1/2-line increments, to line 12.5. You just inserted 16 half-lines of space into the document. With this blank area established, you can move the cursor around without affecting other characters or the spacing.

6. Press F7 to return to the document.

7. Press ↑ until the cursor is on line 8, then press Home ← to reach the left margin.

8. Press the Ins key. The word *Typeover* appears on the status line.

9. Type **(S**.

10. Press ↓. Even though the cursor appears one entire line down on the screen, the Ln indicator shows 8.5. The printed formula will appear with this half-line spacing.

11. Press **6**. Your screen should look like this:

(S
6

12. Press ↑ once to return to line 8.

13. Type = then press the space bar. The screen displays

(S =
6

14. Press ↑ once to reach line 7.5.

15. Press F8 to turn on underlining.

16. Type **1 [-(1/2)]**. Remember to press Ctrl-2 4,17 → for the 1/2 sign and to leave a space before the last bracket. Type the entire line without worrying, at least for the time being, about the superscripted 6. The screen now displays

1 [-(1/2)]
(S = ‾‾‾‾‾‾‾‾‾‾‾
6

17. Press ↓ to move the cursor down one line, then press → to move to the space after the bracket.

18. Type). Now your screen shows

1 [-(1/2)]
(S = ‾‾‾‾‾‾‾‾‾‾‾   )
6

19. Press ↑ to reach line 7, then move the cursor to the space before the closing bracket in the line below.

20. Type **6**. The formula so far appears as

6
1 [-(1/2)]
(S = ‾‾‾‾‾‾‾‾‾‾‾   )
6

21. Press ↓ to reach line 8.5.

22. Line up the cursor under the opening bracket, then type (**1-r**). The completed formula appears as

$$(S = \frac{1\,[\,-(1/2)\,]}{6\quad(1-r)}^{6}\,)$$

23. Press Shift-F7 1 to print the document. Notice that although full-line spacing appears on the screen, the half-line spacing on paper makes the formula appear correctly formatted (that is, if your printer is capable of printing half-line spacing).

24. Press F7 N Y if you want to exit WordPerfect.

Changing to half-line spacing, inserting an area of blank spaces, and turning on Typeover mode are necessary for this kind of typing. The blank area provides a working space in which you can move the cursor freely. Just be sure to insert enough blank lines to hold the entire formula. And be aware that not all printers are capable of half-line spacing.

RETURNING THE STATUS LINE DISPLAY TO THE DEFAULT

Before going on, let's return the status line to the default display.

New Feature
Additional related features in version 5.1 are discussed under "The Equation Editor," page 342.

1. Press Shift-F1 for the Setup menu.

2. Press **8** or **u** to display the Units of Measure menu.

3. Press **2** or **s** to change the status line display.

4. Press " then press Return twice.

MATHEMATICAL TYPING WITH MULTIPLE FONTS

If your printer uses small characters for superscripts and subscripts, then you can produce the two sample formulas using different techniques. For the formula that has the integral sign, change to half-line spacing and type the formula using all normal characters (not superscripts or subscripts) as shown in Figure 15.5.

The integral sign will appear together when printed, with the main line of the formula properly centered.

Create the multiple-level formula as explained in the last section except for steps 10 through 12 and 19 through 21. These are the steps that use half-line spacing to create the subscript 6 and superscript 6.

Instead, you should create the subscript 6 and superscript 6 by using the following instructions:

10. Press Ctrl-F8 1 2.

11. Type **6**.

12. Press → to move off of the [subscpt] code.

Create the superscript 6 using these steps:

19. Press Ctrl-F8 1 1.

20. Type **6**.

21. Press → to move off of the [suprscpt] code.

Figure 15.4 compares the two methods.

USING LINE ADVANCE

If you are entering a formula with only one level of subscripts and superscripts, then you can use either the Subscript and Superscript commands—Ctrl-F8 1 1 or Ctrl-F8 1 2—or change to half-line spacing. The latter technique has the advantage of displaying the document on the screen in the same general format as it will appear when it is printed. This allows you to judge how the finished text will look before actually printing it.

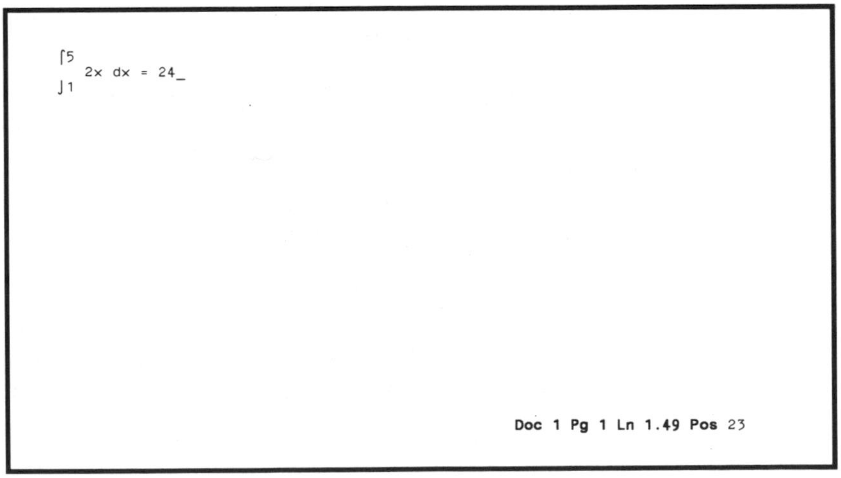

```
⌠5
⌡1   2x  dx  =  24_

                                      Doc 1 Pg 1 Ln 1.49 Pos 23
```

■**FIGURE 15.5:** *Integral formula with graphic printers*

If your formula requires more than one level of subscripting or superscripting, as in the equation

$$Z^{(n)} = X^{(y^n)} - 2Y^{(3^n)}$$

then half-line spacing is the obvious choice between the two methods since the Subscript and Superscript commands will only move one half-space above the line.

Another method of typing such formulas is to use the Advance Up and Advance Down commands on the Format Other menu. The Advance command instructs the printer to position characters either higher (Advance Up) or lower (Advance Down) than the line you're typing on. As with the Superscript and Subscript keys, the screen display shows the text on the same line as the other parts of the formula on the screen, so you won't know exactly how the finished formula looks until you print or preview it. However, the Advance Up and Advance Down commands can move text as far above or below the line as necessary. The only particular difficulty is in calculating the amount of movement needed to return to the starting line position.

Just as with half-line spacing, you can prepare the text using this feature, but your printer may not be able to print it. Your printer must be capable of reverse line feeding for these commands to take effect. Many printers capable of superscripting and subscripting cannot perform reverse line feeds. In fact most dot-matrix printers won't work this way.

Let's use the Advance commands to type the above formula.

1. If necessary, start WordPerfect.

2. Press Return three times. These extra lines are necessary to maintain the proper top margin, since the formula will take up more than one actual line on the page.

    The line you're now on is called the *base* line. As you advance up or down from the base line, you should keep track of the total distance away so you can return to it. You must advance the same distance but in the opposite direction to return to the original base line.

3. Type **Z**.

4. Press Shift-F8 4 1 to select Advance from the Format Other menu and display the prompt line

    Advance: 1 Up; 2 Down; 3 Line; 4 Left; 5 Right; 6 Column:0

5. Press **1** or **u** for Advance Up. You'll see the prompt

    Adv. up 0"

Here is where you enter the amount of space, in inches, that you want the next characters to appear in relation to the current line position.

6. Type **.08** then press Return three times to return to the document. The code [AdvUp:0.08"] is inserted into the text.

7. Type (**n**). The characters appear on the same line, but they will be printed about 1/2 line above the starting line.

   These measurements are absolute from the last position, not relative to the original base line. For example, you just moved the position up 0.08" from the base line. If you give the same command again, you'll move it 0.08" farther up, a total of 0.16" above the base line.

8. Press Shift-F8 4 1 2 to select Advance Down.

9. Type **.08** then press Return three times. This returns the typing line to the base line.

10. Type =**X**.

11. Press Shift-F8 4 1 1.

12. Type **.08** then press Return three times.

13. Type (**y**.

14. Press Shift-F8 4 1 1.

15. Type **.08** then press Return three times. This second Advance Up command moves the printing position another half-line up—now about one full line from the starting line.

16. Type **n**.

17. Press Shift-F8 4 1 2 to move down 1/2 line.

18. Type **.08** then press Return three times.

19. Type). Your screen should now look like this:

    Z(n)=X(yn)

20. Press Shift-F8 4 1 2.

21. Type **.08** then press Return three times to return to the original base line.

22. Type −**2Y**.

23. Press Shift-F8 4 1 1.

24. Type **.08** then press Return three times.

25. Type **(3**.

26. Press Shift-F8 4 1 1.

27. Type **.08** then press Return three times.

28. Type **n**.

29. Press Shift-F8 4 1 2.

30. Type **.08** then press Return three times.

31. Type **)**.

32. Press Shift-F8 4 1 2.

33. Type **.08** then press Return three times to return to the original base line. On the screen, the completed equation looks like this:

Z(n)=X(yn)–2Y(3n)

The equation with its codes revealed is shown in Figure 15.6. Notice that you must enter the proper measurements to restore the cursor to the base line. You can make sure that you've returned the cursor to the original line by placing the cursor on the first character of the equation, then on the space following the formula. The Ln indicator should show the same number at both positions.

In our example, we used the Advance Up and Advance Down commands to place text several levels above the original line. You can use the same techniques to print text below the starting line.

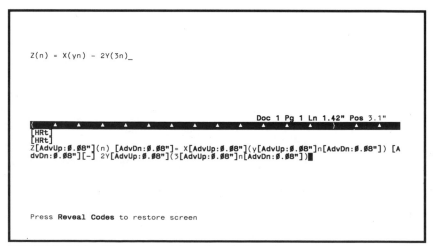

■**FIGURE 15.6:** *The completed formula with the codes revealed*

ADVANCE MACROS

You can save yourself keystrokes by creating macros to issue the Advance Up and Advance Down commands. For example, create a named macro—called *Up*—with the keystrokes

Ctrl-F10 Up Return Return Shift-F8 4 1 1 .08 Return Return
Return Ctrl-F10

The Advance Down macro would be

Ctrl-F10 Down Return Return Shift-F8 4 1 2 .08 Return Return
Return Ctrl-F10

When you want to advance up, type Alt-F10 Up Return; type Alt-F10 Down Return to move down.

■ PRINTER PROBLEMS

If you have difficulty printing your technical documents, start with a small practice exercise. First, experiment to determine how many of the special characters your printer can handle. Then, test the Superscript and Subscript features. Follow that with a test of half-line spacing and the Advance Up and Advance Down commands. If you still have trouble, type a few characters at a time, then reveal the codes. Look carefully to make that sure that the proper commands are in place.

Unfortunately, even if your printer was named specifically in the printer selection process, there is still a chance that you won't be able to print all of the special characters that can be displayed on the screen. You should check your printer manual or any instructions that came with your type element or cartridge. Somewhere there will be a chart showing all of the printable characters. If there is a code given for the character, use it as a printer command from Printer Functions on the Format Other menu.

If some important character is not available, determine whether it can be created by overstriking two characters. For example, accented characters can be created by typing both characters in the Overstrike mode, as long as the accent itself is available on your printer.

If all else fails, determine whether your printer is compatible with any of those listed. Many dot matrix printers, for example, share common features. There are several compatible groups of letter-quality and laser printers as well. Some printers have controls or switches that can be adjusted to make them compatible with other printers. Check your manual and adjust the switches if you find a compatible printer listed. Then set WordPerfect for the compatible machine and print a sample list of special characters.

VERSION 5.1 FEATURES

WORDPERFECT CHARACTERS

Earlier versions of WordPerfect could only print special characters if they were supported by your printer, even though they might have appeared on the screen.

With version 5.1, however, you need not have special font elements, cartridges, or soft fonts to print the 1500-plus characters in the WordPerfect character sets. Instead of relying on your printer for support, during setup WordPerfect creates a file called WP.DRS that contains the commands necessary to produce the special characters on your printer as graphic images and display them in View mode on your monitor. Of course, your printer must have graphic capabilities.

When you print a special character, WordPerfect first determines whether it is supported by your printer's own fonts. If it is supported, WordPerfect transmits the ASCII code for that character. However, if your printer does not support the character, WordPerfect uses the information in WP.DRS to produce it as a graphic image.

The size of the character is determined by the Base Font and Size settings. So laser printers can print special characters in all of the sizes of their internal fonts, cartridges, and available soft fonts. Depending on your printer, several different fonts may be supported by WP.DRS. Using laser printers, for instance, Word-Perfect will automatically select between fonts similar to Courier, Helvetica, or Times Roman to most closely match the base font.

WordPerfect will also try to match the Appearance setting being used—for example, creating italic, bold, outline, or shadow characters to match the style of the surrounding text. Figure 15.7 illustrates how special characters can be used.

THE EQUATION EDITOR

With version 5.1, WordPerfect is as much at home with math and technical typing as it is with business typing. Through the Equation Editor, 256 symbols,

54 Greek characters, and 60 mathematical commands and functions can be combined easily into even the most complex formulas.

The Equation Editor lets you enter an equation using special instructions, and then it translates the equation into a graphic image that can be printed on supported printers. Note that the Equation Editor is just used to form equations; it cannot perform the actual calculations.

Many of the steps in creating and formatting the overall appearance of equations are similar to those for graphic images, as discussed in Chapters 17 and 18. So in this chapter we'll concentrate on constructing the actual equation. Refer to Chapters 17 and 18 for detailed explanations of options and commands not discussed here.

Equation Keyboard   Before using the Equation Editor, however, let's look at a way of streamlining your work. WordPerfect 5.1 is packaged with six alternate keyboard layouts. Each layout contains special characters, commands, or macros that are *mapped* to Alt and Ctrl key combinations. The keyboard layout called Equation assigns 37 key combinations for frequently used equation symbols and commands. All of the prepackaged keyboards and their key assignments are detailed in Appendix H of the WordPerfect manual.

You activate an alternate keyboard such as Equation by selecting it in the Setup menus. Of course, you have to have copied the keyboards from the master disks during the installation process. If you set up WordPerfect without the keyboards, exit at this point and rerun the Install program, answering Yes when asked if you want to install the keyboard layouts.

Now follow these steps to use the Equation keyboard:

1. Press Shift-F1 5 or select **F**ile **S**etup **K**eyboard Layout to select the Keyboard Layout option on the Setup menu. A list of available keyboards

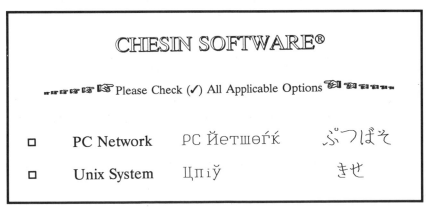

■**FIGURE 15.7:** *Using special characters*

will appear on the screen, along with the prompt line

1 Select; 2 Delete; 3 Rename; 4 Create; 5 Copy; 6 Original;
7 Edit; 8 Map; N Name Search: 1

2. Press the arrow kcys to highlight EQUATION, the name of the keyboard you want to use.

3. Press *1* or *s* to select it.

4. Press F7 to return to the document.

When you use the Equation keyboard, however, you can no longer access the pull-down menus with Alt-=. To return to the default keyboard assignment, press Shift-F1 5 and select Original from the prompt line. You can temporarily return to one original keyboard by pressing Ctrl-6. But unlike when you select Original, the alternate keyboard will be in effect the next time you start WordPerfect.

Now let's see how the Equation keyboard and the Equation Editor work.

Creating Equations   Let's create and print the equation shown in Figure 15.8. I'm sure you'll recognize it as the equation for computing the loss in decibels over an unbalanced attenuator network. Follow these steps:

1. Press Alt-F9 or select **Graphics** to display the options

1 Figure; 1 Table Box; 3 Text Box; 4 User Box; 5 Line;
6 Equation:0

2. Press **6** or **e**, or select **Equation**, to display the options

Equation: 1 Create; 2 Edit; 3 New Number; 4 Options: 0

3. Press **1** or **c**, or select **Create**, to show the Equation Definition menu (Figure 15.9).

4. Press **9** or **e**. The Equation Editor screen is displayed (Figure 15.10).

$$db\ loss = 20\ \log_{10}\left(\sqrt{\frac{Z_1}{Z_2}} + \sqrt{\frac{Z_1}{Z_2} - 1}\right)$$

■**FIGURE 15.8:** *Equation*

The Equation Editor screen contains three major sections:

- The Editing Window, along the bottom, is where you create the equation by entering characters, symbols, and keywords—Equation commands. The double border along the right side shows that it is currently the active window.

```
Definition: Equation

      1 - Filename

      2 - Contents              Equation

      3 - Caption

      4 - Anchor Type           Paragraph

      5 - Vertical Position     Ø"

      6 - Horizontal Position   Full

      7 - Size                  6.5" wide x Ø.333" (high)

      8 - Wrap Text Around Box  Yes

      9 - Edit


Selection: Ø
```

■**FIGURE 15.9:** *Equation Definition menu*

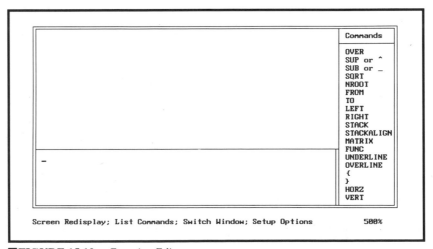

■**FIGURE 15.10:** *Equation Editor*

- The Equation Palette, along the right of the screen, shows the commands, functions, and symbols that are available. You'll soon learn how to scroll the palette to display additional selections. Table 15.1 lists the eight sets of options available in the Palette.

- The Display Window, above the Editing Window, will show a graphic representation of the equation. When you activate the Display Window, the double border is removed from the Editing Window and placed here. The image in the Display Window is not updated automatically as you create the equation in the Editing Window. To display the equation, you must use the Ctrl-F3, F9, or Shift-F3 keystrokes explained below.

When working on equations, use these commands:

- Press Shift-F3 to move between the Editing Window and the Display Window. When you switch to the Display Window, the equation is updated to conform to recent changes in the Editing Window. From the Display Window you can scale and move the equation.

■TABLE 15.1:   *The Eight Equation Palette Sets*

Palette	Function
Commands	Common formats and symbols. All have keyword equivalents.
Large	Popular math symbols in two sizes from character set 7. All have keywords and can be accessed using Compose.
Symbols	Miscellaneous symbols from character sets 3, 4, 5, and 6. All have keywords and can be accessed using Compose.
Greek	Greek characters from set 10. All have keywords and can be accessed using Compose. The keywords are case-sensitive. Type *ALPHA* for A, *alpha* for α.
Arrows	Arrows, triangles, squares, and circles. None have keyword equivalents, but they can be accessed using Compose.
Sets	Set symbols, relational operators, Fraktur, and hollow letters. Some of the symbols have keywords but all can be accessed with Compose.
Other	Diacritical marks and ellipses, with keyword equivalents.
Functions	Mathematical functions, with keyword equivalents.

- Press Ctrl-F3 or F9 to update the graphic image in the Display Window without leaving the Editing Window.

- Press F5 to enter the Equation Palette for selecting commands.

- Press Shift-F1 to change the horizontal and vertical alignment or the default font size, or to change between graphic and text printing of the final equation.

The figure 500% at the bottom right of the screen is the *scale factor*. When you first start to enter an equation and update the screen, the graphic image shown in the Display Window is five times the actual size. As your equation gets larger, however, WordPerfect will scale the image down so it fits in the Display Window. Once WordPerfect scales the image, the exact scale factor shown will vary between display adapters.

Entering Equations   There are several ways to enter the symbols and equation commands in the Editing Window. Most symbols can be entered using the Ctrl-2 Compose key as explained earlier in this chapter. (Ctrl-V, by the way, will not work in the Equation Editor.) In addition, many symbols can be entered as *keywords*, special commands recognized by the Equation Editor.

For example, you can enter the capital sigma (Σ) into an equation by typing the keyword SIGMA, SUM, or SMALLSUM, by pressing Ctrl-2 7,6 or by pressing Ctrl-S when the Equation keyboard is active. Using the Compose key, the symbol itself appears in the Editing Window. The keywords will appear in the Editing Window if you type them in, and the word *SUM* will appear if you press Ctrl-S. But in all cases, the symbol will appear in the Display Window and in the printed equation.

There is still another way to enter symbols and keywords: selecting them from the Equation Palette. When you select a symbol from the palette, pressing Return inserts the highlighted symbol's keyword into the Editing Window, and pressing Ctrl-Return inserts the symbol itself. But again, the symbol will appear in the Display Window and in the printed equation.

Figure 15.11 shows the sigma character entered seven ways. The figure shows one of the other menus of options available in the Equation Palette. Left to right, they have been entered by using Compose, by typing the three keywords, by pressing Ctrl-S, and twice by using the palette—first by selecting the symbol and pressing Return, and then by selecting the symbol again and pressing Ctrl-Return. No matter how the character appears in the Editing Window, all methods produce the character itself in the Display Window and in print. The Large palette contains two sizes of most characters in the set. The first and fourth symbols in Figure 15.11 represent the smaller size compared with its larger counterpart created by the keyword SUM and by selecting the larger Σ symbol in the palette. The smaller—second—character is taken from the Greek palette using the keyword SIGMA, differentiating between the Greek and mathematical applications.

If you make a mistake typing in the Editing Window, delete characters using either the Del or Backspace key. Press Ctrl-PgDn Y to delete everything from the cursor to the end of the equation, or Ctrl-End to delete to the end of the line. You can use the arrow keys to move the cursor and insert characters. Pressing Ins places the editor in Typeover mode.

Now let's begin entering the equation.

5. Type **db loss** =. Nothing yet appears in the Display Window. Let's take care of that now.

6. Press Ctrl-F3 or F9. The characters in the Editing Window now appear enlarged in the Display Window (Figure 15.12).

The Display Window is not updated automatically as you form the equation. To see how the equation looks at any time, press Ctrl-F3 or F9. This *updates* the Display Window.

If the message

Error: Incorrect Format

appears when you try to update the Display Window, something is wrong with your equation. Correct the equation and try updating the Display Window again.

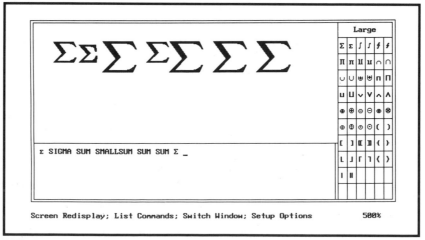

■FIGURE 15.11: *Sigma character entered seven ways*

You should notice two things about the format of the equation in the Display Window.

First, the words *db loss* are in italic. When you enter words that are not Equation commands, functions, or keywords, WordPerfect assumes they are the *variables* of the equation and prints them in italic.

Second, although you typed spaces in the Editing Window, no spaces appear in the Display Window. That's because spaces that you type or see in the Editing Window are ignored when the display is updated. Spaces, in fact, are reserved for a special purpose—as *delimiters* identifying Equation commands. You'll see how spaces work this way in a moment. But for now, let's solve the spacing problem.

7. Press ← to place the cursor immediately after *db*.

8. Type ~, the tilde symbol. WordPerfect uses the tilde to indicate a full space, and the backward accent (`) for a quarter space.

9. In the same way, enter a tilde after the word *loss*, and press End to reach the end of the equation

10. Press F9 to update the screen. Spaces now appear where you typed tildes in the Editing Window.

11. Type **~20~log**.

12. Press F9 to update the display.

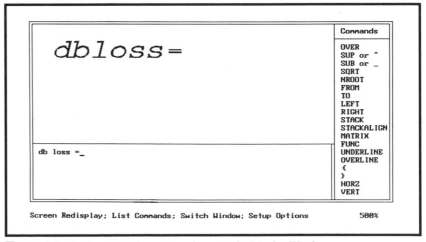

■**FIGURE 15.12:** *Partial equation shown in the Display Window*

WordPerfect automatically scales the image so the entire formula fits in the Display Window. The word *log* does not appear in italics because it is a mathematical function.

13. Enter the Subscript command using one of these methods:

> If you have activated the Equation keyboard, press Ctrl-Z. The word *SUB* appears with a space before and after.

> Type the word **SUB**, leaving a space before and after.

With the spaces, WordPerfect will interpret the word SUB as the keyword for subscript. Without the spaces, WordPerfect will interpret it as a variable, and the characters *S U B* will appear in the display and in print, like this:

db loss = 20 log SUB10

You can also enter the Subscript command by typing an underline character, as in

db~loss~=~20 log_

Any spaces you enter before the underline will be ignored.

14. Type **10**, making sure there is at least one space after the word SUB.

15. Press F9 to update the display. WordPerfect subscripted the number *10*.

All numeric characters following a SUB or _ (or SUP or + for a superscript) will be formatted correctly. The subscript or superscript stops with the first non-numeric character. So, for example, the command *log SUB 10x* would result in:

$\log_{10} x$

If you want to subscript or superscript nonnumeric characters, they all must be classified as a group. Groups are surrounded by { and } characters, either entered from the keyboard or selected in the palette. Using groups, *log SUB {10x}* would result in:

$\log_{10x}$

If you typed the (character into the equation now on your screen, it would appear in its normal size instead of enlarged to enclose the remainder of the equation. To format the equation properly, we'll use a special equation function—Left. The Left command tells WordPerfect to print the next enclosing character, such as a bracket or parenthesis, large enough for the subgroup that follows.

While you could type the word directly into the Editing Window, let's see how the Equation Palette operates.

16. Press F5 to enter the Equation Palette, which contains the first of the eight sets of options.

The first command, Over, is highlighted, and the prompt line shows

Fraction: x OVER y

When in the Equation Palette, the prompt line lists the name of the selected command and shows a sample of its use.

Use ↓ and ↑ to scroll through the list of options. Use PgDn and PgUp to move from one list of options to the next. To exit the palette without making a selection, press Esc.

Appendix D in the WordPerfect manual lists the contents of each option set and their corresponding keywords. In most cases, the keyword selected is entirely logical, such as NRoot for the *n*th root or Alpha for the Greek letter.

17. Press the ↓ key to highlight the word *LEFT*, and then press Return. The word *LEFT* appears in the Editing Window, with spaces automatically inserted before and after. (If you type the word yourself, you must insert the spaces.)

If you tried to update the display at this point, you'd get the Incorrect Format error message. That's because each Left command requires a corresponding Right command.

18. Press the space bar and then type (

19. Enter the square-root symbol using any of these methods:

If you are using the Equation keyboard, press Ctrl-Q to insert the characters *SQRT* surrounded by spaces.

Type *SQRT* surrounded by spaces.

Press F5 to enter the palette, highlight *SQRT*, and press Return.

Before entering the rest of the equation, make sure you understand the concept of groups, as mentioned earlier. Now that the square-root symbol is inserted, WordPerfect needs some way to determine which of the next characters entered to put under it. The plus sign, for example, does not belong under that square-root symbol. WordPerfect also has to determine which characters are above the division line—Z SUB 1—and which are under it—Z SUB 2.

This is all done with the group indicators { and }.

The Equation commands to create the text inside the square root are *Z SUB 1 OVER Z SUB 2*. This means, "Place Z SUB 1 on a line over Z SUB 2." But if we entered

SQRT Z SUB 1 OVER Z SUB 2

only the Z_1 would appear under the square-root sign in the display window. To solve this problem, you have to surround the entire group with brackets.

Commands such as SUB and OVER are not case-sensitive. They can be entered in any combination of uppercase and lowercase letters. Variables such as Z, however, will appear in the exact case in which you enter them.

20. Type **{ Z SUB 1 OVER Z SUB 2 }**

Enter the braces by typing them or by selecting them from the palette. *OVER* can be typed, selected from the palette, or inserted with Ctrl-O on the Equation keyboard. Make sure that at least one space surrounds each SUB and OVER.

21. Enter **+ SQRT { Z SUB 1 OVER Z SUB 2 - 1 } right**).

The -1 will not be subscripted, because it starts with a nonnumeric character. Yet it appears under the second square root because it is within its group—the opening and closing braces.

22. Press F9 to update the display (Figure 15.13). Notice that the scale factor has been decreased to fit the equation into the window.

So far, you've been working only in the Editing Window and the Equation Palette, updating the Display Window but not switching to it. By moving into the Display Window, however, you can adjust the scale and position of the equation. Let's try that now.

23. Press Shift-F3. The Display Window is updated and the double border appears at its right side. The prompt line is now

Arrow Keys Move; PgUp/PgDn Scale; GOTO Reset; Switch Window.

These commands are used to manipulate the image in the Display Window. For example, Figure 15.14 shows the equation after being scaled down by pressing the PgDn key three times. Each time you press PgDn, the scale factor changes by 25%. The arrow keys were used to move the equation within the window.

24. Press Shift-F3 to return to the Editing Window.

Before leaving this screen, look carefully at the final form of the equation:

db~loss~=~20~log SUB 10 LEFT (SQRT { Z SUB 1 OVER Z SUB 2} + SQRT {Z SUB 1 OVER Z SUB 2 -1} RIGHT)

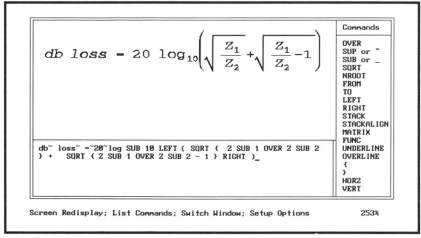

■FIGURE 15.13: *Updated equation*

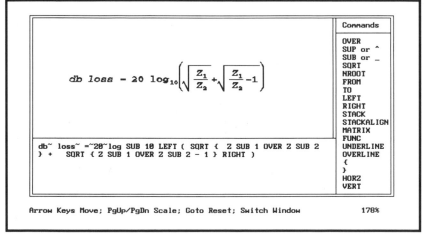

■FIGURE 15.14: *Equation scaled down and moved within the window*

Spaces inserted in the equation (except with the ~ and backward accent symbols) were ignored when WordPerfect compiled it into its graphic form as shown in the Display Window.

25. Press F7 to accept the equation and return to the Equation Definition menu.

26. Press F7 twice to return to the document. All that's displayed on the screen is the top of an equation box labelled *EQU 1* (Figure 15.15). This means that it is the first equation box in the document. You'll learn more about graphic boxes like this equation box in Chapters 17 and 18.

27. Press Shift-F7 1 or select **F**ile **P**rint **F**ull to print the equation, or if you prefer, press Shift-F7 6 or select **F**ile **P**rint **V**iew Document to see it in View mode.

SAVING AND RETRIEVING EQUATIONS

While you're working on an equation, you can save it in its own file, separate from the document. This is useful when you're constructing complex equations and you don't want to exit the Equation Editor to save the file, or when you plan to use the equation in other documents.

From within the Equation Editor, press F10 to see the prompt:

Equation file to save:

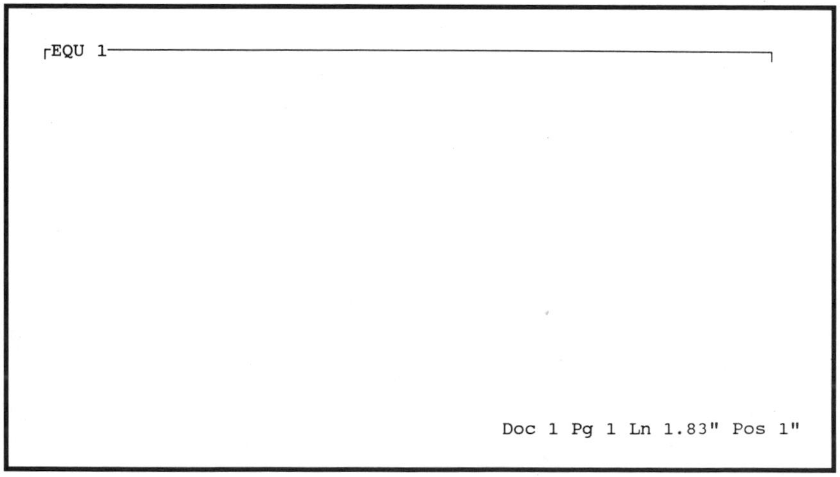

```
┌EQU 1──────────────────────────────────────────────────┐






                                              Doc 1 Pg 1 Ln 1.83" Pos 1"
```

■**FIGURE 15.15:** *Equation box displayed on the screen*

Type a file name, and press Return. If a file with that name already exists, you'll be asked to confirm the replacement.

To recall the file into the Equation Editor, press Shift-F10 for the prompt

Equation file to retrieve:

Type the name and press Return.

EQUATION OPTIONS

In Chapters 17 and 18 you'll learn how to use the Equation Definition and Equation Options menus to control equation boxes. From within the Equation Editor, however, you can control four aspects of how the final equation will appear. Press Shift-F1 to display the Equation Options menu (Figure 15.16).

Print as Graphics   Using the default setting, WordPerfect creates the equation as a graphic image. Set this option to No to have WordPerfect use your printer's available fonts instead. Users of laser printers, for example, might have technical cartridge fonts or soft fonts that contain all of the symbols required for the equation. The equation would appear in a higher resolution using these fonts rather than printed as a graphic. However, if you select No for this option, blank spaces will appear at each location where no matching symbol exists in your font.

Graphical Font Size   Equation characters will be printed in the same size as the default document font. Like special characters, WordPerfect will attempt

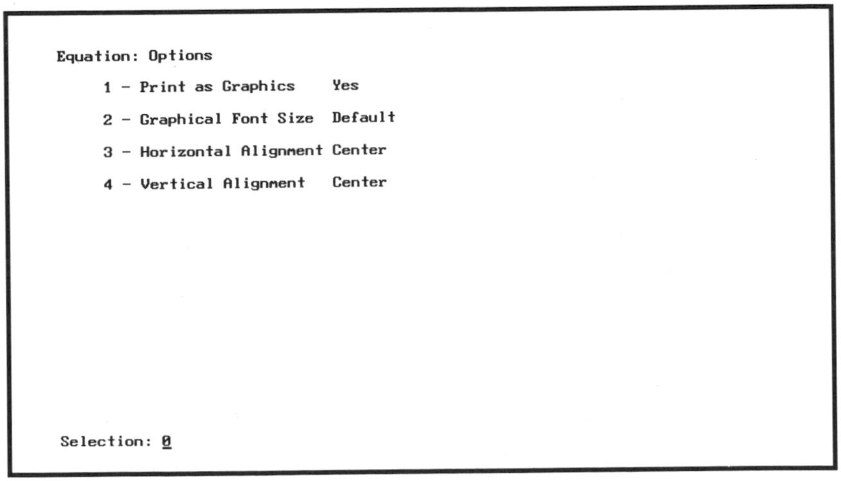

```
Equation: Options
        1 - Print as Graphics     Yes
        2 - Graphical Font Size   Default
        3 - Horizontal Alignment  Center
        4 - Vertical Alignment    Center




        Selection: 0
```

■**FIGURE 15.16:**   *Equation Options menu*

to match the font as closely as possible using styles similar to Courier, Helvetica, and Times Roman.

You can change the size of the font used, and thus the overall size of the equation, by selecting this option. You'll see the prompt

> 1 Default Font; 2 Set Point Size: 0

Press *2* or *s*, enter the point size desired, and press Return.

WordPerfect will not confirm that the equation can in fact fit on the line in that point size. If you select a size too large, not all of the equation will be printed. So before printing, display the equation in View mode to make sure it's not too large.

Horizontal Alignment   This option determines whether the equation appears at the left, center (the default), or right of the equation box.

Vertical Alignment   Select this option to determine whether the equation appears at the top, center (the default), or bottom of the equation box.

RECALLING AND EDITING EQUATIONS

If you saved the equation in a separate file from within the Equation Editor and you wish to edit it, display the Equation Editor by pressing Alt-F9 6 1 9 or selecting **G**raphics **E**quation **C**reate **E**dit, and then press Shift-F10, type the file name, and press Return.

If you've saved the equation as a graphic box after exiting the Equation Editor, recall the document, and press Alt-F9 6 2 or select **G**raphics **E**quation **E**dit to see the prompt

> Equation Number? 1

Enter the equation's box number and press Return, or just press Return if its number appears at the prompt. Then select Edit from the menu.

Change or add to the equation as required, and resave your changes.

We touched on only a few of the 370 symbols and commands recognized by the Equation Editor. Once you understand how the Equation commands operate, however, you should be able to construct complex equations—even if you don't understand the mathematical concepts involved.

MOUSE AND MENU EQUIVALENTS

Function	Keyboard	Pull-Down Menus
Compose	Ctrl-2 (or Ctrl-V)	Font Characters
Line Draw	Ctrl-F3 2	Tools Line Draw
Advance	Shift-F8 4 1	Layout Other Advance
Equation	Alt-F9 6	Graphics Equation

PART 3

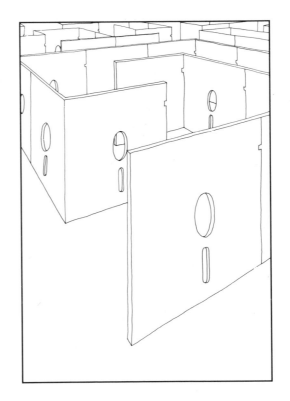

WORDPERFECT AS MULTIPURPOSE SOFTWARE

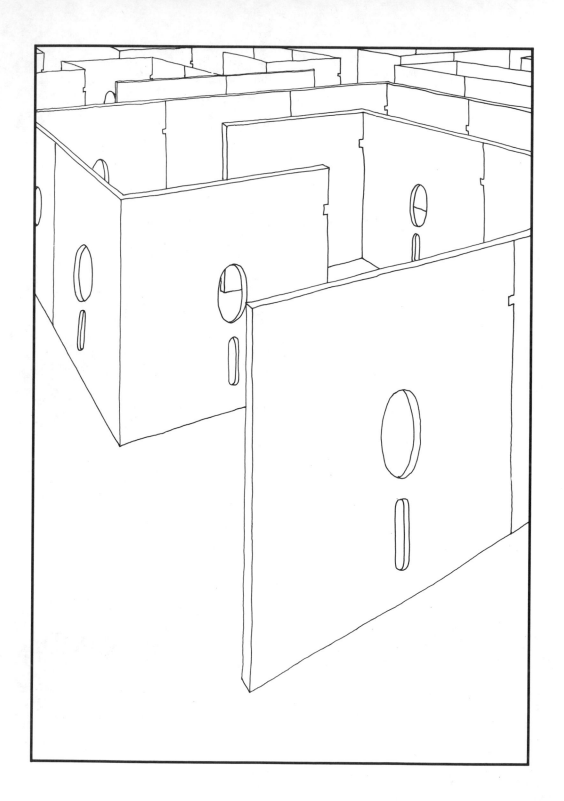

16

USING WORDPERFECT AS AN OUTLINE AND THOUGHT PROCESSOR

The process of working out an outline is one of refinement—starting at a major point and cultivating the details. Using outlines in this way is called *thought processing* and has spawned numerous computer programs designed for this task. This process can be a prelude to writing a document or the planning stage of any project.

WordPerfect provides an automatic Outline-Numbering function that was probably designed as a writing aid; it provides the outline or paragraph numbers and the formatting for you as you type. But this facility can also be used as an important planning tool.

In this chapter, you will learn how to use the Outlining function both for the mechanical task of typing outlines and for expediting the mental and creative processes.

You'll also learn how to use the Master Document feature to add details to your outline from other documents. This will let you expand and condense your outline to include as much detail as you want.

OUTLINE STYLES

WordPerfect offers four different outline-numbering styles: outline, paragraph, legal, and bullet. You can also design your own numbering style.

OUTLINE

The most common numbering style for outlines includes both numbers (Roman and Arabic) and uppercase and lowercase letters.

```
I.
   A.
      1.
         a.
            (1)
               (a)
                  i)
                     a)
```

The text at each level appears as a hanging indentation, with each level number aligned under the text of the level above. Tab stops can be used for alignment.

PARAGRAPH

The paragraph style is a common format for outlines with lengthy entries. It does not include any uppercase letters or uppercase Roman numerals.

```
1.
   a.
      i.
         (1)
            (a)
               (i)
                  1)
                     a)
```

As with the outline style, hanging indentations and tab stops are usually used to align the text.

LEGAL

Outlines in legal style use numbers separated by periods. Each indentation adds another period and number to the end of the level above. This style is commonly used for legal documents and contracts, in which various points must be refined in detail, clearly associated with the major division, and easily referenced in other parts of the document.

```
1.
   1.1
      1.1.1
```

1.1.1.1
  1.1.1.1.1

Because of the length of the numbers, the indentations cannot be as neatly aligned as in the outline and paragraph styles, but hanging indentations can still be used to distinguish the different levels. You can add the period separators to other styles.

BULLET

This style uses characters other than letters or numbers to indicate outline levels.

CUSTOM STYLES

If the styles provided by WordPerfect are not appropriate, you can design your own numbering system using four different punctuation styles. The style shown below, for example, contains only uppercase and lowercase letters.

A
  A)
    (A)
      a
        a)
          (a)

Later, you'll learn how to define your own numbering style.

AUTOMATIC OUTLINING

Typing an outline requires three distinct tasks: entering the level numbers, indenting the entries, and keeping track of the levels. Fortunately, WordPerfect can take care of these tasks for you. This frees you from the mechanical aspects of creating outlines, allowing you to concentrate on the cerebral.

CREATING AN OUTLINE

The key to using WordPerfect's Automatic Outlining function is to distinguish the uses of the Return, Tab, and F4 keys.

- Return ends one entry and displays the highest level number.

- Tab moves the cursor to the next tab stop and changes the level number.

- F4 indents the text at the next tab stop.
     Thus, in creating a WordPerfect outline, you must remember one simple rule:

- Use the Tab key to change levels, not to indent text.

As an example, we'll enter the outline shown in Figure 16.1 using the default outline style. Follow these steps:

Warning
Users of version 5.1 should follow the special instructions under "Creating an Outline," page 384.

1. Start WordPerfect.

2. Press Shift-F5 to display the prompt line

    1 Date Text; 2 Date Code; 3 Date Format; 4 Outline;
    5 Para Num; 6 Define: 0

3. Press **4** to select Outline. The word

    Outline

   appears on the status line.

4. Press Return. The first level number (I.) appears on the screen, followed by the cursor. Figure 16.2 shows what this looks like with the codes revealed.

Notice that the Roman numeral does not appear with the codes. As with page numbers, WordPerfect uses a numbering code for outline levels so that they can be changed easily.

5. Press F4 to indent the entry, then type **Computer Hardware**.

6. Press Return. The characters *II.* appear automatically. Each time you press Return, the cursor moves to the next line, and the next number on the leftmost level appears.

7. Press Tab. The cursor moves to the first tab stop, and an uppercase *A* appears for the next level, like this:

    I. Computer Hardware
       A.

8. Press F4 to indent the entry, then type **Computers**.

9. Press Return. The characters *II.* appear again.

10. Press Tab twice. The number *1* appears:

    I. Computer Hardware
    A. Computers
       1.

11. Press F4, then type **Mainframes**.

```
          I.    Computer Hardware
                A.    Computers
                      1.    Mainframe
                      2.    Mini
                      3.    Micro
                            a.    Single-user
                            b.    Multi-user
                B.    Storage Devices
                      1.    Tape
                      2.    Disk
                            a.    Flexible
                            b.    Rigid
                                  (1)   Fixed
                                  (2)   Removable
                C.    Printers
                D.    Monitors

          II.   Computer Software
                A.    Word Processing
                B.    Database
                C.    Spreadsheet
                D.    Graphic
                E.    Integrated
                F.    System

          III.  Peripherals
```

■**FIGURE 16.1:** *Sample outline*

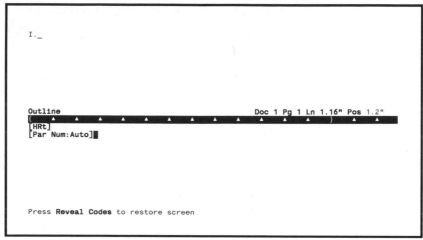

```
    I._




Outline                                    Doc 1 Pg 1 Ln 1.16" Pos 1.2"
(  ▲    ▲    ▲    ▲    ▲    ▲    ▲    ▲    ▲    ▲    ▲  )   ▲    ▲
[HRt]
[Par Num:Auto]█




Press Reveal Codes to restore screen
```

■**FIGURE 16.2:**   *The first level of the outline displayed with the codes revealed*

12. Press Return, then press Tab twice to display level number 2.

13. Press F4, then type **Mini**.

14. Press Return, press Tab twice, press F4, then type **Micro**.

15. Press Return, press Tab three times, press F4, and type **Single-user**.

16. Press Return, press Tab three times, press F4, and type **Multi-user**.

17. Press Return, press Tab once, press F4, and type **Storage Devices**.

18. Press Return, press Tab twice, press F4, and type **Tape**.

19. Press Return, press Tab twice, press F4, and type **Disk**.

20. Press Return, press Tab three times, press F4, and type **Flexible**.

21. Press Return, press Tab three times, press F4, and type **Rigid**.

22. Press Return, press Tab four times, press F4, and type **Fixed**.

23. Press Return, press Tab four times, press F4, and type **Removable**.

24. Press Return, press Tab once, press F4, and type **Printers**.

25. Press Return, press Tab once, press F4, and type **Monitors**.

26. Press Return twice. Notice that the *II* appeared both times. If you do not type text following a level number, the same number appears after you press Return.

27. Press F4, then type **Computer Software**.

28. Type the entries under the second main heading. They are all at the same level, so press Return, press Tab once followed by F4, then type each of the following entries:

    Word Processing
    Database
    Spreadsheet
    Graphic
    Integrated
    System

29. Press Return twice.

30. Press F4, then type **Peripherals**.

31. Press Shift-F5 4 to turn off the Outlining function. This command acts as a toggle.

32. Press Shift-F7 1 if you want to print the outline.

33. Press F7 Y, type **OUTLINE**, and press Return to save the document.

34. Press **Y** if you want to exit WordPerfect.

■ EDITING OUTLINES

The only special aspect of editing outlines is changing the levels of the entries. Figure 16.3 shows an edited version of the outline that we just created. A few entries have been changed, and several existing entries are at new levels. Let's make these revisions.

Warning
Users of version 5.1 should follow the special instructions under "Editing an Outline," page 386.

1. Start WordPerfect if you exited after the last section.

2. Press Shift-F10, type **OUTLINE**, and press Return.

3. Press Shift-F5 4 (in version 4.2: Alt-F5 1) to turn on the Outlining function.

4. Place the cursor on the line

    A. Computers

5. Press Ctrl-F4 2 3 (in version 4.2: Ctrl-F4 2 1) to delete the line and move up the remainder of the outline. Your screen looks like this:

> I. Computer Hardware
>   1. Mainframes
>   2. Mini

6. Press Del to move the level one tab stop to the left, like this:

> I. Computer Hardware
>   1. Mainframes
>   2. Mini

7. Press ↓. If the outline did not adjust automatically after step 6, it will now.

> I. Computer Hardware
>   A. Mainframes
>   2. Mini

8. Press Del ↓ to change the *2* to *B*.

9. Press Del ↓ to change the *3* to *C*.

10. Press Del ↓ to change the *a* to *1*.

11. Press Del ↓ to change the *b* to *2*.

12. Press the arrow keys to place the cursor on the *P* in *Printers*. Notice that the letter for Storage Devices automatically changed from *B* to *D*, and the *C* changed to *E*.

```
I.    Computer Hardware
      A.    Mainframe
      B.    Mini
      C.    Micro
            1.    Single-user
            2.    Multi-user
      D.    Storage Devices
            1.    Tape
            2.    Disk
                  a.    Flexible
                  b.    Rigid
                        (1)   Fixed
                        (2)   Removable
      E.    Other
            1.    Printers
            2.    Monitors
```

■**FIGURE 16.3:**   *The edited outline*

13. Type **Other**.

14. Press Return to move *Printers* to the next line. It is entered as level II.

15. Press Tab twice, then press F4 to adjust the level number. Your screen should look like this:

> E. Other
>   1. Printers

16. Press ↓, then press Home ← to reach the left margin of the next line.

17. Press Tab, then press ↓ to adjust the level number, like this:

> E. Other
>   1. Printers
>   2. Monitors

18. Press Shift-F5 4 to turn off the Outlining function.

19. Press Shift-F7 1 if you want to print the edited document. Leave the document on the screen for the next example.

New Feature
Additional related features in version 5.1 are discussed under "Outline Families," page 387.

We could have made most of the level changes in our sample outline without turning on the Outlining function. Once the [Par Num: Auto] codes are in the text, the levels will adjust automatically when you insert or delete tab stops. However, in order to have any new levels numbered when you press Return, you must first turn on the Outlining function.

DEFINING AND CHANGING STYLES

You may prefer using the paragraph or legal style or a format of your own design instead of the default outline style. You can either enter the outline in the other style or change the style of an existing outline.

To define or change an outline's style, press Shift-F5 6 to display the Paragraph Number Definition menu, shown in Figure 16.4. The four defined styles and examples of their numbering schemes are shown at the top of the menu. The format currently in force is shown in the middle, and the possible numbering styles and punctuation for each level are at the bottom. Option 1 shows that outlines will start numbering at 1, I, or • depending on the style.

If you press *2* through *5,* you'll select the numbering style shown, and it will appear as the current definition. To define your own style, press *6* or *u* for User-defined. The cursor moves to the Current Definition line. Under each level, type the numbering style you want (1, A, a, I, i, or some other character) and the

Note
The appearance
of the version
5.1 screen is
slightly dif-
ferent, but the
steps listed here
still apply.

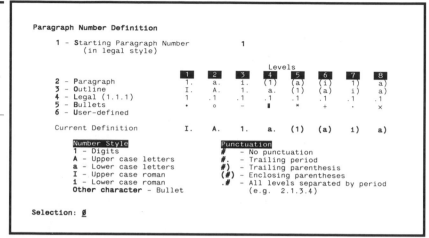

```
Paragraph Number Definition

        1 - Starting Paragraph Number          1
            (in legal style)

                                        Levels
                                  1   2   3   4   5   6   7   8
        2 - Paragraph            1.  a.  i.  (1) (a) (i) 1)  a)
        3 - Outline              I.  A.  1.  a.  (1) (a) i)  a)
        4 - Legal (1.1.1)        1   .1  .1  .1  .1  .1  .1  .1
        5 - Bullets              •   o   -   ■   *   +   ·   ×
        6 - User-defined

        Current Definition       I.  A.  1.  a.  (1) (a) 1)  a)

            Number Style                Punctuation
            1 - Digits                  #    - No punctuation
            A - Upper case letters      #.   - Trailing period
            a - Lower case letters      #)   - Trailing parenthesis
            I - Upper case roman        (#)  - Enclosing parentheses
            1 - Lower case roman        .#   - All levels separated by period
            Other character - Bullet          (e.g. 2.1.3.4)

        Selection: 0
```

■**FIGURE 16.4:**   *The Paragraph Numbering Definition menu*

type of punctuation desired, if any. If you enter a period before the number, all
levels will be separated with periods—like the legal style, but with your own
letters or numbers repeated. Level separators can only be used with letter or
number styles, not with bullets.

Let's change the text already on the screen in outline style to paragraph style,
as shown in Figure 16.5.

1. Press Home Home ↑ to place the cursor at the start of the document.

2. Press Shift-F5 6 to display the Paragraph Numbering Definition menu.

3. Press **2** to select the paragraph style.

4. Press Return twice, once to return to the document, a second time to clear
   the Date/Outline prompt line.

5. Press Ctrl-F3 Return to rewrite the screen. The level numbers automatically conform to the new style. If you reveal the codes, you'll see the
   code [Par Num Def] in the text.

6. Press Shift-F7 1 if you want to print the paragraph-style outline.

7. Press F7 N Y if you want to exit WordPerfect.

To check on an outline's current numbering and punctuation styles, press
Shift-F5 6 to display the Paragraph Number Definition menu. The Current

```
          1.   Computer Hardware
               a.   Mainframe
               b.   Mini
               c.   Micro
                    i.    Single-user
                    ii.   Multi-user
               d.   Storage Devices
                    i.    Tape
                    ii.   Disk
                          (1)  Flexible
                          (2)  Rigid
                               (a)   Fixed
                               (b)   Removable
               e.   Other
                    i.    Printers
                    ii.   Monitors

          2.   Computer Software
               a.   Word Processing
               b.   Database
               c.   Spreadsheet
               d.   Graphic
               e.   Integrated
               f.   System

          3.   Peripherals
```

■**FIGURE 16.5:** *An outline in paragraph style*

Definition line always indicates the outlining format in effect at the position of the cursor. Press Return when you want to return to the document.

If you want to return to the default outline style, reveal the codes and delete the [Par Num Def] code.

■ THOUGHT PROCESSING

Once you have mastered the mechanics of defining and typing outlines, you can use WordPerfect's Outlining function as a thought processor for developing projects.

An outline form on the screen creates a work space where you can arrange ideas and visualize the project taking shape. The Automatic Numbering function allows you to refine ideas, adding or deleting thoughts while maintaining organization. This visual reference makes it easier to identify weak areas—you can see that points are missing or that some subjects are not in the correct sequence.

As the outline takes shape, you can turn it into a master document linked with subdocuments that contain details. You can then view just the outline—the condensed mode—or the expanded document containing all of the associated text.

To organize such an undertaking, we can divide the task into five distinct steps:

1. Create a basic outline template.

2. Add the major points.

3. Refine the major levels into sublevels.

4. Link the entries with more detailed files or boilerplate text.

5. Print the outline and the expanded master document.

As an example, we'll follow this procedure to develop a plan for a community fund-raising project.

CREATING A BASIC TEMPLATE

The outline template is actually a blank outline form. Why create an outline with no entries? It creates an uncluttered workspace, just like a clear workbench, where your ideas can be tested and clarified. The template provides a starting point. As you develop your thoughts, you'll enter information and add sublevels.

We'll use the default outline style for our example, but any format could be used. Follow these steps to create the template:

1. Start WordPerfect if you exited after the last section.

2. Press Shift-F5 4 to turn on the Outlining function.

Warning
Step 2: Users of version 5.1 should press Shift-F5 4 1.

3. Press Return to display the first level, then press F4. You're adding the Indent code now so you can enter text later without worrying about formatting.

4. Press Return Tab F4 to enter the A level.

Warning
Steps 5 and 6: Users of version 5.1 should not press Tab.

5. Press Return Tab F4 to enter the B level.

6. Press Return Tab F4 to enter the C level. This establishes three divisions for the first major point:

    I.
      A.
      B.
      C.

If you think most of your projects will require more divisions, just enter them now as you did the first three.

7. In the same manner, create three divisions for the second and third major levels:

    I.
        A.
        B.
        C.
    II.
        A.
        B.
        C.
    III.
        A.
        B.
        C.

Warning
Step 8: Users of version 5.1 should press Shift-F5 4 2.

8. Press Shift-F5 4 to turn off the Outlining function.

9. Press F7 Y, type **PLAN**, and press Return.

10. Press **N** to clear the screen.

ADDING THE MAJOR POINTS

The next step starts the development process by establishing the major components of the project.

Since we are entering text into a template, we don't need to worry about formatting. We'll use the arrow keys to move among existing levels and the Return, Tab, and F4 keys to insert new levels.

1. Press Home Home ↑.

Warning
Step 2: Users of version 5.1 should press Shift-F5 4 1.

2. Press Shift-F5 4 to turn on the Outlining function.

3. Press ↓ to move the cursor to the indented position following the *I*, then type **Financial Needs**.

4. Press ↓ four times to place the cursor at the indented position following the *II*, then type **Current Resources**.

5. Press ↓ four times to place the cursor at the indented position following the *III*, then type **Possible Income Sources**.

6. Take a look at the three topics now in the outline. Are there any other major subjects that should be included? The outline includes making assessments of the financial needs, resources at hand, and possible sources of income—three initial planning steps in a typical fund-raising effort. But several key steps are missing. Let's add them now.

7. Place the cursor on level C under *Possible Income Sources* and press End.

Warning

Steps 8 and 10:
Users of version
5.1 should press
Return Shift-
Tab F4 before
typing the entry.

8. Press Return F4 to add number IV, then type **Plan of Action**.

9. Add blank levels A, B, and C.

10. Press Return F4 to insert number V, then type **Evaluation of Project**.

11. Add blank levels A, B, and C. The outline now looks like this:

   I. Financial Needs
      A.
      B.
      C.
   II. Current Resources
      A.
      B.
      C.
   III. Possible Income Sources
      A.
      B.
      C.
   IV. Plan of Action
      A.
      B.
      C.
   V. Evaluation of Project
      A.
      B.
      C.

Again, take some time to look at the outline. Are there any other major areas that should be added? Are the areas listed in the correct order? Are they of equal importance? Do they belong on the same level? If any major division is missing, decide where it belongs, place the cursor at the end of the line before the point of insertion, and press Return. WordPerfect will insert a new number and adjust the following ones.

REFINING THE MAJOR POINTS INTO SUBLEVELS

Once the major divisions seem in order, you should refine the outline by adding details under each level. Start by entering the first thoughts that come to mind. Don't worry too much at this point about their order, since they can be rearranged easily. If you need additional numbers or levels, place the cursor on the end of the line above where they should be inserted and press Return. Press the Tab key the appropriate number of times to reach the level, then press F4 to indent.

Follow these steps to refine our sample outline:

1. Add the following second-level entries to the outline on the screen. Remember to use the arrow keys to move within the outline. Do not press Return, or Tab when you're at the start of a line, unless you want to insert a new level or change an existing one.

   I. Financial Needs
      A. Deficit this year
      B. Increased costs
      C. Need new building and equipment
   II. Current Resources
      A. Community members
      B. Annual fund-raising dinner
      C.
   III. Possible Income Sources
      A. Neighborhood businesses
      B. Government
      C. Private foundations
   IV. Plan of Action
      A. Set up meetings with key individuals
      B. Formally announce fund-raising drive
      C. Mail out pledge cards
   V. Evaluation of Project
      A. Goal met?
      B.
      C.

Warning
Step 2: Users of version 5.1 should press Shift-F5 4 1.

2. Place the cursor at the end of the word *Government* under Level III. The Outlining function should still be turned on. If the word Outline is not on the status line, press Shift-F5 4.

Warning
Users of version
5.1 should fol-
low the special
instructions
under "Refining
the Major Points
into Sublevels,"
page 388.

3. Press Return, press Tab twice, then press F4 to insert *1.* under that level, like this:

> III. Possible Income Sources
>   A. Neighborhood businesses
>   B. Government
>   1.
>   C. Private foundations

4. Type **State**.

5. Press Return, press Tab twice to insert *2.*, then press F4.

6. Type **Local**.

7. Press Return, press Tab three times, then press F4. Your screen should look like this:

> III. Possible Income Sources
>   A. Neighborhood businesses
>   B. Government
>   1. State
>   2. Local
>   a.
>   C. Private foundations

8. Type **City Council Block Grant**.

9. Press Return, press Tab three times, and press F4.

10. Type **Community Development Funds—Recreation Department**.

11. Place the cursor on the line *Mail out pledge cards* under level IV, then press End.

12. Press Return Tab F4.

13. Type **Follow-up phone calls**.

14. Press Return Tab F4.

15. Type **Mail pledge reminders**.

16. Press Return Tab F4.

17. Type **Send thank you's and receipts**.

18. Place the cursor on the line following *Goal met?* under Level V.

19. Type **Percent of receipts vs. pledge**?

20. Place the cursor on the line *Formally announce fund-raising drive* under Level IV, then press End.

21. Press Return Tab F4.

22. Type **Hold rally**.

The refined outline is shown in Figure 16.6.

Look at the outline and consider the same questions that you asked after entering the major divisions. Did you leave anything out? Are the steps in the right order? If anything is missing, move the cursor and insert text or a new level. You can delete unused numbers or leave them for further additions later on.

Don't rush through the refinement stage and don't hesitate to add or delete entries from the outline at any time. The outline is a tool, not a finished product. It is designed to stimulate your thinking and provide a framework for developing ideas.

23. Press F7 Y Return Y N to clear the screen.

```
I.    Financial Needs
      A.   Deficit this year
      B.   Increased costs
      C.   Need new building and equipment
II.   Current Resources
      A.   Community members
      B.   Annual fund raising dinner
      C.
III.  Possible Income Sources
      A.   Neighborhood businesses
      B.   Government
           1.   State
           2.   Local
                a.   City Council Block Grant
                b.   Community Development Funds  --  Recreation
                     Department
      C.   Private foundations
IV.   Plan of Action
      A.   Set up meetings with key individuals
      B.   Formally announce fund raising drive
      C.   Hold rally
      D.   Mail out pledge cards
      E.   Follow-up phone calls
      F.   Mail pledge reminders
      G.   Send thank you's and receipts
V.    Evaluation of Project
      A.   Goal met?
      B.   Percent of receipts vs. pledge?
      C.
```

■**FIGURE 16.6:** *The refined outline*

■ LINKING THE ENTRIES WITH OTHER FILES—MASTER DOCUMENTS

As you perfect your plan, certain subjects require greater detail: sentences, paragraphs, or even pages of text. If you include all of this detail in your outline, it becomes cumbersome to edit and the structure becomes difficult to visualize.

Instead of cluttering up your outline, include these details in a separate document. Other subjects might relate to documents already on the disk, such as a mailing list, a letter, or another file that describes an outline entry in detail.

Instead of duplicating these details in the outline itself, you can link the files containing them as *subdocuments*. Using this method, you can view the outline in the *Condensed* mode, which keeps the text of the other documents off the screen. But you can *expand* the document to see, and print, all of the associated text.

First we'll create two files that are associated with points in our outline, then we'll add them as subdocuments to the outline. You'll expand and condense the document to print and view the outline both ways. Follow these steps:

1. Type the following list of key individuals:

    Arlene Casey
    Recreation Commissioner
    Room 405
    City Hall
    555-9876

    Samuel P. Tobias
    Assistant to Council President
    Room 405
    City Hall
    555-9854

    Robert Gilardi
    Block Grant Program
    Room 456
    City Hall
    555-7643

    Marla Morrison
    State Representative
    (716) 654-9812

2. Press Return.

3. Press F7 Y, type **KEYLIST**, and press Return N to save the document and clear the screen.

4. Type the following list of printers:

    Printers for pledge cards:

    Almo Printing
    Eastham Lithographers
    Merrimac Offset
    Colonial Printers

5. Press Return.

6. Press F7 Y, type **PRINTERS**, and press Return N to save the document and clear the screen.

7. Press Shift-F10, type **PLAN**, then press Return to retrieve the outline. Make sure the Outlining function is off.

8. Place the cursor on the line *Set up meetings with key individuals* under level IV, then press End.

9. Press Return.

10. Press Alt-F5 to display the prompt

    1 Auto Def; 2 Subdoc; 3 Index; 4 ToA Short Form;
    5 Define; 6 Generate:0

Note
The appearance of the version 5.1 screen is slightly different, but the steps listed here still apply.

11. Press **2** or **s** for the Subdoc option and display

    Subdoc Filename:

12. Type **KEYLIST** and press Return. The code [Subdoc: Keylist] is inserted in the text and a Subdocument comment box appears on the screen (Figure 16.7).

    When you later expand the master document, WordPerfect will retrieve the KEYLIST file and insert it at this point.

13. Place the cursor on the line *Mail out pledge cards* under level IV, then press End.

14. Press Return.

15. Press Alt-F5 2, type **PRINTERS**, and press Return. A code is inserted and a Comment box appears.

16. Press F10 Return Y to save the outline—now called a *master document*.

```
    I.   Financial Needs
         A.   Deficit this year
         B.   Increased costs
         C.   Need new building and equipment
   II.   Current Resources
         A.   Community members
         B.   Annual fund raising dinner
         C.
  III.   Possible Income Sources
         A.   Neighborhood businesses
         B.   Government
              1.   State
              2.   Local
                   (a)  City Council Block Grant
                   (b)  Community Development Funds -- Recreation
                        Department.
         C.   Private foundations
   IV.   Plan of Action
         A.   Set up meetings with key individuals

   Subdoc: KEYLIST

C:\WP5\PLAN                              Doc 1 Pg 1 Ln 4.18" Pos 1"
```

■**FIGURE 16.7:**   *Subdocument comment box*

EXPANDING AND CONDENSING MASTER DOCUMENTS

You now can work with two different types of documentation: the outline itself in Condensed mode and an expanded document including the outline and all of the subdocuments. The outline can be recalled and printed just like any other document. To print all of the detail you must expand the master document.

Follow the steps below to print our sample outline and its associated documents. The outline should still be on the screen.

1. Press Alt-F5 6 to display the Mark Text Generate menu.

2. Press **3** or **e** to select Expand Master Document. The message

   Expanding master document

   appears at the status line while the subdocuments are recalled and inserted into the text. Each subdocument is surrounded by Subdoc Start and Subdoc End comment boxes.

3. Press Shift-F7 1 to print the expanded document—the outline and the two subdocuments.

   With the subdocuments displayed, it is difficult to visualize the overall structure of the document. So let's condense the master document.

4. Press Alt-F5 6 4 to select the Condense Master Document option on the Mark Text Generate menu. The prompt changes to

Save Subdocs? (Y/N) Yes

If you edited the text in the subdocuments while they appeared in the expanded outline, select the default Yes from this prompt line. The subdocuments will be saved on the disk before being removed from the master document. If you didn't change the subdocuments, press *N*.

Even though you made no changes to the subdocuments, let's save them to see what happens.

5. Press Return to accept the default Yes. Since the subdocuments already exist on the disk, the prompt line changes to

Replace KEYLIST? 1 Yes; 2 No; 3 Replace All Remaining: 0

■ Press *1* or *y* to replace the subdocument named at the prompt. You will see this prompt again when the next subdocument is encountered in the master document.

■ Press *2* or *n* if you want to save the subdocument under a different name. The prompt will change to

Document to be saved

Enter the name you now wish to call the subdocument, then press Return. The subdocument will be saved under that name and the Subdoc codes will be changed in the text to include that new name.

■ Press *3* or *r* to replace all of the subdocuments without being prompted.

If you try to save or exit an expanded master document, you'll see the prompt

Document is expanded, condense it? (Y/N) No

Press Return to exit and save the document in its expanded form, or *Y* to condense it first.

6. Press F7 N N to exit WordPerfect without saving the document.

Subdocuments can be added to any text and are particularly useful when you're producing a long document. If either the master document or the subdocuments contain Index or Table of Contents codes, expand the document before generating the table. In fact, if you try to generate tables in a condensed

Note

The appearance
of the version
5.1 screen is
slightly dif-
ferent, but the
steps listed here
still apply.

master document, WordPerfect will expand it for you. When the generation is complete, you'll see the prompt

Update Subdocs (Y/N)? No

Press *N* to condense the master document without saving any index or table of contents that may have been placed in a subdocument. Press *Y* to save the subdocuments before they are condensed out.

USING SUBDOCUMENTS FOR BOILERPLATE TEXT

If you have documents that regularly use standard clauses, paragraphs, or entire sections, consider saving these common elements in their own subdocument files. Include a Subdocument code in the master document, rather than the text itself. This saves quite a bit of disk space, compared to saving duplicate copies of common sections with each master document. In addition, if you update or otherwise edit the subdocument, the latest version will always be used when you expand and print the master document.

PARAGRAPH NUMBERING

You can also use the Automatic Numbering feature to enter a series of numbered paragraphs. Like outlining, the Paragraph Numbering function will insert the level number for you and keep track of which numbers have been used. But, unlike with outlining, new level numbers do not appear each time you press the Return key.

This feature is most useful when your entries are more than one paragraph long. You can type as many paragraphs as you want, or press Return as many times as needed, before inserting another number.

When you want to insert a number, press Tab or F4 to reach the desired indentation level, then press Shift-F5 5 to select the Para·Num option. The status line displays the prompt

Paragraph Level (Press Enter for Automatic):

To insert the number associated with that tab stop, press Return for automatic numbering. To enter another number, type a number from 1 to 8, then press Return. The default numbering and punctuation style will be used unless you change the style setting in the Paragraph Numbering Definition menu.

If working with an outline seems too rigid to activate your creativity, just type your ideas using the Paragraph Numbering function instead.

■ ANOTHER NOTE FOR TEACHERS

In Chapter 12 you learned how to sort paragraphs of a test. Now you can take that one step further to automatically renumber your test for you.

Create your test using automatic paragraph numbering. Rearrange the questions using a paragraph sort with some random word as the key. The numbers will automatically adjust to sequential order.

■ MACROS AND STYLES FOR OUTLINING

Because formatting outlines can require a large number of keystrokes, plan on using macros or styles as much as possible. For example, here is a macro that selects the outline style and turns on the Outlining function:

Ctrl-F10 Alt-V Return Shift-F5 6 3 Return 4 Ctrl-F10

Warning
Users of version 5.1 should press Ctrl-F10 Alt-V Return Shift-F5 6 3 Return 4 1 Ctrl-F10.

New Feature
Additional related features in version 5.1 are discussed under "Custom Outline Styles," page 389.

If you plan to use an outline template to develop papers and ideas, add the basic outline to a style. Although you could create a document that contains the outline template, you'd have to remember not to save the developed outline under the same name or you'd delete the blank template. When you add the codes and text to a style on a style sheet, however, saving the document will not affect the style itself; the blank template will be ready whenever you need it. Just retrieve the style sheet and turn on the style. The blank outline will appear. To create an outline style, press Alt-F8 3, then select an open type from the Styles Edit menu. Press *4* or *c* from the same menu to enter the codes, then follow the steps in "Creating a Basic Template" earlier in this chapter. Save the style sheet after you've entered all of the codes.

■ VERSION 5.1 FEATURES

Several new outlining features have been added to WordPerfect 5.1. You can create your own custom outline styles, much like the formatting styles discussed in Chapter 5, and then recall them by name when needed.

The other major change is the function of the Return key in Outline mode. In version 5.0, when you press Return, the cursor moves to the left margin of the next line and inserts the highest level number, such as II or III. With version 5.1, the cursor moves to the next line but at the same indentation or outline level of the previous entry. For example, if you just completed entering the (1) outline level, pressing Return inserts *(2)*. To move the cursor to outline levels on the left, press Shift-Tab.

You can set the Return key to act as it does in previous versions using the Paragraph Number Definition menu, as discussed shortly.

CREATING AN OUTLINE

Follow these steps to create the outline shown in Figure 16.1.

1. Start WordPerfect.

2. Press Shift-F5 4 or select **T**ools **O**utline to see the options

    Outline: 1 On; 2 Off; 3 Move Family; 4 Copy Family; 5 Delete Family:0

(The same options appear but in the form of a submenu if you use the pull-down menus.) Options 1 and 2 turn the Outline function on and off. The other options on the prompt line relate to the new Outline Family feature, which will be discussed later.

3. Press **1** or **O** or select On to turn on outlining. The word *Outline* appears in the status line.

4. Press Return to insert the first level number, *I*.

5. Press F4 to indent the entry, and type **Computer Hardware**.

6. Press Return. You want the next entry to appear at the first indented position, A.

7. Press Tab to move to the first tab stop and display *A*.

8. Press F4 and type **Computers**.

9. Press Return. The cursor moved to the next line but at the same indented position as the line before, inserting an uppercase *B* for that outline level.

10. Press Tab. The number *I* appears.

11. Press F4 and type **Mainframe**.

12. Press Return to display level number *2*.

13. Press F4 and type **Mini**.

14. Press Return F4 and type **Micro**.

15. Press Return Tab F4 and type **Single-user**.

16. Press Return, F4, then type **Multi-user**.

17. Press Return. The next entry should be at the B outline level, two tab stops to the left of the current position.

18. Press Shift-Tab. The cursor moves one tab stop to the left, increasing the outline number by one level and inserting the number *4*.

19. Press Shift-Tab again to insert *B*.

20. Press F4 and type **Storage Devices**.

21. Press Return Tab F4 and type **Tape**.

22. Press Return F4 and type **Disk**.

23. Press Return Tab F4 and type **Flexible**.

24. Press Return F4 and type **Rigid**.

25. Press Return Tab F4 and type **Fixed**.

26. Press Return F4 and type **Removable**.

27. Press Return, press Shift-Tab three times, press F4, and type **Printers**.

28. Press Return F4 and type **Monitors**.

29. Press Return twice. If you do not type text following a level number, the same number appears after you next press Return.

30. Press Shift-Tab F4 and type **Computer Software**.

31. Press Return Tab F4 and type **Word Processing**.

32. Type the remaining entries. Since they are all at the same level as the current entry, press Return F4 and type each of the following entries:

    Database
    Spreadsheet
    Graphic
    Integrated
    System

33. Press Return twice, and then press Shift-Tab to display *III*.

34. Press F4 and type **Peripherals**.

35. Press Shift-F5 4 2 or select **T**ools **O**utline **O**ff to turn off the Outline function.

36. Press Shift-F7 1 or select **F**ile **P**rint **F**ull to print the outline.

37. Press F7 or select **F**ile **E**xit, press **Y**, type **OUTLINE**, and press Return to save the document.

38. Type **Y** to exit WordPerfect.

EDITING AN OUTLINE

Follow these steps to edit the outline as shown in figure 16.3:

1. Start WordPerfect.

2. Press Shift-F10 or select **F**ile **R**etrieve, type **OUTLINE**, and press Return.

3. Press Shift-F5 4 1 or select **T**ools **O**utline **O**n to turn on the Outline function.

4. Place the cursor on the line

   A. Computers

5. Press Ctrl-F4 2 3 or select **E**dit **S**elect **P**aragraph **D**elete to delete the line and move up the remainder of the outline. Your screen looks like this:

   I. Computer Hardware
     1. Mainframes
     2. Mini

6. Press Del to move the level one tab stop to the left, adjusting the level numbers like this:

   I. Computer Hardware
     A. Mainframes
       1. Mini

7. Press ↓ Del to change the next level to *B*.

8. Press ↓ Del to change the next level to *C*.

9. Press ↓ Del to change the next level to *1*.

10. Press ↓ Del to change the next level to *2*.

11. Press the arrow keys to place the cursor on the *P* in *Printers*. Notice that the letter for storage devices automatically changed to *D*, and printers to *E*.

12. Type **Other**.

13. Press Return to move the word *Printers* to the next line. It is entered as level *F*.

14. Press Tab and press F4 to adjust the level number. Your screen should look like this:

    E. Other
    　　1. Printers

15. Press ↓ and then press Home ← to reach the left margin of the next line.

16. Press Tab and then press ↓ to adjust the level number, like this:

    E. Other
    　　1. Printers
    　　2. Monitors

17. Press Shift-F5 4 2 or select **T**ools **O**utline Off to turn off the Outline function.

18. Press Shift-F7 1 or select **F**ile **P**rint Full Document to print the edited document. Leave the document on the screen for the next example.

OUTLINE FAMILIES

An *outline family* consists of the outline level on which the cursor is placed, along with all sublevels under it. For example, look at this outline:

    I. Health Science
    　A. Nursing
    　　1. Undergraduate
    　　2. Graduate
    　B. Medical Technology
    　C. Physical Therapy
    II. Science
    　A. Biology
    　B. Chemistry
    　C. Physics

When the cursor is on level *1*, Health Science, the family contains that line and all entries up to level *II*. If the cursor is on the line *Nursing*, then the family just contains that line and the *1* and *2* levels beneath it.

The Move, Copy, and Delete Family options on the Outline prompt line let you quickly manipulate families of outline levels, automatically adjusting level numbers.

Moving and Copying Families   To move or copy a family, place the cursor anywhere in the first line of the family, and press Shift-F5 4 3 (**T**ools **O**utline **M**ove Family) or Shift-F5 4 4 (**T**ools **O**utline **C**opy Family). The entire family becomes highlighted on the screen and the prompt line changes to

Press Arrows to Move Family; Enter when done

Each time you press the ↓ or ↑ key, the entire family—if you selected Move—or a copy of it moves up or down one line in the outline, with the level numbers adjusting to the new position. Press Home ↑ to quickly reach the start of the outline, or Home ↓ to reach the bottom.

When the family is where you want it, press Return.

While the family is highlighted, you can press → to move all of its entries one step lower, or press ← to make them one step higher.

Deleting Families   To delete a family, place the cursor anywhere in the first line of the family, and then press Shift-F5 4 5 or select **T**ools **O**utline **D**elete Family to see the prompt

Delete Outline Family? No (Yes)
Select Yes to delete the family from the outline.

REFINING THE MAJOR POINTS INTO SUBLEVELS

Follow these steps in place of those earlier in the chapter to refine the major outline points:

3. Press Return Tab F4 to insert *1.* under that level.

4. Type **State**.

5. Press Return F4 to insert *2*.

6. Type **Local**.

7. Press Return Tab F4.

8. Type **City Council Block Grant**.

9. Press Return F4.

10. Type **Community Development Funds—Recreation Department**.

11. Place the cursor on the line *Mail out pledge cards* under level *IV*, then press End.

12. Press Return F4.

13. Type **Follow-up phone calls**.

14. Press Return F4.

15. Type **Mail pledge reminders**.

16. Press Return F4.

17. Type **Send thank you's and receipts**.

18. Place the cursor on the line following *Goal met?* under Level *V*.

19. Type **Percent of receipts vs. pledge?**

20. Place the cursor on the line *Formally announce fund-raising drive* under level *IV*, then press End.

21. Press Return F4.

22. Type **Hold rally**.

23. Press F7 Y Return Y N to clear the screen.

CUSTOM OUTLINE STYLES

While WordPerfect's outline formats are surely timesaving, they make certain assumptions about the way you outline. All levels are indented 1/2 inch from the next, using hanging indentations and normal character styles for level numbers. With the Paragraph Number Definition menu, however, you can quickly create your own custom outline styles.

Actually, two different types of styles are available. The *user-defined* style uses the same indentation levels but lets you quickly change the level-numbering scheme. But by creating custom styles, much like those discussed in Chapter 5, you can create any number of outlining methods.

Start by pressing Shift-F5 6 or selecting **T**ools **D**efine to display the Paragraph Number Definition menu (Figure 16.8).

Automatic Levels   As you know, pressing Return in Outline mode moves the cursor to the next line but at the same indentation level as the line above. If you prefer to have the cursor move to the left margin and insert the highest outline level number, press *8* or *a* to select Automatically Adjust to Current Level, and then press *N*.

User-Defined Style   If you want to maintain the same indentation levels, but want your own style of numbering, press *6* or *u* to display the numbering choices shown in Figure 16.9. The cursor is under Level 1 at *Current Definition*.

For each level, enter the letter or number corresponding to the type of numbering desired, and press Return to reach the next level. For example, press *A* if you want to start your outline with uppercase letters, *i* for lowercase Roman

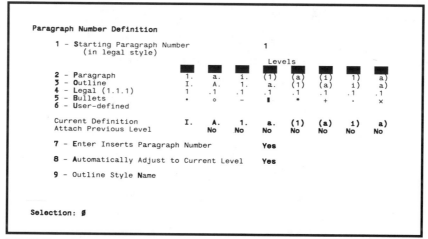

■**FIGURE 16.8:**   *Version 5.1 Paragraph Number Definition menu*

■**FIGURE 16.9:**   *User-defined options*

numerals. Press Return by itself if you want to keep the default scheme for that level.

When you've selected all of the level numbers, the cursor moves to the Attach Previous Level prompt line, and the second level changes to *N (Y)*.

Press *Y* if you want the level attached, as in the legal outline style illustrated at the beginning of this chapter.

You can move between the two prompt lines using the ↑ and ↓ keys, and to levels on the right using →, Tab, or Return. Press Shift-Tab to move to the left.

When you are done defining the style, press F7.

Custom Styles   The user-defined outline styles maintain the same indentation formats as the default styles. By creating a custom style you can define exactly what occurs at each outline level. You determine the codes that will be inserted before and after each outline number. The numbers themselves are determined from the other settings on the Paragraph Number Definition menu.

To create an outline style from the Paragraph Number Definition menu, press *9* or *n* to select Outline Style Name and display the Outline Styles menu (Figure 16.10).

This menu, which lists any previously defined outline styles, includes a prompt line much like the Styles menu. (If necessary, refer to Chapter 5 to refresh your memory.) The main difference is that the On and Off options have been replaced with Select. Once you select a style, it turns on and off when you turn the Outline feature on and off.

Press *2* or *c* to create an outline style and display the Outline Styles Edit menu (Figure 16.11).

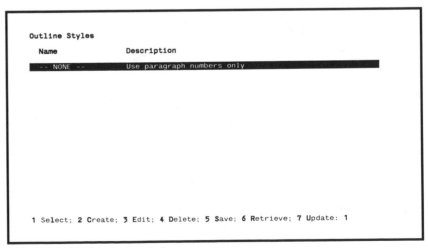

```
Outline Styles
   Name                    Description

 -- NONE --               Use paragraph numbers only
```

```
 1 Select; 2 Create; 3 Edit; 4 Delete; 5 Save; 6 Retrieve; 7 Update: 1
```

■**FIGURE 16.10:**   *Outline Styles menu*

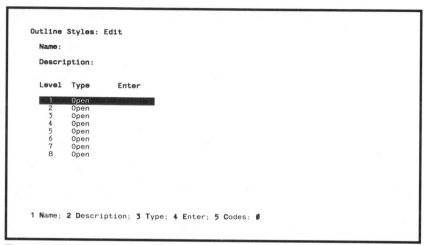

■FIGURE 16.11:   *Outline Styles Edit menu*

In this menu, you name the style, give it a brief description, and enter the codes to be associated with each of the levels. As with other styles, Type determines whether it is an open or paired style, Enter selects the action of the Return key for paired styles, and Codes lets you enter formatting codes for the level.

WordPerfect ignores the default indentation format when using a custom outline style. So if you want a level indented, be sure to insert one or more Indent codes (and a margin release for hanging indentations).

Once you define a style, its name appears on the Outline Styles menu (Figure 16.12). To select it, highlight the name of the style, press Return to display the Paragraph Number Definition menu, and press F7 4 1 to turn on Outline mode using that style.

The style will be saved along with the document in which it is used. To save your style as a separate file so it can be used with other documents, save it from the Outline Styles menu. Remember, save it in the file LIBRARY.STY to have it automatically available when you start WordPerfect.

You can also create and save outline styles from the Style function initiated by pressing Alt-F8 or selecting **L**ayout **S**tyles. When you select Outline as the Type, you'll be prompted to enter a name and level number, then placed in the Outline Styles Edit menu.

```
Outline Styles

  Name                 Description

  -- NONE --           Use paragraph numbers only
  Budget               Outline for budget requests
  English              Outline for English Lit class
```

```
1 Select; 2 Create; 3 Edit; 4 Delete; 5 Save; 6 Retrieve; 7 Update: 1
```

■**FIGURE 16.12:** *Custom outline styles listed in the menu*

MOUSE AND MENU EQUIVALENTS

Function	Keyboard	Pull-Down Menus
Outline On	Shift-F5 4 1	**T**ools **O**utline **O**n
Outline Off	Shift-F5 4 2	**T**ools **O**utline Off
Define Outline	Shift-F5 6	**T**ools **D**efine
Subdocument	Alt-F5 2	**M**ark **S**ubdocument

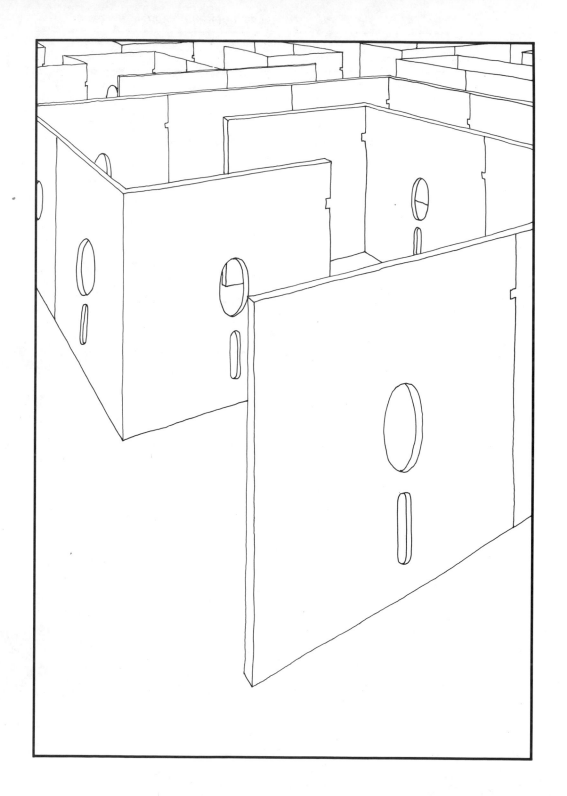

17

USING WORDPERFECT AS
A GRAPHICS TOOL

WordPerfect has the capabilities to incorporate a wide range of graphic elements within your documents. Using *Line Draw*, you can create custom charts, graphs, and forms. Through *Graphics* commands, you can enclose text in boxes, insert lines between columns, and merge drawings and scanned images from other programs.

In this chapter, we'll take a look at lines and text boxes. We'll discuss graphic images in Chapter 18.

Just keep in mind that your ability to print graphics, just like fonts and type sizes, is based entirely on your printer. If you have a daisy-wheel printer, or a dot-matrix printer without graphic capabilities, then many of the features here and in Chapter 18 will not be very useful to you.

■ DESIGNING FORMS

New Feature
Additional related features in version 5.1 are discussed under "Ruled Forms with the Table Editor," page 420.

Most businesses and organizations use forms of some type. Academicians require questionnaires for research. Clubs need applications, membership and attendance forms, scorecards, and dues records. Businesses use invoices and sales forms, interoffice forms, and inventory records.

The Line Draw feature produces vertical and horizontal lines that can be combined to produce boxes. To use Line Draw, press Ctrl-F3 2. You see the prompt

   1 |; 2 ||; 3 *; 4 Change; 5 Erase; 6 Move: 1

The first three options present three drawing choices: single lines, double lines, or asterisks. Although your screen can display lines created with any of these options, your printer may not be able to produce continuous vertical double lines.

It may print them with spaces between each line, or it may just print a continuous single line in their place. Option *4* provides additional drawing choices, option *5* erases existing lines, and option *6* moves the cursor around the screen quickly.

As an example, we'll use the Line Draw feature to produce the membership form shown in Figure 17.1.

1. Start WordPerfect.

2. Press Ctrl-F3 to display the prompt

       0 Rewrite; 1 Window; 2 Line Draw: 0

Note

The appearance of the version 5.1 screen is slightly different, but the steps listed here still apply.

3. Press **2** to display the Line Draw prompt line.

4. Press Esc, type **64**, and then press → once. A line 64 characters wide is drawn across the screen. (The small arrows displayed on the screen indicate the end of a line and will not be printed.) If you reveal the codes you'll see the code [-:3,48] at the right end of the line, representing the character set and number of the default drawing character, a single line.

5. Press Esc, type **10** and press ↓ once. This draws a vertical line down the right edge of the screen. Wait for the line to stop.

6. Press Esc, type **64** and press ← once to draw the line at the bottom of the form.

7. Press Esc, type **10** and press ↑ once to close off the box. The cursor stops on line 1", position 1".

8. Press F7 to turn off the Line Draw function.

9. Press ↓ twice to reach line 1.17".

Warning

Depending on your printer, the line positions on your status line may differ slightly from those shown in these steps.

10. Press Ins to enter Typeover mode. If you entered text in Insert mode, the lines would shift, so always enter text into drawings in Typeover.

```
┌──────────────────────────────────────────────────────────┐
│  ┌──────────────────────────────────────────────────────┐ │
│  │                    Membership Form                     │ │
│  ├──────────────────────────────────────────────────────┤ │
│  │  Name:                                                 │ │
│  ├──────────────────────────────────────────────────────┤ │
│  │  Address:                                              │ │
│  ├───────────────────────┬──────────────┬───────────────┤ │
│  │  City:                 │ State:       │ Zip code:     │ │
│  ├───────────────────────┴──────────────┴───────────────┤ │
│  │  Dues Paid:                                            │ │
│  └──────────────────────────────────────────────────────┘ │
└──────────────────────────────────────────────────────────┘
```

■**FIGURE 17.1:** *Sample membership form*

Note: Throughout this example, when a step says to move or position the cursor, always use the arrow keys. Do not press the Return key or the space bar unless specifically instructed to do so.

11. Use → to move the cursor to position 3.2" and type **Membership Form.**

12. Move the cursor to line 1.33", position 1" and press Ctrl-F3 2.

13. Press Esc, type **64** and press →.

14. Press F7 to turn off the Line Draw function.

15. Move the cursor to line 1.5", position 1.2" and type **Name:**

16. Move the cursor to line 1.67", position 1" and press Ctrl-F3 2.

17. Press Esc, type **64** and press → once.

18. Press ↓ twice to reach line 2".

19. Press Esc, type **64** and press ← once.

20. Press ↓ twice to reach line 2.33".

21. Press Esc, type **64** and press → once.

22. Press F7. Make sure the word *Typeover* still appears on the status line; if not, press Ins.

23. Move the cursor to line 1.83", position 1.2" and type **Address:**

24. Move the cursor to line 2.17", position 1.2" and type **City:**

25. Move the cursor to position 4" on the same line and type **State:**

26. Move the cursor to position 5.5" on the same line and type **Zip code:**

27. Move the cursor to line 2.33", position 5.3" and press Ctrl-F3 2.

28. Press ↑ twice.

29. Press Esc, type **15** and press ←.

30. Press ↓ twice.

31. Press F7.

32. Move the cursor to line 2.5", position 1.2" and type **Dues Paid:**. Figure 17.2 shows the completed form on the screen.

33. Press Shift-F7 1 to print the form.

34. Press F7 Y, type **FORM** and press Return Y to save the document and exit WordPerfect.

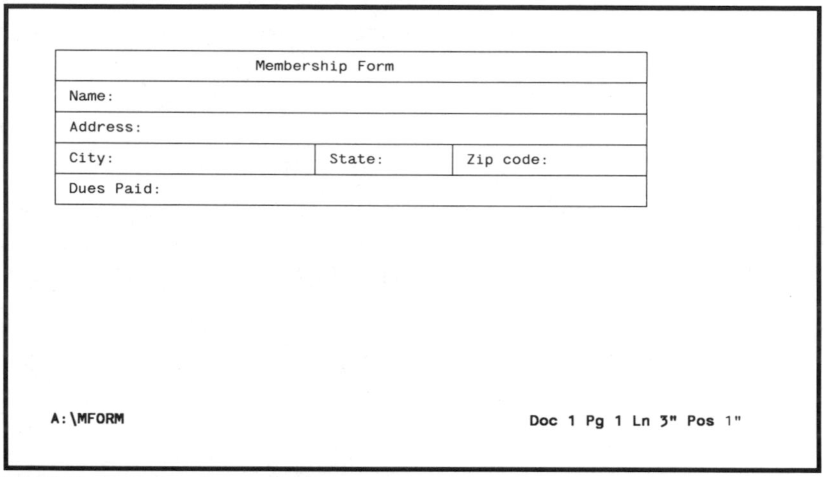

```
┌────────────────────────────────────────────────────────────────┐
│                                                                  │
│    ┌──────────────────────────────────────────────────────┐     │
│    │                    Membership Form                    │     │
│    ├──────────────────────────────────────────────────────┤     │
│    │  Name:                                                │     │
│    ├──────────────────────────────────────────────────────┤     │
│    │  Address:                                             │     │
│    ├───────────────────────┬───────────────┬──────────────┤     │
│    │  City:                │  State:       │  Zip code:    │     │
│    ├───────────────────────┴───────────────┴──────────────┤     │
│    │  Dues Paid:                                           │     │
│    └──────────────────────────────────────────────────────┘     │
│                                                                  │
│                                                                  │
│                                                                  │
│                                                                  │
│    A:\MFORM                              Doc 1 Pg 1 Ln 3" Pos 1" │
└────────────────────────────────────────────────────────────────┘
```

■**FIGURE 17.2:**   *Completed form on the screen*

If your printed form does not look like Figure 17.1, then either your printer cannot produce line drawings or you have not selected the proper printer. Press Shift-F7 to confirm that your printer is selected. If you have made the proper printer selection, then it's time to use a different printer or skip to Chapter 19.

■ # TYPING TEXT IN GRAPHIC DOCUMENTS

As you just saw, you can type characters anywhere in a graphic document. However, there are some simple rules that you must follow when entering the text.

- Use the Move option on the Line Draw prompt line (Ctrl-F3 2 6) to create a blank drawing area.

- Make sure that Typeover mode is turned on. (Look for the word *Typeover* on the status line; press Ins if it is not there.)

- Do not press the Del key to erase characters. Instead, use the space bar to type a blank space over characters that you want to delete. If you use Del by mistake, turn off the Typeover mode by pressing the Ins key, then press the space bar until the lines are realigned.

LINE DRAWING WITH MACROS

To repeat a graphic figure, you can copy it from one location to another or create it with a macro. Stored macros are very handy for duplicating shapes and boxes that you will be using frequently.

Organizational charts, family trees, and flow diagrams are examples of the types of line drawings that can be created with graphic macros. These typically consist of many boxes connected by lines. If you have macros containing the keystrokes required to create the right size boxes, then drawing these charts is simple.

DRAWING SQUARES

When you're drawing a square box, you must first consider the ratio of lines on the screen. (Depending on your hardware, your own screen may differ slightly from the figures shown in this section.) Each vertical line is the height of one complete screen line, but each horizontal line is only the width of a character. Box 1 in the top portion of Figure 17.3 is 3 lines wide and 3 lines high, but it is far from a square. Box 2 is 10 lines wide and 4 high, and box 3 is 5 lines wide and 2 high. Both of these boxes have a ratio of 5 to 2 and appear square on the

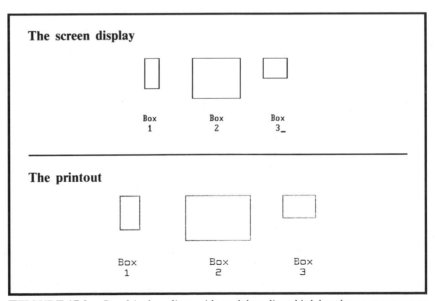

■**FIGURE 17.3:** *Box 1 is three lines wide and three lines high but does not appear as a square on the screen; boxes 2 and 3 use a 5 to 2 ratio and appear as squares on the screen, but not in the printout*

screen. To draw a square on the screen, create the box with this ratio of width lines to height lines. For example, a box 15 lines wide and 6 high will also be a square.

Unfortunately, the screen and your printer may not have the same vertical to horizontal ratio. The bottom of Figure 17.3 shows a printout of the document above it. Although boxes 2 and 3 appear as squares on the screen, they are printed as rectangles. Thus, you may need to use some other ratio to print squares. On many dot matrix printers, the ratio for a printed square is 5 to 3. So a 5-line by 3-line box will appear as a rectangle on the screen, but it will be a square when printed. Figure 17.4 shows several boxes with a 5 to 3 ratio as they appear on the screen and as they appear when printed.

So, when you are planning line drawings that include squares, decide whether you want them to appear properly on the screen or when printed—you can't have it both ways.

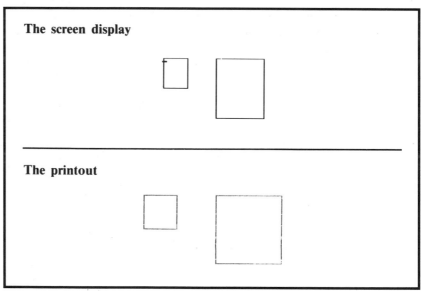

The screen display

The printout

■**FIGURE 17.4:**   *Boxes with a 5 to 3 ratio that appear as rectangles on the screen and as squares when printed*

■ CREATING A GRAPHIC MACRO LIBRARY

Let's create a new document containing the following library of graphic macros for use later on. After you create each macro, press Home Home ↓ to place the cursor at the end of the document, then press Return before defining the next macro.

Note: In the Macro column below, the spelled-out number and directional arrow (e.g., five-↑) means to press that arrow key that number of times to draw the line.

These macros use a 5 to 3 ratio to draw squares.

Function	Name	Macro
Draws a small printed square (a rectangle on the screen) to hold four characters	Smallsq	Ctrl-F10 Smallsq Return Return Ctrl-F3 2 1 five-→ three-↓ five-← three-↑ F7 Ctrl-F10
Draws a large printed square (a rectangle on the screen) to hold up to five lines of nine characters each	Largesq	Ctrl-F10 Largesq Return Return Ctrl-F3 2 1 ten-→ six-↓ ten-← six-↑ F7 Ctrl-F10
Draws a small rectangle to hold one line of up to fourteen characters	Smallbox	Ctrl-F10 Smallbox Return Return Ctrl-F3 2 1 Esc 15 one-→ two-↓ Esc 15 one-← two-↑ F7 Ctrl-F10
Draws a large rectangle to hold two lines of nineteen characters each	Largebox	Ctrl-F10 Largebox Return Return Ctrl-F3 2 1 Esc 20 one-→ three-↓ Esc 20 one-← three-↑ F7 Ctrl-F10
Draws a large rectangle with a wide drawing character	Thickbox	Ctrl-F10 Thickbox Return Return Ctrl-F3 2 4 4 Esc 45 one-→ four-↓ Esc 45 one-← three-↑ F7 Ctrl-F10

Draws a box   Starbox   Ctrl-F10 Starbox
with asterisks   Return Return
                                                Ctrl-F3 2 4 9 * Esc
                                                45 one-→ four-↓
                                                Esc 45 one-←
                                                four-↑ F7 Ctrl-F10

After the macros are created, press F7 N N to clear the screen in preparation for the next section.

Figure 17.5 shows how these boxes appear on the screen.

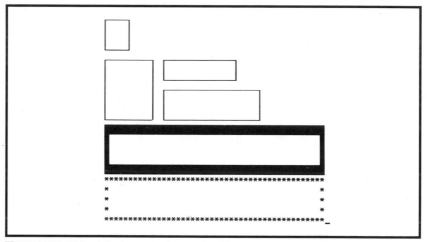

■**FIGURE 17.5:**   *The boxes in the graphic library as they would appear on the screen*

■ ERASING LINES

You can erase lines in two ways: with the Line Draw function off, or with it on. When the function is off, delete lines by pressing the space bar in Typeover mode to type over the line with spaces or by pressing Del or Backspace. You can also work with a series of lines as a block. With the Line Draw function on, press 5 to select the Erase option. Then move the cursor back over the lines that you want to delete. Press *1* to draw again.

PLANNING LINE DRAWINGS

Since line drawings can get complicated, it's best to first outline the drawing on paper. Use graph paper and number the boxes along the top and left sides. Make sure that the numbers on the graph paper correspond to the margins and size of the document page, which is 65 boxes wide and 51 high. With a pencil, sketch out the drawing and adjust it until it appears neatly arranged, making sure it fits within the margins of the document page.

For a drawing that is too wide to fit within the default margins, draw it larger, but count the width in boxes and change the margins as soon as you start WordPerfect. If the chart is wider than 80 characters and you have a dot matrix printer, select the small or condensed font, then widen the margins. Most 80-character dot matrix printers can print up to 132 characters per line in Condensed mode.

If you plan to include text within the drawing, leave enough room for the characters. In fact, you should pencil in the text on the rough copy to make sure that the boxes or blank spaces are wide enough.

At important locations in the drawing, such as the upper left corner of a box and the intersection of two lines, mark down the line and position numbers on the graph paper. Use these markings to position the cursor on the screen and to count the length of lines.

When you're actually entering the drawing, save the document at frequent intervals. If some complicated box or series of lines is incorrect, press F7 N N, then recall the last correct version that you saved and redraw that portion of the chart.

PAGE COMPOSITION

When you decide on the layout of the page and arrange the text and graphics, you are *composing* the page. In Chapter 9, for example, you composed a newsletter page with three elements—a masthead across the top of the page, a single-column introductory paragraph, and two-column text on the remainder of that page.

If your printer has graphics capabilities, the layout might also include lines, charts, line drawings, or pictures. Because it is difficult to visualize the final printed page, it's helpful if you're able to move the elements to different positions then use View mode to see how the page will appear each way. Print the page only when you're pleased with the composition. Figure 17.6, for example, shows alternative layouts for the first page of a newsletter.

The layout on the left is two columns with a graphic image in column 2. The other layout is three columns with two graphics, one surrounded by a box, the other with lines on top and bottom. Once the text is entered, you can change the layout of the page with a few keystrokes—by changing the column definition and the positions of the figures. You already know how to format columns, so the only new elements concern the graphics.

■ GRAPHIC INTERFACING

Some of the graphic types available are illustrated in Figure 17.6. The masthead, for example, is contained in a shaded text box. A horizontal line has been placed under the dateline, and line drawings have been inserted in the columns. These two line drawings, by the way, are among those supplied as samples on your WordPerfect Graphics disk.

You create text boxes and horizontal and vertical lines by simply telling WordPerfect where to place them, then—in the case of a text box—entering or recalling the text to be included in the box.

Graphic images can be obtained from a number of sources. Some, like the flag and inkwell shown in the figure, are in WordPerfect's own WordPerfect Graphic format (WPG). But you can also use graphics produced by a number

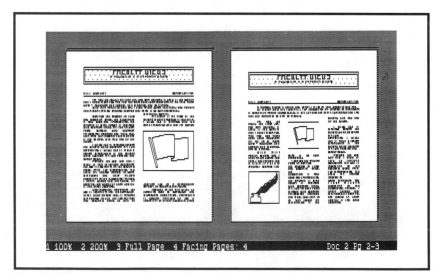

■**FIGURE 17.6:**   *Alternative layouts in View mode*

of other programs, such as charts developed with Lotus 1-2-3, or drawings created with PC Paintbrush or GEM Paint.

Graphics such as these are divided into two types—line drawings and bitmap images. WPG, Lotus, and AutoCAD files, for example, are line drawings consisting of solid lines or dots. You can use WordPerfect's Graphic Edit function to scale, rotate, and mirror-image these.

Bitmap drawings, created with painting programs, have a wider range of shades and densities. Depending on your printer, all graphic types can be rotated and printed in landscape.

In this chapter and the next, you'll learn how to create documents using a variety of graphic images, and how to grab screens from other applications.

BOX TYPES

Graphics are inserted into documents in boxes, which don't necessarily have to be surrounded by borders. The boxes are all created using Alt-F9, the Graphics key, which displays the prompt line:

Note
The appearance of the version 5.1 screen is slightly different, but the steps listed here still apply. Refer to "Graphic Options," page 421.

1 Figure; 2 Table; 3 Text Box; 4 User-defined Box; 5 Line: 0

Option 5 is used to add horizontal and vertical lines to your document. Use the other options to incorporate either boxed text or graphic images.

Options 1 to 4 refer to four different types of boxes you can have in a document—figure, table, text, and user-defined boxes. However, you can use any box type to hold any type of image—text or graphics. For example, you can insert text in a figure box, a table in a user-defined box, or a Lotus 1-2-3 chart in a text box.

The different types are just there to help you coordinate your graphics, and each one starts out with slightly different default values, listed in Figure 17.7.

Because the Graphics functions can be rather complicated, you'll create several different documents in this chapter and the next. First you'll create an announcement containing lines and a text box. Then in Chapter 18 you'll produce a newsletter, like those illustrated in Figure 17.6, with a masthead and graphic images. The last example will be a report containing a Lotus 1-2-3 chart. Don't worry if you don't have any Lotus picture files. You can use one of the WPG files in its place.

Note

Equation boxes
(version 5.1
only) have no
borders, 0.083"
spacing inside
and outside,
bold caption
numbers on the
right side, and
no shading.

```
Text  Box:          Thick top and bottom border lines; 0.16"
                    outside and inside border space; captions use
                    bold numbers only, below the box and outside
                    the borders; 10% shading

Figure  Box:        Single line border on all sides; 0.16"
                    outside and no inside border space; captions
                    use bold figure numbers below the box and
                    outside the borders; no shading

Table  Box:         Thick top and bottom border lines; 0.16"
                    outside and inside border space; captions use
                    bold table numbers in Roman numerals above
                    the box and outside the borders; no shading

User-Defined Box:   No border; 0.16" outside and no inside border
                    space; captions use bold numbers below the
                    box and outside the borders; no shading
```

■**FIGURE 17.7:**   *Box default values*

■ USING LINES AND TEXT BOXES

Lines and text boxes are perhaps the simplest of the Graphics functions to use. Still, and perhaps because of their visual simplicity, they can be used quite effectively.

You can use horizontal and vertical lines to separate text on the page or simply to add some visual perspective. Using the Graphic Lines command, you insert lines before and after text, between columns, or along the margins. Lines do not appear on the screen, but only when the document is printed or displayed in View mode.

In this exercise, you'll create a template for preparing an announcement. Suppose your organization holds regular meetings, each featuring a different speaker or featured event. Rather than create a new announcement each month, you will design a template to hold the basic elements, then add the specific information for each meeting.

1. Start WordPerfect.

    If you have a laser printer, for maximum impact make sure you're in a base font that provides a number of type sizes. Check by pressing Ctrl-F8 4 or F. The current base font is marked with an asterisk. If you have to select another font, highlight it using the ↑ or ↓ key, then press Return.

    Now you'll type and save a small document containing the specifics about the next meeting.

2. Press Shift-F6 to center the cursor.

3. Press Ctrl-F8 1 6 for very large type.

4. Type

   Master Sam Wilson

5. Press → to move past the Very Large code then press Return twice.

6. Press Shift-F6 to center the cursor, then Ctrl-F8 1 5 to select large type.

7. Type

   Of Kim's Martial Arts

8. Press → to move past the Large code, then press Return twice.

9. Using Shift-F6 to center the cursor, type

   Speaking on Martial Arts
   training for teenagers and young children
   Tuesday, May 12, 1991
   7:30 P.M.

10. Press F7 Y, type **MAY**, then press Return N to save the document and clear the screen.

Now let's create a template to use for the monthly announcements. Again, make sure you're using a base font that provides a variety of type sizes.

1. Press Shift-F6 to center the cursor.

2. Press Ctrl-F8 1 7 for the extra large font, then type

   HFC Faculty Club

Note
The prompts, menus, and options lines are different in version 5.1. Refer to "Line Options" on page 421 and to the margin notes. (Later releases of version 5.0 contain the Edit Line options discussed under "Version 5.1 Features.")

3. Press → to move past the Extra Large code, then press Return twice.

Let's add a horizontal line across the page at this point.

4. Press Alt-F9 to display the prompt

   1 Figure; 2 Table; 3 Text Box; 4 User-defined Box; 5 Line: 0

5. Press **5** or **l** for the Line option to display

   1 Horizontal Line; 2 Vertical Line: 0

6. Press **1** or **h** to select a horizontal line. The screen will show the Horizontal Line menu (Figure 17.8).

These options are used to set the position and size of the line. The default settings call for a single solid horizontal line between the left and right margins.

If you just press Return here, that's what you'll get printed. But let's change this to a 5-inch shaded line, 1/4 inch thick.

7. Press **1** or **h** to set the horizontal position. The prompt line changes to

   Horizontal Pos: 1 Left 2 Right 3 Center 4 Both Left & Right 5 Set Position: 0

8. Press **3** or **c** to center the line. The word *Center* appears at the first prompt on the menu. The Left and Right options place the line closest to the corresponding margin; Set Position lets you determine the exact distance from the left edge of the paper.

9. Press **2** or **l** to set the length of the line. Selecting this option has no effect if the horizontal position is set at Left and Right, in which case the line extends between both margins.

10. Type **5** then press Return.

11. Press **3** or **w** for the Width of Line option.

12. Type **.25** then press Return.

13. Press **4** or **g** for the Gray Shading option.

14. Type **50** (for 50 percent) then press Return.

Warning
Users of version 5.1: In step 9, press *3* or *1*. In step 11, press *4* or *w*. In step 13, press *5* or *g*.

```
Graphics: Horizontal Line

    1 - Horizontal Position          Left & Right

    2 - Length of Line

    3 - Width of Line                0.01"

    4 - Gray Shading (% of black)    100%




    Selection: 0
```

■**FIGURE 17.8:** *Horizontal Line menu*

15. Press Return to return to the document. The code [HLine:Center, 5", 0.25", 50%] will be inserted in the text, showing the line type and specifications. Remember, you won't see the line on the screen.

16. Press Return twice.

17. Using Shift-F6 to center the cursor, type

The Holy Family College Faculty Club
invites all staff and faculty
to the next monthly meeting

18. Press Return twice. Figure 17.9 shows the page at this point in View mode. It's now time to create a text box that will contain the specifics of the meeting, saved in the file MAY.

    You can enclose any amount of text in a box, and even retrieve a document on the disk into a box. As with all graphics, however, you'll only see the box when it's viewed or printed. But you can easily edit and format the text in the box.

19. Press Alt-F9 for the Graphics prompt line. Notice the options other than Line. Each of these represents a type of graphic box that can be included in your document. As you learned before, the option names really have nothing to do with the type of text or graphics you place in the box.

    For consistency, however, let's use a text box to hold text.

20. Press **3** or **b** to select Text Box and show the prompt line

    Text Box: 1 Create; 2 Edit; 3 New Number; 4 Options: 0

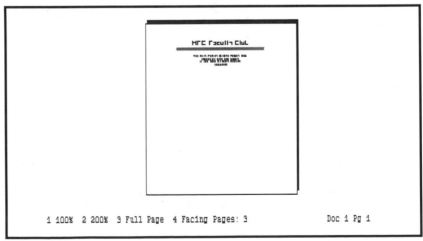

■**FIGURE 17.9:** *The composition of the flyer before the text box is added*

Before creating a box, you should set any specific options you want.

21. Press **4** or **o** for Options to display the Text Box Options menu (Figure 17.10).

    The menu shows the default values used for text boxes—thick border lines on the top and bottom, nothing on the sides, and a 10-percent shade. To make it a complete box, you have to add lines on the sides.

22. Press **1** for the Border Style option. The cursor moves to the word *None* next to the left border style and the prompt line changes to

    1 None; 2 Single; 3 Double; 4 Dashed; 5 Dotted;
    6 Thick; 7 Extra Thick: 0

23. Press **7** to select Extra Thick for the left border.

24. Press **7** three more times to select the extra thick border for the remaining sides.

Take a moment to review the other options. They determine the space between the text and the border, and the numbering used to reference the boxes. The last option is used to shade the inside of the box, such as the light shading selected for the horizontal line. On dot matrix printers, shading takes a long time to print. So if you didn't want any shading, you'd press *9* to select the option, type *0*, then press Return.

Note

The appearance of the version 5.1 screen is slightly different, but the steps listed here still apply.

```
Options:     Text Box

         1 - Border Style
                 Left                        None
                 Right                       None
                 Top                         Thick
                 Bottom                      Thick
         2 - Outside Border Space
                 Left                        Ø.16"
                 Right                       Ø.16"
                 Top                         Ø.16"
                 Bottom                      Ø.16"
         3 - Inside Border Space
                 Left                        Ø.16"
                 Right                       Ø.16"
                 Top                         Ø.16"
                 Bottom                      Ø.16"
         4 - First Level Numbering Method    Numbers
         5 - Second Level Numbering Method   Off
         6 - Caption Number Style            [BOLD]1[bold]
         7 - Position of Caption             Below box, Outside borders
         8 - Minimum Offset from Paragraph   Ø"
         9 - Gray Shading (% of black)       1Ø%

Selection: Ø
```

■**FIGURE 17.10:**   *Text Box Options menu*

25. Press Return to return to the document. The code [Txt Opt] is inserted into the text. Now any text boxes that you define after this point will be formatted according to those options—that is, unless you select other options later on or delete the [Txt Opt] code.

Now that the box options are selected, let's define the box itself.

26. Press Alt-F9 3 to select Text Box again.

27. Press **1** or **c** to create the box and display the Text Box Definition menu (Figure 17.11).
    Graphics can be a complicated process, so let's briefly review the options on this menu.

Note
Version 5.1
graphic-box
menus include a
new option:
Contents. Refer
to "Graphic-
Box Options,"
page 421.

- **Filename**—allows you to recall a document or graphic image to be inserted into the box.

- **Caption**—allows you to enter a caption to be printed with the box.

- **Type**—allows you to choose paragraph, page, or character. Paragraph boxes align with the paragraph where the box is defined; page boxes can be placed anywhere on the page; character boxes can be placed within lines.

- **Vertical Position**—allows you to move the position of the box in relation to the text or the top margin.

```
Definition: Text Box
        1 - Filename
        2 - Caption
        3 - Type                    Paragraph
        4 - Vertical Position       Ø"
        5 - Horizontal Position     Right
        6 - Size                    3.25" wide x Ø.72" (high)
        7 - Wrap Text Around Box    Yes
        8 - Edit




    Selection: Ø
```

■**FIGURE 17.11:** *Text Box Definition menu*

- **Horizontal Position**—allows you to position the box where desired between the right and left margins.

- **Size**—allows you to change the size of the box. The default width of the text box is 3.25". The height will vary, depending on the base font you're using.

- **Wrap Text Around Box**—in the default mode, prevents text outside of the box from being printed over the box and its contents.

- **Edit**—allows you to add, edit, or format text in the box. With graphics boxes, this allows you to scale, move, or invert the image.

28. Press **1** or **f** to select the Filename option. The status line changes to

    Enter filename:

29. Type **MAY** then press Return. The words *May (Text)* appear at the prompt, informing you that the text from the document MAY will be inserted in the box. The file on the disk is unchanged, since it is only a copy that is added to the document on the screen.

Also notice that the box height has increased to accommodate the amount of text in the file, but the width stayed the same.

30. Press **5** to set the horizontal position. The prompt line changes to

    Horizontal Position: 1 Left; 2 Right, 3 Center; 4 Both
    Left & Right: 0

Warning
Step 30: Users of version 5.1 should press *6*.

31. Press **3** or **c** to center the box between the margins.

32. Press Return to return to the document. No indication of the text box appears yet on the screen.

33. Press Return eleven times to reveal the outline of the box with *TXT 1* in the upper left corner, indicating the presence of text box 1 (Figure 17.12).

34. Press Shift-F7 V to view the document (Figure 17.13).
    Notice that two lines of the document are too long to fit in 3.25 inches and were therefore divided in two. This just won't do, so let's investigate ways to correct the situation.

35. Press F7 to return to the document.

36. Press Alt-F9 3 2 to select the Edit Text Box option. The prompt line shows:

    Text Box number? 2

37. Press **1** to edit the first—and in our case the only—text box, then press Return. If you had pressed Return to accept the second box, you'd have seen the warning *Not Found* and the document would have returned to the screen.

The Definition menu reappears.

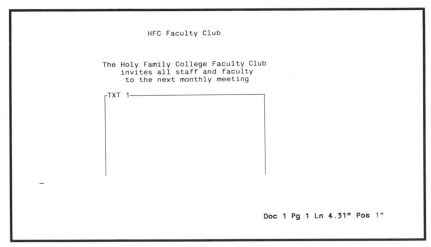

■**FIGURE 17.12:** *Text box as it appears on the screen*

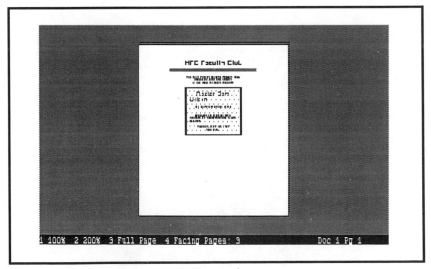

■**FIGURE 17.13:** *The document in View mode*

38. Change the position of the box so it spreads across the page.

    a. Press **5** or **h** for the Horizontal option.

    b. Press **4** or **b** for Both Left & Right.

Warning
Users of version
5.1, step 38a
and b: Press *6* or
h, and then
press *4* or *f*
for Full.

39. Press Return to return to the document. The box indicator is now as wide as the screen.

40. Press Shift-F7 V to view the document (Figure 17.14). With the wider box, all of the lines fit. However, there's a lot of extra space around the text, and the two lines that were previously divided are no longer centered.

Warning
Step 43: Users
of version 5.1
should press *6 3*.

41. Press F7 to return to the document.

42. Press Alt-F9 3 2 1 Return to edit the text box and display the menu.

Warning
Step 44: Users
of version 5.1
should press *7*
or *s*.

43. Press **5 3** to select Center from the Horizontal Position option. You cannot manually adjust the width of the box if it is defined as Both Left and Right.

44. Press **6** or **s** for the Size option, to display

    1 Width (auto height); 2 Height (auto width); 3 Both Width and Height: 0

45. Press **1** or **w** to change the width of the box, allowing the height to adjust automatically for the proper proportions. The prompt changes to

    Width = 6.16"

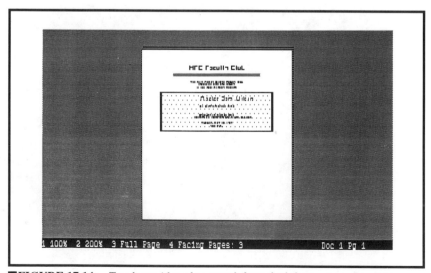

■**FIGURE 17.14:** *Text box widened to stretch from the left margin to the right*

Your own prompt may differ depending on your base font.

46. Type **4.5** then press Return.

Warning
Step 47: Users
of version 5.1
should press 9
or *e*.

47. Press **8** or **e** to edit the text in the menu. The Text Box Edit screen appears (Figure 17.15). The line and position indicators on your own screen may be different.

48. Place the cursor at the start of the first line.

49. Press Del Ctrl-F3 Return to delete the original Center code and rewrite the line, then Shift-F6 to recenter it.

50. Place the cursor at the start of the line beginning with the word *training*.

51. Press Del Ctrl-F3 Return to delete the original Center code and rewrite the line, then Shift-F6 to recenter it.

52. Press F7 twice to display the document.

53. Press Shift-F7 V to view the document. The lines are centered, and the text box is slightly smaller than the horizontal line on top of the page.

54. Press F7 to return to the document.

55. Finally, let's center the entire announcement on the page.

    a. Press Home Home ↑ to reach the top of the document.

    b. Press Shift-F8 2 1 Return Return to insert the [Center Pg] code.

Warning
Step 55b: Users
of version 5.1
should press
Shift-F8 2 1 Y
Return Return.

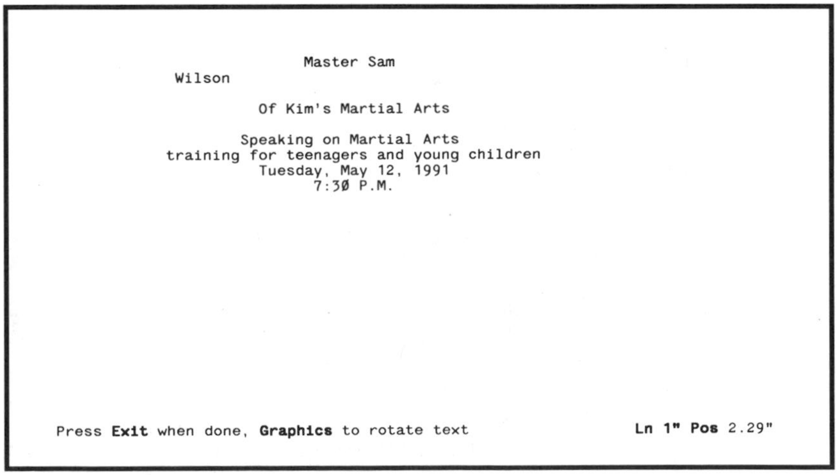

```
                              Master Sam
                Wilson

                      Of Kim's Martial Arts

                    Speaking on Martial Arts
              training for teenagers and young children
                      Tuesday, May 12, 1991
                           7:3Ø P.M.










     Press Exit when done, Graphics to rotate text          Ln 1" Pos 2.29"
```

■**FIGURE 17.15:** *Text Box Edit screen*

56. Press Shift-F7 1 to print the final document (Figure 17.16).

57. Press F7 Y, type **Flyer**, then press Return N to save the document and clear the screen.

You can use the Edit mode to enter text into a box. The length of the line you'll be able to type is controlled by the box width. The height will automatically adjust to fit the text that you enter. You can make the box larger than the text by using the Size option on the Text Box Definition menu.

USING THE TEMPLATE

You just completed a template for a monthly meeting announcement. The template stores the text and graphics that you want to include every month. Now that it is created, you can easily change the contents of the box by recalling a different file or by entering text directly with the Edit option. For example, suppose it's time to announce the June meeting with the monthly flyer we created in this chapter.

Start by typing a document called JUNE, containing the particulars of the June meeting. Save that document and clear the screen. Retrieve FLYER, then press Alt-F9 3 2 1 Return to edit text box 1. Press *1* to select Filename then type JUNE as the document to be included in the box. You'll see the prompt

> **Note**
> The appearance of the version 5.1 screen is slightly different, but the steps listed here still apply.

Replace contents with JUNE? (Y/N) No

HFC Faculty Club

The Holy Family College Faculty Club
invites all staff and faculty
to the next monthly meeting

Master Sam Wilson

Of Kim's Martial Arts

Speaking on Martial Arts
training for teenagers and young children
Tuesday, May 12, 1991

■**FIGURE 17.16:**   *Completed monthly announcement*

Press *Y* to replace the contents of the box (the document MAY) with the June information. Press F7 to return to the document then Shift-F7 1 to print it.

OTHER TEXT BOX FEATURES

Using the options on the Text Box Definition menu, you can adjust the size and position of text boxes, or even add a border around the entire page. The border is really just a large box, the full size of the page. You can add text within the border, or a graphic image, as you'll soon see.

Here's how to place a border around a page, as illustrated in Figure 17.17. You must add the border first, then write or recall a file into it.

1. Press Alt-F9 3 4 to display the Text Box Options menu.

2. Press **1** or **b** to set the border type.

3. Press **3** four times to create a double-line border.

4. Press **9** or **g** for the Shading option.

5. Press **0** then Return to eliminate the shading in the box.

6. Press Return to exit the menu.

7. Press Alt-F9 3 1 to create the text box.

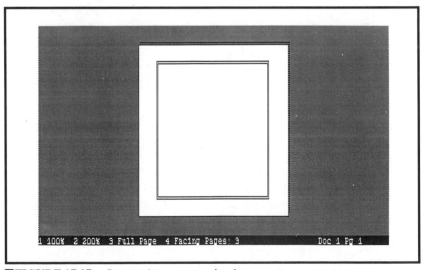

■**FIGURE 17.17:** *Box serving as a page border*

Warning
Step 8: Users of
version 5.1
should press *4*
or *t* for the
Anchor Type
option.

Warning:
Step 9: Users of
version 5.1
should press *2*
or *a*, and then
Return. Refer to
"Page Anchors,"
page 423.

Warning
Users of version
5.1: In step 10,
press *5* or *v*. In
step 12, press *6*
or *h*.

Warning
Step 14: Users
of version 5.1
should press *4*
or *f* for the Full
option.

8. Press **3** or **t** for the Type option. The status line changes to

   Type: 1 Paragraph; 2 Page; 3 Character: 0

9. Press **2** or **a** for a page box. The Vertical option changes to Top, the Horizontal option to Margin, Right.

10. Press **4** or **v** for the Vertical option to display the prompt line

    Vertical Position: 1 Full Page; 2 Top; 3 Center;
    4 Bottom; 5 Set Position: 0

11. Press **1** or **f** for Full Page.

12. Press **5** or **h** for the Horizontal option to display

    Horizontal Position: 1 Margins; 2 Columns; 3 Set Position: 0

13. Press **1** or **m** to display

    Horizontal Position: 1 Left; 2 Right; 3 Center; 4 Both
    Left & Right: 0

14. Press **4** or **b** so the box stretches across the page between the left and right margins.

15. Press Return to return to the document.

16. Press Return several times. The page break line appears with the top border of the text box showing. You'd press *1* and enter a file name to insert a document on disk into the box, or press *8* to display the Edit screen and type the document.

17. Press Shift-F7 V to view the box.

18. Press F7 then F7 N N to clear the screen.

VERTICAL LINES

Vertical lines are used to separate columns on the page or to highlight the left or right margin. They can provide a pleasing visual effect that breaks up large sections of text, particularly in bound books.

To enter vertical lines, press Alt-F9 5 2 to select Vertical Lines. You'll see the Vertical Line menu (Figure 17.18).

The options on this menu are similar to those for horizontal lines, but there are some important differences. The Length of Line setting determines the height of the line. Use the Horizonal Position option to place the lines either at the right or left margin, between columns, or at some specific position. Vertical

```
Graphics: Vertical Line

    1 - Horizontal Position          Left Margin

    2 - Vertical Position            Full Page

    3 - Length of Line

    4 - Width of Line                0.01"

    5 - Gray Shading (% of black)    100%




Selection: 0
```

■FIGURE 17.18:   *Vertical Line menu*

Position controls where at that position the line appears: along the full length of the page, near the top, center, or bottom, or at a specific position that you can set.

You can only enter a line length if the vertical position is something other than Full Page.

Vertical lines can also be used to separate columns. Start by defining the columns as you did in Chapter 9, then create the line by selecting the Horizontal Position option to see the prompt

Horizontal Position: 1 Left; 2 Right; 3 Between
Columns; 4 Set Position: 0

Press *3*, Between Columns, for the prompt

Place line to the right of column: 1

Press Return if you want a line down the center of the page between two columns, then Return again to return to the document. Turn Columns on and enter your columns.

By adjusting the vertical position and length, you can insert lines anywhere on the page, even between uneven parallel columns surrounded by regular paragraphs.

VERSION 5.1 FEATURES

RULED FORMS WITH THE TABLE EDITOR

If you are faced with designing a ruled form, I recommend using the Table Editor instead of Line Draw. The Table Editor has many advantages over Line Draw, not only in the design stage, but also when actually entering text into the completed form. For example, columns and rows can easily be expanded as needed.

Figure 17.19 shows a form created using the Table Editor. It was a simple task to start with a basic form (table) of 15 rows and three columns: Alt-F7 2 1 Return 15 Return. The table was then modified using the Join, Split, and Lines commands—the most useful commands for form design.

For example, two cells were joined to make one large one for the name, and three cells were joined for the street address. The next line—three different-sized "boxes" to hold the remaining parts of the address—was created by splitting the center cell into two, and then joining the resulting first two cells. A wide variety of boxes can be created using similar methods.

Employee Status Report		
Name:		SS #:
Address:		
City:	State:	Zip:
Class 1:	Description:	
Salary 1:		
Class 2:	Description:	
Salary 2:		
Annual Rating:		
1991	1992	1993
(Cut here and return to personnel upon termination)		
Name:		SS #:
Date:	Termination Code:	
Comments:		

■**FIGURE 17.19:**   *Form created with the Table Editor*

GRAPHIC OPTIONS

In version 5.1, the Graphics prompt line appears as

1 Figure; 2 Table Box; 3 Text Box; 4 User Box; 5 Line; 6 Equation: 0.

LINE OPTIONS

When you press *5* or *L* from the Graphics prompt line, the options change to

Create Line: 1 Horizontal; 2 Vertical; Edit Line: 3 Horizontal; 4 Vertical: 0

The Horizontal Line menu in WordPerfect 5.1 appears as in Figure 17.20. Vertical Position has two settings: *Baseline*, the default, positions the line on the current baseline of the text. *Set Position* allows you to enter a specific position on the page.

In the Horizontal Position options, *Both Left & Right* has been replaced by *Full*, but this option works the same way, producing a line that stretches from margin to margin across the page. The Edit Line options allow you to edit a line you already created.

GRAPHIC-BOX OPTIONS

Graphic boxes now include an option for determining the type of content to be inserted into the box, as shown in Figure 17.21 for a text box. By default, this

```
Graphics: Horizontal Line

        1 - Horizontal Position       Full

        2 - Vertical Position         Baseline

        3 - Length of Line

        4 - Width of Line             0.013"

        5 - Gray Shading (% of black) 100%




    Selection: 0
```

■**FIGURE 17.20:** *Horizontal Line menu in version 5.1*

option is set to *empty* for figure, table, and user boxes; *Text* for text boxes; and *Equation* for equation boxes.

When you import a graphics file, as you'll do in Chapter 18, the option changes to Graphics. However, you can designate another type of contents by pressing *2* or *o* to display the prompt line:

Contents: 1 Graphics; 2 Graphic on Disk; 3 Text; 4 Equation: 0

The options are:

Graphics	A graphic file is merged into the document and saved along with it. You can later load and print the document without having the original graphic available on disk.
Graphic on Disk	The graphic is linked with the document rather than merged with it. When printed, the graphic file is located on disk and used. The graphic file must be available whenever you access the document. As you'll learn in Chapter 18, using this option results in smaller disk files and ensures that the most recent version of your graphic file is printed with the document.
Text	The box will contain text and formatting codes. Any codes used to format box text do not affect other characters in the document.

```
Definition: Text Box
      1 - Filename
      2 - Contents          Text
      3 - Caption
      4 - Anchor Type        Paragraph
      5 - Vertical Position  Ø"
      6 - Horizontal Position Right
      7 - Size               3.25" wide x Ø.625" (high)
      8 - Wrap Text Around Box Yes
      9 - Edit



Selection: Ø
```

■**FIGURE 17.21:** *Text Box menu in version 5.1*

Equation   Allows you to create an equation graphic, as explained in Chapter 15.

You can select any type of content for any box.

PAGE ANCHORS

When you select a page anchor in version 5.1, the prompt line changes to

Number of pages to skip: 0

This option allows you to place the box on a specific page. If you're on page 1 and you want to place the box on the third page, for example, enter *2*. Press Return by itself to insert the box on the current page.

Page-anchored boxes will be bumped to the next page if there is not sufficient room on the current (or selected) page.

MOUSE AND MENU EQUIVALENTS

Function	Keyboard	Pull-Down Menus
Line Draw	Ctrl-F3 2	Tools Line Draw
Lines	Alt-F9 5	Graphics Line
Figure Box	Alt-F9 1	Graphics Figure
Table Box	Alt-F9 2	Graphics Table Box
Text Box	Alt-F9 3	Graphics Text Box
User Box	Alt-F9 4	Graphics User Box
Equation Box	Alt-F9 5	Graphics Equation

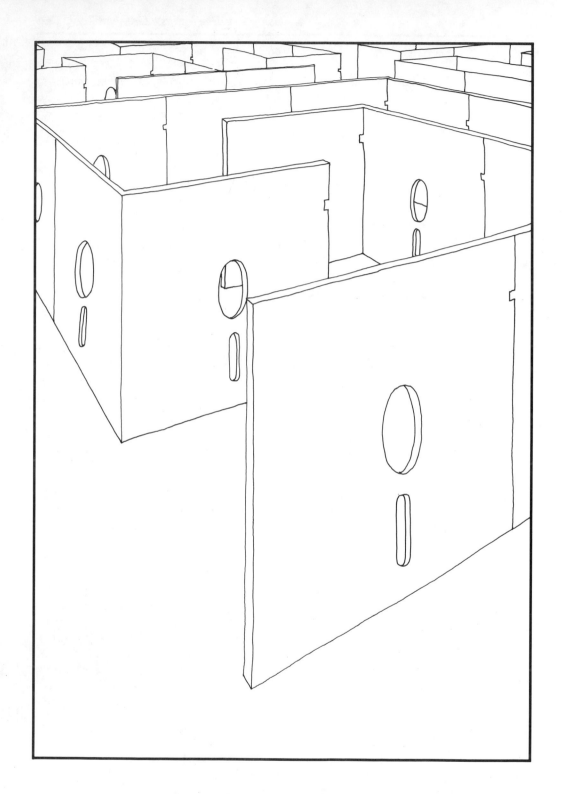

18

ENHANCING DOCUMENTS WITH GRAPHICS

WordPerfect has been programmed to recognize a number of graphic formats and can use them in a document without any special conversion. Graphics created with some other programs, however, must be saved in some special way before WordPerfect can use them. Many of these images, however, can be captured directly using GRAB. This WordPerfect program "photographs" the image on the screen directly into the WPG format. Once "grabbed," it can be used just like the WPG samples provided.

■ IMPORTING GRAPHICS INTO DOCUMENTS

The techniques for using line drawings and bitmap graphics are almost identical to those for creating a text box, so most of these steps will be familiar to you from Chapter 17. If the graphic is in a format directly readable by WordPerfect, just create the box and enter the graphic's file name.

As an example of the page composition powers of WordPerfect, let's create a newsletter format similar to those you saw in Figure 17.1. We'll create a text box to contain the masthead, and single- and two-column text. For graphics, we'll use a WPG file that you have on your WordPerfect graphics disk and a bitmap graphic file created with PC Paintbrush. If you don't have any bitmap files available to you, read the instructions given but select a WPG image instead. You just won't be able to perform some of the editing explained.

For the text of the newsletter, select any of the documents you've already created. The actual text doesn't matter here, just the technique. If you want, you can use the text shown in Figure 18.1 when called for. Otherwise, just recall some existing document.

How text and graphics appear on your screen will depend on your graphics display card and the base font you select. Your own screen may, therefore, appear different from the figures shown in this chapter, and there may be some slight variations in the settings and measurements shown in some prompts. Even so, continue following the instructions given here. If any of your printouts differ substantially, then you'll have to make some minor adjustments to the settings selected, but you'll learn how to make such adjustments in this section.

Let's start with the masthead, a single-column text box. Follow these steps:

1. Press Alt-F9 3 4 to display the Text Box Options menu. We want to display the masthead in a shaded box bordered by single-thickness lines.

2. Press **1** for the Border option then press **2** (the single-thickness selection) four times.

3. Press Return to accept the remaining defaults.

```
        The largest computer systems are called mainframes. These are
    large centralized computer systems that can be accessed by a great
    many users at one time, performing many different tasks.
        The next size computers are called minicomputers. These are
    still centralized systems that can be used by a number of persons.
    However, they have less processing capability than mainframes and
    can accommodate fewer users.
        Supermicros are smaller than minicomputers. These are smaller
    computer systems, based on microcomputers, which serve a number of
    persons at a time. These are called multi-user, multi-tasking
    microcomputers.
        A microcomputer, also called a personal or desktop computer,
    can be used by only one individual at a time. Compared to the other
    types of computers, the microcomputer has limited processing
    capabilities.
        The special purpose computer is designed to perform a very
    specific task. It can be large or small, but is "dedicated" to the
    one job for which it was made. Special purpose computers can be
    found in automobiles, industrial equipment, and even home
    appliances.
        Every computer system, no matter what the size, has the same
    basic parts. These include input and output devices, and some type
    of storage.
        The most common input device today is the keyboard. This is
    used to get data and instructions into the computer itself. Other
    input devices include the mouse, drawing tablet, and punch cards.
        The video display, or Cathode Ray Tube, is the most common
    output device. These may be color or black and white. Other types
    of output devices are printers and voice synthesizers.
        Computer storage can be classified into two categories: main
    and auxiliary. Main storage includes Random Access Memory (RAM) and
    Read Only Memory (ROM). Auxiliary storage devices are disk and tape
    drives.
```

■**FIGURE 18.1:** *Text for newsletter*

4. Press Alt-F9 3 1 to create a text box and display the Text Box Definition menu.

Warning
Users of version
5.1: In Step 5:
Press **4** or **t**. In
Step 6: Press **2**
or **a**, then
Return to skip
no pages. In
Step 7: a. Press
6 or **h**; b. Press
1 or **m**; c. Press
4 or **f**. In Step 8:
Press **9** or **e**.

5. Press **3** or **t** for the type option.

6. Press **2** or **a** for a page box. We're using this type because, in this case, we are positioning the box in relation to the entire page, not a single paragraph.

7. We want the box to appear only on the top of the page, the default vertical position option. But we have to change the horizontal position to Both Left and Right so it spans the page, just as you did for the full border previously.

   a. Press **5** or **h** for the Horizontal option.

   b. Press **1** or **m** to select Margins.

   c. Press **4** or **b** so the box spans the page.

   Now enter text into the box. If you're using a laser printer, be sure the base font is set correctly.

8. Press **8** or **e** for the Edit screen.

9. Press Return to give an extra line between the top of the box and the first line of text. This saves you from changing the box size to insert this space.
   If you want to select a new base font to be used for the text in the box, do so now—even if you selected a base font before defining the box. Any new Base Font code in the document will not affect text in the box.

10. Now enter the masthead.

    a. Press Shift-F6 to center the cursor.

    b. Press Ctrl-F8 1 7 for the extra large font.

    c. Type **Industry Newsletter**.

11. Press the → key to move past the Extra Large code, then press Return twice.

12. Press Shift-F6 to center the cursor, then Ctrl-F8 1 5 for large printing.

13. Type **A public service of the Aardvark Corporation**.

14. Press → to move past the Large code, then press Return twice.

15. Press F7 to return to the Definition menu, then F7 again to display the document.

Now enter and format the text of the newsletter.

1. Press Return for some extra space, then type

   This newsletter is distributed without charge to companies and individuals interested in any aspect of the computer industry. For additional copies, contact Alvin Aardvark, President, Aardvark Corporation.

2. Press Return twice to see the screen shown in Figure 18.2.

3. Now type the text shown in Figure 18.1, or press Shift-F10, type the name of a file on your disk that you can use as the sample, and press Return.

Warning
Users of version
5.1: In Step 4:
Press Alt-F7 1 3
Return. In Step
5: Press **1** or **O**.

4. Place the cursor at the start of the text you just typed or recalled, then press Alt-F7 4 Return to define a two-column newspaper format. Because that is the default style, you only have to display the Column Definition menu and press Return.

5. Press **3** to turn on Columns.

6. Press Ctrl-F3 Return to rewrite the screen so the text is formatted into the columns (Figure 18.3).

Let's add two graphics to this document. The first will be a WPG file in a box between the two columns. The cursor should still be at the start of the text.

1. Press Alt-F9 1 to select a figure box. Remember, any box type could really be used.

```
┌TXT 1─────────────────────────────────────────────────┐

        This newsletter is distributed without charge to companies and individual
   interested in any aspect of the computer industry. For additional copies, cont
   Alvin Aardvark, Present, Aardvark Corporation.


   _




                                              Doc 1 Pg 1 Ln 3.93" Pos 1"
```

■FIGURE 18.2:   *The masthead and introductory paragraph as they appear on screen*

2. Press **4** or **o** to display the Figure Options menu. It is just like the Text Box Options menu that you saw in Figure 17.5 except for some different default values: figure boxes are already formatted for a single-line border but with no shading. So let's add a 10-percent shading to really make it stand out on the page.

3. Press **9** for the Gray Shading option.

4. Type **10** and press Return twice to return to the document. Now let's define the box itself.

New Feature
Additional related features in version 5.1 are discussed under "Graphic Contents," page 442.

5. Press Alt-F9 1 1 to create a figure box. The Figure Box Definition menu appears. It is identical to the Text Box Definition menu shown in Figure 17.11 except for the title.

6. Now insert the graphic file GAVEL.WPG supplied on the WordPerfect Graphics disk. If you have a floppy drive system, insert this disk in drive B.

   a. Press **1** to select Filename.

   b. Type **GAVEL.WPG** then press Return. You'll see the message

      Please wait – Loading WP Graphics File

      as the file is retrieved.

   Now we have to position the box so it appears between the two columns.

Warning
Step 7: Users of version 5.1 should press 4 2 Return.

7. Press **3 2** to select a page box.

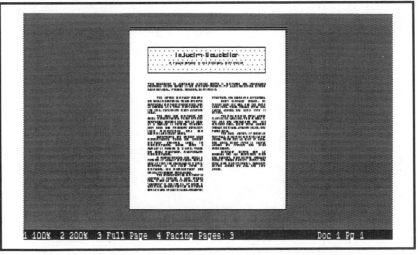

■**FIGURE 18.3:** *Newsletter with text in View mode*

8. We'd like the box to start below the single-column text, centered between the columns.

a. Press **4** or **v** for the Vertical Position option.

b. Press **5** or **s** to set the position. The prompt changes to

> Offset from top of page: 3.92

Your own offset might be different.

c. Press Return to accept the box's offset from the top of the page.

d. Press **5** or **h** for the Horizontal option.

e. Press **2** or **c** for Columns, displaying the prompt

> Enter column(s): 1

f. Type **1–2** followed by Return to position the box between the two columns.

g. Press **3** or **c** to center the horizontal position.

9. Enter a caption under the box.

a. Press **2** or **c** for the Caption option. The screen clears, and *Figure 1* appears on the top. If you want the caption text to use a different base font, select it before entering the text.

b. Type **Only you can judge if computers can help your business**.

c. Press F7.

The caption will be the same width as the box, and the figure number itself will be inserted as a code. If you add or delete other boxes of that type, the number will adjust.

Let's see what the figure will look like and how we might be able to edit or change it.

10. Press **8** or **e** for the Edit option. Because this box holds a graphic figure, you'll see the screen in Figure 18.4.

There are two lines of options on this menu, so let's review them before going on. The top line shows commands that are performed by single keystrokes:

- Press the directional arrows to move the image in the box.

- Press PgUp and PgDn to change the scale of the drawing.

New Feature
Additional related features in version 5.1 are discussed under "Editing Graphics," page 443.

■   Press the – or + key (on the numeric keypad) to rotate the image—the plus key rotates counterclockwise, minus rotates clockwise.

■   Press Ins to adjust the percentage of change made with each of the commands just listed. The amount is shown in the bottom right corner of the screen; it can be either 1 percent, 5 percent, 10 percent, or 25 percent with each keystroke.

■   Press Ctrl-Home (Goto) to reset the image to its original state.

The commands in the bottom prompt line perform similar changes but allow you to enter a specific amount. If you select *l* or *s,* compared to PgUp or PgDn, you can enter a separate scale factor for both the X- and Y-axes. If you elect to rotate the image—by pressing *3* or *r*—you can enter the degrees of rotation and select whether or not you want to mirror-image the graphic. The Invert command has no effect on line drawings, just bitmap images.

When you load a graphic into a box, the size of the box adjusts so the image fills it. If you move, scale, or rotate the image, some of it may move out of the box and will not appear when printed. It is not lost, however, and it can be moved, scaled, or rotated back into view. So if you want to enlarge the image, as we'll do later for the bitmap graphic, change the size of the box on the Definition menu then scale it in the Edit screen.

No matter what you do to the image in Edit mode, the original file is not affected.

11.   Press **3** or **r** to select Rotate. The prompt changes to

Note
The appearance of the version 5.1 screen is slightly different, but the steps listed here still apply.

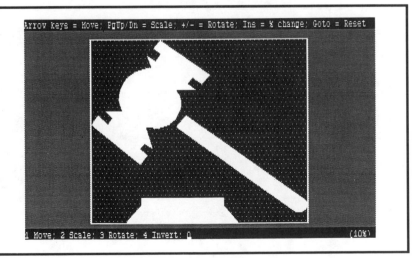

■**FIGURE 18.4:**   *GAVEL.WPG in the Graphic Edit screen*

Enter number of degrees (0-360): 0

12. Press Return to bypass any rotation and display

Mirror Image? (Y/N) No

13. Press **Y**. The gavel is mirror-imaged.

14. Press + (on the numeric keypad) to rotate the image clockwise 10 percent.

15. Press – (on the numeric keypad) to rotate it counterclockwise to its original position.

16. Press Return to return to the Definition menu.

17. Press Return to return to the document.

18. Press Shift-F7 V 3 to view the document (Figure 18.5). Make sure the placement of the box is correct. If it is too low, you'll have to decrease the vertical position offset using the Text Box Definition menu. If the graphic box doesn't appear at all, it is probably set too high and is conflicting with the text box. In this case, increase the vertical position.

19. Press F7 to return to the document.

Now let's add another graphic to the document. In this example I'll use a bitmap drawing to demonstrate how these can be edited. If one isn't available to you, select one of the other WPG files on your disk. Try PC.WPG if you want.

This graphic will be placed at the bottom of the second column.

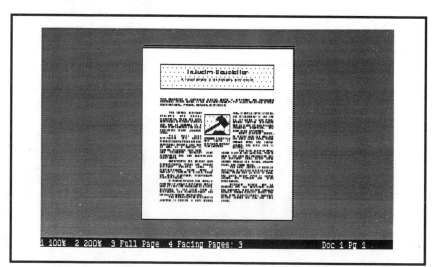

■**FIGURE 18.5:**   *Newsletter with graphic box added*

1. Press Alt-F9 1 to select a figure box.

2. Press **4** or **o** to display the Figure Options menu. The options reflect the 10-percent shading you added for the last picture. So let's remove this for the next box.

3. Press **9** for the Gray Shading option.

4. Type **0** then press Return twice to return to the document. Now let's define the box itself.

5. Press Alt-F9 1 1 to create a figure box. The Figure Box Definition menu appears.

6. Insert the name of a graphic file.

   a. Press **1** to select Filename.

   b. Type the name of the bitmap file or **PC.WPG** if you don't have one. Mine is called *MAP.PCX*. It contains the drawing of a map made using PC Paintbrush.

   c. Press Return and wait until the file is retrieved.

   We have to position the box so it appears at the bottom right. Since it isn't related to a specific paragraph, we'll use a page box.

Warning
Users of version 5.1: In Step 7: Press 4 2 Return. In Step 8: a. Press **5** or **v**; b. Press **4** or **b**; c. Press **6** or **h**; d. Press **2** or **c**; e. Type **2** Return; f. Press **4** or **f**, for Full. In Step 9: Press **9** or **e**.

7. Press **3 2** to select a page box.

8. Position the box at the bottom of the second column.

   a. Press **4** or **v** for the Vertical Position option.

   b. Press **4** or **b** for the bottom of the page.

   c. Press **5** or **h** for the Horizontal option.

   d. Press **2** or **c** for Columns.

   e. Type **2** then press Return for the second column.

   f. Press **4** or **b** for Both Left and Right.

9. Press **8** or **e** to edit the figure (Figure 18.6).
   The same options are available as before. You can use either the keypad or the selections on the prompt line to scale, rotate, move, or invert the image.
   In this specific example, the PC Paintbrush image is wide but narrow, and a little difficult to read. The image is also reversed—that is, the background will be printed black and the lines white.
   Let's see how the image will look inverted, then adjust the size.

10. Press **4** or **i** (you could also press Shift-F3) to invert the image.

11. Press F7 to return to the Edit menu.

12. Press **6** or **s** to change the size.

Warning
Step 12: Users
of version 5.1
should press **7**
or **s**.

13. Press **2** or **h** for Height.

14. Type **2** then press Return.

Even though you elected to change the height with the width adjusting automatically, the width didn't change. That's because the Horizontal Position option is set to position the box from the left margin to the right in the second column, 3 inches wide. The Horizontal Position option overrides any manual changes to the size.

Warning
Step 15: Users
of version 5.1
should press **9**
or **e**.

15. Press **8** or **e** to return to Edit mode. The proportions of the box and image have been adjusted, so there is no need, in this case, to use the Scale setting (Figure 18.7).

16. Press F7 to return to the Definition menu, then F7 again to display the document. The text and boxes do not appear properly arranged, but let's look at the document in View mode and print a copy.

17. Press Shift-F7 V to view the document. The figures are in the correct places.

18. Press F7, then Shift-F7 1 to print the newsletter. Figure 18.8 shows the

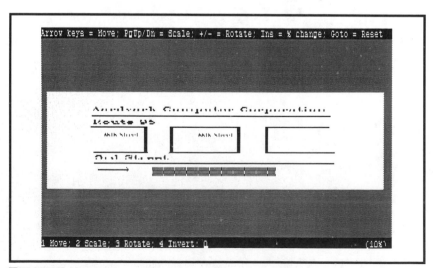

■FIGURE 18.6: *Bitmap picture file image on the Edit screen*

newsletter printed on a LaserJet printer. The base font selected in the text box and for the document was Century Schoolbook 12 pt. Notice that the caption for Figure 1 is in a different font—Courier—because the new base font was not selected when the caption was entered.

19. Press F7 N Y to exit WordPerfect.

Because the appearance of the document in the typing window may be somewhat off, you should view documents with complex layouts frequently. Make minor adjustments in position and size until the composition is just how you want it. Keep in mind a quirk about the Graphics feature: If a box will not fit on the page, WordPerfect will move it to the next. So don't be too surprised if you don't see a box when viewing the document—it may have been moved to the next page. This is particularly common with page boxes and all types of large boxes.

USING LOTUS GRAPHS WITH WORDPERFECT

We've now worked with three types of images—text boxes, line drawings (WPG files), and bitmap images. Another potent use of the Graphics commands is to merge charts developed with spreadsheet programs like Lotus 1-2-3 with your documents. Create and save the graph file using the spreadsheet program. Be sure to format it for black and white unless you have a color printer. Then copy the PIC file to your WordPerfect directory or document disk. Start WordPerfect and, when ready, enter the name of the PIC file as the file name when defining the box.

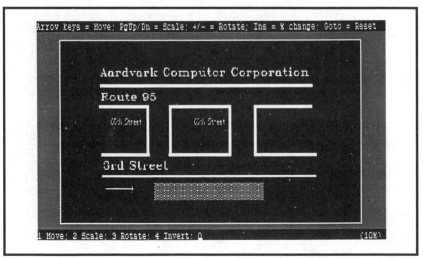

■**FIGURE 18.7:** *Map graphic resized*

Industry Newsletter

A public service of the Aardvark Corporation

This newsletter is distributed without charge to companies and individuals interested in any aspect of the computer industry. For additional copies, contact Alvin Aardvark, Present, Aardvark Corporation.

The largest computer systems are called mainframes. These are large centralized computer systems that can be accessed by a great many users at one time, performing many different tasks.

The next size computers are called minicomputers. These are still centralized systems that can be used by a number of persons. However, they have less processing capability than mainframes and can accommodate fewer users.

Supermicros are smaller than minicomputers. These are smaller computer systems, based on microcomputers, which serve a number of persons at a time. These are called multi-user, multi-tasking microcomputers.

A microcomputer, also called a personal or desktop computer, can be used by only one individual at a time. Compared to the other types of computers, the microcomputer has limited processing capabilities.

The special purpose computer is designed to perform a very specific

Figure 1 Only you can judge if computers can help your business.

task. It can be large or small, but is "dedicated" to the one job for which it was made. Special purpose computers can be found in automobiles, industrial equipment, and even home appliances.

Every computer system, no matter what the size, has the same basic parts. These include input and output devices, and some type of storage.

The most common input device today is the keyboard. This is used to get data and instructions into the computer itself. Other input devices include the mouse, drawing tablet, and punch cards.

The video display, or Cathode

■FIGURE 18.8: *Completed newsletter*

Figure 18.9 illustrates a document containing a Lotus 1-2-3 chart. In this particular example, I selected a page box with Bottom vertical position and Both Left and Right horizontal position.

■ USING GRAB

GRAB is WordPerfect's screen capture utility; it saves any screen image that's in the graphic mode to a WPG format file. The file can then be used in boxes just like the samples provided.

To load the utility, you must be at the DOS prompt. Type *GRAB* and press Return to see the message:

> Screen capture utility successfully installed
> Activation (hot key) sequence is "<ALT><SHIFT><F9>"
> Output goes to active directory at time of capture
> Output file name is "GRAB.WPG"
> For help, type "grab /h"

If you type *GRAB/H* you'll see several screens of information explaining how the program operates.

It is loaded as a *resident* program, which means that after it is installed you can continue using your computer normally. When you want to capture a screen, just press Alt-Shift-F9.

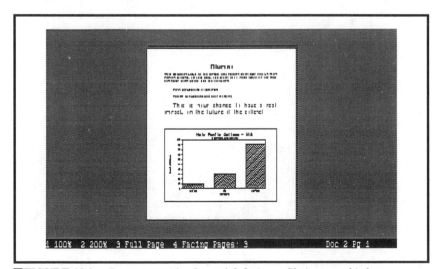

■FIGURE 18.9: *Document with a Lotus 1-2-3 picture file in a graphic box*

If your screen is in a mode that GRAB does not recognize, you'll hear a beep. Otherwise you'll hear two beeps, and a box will appear as shown in Figure 18.10.

When you press Return, the image in the box will be saved to a WPG file, and your screen will return to normal.

Press any of the directional arrows to move the box or press Shift with any of the arrow keys to resize the box. When a box is resized, only the bottom and right sides move. So if you want to capture the entire screen, for example, first use the arrow keys to place the box in the upper left corner, then use Shift-↓ and Shift-→ to expand the box to cover the entire screen.

Press Esc if you decide not to capture the screen.

The first image you capture is saved under the name GRAB.WPG. Subsequent captured images will be numbered GRAB1.WPG to GRAB999.WPG.

To remove the resident program from memory, type *GRAB/T* from the DOS prompt.

WORDPERFECT AND DESKTOP PUBLISHING SOFTWARE

Even with these Graphics functions, you might still be using WordPerfect as just a word processor and merging the document into a separate desktop publishing program. The most difficult task, in this case, is to save your file in a format

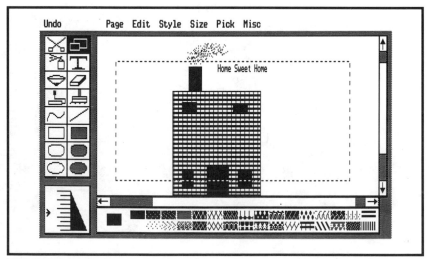

■**FIGURE 18.10:** *The box that appears so you can enclose the area to be grabbed*

readable by the desktop publisher, so start by referring to your publisher's documentation.

In almost all cases, you could save the document in a generic format. All of your character codes (such as boldface and font changes) will be lost, unfortunately, but your desktop publisher will be able to read the text.

Some desktop publishers may be able to accept a document directly in WordPerfect format. If yours does, check the documentation carefully to see which version of WordPerfect it accepts. If it doesn't say, import a WordPerfect file from your version just to see what happens.

You may be fortunate enough to have a program that works directly with version 5.0. But if not, here are some tips for working with a desktop publisher that only accepts documents from earlier versions or as generic text files.

You'll eventually have to save your file in either generic or earlier version format, if your software accepts it. Press Ctrl-F5 then select the format desired. Type a document name, then press Return. Any boxes and graphic lines will be deleted along with all other codes. If you're saving the document in an earlier format, newer codes will be converted whenever possible.

But most desktop publishers allow you to enter formatting codes as special text in the word processor. This text is saved, along with the regular document, and transferred to the publisher, which converts the codes to its own format. Our goal is to easily convert your WordPerfect codes into the publisher's codes before saving.

The codes illustrated in this section are those used by Xerox's Ventura Publisher. While this software does accept some WordPerfect codes, let's assume that you have to convert all of your codes to Ventura format. This way, the techniques can be used to transfer your document to any desktop publishing program—only the specific codes will be different.

First refer to your publishing program's documentation and make a list of the codes that it will recognize. For instance, with Ventura publisher:

This code in the text:	**Will perform this format:**
<B>	Boldface
<N>	Required space
<O>	Overstrike
<D>	Normal type
<X>	Strikeout
<v>	Subscript
<^>	Superscript

<U>	Underline
<=>	Double underline
<F*nnn*>	Font number *nnn*
<P*nnn*>	Point size *nnn*

Then convert the WordPerfect codes (such as [BOLD]) in your document to their corresponding desktop publisher's codes (such as <B>).

While you may think you can do this easily with the Replace command, it is a little more complex because of the way WordPerfect handles paired codes such as [BOLD] and [bold]. Say you use Alt-F2 to replace all instances of [BOLD] with <B>. When the Bold code is replaced with the text <B>, the corresponding [bold] code is deleted. So your desktop publisher will turn on boldfacing but never turn it off. Since the code is gone, it is too late to try to replace [bold] with <D>.

If you try to start by replacing [bold] with <D>, then the [BOLD] code is deleted so you won't be able to replace it with <B>.

You have to make the replacement in a very specific way. Here's an example using the Bold codes.

1. Press Home Home ↓ to reach the end of the document you're working on. If you press Home Home ↑, the cursor is placed at the first character, which may be after the first codes.

2. Press Alt-F2 Return for an unconfirmed replacement, displaying the prompt:

   -> Srch:

3. Press ↑ to change the direction of the search:

   <- Srch:

4. Press F6 to display

   <- Srch: [BOLD]

5. Press F2 to display

   Replace with:

6. Press F6 then type **<B>** or your publisher's text code for bold printing.

   Replace with: [BOLD]<B>

7. Press F2 to perform the replacement. Because you are inserting another [BOLD] code in the text along with the <B> code, the concluding [bold] is not deleted.

8. Press Home Home ↓.

9. Press Alt-F2 Return for an unconfirmed replacement.

10. Press ↑ for a backward search and replacement.

11. Press Del then press F6 twice. Because the [BOLD] code was already at the prompt, it now appears as

    <- Srch: [BOLD][bold]

12. Press ← then Backspace to delete the [BOLD] code.

13. Press F2 for the *Replace with* prompt.

14. Type **<D>** or your system's code for normal text.

15. Press F2. As the [bold] codes are replaced, the initial [BOLD] codes are deleted. But the text to be boldfaced is now surrounded by your publisher's codes. For example,

    [BOLD]this is boldfaced[bold]

is replaced by

    <B>this is boldfaced<D>

Do not try to do this in reverse—by first replacing the [bold] codes with [bold]<D>. It doesn't work. When the replacement is made, the initial [BOLD] codes are deleted and the closing [bold] is never reinserted. So you're stuck with

    this is boldfaced<D>

Once you've converted all the Bold codes, repeat the procedure for [UND] and [und], and any other codes that you've used, such as [ITALC] and [italc].

Font and Point codes can be replaced in the same way. For example, say you selected a base font of 12-point Times Roman. Delete that code and insert <F014><P012>, the Ventura codes for 12-point Times Roman.

When you select other sizes of that type, replace the appropriate codes. Using the techniques described above, replace all of the beginning codes with the appropriate point sizes, such as:

Replace this:	With this:
[FINE]	[FINE]<P006>

[SMALL]	[SMALL]<P010>
[LARGE]	[LARGE]<P014>
[VRY LARGE]	[VRY LARGE]<P018>
[EXT LARGE]	[EXT LARGE]<P024>

Then replace all ending codes, such as [large] and [small], with <P012>.

VERSION 5.1 FEATURES

GRAPHIC CONTENTS

In Chapter 17 you learned that the Contents option determines the type of materials in the Graphics box. When you insert a graphic file, the Contents option changes from *Empty* to *Graphics*. This means that the graphic file is merged into the document, and saved along with it.

The advantage of merging the graphic file into the document is that you no longer have to worry whether the file is on the same drive or directory. In fact, you could even delete the graphic file entirely, since a copy of it is in the document.

There are disadvantages to this method, however. The major disadvantage is that merged graphics can make for a very large document file; moreover, if you use a graphic file in more than one document, you are using disk space for each copy of it. Also, the graphic will not be updated if you later change it with the program that created it originally. For example, suppose you merge a Lotus chart into a document. Later in the week you change the data in the spreadsheet and save an updated copy of the chart. When you print the document, the original chart—the version added to the file earlier—will appear.

To avoid this problem, you can select Graphics on Disk as the contents. That way, only a small "link" to the file is maintained in the document—not the entire graphic file itself. Of course you have to ensure that the graphic is on the proper drive and directory when you recall the document. If the file isn't found, a warning message will appear, and an empty box will be printed. But then only one copy of the graphic will be on disk, and the newest version will be used when the document is viewed or printed.

EDITING GRAPHICS

The editing screen now includes the *Black & White* option to determine how the image is displayed on the screen and printed (Figure 18.11).

By default, graphic images will be displayed in color—on a color monitor. To display the image in black and white, press *5* or *B* for the prompt line

Print/display image in black & white? No (Yes)

Press Y to have the image appear in black and white.

This setting also determines how the image is printed (Figure 18.12). When set for color, patterns and shades of gray are printed to represent the colors. Select black and white for all colors to appear as solid black.

If you have a dot matrix printer, try printing a sample graphic image both ways to determine the best appearance.

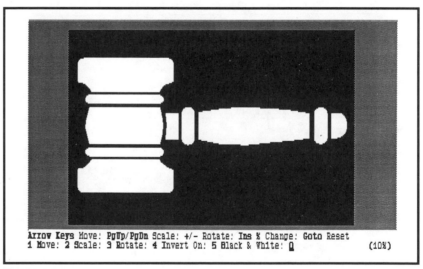

■**FIGURE 18.11:**   *Version 5.1 graphic editing screen*

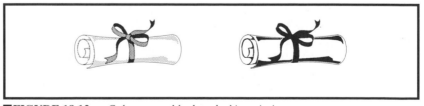

■**FIGURE 18.12:**   *Color versus black and white printing*

MOUSE AND MENU EQUIVALENTS

Function	Keyboard	Pull-Down Menus
Equation Box Options	Alt-F9 5 4	**Graphics Equation Options**
Figure Box Options	Alt-F9 1 4	**Graphics Figure Options**
Table Box Options	Alt-F9 2 4	**Graphics Table Box Options**
Text Box Options	Alt-F9 3 4	**Graphics Text Box Options**
User Box Options	Alt-F9 4 4	**Graphics User Box Options**

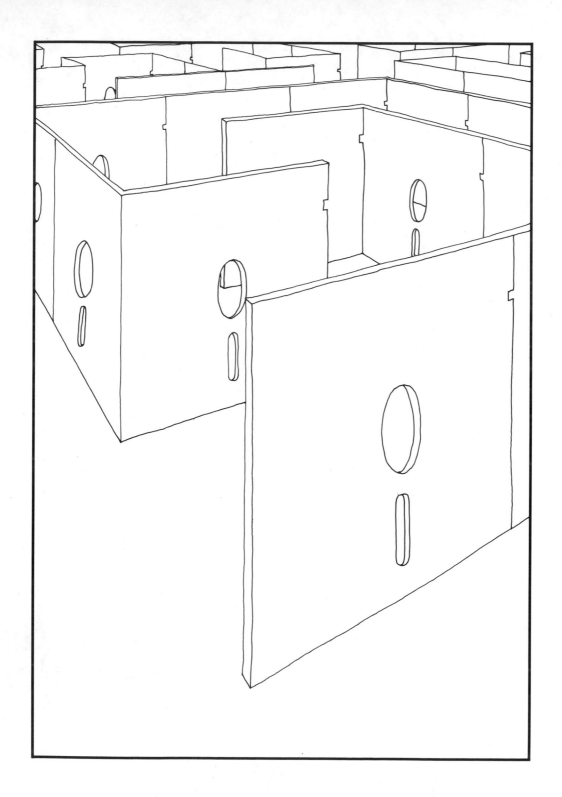

19

USING WORDPERFECT AS A SPREADSHEET

New Feature
Additional re-
lated features in
version 5.1 are
discussed under
"Creating
Spreadsheets
as Tables,"
page 472.

Many word processing documents contain numbers as well as words. Invoices and orders, for example, often include columns of numbers. Many reports incorporate statistical data in tabular form. As you learned in earlier chapters, entering columns of numbers is easy. But these types of documents frequently require an additional task: performing mathematical operations on the numbers themselves. They may need simple arithmetic, such as calculating the total of a column of numbers, or they may even involve complicated what-if problems.

WordPerfect provides a number of mathematical functions which can be used to perform arithmetic on columns of numbers, and even incorporate small spreadsheets into the text, complete with formulas. You can also recalculate figures for a what-if simulation. This chapter will show you how to use these mathematical functions and integrate the results into typical word processing documents.

COLUMNAR MATHEMATICS

The simplest of WordPerfect's mathematical operations is computing subtotals and totals of columns of numbers. You can total up to 24 columns without using a formula.

The basic procedure for totaling columns consists of these five steps:

1. Delete all default tab stops and set only those necessary for the document.

2. Turn on the Math function by pressing Alt-F7 1.

3. Type the column entries.

4. Calculate the subtotals and totals.

5. Turn off the Math function.

By default, all the columns are defined as numeric. Later in this chapter, you'll learn how to redefine columns as text and use them for labels or formulas.

SETTING TAB STOPS

While the Math function is on, the Tab key functions like a decimal tab or the Ctrl-F6 Tab Align key. That is, it aligns the numbers to the left of the decimal point.

Each of the tab stops in the document represents a column (from A to X), and each line is a row. The first column of the spreadsheet, column A, is the one at the first tab stop, not the one at the left margin.

Because tab stops are so critical to the mathematical operations, you should always delete all the tab stops, then set only those that are necessary for the table. For example, if you used the default tab stops in this table:

Item	Amount	% Change
Accounts Receivable	0,000.00	+.1
Accounts Payable	12,000.00	−.2
Cash on Hand	15,000.00	+.3

the three columns would actually span nine columns, A to I, as shown in Figure 19.1. If you deleted all the tab stops and set only the two needed for the table, the document would appear the same, but WordPerfect would define the columns as shown in Figure 19.2.

If you wanted the Item column to be column A, you would have to define it as a text column and set three tab stops. Then you would press the Tab key to reach the first column, and the entire table would be indented. Remember, column A is always at the position of the first tab stop, not at the left margin. You'll learn how to format columns later in this chapter.

```
                A    B    C    D    E    F    G    H    I
            Item                        Amount              % Change
     1      Accounts Receivable        50,000.00              +.1
     2      Accounts Payable           12,000.00              -.2
     3      Cash on Hand                5,000.00              +.3
     4
     5
     6
     7
     8
     9
    10
    11
    12
```

■**FIGURE 19.1:** *A three-column table spanning nine math columns using the default tab stops*

MATHEMATICAL OPERATORS

Wherever you want WordPerfect to insert a total, you enter the appropriate mathematical operator. The following operators are available:

+	Inserts the subtotal of all numbers following the previous subtotal
t	Followed by a number, inserts an additional subtotal
=	Totals all of the subtotals
T	Followed by a number, inserts an additional total
*	Inserts the grand total all of the totals
N	Treats the number as negative

The actual calculations must be performed while the Math function is turned on.

USING COLUMNAR MATH

Figure 19.3 shows an example of how the Columnar Math function can be used with a typical word processing document. Let's create that letter.

```
                                      A                    B
            Item                    Amount             % Change
     1      Accounts Receivable    50,000.00             +.1
     2      Accounts Payable       12,000.00             -.2
     3      Cash on Hand            5,000.00             +.3
     4
     5
     6
     7
     8
     9
     10
     11
     12
```

■**FIGURE 19.2:**   *A three-column table containing only two math columns with the tab stops deleted and reset*

```
     Siravo Hobby and Craft Company
     456 Tudor Drive
     Philadelphia, PA 19116

     Dear Sirs:

          Please ship us the following items and bill our account:

     Items              Amount              Price

     Balsa Wood

     1" by 1" by 2'     10 pieces            5.00
     2" by 2" by 2'     20 pieces           18.00
     1" by 4" by 2'     10 pieces           12.00
     Subtotal                               35.00

     Paint

     Red                4 boxes             18.00
     Blue               4 boxes             16.00
     White              4 boxes             18.00
     Subtotal                               52.00

     Total of Items                         87.00
     Credit                                  5.00

     Amount of Charge                       82.00

          Your  prompt  attention  to  this  order  will  be  greatly
     appreciated.

                           Sincerely,


                           William W. Watson
```

■**FIGURE 19.3:**   *Sample document created using the Columnar Math function*

1. Start WordPerfect.

Warning

With version 5.1, set tabs to absolute or subtract 1 inch from each of the tab stops set in this chapter.

2. Type the following text:

> Siravo Hobby and Craft Company
> 456 Tudor Drive
> Philadelphia, PA 19116
>
> Dear Sirs:
>   Please ship us the following items and bill our account:

3. Press Return twice.

4. Type the column headings.

    a. Type **Items**, then press Tab three times to reach position 30.

    b. Type **Amount**, then press Tab four times to reach position 50.

    c. Type **Price**, then press Return twice.

5. Delete the default tab stops and set the two needed for this document.

    a. Press Shift-F8 1 8.

    b. Press Ctrl-End to delete all the tab stops.

    c. Type **3.8** then press return.

    d. Type **5.8** then press Return.

    e. Press F7 twice.

Warning

Step 6: Users of version 5.1 should press Alt-F7 3 1.

6. Press Alt-F7 to display the prompt line

    1 Math On; 2 Math Def; 3 Column On/Off; 4 Column Def: 0

7. Press **1** to turn on the Math function. The word

    Math

will appear on the status line.

8. Type **Balsa Wood** then press Return twice.

9. Type **1" by 1" by 2'**.

10. Press Tab. Notice that the status line now displays the Align Character prompt.

11. Type **10 pieces**.

12. Press Tab. The Align Character prompt reappears.

13. Type **5.00** then press Return.

14. Type **2" by 2" by 2'**.

15. Press Tab, then type **20 pieces**.

16. Press Tab, type **18.00**, and press Return.

17. Type **1" by 4" by 2'**.

18. Press Tab, then type **10 pieces**.

19. Press Tab, type **12.00**, and press Return. This is the last order of balsa wood. We now need a subtotal for that category.

20. Type **Subtotal**.

21. Press Tab twice to reach position 58 (under the Price column).

22. Type + (the plus sign) to tell WordPerfect to calculate a subtotal here.

23. Press Return twice.

24. Enter the second category of items.

    a. Type **Paint** then press Return twice.

    b. Type **Red**, press Tab, type **4 boxes**, press Tab, type **18.00**, and press Return.

    c. Type **Blue**, press Tab, type **4 boxes**, press Tab, type **16.00**, and press Return.

    d. Type **White**, press Tab, type **4 boxes**, press Tab, type **18.00**, and press Return.

25. Type **Subtotal**, press Tab twice, and type +. This plus sign will insert the subtotal of every number in the column following the last plus sign.

26. Press Return twice.

27. Type **Total of Items**.

28. Press Tab twice.

29. Type = to have WordPerfect place the total of all of the subtotals here.

30. Press Return.

31. Type **Credit** and press Tab twice.
    We now want to subtract a $5.00 credit from the amount owed. You could enter the credit amount as a negative number, either as *–5.00* or *(5.00)*. However, credits are always subtracted from the bill, and using a

(5.00). However, credits are always subtracted from the bill, and using a negative might give the impression of a negative credit (a sort of double negative). So let's use the N operator to avoid having a negative appear in the final document but still subtract the credit.

32. Type **TN5.00**. The uppercase *T* preceding the number means that it should be treated as an additional total in the calculations. A number preceded by a lowercase *t* is an additional subtotal. Use these operators when you have numbers to include in totals and grand totals that are not calculated with the + or = operators.

33. Press Return twice and type **Amount of Charge**.

34. Press Tab twice and type * (an asterisk). The asterisk is the grand total operator that calculates the sum of all the totals. In this case, there are two totals: the number calculated with the = operator and the number preceded by the *T*. Your screen should now look like Figure 19.4.

Warning

Step 36: Users of version 5.1 should press Alt-F7 3 4.

35. Press Return twice.

36. Press Alt-F7 2 to calculate the subtotals, totals, and grand total. The message

    Please Wait

appears for a few seconds, then WordPerfect inserts the calculated values, as shown in Figure 19.5. Although the operators are still displayed on the

```
Items                Amount              Price

Balsa Wood

1" by 1" by 2'       10 pieces            5.00
2" by 2" by 2'       20 pieces           18.00
1" by 4" by 2'       10 pieces           12.00
Subtotal                                  +

Paint

Red                  4 boxes             18.00
Blue                 4 boxes             16.00
White                4 boxes             18.00
Subtotal                                  +

Total of Items                            =
Credit                                   TN5.00

Amount of Charge                          *_


Math                          Doc 1 Pg 1 Ln 5.52" Pos 5.9"
```

■**FIGURE 19.4:** *The columns, entered and ready for calculation* screen, they will not be printed with the document. To calculate totals while you're entering the numbers, press Alt-F7 2 each time you enter an operator. WordPerfect will display the results immediately.

Warning

Step 37: Users of version 5.1 should press Alt-F7 3 2.

37. Press Alt-F7 1 to turn off the Math function.

38. Press Shift-F8 1 8 Ctrl-End 0,.5 Return to reset the default tab stops.

39. Press F7 twice to return to the document.

40. Type the final paragraph and closing.

> Your prompt attention to this order will be greatly appreciated.
>
> Sincerely,
>
> William W. Watson

41. Press Shift-F7 1 if you want to print the document.

42. Press F7 N Y if you want to exit WordPerfect.

This example shows that totaling columns of numbers requires only a few extra steps. Just be sure to delete all the tab stops and set only the necessary ones before entering the columns. Tab to the correct spot, then enter the appropriate operator. Reinsert the default tab stops when you are finished.

```
        Please ship us the following items and bill our account:

    Items                Amount                Price

    Balsa Wood

    1" by 1" by 2'       10 pieces               5.00
    2" by 2" by 2'       20 pieces              18.00
    1" by 4" by 2'       10 pieces              12.00
    Subtotal                                    35.00+

    Paint

    Red                  4 boxes                18.00
    Blue                 4 boxes                16.00
    White                4 boxes                18.00
    Subtotal                                    52.00+

    Total of Items                              87.00=
    Credit                                      TN5.00

    Amount of Charge                            82.00*_


    Math                                Doc 1 Pg 1 Ln 5.52" Pos 6.2"
```

■**FIGURE 19.5:**   *The completed calculations, with operators appearing next to the numbers on the screen, but not in print*

EDITING COLUMNAR MATH

If you need to change a number in a column, just move the cursor to it and use the standard editing procedures. When the cursor is in the calculation area, the word *Math* will appear on the status line. After you change the number, recalculate the totals by pressing Alt-F7 2. The computed values will reflect the change.

Warning
Users of version 5.1 should press Alt-F7 3 4.

Use this same approach if you must add or delete lines. Make whatever changes are required, then recalculate the totals.

■ MATHEMATICS WITH FORMULAS

WordPerfect can incorporate mathematical formulas in tables, with some limitations. Only four formulas are allowed per table. WordPerfect formulas can only be used to perform calculations on the numbers in a row, not down a column.

You can overcome these limitations and create some useful spreadsheets by planning in advance. As an example, take a look at this spreadsheet arrangement:

	John	Paul	Ringo	George
Sales				
Salary				
Commissions				
Totals				

The items in the third row, Commissions, are calculated as 7 percent of the entries in sales, and the fourth row will be the sum of the second and third rows. While this setup is quite appropriate for spreadsheet programs, it won't work with WordPerfect because the program can only use formulas that perform calculations on the numbers across a row.

The solution is to rotate the table so that the calculated figures appear in columns, like this:

	Sales	Salary	Commissions	Total
John				
Paul				
Ringo				
George				
Totals				

The Commissions column will use one formula (the item in column A multiplied by 7 percent), and the Total column will be the sum of the Salary and Commissions columns. The Totals row uses the + operator, not a formula.

If you need to use more than four formulas, you might be able to divide the spreadsheet into two or three smaller ones. You would define each table separately and use different formulas in them. Then you would just have to enter some numbers manually to carry results from one table to another.

PLANNING THE DETAILS

If you're creating a spreadsheet with WordPerfect, the planning stage is critical. In fact, you should be fully prepared before you turn on your computer.

As an example, we will create the quarterly report shown in Figure 19.6. Listed below are the initial steps we must take before we start.

- Write down the type of item that will go in each column and label all but the one at the left margin with letters, starting with A.

    Left margin: Detail name

```
                    Quarterly Report

        This past year was marked by an aggressive marketing
    campaign combined with cost-saving programs in every aspect of
    the corporation. The following chart illustrates the overall
    operating statistics for 1991 and presents a comparison with
    fiscal 1990.


            Quarters
              First    Second    Third    Fourth     1991      1990     Change
                                                    Average   Average

    Income

    Sales      65,000   60,000    55,000   75,000    63,750    62,000    0.03
    Rental      5,000    5,500     6,000    4,500     5,250     4,000    0.31
    Total      70,000   65,500    61,000   79,500    69,000    66,000    0.05

    Expenses
    Salaries   22,000   22,000    24,000   24,000    23,000    21,000    0.10
    Supplies      500      450       350      400       425       375    0.13
    Total      22,500   22,450    24,350   24,400    23,425    21,375    0.10

    Net        47,500   43,050    36,650   55,100    45,575    44,625    0.02


        We hope you find this information useful. Please do not
    hesitate to contact us with any comments or questions.
```

■**FIGURE 19.6:** *Sample document created using formulas*

A: First quarter

B: Second quarter

C: Third quarter

D: Fourth quarter

E: 1991 average

F: 1990 average

G: Change

■ Count the number of characters that will be in the longest entry in each column and add the numbers to the list.

Left margin: Detail name 8

A: First quarter 6

B: Second quarter 6

C: Third quarter 6

D: Fourth quarter 6

E: 1991 average 6

F: 1990 average 6

G: Change 4 (two decimals)

■ Decide how many spaces there should be between columns and write the numbers between the column descriptions.

Left margin: Detail name 8
4

A: First quarter 6
4

B: Second quarter 6
4

C: Third quarter 6
4

D: Fourth quarter 6
4

E: 1991 average 6
4

F: 1990 average 6
4

G: Change 4 (two decimals)

■ Add the type of each column to the list. If it's a calculated column, include the formula.

Left margin: Detail name 8
4

A: First quarter 6 numeric
4

B: Second quarter 6 numeric
4

C: Third quarter 6 numeric
4

D: Fourth quarter 6 numeric
4

E: 1991 average 6 calculated (A+B+C+D)/4
4

F: 1990 average 6 numeric
4

G: Change 4 (two decimals) calculated (E-F)/F

■ Calculate the space required by adding all of the column widths and the spaces between columns, then adding the margins.

If the table is small enough to fit across your standard form, then just set the margins and tab stops and enter the data.

However, our table takes up to 76 characters. If we use a 10-pitch typeface (10 characters per inch) this would be in addition to the 10-character right and left margins, for a total of 96. On standard 8 1/2" by 11" paper, this is 96 characters, or 9.6", which is longer than the page.

If you have a wide-carriage printer, just set the margins and select the proper wide form. With a laser printer, use a landscape orientation and the appropriate form.

If you have a dot matrix printer, or want to use portrait orientation on a laser printer, then you have two options. You could set margins of about 1/2 inch or select a smaller font. Changing margins may seem easier but may also create an unattractive page. However, a smaller font creates complications when you're setting tab stops for the columns.

Tab stops are set across the page at inch positions, not character positions. So to properly align the columns you have to know the pitch of your typeface and convert the character spacing into inch positions on the tab scale line.

As an example, let's try to use a small type size (twelve characters per inch) on standard 8 1/2" by 11" paper, keeping 1-inch left and right margins. Your own small type may be different, so this procedure may not work the same for you.

■ Start by adding the character positions where the tab stops should be set. If the numeric columns will not show decimal places, place the tab stop in the first space between each column. (For this step, you could draw a sample of the chart on graph paper and actually count the number of blocks.) If you get confused, it's better to leave a few extra spaces than not enough.

Left margin: Detail name 8		tab stop: none
4		
A: First quarter 6 numeric		30
4		
B: Second quarter 6 numeric		40
4		
C: Third quarter 6 numeric		50
4		

D: Fourth quarter 6 numeric   60
    4

E: 1988 average 6 calculated (A+B+C+D)/4   70
    4

F: 1987 average 6 numeric   80
    4

G: Change 4 (two decimals) calculated (E-F)/F   86

■ Now divide by 12 (the pitch) to convert the character positions to inch positions. Round off the measurements and add them to the chart.

Left margin: Detail name 8   tab stop: none
    4

A: First quarter 6 numeric   30 2.5
    4

B: Second quarter 6 numeric   40 3.3
    4

C: Third quarter 6 numeric   50 4.2
    4

D: Fourth quarter 6 numeric   60 5.0
    4

E: 1988 average 6 calculated (A+B+C+D)/4   70 5.8
    4

F: 1987 average 6 numeric   80 6.7
    4

G: Change 4 (two decimals) calculated (E-F)/F   86 7.2

Now that these calculations are completed, it's time to begin entering the spreadsheet.

■ SETTING UP THE SPREADSHEET

The next stage of creating a complicated spreadsheet involves entering any preliminary text, setting margins and tab stops, and defining the types of columns.

Our sample spreadsheet has two types of columns: numeric (columns A, B, C, D, and F), and calculated (columns E and G). The default column type is numeric, so we only need to define the calculated columns. This is done through the Math Definition menu, shown in Figure 19.7.

The column letters are listed across the top of this menu. The lines that follow indicate the type of column to be used, how negative calculated numbers will be displayed (the default setting is to display them in parentheses), and the number of decimal places. The types of columns are indicated with numbers: 0 for Calculation, 1 for Text, 2 for Numeric, and 3 for Total. (Total columns hold the subtotals, totals, and grand totals of the columns to the left.) To change a column from the default numeric to another type, move the cursor under the appropriate column letter and enter the corresponding number.

Although we've already planned the column types and spacing, we have not considered the spacing for the column headings. The most efficient method is to leave an extra line before changing the tab stops. After we enter the spreadsheet itself, we'll move the cursor to that extra line and add the headings.

Now let's do the preliminary work.

1. If necessary, start WordPerfect.

2. Type the text that precedes the spreadsheet, using the default settings.

Quarterly Report

This past year was marked by an aggressive marketing campaign combined with cost-saving programs in every

```
Math Definition            Use arrow keys to position cursor

Columns                    A B C D E F G H I J K L M N O P Q R S T U V W X

Type                       2 2 2 2 2 2 2 2 2 2 2 2 2 2 2 2 2 2 2 2 2 2 2 2

Negative Numbers           ( ( ( ( ( ( ( ( ( ( ( ( ( ( ( ( ( ( ( ( ( ( ( (

Number of Digits to        2 2 2 2 2 2 2 2 2 2 2 2 2 2 2 2 2 2 2 2 2 2 2 2
  the Right (0-4)

Calculation     1
  Formulas      2
                3
                4

Type of Column:
     0 = Calculation    1 = Text      2 = Numeric    3 = Total

Negative Numbers
     ( = Parentheses (50.00)          - = Minus Sign  -50.00


Press Exit when done
```

■**FIGURE 19.7:** *The Math Definition menu*

aspect of the corporation. The following chart illustrates the overall operating statistics for 1991 and presents a comparison with fiscal 1990.

3. Press Return twice.

4. Press Ctrl-F8 1 4 to select small characters for the table.

5. Press Shift-F8 1 8 to reset the tab stops.

6. Press Ctrl-End to delete all the default tab stops.

7. Set the tab stops that we calculated and added to our list. Press Return after typing each of the following numbers:

    2.5
    3.3
    4.2
    5
    5.8
    6.7
    7.2

8. Press F7 twice to return to the document.

9. Press Return five times to leave several blank lines for the column headings to be added later.

Warning
Step 10: Users
of version 5.1
should press Alt-
F7 3 3.

10. Press Alt-F7 2 to display the Math Definition menu.

11. Press → four times to reach column E.

12. Press **0**. The cursor moves next to the Calculation Formulas option, and *E* appears next to the first formula.

13. Column E will contain the average of the four quarters of the fiscal year. This is computed by adding the four quarters and dividing the sum by four. Thus, the formula you should type now is **(A+B+C+D)/4**. Note that spaces are not allowed in formulas. The letters represent the columns in the table, and the parentheses are critical here. WordPerfect's order of calculations is like that of most computer math: divisions and multiplications first, then any additions and subtractions. If the formula were written as *A+B+C+D/4,* the program would first calculate D/4, then add the values of columns A, B, and C. The parentheses change this order. WordPerfect will first compute the value of the formula inside the parentheses and then

continue. (You can have more than one set of parentheses in a formula, but they cannot be nested within each other.)

14. Press Return. The cursor returns to the Type option for the next column.

15. Press → once to place the cursor on column G, then press **0** to enter a second formula. The cursor moves to the formula area.

16. Type **(E-F)/F** and press Return.

17. Press ↓ twice, then press ← seven times to place the cursor on the Number of Digits to the Right option under column A. The default number of digits to the right of the decimal point is two. In our spreadsheet, every column except G should be formatted without decimal places. Press **0** six times to make this change. Figure 19.8 shows the completed Math Definition menu.

18. Press F7. The code [Math Def] will be inserted into the text.

19. Press **1** to turn on the Math function. Note that we turned on the Math function only after leaving extra lines for the column headings. This way, headings such as *1990* will not be added into the column totals.

20. Press F10, type **REPORT**, and press Return to save the document.

The spreadsheet format is now set.

```
Math Definition          Use arrow keys to position cursor

Columns                  A B C D E F G H I J K L M N O P Q R S T U V W X

Type                     2 2 2 2 Ø 2 Ø 2 2 2 2 2 2 2 2 2 2 2 2 2 2 2 2 2

Negative Numbers         ( ( ( ( ( ( ( ( ( ( ( ( ( ( ( ( ( ( ( ( ( ( ( (

Number of Digits to      Ø Ø Ø Ø Ø Ø 2 2 2 2 2 2 2 2 2 2 2 2 2 2 2 2 2 2
  the Right (Ø-4)

Calculation   1    E     (A+B+C+D)/4
  Formulas    2    G     (E-F)/F
              3
              4

Type of Column:
      Ø = Calculation   1 = Text    2 = Numeric    3 = Total

Negative Numbers
      ( = Parentheses (5Ø.ØØ)       - = Minus Sign  -5Ø.ØØ


Press Exit when done
```

■FIGURE 19.8: *The completed Math Definition menu*

ENTERING THE SPREADSHEET

Now we're finally ready to type the spreadsheet. Follow these steps:

1. You should still be in WordPerfect with the prepared document on the screen. If not, start WordPerfect and retrieve the REPORT document. Press Home Home ↓ to reach the end of the document.

2. Type **Income** then press Return twice.

3. Type **Sales**.

4. Enter the numbers in columns A through D. Press Tab before each entry.

    65,000
    60,000
    55,000
    75,000

5. Press Tab to reach column E, the first calculated column. An exclamation point (!) appears in that column. The ! indicates that a value will be computed when the Calculate option is selected. Just like Columnar Math operators, this symbol will appear on the screen, but it will not be printed. Just keep in mind that, unlike the other operators, the ! is inserted for you automatically; you do not have to type it yourself.

6. Press Tab to reach column F, and type **62,000**. The columns now extend far to the right of the text above. When printed, however, the compressed-character spreadsheet will be under the text.

7. Press Tab to reach column G, the second calculated column. Another ! will appear at that location.

8. Press Return.

9. Type the label and the first four numeric columns, pressing Tab before each column.

    Rental
    5,000
    5,500
    6,000
    4,500

10. Press Tab to display the ! in column E.

11. Press Tab, then type **4,000**.

12. Press Tab to display the ! in column G, then press Return. Figure 19.9 shows how your screen should look at this point. This figure was created for a laser printer with a proportionally spaced font. With this font, more characters will fit in each line than will appear on the screen, so the text has scrolled off the right edge.

13. Type **Total** to begin the subtotal line.

14. For columns A through D, press Tab, then type **+**.

15. Press Tab to display the ! in column E.

16. Press Tab, then type **+**.

17. Press Tab to display the !, then press Return. We didn't need to enter + to compute the sums of columns F and G because the formulas will calculate the same figure.

18. Press Return to add an extra line between the Income and Expenses sections.

19. Type **Expenses** then press Return twice. Since formulas cannot be used for columns, how will we compute the net figure at the end of the spreadsheet? This figure should be the total income minus the total expenses. The solution is to enter all expense figures as negative numbers using the N operator.

20. Enter the first Expenses row. After you enter the label *Salaries,* press Tab to enter each column.

```
                      Quarterly Report
          This past year was marked by an aggressive marketing campaign
       combined with cost-saving programs in every aspect of the
       corporation. The following chart illustrates the overall operating
       statistics for 1990 and presents a comparison with fiscal 1991.




       Income

       Sales    65,000  60,000   55,000 75,000       !   62,000   !
       Rental    5,000   5,500    6,000  4,500       !    4,000   !




       Math                                  Doc 1 Pg 1 Ln 3.67" Pos 1"
```

■**FIGURE 19.9:** *The spreadsheet after the second row has been entered*

Salaries
N22,000
N22,000
N24,000
N24,000

On some systems with version 5.0, you'll notice that there are no spaces between the Salaries label and the number following it. We'll take care of this in a moment.

21. Press Tab to display the ! in column E.

22. Press Tab, then type **N21,000**.

23. Press Tab to display the ! in column G, then press Return.

    While your spacing may not appear correctly on the screen, it will when printed. That's caused by the difference between the character pitch when printed and when displayed on the screen. Remember that the tab stops were set according to a typeface that prints 12 characters per inch. But the text on the screen is in 10 pitch. You could leave the screen like this and continue typing or change the displayed screen to adjust for the pitch difference. Let's change the display before continuing.

24. Press Shift-F8 3 to see the Format Document menu.

25. Press **1** for the Display Pitch option. The cursor moves to the Automatic prompt.

26. Press **N** for No. The cursor moves to the Width prompt. The width measurement determines the amount of screen space that represents each character on the printed document. The default is .1", for a standard 10-pitch font.

    By making the width smaller, you're telling WordPerfect that each space on the screen represents a smaller space on the paper. This will also spread out your line horizontally on the screen, simulating the spacing on the printout.

27. Type **.08** then press Return three times. Your lines are now spaced so the columns do not run together (Figure 19.10).

28. Enter the next row, pressing Tab between entries.

Supplies
N500
N450

N350
N400

29. Press Tab to display the ! in column E.

30. Press Tab, then type **N375**.

31. Press Tab to display the ! in column G, then press Return.

32. Type **Total** to begin the subtotal line.

33. For columns A through D, press Tab, then type +.

34. Press Tab to display the !.

35. Press Tab, then type +.

36. Press Tab to display the !, then press Return.

37. Press Return to insert a blank line.

38. Type **Net** to begin the final row.

39. For columns A through D, press Tab, then type =.

40. Press Tab to display the !.

41. Press Tab, then type =.

42. Press Tab to display the !, then press Return.

43. Press Alt-F7 2 to calculate the values. The message

Warning
Step 43: Users of version 5.1 should press Alt-F7 3 4.

```
                              Quarterly Report

              This past year was marked by an aggressive marketing campaign
          combined with cost-saving programs in every aspect of the
          corporation. The following chart illustrates the overall operating
          statistics for 1990 and presents a comparison with fiscal 1991.




          Income

          Sales      65,000    60,000    55,000    75,000        !      62,000     !
          Rental      5,000     5,500     6,000     4,500        !       4,000     !
          Total         +         +         +         +          !         +       !

          Expenses
          Salaries   N22,000   N22,000   N24,000   N24,000       !     N21,000     !




          Math                                    Doc 1 Pg 1 Ln 4.33" Pos 1"
```

■**FIGURE 19.10:** *The screen adjusted for the 12-pitch font*

Please Wait

appears for a few seconds while WordPerfect performs the calculations. Then your screen should look like Figure 19.11.

There are still a few final steps. We must turn off the Math function, reset the default values, and complete the text. We must also add the column headings and delete the parentheses around the calculated negative numbers.

Warning

Step 44: Users of version 5.1 should press Alt-F7 3 2.

44. Press Alt-F7 1 to turn off the Math function.

45. Press Ctrl-F8 3 to select the normal font.

46. Press Shift-F8 1 8 to select the Tab Set form.

47. Press Ctrl-End to delete the custom tab stops.

48. Type **0.0,.5** to reset the default tab stops.

49. Press F7 twice to return to the document.

50. Type the closing paragraph.

   We hope you find this information useful. Please do not hesitate to contact us with any comments or questions.

51. Press the ↑ key to move the cursor back through the table. When you're in the table, the word MATH appears in the status line. Press ↑ until the

```
Sales      65,000    60,000    55,000    75,000    63,750!    62,000    0.
Rental      5,000     5,500     6,000     4,500     5,250!     4,000    0.
Total      70,000+   65,500+   61,000+   79,500+   69,000!    66,000+   0.

Expenses
Salaries  N22,000   N22,000   N24,000   N24,000   (23,000)!  N21,000    0.
Supplies     N500      N450      N350      N400      (425)!     N375    0.
Total     (22,500)+ (22,450)+ (24,350)+ (24,400)+ (23,425)!  (21,375)+  0.

Net        47,500=   43,050=   36,650=   55,100=   45,575!    44,625=   0.
```

```
Math                                        Doc 1 Pg 1 Ln 5" Pos 1"
```

■**FIGURE 19.11:**   *The calculated spreadsheet (the operators remain on the screen but will not be printed)*

word MATH disappears, then press ↑ twice more. This is within the area containing the new margins and tab stops but not the math.

If you tried to type the headings with Math on, you wouldn't be able to type the letter N without WordPerfect taking it as the negative operator.

52. Enter the following column headings. Use Ctrl-F6 to position the cursor at a correct location, then enter the heading.

    Quarters
    First Second Third Fourth 1991 1990 Change

53. Press ↓ then type the two entries in the second row of headings.

    Average Average

54. Use Replace to delete the parentheses surrounding the negative calculated numbers, making them consistent with the numbers you entered.

    a. Press Home Home ↑.

    b. Press Alt-F2 Return for an unconfirmed replacement.

    c. Press (F2 F2.

    d. Press Home Home ↑.

    e. Press Alt-F2 Return.

    f. Press) F2 F2.

55. Press Shift-F7 1 if you want to print the document.

56. Press F7 Y Return Y Y to save the document and exit WordPerfect.

Using just a word processing program, we now have a very informative document that includes a spreadsheet.

SPECIAL OPERATORS

WordPerfect also offers several special operators for computing the totals and averages of rows. You can use these built-in operators instead of writing your own formulas. They are intended for use by themselves, without any other computations in the same formula.

Warning
Users of ver-
sion 5.1 should
press Alt-F7 3 3.

To use a special operator, press Alt-F7 2 to display the Math Definition menu, select type 0 for the column that will use it, then enter one of the following operators, by itself, next to the Calculation Formulas option:

+   Calculates the total of all numeric figures in the row

+/   Calculates the average of all numeric figures in the row

=   Calculates the total of all figures in the row that are in Total columns

=/   Calculates the average of all figures in the row that are in Total columns

For example, if you wanted column E of your spreadsheet to use the total operator to display the sum of all numeric columns, and column F to use the average operator to compute the average of those same columns, the formula area of the Math Definition menu would look like this:

```
Calculation      1 E +
Formulas         2 F +/
                 3
                 4
```

Why didn't we use the average operator +/ in the application above instead of the formula (A+B+C+D)/4? Because the average operator (just like the row total operator +) calculates the value using all numeric columns in the table, not just those to the left. In our spreadsheet, we had the additional numeric column F, which we did not want to be included in the calculation of the average.

The special operators ignore calculated and text columns in their computations. They are very useful when you want the total or average of all the numeric columns in your spreadsheet, including those to the left and right of the operator.

■   LIMITED CALCULATIONS

While a column cannot have more than one formula, you don't have to use that formula in every row of the column. If you don't want a row to be calculated, just delete the ! operator before selecting the Calculation option. You can manually insert some other figure or text in place of the deleted ! operator.

■ CONSTRUCTING WHAT-IF PROBLEMS

The ability to recalculate as figures change makes spreadsheets powerful planning and projecting tools. Although WordPerfect does not recalculate automatically, you can have it perform the same action by pressing Alt-F7 2 while the Math function is turned on. This works well for simple what-if problems that only require some of the values in numeric columns to change.

Warning
Users of version 5.1 should press Alt-F7 3 4.

But some what-if problems also use a program's ability to reference a specific cell in a number of formulas. Changing that one cell could result in changes throughout the spreadsheet.

WordPerfect does not use the cell-reference method, but you can obtain the same results by editing a formula. For example, suppose that a sales manager has a WordPerfect spreadsheet with each salesperson's sales in column A and the base pay in column B. She uses the formula *A*.1* in column C to calculate commissions and the formula *C+B* in column D to calculate total salary. To see what happens if commissions are increased to 12 percent, she could change the formula in column C to *A*.12* and then recalculate the spreadsheet.

■ EDITING FORMULAS

Here's the procedure for changing formulas:

1. Press Home Home ↑ to reach the start of the document.

2. Press F2 to display the Search prompt.

Warning
Step 3: Users of version 5.1 should press Alt-F7 3 1.

3. Press Alt-F7 1 to search for Math Definition codes.

4. Press F2 to start the search. The cursor will move to the space following the Math Definition code, like this:

   [Math Def][Math On]

Warning
Step 5: Users of version 5.1 should press Alt-F7 3 3.

5. Press Alt-F7 2 to display the Math Definition menu.

6. Move the cursor to the column that you want to edit. If it is already a calculated column, its type will be 0.

7. Press **0**. The cursor will move to the formula area.

8. Revise the formula using standard editing techniques, then press Return.

9. Press F7 to set the new definition.

Although there are actually two definition codes now in place, the edited one will take effect during recalculation. To delete the original code, press Alt-F3 to reveal the codes, press ← twice, and then press Del. You can use the same procedure to add or change any of the column definitions.

VERSION 5.1 FEATURES

MATH PROMPT LINES

Press Alt-F7 3 to select Math from the prompt line, or select **Layout Math**, for the options

> Math: 1 On; 2 Off; 3 Define; 4 Calculate: 0

Press **1** or **o** to turn on the Math function, **2** or **f** to turn it off, **3** or **d** to define math columns, or **4** or **c** to calculate math columns you've entered.

CREATING SPREADSHEETS AS TABLES

All of the math operators and functions discussed in this chapter apply to version 5.1. But if you're creating a document that relies heavily on math, one that resembles a spreadsheet in format, or one that requires more than four formulas, then you should create it as a table.

In earlier chapters you learned how easy it is to use the Table Editor. You created tables, inserting headings and numbers in various cells.

The Math feature of the Table Editor provides more familiar spreadsheet-like functions, including the ability to perform math using cell references. In this section, let's create the spreadsheet shown in Figure 19.12. However, remember that tables do not necessarily have to have lines separating cells. So procedures similar to the ones in this section can be used to create letters, invoices, and any type of document that requires mathematical operations (Figure 19.13).

Follow these steps to create the spreadsheet.

1. Press Alt-F7 2 1, or select **Layout Tables Create** to display the Number of Columns prompt.

2. Type **6** and press Return to display the Number of Rows prompt.

3. Type **10**, the number of rows required to hold the table title and column headings along with the data, and press Return. The Table Editor appears.

Before entering the data and mathematical formulas, let's format the first two rows. The cursor is in cell A1.

4. Combine the cells in row 1.

Sales Points Per Period					
Name	Points				
	1	2	3	Total	Average
Joan Emery	982	346	456	1,784.00	594.67
Pete Fulton	433	23	45	501.00	167.00
Adam Chesin	543	34	34	611.00	203.67
Nancy Riser	765	765	344	1,874.00	624.67
Totals	2,723.00	1,168.00	879.00	4,770.00	
Averages	680.75	292.00	219.75	1,192.50	

■**FIGURE 19.12:** *Spreadsheet created as a table*

Siravo Hobby and Craft Company 456 Tudar Drive Philadelphia, PA 19116				
TO: William Watson 102 Flagstaff Lane Norwalk, NJ 08751			Date: 4/6/91	
			Invoice #: 19865	
Net: 30 days				
Item	Ordered	Shipped	Price	Amount
Balsa 1 x 1 x 2	10	10	.50	5.00
Balsa 2 x 2 x 2	20	10	.60	18.00
Balsa 1 x 4 x 2	10	10	1.20	12.00
Paint Red	4	4	4.50	18.00
Paint Blue	4	4	4.00	16.00
Paint White	4	4	4.50	16.00
		Subtotal		87.00
		Sales Tax 6%		5.22
		Less Credit		-5.00
		Invoice Total		87.22

■**FIGURE 19.13:** *Invoice created as a table*

    a. Press Alt-F4 to turn on the Block mode.

    b. Press → five times to select the entire first row.

    c. Press **7** or **j**, then **y**.

5. Combine the last five cells in the second row.

    a. Place the cursor in cell B2.

    b. Press Alt-F4 to turn on the Block mode.

    c. Press → four times.

    d. Press **7** or **j**, then **y**.

6. Press F7 to return to the document.

7. Enter the Table title.

    a. Place the cursor in cell A1.

    b. Press Shift-F6, or select **L**ayout **A**lign Center.

    c. Type **Sales Points Per Period**

8. Enter the column headings in the second row.

    a. Press ↓ to place the cursor in cell B1.

    b. Type **Name**

    c. Press Tab to reach cell B2.

    d. Type **Points**

9. Enter the column headings in the third row.

    a. Press ↓ to place the cursor in cell B3.

    b. Press Shift-F6, or select **L**ayout **A**lign Center.

    c. Type **1**

    d. Press Tab to reach cell C3.

    e. Press Shift-F6, or select **L**ayout **A**lign Center.

    f. Type **2**

    g. Press Tab to reach cell D3.

    h. Press Shift-F6, or select **L**ayout **A**lign Center.

    i. Type **3**

    j. Press Tab to reach cell E3.

    k. Press Shift-F6, or select **L**ayout **A**lign **C**enter.

    l. Type **Total**

   m. Press Tab to reach cell F3.

    n. Press Shift-F6, or select **L**ayout **A**lign **C**enter.

    o. Type **Average**

10. Enter the names and labels in the the first column.

    a. Press → to reach cell A4.

    b. Type **Joan Emery**. The name was too long for the column, so it wrapped to the next line, expanding the cell height. We'll widen the first column later on in the Table Editor.

    c. Press ↓ to reach cell A5.

    d. Type **Pete Fulton**

    e. Press ↓ to reach cell A6.

    f. Type **Adam Chesin**

    g. Press ↓ to reach cell A7.

    h. Type **Nancy Riser**

    i. Press ↓ twice to reach cell A9.

    j. Type **Totals**

    k. Press ↓ to reach cell A10.

    l. Type **Averages**. Figure 19.14 shows the table at this point.

11. Press Alt-F7 or select **L**ayout **T**ables **E**dit to enter the Table Editor. Expand the first column so each name fits on one line. The cursor should be in cell A10.

12. Press Ctrl-→ three times.

   You could have entered the numbers at the same time as the titles, headings, and labels, then entered the Table Editor to format cells and add formulas. Instead, we'll enter all of the formulas then exit the Table Editor to insert the numbers. This way you'll see how the entire table can be calculated at one time.

13. Place the cursor in cell E4.

14. Press **5** or **m** to display the prompt line

    Math: 1 Calculate; 2 Formula; 3 Copy; 4 +; 5 =; 6 *:0

As with math functions outside of tables, the +, = and * operators perform math on columns: + computes the subtotal, = the total, and * the grand total. While row operators are available to compute totals and averages across rows using math columns, they cannot be used inside tables. So we must add formulas for computing the total and average number of points in each row.

15. Press **2** or **f** to display the prompt line

    Enter formula:

16. Type **B4+C4+D4**, then press Return. WordPerfect performs the calculation and inserts the total—now zero—in the cell. The cell's formula is shown on the left side of the status line.

17. Insert the formula for the average in cell F4.

    a. Press → to reach the cell.

    b. Press **5** or **m**.

    c. Press **2** or **f**.

    d. Type **E4/3**

    e. Press Return.

Sales Points Per Period					
Name	Points				
	1	2	3	Total	Average
Joan Emery					
Pete Fulton					
Adam Chesin					
Nancy Riser					
Totals					
Averages					

Cell A1Ø Doc 1 Pg 1 Ln 4.16" Pos 1.92"

■**FIGURE 19.14:**   *Title and headings inserted in table*

The totals and averages for the other rows require similar formulas. The formulas are basically repeated down the column with only the row number changing. Each total is a sum of the three cells before it:

Cell	Contents
E4	B4+C4+D4
E5	B5+C5+D5
E6	B6+C6+D6
E7	B7+C7+D7

Each average is the total divided by three:

Cell	Contents
F4	E4/3
F5	E5/3
F6	E6/3
F7	E7/3

Since each formula only changes by the row references, we can copy the formula down the table. When you copy a formula down a column, the row referenced adjusts automatically. When you copy a formula across a row, the column referenced adjusts automatically. This is called *relative* copying.

You can copy the formula two ways—using the Ctrl-F4 function key or through the math options. Let's use the math option. The cursor should still be in cell F4.

18. Press **5** or **m**, then **3** or **p** to select Copy and display the prompt line

    Copy Formula To: 1 Cell; 2 Down; 3 Right: 0

19. Copy the formula:

    a. To copy the formula to an individual cell, press **1** or **c**, move the cursor to the destination cell, then press Return.

    b. To copy the formula down a column, press **2** or **d**.

    c. Press **3** or **r** to copy the formula to cells on the right.

20. Press **2** or **d** to see the prompt

    Number of times to copy formula: 1

21. Press **3**, then Return. The formula E4/3 is copied to the next three cells but adjusted to E5/3, E6/3, and E7/3.

22. Copy the total formula in the same way.

    a. Place the cursor in cell E4.

    b. Press 5 3 2 (Math Copy Down).

    c. Press **3**, then Return. The formula B4+C4+D4 is copied to the next three cells but adjusted to B5+C5+D5, B6+C6+D6, and B7+C7+D7.

The next formulas needed are the totals and averages of the columns. For the totals, we can use the + column operator.

23. Place the cursor in cell B9.

24. Press **5** or **M**, then **4** or **+**. This operator inserts the total of all numeric cells in the column.

25. Press 5 3 3 3 Return to copy the formula across the row, to the next three cells. While no cell references are involved, it is faster to copy the + operator than it is to enter it three more times.

26. Enter the formula for averages in cell B10.

    a. Place the cursor in cell B10.

    b. Press 5 2.

    c. Type B9/4

    d. Press Return.

27. Press 5 3 3 3 Return to copy the formula across the row, to the next three cells.

28. Press F7 to exit the Table Editor.

When the cursor is in a cell that contains a formula, the formula is shown on the status line. This is WordPerfect's way of differentiating between the cell's contents—the formula—and its value—the currently calculated and displayed results.

29. Enter the numbers in the following cells:

Cell	Contents
B4	982
C4	346
D4	456
B5	433
C5	23
D5	45
B6	543
C6	34
D6	34
B7	765
C7	765
D7	344

Now calculate the totals and averages.

30. Press Alt-F7, or select **L**ayout **T**ables Edit.

31. Press 5 1 (Math Calculate). The message *Please wait* appears on the bottom of the screen while WordPerfect calculates all of the formulas in the table.

    Calculated numbers appear with two decimal places, which can be adjusted using the # of Digits option on the Format Column prompt line.

32. Finally, format the numbers so they are decimal-aligned.

    a. Place the cursor in cell B4.

    b. Press Alt-F4.

    c. Press ↓ six times to reach cell B10.

    d. Press 2 1 3 5 (Format Cell Justify Decimal Align).

    e. Press → to place the cursor in cell C10.

    f. Press Alt-F4.

g. Press ↑ six times to reach cell C4.

h. Press 2 1 3 5 (Format Cell Justify Decimal Align).

i. Press → to place the cursor in cell D4.

j. Press Alt-F4.

k. Press ↓ six times to reach cell D10.

l. Press 2 1 3 5 (Format Cell Justify Decimal Align).

m. Press → to place the cursor in cell E10.

n. Press Alt-F4.

o. Press ↑ six times to reach cell E4.

p. Press 2 1 3 5 (Format Cell Justify Decimal Align).

q. Press → to place the cursor in cell F4.

r. Press Alt-F4.

s. Press ↓ three times to reach cell F7.

t. Press 2 1 3 5 (Format Cell Justify Decimal Align).

33. Press F7 to exit the Table Editor.

34. Press Shift-F7 1 or select **F**ile **P**rint **F**ull Document.

Tips with Formulas   Here are some tips for using formulas in tables:

- Formulas need not contain cell references. You can enter a mathematical equation directly, such as 467 * 12 / 3, then display the results by selecting Math Calculate.

- As a shortcut, omit row numbers when entering formulas—WordPerfect assumes you're referencing the row of the current cell. For example, the formula B4+C4+D4 in row 4 could have been entered as B+C+D.

- Deleting calculated numbers from a cell outside of the Table Editor does not delete the formula. Delete a formula from within the Table Editor. Position the cursor in the cell, press 5 2 (Math Formula) Del until you erase the formula at the prompt, then Return. Any calculated numbers will still appear in the cell, so press F7 to exit the Table Editor, then press Del to delete the numbers.

- To copy a formula from one cell to another without changing row or column references, often called an absolute copy, enter the cell reference (such as E10) as the formula.

- When you enter a formula, only that cell is calculated. To recalculate the entire table, press 5 2 (Math Calculate).

- After calculating the table, make sure cells are wide enough to store the results in one line.

- Formulas are calculated from left to right so *100+100+100/3* results in 100. Use parentheses to change the order of operations.

- Formulas may not adjust correctly when you insert or delete rows and columns. After inserting or deleting, check any formulas that may no longer be accurate. For example, if we added a new Column B (between the names and period 1) in our sample table, the formulas would correctly change to C4+D4+E4. However, if you insert a new Column C (between Period 1 and Period 2), perhaps to add some notation or comment, the formula would also change to C4+D4+E4 even though it should be B4+D4+E4.

- Be careful referencing a cell containing words, not numbers, in a formula. In some cases, the cell will be ignored or treated as a zero. Other times, particularly if it used as a divisor, questions marks will appear in the referencing cell.

SPREADSHEET PUBLISHING

While WordPerfect has a wide range of font and graphic commands to produce high-quality tables, its mathematical functions are limited compared to full-featured programs such as Lotus 1-2-3. By combining the best features of both programs, however, you can create professionally published documents including text, tables, and graphics (Figure 19.15).

In addition to the capability of importing charts, such as Lotus PIC files, into graphic boxes, WordPerfect lets you merge spreadsheets directly into the Table Editor where they can be edited and formatted. Spreadsheets can be merged from Lotus 1-2-3, Excel, and PlanPerfect.

There are two ways to merge spreadsheets—by importing and by linking. When you *import* a spreadsheet, a copy of it is placed in the document, much like retrieving one document into another. But when you *link* a spreadsheet, a special code is inserted that lets you update the document at any time with the speadsheet's latest version.

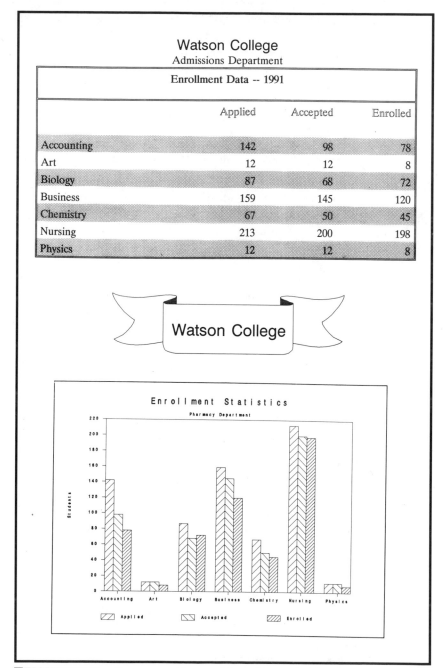

■FIGURE 19.15:   *Document with spreadsheet chart and table*

In both cases, WordPerfect calculates any formulas before merging the spreadsheet.

To merge a spreadsheet file, press Ctrl-F5 5, or select **F**ile **T**ext **In Sp**readsheet to see the options

Spreadsheet: 1 Import; 2 Create Link; 3 Edit Link; 4 Link
Options:0

Importing Spreadsheets   To import the spreadsheet, press **1** or **I** from the prompt line to see the Spreadsheet Import menu (Figure 19.16). After selecting the options from the menu, you must press **4** or **P** to actually import the file.

Press **1** or **f** to enter the filename.

Press **2** or **r** to designate the range of the spreadsheet you want to import. You can enter the range by designating starting and ending cells (such as A1..D10 or A1:D10) or press F5 to see a list of named ranges, if any exist for that spreadsheet.

Press **3** or **t** to specify whether to import the spreadsheet as a WordPerfect table or as plain text.

Press **4** or **p** to import the named file.

You can import spreadsheets up to 32 columns into tables, or 20 columns as text.

```
Spreadsheet: Import
     1 - Filename
     2 - Range
     3 - Type                        Table
     4 - Perform Import




     Selection: 0
```

■**FIGURE 19.16:**   *Spreadsheet Import menu*

When you import a spreadsheet as a table, WordPerfect creates a table with the appropriate number of rows and columns. You can then enter the Table Editor to format cells.

As an alternative, you can create and format the table first, then place the cursor in cell A1 and import the spreadsheet. Entries in the spreadsheet will fill in table cells. No matter what the range specified in the Import menu, however, WordPerfect will only import enough cells to fill in the table.

Delete an imported spreadsheet as you would any regular text.

Linking Spreadsheets   To link a spreadsheet, press **2** or **c** from the prompt line to see the Spreadsheet Create Link menu that contains similar options as in Figure 19.16. Select from the menu, then press **4** or **P** to create the link.

The spreadsheet is merged into the document exactly as when imported, except Link and Link End codes are inserted as comments (Figure 19.17). These codes are used for updating the link, retrieving the current version of the spreadsheet file at a later time.

To update the link, press Ctrl-F5 5 4, or select **F**ile **T**ext **I**n **Sp**readsheet **L**ink Options, to display the Link Options menu (Figure 19.18). The options are:

Update on Retrieve   Set this option at *Yes* to automatically update the link whenever you recall the document. Use this option if you are making frequent changes to the spreadsheet.

	1989	1990	1991
Applied	512	592	549
Accepted	462	465	470
Enrolled	397	420	388

Link: B:\ENROLL.WK1   <Spreadsheet>

Link End

Doc 1 Pg 1 Ln 1" Pos 1"

■**FIGURE 19.17:**   *Link and End Link codes*

Show Link Codes	Make the Link and Link End comments invisible.
Update All Links	Retrieve the current version of all spreadsheets linked with the document.

To delete the spreadsheet from the document, delete the Link or End Link code.

If you want to change any of the Link menu options, press Ctrl-F5 5 3, or select **F**ile **T**ext **I**n **Sp**readsheet **E**dit Link, to display the Link menu. Change the file name, range, or type, then press **4** or **p**.

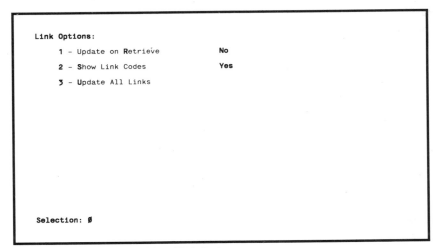

```
Link Options:
    1 - Update on Retrieve          No
    2 - Show Link Codes             Yes
    3 - Update All Links




    Selection: 0
```

■FIGURE 19.18: *Spreadsheet Link Options menu*

MOUSE AND MENU EQUIVALENTS

Function	Keyboard	Pull-Down Menus
Math	Alt-F7 3	Layout **M**ath
Import Spreadsheet	Ctrl-F5 5 1	**F**ile **T**ext **I**n **Sp**readsheet Import
Link Spreadsheet	Ctrl-F5 5 2	**F**ile **T**ext **I**n **Sp**readsheet Create Link

Function	Keyboard	Pull-Down Menus
Edit Link	Ctrl-F5 5 3	File Text In Spreadsheet Edit Link
Link Options	Ctrl-F5 5 4	File Text In Spreadsheet Link Options

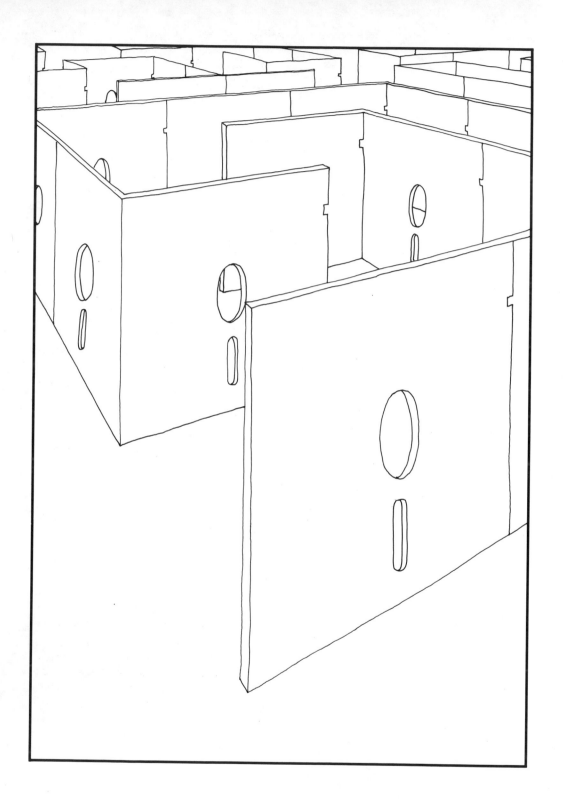

20

USING WORDPERFECT AS
A DATABASE MANAGER

To WordPerfect, a database is just another table—a listing of individual records (rows) and fields (columns)—and many of the program's database management features are the same as those for tables, but on a grander scale. This view of a database is called *relational* because every record belongs to one common group and has the same type and number of fields.

In this chapter, we will create and manipulate a typical database, and even write a menu-driven application in WordPerfect for selecting from a list of data reports. You'll also learn how to write macros using WordPerfect's macro programming language.

In the next chapter, you'll see how these same techniques can be used to produce form letters.

THE DATABASE APPROACH

The benefit of a database approach is the ease with which information is handled. A database format facilitates the tasks of data maintenance and reporting.

Data maintenance includes adding, editing, and deleting data from the database. The data maintenance tasks can be accomplished by using the standard editing techniques to change or delete records. The Search and Replace functions are also extremely useful for updating records.

Data reports provide useful information from the database, such as a list of clients, a student honor roll, or the stock on hand of a particular part. Reporting involves retrieving selected records, performing mathematical manipulations, and printing the results. Reporting is based on techniques of selection and projection.

Selection, as discussed in Chapter 12, is used to retrieve records that meet certain criteria. For example, a store manager may want a database report listing all the information about any items that need to be reordered.

Projection, on the other hand, is used to retrieve only the fields that meet the criteria. If a particular vendor went bankrupt, for example, the store manager might want a report listing only the items that the vendor supplied and the stock remaining.

WordPerfect can produce such reports, but it sets up a database differently from a specialized database manager. It creates a file containing just the data, field after field, record after record. Then merging, sorting, selection, and mathematical techniques are used to simulate the actions of a relational database. Because this function is integrated into a word processor, the database can also be used to create form letters and other assembled documents.

■ PLANNING A DATA FILE

The first step in data management is to identify which fields will comprise the record and what format each field will take. Let's use a customer file as an example in this chapter. What information would you keep on file for a customer? You would certainly list the name and address. But you can break these down even further: the customer's first and last name, street address, city, state, and zip code. The record might even include an office or box number, or some other address element, even though not every client would have one. You would also want the telephone number, perhaps a credit rating, the last date that the client made a purchase, and the total amount due. These items seem to be the minimum for a good client list.

Next you must decide on the format. Should the first and last names be together in one field? Should the entire address be one field, or should it be separated into several? You have to base these decisions on how you'll be using the data. For example, if you include both the first and last names as one field, and the entire address as another, then you could not print a report with only the last name or only the city or zip code.

It is usually a good idea to separate the address into four fields: the street number and name, the city, the state, and the zip code. This gives you the greatest flexibility. It is also good practice to set aside one additional line for other address elements, such as box numbers.

For our client list example, some thought also must be devoted to two other types of fields: telephone numbers and dates. Telephone numbers are usually entered as one field, but you may want to group clients by area code. Dates may take a little more consideration since they can be entered in so many different ways.

Dates such as *July 3, 1990* are in the proper format for letters and documents, but can they serve any other purpose? You could use the last "word" of the date as a key in the selection process. For example, the selection criterion key1 <1990 would display clients who haven't purchased anything in that year.

If that isn't useful enough, you can enter dates in a six- character format showing the year, month, and day: 900703. Now the criterion key1<900603 could identify clients who haven't ordered in 30 days. This format also allows you to sort the list by purchase date, not just year. Again, your final decision must be based on how you'll use the data.

For our sample database, we'll use the following fields:

Name (first then last)

Street address

City

State

Zip code

Telephone

Credit

Date of last order

Amount due

CREATING A DATA FILE

The only difference between entering a WordPerfect data file and typing an ordinary client list is that you must mark the end of each field and each record. The end of each field is marked by the ^R code, which is entered by pressing F9. The end of each record is shown by the ^E code, which is entered by pressing Shift-F9. In WordPerfect parlance, the data file is a *secondary merge file*.

Follow these steps to enter our sample client database:

1. Start WordPerfect.

Note
Version 5.1
merge codes
and prompt
lines are dif-
ferent than in
earlier versions,
although the
steps listed here
still apply. Fol-
low the steps,
except where
otherwise noted,
but refer to "Ver-
sion 5.1 Merge
Codes."

2. Type **Frederick Rogers** then press F9. Do not press Return. WordPerfect displays the code ^R following the name and moves the cursor to the next line. (If you press Return, you'll insert extra lines in the record.)

3. Type **431 Broad Street** then press F9. Another ^R follows this line. As you can tell by now, you must press the F9 key immediately after each field.

4. Type the following fields, pressing F9 after each one. Remember, do not press Return.

   Philadelphia
   PA
   19101
   (215) 555-7654
   500
   January 2, 1990
   45.67

Note
The appearance
of the version
5.1 screen is
slightly dif-
ferent, but the
steps listed here
still apply.

5. Press Shift-F9. With version 5.0, the prompt line changes to

   ^C; ^D; ^E; ^F; ^G; ^N; ^O; ^P; ^Q; ^S; ^T; ^U; ^V:

   These are all of the Merge codes that you can use with data files. You'll learn about most of these codes in this and the next several chapters.

6. Press **E**. The ^E code is placed after the last field to mark the end of the record, and a hard page break is inserted. The first record should look like this on your screen:

Note
With version 5.1,
throughout this
chapter, {END
FIELD}
replaces ^R,
{END
RECORD}
replaces ^E, and
{FIELD}
replaces ^F.

   Frederick Rogers^R
   431 Broad Street^R
   Philadelphia^R
   PA^R
   19101^R
   (215) 555-7654^R
   500^R
   January 2, 1990^R
   45.67^R
   ^E

   ===

7. In the same manner, enter the following record as shown. Notice that this client does not have a telephone number. However, since every record must have the same number of fields, F9 is pressed by itself as a placeholder.

```
Adam Chesin^R
231 Lockhaven Road^R
Freeport^R
NY^R
10109^R
^R
100^R
December 4, 1990^R
0^R
^E
```

8. Enter the records for two more clients.

```
Herman Gringold^R
45th Street and Osage Avenue^R
El Paso^R
TX^R
23123^R
(543) 765-0908^R
500^R
May 5, 1990^R
21.76^R
^E
Jean Kohl^R
Northwest Avenue^R
Margate^R
NJ^R
71652^R
(609) 657-8767^R
50^R
February 1, 1990^R
0^R
^E
```

9. Press F7 Y, type **LIST1**, press Return, and press **Y** to save the client list and exit WordPerfect.

DATA MAINTENANCE

Database management programs give names like *append, delete,* and *update* to data maintenance functions. WordPerfect performs these same functions using the standard editing techniques. Here's how to maintain your WordPerfect database:

- To append data—which simply means to add data to the file—recall the document and press Home Home ↓ to reach the end. Enter all of the fields for the new record, making sure to add the ^R code at the end of each field and the ^E code at the end of the record. Be sure that the new record has the same fields as the other records.

- Updating is a two-step procedure: first locate the record to be changed, then edit it. To locate a particular record, use the Search function. For example, suppose that our client Jean Kohl's telephone number has changed. Press F2 to display the Search prompt, then type *Jean Kohl.* Press F2 again. The cursor is now on that client's record. Use the deletion and insertion techniques to update the telephone number.

- You can delete records individually or in groups by using selection techniques. We'll discuss selection a little later in the chapter. Individual records can be erased with the aid of a macro, as described below.

DELETING RECORDS WITH MACROS

To delete a record, you must first locate it. For this purpose, we'll create two macros and link them together. The first macro will request the name of the person whom you wish to delete and locate that person's record in the data file. If the name is not found, the message

Not Found

will appear on the status line. If the record is found, the macro will activate the second macro, which will automatically erase the record by deleting ten lines (a successful search will place the cursor in the first line of a ten-line record).

First, start WordPerfect. Press Shift-F10, type **LIST1**, then press Return to recall the data file. Now enter the following macros.

Request Record Macro—Delete   This macro requests the name of the person to be deleted, searches the list, then calls the Erase macro.

    Ctrl-F10 Delete Return Return Home Home ↑ F2 Ctrl-PgUp
    1 Return F2 Alt-F10 Erase Return Ctrl-F10

When you pressed Ctrl-PgUp in defining this macro, you saw the prompt

1 Pause; 2 Display: 0

instead of the programming command box seen when you press Ctrl-PgUp while editing a macro. The Pause option, which you selected by pressing *1*, lets the macro stop long enough for you to enter data from the keyboard—in this case the name of the person you wish to locate. The Display option determines whether you want to display the keystrokes as they appear. When you select that option (2), you see the prompt

Display Execution? (Y/N) No

Press Return or *N* to accept the default No, or *Y* to display the keystrokes. If you press Ctrl-PgUp at other times, you might see these four choices:

1. Pause; 2 Display; 3 Assign; 4 Comment: 0

Option 3 lets you assign a value to an Alt-number variable, and option 4 allows you to add comments that are displayed when the macro is running.

Delete Record Macro—Erase   This macro deletes ten lines from the file. Note that *ten-↓* means press ↓ ten times.

Ctrl-F10 Erase Return Return Home ← Alt-F4 ten-↓ Del
Y Ctrl-F10

When you want to delete a record, press Alt-F10, type *Delete,* then press Return. The Search prompt will appear on the status line. The macro will pause (that's what the Ctrl-PgUp code does). Type the name that you want to delete, then press Return (not F2). If the search item exists, WordPerfect will locate and delete the record.

These macros are designed for our sample data file. They delete a ten-line record starting from the first line where the name is found. To use them for other data files in which the search string is in the first line of the record, press ↓ the appropriate number of times when creating the second macro. If the search string is in another line, press ↑ enough times to place the cursor in the first line. For example, suppose that you want to delete a six-line record where the search string will always be in the second line. Before highlighting the block, you must move the cursor up one line, then to the left margin. The Erase macro would be

Ctrl-F10 Erase Return Return ↑ Home ← Alt-F4 six-↓ Del
Y Ctrl-F10

When you're done entering the macros, press F7 N Y to exit WordPerfect.

■ SELECTING AND SORTING DATA FILES

You can sort and select the records in a data file independently of any report-writing function. But for most reports, these procedures are an important prelude to producing useful summaries of your data.

The same sorting and selection techniques discussed in Chapter 11 can be applied here. As with tables, the fields for the sorting and selection criteria must be defined. And, as with a paragraph sort, the sorting keys include the type, field, line, and word of the record.

In our sample data file, each field has only one line:

Field

1	Herman Gringold
2	45th Street and Osage Avenue
3	El Paso
4	TX
5	23123
6	(543) 765-0908
7	500
8	May 5, 1990
9	21.76

So to sort by zip code, for example, the key would be type n, field 5, line 1, and word 1. The last name would be type a, field 1, line 1, and word −1.

If the full name and address were one field, then the key would be different:

Field

1	Herman Gringold 45th Street and Osage Avenue El Paso, TX 23123
2	(543) 765-0908
3	500

4   May 5, 1990

5   21.76

Having the name and address as one field can expedite merging with form letters and envelopes. In this case, the key to sort by zip code would now be type n, field 1, line 3, word -1.

As an example of database sorting and selection techniques, let's create a new data file containing the records of clients who owe money, sorted alphabetically. We'll use two keys, one for sorting and the other for the selection criteria. Follow these steps:

1. Start WordPerfect.

2. Press Ctrl-F9 2 to select the Sort option and display the prompt

   Input file to sort: (Screen)

3. Type **LIST1** then press Return. The status line changes to

   Output file for sort: (Screen)

4. Press Return. The Sort by Line menu appears on the screen.

5. Press **7 1** to select a merge sort. The Sort Secondary Merge File menu appears at the bottom of the screen, as shown in Figure 20.1.

6. Press **3** to change the keys. The cursor moves to the key 1 area.

7. Press Return three times to accept the default type, field, and line.

8. Type **–1** to use the last name as the key.

9. Press Return to reach key 2.

10. Press **N** for a numeric sort. The cursor moves to the Field option.

11. Press **9** to select the ninth field as the second key.

12. Press F7 to return to the Sort menu prompt line.

13. Press **4** to choose the Selection option.

14. Type **key2>0**.

15. Press F7. The completed menu is shown in Figure 20.2.

16. Press **1** to sort and select the records. There are two clients that meet the criteria: Gringold and Rogers. They appear on the screen alphabetized by last name.

17. Press F7 Y, type **LIST2**, press Return, and press **Y** to save the new data file and exit WordPerfect.

The original file, LIST1, is the permanent database. Any databases produced by sorting and selection should be considered temporary files created for a

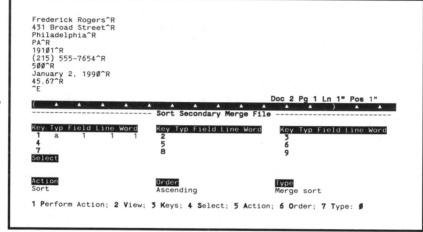

■**FIGURE 20.1:** *The Sort Secondary Merge File menu*

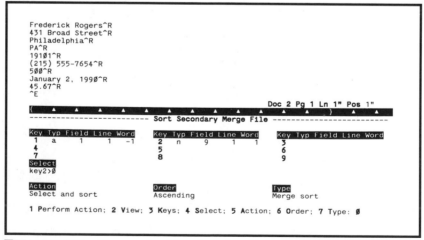

■**FIGURE 20.2:** *The completed Sort Secondary Merge File menu*

specific report or function. If you always save such files under the name LIST2, then you can use either the original or the sorted list for printing reports.

DESIGNING REPORT FORMS—THE PRIMARY FILE

The sorted and selected database is useful but not very presentable in its current format. You wouldn't distribute that document, with all of the ^R and ^E codes, at a board of directors meeting. What would be useful, however, would be neat listings, such as the one shown in Figure 20.3, and reports, such as the client profile shown in Figure 20.4.

You can design such reports in a primary file, then merge data from the secondary file. The primary file contains codes showing which fields should be included and their placement on the page. It can also include Math columns so that you can total columns or use formulas after the report has been created.

```
      Client              Last Order           Amount Due

   Frederick Rogers     January 2, 1990           45.67
   Adam Chesin          December 4, 1988          0
   Herman Gringold      May 5, 1990               21.76
   Jean Kohl            February 1, 1990          0
```

■**FIGURE 20.3:** *A client listing created from the sample database*

```
           Name: Adam Chesin
           Address: 231 Lockhaven Road
           City: Freeport
           State: NY            Zip Code: 10109

           Telephone:

           Amount Due: 0        Total Credit: 100

           Date of last order: December 4, 1990
```

■**FIGURE 20.4:** *A report created from the sample database*

As an example, let's use our LIST1 data file to prepare a client report showing the name (field 1), credit limit (field 7), amount due (field 9), and credit remaining. The credit remaining column must be calculated from fields 7 and 9. Follow these steps to create the report:

1. Start WordPerfect.

2. Press Shift-F8 1 8 to set tab stops.

3. Press Ctrl-End to delete all of the default tab stops.

Warning
With version 5.1, set tabs to absolute or subtract one inch from each of the tab stops set in this chapter.

4. Set new tab stops for three columns.

   a. Type **3.5** then press Return.

   b. Type **5** then press Return.

   c. Type **7** then press Return.

   d. Press F7 twice.

Warning
Step 5: With version 5.1, press Alt-F7 3 3.

5. Press Alt-F7 2 to display the Math Definition menu.

6. Move the cursor to column C and press **0**. The cursor moves to the formula area.

7. Type **A-B**.

8. Press Return F7 1 to turn on the Math function.

9. Press Shift-F9 to display the Merge codes.

Note
In version 5.1, the prompt reads *Enter Field:*

10. Press **F** for Field (the other codes are discussed later in this chapter and in other chapters). The prompt changes to

  Field:

11. Press **1** then press Return. The screen displays

  ^F1^

Note
With version 5.1, the Field code appears as {FIELD}1.

When the documents are merged, the first field will appear at this location on the row.

12. Press Tab. Since the Math function is on, the Alignment Character prompt appears on the status line.

13. Press Shift-F9 F 7 Return to display field 7 at this position.

14. Press Tab Shift-F9 F 9 Return to display field 9 at this position.

15. Press Tab to reach the last column. The character ! appears because we defined this as a calculated column.

16. Press Return to reach the next line. These codes will print the name, credit, amount due, and difference for the first person in the data file. Now we must instruct WordPerfect to continue this format for every record in the file.

Warning
Steps 17 and 18:
Users of version 5.1 should skip step 17 and in step 18 press Shift-F9 P to insert the {Page Off} code.

17. Press Shift-F9 N to display the ^N code on the screen. This code tells WordPerfect to get the next record.

18. Press Shift-F9 P Shift-F9 P to display two ^P codes. Your screen should look like Figure 20.5. WordPerfect will use the primary file named between the two ^P codes. But, since no file name was entered, the same primary file will be repeated for each record in the database.

19. Press F7 Y, type **REPORT1**, press Return, and press **N** to save the document and clear the screen.

You can use this procedure to design a variety of database reports. Since these reports are in the format of a table or spreadsheet, follow the same basic rules to plan them: set only the tab stops that are necessary and leave enough room for the widest entry in each column. If a column is aligned on the decimal point, set the tab stop so that there is sufficient room to the left for the longest number.

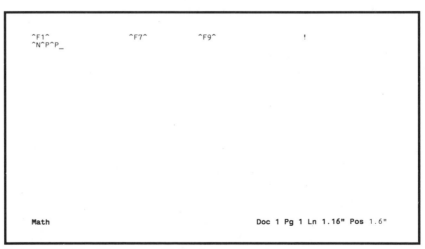

■**FIGURE 20.5:** *The primary file for the report*

PRINTING REPORTS—MERGING PRIMARY AND SECONDARY FILES

To produce our sample report, we must merge both the primary and secondary files, then complete the math operation. Follow these steps:

Note
The appearance of the version 5.1 screen is slightly different, but the steps listed here still apply.

1. Press Ctrl-F9 to display the prompt

    1 Merge; 2 Sort; 3 Sort Order: 0

2. Press **1**. The prompt changes to

    Primary file:

3. Type **REPORT1** then press Return. The prompt shows

    Secondary file:

4. Type **LIST1** (the name of the data file), then press Return. After a few seconds, the three fields appear on the screen in columns. The fourth column contains the ! operators, and the word *Math* is on the status line, as shown in Figure 20.6. Notice that nothing appeared on the screen until the entire merge operation was completed.

Warning
Step 5: Users of version 5.1 should press Alt-F7 3 4.

5. Press Alt-F7 2 to calculate the difference for the last column. Now we'll add the column headings.

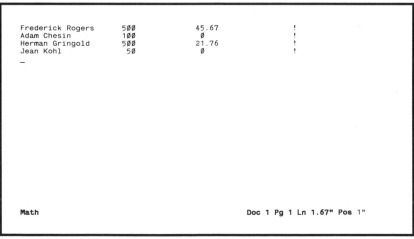

```
Frederick Rogers    500        45.67           !
Adam Chesin         100        0               !
Herman Gringold     500        21.76           !
Jean Kohl            50        0               !
—
```

Math   Doc 1 Pg 1 Ln 1.67" Pos 1"

■**FIGURE 20.6:** *The primary file merged with the data file*

6. Press Home Home ↑, then ← three times to move the cursor beyond the Math and Tab codes.

7. Press Return twice.

8. Press ↑ twice to reach line 1".

9. Type **Name** and press Tab four times.

10. Type **Credit** and press Tab twice.

11. Type **Amount Due** and press Tab twice.

12. Type **Remaining**.

13. Press Shift-F7 1 to print the document. Figure 20.7 shows the printed report.

14. Press F7 N Y to exit WordPerfect.

```
Name                 Credit        Amount Due        Remaining

Frederick Rogers      500            45.67             454.33
Adam Chesin           100             0                100.00
Herman Gringold       500            21.76             478.24
Jean Kohl              50             0                 50.00
```

■**FIGURE 20.7:**   *The finished report*

The database and REPORT1 are always on disk, ready to be generated and printed.

Our sample report uses a calculated column to compute a value across the rows. To display the total of a column, press Tab to reach the appropriate tab stop, then enter the proper operator: subtotal (+), total (=), or grand total (*).

You can also display the completed table sorted or based on some selection criteria. For example, if many clients don't owe anything, you might want to omit them from this report. Select and sort the database using the appropriate keys, then enter the name of that new file (LIST2) at the Secondary File prompt. An alternative is to use the Sort by Line menu to select or sort the completed table on the screen.

Any other text that should be part of the report can be added after the merge operation. If the completed report is longer than one page, you might want to include page numbers, headers, or footers.

A DATA-REPORTING SYSTEM

Hold on—now we're going to put all this together to form a custom application that allows you to select from a menu of reports. All this from just a word processing program, without writing one line of BASIC or Pascal or using a database program.

Some of the reports will be tables, some will contain multiline records, and others will list the full client data on individual pages.

We'll first create the primary files for the reports; then we'll write a special primary file that displays the menu and lets you enter your selections.

DESIGNING THE REPORTS

The first report, REPORT1, is already saved on disk. Our example will include three other reports; your own application could have more. Follow these steps to create the other primary files:

1. Start WordPerfect.

Warning
With version 5.1, refer to "Report Forms" for the format of these reports.

2. Type the following primary file, using Shift-F9 to enter the codes just as you did for REPORT1. This file will create a complete address and telephone list. Each record will be four lines long, separated from the next record by one blank line.

```
^F1^
^F2^
^F3^, ^F4^^F5^
^F6^
^N^P^P
```

3. Press F7 Y, type **REPORT2**, press Return, and press **N** to save the primary file and clear the screen.

4. Type the next primary file. This file creates a table listing each client's name and the date of the client's last order. Before you enter the file, clear all the tab stops, then set one at the 5" position.

```
^F1^                              ^F8^
^N^P^P
```

5. Press F7 Y, type **REPORT3**, press Return, and press **N** to save the primary file and clear the screen.

6. Type the last new primary file. This file creates a full report on each client, one per page.

Name: ^F1^
Address: ^F2^
City: ^F3^
State: ^F4^   Zip Code: ^F5^

Telephone: ^F6^

Amount Due: ^F9^   Total Credit: ^F7^

Date of last order: ^F8^

7. Press F7 Y, type **REPORT4**, press Return, and press **N** to save the primary file and clear the screen.

We did not include the ^N^P^P codes at the end of the last primary file because we want each record to appear on a separate page. When it merges the files, WordPerfect will repeat the process until all of the records have been used, inserting a page break after each report. The ^N^P^P codes actually prevent WordPerfect from placing each record on a separate page.

Now we have four reports saved on disk: REPORT1, REPORT2, REPORT3, and REPORT4. Their names may not be very informative, but you'll soon understand why we used them.

CREATING THE MENU

WordPerfect will display a custom prompt or message that is enclosed in ^O codes. We'll use this technique to create the menu, which is another primary file. Follow these steps:

Warning
Users of version 5.1 should follow the special instructions under "Creating The Menu."

1. Press Shift-F9.

2. Press **O**.

3. Type **Database Reports**.

4. Press Return twice.

5. Type the menu.

    1   Credit Remaining
    2   Address and Phone List
    3   Last Order Date
    4   Full Client List

    Please enter number of the report desired

6. Press the space bar several times after entering the last line.

7. Press Shift-F9 P.

8. Type **REPORT**.

9. Press Shift-F9 C.

10. Press Shift-F9 P.

11. Press Shift-F9 O. Figure 20.8 shows the completed menu.

12. Press F7 Y, type **MENU**, press Return, and press **N** to save the primary file and clear the screen.

The two ^P codes at the end of the menu designate the name of a primary file. The word REPORT after the first ^P means that each primary file must begin with this word. The ^C code temporarily pauses the merge operation and allows the user to enter text from the keyboard. Because the ^C code is between two ^P codes, the text entered will be taken as the name of the primary report file. The final ^O code ends the custom message.

To use this menu, you just enter the number of the report, 1 through 4. WordPerfect adds the number to the end of the word REPORT, then recalls and starts that primary file.

RUNNING THE APPLICATION

Let's go through the process of printing a client address and telephone list.

```
^ODatabase Reports

1   Credit Remaining
2   Address and Phone List
3   Last Order Date
4   Full Client List

Please enter number of the report desired ^PReport^C^P^O
_




                                                   Doc 1 Pg 1 Ln 2.34" Pos 1"
```

■**FIGURE 20.8:** *The completed Database Reports menu*

Here's the procedure:

1. Start WordPerfect.

2. Press Ctrl-F9 1 and type **MENU** at the Primary File prompt.

3. Press Return.

4. Type **LIST1** at the Secondary File prompt. If you want to use a sorted or selected database that's in a temporary file, you can enter **LIST2** (or whatever name you've given that file) at this point.

5. Press Return. Our menu of choices appears at the bottom of the screen.

6. Press the appropriate number, then press Return. WordPerfect will merge the files and display the report on the screen. Figure 20.9 shows the report produced by pressing *4*.

After the files are merged, you can add column headings or other text, or simply print the finished report.

■ LONG MENUS

A single menu should not be longer than one screen, since it would just scroll out of view. However, there are ways of handling long menus. One method is

```
Name: Herman Gringold
Address: 45th Street and Osage Avenue
City: El Paso
State: TX          Zip Code: 23123

Telephone: (543) 765-0908

Amount Due: 21.76      Total Credit: 500

Date of last order: May 5, 1990
================================================================================
Name: Jean Kohl
Address: Northwest Avenue
City: Margate
State: NJ          Zip Code: 71652

Telephone: (609) 657-8767

Amount Due: 0      Total Credit: 50

Date of last order: February 1, 1990



                                        Doc 1 Pg 4 Ln 2.63" Pos 4.6"
```

■**FIGURE 20.9:** *The report created by option 4 of the Database Reports menu* to make two columns of menu options. For example, ten report options could be listed on screen like this:

1	Credit Remaining	6	PhoneList
2	Address List	7	ItemsPurchased
3	Last Order Date	8	Last Invoice Paid
4	Full Client List	9	SpecialNotes
5	Names	10	Discount Categories

The other method is to have several menus chained together. The first menu would be named REPORT0 instead of MENU. The options could look like this:

1   Cred it Remaining
2   AddressList
3   Last Order Date
4   Full Client List
5   Names

99   Additional Reports

REPORT99 would be another separate menu that would look something like this:

Page 2 – Database Reports
0   Page 1 of report

6   PhoneList
7   ItemsPurchased
8   Last Invoice Paid
9   SpecialNotes
10   Discount Categories

Please enter number of the report desired ^PReport^C^P^O

Warning
Users of version 5.1 should replace the commands ^P-Report^C^P^O with the Chain Primary and Keyboard commands. Refer to "Creating The Menu."

If you typed *99* from the first menu, the REPORT99 primary file with the additional options would be recalled. To return to the first menu from here, you would enter *0,* and REPORT0 would be recalled.

Since file names cannot be longer than eight characters, you can have a maximum of 99 reports—REPORT99 is eight characters long.

PROGRAMMED MACROS

There is one other way to create a menu-driven application in WordPerfect if you are at least familiar with the basics of computer programming—you can write a *programmed macro.*

In addition to keystrokes, editing, and formatting commands, a programmed macro can include special commands not found on the keyboard. These commands—a *macro language*—let you perform tasks in WordPerfect much as a computer programmer can perform using BASIC or some other computer language.

To write these macros, you should be at least familiar with the logic and structure of some computer language. If you are, then you'll find the macro language a powerful tool.

In this section, we'll create a programmed macro to perform the same application you just created. The program will present two menus, one to select the report, another for the database. After you enter the report and database numbers, the program will perform the merge sort.

We'll enter two versions of this program to demonstrate the use of macro commands. The more sophisticated version will use the CASE structure, a common method used in many programming languages to select a course of action. The WordPerfect CASE structure is very much like its counterpart in Pascal and many structured BASIC languages.

Now let's create the program.

ENTERING THE INITIAL MACRO

Since this program will include text and formatting commands, we'll start by entering these using the regular macro definition procedures. This is necessary because you can only add programming commands from the Macro Edit menu, so a macro with the name desired must be on the disk before you start.

1. Start the macro definition.

    a. Press Ctrl-F10.

    b. Type **MENU**.

    c. Press Return.

d. Type **Database Application**.

e. Press Return.

2. Type the text of the first menu.

Database Reports

1   Credit Remaining
2   Address and Phone List
3   Last Order Date
4   Full Client List

3. Press Return three times.

4. Type the text of the second menu.

Databases Available

1   Master File
2   Sorted File

5. Press Return then Ctrl-F10 to end the macro definition.

6. Press F7 N N to clear the screen.

7. Now enter the Macro Edit menu by defining the same macro.

a. Press Ctrl-F10.

b. Type **MENU**.

c. Press Return to display the prompt

MENU.WPM is Already Defined. 1 Replace; 2 Edit: 0

d. Press **2** or **e**. The Macro Edit menu appears with the text of the macro displayed in the box (Figure 20.10).

The macro starts with the {DISPLAY OFF} code. Because of the commands we are going to enter, we must delete that code so the menus appear when you run the application.

8. Press **2** or **a** for the Action program; the cursor is placed in the box.

9. Press Del to delete the {DISPLAY OFF} code. The program will now appear as in Figure 20.11.

10. Press F7 twice to save the macro and return, for now, to the document window.

New Feature
Additional related features in version 5.1 are discussed under "Editing Macros."

Note
The appearance of the version 5.1 screen is slightly different, but the steps listed here still apply.

Warning
Step 8: Users of version 5.1 should skip this step.

MACRO LANGUAGE COMMANDS

Before adding the commands to the Menu macro, let's review the statements (commands) we'll be using—CHAR, CASE, LABEL, and RETURN. These are just a few of the commands available in the language.

The commands are not typed in but are selected from a list that's displayed when you press Ctrl-PgUp while editing a macro. Most commands are followed by arguments which are separated by the tilde character (~).

```
Macro: Edit

        File          MENU.WPM

  1 - Description      Database Application

  2 - Action

        ┌──────────────────────────────────────────────┐
        │{DISPLAY OFF}{Center}Database·Reports{Enter}    │
        │{Enter}                                         │
        │1{Tab}Credit·Remaining{Enter}                   │
        │2{Tab}Address·and·Phone·List{Enter}             │
        │3{Tab}Last·Order·Date{Enter}                    │
        │4{Tab}Full·Client·List{Enter}                   │
        │{Enter}                                         │
        │{Enter}                                         │
        │{Center}Databases·Available{Enter}              │
        │{Enter}                                         │
        │1{Tab}Master·File{Enter}                        │
        │2{Tab}Sorted·File{Enter}                        │
        └──────────────────────────────────────────────┘

  Selection: 0
```

■**FIGURE 20.10:** *Macro Edit menu*

```
Macro: Edit

        File          MENU.WPM

  1 - Description      Database Application

  2 - Action

        ┌──────────────────────────────────────────────┐
        │{Center}Database·Reports{Enter}                 │
        │{Enter}                                         │
        │1{Tab}Credit·Remaining{Enter}                   │
        │2{Tab}Address·and·Phone·List{Enter}             │
        │3{Tab}Last·Order·Date{Enter}                    │
        │4{Tab}Full·Client·List{Enter}                   │
        │{Enter}                                         │
        │{Enter}                                         │
        │{Center}Databases·Available{Enter}              │
        │{Enter}                                         │
        │1{Tab}Master·File{Enter}                        │
        │2{Tab}Sorted·File{Enter}                        │
        └──────────────────────────────────────────────┘

  Selection: 2
```

■**FIGURE 20.11:** *Program divided into lines*

In the definitions that follow, the word *variable* represents a number from 0 to 9, and the word *value* represents the Alt-number command using that number. *Value* will be seen in the macro as the code {VAR *n*} where *n* is the variable number.

CHAR

Purpose:

The Char instruction is a method of getting information into the macro while it is running. It is like the Input command in BASIC or the Read command in Pascal, but it only lets the operator enter a single character.

Syntax:

{CHAR}variable~prompt~

Sample:

{CHAR}1~Please enter your selection~

You can retrieve the value of your selection by pressing Alt-1.

CASE

Purpose:

This structure directs the program to perform one of a selection of tasks based on the value of a variable.

Syntax:

{CASE}value~case1~label1~case2~label2~ ... ~casen~labeln~~

Case1, case2, and *casen* represent one specific value. The labels represent a later subroutine that contains the tasks to be performed. Look at the sample below.

Sample:

{CASE}{VAR 1}~1~add~2~delete~3~end~~

If the value of {VAR 1} is 1, then the macro will go to the subroutine called *add* and perform the instructions given. If the value is 2, *delete* will be performed, or if 3, *end.*

If the value is neither 1, 2, nor 3, then the macro will continue with the instruction following the CASE command.

LABEL

Purpose:

Marks the beginning of a subroutine (a series of instructions) to be performed from CASE or another command.

Syntax:

{LABEL}name~instructions

Sample:

{LABEL}delete~{MOVE}13{RETURN}

When control is passed to the task called *delete,* WordPerfect performs the Move command (pressing Ctrl-F4) then the keystrokes 1 and 3. Ctrl-F4 1 3 deletes a sentence.

After the task is performed, in this case, the {RETURN} instruction ends the macro.

RETURN

Purpose:

Returns from the current subroutine or ends the macro. When you're using the CASE structure, this ends the macro

The syntax and an example were discussed above.

CREATING A PROGRAMMED MACRO

Now let's add the macro commands to the Menu macro.

1. Display the Macro Edit screen.

    a. Press Ctrl-F10.

    b. Type **MENU**.

    c. Press Return.

    d. Press **2** or **e**.

Warning
Step 2: Users of
version 5.1
should skip this
step.

2. Press **2** or **a** to place the cursor in the box on the screen.

3. Place the cursor after the {ENTER} code following the first menu and press Return. This inserts a blank line (not an {ENTER} code) so you can add a command.

4. Press Ctrl-PgUp. A window showing macro commands appears on the right (Figure 20.12).

5. Press ↓ to scroll down the commands until you highlight the {CHAR} command (Figure 20.13).

Note

The appearance of the version 5.1 screen is slightly different, but the steps listed here still apply.

■**FIGURE 20.12:**   *Macro Command box*

■**FIGURE 20.13:**   *CHAR command selected*

6. Press Return. The {CHAR} command is inserted in the macro. (See Figure 20.14.)

7. Type

   1~Enter Report Number:~

   Small bullets appear whenever you press the space bar.

8. Place the cursor after the {ENTER} code following the second macro and press Return.

9. Enter another {CHAR} command.

   a. Press Ctrl-PgUp. The {CHAR} command is still selected.

   b. Press Return to insert the command in the macro.

   c. Type

      2~Enter Database Number:~

10. Press Return to insert a blank line. At this point in the application you will have entered the two variables using {CHAR} commands—the number of the report desired and the database to use for the report.

    Before actually merging the files to the screen, however, you should clear the menus so they do not appear with the reports.

11. Press Ctrl-F10. The prompt changes to

    Press Macro Define to enable editing

```
Macro: Edit                                  {CHAIN}file~
                                             {CHAR}variable~message~
        File            MENU.WPM             {DISPLAY OFF}
                                             {DISPLAY ON}
   1 - Description    Database Application    {ELSE}
                                             {END IF}
   2 - Action                                {GO}label~

        {Center}Database-Reports{Enter}
        {Enter}
        1{Tab}Credit-Remaining{Enter}
        2{Tab}Address-and-Phone-List{Enter}
        3{Tab}Last-Order-Date{Enter}
        4{Tab}Full-Client-List{Enter}
        {Enter}
        {CHAR}
        {Enter}     .
        {Center}Databases-Available{Enter}
        {Enter}
        1{Tab}Master-File{Enter}
        2{Tab}Sorted-File{Enter}
```

■**FIGURE 20.14:** *Command inserted in the macro*

In this mode, any editing, formatting, or function keys inserted will insert codes. So if you make a mistake and use any of the directional arrows or editing commands to correct it, the codes will be inserted in the text. If this happens, press Ctrl-F10 to return to Edit mode, make your corrections, then press Ctrl-F10 to continue.

12. Press F7 to insert the {EXIT} code, then press **N N**. These are the keystrokes needed to clear the screen.

13. Press Ctrl-F10 to return to Edit mode. If you don't return to Edit mode, every time you press Return to insert a blank line you'll actually be inserting an {ENTER} code in the text.

14. Press Return to move to the next line.

15. Press Ctrl-F10 then Ctrl-F9 to insert the {Merge/Sort} code.

    If you were running the application, this would display the Merge/Sort prompt line on the screen so you could enter *1* for a merge operation. Enter that keystroke now.

16. Type **1**. The prompt would now ask for the name of the primary file.

17. Type **report**. Remember that each database report started with the word *report* and was followed by a number. The number corresponds to the number in the menu.

    Since we do not know what selection we'll be making when we run the macro, we can't enter the number here. But we can enter the {VAR} command that contains the value selected.

18. Press Alt-1, the variable that holds the report number. The command line looks like this so far:

    {Merge/Sort}1report{VAR 1}

19. Press Return to insert the {ENTER} command. The prompt line would now ask for the name of the secondary file.

20. Type **list**, the name that starts each of our secondary files.

21. Press Alt-2, the variable that holds the number of the database to use for the merge.

22. Press Return to add the {ENTER} command. The completed line is shown in Figure 20.15.

23. Press Ctrl-F10 to return to Edit mode.

24. Press F7 twice to accept the changes and return to the document.

By the way, you can add certain commands into a macro directly from Edit mode, without pressing Ctrl-F10. Press Ctrl-V then the keystroke. For instance, in Edit mode—when the prompt

Press Macro Define to enable editing

is not displayed—pressing Return will insert a blank line. But if you press Ctrl-V Return, the {ENTER} code will be inserted. So if you don't need to enter the programming commands, you can stay in Edit mode and insert function keys, cursor movement keys, and many editing commands directly.

RUNNING THE APPLICATION

The programmed macro is now complete. Let's run it and see exactly how it operates.

1. Press Alt-F10 to see the prompt

Macro:

2. Type **MENU** and press Return. The first menu will be displayed on the screen and the prompt line will change to

Enter Report Number:

3. Press **2**, the number of one of our reports. This will insert the value 2 into

```
Macro: Edit

        File            MENU.WPM

   1 - Description    Database Application

   2 - Action

        3{Tab}Last-Order-Date{Enter}
        4{Tab}Full-Client-List{Enter}
        {Enter}
        {CHAR}1~Enter-Report-Number:~
        {Enter}
        {Center}Databases-Available{Enter}
        {Enter}
        1{Tab}Master-File{Enter}
        2{Tab}Sorted-File{Enter}
        {Enter}
        {CHAR}2~Enter-Database-Number~
        {Exit}nn
        {Merge/Sort}1report{VAR 1}{Enter}list{VAR 2}{Enter}_

   Selection: 2
```

■**FIGURE 20.15:** *Completed Merge/Sort command*

the variable Alt-1. The second menu appears. You did not have to press Return after the number, since the {CHAR} command accepts just one character then continues the macro.

4. Press **1**, the number of our list, to insert the value 1 into the variable Alt-2. The macro now performs the line

{Merge/Sort}1report{VAR 1}{ENTER}list{VAR 2}{ENTER}

which is actually interpreted as

{Merge/Sort}1report2{ENTER}list1{ENTER}

So you understand exactly what's happening, let's break down the line and show what keystrokes are being repeated.

In Macro:	Performs:
{Merge/Sort}	Ctrl-F10
1	selecting 1 (Merge) from the prompt line
report{VAR 1}	report2
{ENTER}	Return
list{Var 2}	list1
{ENTER}	Return

This merges the primary file REPORT1 with the secondary file LIST1.

If you enter a number of a report or list that doesn't exist, you'll see the message

Error - File Not Found

and the macro will end.

USING THE CASE STRUCTURE

If you are more familiar with programming, then you might be interested in seeing how the CASE structure works. While the Menu macro works fine the way it is, here's how you could use CASE to perform the same function:

{CENTER}Database Reports{ENTER}
{ENTER}
1{TAB}Credit Remaining{ENTER}

```
2{TAB}Address and Phone List{ENTER}
3{TAB}Last Order Date{ENTER}
4{TAB}Full Client List{ENTER}
{ENTER}
{CHAR}1~Enter Report Number~
{ENTER}
{CENTER}Databases Available{ENTER}
{ENTER}
1{TAB}Master File{ENTER}
2{TAB}Sorted File{ENTER}
{ENTER}
{CHAR}2~Enter Database Number~
{EXIT}nn
{CASE}{VAR 1}~1~credit~2~address~3~last~4~full~~

{LABEL}credit~{Merge/Sort}1report1{ENTER}list{VAR
2}{ENTER}{RETURN}
{LABEL}address~{Merge/Sort}1report2{ENTER}list{VAR2}{ENTER
}{RETURN}
{LABEL}last~{Merge/Sort}1report3{ENTER}list{VAR
2}{ENTER}{RETURN}
{LABEL}full~{Merge/Sort}1report4{ENTER}list{VAR
2}{ENTER}{RETURN}
```

Let's review how this works after the two variables are entered and the screen is cleared.

The {CASE} command uses the value in variable 1 to determine which label, or subroutine, is performed. If the value is 1, then the macro will execute the subroutine labeled *credit;* if the value is 2, *address;* 3, *last;* 4, *full.*

The macro will move to the subroutine, perform the keystrokes, then {RETURN}. With the {CASE} command, this ends the macro.

One advantage of using the CASE structure is that you could name the files something that clearly identifies their purpose, other than REPORT1, REPORT2, etc.

For instance, if you rename the primary files, then you have the following subroutines:

```
{LABEL}credit~{Merge/Sort}1credit{ENTER}list{VAR
2}{ENTER}{RETURN}
{LABEL}address~{Merge/Sort}1address{ENTER}list{VAR2}
{ENTER}{RETURN}
{LABEL}last~{Merge/Sort}1orderdt{ENTER}list{VAR
2}{ENTER}{RETURN}
```

{LABEL}full~{Merge/Sort}1fulllist{ENTER}list{VAR 2}{ENTER}{RETURN}

VERSION 5.1 FEATURES

MERGE CODES

The merge codes and prompt lines are different in version 5.1.

Ending Fields   To end a field, press F9, or select **T**ools **M**erge Codes **E**nd Record, to insert the code {END FIELD} instead of ^R. The prompt FIELD: appears on the left side of the status line followed by the number of the next field to be entered. After typing the first field of the record, you'll see

FIELD: 2

As you use the arrow keys to move through a record, the number at the prompt indicates the field number where the cursor is placed. This is particularly useful with long records, and to insure that each record has the same number of fields.

Ending Records   To end the record, press Shift-F9, or select **T**ools **M**erge Codes, to display the options:

1 Field; 2 End Record; 3 Input; 4 Page Off; 5 Next Record; 6 More:0

Notice that fewer codes are shown on the version 5.1 prompt line. Some of these are direct replacements for earlier merge codes and will be discussed later in this and other chapters.

Press **2** or **E** to insert {END RECORD}, which replaces ^E used in earlier versions of WordPerfect.

Inserting Fields   To insert a field, press Shift-F9 1, or select **T**ools **M**erge Codes **F**ield to insert {FIELD}, which replaces ^F used in earlier versions.

For more information comparing version 5.0 and 5.1 merge codes, refer to "Converting Merge Codes."

REPORT FORMS

Using version 5.1 merge codes, the report forms will appear as:

Report2

```
{FIELD}1~
{FIELD}2~
{FIELD}3~, {FIELD}4~ {FIELD}5~
{FIELD}6~

{PAGE OFF}
```

Report3

```
{FIELD}1~ {FIELD}8~
{PAGE OFF}
```

Report4

```
Name: {FIELD}1~
Address: {FIELD}2~
City: {FIELD}3~
State: {FIELD}4~                              Zip Code: {FIELD}5~
Telephone: {FIELD}6~

Amount Due: {FIELD}9~                         Total Credit: {FIELD}7~

Date of last order: {FIELD}8~
```

CREATING THE MENU

The menu shown in the chapter will not operate correctly in version 5.1. Instead, follow these steps:

1. Press Shift-F9 6, or select **T**ools **M**erge Codes **M**ore, to display a list of merge commands in the top right of the screen (Figure 20.16).

Version 5.1 provides many powerful commands that can be used to create entire computer programs in merge and macro operations. All of these commands can be displayed in this window, and explained in detail in Appendix K of the WordPerfect manual.

While a number of these commands will be discussed in this chapter and in later chapters, they offer some sophisticated and complex capabilities that require knowledge of computer programming.

2. Press ↓ or PgDn to scroll down the commands until you highlight the command

{PROMPT}message~   ^O

The notation on the left shows an example of the syntax for using the command. In this case, {PROMPT} is followed by some message you want to appear on the screen, then the tilde character that closes off merge commands.

The ^O on the right is the code's equivalent in earlier versions. Refer to "Converting Merge Codes" to see how these earlier codes can be used.

3. Press Return to see the prompt

Enter Message:

Since this code is normally used to insert a one-line message on the screen, you'd enter the message, then press Return. In our case, however, we want an entire menu to appear, not a single line.

4. Press Return to display

{PROMPT}~

on the screen.

We have to insert the entire text of the menu between the {PROMPT} command and the ~.

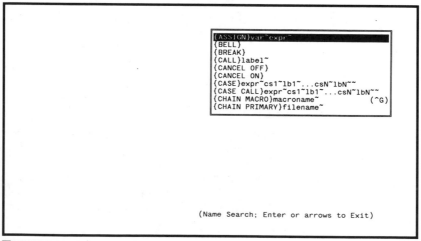

■**FIGURE 20.16:**   *Merge codes*

5. Press ←, then type Database Reports.

6. Press Return twice.

7. Type the menu.

   1 Credit Remaining
   2 Address and Phone List
   3 Last Order Date
   4 Full Client List

Please enter number of the report desired

8. Press the space bar after entering the last line.

9. Press Shift-F9 6, or select **T**ools Me**r**ge **C**odes **M**ore.

10. Press ↑ or PgUp to scroll the list until you highlight the command {CHAIN PRIMARY}. This command passes control from one primary file to another.

11. Press Return to display the prompt

Enter Filename:

12. Type **Report**, then press Return. The line appears on the screen as

Please enter number of the report desired {CHAIN PRIMARY}report~~

If we left the line like this, during the merge operation WordPerfect would try to pass control to a primary file called REPORT. Instead, we want to enter the report number from the keyboard, adding it onto the filename.

13. Press ← to place the cursor under the first tilde.

14. Press Shift-F9 6, or select **T**ools Me**r**ge **C**odes **M**ore.

15. Press ↓ or PgDn to scroll the list until you highlight the command {KEYBOARD}. This command pauses the execution of the merge operation to allow you to enter characters from the keyboard. Additional methods of inputting to merge and macro operations are discussed in Chapter 21.

16. Press Return. The line now appears as:

Please enter number of the report desired {CHAIN PRIMARY}report{KEYBOARD}~~

17. Press F7, or select **File Exit, Y,** type **MENU**, press Return, and press N to save the primary file and clear the screen.

The command {CHAIN PRIMARY} at the end of the menu designates the name of a primary file. The word REPORT following the command means that each primary file must begin with this word. The command {KEYBOARD} temporarily pauses the merge operation and allows the user to enter text from the keyboard. Because the {KEYBOARD} command is before two tildes, the text entered will be added to the word REPORT and taken as the name of the primary report file.

To use this menu, you just enter the number of the report, 1 through 4. WordPerfect adds the number to the end of the word REPORT, then recalls and starts that primary file.

CONVERTING MERGE CODES

In many instances, version 5.1 can run merge files and macros created with version 5.0. It will correctly recognize ^F^, ^E, and ^R codes and merge most simple form documents without conversion. For example, the version 5.0 secondary file and four report forms discussed in this chapter could be used directly in version 5.1.

In fact, in some instances, you might find it more convenient to use the older codes. For example, it is easier to press Ctrl-D to insert the version 5.0 date code ^D, than it is to insert the version 5.1 {DATE} code—press Shift-F9 6, scroll the list of commands to highlight {DATE}, then press Return. To enter any version 5.0 code, press Ctrl then the code letter.

But if you want to convert your version 5.0 merge files to version 5.1, you can change the codes yourself using this chart as a guide:

Version 5.0:	Press:	To Insert
^R	F9	{END FIELD}
^E	Shift-F9 2	{END RECORD}
^N^P^P	Shift-F9 4	{PAGE OFF}
^F^	Shift-F9 1	{FIELD}
^O	Shift-F9 6, select {PROMPT}, press Return	{PROMPT}~

Version 5.0:	Press:	To Insert
^C	Shift-F9 6, select {KEYBOARD}, press Return	{KEYBOARD}
^D	Shift-F9 6, select {DATE}, press Return	{DATE}

WordPerfect 5.1 can even convert the codes automatically for you. Retrieve the version 5.0 file, then press Ctrl-F9 3 to select Convert Old Merge Codes. All of the Ctrl codes will be replaced with their version 5.1 counterparts.

In some cases, the converted codes will be different than the equivalents shown above. For example, ^N^P^P is converted into

{NEXT RECORD}{NEST PRIMARY}~

instead of the simpler {PAGE OFF}, but it will still operate properly—all of the version 5.0 report forms in this chapter could be converted and used without problem.

Like {CHAIN PRIMARY}, {NEST PRIMARY} passes control of the program to another primary file. With {CHAIN PRIMARY}, the current primary file is completed, then the chained primary file is executed. {NEST PRIMARY}, on the other hand, first passes control to the named file, then returns to complete the original one.

Unfortunately, more complicated version 5.0 merge files, such as MENU, will not operate correctly either before or after automatic conversion. For example, the final line of the MENU merge file is converted into

Please enter number of the report desired {NEST
PRIMARY}report{KEYBOARD}~~

instead of the {CHAIN PRIMARY} command.

WordPerfect replaced the two ^P codes with {NEST PRIMARY} as it did when used in ^N^P^P. While the replacement worked in the simpler report forms, the MENU file will not operate as converted. The merge operation stops after the first record is merged.

This makes it difficult to present any general rules about which version 5.0 codes—beyond ^D, ^R, ^E, and ^F—will work before or after conversion. While most of the other codes will work when used in simple form documents, some must be replaced with version 5.1 equivalents when used in more complex operations.

Try your merge operations several times after converting them. If they do not work correctly, look for new version 5.1 codes that might be substituted.

EDITING MACROS

Version 5.1 provides a quick way to enter the Macro Editor:

1. Press Home Ctrl-F10.

2. Type the name of the macro and press Return.

The Macro Editor will appear on the screen.

MOUSE AND MENU EQUIVALENTS

Function	Keyboard	Pull-Down Menus
Merge	Ctrl-F9 1	Tools Merge
Merge Codes	Shift-F9	Tools Merge Codes

PART
4

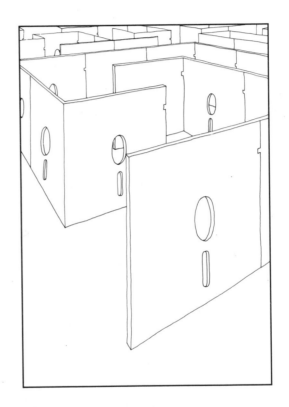

TIMESAVING TECHNIQUES FOR CORRESPONDENCE AND RECORD-KEEPING

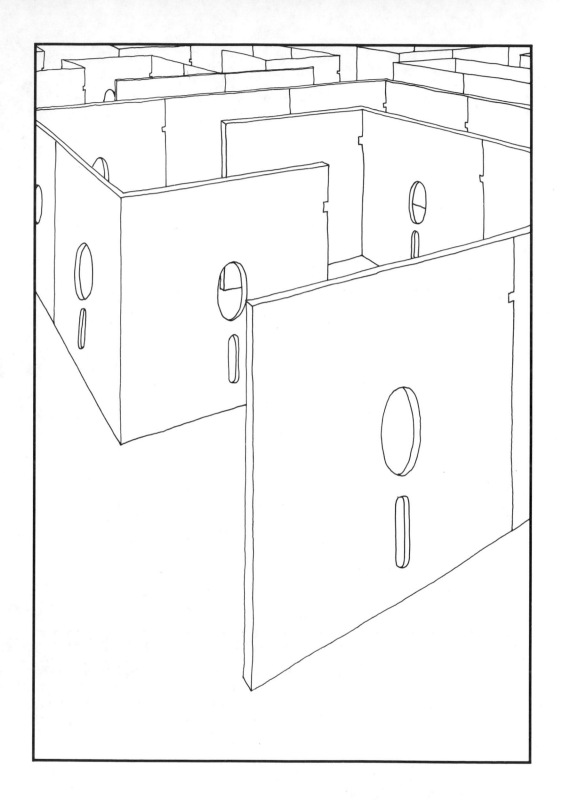

21

STREAMLINING FORM DOCUMENTS

You know the typical uses of form documents: advertisements, account statements, invoices, and announcements. But there are many other applications that you may not have considered. How many project bids, requests for proposals, and contracts that you produce have paragraphs in common? Are you a job-seeker answering classified ads in the newspaper or a student requesting college applications? Even if you only send one such document a week, you actually produce the same letter 52 times in a year!

Form documents can also serve as a sales tool. By using sorting and selection techniques, you could send special announcements to good customers and incentive letters to bad ones. Customers who pay on time could receive your regular price list, and the rest could get one with a 1-percent built-in markup. Or, if you would like to save money by sending a catalog third-class mail, your labels can be printed from a data file sorted by zip code instead of by customer name.

In Chapter 6 you learned how to produce a small number of form documents by using a template and manually copying or typing in the variable information. In this chapter, however, you'll see how any number of form documents can be created automatically—hundreds of them if necessary. You'll also see how to use menus and macros to streamline the entire process.

FORM DOCUMENTS FROM DATA FILES

In the last chapter, you learned how to merge a database (the secondary file) with a report format (the primary file) to produce various types of data reports. The same general procedure is used to produce form documents, with the shell text as the primary file. During merging, WordPerfect replaces the codes in the shell text with variable information from selected fields in the data file. The same data file used for data management tasks can now serve as a mailing list. It doesn't matter if you combined the name and address in one field or divided the address elements into several fields. The label (or envelope) and inside address for the document can be merged from either format.

However, the name field in a data file that will be used as a mailing list requires special consideration. Look at the typical form letter shown in Figure 21.1. This letter is designed for customers who have not purchased after a certain date and who owe no money. You could easily select this information from the data file that we created in the last chapter. But where did the letter get the name *Mr. Rogers* in the salutation?

The client's full name was the first field. Although a specific word in the field can be used as a key in this format, there is no way to print the last name separately from the first.

There are two ways to set up the database so that it can be used to insert the names into the salutation. One method is to separate the name field, like this:

Note

Throughout this chapter, remember that with version 5.1, {END FIELD} replaces ^R, {END RECORD} replaced ^E, and {FIELD} replaces ^F.

Mr.^R
Adam^R
Chesin^R

The other way is to add another field to each record. In fact, you could add two fields so that either a formal (Mr. Chesin) or familiar (Adam) name can be

```
March 18, 1991

Frederick Rogers
431 Broad Street
Philadelphia,   PA   19101

Dear Mr. Rogers:

     Have we done anything wrong? Our records show that your last
order from us was made on January 2, 1990. We hope that you were
pleased with the purchase and our high quality of merchandise.
     Because you are such a good customer, we are making this
special effort to serve you again. Include this letter with your
next order and subtract $10.00 from the total price. This discount
is good on any product from our catalog but, because of bookkeeping
requirements, can only be valid until September 1, 1991.

                         Sincerely,

                         Alvin A. Aardvark
                         President
                         Aardvark International
```

■**FIGURE 21.1:** *A typical form letter*

inserted at the appropriate places.

Let's use the second technique to make our sample data file more suitable for use with form documents. Follow these steps to add two new fields to the file LIST1 you created in Chapter 20. If you didn't enter that file, but want to perform the exercises in this chapter, go back to Chapter 20 and type the data file shown. Then return here and follow the instructions.

1. Start WordPerfect.

2. Press Shift-F10, type **LIST1**, and press Return.

3. Move the cursor down nine lines to the ^E code after the first record and type **Fred**.

4. Press F9 to insert the ^R code and a carriage return.

5. Type **Mr. Rogers**.

6. Press F9 to insert the ^R code.

7. Move the cursor down to the ^E code following the next record. In the same manner, add the names below to each record.

   Adam
   Mr. Chesin

   Herman
   Mr. Gringold

   Jean
   Dr. Kohl

   Figure 21.2 shows the data file with the two new fields.

8. Press F7 Y Return Y Y to save the file and exit WordPerfect.

THE DATA DICTIONARY—PREPARING FOR FORM DOCUMENTS

In order to create the primary file for form documents, you must know the field number for each variable item. You can make this information easily accessible by creating a *data dictionary* that lists the fields and their numbers. You can either print the dictionary and keep it by the computer or divide the screen into windows and display the dictionary for reference.

Let's create a data dictionary for our sample data file. In this example, we'll divide the screen into windows and display the data file as a guide. Follow these steps:

1. Start WordPerfect.

2. Press Ctrl-F3 1, type **12**, and press Return to divide the screen into two windows.

```
                     Frederick Rogers^R
                     431 Broad Street^R
                     Philadelphia^R
                     PA^R
                     19101^R
                     (215) 555-7654^R
                     500^R
                     January 2, 1990^R
                     45.67^R
                     Fred^R
                     Mr. Rogers^R
                     ^E
                     Adam Chesin^R
                     231 Lockhaven Road^R
                     Freeport^R
                     NY^R
                     10109^R
                     ^R
                     100^R
                     December 4, 1990^R
                     0^R
                     Adam^R
                     Mr. Chesin^R
                     ^E
                     Herman Gringold^R
                     Osage Avenue^R
                     El Paso^R
                     TX^R
                     23123^R
                     (543) 765-0908^R
                     500^R
                     May 5, 1990^R
                     21.76^R
                     Herman^R
                     Mr. Gringold^R
                     ^E
                     Jean Kohl^R
                     Northwest Avenue^R
                     Margate^R
                     NJ^R
                     71652^R
                     (609) 657-8767^R
                     50^R
                     February 1, 1990^R
                     0^R
                     Jean^R
                     Dr. Kohl^R
                     ^E
```

■**FIGURE 21.2:**   *The data file with the extra fields for the mailing list*

3. Press Shift-F3 to move the cursor to the bottom window.

4. Press Shift-F10, type **LIST1**, and press Return to recall the data file.

5. Press Shift-F3 to move the cursor to the top window.

6. Using the data file as a guide, type each field number and a description of its contents. Your screen should look something like this:

F#	Item
1	Client's full name
2	Street address
3	City
4	State
5	Zip code
6	Area code and phone number
7	Credit
8	Date of last order
9	Amount outstanding
10	Client's first name
11	Salutation—title and last name

7. Press Shift-F7 1 to print the data dictionary.

8. Press F7 Y, type **DATADICT**, and press Return Y to save the file, clear the window, and place the cursor in the bottom window.

9. Press Ctrl-F3 1, type **24**, and press Return to remove the second window.

10. Press F7 N Y if you want to exit WordPerfect.

USING FIELD NAMES

Warning
Users of version 5.1 should follow the special instructions under "Using Field Names."

If you still find it difficult to remember fields by their numbers, you can reference them with names instead. To do this, create a special record at the start of the data file, prior to the first record, assigning a name to each of the fields. Each field must be given a name. The format of the naming record is quite different from data records, as this example shows:

^N
name
address
city

```
        state
        zip
        phone
        credit
        date
        due
        first
        salutation
        ^N^R
        ^E
```

Start the record by pressing Shift-F9 N. After the last field name, press Shift-F9 N F9 to insert the ^N^R codes. Then end the record with Shift-F9 E.

When you write the primary file and want to enter a field code, press Shift-F9 F for the prompt

    Field:

Type the field name, then press Return to insert the field name code in the text, as in

        ^Fname^F

■   # WRITING THE PRIMARY DOCUMENT

The primary document contains the shell text used in every copy of the letter. It also includes the field codes to insert variable information from each record of the data file. The fields can appear in any order, and the same field can be used more than once in a primary file.

As an example, we'll create the form letter shown in Figure 21.1. Use your printed data dictionary as a guide and follow these steps to enter the primary document:

1. Start WordPerfect.

Warning
Step 2: With version 5.1, press Ctrl-D, or press Alt-F9 6, select {DATE}, then press Return.

2. Press Shift-F9 D to insert ^D, the Date code. During merging, WordPerfect will insert the system date at this location in either the default format or another format that you selected from the Date Format menu displayed by pressing Shift-F5 3.

3. Press Return twice.

4. Press Shift-F9 F 1 Return to have field 1 (the client's name) inserted at this location.

5. Press Return.

6. Press Shift-F9 2 Return to insert the ^F2^ code for the street address.

7. Press Return.

8. Press Shift-F9 F 3 Return.

9. Type **,** (a comma) then press the space bar twice.

10. Press Shift-F9 F 4 Return Tab Shift-F9 F 5, then press Return three times.

11. Type **Dear**, press the space bar twice, and press Shift-F9 F 11 Return.

12. Type **:** (a colon) then press Return twice.

13. Type the beginning of the letter.

> Have we done something wrong? Our records show that your last order from us was made on

14. Press the space bar once after typing the word *on,* then press Shift-F9 F 8 Return to insert the code for the last order date.

15. Type **.** (a period) then press the space bar and continue typing the letter.

> We hope that you are pleased with the purchase and our high quality of merchandise.
> Because you are such a good customer, we are making this special effort to serve you again. Include this letter with your next order and subtract $10.00 from the total price. This discount is good on any product from our catalog but, because of bookkeeping requirements, can only be valid until September 1, 1991.
>
> Sincerely,
>
> Alvin A. Aardvark
> President
> Aardvark International

16. Press Return.

17. Press F7 Y, type **FORM**, and press Return N to save the primary file and clear the screen. Figure 21.3 shows the completed form letter with its Merge codes.

```
^D

^F1^
^F2^
^F3^,    ^F4^   ^F5^

Dear ^F11^:

     Have we done anything wrong? Our records show that your last
order from us was made on ^F8^. We hope that you were pleased with
the purchase and our high quality of merchandise.
     Because you are such a good customer, we are making this
special effort to serve you again. Include this letter with your
next order and subtract $10.00 from the total price. This discount
is good on any product from our catalog but, because of bookkeeping
requirements, can only be valid until September 1, 1991.

                    Sincerely,

                    Alvin A. Aardvark
                    President
                    Aardvark International

                              Doc 1 Pg 1 Ln 4.5" Pos 6.2"
```

■FIGURE 21.3:   *The completed form letter with Merge codes*

■   DIRECTING MERGED OUTPUT

By default, the results of merging primary and secondary files are displayed on the screen. After the files are merged on the screen, the form documents can be printed immediately, saved on disk, or edited. This way, a large group of form letters can be added to the queue and printed while you work on another document.

If your data file is long, however, the resulting merged document may be too large for your computer's memory and available disk space. In this case, you have two alternatives (other than running out to the computer store for more memory): you can break the one large data file down into smaller ones, then merge and save each file individually; or you can direct the output of the merged files to the printer, instead of to the screen, so that each document is printed as soon as it is generated.

First we'll use the default setting to display the merged documents on the screen, then we'll see how to display each document as it is merged, and finally we'll send the output directly to the printer.

MERGING FORM DOCUMENTS ON THE SCREEN

As you discovered in the previous chapter, merging the secondary and primary files and displaying the finished document on the screen is a simple task. We'll use the same procedure to merge all the records into our sample form letter. You should still be in WordPerfect. If not, start the program and follow these steps:

1. Press Ctrl-F9 1 to select the Merge option and display the Primary File prompt.

2. Type **FORM**, then press Return to display the Secondary File prompt.

3. Type **LIST1** then press Return. The word

   Merging

   appears on the status line as the letters are generated. The merged letters will be displayed on the screen.

4. Press F7 N N to clear the screen.

DISPLAYING EACH MERGED DOCUMENT AS IT IS GENERATED

If your data file is long, you may find yourself staring at a blank screen for some time during the merge operation. Remember that nothing appears on the screen until the entire secondary file has been merged. If you would like to see each letter as it is generated, add the ^U code to the primary file. Here's how:

1. Press Shift-F10, type **FORM**, and press Return to recall the primary file.

2. Press Home Home ↓ to reach the end of the document.

3. Press Shift-F9 U to insert the ^U code.

4. Press F7 Y Return Y N to save the edited form letter and clear the screen.

5. Press Ctrl-F9 1.

6. Type **FORM** at the Primary File prompt, then press Return.

7. Type **LIST1** at the Secondary File prompt, then press Return to merge the files.

Each letter is displayed on the screen as it is generated. The ^U code also can be used in merging database reports to display each row of the report as it is created.

Warning
Step 3: Press Ctrl-U or insert the {REWRITE} code—press Shift-F9 6, or select **Tools** Merge Codes **More**, highlight {REWRITE}, and press Return.

DIRECTING MERGED OUTPUT TO THE PRINTER

You can direct the results of the merge operation to the printer by adding the ^T code to the end of the primary file. Unfortunately, using this code changes the use of the ^N and ^P codes.

Most of the data reports that we created in Chapter 20 included the ^N^P^P codes at the end of the primary file to display the records successively on the page. These codes were not used in REPORT4 because we wanted each record to end with a page break.

When you direct the output of a merge operation to the printer, each record is automatically printed on a separate page. This means that you cannot create tablelike reports, in which the records are listed on the same page, and print them at the same time. You must generate such reports on the screen.

But this doesn't mean that you don't have to use the ^N^P^P codes with form documents that you want to direct to the printer. In fact, if you use the ^T code to print form letters or other reports, you must also use ^N^P^P in the primary file. Without these codes, the printed output will have improper page breaks or only the first record will be merged and printed.

So, to direct merged output to the printer, add ^T^N^P^P to the end of your primary file.

Let's use this technique to merge our sample letters and print them at the same time. Follow these steps:

1. Press Shift-F10, type **FORM**, and press Return.

2. Press Home Home ↓ to reach the end of the document.

3. Delete the ^U code. (It has no effect when you send output to the printer.)

4. Press Shift-F9 T Shift-F9 N Shift-F9 P Shift-F9 P.

5. Press F7 Y Return Y N to save the edited form letter and clear the screen.

6. Press Ctrl-F9 1.

7. Type **FORM** at the Primary File prompt, then press Return.

8. Type **LIST1** at the Secondary File prompt, then press Return. The merged form letters are printed; they do not appear on the screen at all.

9. Press F7 N Y to exit WordPerfect.

Warning

Step 3: With version 5.1, delete ^U or {REWRITE}.
Step 4: The version 5.1 equivalents are {PRINT}{PAGE OFF}—press Shift-F9 6, or select **T**ools **M**erge Codes **M**ore, highlight {PRINT}, press Return, press Shift-F9 4.

SORTING AND SELECTING RECORDS FOR FORM DOCUMENTS

Sorting and selecting are not new issues, but these functions are extremely useful for producing effective form documents. Here are some examples:

- The sales manager is planning a trip to California. So why not send a letter to customers in that state scheduling visits (key1=CA)?

- Business is slacking off. So why not send a special mailing to customers who haven't ordered for some time (key2<870312)?

- A new salesperson was hired to cover a territory of specific zip codes in the Philadelphia area. Why not send a letter just to those customers announcing the personnel change (key2=> 19114*key2=<19116)?

In all of the examples, the main data file is put through a selection process, then the selected records are used as the secondary file in the merge operation.

As mentioned in the last chapter, it is a good idea to save the selected files in a temporary data file. Why not sort the file in several ways and keep all the versions on disk? Because this practice would lead to the problem of *data redundancy.* Not only do the files take up a great deal of disk space, but they can result in inaccurate mailings. If you make a change in a record on the master data file, you would have to update every sorted version. By maintaining one master file and using temporary files for other versions, you can ensure that all your mailings and data reports contain current data. However, if you use another version of the entire file frequently, it might be more efficient to have another copy of the list in that order.

As an example, let's sort our sample data file by zip code. Follow these steps:

1. Start WordPerfect.

2. Press Ctrl-F9 2 to select the Sort option.

3. Type **LIST1** at the Input File prompt.

4. Press Return to display the Output File prompt, then type **LIST2**.

5. Press Return to display the Sort by Line menu.

6. Press **7 1** to select a merge sort and display the Sort Secondary Merge File menu.

7. Press **3** to change the key.

8. Press Return to accept the default type *a.*

9. Press **5** for the Field option. Figure 21.4 shows the completed menu.

10. Press F7 1 to sort the file.

In a few seconds, the screen will clear. A duplicate of the data file is now on the disk in zip code order.

▪ MANAGING FORM DOCUMENTS—A MENU AND MACRO

If you produce a number of form documents, you may eventually have several primary files and a few data files accumulated on the disk. To save time, you can create a macro to make the merging process faster and add the form letter options to your database management menu. If you have several secondary files on the disk, you can also add these to the menu.

Let's create a new menu and macro for handling form letters. The screen should now be clear so that you can create the menu. Follow these steps:

1. Type the following, using Shift-F9 to enter the Merge codes, and the space bar (not Tab) to separate the columns:

   ^OForm Document Menu

   Primary Files   Secondary Files

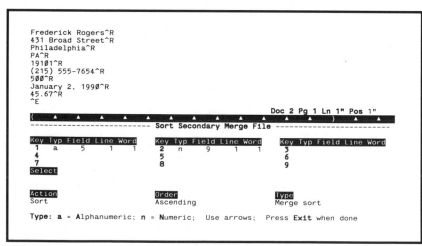

▪**FIGURE 21.4:** *The Sort Secondary Merge File menu for sorting by zip code*

FORM: discount letter   LIST1: master file
REPORT1: credit remaining   LIST2: zip code order
REPORT2: address list
REPORT3: last order date
REPORT4: full client list

Enter the name of the secondary file for this run:
^S^C^S^O

^OEnter the name of the primary file: ^P^C^P^O

Unlike the menu in Chapter 20, which received the name of the secondary file from the Merge prompt, this menu requests both file names. Note that the first message code ends after the first request, and another ^O surrounds the second prompt. Also note that, using this technique, you must request the name of the secondary file first. If the primary file were entered first, that file would be executed immediately, and the secondary file would never be requested.

2. Press F7 Y, type **MENU1**, and press Return Y N to save the menu and clear the screen.

3. Press Ctrl-F10 to create a macro to start the merge process.

4. Type **Start** then press Return twice.

5. Press Ctrl-F9 1 to select the Merge option.

6. Type **MENU1** at the Primary File prompt, then press Return.

7. Press Return at the Secondary File prompt. MENU1 is displayed on the screen.

8. Press Shift-F9.

9. Press F7 N N to clear the screen.

USING THE MENU

When you are ready to produce some form letters or a data report, use the Menu macro. Here's how:

1. Press Alt-F10 to display the Macro prompt.

2. Type **Start** then press Return. The menu and the request for the secondary file name appear on the screen, as shown in Figure 21.5.

```
Form Document Menu

Primary FilesSecondary Files

FORM: discount letter      LIST1: master file
REPORT1: credit remaining  LIST2: zip-code order
REPORT2: address list
REPORT3: last order date
REPORT4: full client list

Enter the name of the secondary file for this run:
_
```

■**FIGURE 21.5:**   *The menu and the request for the secondary file name, which appear when you activate the Menu macro*

3. Type the name of one of the secondary files listed on the menu, then press Return. The Primary File prompt now appears.

4. Type the name of one of the primary files, then press Return to merge the documents.

5. Print or save the forms as desired.

6. Press F7 N Y to exit WordPerfect.

ADDING OPTIONS

You can add other secondary and primary files to the menu. You may find that one primary file is useful with more than one secondary file. For example, you may want to print an address list (REPORT2) for friends and relatives, as well as for clients.

Warning
Users of version 5.1 should follow the special instructions under "Adding Options."

Also, if you want the option of sometimes merging to the printer and sometimes to the screen, you can create two versions of the primary file. At the end of one version, place the codes ^T^N^P^P, and name that file FORMLPT. Name the version without the codes FORMCRT.

A menu with these additional options might look like this:

^OForm Document Menu

Primary Files   Secondary Files

FORMLPT: discount letter to the printer
FORMCRT: discount letter to the screen
REPORT1: credit remaining
REPORT2: address list
REPORT3: last order date
REPORT4: full client list
PART1: stock report
ORDER: items in need of reorder

LIST1: master client
LIST2: zip code order
LIST3: friends

LIST3: family members
LIST4: inventory

Enter the name of the secondary file for this run: ^S^C ^S^O

Enter the name of the primary file: ^P^C^P^O

MAINTAINING MAILING LISTS

While it is easy to recall a secondary file and add new records, it is also easy to forget to include a field when you are using large records. Here is a technique that will streamline this task. It uses a special primary file and macro to append new records to the list, automatically inserting the ^R and ^E Merge codes. You are prompted for each field so that you cannot accidentally leave one out. Follow these steps to create the menu:

1. Start WordPerfect.

Warning
Users of version 5.1 should follow the special instructions under "Maintaining Mailing Lists."

2. Type the following, using Shift-F9 to enter all of the Merge codes, including ^R. Do not use the F9 key by itself because we do not want to insert carriage returns. The ^V codes are used to transfer other Merge codes into a record. Instead of being part of this primary file, the ^R and ^E codes will be placed in the new records.

        ^OEnter the client's full name: ^O^C^V^R^V
        ^OEnter the street address:^O^C^V^R^V
        ^OEnter the city:^O^C^V^R^V
        ^OEnter the state: ^O^C^V^R^V
        ^OEnter the zip code:^O^C^V^R^V
        ^OEnter the phone number: ^O^C^V^R^V
        ^OEnter the credit limit:^O^C^V^R^V
        ^OEnter the date of last order:^O^C^V^R^V

^OEnter the amount outstanding:^O^C^V^R^V^OEnter the
client's first name:^O^C^V^R^V
^OEnter the salutation: Dear ^O^C^V^R^V
^V^E^V
^GAppend^G

3. Press F7 Y, type **NEWNAMES**, and press Return N to save the file and clear the screen.

Now let's create the Append macro to automatically add the new names to the current data file. Since creating this macro will actually add a name to the list, you would normally wait until the first time that you want to use this macro to create it.

1. Press Ctrl-F9 1 to select the Merge option.

2. Type **NEWNAMES** at the Primary File prompt.

3. Press Return at the Secondary File prompt. The menu appears, and the first prompt is displayed at the bottom of the screen, as shown in Figure 21.6.

4. Type **William Watson**.

5. Press F9. Do not press Return unless you are typing a multiline field. If you press Return by mistake, move the cursor to the end of the field that you just entered and press Del. Then press F9 and continue. The name appears at the top of the menu, followed by the ^R code. The ^V codes

```
^V^R^V
^OEnter the street address:^O^C^V^R^V
^OEnter the city:^O^C^V^R^V
^OEnter the state: ^O^C^V^R^V
^OEnter the zip code:^O^C^V^R^V
^OEnter the phone number: ^O^C^V^R^V
^OEnter the credit limit:^O^C^V^R^V
^OEnter the date of last order:^O^C^V^R^V
^OEnter the amount outstanding:^O^C^V^R^V
^OEnter the client's first name:^O^C^V^R^V
^OEnter the salutation: Dear ^O^C^V^R^V
^V^E
==========================================================================
^V
^GAppend^G




        Enter the client's full name:              Doc 1 Pg 1 Ln 1" Pos 1"
```

■**FIGURE 21.6:** *The Primary File menu for appending records* have disappeared, and the ^R code that was between them is inserted into the record itself. The second prompt appears on the screen. Figure 21.7 shows how the screen appears at this point.

6. Enter the rest of the record. Remember to press F9 after entering each field. If you make a mistake, use normal editing techniques to correct it. You can even move the cursor up to correct an earlier entry. The prompt will disappear from the screen until you return the cursor to the current line and continue entering fields.

> 35 Oak Drive
> Freeport Long Island
> NY
> 01877
> (212) 654-8765
> 500
> September 6, 1990
> 0
> William
> Mr. Watson

7. When you press F9 after entering the last field, the system will attempt to find the Append macro, which has not yet been created. The message

> Error File Not Found

appears on the status line.

```
William Watson^R
^V^R^V
^OEnter the city:^O^C^V^R^V
^OEnter the state: ^O^C^V^R^V
^OEnter the zip code:^O^C^V^R^V
^OEnter the phone number: ^O^C^V^R^V
^OEnter the credit limit:^O^C^V^R^V
^OEnter the date of last order:^O^C^V^R^V
^OEnter the amount outstanding:^O^C^V^R^V
^OEnter the client's first name:^O^C^V^R^V
^OEnter the salutation: Dear ^O^C^V^R^V
^V^E
==================================================================
^V
^GAppend^G




Enter the street address:                    Doc 1 Pg 1 Ln 1.16" Pos 1"
```

■**FIGURE 21.7:** *The menu after the first new field is entered*

8. Press Ctrl-F10 to define the macro.

9. Type **Append** then press Return twice.

10. Press the ↑ key once; otherwise you'd have an extra line inserted into the data file.

11. Press Alt-F4 to turn on the highlighting.

12. Press Home Home ↑ to highlight the entire record.

13. Press Ctrl-F4 1 4 to select the Append option.

14. Type **LIST1** then press Return. The new record is appended to the end of the data file.

15. Press Ctrl-F10 to end the macro definition.

16. Press F7 N Y to exit WordPerfect.

When you want to add names to the data file, follow steps 1 to 7 above. Because the Append macro is now created, the data will be added to the file.

■ ENTERING MULTIPLE NAMES WITH PROGRAMMED MACROS

If you want to enter more than one name into the list, create a programmed macro that repeats the NEWNAMES merge operation until you're done.

Programmed macros were introduced in Chapter 20. They provide a way of performing rather sophisticated functions. If you didn't read the section on programmed macros in that chapter and have no experience with computer programming, then you'll have some difficulty understanding the concepts discussed in this section. In this case, keep in mind that you do not have to use programmed macros to create form letters and documents. So skip ahead to the section "Entering Data into Form Documents from the Keyboard."

First review some new commands that you'll need for this macro.

ASSIGN

Purpose:

To assign a value to a variable from within the macro, like the LET statement in BASIC.

Syntax:

{ASSIGN}variable~value~

Sample:

{ASSIGN}1~25~

Pressing Alt-1 (variable 1) will now display 25.

IF ELSE END IF

Purpose:

This instruction, called a *conditional*, makes a determination—while the macro is running—regarding which instructions are to be executed. This is just like the IF THEN instruction in BASIC.

Syntax:

{IF}{VAR n}condition~command{ELSE}command{END IF}

The command itself may require a terminating tilde as in the sample below. The {ELSE} is optional.

Sample:

{IF}{VAR 1}=1~{BELL}{ELSE}{DEL}{END IF}

If the condition is true then the macro performs whatever follows until the {ELSE} command. If the value is not true, then the macro performs the commands between the {ELSE} and the {END IF}. In this case, if {VAR 1}—which is Alt-1 here—is equal to 1, a beep will sound (the {BELL} command does that); otherwise a Delete is executed.

GO

Purpose:

Passes control of the macro to a subroutine, like GOTO in BASIC.

Syntax:

{GO}label

Sample:

{GO}report1

When the macro encounters this command, it performs the subroutine (label) called *report1,* then continues from that point. Any lines between {GO} and the subroutine would not be executed.

PERFORMING REPETITIONS WITH PROGRAMMED MACROS

Here is the macro that can be used to enter any number of names into your data file. To enter it, first create an empty macro, called *Repeat,* like this:

1. Press Ctrl-F10 to start the macro definition.

2. Type **Repeat** then press Return twice.

3. Press Ctrl-F10 to end the definition.

You now have a macro called Repeat that you can edit this way:

Note

With version 5.1, to quickly enter the macro editor, press Home Ctrl-F10, type Repeat, then press Return twice.

1. Press Ctrl-F10.

2. Type **Repeat** then press Return. The Already Defined prompt appears.

3. Press **2** or **e** to edit the macro and display the Edit screen.

4. Enter the macro shown below, then press F7 twice to return to the document.

New Feature

Additional related features in version 5.1 are discussed under "Repeating Macro Instructions."

```
{ASSIGN}1~1~
{LABEL}repeat~
{IF}{VAR 1}=1~{GO}get~{ELSE}{GO}end~{END IF}

{LABEL}get~
{Merge/Sort}1newnames{ENTER}{ENTER}
{CHAR}1~Enter 1 to continue or 0 to end~
{EXIT}nn
{GO}repeat~
{LABEL}end~
```

The first line assigns the value of 1 to the variable 1 (Alt-1). This is necessary for the *repeat* to start working.

The subroutine *repeat* starts the entry process and determines when it ends. That work is done in the {IF} instruction. Since the variable was just assigned the value of 1, the macro goes to the subroutine *get.*

Everything between the lines *{LABEL}get~* and *{GO}repeat~* represents the loop—the section of the program that will be repeated until there are no more names to enter. It performs the Merge/Sort using NEWNAMES, then clears the screen. It then displays the prompt

Enter 1 to continue or 0 to end

and accepts a character into variable 1 before the macro goes back to the subroutine *repeat*.

The {IF} condition is again tested. As long as you enter *1* to the prompt, the condition is true and the cycle is repeated. But when you enter *0* at the prompt, the {IF} condition is false and the program goes to the subroutine *end*. Since this is the last line in the macro, the macro ends.

ENTERING DATA INTO FORM DOCUMENTS FROM THE KEYBOARD

The greatest benefit of merging documents is that form letters can be generated automatically with no additional typing. But not all form letters are mass-produced. For example, suppose that you send the same letter to each new client or new employee. Perhaps you have a contract, lease, or cover letter that is in a standard format, but is personalized each time that you use it.

Warning
Users of version 5.1 should follow the special instructions under "Inputting Data."

In these cases, creating a secondary file with only one or two records is not the most efficient way to produce the document. Instead, you can use the ^C codes to input the variable information from the keyboard just before printing the document, as in this form letter:

Dear ^OEnter salutation^O^C:

Enclosed is my application for acceptance into the graduate program at ^OEnter name of grad school^O^C. Copies of my transcripts and letters of recommendation are being forwarded by the campus placement office.
Please contact me if you need any additional information.

Sincerely,

Samantha Wilkowski

When Samantha selects the Merge option (by pressing Ctrl-F9 1) and names this letter as the primary file, she will be prompted for the name of the secondary file. She will press Return at the Secondary File prompt, and then be prompted for the variable information to be entered from the keyboard.

Keyboard entry can be combined with field insertion from secondary files. If there is some variable information that is not part of the permanent record, use a ^C code to request it during the merge operation. For example, this primary file creates form letters for every client but allows the user to add a personal message if desired:

Warning

Users of version 5.1 should press Ctrl-D or insert the {DATE} macro command from the More menu.

^D

^F1^
^F2^
^F3^, ^F4^ ^F5^

Dear ^F10^:

All of us at Aardvarks Are Us want to wish you, your family, and staff a wonderful holiday season. It is during this time of the year that we realize that we share a common bond beyond a business relationship.

Aardvarks Are Us is planning its traditional holiday party for Monday, December 21, and we would be pleased if you and your family could join us. The festivities begin at 1:30, and ample parking will be provided.

RSVP to my office, 888-8765. ^OEnter any personal note here ! include punctuation:^O^C

Sincerely,

Alvin A. Aardvark
President
Aardvark International

As you have learned in this chapter, WordPerfect's Merge function can be used in a variety of ways for personal, academic, and business applications. You'll discover more uses for the Merge codes as you continue to experiment with WordPerfect.

VERSION 5.1 FEATURES

USING FIELD NAMES

The ^N code cannot be used to name fields in version 5.1. (It can still be used for the *next record* function in primary files, however.) In its place, this version provides an automatic-entry system.

If you want to name your fields, follow these steps to create the initial record:

1. Press Shift-F9 6, or select **T**ools **M**erge Codes **M**ore.

2. Highlight {FIELD NAMES} then press Return. The prompt line displays

   Enter Field 1:

2. Type **name**, then press Return. The prompt changes to

   Enter Field 2:

3. In the same way, enter the remainder of the field names, pressing Return after each:

   address
   city
   state
   zip
   phone
   credit
   date
   due
   first
   salutation

4. Press Return when the prompt

   Enter Field 12:

   appears.When you press Return without entering a field name, Word-Perfect assumes you've completed the list, clears the code window from the screen and displays the record. In this case, the record appears as

   {FIELD NAMES}name~address~city~state~zip~phone~cred-
   it~date~due~first~salutations~~{END RECORD}

   followed by a page break line.

To use the field names in the form document, press Shift-F9 1, or select **Tools Merge Codes Field**, type a field name, and press Return. Fields will appear as *{FIELD}name~*.

MANAGING FORM DOCUMENTS

The version 5.0 MENU1 macro file shown in this chapter will not work correctly with version 5.1, even after automatic conversion. Enter the following merge file in its place, using the More command menu to insert the merge codes. When done, continue with step 2 in the chapter to save the file and create the START macro.

{PROMPT}Client Lists and Reports

Primary Files	Secondary Files
FORM: discount letter	LIST1: master file
REPORT1: credit remaining	LIST2: zip code order
REPORT2: address list	
REPORT3: last order date	
REPORT4: full client list	

Enter the name of the secondary file: {SUBST SECONDARY}{KEYBOARD}~~

{PROMPT}Enter the name of the primary file: {CHAIN PRIMARY}{KEYBOARD}~~

The (SUBST SECONDARY} merge command tells WordPerfect to use the name of the file entered as the secondary file.

ADDING OPTIONS

Remember to replace the version 5.0 codes ^T^N^P^P with {PRINT}{PAGE OFF}, use {SUBST SECONDARY}{KEYBOARD}~~ in place of ^S^C^S^O, and {CHAIN PRIMARY}{KEYBOARD}~~ in place of ^P^C^P^O.
    Use the merge file shown above as a guide.

MAINTAINING MAILING LISTS

The merge file shown in this chapter will operate correctly under version 5.1. In fact, because of all of the merge codes that must be selected, it would actually be more efficient to create the file as shown in the chapter—entering the version 5.0 codes with the Ctrl key—then convert it to version 5.1 using Ctrl-F9 3.

However, if you want to use version 5.1 codes, create the merge file like this:

```
{PROMPT}Enter the client's full name: ~{KEYBOARD}{MRG
   CMND}{END FIELD}{MRG CMND}
{PROMPT}Enter the street address:~{KEYBOARD}{MRG
   CMND}{END FIELD}{MRG CMND}
PROMPT}Enter the city:~{KEYBOARD}{MRG CMND}{END
   FIELD}{MRG CMND}
{PROMPT}Enter the state: ~{KEYBOARD}{MRG CMND}{END
   FIELD}{MRG CMND}
{PROMPT}Enter the zip code:~{KEYBOARD}{MRG
   CMND}{END FIELD}{MRG CMND}
{PROMPT}Enter the phone number: ~{KEYBOARD}{MRG
   CMND}{END FIELD}{MRG CMND}
{PROMPT}Enter the credit limit:~{KEYBOARD}{MRG
   CMND}{END FIELD}{MRG CMND}
{PROMPT}Enter the date of last order:~{KEYBOARD}{MRG
   CMND}{END FIELD}{MRG CMND}
{PROMPT}Enter the amount outstanding:~{KEYBOARD}{MRG
   CMND}{END FIELD}{MRG CMND}
{PROMPT}Enter the client's first name:~{KEYBOARD}{MRG
   CMND}{END FIELD}{MRG CMND}
{PROMPT}Enter the salutation: Dear ~{KEYBOARD}{MRG
   CMND}{END FIELD}{MRG CMND}
{MRG CMND}{END RECORD}
==================================================
{MRG CMND}
{CHAIN MACRO}Append~
```

REPEATING MACRO INSTRUCTIONS

The technique used to repeat instructions in the chapter uses a GOTO-like structure. While effective, it requires quite a few program lines to implement and is contrary to newer principles of structured programming.

Version 5.1 provides additional ways to repeat instructions.

WHILE   The general syntax of the WHILE command is:

```
{WHILE}condition~
....instructions
{END WHILE}
```

In essence, it says that "while the condition is true, repeat all the following instructions up to the command {END WHILE}."

Using this command, the Repeat macro shown in the chapter can be created like this in version 5.1:

```
{ASSIGN}1~1~
{WHILE}{VARIABLE}1~=1~
{Merge/Sort}1newnames{ENTER}{ENTER}
{CHAR}1~Enter 1 to continue, 0 to end~
{EXIT}nn
{END WHILE}
```

The first line assigns the value of 1 to the variable 1 (ALT-1). This *primes* the variable so the repetition works at least one time. The second line starts the WHILE loop with the condition, meaning that "while the variable 1 is equal to 1, repeat all the following instructions up to the command {END WHILE}."

As long as you enter 1 at the prompt, the WHILE condition is true and the loop repeats.

FOR

The FOR loop also repeats instructions but for a fixed number of times, much like repeating operations using the ESC key. The basic syntax is

```
{FOR}VARIABLE~start~stop~step
....instructions
{END FOR}
```

Using this structure, you could create the following macro that repeats the NEWNAMES merge a specific number of times:

```
{TEXT}number~How many names do you want to add ~
{FOR}count~1~{VARIABLE}number~~1~
{Merge/Sort}1newnames{Enter}{Enter}
{Exit}nn
{END FOR}
```

The FOR command performs the repetition in sequence, counting from the starting number to the stopping number in steps.

{TEXT} is another command to input characters from the keyboard. Like {KEYBOARD} and {CHAR}, it pauses the operation so you can enter characters. We'll compare the three methods later on.

Since the FOR command can be confusing if you're just learning how to program, let's look at a few additional examples.

Here's a simple FOR program that prints the numbers 1 to 50 down the left side of the page:

```
{HOME}{LEFT}
{FOR}TIME~1~50~1~
{VARIABLE}TIMES~{ENTER}
{END FOR}
```

So you understand exactly what's happening, let's break down the program:

Command:	Purpose:
{HOME}{LEFT}	Moves the cursor to the left margin.
{FOR}TIME~1~50~1~	Starts the FOR loop by initializing the variable TIMES to 1, the starting value. It sets the stopping or ending value to 50, and the step value to 1.
{VARIABLE}TIMES~{ENTER}	Prints the value of the variable TIMES, then performs a carriage return.
{END FOR}	As long as the value of TIMES has not reached the stopping value (50), the current value is incremented by 1—the step value—and the loop is repeated. When the value reaches 50, the repetition stops.

If you wanted to print all odd numbers, from 1 to 49, enter the FOR instruction as

```
{FOR}TIME~1~50~2~
```

By *nesting* multiple FOR loops, you can create some interesting effects. For example, this macro

```
{FOR}row~1~10~1~
{FOR}col~1~{VARIABLE}row~~1~
*
{END FOR}
```

```
{Enter}
{END FOR}
```

creates this design:

```
*
**
***
****
*****
******
*******
********
*********
**********
```

The first FOR loop sets up 10 rows of lines. For each of these lines, the second FOR loops prints as many asterisks as the row number. The {Enter} command between the {END FOR} commands causes each row of asterisks to print on a separate line.

This same design could be created using a variation of the {FOR} command, {FOR EACH}, in this program

```
{FOR EACH}row~1~2~3~4~5~6~7~8~9~10~~
{FOR}col~1~{VARIABLE}row~~1~
*
{END FOR}
{Enter}
{END FOR}
```

Here, the syntax is

```
{FOR EACH}VARIABLE~first~second~third~...last~~
....instructions
{END FOR}
```

With this loop, the variable is assigned each of the specified values in turn, rather than using a sequential value. During the first repetition, the variable is assigned the first value in the list, during the second repetition the second value, etc.

The best use of FOR EACH is when there is no sequential step value or definite pattern in the repetition, or to count down, such as

```
{FOR EACH}row~10~9~8~7~6~5~4~3~2~1~~
```

Substituting this line in the program would create:

```
*********
********
*******
******
*****
****
***
**
*
```

Finally, consider this macro that asks for a name then prints it backwards:

```
{TEXT}name~Please enter a name ~
{ASSIGN}times~{LEN}name~~
{FOR}counter~1~{VARIABLE}times~~1~
{ASSIGN}position~{LEN}name~-{VARIABLE}counter~~
{ASSIGN}letter~{MID}name~{VARIABLE}position~~1~~
{VARIABLE}letter~
{END FOR}
```

While some of the lines in the program could have been combined, in this format it is easier to see what each line does. Because these commands are new, and might at first seem complex, let's break down each line with an example. The command

```
{TEXT}name~Please enter a name ~
```

displays the prompt *Please enter a name* on the screen. (Sample Input: BARBARA)

```
{ASSIGN}times~{LEN}name~~
```

assigns the number of characters in the variable *name*, 7, to the variable *times*.

```
{FOR}counter~1~{VARIABLE}times~~1~
```

sets up a FOR loop with 7 repetitions. At each repetition, the variable counter will have values 1, 2, 3, 4, 5, 6, then 7.

```
{ASSIGN}position~{LEN}name~-{VARIABLE}counter~~
```

assigns to the variable *position* the value 7 less the value of counter.

```
{ASSIGN}letter~{MID}name~{VARIABLE}position~~1~~
```

assigns to the variable letter, the *mid* section of name, starting at *position* for one character. Character positions start with number 0, not 1. So if *name* is *Barbara*, position 0 is B, position 1 is A, position 2 is R, and so on.

In the first repetition, the starting position is 6—the last character. At the second repetition, the starting position is 5, the next to the last character, and so on until at the final repetition the position is the first character.

The general syntax of the mid command is

{MID}variable~start position~count

So {MID}name~4~3~ would return ARA—three characters starting at position four, the fifth character in the variable.

Here are the values of the variables counter, position, and letter during each of the repetitions:

Repetition	Counter	Position	Letter
1	1	6	A
2	2	5	R
3	3	4	A
4	4	3	B
5	5	2	R
6	6	1	A
7	7	0	B

{VARIABLE}letter~

prints the character in the variable letter.

{END FOR}

repeats the loop until all the characters have been printed.

INPUTTING DATA

While you can use the version 5.0 codes for inputting data directly into form documents, the equivalent version 5.1 codes would be:

Dear {INPUT}Enter Salutation~

To insert the input command, press Shift-F9 3, or select **T**ools **M**er**g**e Code **I**nput, to see the prompt

Enter message:

Type the prompt you want to appear, then press Return. When you run the merge file, the prompt will appear on the status line but the cursor remains after the text in the document. Type the text you want to include in the document then press F9.

This is an excellent means of entering data into standard forms, such as memos. The following merge file, for example, can be used to quickly create memos:

```
TO:      {INPUT}Enter Recipient~
FROM:    {INPUT}Enter Sender~
SUBJECT: {INPUT}Enter Subject~
DATE:    {DATE}


{INPUT}Enter text of memo.
```

As an alternative, you can use the Keyboard command, but no prompt will appear on the status line.

Other Methods of Inputting Data   You've seen examples of four ways to input information into a merge or macro operation—CHAR, KEYBOARD, TEXT, and INPUT. While in some ways the commands are interchangeable, there are important differences between them.

CHAR can be used both in merge files and macros. It accepts only one character into a variable, and displays a prompt or message. Entering the character continues the operation, you do not have to press Return.

KEYBOARD accepts any number of characters into the document rather than a variable, but can only be used in merge files, not macros. No prompt is displayed. When you're done entering text, press F9 to continue the operation (although you can press Return in applications such as the MENU merge file).

TEXT accepts up to 129 characters into a variable and is terminated by pressing Return. It includes a prompt and can be used in both macros and merge files.

INPUT accepts any number of characters into the document, not a variable, in both merge file and macros. It includes a prompt and is terminated by Return in macros and F9 in merge files. Use it when you would CHAR but have more than one character to input.

Version 5.1, however, provides three additional ways to input data:

PAUSE works only in macros and accepts any number of characters into the document. It has no prompt and is terminated with Return. The syntax is

```
{PAUSE}
```

PAUSE KEY is like pause except you specify what key terminates input. The syntax is

{PAUSE KEY}key~

For example, the commands

{PROMPT}Please enter a name, press F7 when done~ {PAUSE
KEY}{Exit}

accept input until F7 is pressed.

LOOK is a much different command. It accepts a maximum of one character into a variable but without stopping the merge or macro operation. Use it in loop operations when you want to type a one-character response without having to press Return or F9 to terminate input. The syntax is

{LOOK}variable~

For example, the following macro inserts numbers down the left margin until you press any key:

{ASSIGN}num~1~
{LABEL}number~
{LOOK}char~
{IF}'{VARIABLE}char~'!=''~
{GO}end~
{END IF}
{VARIABLE}num~
{Enter}
{ASSIGN}num~{VARIABLE}num~+1~
{GO}number~

Notice that the expression {VARIABLE}char~ is quoted because the comparison deals with strings, not numbers. *!=* is WordPerfect's symbol for "does not equal."

VERSION 5.0 CODE EQUIVALENTS

As a summary, here are the version 5.1 equivalents for the version 5.0 merge codes discussed in the last two chapters.

Version 5.0:	Version 5.1:
^C	Keyboard
^D	Date

Version 5.0:	Version 5.1:
^E	End Record
^F	Field
^N	Next Record—in primary files Field Names—in secondary files
^N^P^P	Page Off
^O	Prompt
^Pfilename^P	Chain Primary
^R	End Field
^S	Subst Secondary
^T	Print
^U	Rewrite

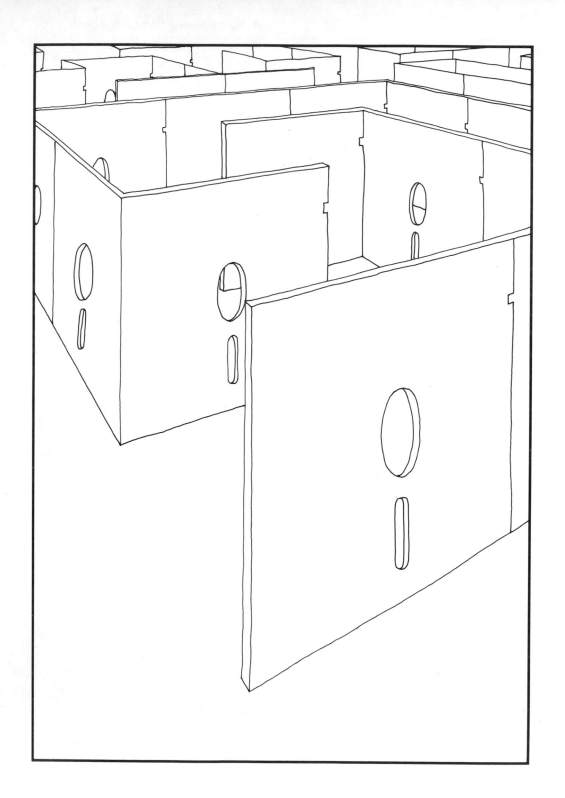

22

USING WORDPERFECT TO AUTOMATE MASS-MAILINGS

There seems something absurd about using a computer to generate a large set of form letters, only to type the envelopes by hand. As you've already learned, WordPerfect and your printer can be used to produce form documents quickly and easily. But what happens once the letters are printed?

Some companies have secretaries type the addresses; others contract with commercial services to maintain mailing lists and supply printed envelopes or labels.

There is an alternative. With a proper printer and the correct supplies, you can have WordPerfect produce addressed envelopes or labels for you. This chapter describes the requirements and procedures for this application.

HARDWARE AND SUPPLIES

The supplies that you'll need to produce printed envelopes or labels depend on the capabilities of your printer.

ENVELOPE SUPPLIES

If your printer cannot handle single sheets of paper (i.e., it has only a tractor feed), then you must purchase envelopes attached to continuous backing. The backing has tractor holes, just like continuous paper. Unfortunately, these envelopes are expensive. You might think that you could attach some envelopes to continuous paper, but you'll have nightmares trying to align them correctly.

If your printer has only a friction feed, then you can print on individual envelopes with WordPerfect in the Hand-Fed mode. This means that you'll have to insert and align each envelope individually—a tiresome task when you're producing many form letters, especially since you'll have to press *G* from the Print menu after aligning every envelope. And if you can't reach your printer and keyboard from one location, you will need roller skates to move between them. The best solution is to use a special envelope-feeder attachment. That way, you can set WordPerfect for sheet-feeder operation and not have to assign someone to sit by the computer.

LABEL SUPPLIES

Printing on labels doesn't present the same kind of problems as printing on envelopes. All labels are supplied on backing sheets, most of which are continuous, but some of which are on individual 8 1/2-inch by 11-inch paper. You can print either type of labels on a friction feed printer. Just keep in mind that continuous stock tends to slide on friction feed printers, so watch for alignment problems. With a tractor feed printer, you'll need to use continuous labels.

After you've selected your supplies, you'll need to adjust WordPerfect for the size of the form and the type of feed—continuous, manual, or sheet feeder. You'll also have to have a properly created data file (secondary file).

■   DATA FILE REQUIREMENTS

Each record in the data file should have the fields necessary for printing a complete address: name, street address, city, state, and zip code. The name could be a person's, a company's, or both, and it may include a title. If the elements in the addresses vary, you can make each one a separate field:

Note
Throughout this chapter, remember that with version 5.1, {END FIELD} replaces ^R, {END RECORD} replaces ^E, and {FIELD} replaces ^F.

Ms. Barbara Elayne^R
Director^R
Philadelphia School of Medical Technology^R
43rd and Kingsessing Mall^R
Philadelphia^R
PA^R
19101^R
^E

or have one name field with several lines:

Ms. Barbara Elayne
Director^R
Philadelphia School of Medical Technology^R
43rd and Kingsessing Mall^R
Philadelphia^R
PA^R
19101^R
^E

or have the name, title, and company elements as one field:

Ms. Barbara Elayne
Director
Philadelphia School of Medical Technology^R
43rd and Kingsessing Mall^R
Philadelphia^R
PA^R
19101^R
^E

However, setting up each element as a separate field could create problems. For example, the following are typical records:

Ms. Barbara Elayne^R
Director^R
Philadelphia School of Medical Technology^R
43rd and Kingsessing Mall^R
Philadelphia^R
PA^R
19101^R
^E
Mr. Mike Clarke^R
^R
Smith's Incorporated^R
23 Walnut Lane^R
El Paso^R
TX^R
87654^R
^E

```
Ms. Lois Schnieder^R
^R
^R
198 Watersdown Street^R
Tampa^R
FL^R
09815^R
^E
```

Notice that not every person has a title or company name. So how do you design the primary file if you would like to include the title and company name if they are available? This way *won't* work:

```
^F1^
^F2^
^F3^
^F4^
^F5^, ^F6^ ^F7^
```

because the addresses would appear like this when printed:

Ms. Barbara Elayne
Director
Philadelphia School of Medical Technology
43rd and Kingsessing Mall
Philadelphia, PA 19101

Mr. Mike Clarke

Smith's Incorporated
23 Walnut Lane
El Paso, TX 87654

Ms. Lois Schnieder

198 Watersdown Street
Tampa, FL 09815

Note
With version 5.1, place the question mark before the closing tilde—{FIELD2?~—to omit a blank field.

The extra lines appear in two of the addresses because the fields were empty. In this case, use the "omit-if-empty" format by placing a question mark after the field number as in

^F1^
^F2?^
^F3?^
^F4^
^F5^, ^F6^ ^F7^

New Feature
Additional re-
lated features in
version 5.1 are
discussed under
"Handling
Blank Fields in
Merge Files."

If the field is empty, WordPerfect will not enter a blank line. To add the question mark, press Shift-F9 F, type the field number, then press **?** followed by Return.

■ PRINTING ON ENVELOPES

The codes in the primary file are exactly the same for printing on individual envelopes or continuous ones, but the format and form selections are different. The only other consideration is whether you are sending the merged files directly to the printer or to a file to be printed at another time.

If you created a secondary file with all of the address elements in one field, the primary file that's needed to display the merged addresses on the screen would simply be

^F1^

If the elements are in separate fields, then enter the appropriate field numbers, such as

^F1^
^F2^
^F3^, ^F4^ ^F5^

Note
With version
5.1, {PAGE
OFF} replaces
^N^P^P, and
{PRINT}
replaces ^T.

To print on the envelopes directly as the files are merged, add ^T^N^P^P to the end of the primary file.

But no matter when you print the envelope addresses, the primary file must contain the proper page format settings. For hand-fed envelopes, use the format settings described in Chapter 6.

For continuous envelopes, you must measure your exact stock. Measure the distance from the top of one envelope to the top of the next, as shown in Figure 22.1. That's your page height. Then make small lines where you want the address to begin and end on the envelope itself, as shown in Figure 22.2.

If you're using envelopes with the return address already printed, measure the distance between the two lines and subtract that from the page height to get the bottom margin. Multiply that size by 6 lines per inch to get the maximum number of text lines allowed per page. Make sure that none of the addresses in your list has more than this number of lines.

Set the top margin at 0, and the bottom margin and page size as calculated above. Align the first envelope so that the printhead is where you want the first line of the address to appear, as shown in Figure 22.3. Then begin the merge operation.

The procedure is different if you want to print your return address at the same time as the mailing address. Set the top margin at .5" and the page height as you measured above. Then measure the distance from the bottom line you drew to the bottom of the envelope. Set that as the bottom margin. Align the top of the first envelope with the printhead. Now use the techniques

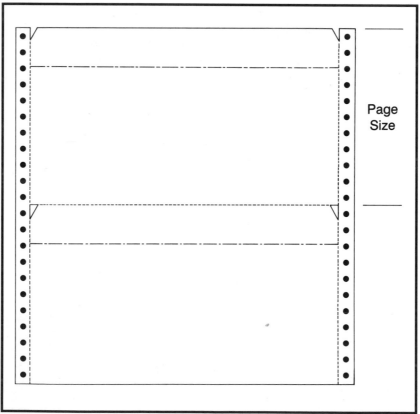

■FIGURE 22.1:   *The distance from the top of one envelope to the top of the next is the page height*

discussed in Chapter 6 to format and enter your return address and type the Merge codes at the position of the mailing address. Start the merge operation.

With some printers, you'll have a feeding problem if you try to print on the first envelope. If this happens, begin the merge with the top of the second envelope at the printhead.

■ PRINTING ON LABELS

New Feature
Additional related features in version 5.1 are discussed under "Formatting and Printing Labels."

A primary file for printing on labels should have the same codes as a file for printing on envelopes. The format settings that you use depend on whether the labels are attached to the backing in a single column or in several columns.

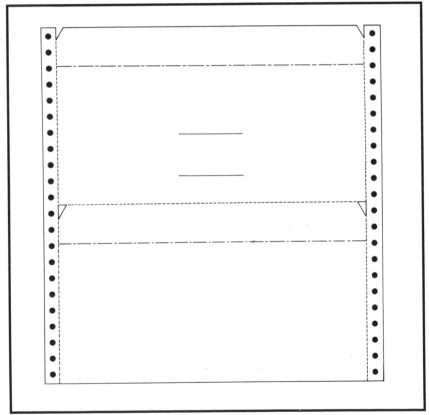

■FIGURE 22.2: *Mark where the printed address should begin and end*

SIZE RESTRICTIONS

One major problem is the size restriction of most labels. Some, for example, provide only enough room for four lines. So, first make sure that your addresses are not longer than the label itself. If you have long addresses, you may have to restructure your address list. This means that you may have to omit extra elements, such as a title line.

The width of labels can also be a problem. If a long address line (such as *The Philadelphia Technical College of Textiles and Science*) is too wide to fit on a narrow label, WordPerfect will break it into two lines during the merge operation. While the adjusted address will fit the label width, the extra line may make it too long!

One-Across Labels   One-across labels (those in a single column) are packaged on narrow continuous form stock. Because the backing is not the standard

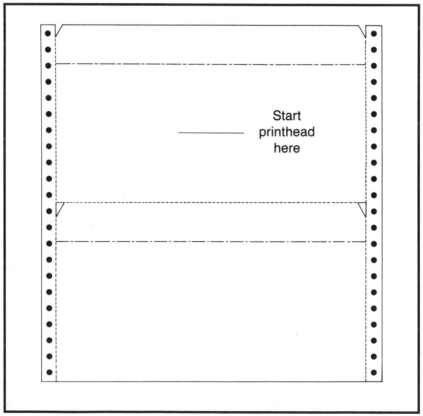

Start
printhead
here

■**FIGURE 22.3:**   *Align the envelope so that the printhead is on the first address line*

8 1/2 inches wide, you must have adjustable tractor pins on your printer to use such labels.

The format settings for one-across labels depend on your label stock. Exact measurements are important. A one-line error is multiplied greatly after 1,000 labels! The margin settings for one-across labels can be calculated using the procedure described below for labels in multiple columns, except that you do not have to define columns.

Multiple-Column Labels   Other labels are supplied two, three, four, or even five across the backing. You might need a wide-carriage printer for the ones that are more than two across, although some three-across labels will fit on 9 1/2-inch tractors used with 8 1/2-inch perforated stock.

Multiple-column labels should be merged into a multicolumn formatted file, then printed afterward.

FORMATTING FOR LABELS

You can use the same basic procedure to determine the proper format settings for labels of any size. First make a test pattern of several lines on a sample page of labels, then use the printed sample to calculate the page size, text lines, and top margin settings.

Because of size restrictions, printing on labels often requires some trial and error. To save stock, use a pencil to outline the labels on a sheet of paper. If your printer accepts friction feed paper, make some photocopies of this to use for the tests. If it only accepts tractor feed, outline the labels directly on your continuous paper.

Follow these steps to print the test pattern:

1. Start WordPerfect.

2. Measure the width of a sheet of label stock.

3. Measure the amount of left and right margin desired. If your labels have tractor holes, be sure not to include that area as part of the margin.

4. Set the left and right margins that you measured in step 3, and the page width that you measured in step 2.

5. Set the top margin to 0.

6. Type several lines of repeating numbers across the screen from margin to margin, starting with the number 1 (the left margin), like this:

   ```
   12345678911234567892123456789312345678941234567895
   12345678911234567892123456789312345678941234567895
   ```

```
12345678911234567892123456789312345678941234567895
12345678911234567892123456789312345678941234567895
12345678911234567892123456789312345678941234567895
```

Instead of typing all of the lines, you can type just one line then copy it several times down the page. Press Ctrl-F4 1 1 to copy the line then press Return to duplicate it. Now press Ctrl-F4 4 1 several times to retrieve additional copies. Enter enough lines to fill at least two complete rows of labels.

7. Insert the test label stock (the copy) and place the printhead where the first line of the address should be printed, about one line down from the top of the label.

8. Print the test pattern using the same typeface that you'll use to print the final labels.

9. Measure from the first line on the top label to the first line on the second one. Record this as the page height.

10. Mark the line that should be the last printed line on the top label.

11. Measure from the top of the first printed line to the line you marked in step 10.

12. Subtract that from the page size calculated in step 9 and record the difference as your bottom margin.

13. Is the position of the left margin acceptable? If not, mark the number where you would like the printing to begin, measure the distance from the edge of the page, and record that as the left margin.

14. Is the right margin correct? If not, mark the position where the last character should be printed and measure the distance. Record that as the new right margin.

15. For each label across the backing paper, mark and measure the left and right margin position from the edges of the page.

16. Press F7 N N to clear the screen.

17. Set the top margin at 0, and the bottom margin, page width, height, and right and left margins as calculated.

18. Enter the codes for the address. Adjust the primary file so the codes ^N^P^P come under the page break line, as in:

    ^F1^
    ^F2^

```
^F3^, ^F4^ ^F5^
_ _ _ _ _ _ _ _ _ _ _ _ _ _ _ _ _ _ _ _ _ _ _ _ _ _ _ _ _ _ _ _
^N^P^P
```

Insert a blank line above or below the codes if you have to.

19. Save the primary file.

20. Check your data file to ensure that each address conforms to the settings. Are there any lines too long to fit within the column margins? Are some records too long for the settings?

21. Merge the primary file with the data file.

22. For multicolumn margins do the following:

    a. Place the cursor at the start of the resulting merged document.

    b. Define the columns by entering the left and right column margins for each label across, as calculated in steps 14 and 15.

    c. Press F7 3 to exit the Column Definition menu and turn on Columns.

23. Print the file on label stock. Remember to align the printhead where you want the first line printed.

Make sure that the left and right edges of each column are printed at the correct position and that the top and bottom of each address fits on the label. Make any minor adjustments, then print the file to your labels.

There are so many different sizes of labels and variations in address styles that printing labels is far from an exact science. It pays to take the time to scan the completed address list carefully after it has been formatted in columns. Keep an eye on the labels during printing—some extra long addresses may have passed your review.

LABELS ON LASER PRINTERS

The formats used above to print labels won't work if you're using sheets of labels in a laser printer. Each time the Page Break code is received, a sheet of labels will feed out of the printer, so you'll only get the top label printed on each sheet.

Instead, use the techniques illustrated in Figure 22.4.

The top of the figure shows the primary document for three-across labels; the codes are revealed in the bottom.

The column definition is set for parallel columns with block protection; the number of labels across the page is the number of columns. The first two columns were entered as

```
^F1^
^F2^
^F3^, ^F4^  ^F5^
^N^
```

Note
With version
5.1, {NEXT
RECORD}
replaces ^N.

Press Ctrl-Return to end these two columns. The ^N^ code tells WordPerfect to get the next record after merging the first into the primary document.

The last column ends with the codes ^N^^P^^P^ and a Return to repeat the merge with the same primary document after three labels are merged across the page.

When the merge is completed, the addresses will appear properly positioned in three columns, and each sheet will end in a page break.

In using this technique, just make sure that each address fits in the label. Because you're using several columns, long addresses may not fit in the label width, and word wrap will create another line in the label. This extra line may push later addresses down so they do not align properly on their labels.

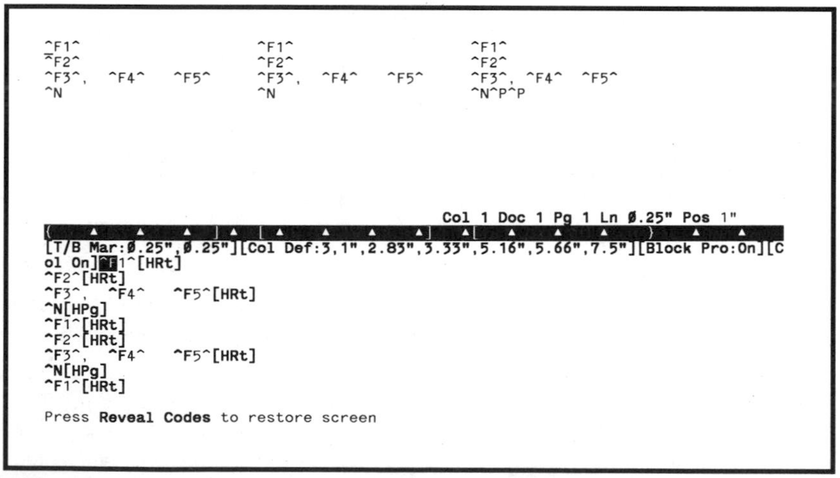

■**FIGURE 22.4:** *Primary document with codes for laser printers*

VERSION 5.1 FEATURES

HANDLING BLANK FIELDS IN MERGE FILES

Two special IF commands are available for dealing with blank fields in macros. IF BLANK specifies actions that should occur if a field is empty, IF NOT BLANK determines actions if the field contains information.

For example, this merge command prints the word President in an inside address if the *name* field is empty:

```
{IF BLANK}name~
President
{ELSE}
{FIELD}name~
{END IF}{FIELD}address~
{FIELD}city~
```

This merge accomplishes the same objective using IF NOT BLANK but with field numbers instead of names:

```
{IF NOT BLANK}1~
{FIELD}1~
{ELSE}
President
{END IF}{FIELD}address~
{FIELD}city~
```

IF BLANK and IF NOT BLANK cannot be used in macros.

FORMATTING AND PRINTING LABELS

Because of the importance of labels in the business world, WordPerfect has taken several steps to streamline their production in version 5.1. A special page style form has been created for labels, along with a new menu to specify their size and spacing. Once you set up the label form, multiple column labels can be easily entered or merged from a secondary list file.

To automate the process even further, WordPerfect supplies a Labels macro that presents a menu of 19 popular label styles then creates the page form for you automatically.

While the macro can save you a great number of keystrokes, it is important to know how to create the label form yourself, since your own labels might not be among those supported by the macro. In addition, the label form can be used effectively for other types of documents, such as parallel columns.

So let's go through the procedure for formatting and using the label form before looking at the Labels macro.

Creating a Label Form   When you create a label form, you will be adding a page style code into the document. Where you place the code depends on whether you plan to type the labels yourself, or you are creating a primary merge file to create the labels from a mailing list.

First, we'll create a label form. Then, we'll look at where to place the code in the document. Many of the menus and procedures you'll be using here will already be familiar to you from Chapter 3.

Follow these steps.

1. Press Shift-F8 2 7 or select **L**ayout **P**age Paper **S**ize, to display the Format Paper Size/Type menu listing available forms.

2. Press **2** or **a** to add a new form, displaying the Format Paper Type menu. Even though there is a Label type on the menu, you can select any of the types listed. However, selecting Labels makes the form easier to recognize when you're ready to enter or merge the labels.

3. Press **L** or **4**, or any of the other options, to display the Edit Paper Definition menu.

4. Press **8** or **a**, for the Labels option, then Y. The Format Labels menu appears (Figure 22.5). Set the options in this menu to fully describe the labels you are using.

```
Format: Labels

    1 - Label Size
                      Width           2.63"
                      Height          1"

    2 - Number of Labels
                      Columns         3
                      Rows            10

    3 - Top Left Corner
                      Top             0.5"
                      Left            0.188"

    4 - Distance Between Labels
                      Column          0.125"
                      Row             0"

    5 - Label Margins
                      Left            0.013"
                      Right           0.193"
                      Top             0"
                      Bottom          0"

    Selection: 0
```

■**FIGURE 22.5:**   *Format Labels menu*

Label Size	Enter the width and height of the individual labels, not including the spaces between labels or margins to the end of the sheet. If you are using a round label, enter the diameter as both the width and height.
Number of Labels	Enter the number of labels across (columns) and down (rows) the page.
Top Left Corner	This setting tells WordPerfect the exact location of the first label on the page. Enter the distance from the top of the page to the top of the first label, and from the left side of the page to the left edge of the labels. When using labels on tractor paper, set the top left corner at 0" and 0" to position the labels so the printer starts at the top of the first label.
Distance Between Labels	Enter the amount of spacing, if any, between labels.
Label Margins	These margin settings control where WordPerfect prints text on the label. For example, the top margin is the amount of space between the top of the label and the first line of text.

5. Make your selections from the menu, then press Return to display the Edit Paper Definition menu.

If your settings conflict with the paper size, one of these warnings may appear on the status line:

Error: Labels will not fit on paper size

This message means that the label size you entered is too large to fit on the page in the quantities shown. You must change the label size before exiting the menu or press F1 to cancel the changes.

Error: Label margins increased due to printer's minimum margins

This message means that you've set the label margins or corner settings too small to accommodate any minimum margins on your printer. This most frequently occurs with laser printers that have small non-printable areas on each side of the page. WordPerfect will automatically increase the label margin settings. If the settings are acceptable, press Return or F7 to exit the menu after the message disappears from the prompt line.

6. Make any necessary selections from this menu, then press Return to display the Paper Size/Type menu. However, if you now change the paper size so the labels no longer fit, you'll see the message

> Error: Label information needs to be updated for this paper size

when you exit the Paper Size menu. Increase the paper size or edit the label definition. From the Edit Paper Definition menu, press 8 Y to redisplay the Format Labels menu.

When you exit the Edit Paper Definition menu, the list of paper sizes and types appears with the label form selected.

7. Press F1 F7 to exit the menu without selecting the form.

When you are ready to use the form, press Shift-F8 2 7, or select **L**ayout **P**age Paper **S**ize, highlight the label form, then press Return three times. The form type code will be inserted in the document.

Typing Labels   If you plan on typing the labels yourself, enter the code at the start of the document. Press Ctrl-Return to insert a page break line after typing each label.

Merging Labels   If you are creating a primary merge file to create labels from a mailing list, the code must be inserted as the document's initial code. To do this, press Shift-F8 3 2, or select **L**ayout **D**ocument Initial Codes, select the label form as described above, then press F7 twice.

Enter the field codes for the label, such as

{FIELD}1~

{FIELD}2~

{FIELD}3~, {FIELD}4~ {FIELD}5~

Save the primary file then merge it with the mailing list.

Logical and Physical Pages   When you create a label form, WordPerfect considers each label a *logical* page. The size and margins of the logical page are determined by the size and margin settings on the labels menu.

The sheet which holds the labels is considered the *physical* page. The Top Left corner setting determines the top and left margins of the physical page. The bottom and right margins are calculated by subtracting the labels and the space between them.

When you have labels on the screen, each will be separated by a page break line, and the page counter will increase as you move from label to label. However, the labels will print in the correct number of rows and columns (Figure 22.6). With multicolumn labels, the labels fill out the physical page row by row. Using three across labels, for example, labels 1, 2, and 3 take up the first row, labels 4, 5, and 6, the second, and so on.

Considering each label a page is useful for several reasons:

- To see how many labels you've entered, press Home Home ↓, then look at the page indicator on the status line.

- To determine how many sheets of labels you have, divide the last page number by the number of labels per page.

- To move from label to label, press PgUp and PgDn.

- To move to a specific label (page), press Ctrl-Home, enter the label number, then press Return.

- To print specific labels use the multiple pages options on the Print menu.

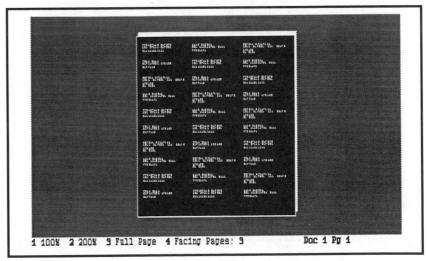

■FIGURE 22.6: *Labels as they appear in View mode*

- To center text on the label, insert the Center Page code. Press Shift-F8 2 1 Y, or select **Layout Page** Center Page **Yes**. When typing labels, insert the code at the top of each. In a primary merge file, insert the code once at the start of the file, not as an initial code.

Using the Labels Macro   The macro LABELS.WPM automates the process of creating a label form for common label layouts. The macro is installed along with the keyboard layout files during the installation process. So if you didn't install the keyboard layouts, run Install again but enter Yes when asked if you want these files installed.

This macro, by the way, is an excellent example of the powerful capabilities of the version 5.1 macro/merge language. You can create your own customized menus, prompts, and command lines just like those used in this macro.

Follow these steps to use the Labels macro, either at the start of the document or from the initial codes screen.

1. Press Alt-F10 or select **Tools Macro Execute**.

2. Type **LABELS**, then press Return. It may take a few moments, but you'll soon see a menu of supported label forms (Figure 22.7).

If your label isn't listed, press PgDn to see additional forms.

```
                    Label Page/Size Definitions
Mnu  Label Sizes        # of labels per..
ltr   H x W             Sheet Row Column   Examples
 A    1" x 2 5/8"         30   3    10      Avery 5160/5260
 B    1" x 4"            20   2    10      Avery 5161/5261
 C    1 1/3" x 4"        14   2     7      Avery 5162/5262
 D    2" x 4"            10   2     5      Avery 5163
 E    3 1/3" x 4"         6   2     3      Avery 5164
 F    2/3" x 3 7/16"     30   2    15      Avery 5266
 G    1/2" x 1 3/4"      80   4    20      Avery 5267
 H    2 3/4" x 2 3/4"     9   3     3      Avery 5196
 I    1 1/2" x 4"        12   2     6      Avery 5197
 J    8 1/2" x 11"        1   0     0      Avery 5165
 K    1" x 2 5/8"        30   3    10      3M 7730
 L    1 1/2" x 2 5/6"    21   3     7      3M 7721
 M    1" x 2 5/6"        33   3    11      3M 7733
 N    2 1/2" x 2 5/6"    12   3     4      3M 7712
 O    3 1/3" x 2 5/6"     9   3     3      3M 7709
 P    11" x 8 7/16"       1   0     0      3M 7701
 (↑↓), (Mnu Ltr), or (*), then Press Enter; More=PgDn
Selection: A
```

■**FIGURE 22.7:** *Menu from LABELS macro*

3. Press the menu letter of your label form, then press Return. You can also use the ↓ key to highlight the label, then press Return. You'll see a message similar to

Setting up (1 1/3 x 4) inch labels

as WordPerfect starts to work through the Format Label menu for you. In a moment, you'll see a prompt line like:

(1 1/3 x 4) inch labels location: 1 Continuous; 2 Bin Number; 3 Manual:3

Select the type of paper feed. If you've selected Manual, you'll see a second prompt line such as

Prompt to load (1 1/3 x 4 inch) labels: Yes (No)

WordPerfect will complete the Edit Paper Definition menu, then display the Paper Size/Type menu with the label form selected. The prompt line will be:

Highlight selection press 1 Select 2 Exit

4. Press **1** or **s** if you want to insert the code at this point. Press **2** or **e** to return to the document. This is a convenient way to insert the label form in your list of available forms for selecting at a later time.

Other Uses for Labels   In addition to mailing labels, label forms can be used to quickly create documents that require parallel columns. While the paragraphs won't appear side-by-side on the screen, the label form allows control over placement and spacing.

Another use of the label form is designing booklets or pamphlets, especially with laser printers that print in landscape. Figure 22.8 shows two pages of a booklet created using a label form designated as standard landscape containing two 5 1/2- by 8 1/2-inch labels (two columns, one row) with 1/2-inch label margins on all sides.

A footer at the start of the document was used to insert the page numbers, and a graphic was inserted on the second page.

To create a similar multipage booklet, make up a "dummy layout" on scrap paper to see which pages print side-by-side on the same sheet of paper. Create the label form, then insert the appropriate text. With a 4-page folder, for example, pages 1 and 4 are on one side of the sheet, 2 and 3 on the other.

Design the label form, then type the pages in this order: **1 4 2 3**. Print the first two pages, turn the paper over then print the next two pages. You'll have to find the correct way to feed and flip the paper for your own printer.

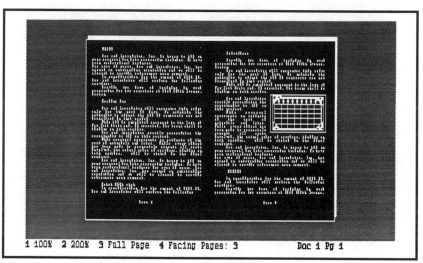

■**FIGURE 22.8:**   *Folder created using label form*

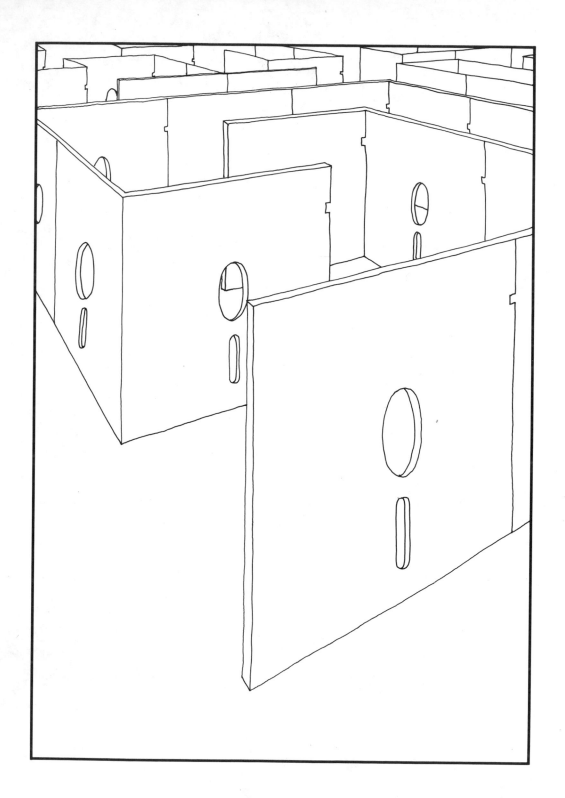

23

ADVANCED DOCUMENT ASSEMBLY

WordPerfect's Merge functions give the program a large capability for combining files. They can be used for managing data files, producing form documents, and inserting boilerplate files. Now you will learn how to take full advantage of these functions.

This chapter concentrates on techniques for document assembly. You will learn how to build complex documents from boilerplate files and from specially constructed secondary files. Our data management and document assembly system example combines WordPerfect's Merge functions into a sophisticated practical application.

■ MASTER DOCUMENT

The longer your document becomes, the more time it takes to load and save, or to move from the first to the last page. To avoid such long documents, you can write and edit the document in smaller sections, each a separate file, then create a *master document* to merge and format it for printing.

For instance, create a document with nothing but the page and document formatting codes, then, for each separate file that will comprise the larger document, press Alt-F5 2 (for the Subdoc option) and enter the file name. Your master document may appear on screen as in Figure 23.1.

When you're ready to print the file (or to create a table of contents or index), press Alt-F5 6 3 to expand the master document.

USING THE ^P CODE

You can also create a master document by surrounding the files to be included in ^P codes. While this doesn't give you the flexibility provided by subdocuments, it illustrates another use of merge codes. For example, here is a file called REPORT:

^PIntroduction^P
^PHypothesis^P
^PMethod^P
^PResults^P
^PSummary^P

Note
With version 5.1 use {NEST PRIMARY} *filename~.*

When you name REPORT as the primary file for a merge operation without naming a secondary file, the five named documents are recalled from disk and assembled into one large document. These files are called boilerplate, yet they are simply individual documents combined by a merge operation.

Whether you are using the ^P codes to merge entire documents or just boilerplate paragraphs, they provide tremendous flexibility. Primary files can be chained together to construct a document from any number of boilerplate files. You can also merge boilerplate text while reading fields from a single secondary file. In fact, you can even transfer the name of a primary file as one of the secondary file fields.

However, there are some limitations. You cannot include another primary file name or use two secondary files when merging files for more than one form

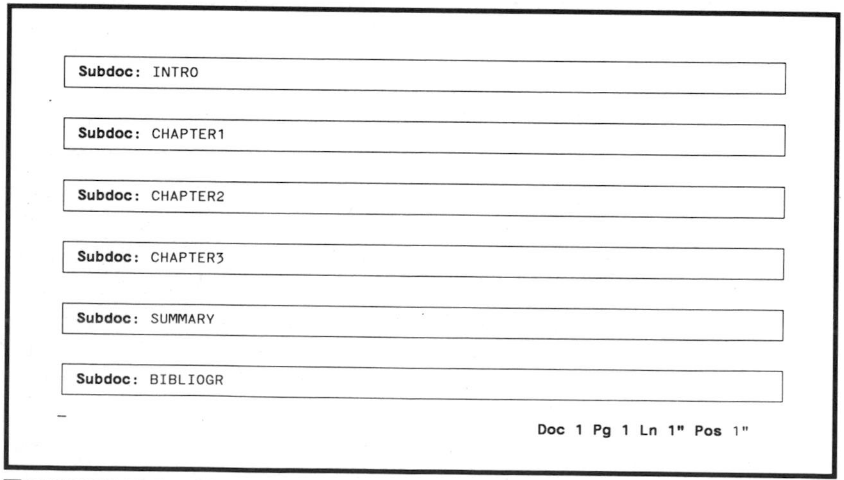

■**FIGURE 23.1:** *Master document containing Subdoc codes*

document. WordPerfect does not have the capability to switch back and forth between secondary files during a merge operation.

New Feature
Additional related features in version 5.1 are discussed under "Nesting Merge Files."

These restrictions do not apply if you are merging a secondary file with only one record. So there are additional options available when you are assembling individual documents rather than mass-producing them.

In the example above, each of the five files in ^P codes that make up the REPORT file could be called a primary file. However, this is a bit misleading in a discussion of document assembly techniques. So, for clarity, I'll call the document being assembled the *master file* to distinguish it from the primary files used as boilerplate and from master documents containing Subdoc codes.

■ DATA MANAGEMENT AND DOCUMENT ASSEMBLY SYSTEMS

In the REPORT example, all of the primary files are specifically named in the master file. In this case, the master file will always be composed of the same combination of primary files, in the same order. But WordPerfect offers much more flexibility in document assembly.

You can construct a small master file that allows you to assemble primary files in any order. Because the files are named at the time of merging, this master file can be used to produce any assembled document.

In this section, you'll learn how to get the most from WordPerfect's Merge functions by actually creating a complete assembly program combined with a database management system. This system is designed for use by the graduate admissions office of a small college. Our sample office maintains a list of applicants. When a student applies, his or her mailing address will be added to a secondary file, called PROSPECT. If the student is accepted, the office will send a form letter welcoming the student and listing certain required courses. This list of courses varies depending on the student's course of study.

To handle the situation, we will construct some primary files containing boilerplate paragraphs for the letter. Then we will create a primary file for automatically adding new applicants to the mailing list. We will also create a series of additional files and macros to recall the mailing address of an accepted student, request the names of the boilerplate files, and complete the letter. Take your time and carefully follow each step.

THE BOILERPLATE AND SECONDARY ADDRESS FILES

Let's begin by entering the boilerplate files and the secondary file listing each student's address.

1. Start WordPerfect.

2. Type the following sentence, then press Return twice:

    The admissions committee has reviewed your credentials and is pleased to offer you a place in our fall class.

3. Press F7 Y, type **ADMIT,** and press Return N to save the file and clear the screen.

4. Type the following sentence, then press Return twice:

    You have met all of the basic entry requirements and should schedule an appointment with your advisor to plan your course of study.

5. Press F7 Y, type **METALL,** and press Return N to save the file and clear the screen.

6. Type the following sentences, then press Return twice:

    However, your acceptance is dependent upon completion of several prerequisite classes. Please contact our admissions advisor within 10 days to discuss your academic program.

7. Press F7 Y, type **PREREQ,** and press Return N to save the file and clear the screen.

8. Type the following, then press Return twice:

    As you know, there are several academic divisions within our college, each having slightly different requirements.

    For your own area, these requirements include:

9. Press F7 Y, type **AREAS,** and press Return N to save the file and clear the screen.

10. Type the following list, then press Return twice:

    Computer Programming

    Introduction to Algorithms
    Developing Algorithms

Pascal Programming
Introduction to C
Advanced C Programming
Cobol Programming
Assembler

11. Press F7 Y, type **PROG**, and press Return N to save the file and clear the screen.

12. Type the following list, then press Return twice:

Computer Technology

Microprocessors
Advanced Microprocessors
Compiler Design
Telecommunications
Digital Techniques

13. Press F7 Y, type **TECH**, and press Return N to save the file and clear the screen.

14. Type the following list, then press Return twice:

Systems and Management

Systems Analysis and Design
Introduction to MIS
Database Management Systems
Computer Resource Management

15. Press F7 Y, type **MIS**, and press Return N to save the file and clear the screen.

16. Type the following list, then press Return twice:

Math

Finite Math I and II
Geometry
Calculus I
Advanced Calculus
Trigonometry

17. Press F7 Y, type **MATH**, and press Return N to save the file and clear the screen.

18. Type the following list, then press Return twice:

    Statistics

    Introductory Statistics
    Business Statistics
    Clinical Laboratory Statistics

19. Press F7 Y, type **STAT**, and press Return N to save the file and clear the screen.

20. Type the following sentence and closing:

    We hope the next year will be a rewarding one for you.

                                    Sincerely,

                                    Dean I. O. Kim

21. Press F7 Y, type **CLOSE**, and press Return N to save the file and clear the screen.

22. Create the following secondary file with two records:

Note

Throughout this chapter, remember that with version 5.1, {END FIELD} replaces ^R, {END RECORD} replaced ^E, {FIELD} replaces ^F, {PAGE OFF} replaces ^N^P^P, and {PRINT} replaces ^T.

    Stephen Chesin^R
    653 Old Farm Road^R
    Houston^R
    TX^R
    08634^R
    Stephen^R
    ^E
    Terry Devlin^R
    520 Popular Street^R
    Detroit^R
    MI^R
    76510^R
    Terry^R
    ^E

23. Press F7 Y, type **PROSPECT**, and press Return Y to save the file and exit WordPerfect.

We will use these sample files to create several assembled documents.

THE ADDRESS PRIMARY FILE

The address primary file is used to input the data for the secondary file. The Save macro, which we will create next, will then actually add the information to the existing address list.

1. Start WordPerfect.

Note

With version 5.1, refer to "The Address Primary File."

2. Type the following text, pressing Shift-F9 to enter the Merge codes, and F9 to enter ^R.

   ^OEnter the name^O^C^V^R^V
   ^OEnter the street address^O^C^V^R^V
   ^OEnter the city^O^C^V^R^V
   ^OEnter the state^O^C^V^R^V
   ^OZip code?^O^C^V^R^V
   ^OEnter the salutation: Dear ^O^C^V^R^V
   ^V^E^V
   ^Gsave^G

   The page break line will separate the ^E and ^V codes.

3. Press F7 Y, type **ADD**, and press Return N to save the file and clear the screen.

THE SAVE MACRO

Note

With version 5.1, refer to "The Save Macro."

The Save macro is called after the variable information has been entered. This macro will add the new applicant to the list of prospective students.

1. Type **Test**. We'll delete this word after we create the macro, but some text is needed for WordPerfect to save a file.

2. Press Ctrl-F10, type **Save**, and press Return twice.

3. Press ↑. Otherwise, you'd save an extra blank line that will be left after the data is entered.

4. Press Alt-F4, then press Home Home ↑ to highlight the text.

5. Press Ctrl-F4 1 4 to select the Append option.

6. Type **PROSPECT** then press Return.

7. Press F7 N N, then press Ctrl-F10 to end the macro.

8. Press Shift-F10, type **PROSPECT**, and press Return to recall the file.

9. Press Home Home ↓, then delete the word *Test*. Do not delete the ^E code.

10. Press F7 Y Return Y N to save the corrected file and clear the screen.

THE SELECT MACRO

When it is time to put together an acceptance letter, the student's address must be selected from the data file. The address will be stored in a temporary file and later merged with the body of the acceptance letter. Using the Select macro, the user will enter the student's last name as part of the selection criteria. (For this system to work, the selection criteria can only be used to retrieve one name—more on that later.)

Note
With version 5.1, refer to "The Select Macro."

1. Type **Test**.

2. Press F7 Y, type **STUDENT**, and press Return N to save this temporary file and clear the screen. (We must have a file called STUDENT on the disk to complete this macro.)

3. Press Ctrl-F10, type **Select**, and press Return twice.

4. Press Ctrl-F9 2 to select the Sort option.

5. Type **PROSPECT** at the Input File prompt, then press Return.

6. Type **STUDENT** at the Output File prompt, then press Return.

7. Press **Y**. The Sort by Line menu appears. As part of the macro, we will enter the appropriate keys and selection criteria for this application. This will ensure that the correct information is on the menu before the file is sorted.

8. Press **7 1** to select a merge sort.

9. Press **3** to select the key.

10. Press A 1 Return 1 Return −1. This selects the last word of the first line—the student's last name. Even though these options may already be selected, you must still enter the exact keystrokes to ensure that the macro will work even if you previously selected another key.

11. Press F7 to return to the Sort by Line menu.

12. Press **4** to choose the Select option.

13. Press Ctrl-End to ensure that any other selection criteria are deleted.

14. Type **key1=**.

15. Press Ctrl-PgUp to insert a pause in the macro.

16. Press **1** followed by Return.

17. Press F7 to exit the Select menu.

18. Press **1** to perform the selection.

19. Press Ctrl-F10 to end the macro.

Selection Criteria Variations   As mentioned before, only one record can be selected for this system to function properly. However, some variations in the selection criteria may be necessary in your own application.

The Select macro selects the student by the last name, using the −1 word in the first field. If necessary, two keys can be established, one for the first name and another for the last name. (You cannot use both names as one key because a key can only be one word long.) For example, to locate the name Frederick Rogers, the selection criteria would be

key1=Rogers*key2=Frederick

If just using the −1 word is not sufficient because your list includes names such as *John Wilkes, Jr.,* you can define three keys, then use them selectively depending on the name. For example, the following keys could be defined:

Key	Typ	Field	Line	Word	Key	Typ	Field	Line	Word
1	a	1	1	-1	2	a	1	1	-2

Key	Typ	Field	Line	Word
3	a	1	1	1

Select key1=

Key1 is the last word in the name, key2 the next to last, and key3 the first word. A combination of these keys should locate any specific record. If you are searching for Richard Needlemyer, the only Needlemyer in the list, the selection criterion can be simply *key1=Needlemyer.* If there is a possibility of two Needlemyers, you would enter

key1=Needlemyer*key3=Richard

Locate John Wilkes, Jr., by entering

key1=Jr.*key2=Wilkes*key3=John

A more efficient alternative, however, is to separate the last name from the Jr., or other ending, with a hard space (Home space bar) and use the −1 word for the search or sort. WordPerfect will treat the ending as part of the word and sort the last names correctly.

At the end of the actual search, a message such as

1 Record Retrieved

will appear on the screen. If no such message is displayed, then no record matched the selection criteria. If more than one record was retrieved, then repeat the selection process using more keys in the criteria.

Another option is to change the macro so that the selected record appears on the screen instead of being sent directly to the file. Another pause could be entered so that if the proper record was displayed, pressing Return would chain to another macro that would write the record to the disk. If the wrong record or more than one record appeared, you would press F1 to cancel the action, then run the Select macro again using different keys.

CREATING THE MASTER FILE

Now the body of the letter must be assembled from boilerplate paragraphs on the disk. We'll create a small generic master file that can be used to assemble any number of documents. It allows you to enter the names of the primary files to be assembled. The Append macro, which we'll create a little later, does the bulk of the work.

Note

With version 5.1, refer to "The Master Primary File."

1. Type the following two lines:

    ^OEnter a primary file name: ^O^V^P^V^C^V^P^V
    ^P^P

2. Press F7 Y, type **MASTER**, and press Return N to save the file and clear the screen.

Here's what all of these codes mean:

■ *^OEnter a primary file name: ^O* displays a message on the screen with each cycle of the master file.

■ *^V^P^V* inserts a ^P code into the completed document after the files are merged.

■ *^C* pauses the merge operation for operator input.

■ *^V^P^V* inserts another ^P code so that the text input will be surrounded by ^P codes and used as a primary file name.

THE SHELL MASTER FILE

Note
With version 5.1, refer to "The Shell Master File."

The SHELL master file will contain the Merge codes to add the inside address and salutation to the assembled letter.

1. Type the following:

   ^D

   ^F1^
   ^F2^
   ^F3^, ^F4^ ^F5^

   Dear ^F6^:

2. Press Return twice after the last line.

3. Press F7 Y, type **SHELL**, and press Return N to save the file and clear the screen.

THE SHELL MACRO

Note
With version 5.1, refer to "The Shell Macro."

If you added data to the SHELL master file for one letter, you would destroy it for use the next time. The Shell macro will create a document called LETTER, which will be the final master file. It recalls the SHELL master file and saves it under the name LETTER, then runs the Master macro, which we will create soon.

1. Type **Test**.

2. Press F7 Y, type **LETTER**, and press Return N.

3. Press Ctrl-F10, type **Shell**, and press Return twice.

4. Press Shift-F10, type **SHELL**, and press Return.

5. Press F7 Y.

6. Type **LETTER** then press Return Y N.

7. Press Alt-F10, type **Master**, and press Return.

8. Press Ctrl-F10 to end the macro definition.

THE APPEND MACRO

The Append macro is essential to this system because it combines the list of primary files with the codes to merge the inside address.

1. Type the following:

   this is a test
   this is a test

   At least two lines of text are needed on the screen for the various parts of the macro to be created.

2. Press Ctrl-F10, type **Append**, and press Return. You already created an Append macro in Chapter 21, so you'll be prompted to either replace or edit the macro.

3. Press **1** to replace the existing macro.

4. Press Return to skip the Description prompt.

After the names of the primary files have been entered, there will be some extra codes on the screen. The next several steps delete these codes.

5. Press ↑ Home ←.

6. Press Alt-F4 to turn on the highlighting.

7. Press Home Home ↓ to highlight the text.

8. Press Del Y to delete the highlighted text.

9. Press Alt-F4 to turn on the highlighting.

10. Press Home Home ↑ to highlight the text on the screen.

11. Press Ctrl-F4 1 4 to select the Append option.

12. Type **LETTER**, then press Return. The master file with the names of the primary files to be merged will be added to the end of the inside address.

13. Press F7 N N.

14. Press Ctrl-F10 to end the macro definition.

THE MASTER MACRO

The Master macro runs the MASTER merge file to allow selection of primary files, then it runs the Append macro.

1. Press Ctrl-F10, type **Master**, and press Return.

2. Press Alt-F10, type **Append**, and press Return.

Warning
Step 5: With version 5.1, press Shift-F9 1. Refer to "Stopping Macro Operations."

3. Press Ctrl-F9 1 to select the Merge option.

4. Type **MASTER** then press Return twice.

5. Press ↓ F9 to end the merge operation and save the macro to the disk.

6. Press F7 N N to clear the screen.

THE PRINT MACRO

Finally, the Print macro merges the LETTER file, which contains the codes for the address and primary files, with the STUDENT secondary file, which contains the variable data.

1. Press Ctrl-F10, type **Print**, and press Return twice.

2. Press Ctrl-F9 1.

3. Type **LETTER** then press Return.

4. Type **STUDENT** then press Return.

5. Press F7 N Y to exit WordPerfect.

SUMMARY OF FILES AND MACROS

All the files and macros that we've created so far amount to fewer than 2,000 bytes (characters) of disk space. And they allow WordPerfect to perform some rather sophisticated tasks for a word processing program. The same application written in a computer programming language would take hundreds of lines of instructions—many thousands of bytes of disk space.

To recap, your disk should now contain the following boilerplate files:

- ADMIT

- PROG

- STAT

- METALL

- TECH

- CLOSE

- PREREQ

- MIS

- AREAS

- MATH

We created the following primary files:

- ADD, which accepts entry of a new record

- STUDENT, which holds the selected name for merging

- MASTER, which requests the names of boilerplate files

- SHELL, which contains the Merge codes for the address

- LETTER, which holds the codes for merging the addresses and the boilerplate files

Our macros include the following:

- Save, which adds the record to the STUDENT file

- Select, which requests and finds the record

- Shell, which transfers the SHELL file into the LETTER file, then runs Master macro

- Append, which adds the boilerplate codes to the LETTER file

- Master, which runs the MASTER merge file, then runs the Append macro

- Print, which merges the LETTER primary file with the STUDENT secondary file to complete the letter

We have one secondary file, PROSPECT, which is the student address list.

USING THE APPLICATION

Now let's use our system to create the document (Figure 23.2) to send to a new student who must also be added to the address list. Of course, any student already in the data file could be used.

1. Start WordPerfect and press Ctrl-F9 1 to select the Merge option.

2. Type **ADD** then press Return twice. The menu for inserting new students is displayed, as shown in Figure 23.3.

3. Enter the entire record for this student. Press F9 after each field.

Eugene Chen
405 East Frankford Avenue
Philadelphia
PA

```
January 1, 1991

Eugene Chen
405 East Franford Avenue
Philadelphia,  PA  19109

Dear Eugene:

     The admissions committee has reviewed your credentials and is
pleased to offer you a place in our fall class.

     As you know, there are several academic divisions within our
college, each having slightly different requirements.

     For your own area, these requirements include:


Computer Programming

Introduction to Algorithms
Developing Algorithms
Pascal Programming
Introduction to C
Advanced C Proqramming
Cobol Programming
Assembler


Systems and Management

Systems Analysis and Design
Introduction to MIS
Database Management Systems
Computer Resource Management


Statistics

Introductory Statistics
Business Statistics
Clinical Laboratory Statistics


We hope the next year will be a rewarding one for you.

                    Sincerely,

                    Dean I. O. Kim
```

■**FIGURE 23.2:** *Sample letter created by the document assembly system*

19109
Eugene

Figure 23.4 shows the completed record. After you enter all the fields, the Save macro will add the record to the PROSPECT file. The next step is to select the record of the student to receive the letter.

4. Press Alt-F10, type **Select**, and press Return. In a few moments, the Sort Secondary Merge File menu will appear, and the cursor will be at the Selection Criteria prompt.

Note

The appearance of the version 5.1 screen is slightly different, but the steps listed here still apply.

```
^V^R^V
^OEnter the street address^O^C^V^R^V
^OEnter the city^O^C^V^R^V
^OEnter the state^O^C^V^R^V
^OZip code?^O^C^V^R^V
^OEnter the salutation: Dear ^O^C^V^R^V
^V^E
==============================================================================
^V
^Gsave^G




Enter the name                                      Doc 1 Pg 1 Ln 1" Pos 1"
```

■**FIGURE 23.3:**   *The menu for adding a new student to the address list*

```
Eugene Chen^R
405 East Frankford Avenue^R
Philadelphia^R
PA^R
19109^R
Eugene^V^R^V
^V^E
==============================================================================
^V
^Gsave^G




Enter the salutation: Dear                    Doc 1 Pg 1 Ln 1.83" Pos 1.6"
```

■**FIGURE 23.4:**   *The new record*

5. Type **Chen** then press Return. The record is located and placed in the STUDENT file, and the screen is cleared. Now the appropriate primary files must be selected.

6. Press Alt-F10, type **Shell**, and press Return. First, the SHELL master file is copied into the LETTER document, then the Primary File prompt appears on the screen, as shown in Figure 23.5.

Warning
Step 8: With version 5.1, press Shift-F9 1.

7. Type each of the following boilerplate file names. Press F9 after each one.

```
ADMIT
AREAS
PROG
MIS
STAT
CLOSE
```

Figure 23.6 shows how the screen looks at this point.

8. Press the ↓ key then F9 to end the selection of primary files. Now the Append macro adds the primary file names, complete with ^P codes, to the LETTER document, which already contains the address codes. The LETTER document is not displayed on the screen, but if you recalled it, the file would appear as shown in Figure 23.7.

Note
The appearance of the version 5.1 screen is slightly different, but the steps listed here still apply.

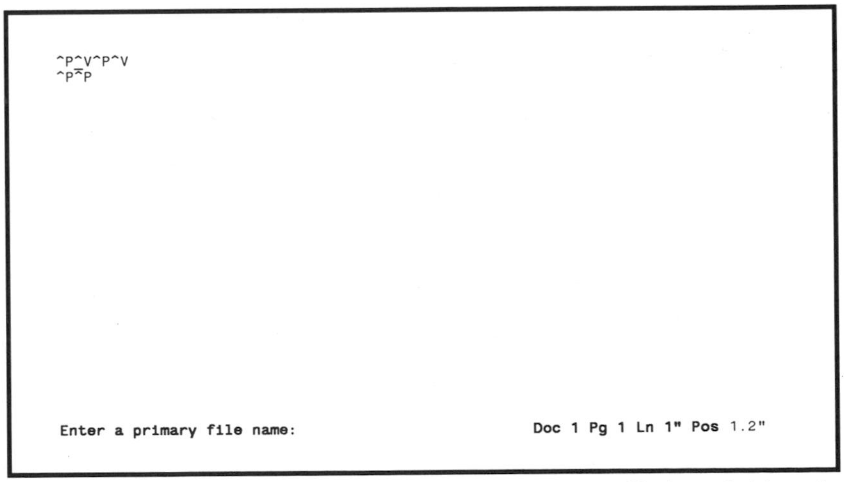

```
^P^V^P^V
^P˜P




                                                                         
Enter a primary file name:                    Doc 1 Pg 1 Ln 1" Pos 1.2"
```

■**FIGURE 23.5:** *The Primary File prompt after the master file is copied into the document*

9. Press Alt-F10, type **Print**, and press Return. The LETTER master file is merged with the STUDENT secondary file and displayed on the screen.

10. Press Shift-F7 1 to print the letter.

RUNNING YOUR OWN SYSTEM

To run your own system, follow this general procedure:

- Use the ADD primary merge file whenever you want to add persons to the master list. (You could create a Delete macro similar to the one shown in Chapter 21 to remove names.)

- When you want to send out a letter, use the Select macro to pick out the subject, then the Shell macro to select the boilerplate paragraphs you want to include in the letter.

- Finally, use the Print macro to merge the final letter to the screen.

■ PROGRAMMED MACRO FOR MULTIPLE ADDITIONS

You can use modified versions of the Save macro, the ADD master file, and the programmed macro illustrated in Chapter 21 to enter as many persons to the list

```
^PADMIT^P
^PAREAS^P
^PPROG^P
^PMIS^P
^PSTAT^P
^PCLOSE^P
^P^V^P^V
^P=P
```

Enter a primary file name: Doc 1 Pg 1 Ln 2" POS 1.2"

■FIGURE 23.6: *The screen after the primary files are entered*

as you want without having to reenter the Merge command.

Change the Save macro by deleting the first {UP} command. The revised macro would appear as

```
{DISPLAY OFF} {Block}{HOME}{HOME}{UP}
{MOVE}14prospect{ENTER}
{EXIT}nn
```

Delete the line *^Gsave^G* from the ADD master file.
The programmed macro would be

```
{ASSIGN}1~1~
{LABEL}repeat~
{IF}{VAR 1}=1~{GO}get~{ELSE}{GO}end~{END IF}
{LABEL}get~
{Merge/Sort}1add{ENTER}{ENTER}
{CHAR}1~Enter 1 to continue or 0 to end~
{Backspace}{GO}repeat~
{LABEL}end~
```

Name the macro *Add*. When you have names to enter, press Alt-F10, then type *Add* followed by Return. The Add primary file will appear. After you enter each name, respond to the prompt

Enter 1 to continue or 0 to end~

```
^D

^F1^
^F2^
^F3^,   ^F4^  ^F5^

Dear ^F6^:

^PADMIT^P
^PAREAS^P
^PPROG^P
^PMIS^P
^PSTAT^P
^PCLOSE^P




A:\LETTER                              Doc 1 Pg 1 Ln 1" POS 1"
```

■**FIGURE 23.7:** *The LETTER file, assembled by several primary files and macros (not displayed as part of the process)*

Press *1* if you have more names to enter. After entering the last person, press *0* then run the Save macro—press Alt-F10, type *Save,* then press Return.

Because of minor differences in the macros, you must set them up one way or the other. If you are going to use the programmed macro shown here, you must use the modified Save macro. Do not use the modified Save macro, however, if you're using the Add primary file directly as explained earlier.

As you can see, once the groundwork has been laid, a complex document assembly and merge procedure can be accomplished with a few keystrokes. The files and macros created here could actually be part of a larger system for maintaining records and assembling form documents.

YOUR OWN PROJECTS

The example in this chapter can serve as a starting point for creating your own applications. Following the basic procedure that we used in the example will make the task easier.

Start by designing the main secondary file that will contain the address list or data file. Think carefully about how fields can be combined or separated to best suit the purposes of the data file. Look ahead to the types of selections and sorts that you will be performing.

Plan what types of assembled documents may be required. Will certain paragraphs always be used with others? If so, combine them in one boilerplate file. If individual paragraphs may be combined in a variety of ways, save each as a separate file.

Create any simple primary files that may be needed. Don't worry about macros yet because they can be created at any time. Test each primary file before trying to link several together.

Add any macros that will stand by themselves or be used with other macros. Then create the macros that will be used for merging with primary files.

Finally, write the macros to combine the merge operations and other macros. Test everything several times.

When you're creating a macro that links another macro with a merge operation, enter the macro first, then enter the merge keystrokes. The macro will not be run until after the files have been merged. As an example, look at the Master macro in this chapter. The Append macro was inserted first, then the merge keystrokes were entered, even though they will be performed in the opposite order.

When combining macros with primary files (such as the ADD file), place the macro in its proper order. Use the Master, Append, and Shell macros that we created in this chapter as examples.

VERSION 5.1 FEATURES

NESTING MERGE FILES

Version 5.1 does allow multiple secondary files to be used in a single merge operation by linking them together with the CHAIN SECONDARY command. Suppose you have two secondary files, LISTA and LISTB. During a merge, you want to use the data in LISTA, then the data in LISTB. Your first record in LISTA would appear like this:

```
{PROCESS}{CHAIN SECONDARY}LISTB~{PROCESS}
Frederick Rogers{END FIELD}
431 Broad Street{END FIELD}
Philadelphia{END FIELD}
PA{END FIELD}
19101{END FIELD}
(215) 555-7654{END FIELD}
500{END FIELD}
January 2, 1991{END FIELD}
45.67{END FIELD}
Fred{END FIELD}
Mr. Rogers{END FIELD}
{END RECORD}
```

The process command tells WordPerfect to complete the current secondary file, then process the Chain Secondary command, which passes the merge operation to LISTB.

THE ADDRESS PRIMARY FILE

Using version 5.1 merge codes, enter the address primary file as follows using Shift-F9 6, or Tools Merge Codes More, to access the merge code window:

```
{PROMPT}Enter the name~{KEYBOARD}{MRG CMND}{END
    FIELD}{MRG CMND}
{PROMPT}Enter the street address~{KEYBOARD}{MRG
    CMND}{END FIELD}{MRG CMND}
{PROMPT}Enter the city~{KEYBOARD}{MRG CMND}{END
    FIELD}{MRG CMND}
{PROMPT}Enter the state~{KEYBOARD}{MRG CMND}{END
    FIELD}{MRG CMND}
```

```
{PROMPT}Zip code?~{KEYBOARD}{MRG CMND}{END
    FIELD}{MRG CMND}
{PROMPT}Enter the salutation: Dear ~{KEYBOARD}{MRG
    CMND}{END FIELD}{MRG CMND}
{MRG CMND}{END RECORD}
{MRG CMND}
{CHAIN MACRO}save~
```

The version 5.0 file shown in the chapter will operate properly before and after automatic conversion.

THE SAVE MACRO

You can create the macro as explained in the chapter, or enter it directly in the macro editor. Follow these steps to use the macro editor:

1. Press Home Ctrl-F10, type **SAVE**, then press Return twice.

2. Press Del to delete the {DISPLAY OFF} code.

3. Press Ctrl-F10 to enter macro commands.

4. Press ↑ Alt-F4 Home Home ↑ Ctrl-F4.

6. Type **14prospect**.

7. Press Return F7 n n.

8. Press Ctrl-F10.

9. Press F7 to save the macro and return to the document window.

THE SELECT MACRO

You can create the macro as explained in the chapter, or enter it directly in the macro editor. You don't have to create the temporary Student file before creating the macro, but it must exist on the disk before executing it for the first time. Follow these steps to use the macro editor:

1. Press Home Ctrl-F10, type **SELECT**, then press Return twice.

2. Press DEL to delete the {DISPLAY OFF} code.

3. Press Ctrl-F10 to enter macro commands.

4. Press Ctrl-F9 2.

5. Type **prospect**, then press Return.

6. Type **student**, then press Return.

7. Press Y 7 1 3 a 1 Return 1 Return -1 F7 4 Ctrl-End.

8. Type **key1=**

9. Press Ctrl-F10 to exit macro commands.

10. Press Ctrl-PgUp, select {PAUSE}, then press Return.

11. Press Ctrl-F10 F7 1.

12. Press Ctrl-F10, then F7 to save the macro.

THE MASTER PRIMARY FILE

Using version 5.1 merge codes, enter the master primary file as follows using Shift-F9 6, or **T**ools Me**r**ge Codes **M**ore to access the merge code window:

```
{PROMPT}Enter a primary file name: ~{MRG CMND}{NEST
     PRIMARY}{MRG CMND}{KEYBOARD}{MRG CMND}~{MRG
     CMND}
{NEST PRIMARY}~
```

The version 5.0 file shown in the chapter will operate properly before and after automatic conversion. To enter ^V, however, you must press Ctrl-V twice.

THE SHELL MASTER FILE

Using version 5.1 merge codes, enter the master primary file as follows using Shift-F9 6, or **T**ools Me**r**ge Codes **M**ore to access the merge code window:

```
{DATE}

{FIELD}1~
{FIELD}2~
{FIELD}3~, {FIELD4}~  {FIELD}5~

Dear {FIELD}6~
```

The version 5.0 file shown in the chapter will operate properly before and after automatic conversion.

THE SHELL MACRO

You can create the macro as explained in the chapter, or enter it directly in the macro editor. You don't have to create the Letter file before creating the macro. Follow these steps to use the macro editor:

1. Press Home Ctrl-F10, type **SHELL**, then press Return twice.

2. Press DEL to delete the {DISPLAY OFF} code.

3. Press Ctrl-F10 to enter macro commands.

4. Press Shift-F10, type **shell**, then press Return.

5. Press F7 Y, type **letter**, press Return Y N.

6. Press Alt-F10, type **master**, then press Return.

7. Press Ctrl-F10, then F7 to save the macro.

THE APPEND MACRO

If you've created the Master primary file using version 5.1 codes, then you must create the Append macro using these steps. You already created an APPEND macro in Chapter 21, so you'll have to delete the keystrokes.

1. Press Home Ctrl-F10, type Append, then press Return twice.

2. Press DEL until you delete the contents of the macro.

3. Press Ctrl-F10 to enter macro commands.

4. Press ↑ ← ←. This moves the cursor past merge codes that you do not want to copy to the letter file.

5. Press Alt-F4 Home Home ↑ ← Ctrl-F4.

6. Type **14letter**.

7. Press Return F7 n n.

8. Press Ctrl-F10, then F7 to save the macro.

STOPPING MERGE OPERATIONS

When creating or using the Master primary file, stop the merge operation from requesting file names by pressing Shift-F9 to display the prompt line:

1 Quit; 2 Next Record; 3 Stop: 0

then press **1** or **q**.

This command line is normally used to insert one of these three commands into a merge operation as it is running.

AUTOMATING WITH PROGRAMMED MACROS

As the Labels macro illustrated, macros can be used to create entire programs—including windows, command lines, and prompts. As another example, Figure 23.8 shows a macro that automates the application created in this chapter by displaying this prompt line on the status line;

1 Add; 2 Select; 3 Shell; 4 Print; 5 Quit: Q

```
{LABEL}repeat~
{CHAR}select~
{^]}1 A{^Q}dd;
{^]}2 S{^Q}elect;
{^]}3 {^Q}S{^]}h{^Q}ell;
{^]}4 P{^Q}rint;
{^]}5 Q{^Q}uit: Q{Left}~

{CASE}{VARIABLE}select~~
     1~doadd~
     A~doadd~
     a~doadd~
     2~doselect~
     S~doselect~
     s~doselect~
     3~doshell~
     H~doshell~
     h~doshell~
     4~doprint~
     P~doprint~
     p~doprint~
     {ELSE}~end}~
~


{LABEL}doadd~
     {Merge/Sort}1add{Enter}{Enter}{GO}repeat~

{LABEL}doselect~
     {NEST}select~{GO}repeat~

{LABEL}doshell~
     {NEST}shell~{GO}repeat~

{LABEL}doprint~
     {NEST}print~{GO}repeat~

{LABEL}end~
```

■**FIGURE 23.8:** *Macro for custom prompt line*

Select an option by pressing its highlighted number or letter—either upper or lower case. The process repeats until you press any character that doesn't select one of the first four options.

If you use this macro, do not make the changes to the Save macro and ADD master file mentioned in the chapter under "Programmed Macro for Multiple Additions."

While most of the commands should look familiar, those that create the prompt line may be new to you. So let's look at the program in detail. First look at this command:

{LABEL}repeat~

This marks the start of the macro so it can be repeated.

Now look at this:

{CHAR}select~

{^]}1 A{^Q}dd;

{^]}2 S{^Q}elect;

{^]}3 {^Q}S{^]}h{^Q}ell;

{^]}4 P{^Q}rint;

{^]}5 Q{^Q}uit: Q{Left}~

This large CHAR command creates the prompt line at the bottom of the screen, accepting input into the variable *select*. The macro was entered on separate lines just to make it easier to read, but it will appear as one line on the screen. The ^ codes are special operators used to format characters on the screen—{^]} turns on boldface, {^Q} returns to the normal text attribute. The {Left} command at the end of the section moves the cursor under the letter Q, the default selection.

Refer to the WordPerfect manual for a complete list of attribute and screen control codes.

The next example is

{CASE}{VARIABLE}select~~
1~doadd~
A~doadd~
a~doadd~
2~doselect~
S~doselect~
s~doselect~
3~doshell~
H~doshell~

```
h~doshell~
4~doprint~
P~doprint~
p~doprint~
{ELSE}~end}~

~
```

This case statement branches to the appropriate label based on the value of the variable *select*. Notice that cases include both numeric entry as well as upper or lower case letters. While the prompt line requests 5 or *q* to quit the macro, the macro will end by jumping to the label end if neither of the first four options are selected. The final tilde closes the case command.

Now look at the last example:

```
{LABEL}doadd~
    {Merge/Sort}1add{Enter}{Enter}{GO}repeat~
{LABEL}doselect~
    {NEST}select~{GO}repeat~
{LABEL}doshell~
    {NEST}shell~{GO}repeat~
{LABEL}doprint~
    {NEST}print~{GO}repeat~
{LABEL}end~
```

These are the five routines jumped to from the case statement. All but the *end* routine jump back to the beginning to redisplay the prompt line and request input.

The {NEST} commands in doselect, doshell, and doprint execute other macros. WordPerfect performs the macro then returns to perform the {GO}repeat~ command.

So far we've just touched on the capabilities of the version 5.1 merge and macro commands. To use them to the fullest, however, you should be familiar with computer programming, or have a great deal of patience and perseverance.

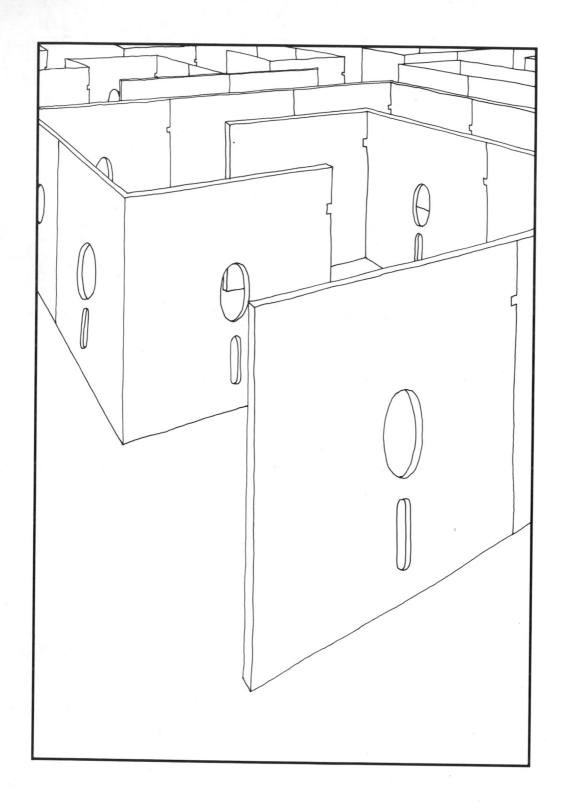

24

COMBINING MACROS, MENUS, AND MERGES

In the last four chapters, you've seen just how versatile WordPerfect can be. We created a menu-driven data management system with client information, including form letters and reports. We also wrote a college admissions program that maintained a prospective student list and assembled form letters.

This chapter will tie all of our efforts together. We will create a series of linked menus and some new macros. These will allow you to move freely from menu to menu to select functions and files.

LINKING MENUS

If an application is large or complicated, it is impractical to try to remember all of the related macros and files. You've learned how to create WordPerfect menus to display such information. However, one on-screen menu can easily become too cluttered. This is particularly true when the menu items really don't relate to each other.

Take a look at the following menu:

```
Menu
ADD             Add inventory items
DELETE          Delete inventory items
REPORT1         Inventory master list
REPORT2         Reorder list
CLIENT          Add client to master list
ERASE           Delete client from list
```

Notice that there are two distinct areas covered in this menu—inventory control and client maintenance. As the menu list grows, the specific tasks performed by each choice will become more and more obscure. The solution is to use several menus linked together. The menu above could be divided into a master menu and two submenus.

Note

With version 5.1, refer to "Linking Menus," page 631.

^OMaster Menu

CLIENT	Perform client maintenance functions
INVEN	Perform inventory functions

Select either CLIENT or INVEN: ^O^G^C^G

^OClient Maintenance Menu

INSERT	Add client to master list
ERASE	Delete client from master list
ADDRESS	Create address and telephone report
LABEL	Create mailing label document
MASTER	Display Master menu
INVEN	Display Inventory Maintenance menu

Enter the name of the function: ^O^G^C^G

^OInventory Maintenance Menu

ADD	Add inventory items
DELETE	Delete inventory items
REPORT1	Inventory master list
REPORT2	Reorder list
VENDOR	Create vendor list
PRICE	Price lists
MASTER	Display Master menu
CLIENT	Display Client Maintenance menu

Enter the name of the function: ^O^G^C^G

BUILDING A COMPLETE MENU-DRIVEN APPLICATION

In the last four chapters, we've created quite a few menus, files, and macros. Now we will tie all of them together in one menu-driven application. You'll need all of them on your disk only if you plan to actually run this application when it is completed. So if you deleted some, you can still complete the exercise in this chapter, but you may not be able to see the final application perform all of its functions.

The system will be started by a macro, called Main, that will display a menu to start a merge operation.

THE MAIN MENU

When you create a macro to start a merge operation, the primary or secondary files named in the macro must already exist on the disk. So we'll create the primary file for the menu first.

Note
With version
5.1, refer to
"The Main
Menu,"
page 631.

1. Type the following menu, using Shift-F9 to enter the codes. Any Center codes or tabs used to format the menu will be ignored when it appears on the screen. Use the space bar instead to position the menu title and application names.

   ^O   Main Menu

   Menu1   Client Lists and Reports
   ADM   Admissions Program

   Please enter your choice
   ^O^G^C^G

2. Press F7 Y, type **MAIN**, and press Return N to save the menu and clear the screen.

This menu requests the name of the next primary file to use. Entering *Menu1* or *ADM* will transfer control to a macro that calls the primary file and displays another menu. Menu1, the Client Lists and Reports menu, should already be on your disk. Soon, we will edit that menu for this application and create the Admissions Program menu.

THE MAIN MACRO

The Main macro will clear the screen, then call the Main menu. This macro will be named in both of the submenus as a way of returning to the Main menu, and it will also be used to start the application.

Note
With version
5.1, refer to
"The Main
Macro,"
page 633.

1. Press Ctrl-F10, type **Main**, and press Return twice.

2. Press F7 N N. This clears the screen so that the menu appears alone.

3. Press Ctrl-F9 1.

4. Type **MAIN**.

5. Press Return twice. The Main menu appears.

6. Press Shift-F9 to exit the menu and end the macro definition.

7. Press F7 N N to clear the screen.

THE CLIENT LISTS AND REPORTS MENU (MENU1)

Menu1 was created in Chapter 19, and you should already have it on your disk. If you deleted it, enter the entire menu again; otherwise, edit it as shown.

Warning
Users of version 5.1 should follow the special instructions under "The Menu1 Primary File," page 632.

1. Press Shift-F10, type **MENU1**, and press Return to recall the file.

2. Edit the menu so that it appears as follows. It has a new title and a revised Secondary File prompt line.

^OClient Lists and Reports

Primary Files   Secondary Files

FORM: discount letter   LIST1: master file
REPORT1:   credit remaining   LIST2: zip code order
REPORT2:   address list
REPORT3:   last order date
REPORT4:   full client list

Enter the name of the secondary file: ^S^C^S^O

^OEnter the name of the primary file: ^P^C^P^O

3. Press F7 Y Return Y N to save the edited file and clear the screen.

All of the selections on this menu are either primary or secondary files.

THE ADMISSIONS PROGRAM MENU

All of the admissions system functions start with macros except the task of appending new students to the file. That was accomplished through a primary master file. Unfortunately, a single menu can allow entry of either file names or macros, not both. So to provide a complete macro menu, we will prepare an Adm macro to call the ADM file. We will also write a Del macro for deleting a student from the address list. Then all of the admissions program functions can be called from a single menu.

To start the MENU1 file from this menu, we also will create a Menu1 macro.

Follow these steps to create the Admissions Program menu:

Note
With version 5.1, refer to "Admissions Program Menu," page 632.

1. Type the following menu, using Shift-F9 to enter the codes:

   ^OAdmissions Program

Add	Add students to mailing list
Del	Delete students from mailing list
Select	Select student to receive letter
Shell	Request paragraphs for the letter—RUN SELECT FIRST
Print	Merge letter to the screen—RUN SHELL FIRST
MAIN	Return to Main menu
MENU1	Client lists and reports

   Please enter the name of desired function
   ^O^G^C^G

2. Press F7 Y, type **ADM**, and press Return N to save the menu and clear the screen.

Notice that the prompt line requests the name of a macro (^G), not a file (^P or ^S).

THE ADM MACRO

The Adm macro is used to transfer control from the Main menu to the Admissions Program menu.

Note
With version 5.1, refer to the "ADM Macro," page 633.

1. Press Ctrl-F10, type **Adm**, and press Return twice.

2. Press F7 N N to clear the screen.

3. Press Ctrl-F9 1.

4. Type **ADM**.

5. Press Return twice. The Admissions Program menu appears.

6. Press Shift-F9 to end the macro definition.

THE ADD MENU

We created the Add menu in Chapter 22, but it needs one additional line to chain it back to the Main menu.

1. Press Shift-F10, type **ADD**, and press Return to recall the menu.

2. Press Home Home ↓.

Warning

With version 5.1, refer to "The Add Menu," page 633.

3. Type **^Gmain^G**. The menu should now look like this:

```
^OEnter the name^O^C^V^R^V
^OEnter the street address^O^C^V^R^V
^OEnter the city^O^C^V^R^V
^OEnter the state^O^C^V^R^V
^OZip code?^O^C^V^R^V
^OEnter the salutation: Dear ^O^C^V^R^V
^V^E^V
^Gsave^G
^Gmain^G
```

If you modified this menu to work from a programmed macro, reenter the *^Gsave^G* line as well. (If you want to enter multiple names, don't change this file—use the programmed macro instead. But after you're done entering records you'll have to run the Save macro and then the Main macro to display the Main menu again.)

4. Press F7 Y Return Y N to save the edited menu and clear the screen.

Adding this link to the Main macro will automatically redisplay the Main menu after a student is added.

THE ADD MACRO

The Add macro clears the screen, then starts the merge of the ADD file, created in Chapter 22.

Note

With version 5.1, refer to "The Add Macro," page 634.

1. Press Ctrl-F10, type **Add**, and press Return.

2. Press **1** to replace the Add macro you created previously.

3. Press Return.

4. Press F7 N N.

5. Press Ctrl-F9 1.

6. Type **ADD**. (There will be an ADD file and an Add macro.)

7. Press Return twice. The Add menu appears.

Warning
With version
5.1, press F9
seven times in
step 8, and skip
step 9.

8. Press ↓ nine times to reach the end of the menu, then press F9. The Main menu appears.

9. Press F9 to end the macro definition. You'll see a File Not Found warning message on the screen; just ignore it for now.

10. Press F7 N N to clear the screen.

THE DEL MACRO

The Del macro is similar to the one that we created in Chapter 18. However, the student record contains a different number of lines from the file used in that chapter, so a new macro must be developed. This macro also has a few extra features. Follow these steps to create the Del macro:

Note
With ver-
sion 5.1, refer
to "The Del
Macro,"
page 335.

1. Press Ctrl-F10, type **Del**, and press Return twice.

2. Press Alt-F10.

3. Type **Main** then press Return. This serves as a "not found" macro. If the search name is not located, the Main macro will be run to redisplay the Main menu. Remember, a macro within a macro is not run until the first macro is completed.

4. Press F7 N N.

5. Press Shift F10, type **PROSPECT**, and press Return to recall the data file.

6. Press F2 to display the Search prompt.

7. Press Ctrl-PgUp 1 Return.

8. Press F2.

9. Press Home ← to place the cursor on the start of the name line.

10. Press Alt-F4 to turn on the highlighting.

11. Press ↓ seven times.

12. Press Del Y.

13. Press F7 Y Return Y N to save the edited file and clear the screen.

14. Press Alt-F10.

15. Type **Main** then press Return. After the file is saved, the Main macro will be called to redisplay the Main menu.

16. Press Ctrl-F10 to end the macro definition.

This macro clears the screen, then recalls the PROSPECT secondary file and starts the search operation. We included a pause at that point to enter the name of the student being deleted from the file. If the name is found, the seven-line record is marked as a block, then deleted. Afterward, the edited file is saved on disk and the Main menu appears. If the name is not found, the Main menu appears immediately.

THE MENU1 MACRO

The Menu1 macro is used from the Admissions Program menu to display the Client Lists and Reports menu.

Note
With version 5.1, refer to "The Menu1 Macro," page 335.

1. Press Ctrl-F10, type **Menu1**, and press Return twice.

2. Press F7 N N.

3. Press Ctrl-F9 1.

4. Type **MENU1**.

5. Press Return.

6. Type **LIST1** as the secondary file. You can change this when you actually run the application. But by adding it here you make it the "default" that is used if you do not enter another choice from the menu.

7. Press Return.

8. Press Shift-F9.

9. Press F7 N N.

SUMMARY OF NEW FILES AND MACROS

We created two new files for the application: MAIN, which is a menu of major selections, and ADM, which is a menu of admissions program functions.
We also created five macros:

■ The Main macro, which runs the MAIN file merge.

- The Adm macro, which starts the ADM file from the Main menu.

- The Del macro, which deletes a student from the student list, then redisplays the Main menu.

- The Add macro, which runs the ADD file merge to append a new student to the list.

- The Menu1 macro, which runs the MENU1 file.

These new files and macros consume less than 1,000 bytes of disk space.

The MENU1 and ADD menu files were created in earlier chapters, but we made some changes to them for the sample application.

RUNNING THE APPLICATION

If you still have all of the files that we created in the last four chapters on your disk, you can control them all with our new series of menus. As an illustration, we'll see how the menus are linked together.

1. Press Alt-F10, type **Main**, and press Return. The screen clears, and then the Main menu appears, as shown in Figure 24.1.

2. Type **ADM** then press Return. The Admissions menu appears as in Figure 24.2.

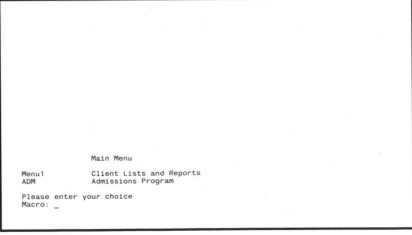

```
                        Main Menu

        Menu1           Client Lists and Reports
        ADM             Admissions Program

        Please enter your choice
        Macro: _
```

■**FIGURE 24.1:** *The Main menu*

3. Type MENU1, then press Return to display the Client Lists and Reports menu as shown in Figure 24.3.

4. Press Return to accept the default List1 data file.

5. Type **Report1** then press Return to merge Report1 with List1. When the merge is complete, the finished report will appear on the screen.

6. Press F7 N Y to exit WordPerfect.

```
Admissions Program

Add             Add students to mailing list
Del             Delete students from mailing list
Select          Select student to receive letter
Shell           Request paragraphs for the letter- -RUN SELECT FIRST
Print           Merge letter to the screen- -RUN SHELL FIRST

MAIN            Return to Main menu
MENU1           Client lists and reports

Please enter the name of desired function
Macro: _
```

■**FIGURE 24.2:**   *The Admissions menu*

```
Client Lists and Reports

Primary Files               Secondary Files

FORM:     discount letter      LIST1: master file
REPORT1: credit remaining      LIST2: zip code order
REPORT2: address list
REPORT3: last order date
REPORT4: full client list

Enter the name of the secondary file: _
```

■**FIGURE 24.3:**   *The Client Lists and Reports menu*

The exercise above demonstrates how you can move from menu to menu. At any point, you could enter the name of a menu option to perform that function. Some, such as the Del option for deleting students from the list, will automatically return you to the Main menu when the function is completed. Others, like the reports from Menu1, will simply end. To return to the Main menu, just run the Main macro (Alt-F10 Main Return).

You could create macros to run every function and add *^Gmain^G* at the end of each. Then change the ^P^C^P prompts in the menus to ^G^C^G. After every function, the Main menu will be redisplayed, completing the chain.

■ YOUR OWN SYSTEMS

Our sample application combined two separate functions, client maintenance and an admissions program, into one system. In your own more practical applications, all of the selections from the Main menu will probably be related. They could be part of your business or personal endeavors.

For example, a collector's Main menu might appear something like this:

Note

With version 5.1, {PROMPT}~ replaces ^O, {CHAIN MACRO} replaces ^G, and {KEYBOARD} replaces ^C.

```
^OMain Menu
INVENT      Inventory report menu
VALUE       Value of each item and totals
LOCAT       Location of each item
CAT         Catalog describing each item in collection
VEND        List of vendors
COLLECT     List of other collectors
SEARCH      Menu of form letters to vendors
ADD         Add item to collection inventory
SOLD        Delete item from collection inventory

Enter the function desired^O^G^C^G
```

A household maintenance system might have a menu that looks like this:

```
^OHousehold Menu
PHONE       Phone list menu
INVEN       Household inventory
DATES       Date reports (birthday, anniversary, etc.)
HOLIDAY     Holiday card and gift reports
COUPON      Store coupon menu

Enter function name:^O^G^C^G
```

Once you have organized your data management system as suggested here, your tasks will be accomplished much more efficiently.

■ USING BOILERPLATE SECONDARY FILES

So far, all of our secondary file examples have contained a series of records, with the same number and type of fields in each record. This is the typical format for secondary files used with form letters.

Another use of secondary files is for boilerplate text. This type of file contains just one record composed of a number of fields. Each field is a boilerplate paragraph or some other text. The ^F codes in the primary file are used to selectively merge text into the main document.

For example, in the file shown in Figure 24.4, there is one record of six

Note
With version 5.1, {END FIELD} replaces ^R, {END RECORD} replaces ^E, {FIELD} replaces ^F, {PAGE OFF} replaces ^N^P^P, and {PRINT} replaces ^T.

```
        The admissions committee has reviewed your credentials and is
pleased to offer you a place in our fall class.^R
        You have met all of the basic entry requirements and should
schedule an appointment with your advisor to plan your course of
study. Among the courses required for this major are:^R
        However, your acceptance is dependent upon completion of
several prerequisite classes. Please contact our admissions advisor
within 10 days to discuss your academic program.^R  We hope the
next year will be a rewarding one for you.

                        Sincerely,

                        Dean I. O. Kim^R

        Computer Programming

        Introduction to Algorithms
        Developing Algorithms
        Pascal Programming
        Introduction to C
        Advanced C Programming
        Cobol Programming
        Assembler

^R

        Systems and Management

        Systems Analysis and Design
        Introduction to MIS
        Database Management Systems
        Computer Resource Management

^R
^E
```

■**FIGURE 24.4:** *A secondary boilerplate file with six fields*

"fields." Each field is composed of some boilerplate text, including any spacing that may be required in the main document. In the figure, there are blank lines before and after the ^R code ending the fifth field (the Computer Programming list), and another blank line before the final ^R. These blank lines are included in the field to provide the required spacing in the merged document.

The primary document used with such a secondary file lists the field numbers in ^F codes. The letter shown in Figure 24.5 can be produced with this primary file:

```
Dear Student:
^F1^
^F2^
^F5^
^F6^
^F4^
```

As you will soon see, ^C and ^U codes can be used in the primary file to allow even greater flexibility.

```
Dear Student:

     The admissions committee has reviewed your credentials and is
pleased to offer you a place in our fall class.
     You have met all of the basic entry requirements and should
schedule an appointment with your advisor to plan your course of
study. Among the courses required for this major are:

     Computer Programming

     Introduction to Algorithms
     Developing Algorithms
     Pascal Programming
     Introduction to C
     Advanced C Programming
     Cobol Programming
     Assembler


     Systems and Management

     Systems Analysis and Design
     Introduction to MIS
     Database Management Systems
     Computer Resource Management

     We hope the next year will be a rewarding one for you.

                    Sincerely,

                    Dean I. O. Kim
```

■**FIGURE 24.5:** *A letter prepared with a secondary boilerplate file*

BUILDING A SECONDARY BOILERPLATE FILE

In Chapter 23, we entered the paragraphs shown in Figure 24.4 as individual documents. Now we will create a single secondary file for them. Here's how:

1. Start WordPerfect.

2. Press Shift-F10, type **ADMIT**, and press Return. The boilerplate paragraph is displayed on the screen.

3. Place the cursor at the end of the sentence and press F9 to insert the ^R code.

4. Press Shift-F10, type **METALL**, and press Return to recall the next paragraph.

5. Place the cursor at the end of the sentence.

6. Type **Among the courses required for this major are:** then press F9.

7. Press Shift-F10, type **PREREQ**, and press Return to recall the next paragraph.

8. Place the cursor at the end of the sentence and press F9.

9. Press Backspace then the space bar to place the cursor one space away from the ^R code.

10. Press Shift-F10, type **CLOSE**, and press Return to recall the next paragraph.

11. Press Home Home ↓ F9.

12. Press Return to insert a blank line.

13. Press Shift-F10, type **PROG**, and press Return to recall the next paragraph.

14. Press Home Home ↓ to place the cursor at the end of the section.

15. Press Return to insert a blank line, then F9 to end the field.

16. Press Return to insert another blank line.

17. Press Shift-F10, type **MIS**, and press Return to recall the next paragraph.

18. Press Home Home ↓ Return F9 to insert a blank line and end the field.

19. Press Shift-F9 E to insert the ^E code, ending the record.

20. Press F7 Y, type **BPLATE**, and press Return N to save the secondary file and clear the screen.

ASSEMBLING BOILERPLATE FILES

The main problem with the primary file that lists field numbers in ^F codes is that the paragraphs will always appear in the same order. This means that different primary files must be created for each possible combination of boilerplate paragraphs. Instead, you can create a small primary file that requests the paragraphs to be assembled and their order. Follow these steps:

Warning
Users of version 5.1 should follow the special instructions under "Assembling Boilerplate Files," page 636.

1. Type the following, using Alt-F9 to enter the codes:

   ^OEnter the paragraph number: ^O^U

2. Press Ctrl-F. This inserts the ^F code into the text.

3. Press Shift-F9 C to insert the ^C code.

4. Press Ctrl-F to insert another ^F code.

5. Press Return.

6. Press Shift-F9 P Shift-F9 P. Your file should look like this:

   ^OEnter the paragraph number:^O^U^F^C^F
   ^P^P

7. Press F7 Y, type **INPUT**, and press Return N to save the file and clear the screen.

This primary file can be used to assemble a document on the screen from any of the paragraphs in the secondary file. The ^U code will display each paragraph as its number is entered.

USING THE INPUT FILE

Now that both the primary and secondary files have been created, the fields can be merged into a finished letter. Try this example:

1. Press Ctrl-F9 1 to display the Primary File prompt.

2. Type **INPUT** then press Return.

3. Type **BPLATE** in response to the Secondary File prompt, then press Return. The Field Number prompt appears.

4. Press **1** then Return. The first field is retrieved, and the Field Number prompt reappears, as shown in Figure 24.6.

5. Complete the letter by entering the appropriate codes. Press 2 Return 5 Return 6 Return 4 Return.

6. Press Shift-F9 to end the merge operation.

7. Press F7 N N to clear the screen.

Note
With version 5.1, a few extra codes will appear when completed. Delete them before printing the document.

CHAINING SECONDARY FILE FIELDS

If certain boilerplate paragraphs always appear together, you can make the input from the secondary file even more efficient. For example, suppose that every student must take the programming classes listed in field 5 of our sample boilerplate file. This would mean that the following two boilerplates are always seen together:

You have met all of the basic entry requirements and should schedule an appointment with your advisor to plan your course of study. Among the courses required for this major are:

Computer Programming

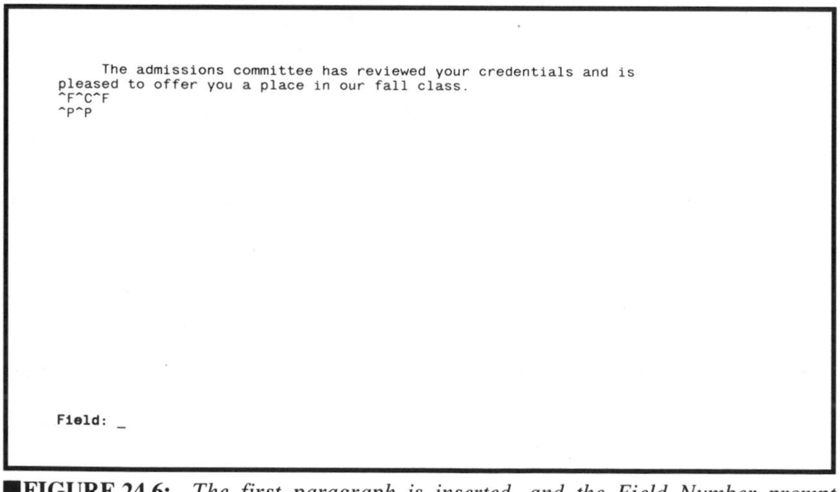

```
        The admissions committee has reviewed your credentials and is
pleased to offer you a place in our fall class.
^F^C^F
^P^P




Field: _
```

■**FIGURE 24.6:** *The first paragraph is inserted, and the Field Number prompt reappears*

Introduction to Algorithms
Developing Algorithms
Pascal Programming
Introduction to C
Advanced C Programming
COBOL Programming
Assembler

Or, if a student needs prerequisite classes, these two boilerplates would always be used together:

However, your acceptance is dependent upon completion of several prerequisite classes. Please contact our admissions advisor within 10 days to discuss your academic program.

We hope the next year will be a rewarding one for you.

Sincerely,

Dean In Ho Kim

These sets of paragraphs could be combined in the secondary file itself, but then the closing paragraph and list of programming classes would have to be repeated separately for use with other letters.

The alternative is to insert field codes in the secondary file itself to chain these boilerplates together. Let's see how this works by revising our boilerplate file.

1. Press Shift-F10, type **BPLATE**, and press Return to recall the secondary file.

2. Place the cursor at the end of the second paragraph, under the ^ of the ^R code, like this:

   Among the courses required for this major are: ^R

3. Press Shift-F9 F 5 Return. This enters a code to insert the fifth field (the second carriage return separates the two paragraphs).

   Among the courses required for this major are: ^F5^^R

4. Place the cursor at the end of the third paragraph, under the ^ of the ^R code.

5. Press Return.

6. Press Shift-F9 F 4 Return. This enters a code to insert the fourth field:

> Please contact our admissions advisor within 10 days to discuss your academic program.
> ^F4^^R

7. Press F7 Y Return Y N to save the edited file and clear the screen.

This new file is now ready to use with the INPUT primary file. However, since certain paragraphs are now chained together, there are fewer field numbers to be entered.

Let's use our revised boilerplate file to create the body of a letter for a student who must take prerequisite classes, as shown in Figure 24.7.

1. Press Ctrl-F9 1.

2. Type **INPUT** at the Primary File prompt, then press Return.

3. Type **BPLATE** at the Secondary File prompt, then press Return.

4. Press **1** at the Field Number prompt, then press Return. The first field is displayed.

5. Press **3** at the Field Number prompt, then press Return. When the third paragraph, which includes the ^F4 code, is recalled from the file, the fourth paragraph (the closing) is automatically recalled as well.

6. Press Shift-F9 to end the merge operation.

7. Press F7 N N to exit WordPerfect.

Use this technique when you know that certain paragraphs will always appear together. It not only saves keystrokes, but also ensures that the required information is entered.

```
        The admissions committee has reviewed your credentials and is
    pleased to offer you a place in our fall class.
        However,  your  acceptance  is  dependent  upon  completion  of
    several prerequisite classes. Please contact our admissions advisor
    within 10 days to discuss your academic program. We hope the next
    year will be a rewarding one for you.

                    Sincerely,

                    Dean I. O. Kim
```

■**FIGURE 24.7:**   *Sample letter created with chained fields*

■ VERSION 5.1 FEATURES

LINKING MENUS

With version 5.1, create a series of menus using this format:

```
{PROMPT}Master Menu
CLIENT       Perform client maintenance functions
INVEN        Perform inventory functions

Select either CLIENT or INVEN:~{CHAIN
MACRO}{KEYBOARD}~
```

{PROMPT}~ replaces the older ^O codes, {CHAIN MACRO} replaces ^G, and {KEYBOARD} replaces ^C.

When you chain a macro, the named macro is executed after the current macro is completed—no matter where in the file you place the Chain command. Only one Chain Macro command can be used in a merge file. If you have more than one, only the last one is executed.

THE MAIN MENU

Using version 5.1 merge codes, enter the Main Menu primary file as follows using Shift-F9 6, or Tools Merge Codes More, to access the Merge Codes window:

```
{PROMPT}            Main Menu

Menu                Client Lists and Reports
ADM                 Admissions Program

Please enter your choice
~{CHAIN MACRO}{KEYBOARD}~
```

The version 5.0 file shown earlier in this chapter will operate properly before and after automatic conversion.

THE MAIN MACRO

You can create the macro as explained earlier in this chapter, or enter it directly in the Macro Editor. Follow these steps to use the Macro Editor:

1. Press Home Ctrl-F10, type **MAIN** and press Return twice.

2. Press Del to delete the {DISPLAY OFF} code.

3. Press Ctrl-F10 to enter Macro Commands.

4. Press F7 N N Ctrl-F9.

5. Type **1main** and press Return twice.

6. Press Ctrl-F10.

7. Press F7 to save the macro and return to the document window.

THE MENU1 PRIMARY FILE

Using version 5.1 merge codes, enter the menu1 primary file as follows using Shift-F9 6, or **T**ools **Me**rge Codes **M**ore, to access the Merge Codes window:

{PROMPT}Client Lists and Reports

Primary Files	Secondary Files
FORM: discount letter	LIST1: master file
REPORT1: credit remaining	LIST2: zip code order
REPORT2: address list	
REPORT3: last order date	
REPORT4: full client list	

Enter the name of the secondary file: {SUBST SECONDARY}{KEYBOARD}~~

{PROMPT}Enter the name of the primary file: {CHAIN PRIMARY}{KEYBOARD}~~

The version 5.0 file shown earlier in this chapter will operate properly before and after automatic conversion.

ADMISSIONS PROGRAM MENU

Using version 5.1 merge codes, enter the Admissions Program Menu primary file as follows using Shift-F9 6, or **T**ools **Me**rge Codes **M**ore, to access the Merge Codes Window:

{PROMPT}Admissions Program
Add   Add students to mailing list
Del   Delete students from mailing list

Select	Select student to receive letter
Shell	Request paragraphs for the letter—RUN SELECT FIRST
Print	Merge letter to the screen—RUN SHELL FIRST

MAIN	Return to Main menu
MENU1	Client lists and reports

Please enter the name of desired function
~{CHAIN MACRO}{KEYBOARD}~

The version 5.0 file shown in the chapter will operate properly before and after automatic conversion.

ADM MACRO

You can create the macro as explained in this chapter, or enter it directly in the Macro Editor. Follow these steps to use the Macro Editor:

1. Press Home Ctrl-F10, type **ADM** and press Return twice.

2. Press Del to delete the {DISPLAY OFF} code.

3. Press Ctrl-F10 to enter Macro Commands.

4. Press F7 N N Ctrl-F9.

5. Type **1adm** and press Return twice.

6. Press Ctrl-F10.

7. Press F7 to save the macro and return to the document window.

THE ADD MENU

Using version 5.1 merge codes, enter the Add Menu primary file as follows using Shift-F9 6, or Tools Merge Codes More, to access the Merge Codes window:

{PROMPT}Enter the name~{KEYBOARD}{MRG CMND}{END FIELD}{MRG CMND}
{PROMPT}Enter the street address~{KEYBOARD}{MRG CMND}{END FIELD}{MRG CMND}

```
{PROMPT}Enter the city~{KEYBOARD}{MRG CMND}{END
    FIELD}{MRG CMND}
{PROMPT}Enter the state~{KEYBOARD}{MRG CMND}{END
    FIELD}{MRG CMND}
{PROMPT}Zip code?~{KEYBOARD}{MRG CMND}{END
    FIELD}{MRG CMND}
{PROMPT}Enter the salutation: Dear ~{KEYBOARD}{MRG
    CMND}{END FIELD}{MRG CMND}
{MRG CMND}{END RECORD}
{MRG CMND}
{NEST MACRO}save~
{CHAIN MACRO}main~
```

The version 5.0 file shown in the chapter will operate correctly before conversion. However, if you convert the file by pressing Ctrl-F9 3, the last two lines will appear as

```
{CHAIN MACRO}save~
{CHAIN MACRO}main~
```

Since only one Chain Macro command can be used in a primary file, the *main* macro will be run, ignoring the *save* macro; your data will not be appended onto the secondary file. If you do convert the 5.0 version, change the command {CHAIN MACRO}save~ to {NEST MACRO}save~.

THE ADD MACRO

You can create the macro as explained in this chapter, or enter it directly in the Macro Editor. Follow these steps to use the Macro Editor:

1. Press Home Ctrl-F10, type **ADD** and press Return twice.

2. Press Del to delete the {DISPLAY OFF} code.

3. Press Ctrl-F10 to enter Macro Commands.

4. Press F7 N N Ctrl-F9.

5. Type **1add** and press Return twice.

6. Press Ctrl-F10.

7. Press F7 to save the macro and return to the document window.

THE DEL MACRO

You can create the macro as explained in this chapter, or enter it directly in the Macro Editor. Follow these steps to use the Macro Editor:

1. Press Home Ctrl-F10, type **DEL** and press Return twice.

2. Press Del to delete the {DISPLAY OFF} code.

3. Press Ctrl-F10 to enter Macro Commands.

4. Press Alt-F10, type **Main** and press Return.

5. Press F7 N N Shift-F10.

6. Type **prospect** and press Return F2.

7. Press Ctrl-F10 to exit Macro Commands.

8. Press Ctrl-PgUp, select {PAUSE}, and press Return.

9. Press Ctrl-F10.

10. Press F2 Home ← Alt-F4.

11. Press ↓ seven times.

12. Press Del Y F7 Y Return Y N.

13. Press Alt-F10, type **Main** and press Return.

14. Press Ctrl-F10.

15. Press F7 to save the macro and return to the document window.

THE MENU1 MACRO

You can create the macro as explained in this chapter, or enter it directly in the Macro Editor. Follow these steps to use the Macro Editor:

1. Press Home Ctrl-F10, type **MENU1** and press Return twice.

2. Press Del to delete the {DISPLAY OFF} code.

3. Press Ctrl-F10 to enter Macro Commands.

4. Press F7 N N Ctrl-F9.

5. Type **1menu1** and press Return.

6. Type **list1** and press Return.

7. Press Ctrl-F10.

8. Press F7 to save the macro and return to the document window.

ASSEMBLING BOILERPLATE FILES

Using version 5.1 merge codes, enter the Input primary file as follows using Shift-F9 6, or **T**ools **M**erge Codes **M**ore, to access the Merge Codes window:

{PROMPT}Enter the paragraph number:~{REWRITE}{FIELD}
{KEYBOARD}~{NEST PRIMARY}~

The version 5.0 file shown in this chapter will not operate as is, but will operate when converted using Ctrl-F9 3.

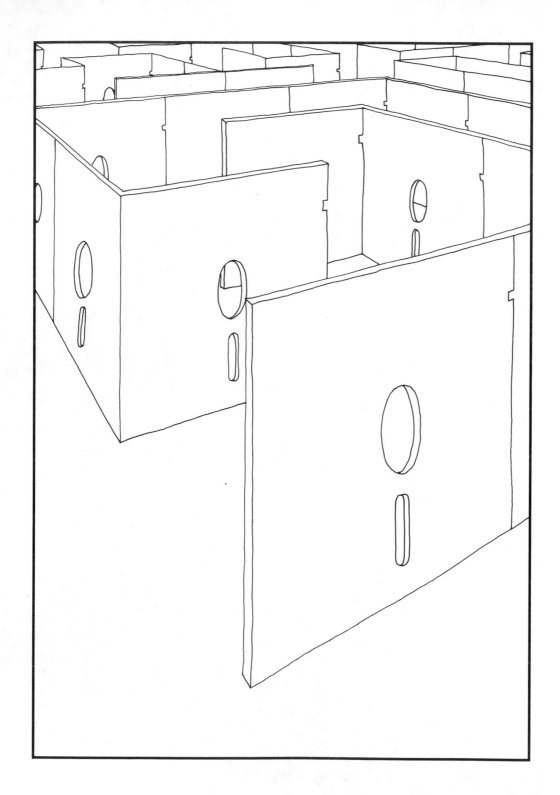

A

CONFIGURING WORDPERFECT FOR YOUR PRINTER

Note: Users of version 5.1 should go right to the section "Version 5.1 Features" later in this appendix.

You must designate which printer you are using before you can print your first document. Use this appendix to configure WordPerfect for your printer, and refer to it later if you want to change your printer definition.

Computers, printers, and software all vary. Sometimes the differences are obvious; at other times they are subtle but equally significant. But nowhere can these differences be as frustrating as when connecting two major pieces of hardware—your computer and your printer.

Luckily, there are some standards for the physical connection. Most personal computers have a printer port, where the cable from your printer is attached to the computer. With IBM-compatible machines, this port is normally a parallel device, which requires no special setup. If your printer is a parallel printer, you can simply connect the cable and tell WordPerfect which printer is being used.

If your printer is a serial printer, then some extra effort is needed. First, the standard printer card adapter in most personal computers will not work; these are parallel cards, so the signals are not correct to operate a serial printer. Instead, you'll need a serial adapter like one used with a telecommunications modem, and you must have the proper cable to link the port to the printer. The cable attached to a modem will not work for a printer because the signals are different. You'll need a special cable called a *null modem*. Also, you must use your operating system's MODE command to establish the communications protocol by which the signals will be transferred from the computer to the printer. All of these considerations require some technical knowledge. So if terms like *baud rate* and *parity* are strange to you, seek advice from the store where you purchased your equipment.

Let's assume, however, that you have your computer and printer attached and both are working. You are just a few steps away from being able to print documents. However, even if your printer works with other programs, you must still set it up to work with WordPerfect. Why?

Well, because WordPerfect is designed to take full advantage of your printer's capabilities. Depending on your printer, you'll be able to print in italics, boldface, and underline, and even draw lines and boxes. You can print foreign-language characters and special graphic and mathematical symbols. But to do so, you need to tell WordPerfect the proper codes to send to the printer.

This setup operation should be performed when you first use WordPerfect. In Appendix B, you will test your printer and, if you have a laser printer, learn how to use downloadable fonts.

SETTING UP WORDPERFECT FOR YOUR PRINTER

To perform these steps you need the WordPerfect Program and Printer disks, either as floppy disks or already installed on a hard disk. The Printer disks (you may have up to four of them) contain the codes and commands required by over 100 different printers.

If you have a hard disk and used the Install program, the files containing the printer definitions were not copied onto the your hard disk. In this case, follow all the instructions below using disk drive A. If you copied the printer files to your disk, however, ignore any instructions that refer to floppy disks.

1. Start WordPerfect.

2. Place one of your Printer disks in drive B (drive A if you have a hard disk).

3. Press Shift-F7. (Press and hold down the Shift key, press and release the F7 key, then release Shift.) You'll see the Print menu shown in Figure A.1.

4. Press **S** for Select Printer. The screen changes to the Select Printer menu (Figure A.2).

5. Press **2** or **a** to select Additional Printers.
   You will see the message shown in Figure A.3.
   Press **2** or **o** for Other Disk, type **B:** (or **A:** if you have a hard disk), then press Return. The Additional Printers screen is displayed (Figure A.4).

This screen lists the various printers WordPerfect has been made to work with. You must select your own printer from the list.

6. Press the ↓ key. As you press the key, the highlight bar will move down the screen from printer to printer. When you reach the bottom of the screen, the list will "scroll" off the top to display more printers at the bottom. You can press the ↑ key to redisplay any names that have scrolled off the top of the screen.

```
Print

    1 - Full Document
    2 - Page
    3 - Document on Disk
    4 - Control Printer
    5 - Type Through
    6 - View Document
    7 - Initialize Printer

Options

    S - Select Printer
    B - Binding                   Ø"
    N - Number of Copies          1
    G - Graphics Quality          Medium
    T - Text Quality              High




Selection: Ø
```

■**FIGURE A.1:**   *Print menu*

```
Print: Select Printer














1 Select; 2 Additional Printers; 3 Edit; 4 Copy; 5 Delete; 6 Help: 1
```

■**FIGURE A.2:**   *Select Printer menu*

7. Press ↓ or ↑ to highlight your printer's name. You might not see your printer's name even after scrolling the entire list. That's because the printer files are divided into several Printer disks. In this case, remove the Printer disk and insert another Printer disk. Then press **2** or **o** to select Other Disk, type **B:** (or **A:** if you have a hard disk), then press Return. Now press ↓ to highlight your printer. If you still cannot find your printer, repeat this procedure with another Printer disk in drive B.

What happens if you don't see your printer listed? Look for a printer that may be compatible or one made by the same manufacturer. For instance, many dot

```
Select Printer: Additional Printers

Printer files not found

        Use the Other Disk option to specify a directory for the printer
        files.  Continue to use this option until you find the disk with the
        printer you want.




















1 Select; 2 Other Disk; 3 Help; 4 List Printer Files; N Name Search: 1
```

■**FIGURE A.3:**   *Message that printer files cannot be found on the current disk*

```
Select Printer: Additional Printers

   Alphacom Alphapro 101
   ALPS ALQ200/300/P2400C
   Alps P2000/P2100
   Apple ImageWriter II
   AST TurboLaser
   Apple Laserwriter Plus
   Blaser
   Brother HR-15XL/20/35
   C.ITOH 8510 Prowriter
   C.ITOH C-310 CP
   C.ITOH C-310 EP/CXP
   C.ITOH C-715F
   C.ITOH C-815
   C.ITOH ProWriter jr. Plus
   C.Itoh D10-40
   Canon LBP-8 A1/A2
   Canon LBP-8II
   Centronics 351
   Centronics GLP II
   Citizen 120D
   Citizen MSP-15

1 Select; 2 Other Disk; 3 Help; 4 List Printer Files; N Name Search: 1
```

■**FIGURE A.4:**   *Additional Printers*

matrix printers are compatible with the Epson MX, Epson FX, Epson FX-85, or IBM Graphics Printer. Many daisy wheel printers can emulate a Diablo 620 or another common printer. If you're not sure, look through your printer's manual to see if it emulates or uses the same commands as some other printer. If you're still unsure, ask the salesperson who sold you the printer.

Nothing drastic will happen if you select and attempt to use the wrong printer definition on the list. You might lose a few sheets of paper, or your printer might just do nothing. So if you don't see yours listed, it's worth trying one that appears close.

8. Press Return when your printer's name is highlighted. You'll see the prompt

    Printer Filename: your printer's name.PRS

    at the bottom of the screen.

9. Press Return. You'll see the message

    Updating font:

    at the prompt line, followed by a font number, while WordPerfect loads the appropriate printer codes onto your disk.

    The Printer Helps and Hints screen will then appear, as shown in Figure A.5. (Don't worry if no Helps or Hints appear for your printer.) Read the screen then press F7.

    After the file is loaded, you'll see the Select Printer: Edit menu (Figure A.6).

    You have to check out two options on this menu: the type of paper feed you're using and the port your printer is attached to. Let's handle the paper feed first, using the Forms option.

10. Press **4** or **f** to select the Forms option. The screen changes to the Select Printer: Forms menu (Figure A.7). Look at the row starting with *Standard,* under the column marked *Location.* If it says *Contin,* then WordPerfect assumes you're using continuous paper and it won't stop to let you insert individual sheets into the printer—manual feed.

    If the location is correct, then skip to step 15. Otherwise continue here.

11. Press **3** or **e** for Edit to display the Select Printer: Forms edit menu (Figure A.8).

12. Press **4** or **l** for the Location option to display the prompt line

    Location: 1 Continuous; 2 Bin Number; 3 Manual: 0

13. Press the number corresponding to the paper source. If you press **2** for Bin Number, you'll see the prompt

   Bin number:

   Enter the number of the paper tray or bin containing the paper you'll be using.

14. Press F7 to display the Select Printer: Forms menu.

```
Printer Helps and Hints:   Epson FX-80

High Quality print is extremely slow but will micro-space and right justify
up to 1/120th of an inch.  If you do not require this high quality we
suggest that you use medium or draft quality. Both of these qualities will
be much quicker.

In the medium or draft modes there will be a slight round off error in
spacing when using 8.5 CPI and 17 CPI.  This is because micro-spacing is
not used.  There will also be a problem right justifying in medium or draft
modes.  The horizontal movement of these modes is 1/10 which creates an
"all or nothing" situation (either there is a space between words or there
is not).  We suggest that the hyphenation zone is decreased or that right
justification is turned off.

The paper feed lever on the printer must be set to friction mode to ensure
correct positioning of graphics and attributes.

When defining forms we suggest a top offset of about -.94"**.  This setting
will enable correct top / bottom margin settings in WordPerfect while the
paper perforation is aligned with the tear-bar on the printer.
    **  This number may vary due to personal preferences.


Press Exit to quit, Cursor Keys for More Text, Switch for Sheet Feeder Help
```

■**FIGURE A.5:**   *Printer Helps and Hints screen*

```
Select Printer: Edit

        Filename              EPFX80.PRS

    1 - Name                  Epson FX-80

    2 - Port                  LPT1:

    3 - Sheet Feeder          None

    4 - Forms

    5 - Cartridges and Fonts

    6 - Initial Font          10 CPI

    7 - Path for Downloadable
        Fonts and Printer
        Command Files



    Selection: 0
```

■**FIGURE A.6:**   *Select Printer: Edit menu*

15. Press F7 to redisplay the Select Printer: Edit menu.

    Look at the Port option. This refers to the port where your printer is attached to your computer. *LPT 1* refers to a standard parallel printer port, the most common in use with PC's. Chances are, you're using a printer attached to that port. If you have a parallel printer and the port listed on the menu says LPT 1, then just press Return and skip to step 18. If you have a serial printer and the port says COM 1, then press Return and skip to step 18.

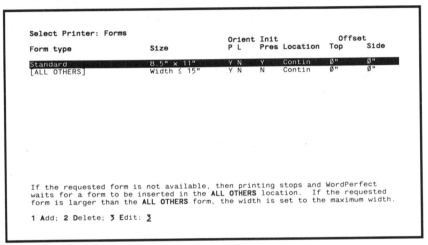

```
Select Printer: Forms
                                        Orient  Init              Offset
  Form type                   Size      P L     Pres  Location   Top    Side

  Standard                    8.5" x 11"  Y N     Y    Contin     Ø"      Ø"
  [ALL OTHERS]                Width ≤ 15"  Y N     N    Contin     Ø"      Ø"










  If the requested form is not available, then printing stops and WordPerfect
  waits for a form to be inserted in the ALL OTHERS location.  If the requested
  form is larger than the ALL OTHERS form, the width is set to the maximum width.

  1 Add; 2 Delete; 3 Edit: 3
```

■**FIGURE A.7:** *Select Printer: Forms menu*

```
Select Printer: Forms

          Filename                EPFX8Ø.PRS

          Form Type               Standard

      1 - Form Size               8.5" x 11"

      2 - Orientation             Portrait

      3 - Initially Present       Yes

      4 - Location                Continuous

      5 - Page Offsets - Top      Ø"
                         Side      Ø"




  Selection: Ø
```

■**FIGURE A.8:** *Select Printer: Forms edit menu*

If you're not sure, read the explanation following the next step.

16. Press **2** or **p** to select the Port option and display the prompt line

Port: 1 LPT 1; 2 LPT 2; 3 LPT 3; 4 COM 1; 5 COM 2; 6 COM 3; 7 COM 4; 8 Other: 0

You can't tell a serial printer from a parallel one just by looking at it. But you might tell by seeing where it's connected to the back of the computer. You'll see a plug—called a *port*—where the printer's cable is attached. If the plug is labeled *Printer, LPT 1,* or *Parallel,* then your printer is a parallel printer. If it's the only port on the back of the computer then it's probably a parallel port as well.

If the port is labelled *COM 1* or *Serial,* you're using a serial printer. However, if you do have a serial printer, you'll have to read your manual for complete instructions.

By the way, if you have more than one port of a type, they are called *LPT 2, LPT 3,* or *COM 2.* You would use these if you have more than one printer attached, such as a dot matrix printer for quick rough copies and a letter quality printer for the final draft. If you do have this type of hardware, repeat this entire procedure for each printer you have.

17. Press the number corresponding to your printer's port.

18. Press F7 to display the Select Printer menu. The printer you just defined is now added to the list and highlighted, although it is not yet selected.

19. Press Return to select the printer and redisplay the Print menu.

20. Press F7 again to return to the document.

CHANGING PRINTER DEFINITIONS

If you purchase a new printer, you must add its definition to the list, then select it. Just follow the steps shown above. If you have more than one printer, follow the steps above so they are all listed. Then, to use a specific one, press Shift-F7 S, highlight the printer you want to use, then press Return twice.

■ VERSION 5.1 FEATURES

SETTING UP WORDPERFECT FOR YOUR PRINTER

You select a printer when you run the Install program to prepare WordPerfect to run on your computer. Follow these steps to install WordPerfect and select a printer:

1. Place the Install/Learning/Utilities 1 diskette in drive A.

2. If you have a hard-disk system, log onto drive A by typing **A:** then pressing Return.

3. Press **Y** when you see the prompt

   Continue?

4. Type **Install** and press Return. You'll see the message

   Installing to a Hard Disk? Yes (No)

   If you have a floppy-disk system, press **N**. You'll be warned that Word-Perfect will not operate on low density 360K 5 1/4-inch disks, and that you'll need nine blank formatted disks available. If you have the disks, continue with the installation, starting with step 6. While these steps are designed for hard-disk systems, follow the prompts as they appear on your screen, using the instructions here as a guide.

5. Press **Y**. The main installation screen will appear as in Figure A.9. Figure A.10 summarizes the options on this menu. Since this is the first time you're installing WordPerfect, however, we'll use the Basic installation procedure.

6. Select Basic installation. In a series of screens, you'll be asked if you want to install specific WordPerfect modules, in this order:

   Utility files

```
Installation
        1 - Basic        Perform a standard installation to C:\WP51.

        2 - Custom       Perform a customized installation.  (User selected
                         directories.)

        3 - Network      Perform a customized installation onto a network.
                         (To be performed by the network supervisor.)

        4 - Printer      Install updated Printer (.ALL) File.

        5 - Update       Install updated program file(s).

        6 - Copy Disks   Install every file from an installation diskette to a
                         specified location.  (Useful for installing all the
                         Printer (.ALL) Files.)




        Selection: 1
```

■**FIGURE A.9:** *Main installation menu*

Learning files

Help files

Keyboard files

Style library

WordPerfect Program

Speller

Thesaurus

PTR program

Graphic drivers

Graphic images

7. Follow the directions on the screen, pressing **Y** for each of the modules you want to install, **N** for those you don't. You'll be prompted to insert specific disks in drive A. You *must* install the WordPerfect program modules to use WordPerfect—the others are optional.

After the modules have been copied, you'll be prompted to insert the Printer 1 disk in drive A to select a printer.

Option	Purpose
Basic	For installing WordPefect on your system for the first time.
Custom	For installing WordPerfect on a hard disk directory other than C:\WP51, for installing individual parts of WordPerfect at a later date, or for installing additional printers.
Network	For installing a network version of WoredPerfect.
Printer	From time to time, WordPerfect releases additional printer files. Use this option to install these files onto your hard disk.
Update	Periodically, WordPerfect provides interim releases that enhance or improve basic program features. Use this option if you receive a program update and wish to install the new features on your system.
Copy Disk	For making copies of the files on your WordPerfect disks.

■**FIGURE A.10:**   *Installation options*

8. Insert the Printer 1 disk in drive A, then press Return to see a list of available printers.

9. Look for the name and model of your printer. If you don't see it, press the PgDn key until your printer is listed.

10. Type the number corresponding to your printer, then press Return to see the prompt

   Select printer (*your printer name*) Yes (No)

11. Press **Y** to see the prompt

   Do you want to install the Printer (.ALL) File? Yes (No)

12. Press **Y**. After the printer information is installed, you'll see

   Do you want to install another printer? No (Yes)

   If you have more than one printer, press **Y**, then repeat steps 8 through 11. Press **N** when all of your printers have been installed. You'll be prompted to enter your registration number.

13. Type your registration number, then press Return. In a moment you'll see a Printer Helps and Hints screen similar to Figure A.5.

14. Read the information then press any key. The installation process finishes and the A> prompt reappears.

CUSTOMIZING PRINTER INFORMATION

In most cases, the printer information copied to your disk during the installation process is complete. But if you're using a laser printer with soft fonts, or have a special hardware configuration, you might have to edit the printer information before taking full advantage of your printer's features.

Follow these steps:

1. Start WordPerfect.

2. Press Shift-F7 S, or select **F**ile **P**rint **S**elect Printer to see the Print: Select Printer menu (Figure A.11).

   All of the printers you installed during the installation process will be listed here. If you later want to change printers to one of these printers, use the arrow keys to highlight the printer you want, then press F7.

3. Press **3** or **E** to display the Select Printer: Edit menu (Figure A.12).

Look at the Port option. If this is correct for your configuration, skip to step 6. If you're unfamiliar with printer ports, read the discussion earlier in this appendix for version 5.0 users.

4. Press **2** or **P** to display the prompt line

Port: 1 LPT 1; 2 LPT 2; 3 LPT 3; 4 COM 1; 5 COM 2;
6 COM 3; 7 COM 4; 8 Other: 0

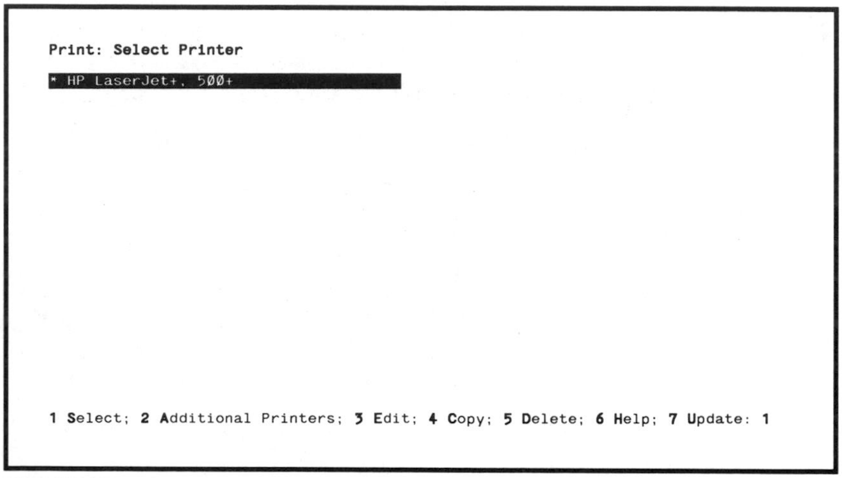

```
Print: Select Printer

* HP LaserJet+, 500+




















  1 Select; 2 Additional Printers; 3 Edit; 4 Copy; 5 Delete; 6 Help; 7 Update: 1
```

■**FIGURE A.11:**   *Print: Select Printer menu*

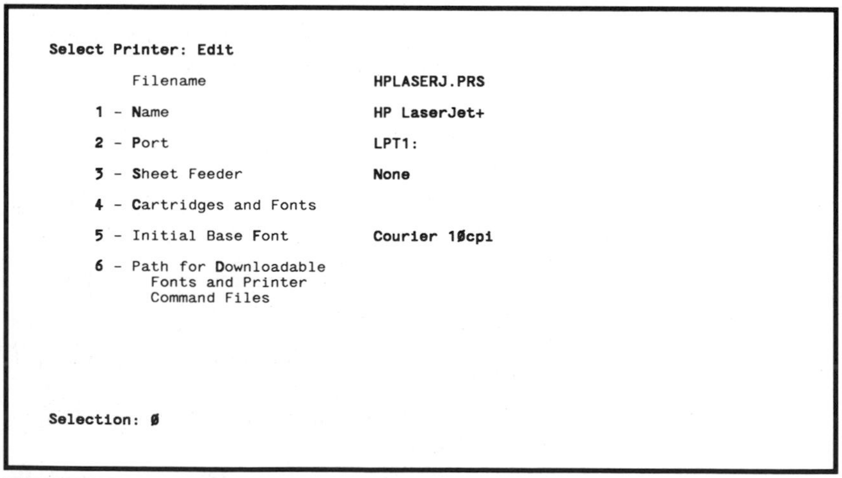

```
Select Printer: Edit

          Filename              HPLASERJ.PRS

     1 - Name                   HP LaserJet+

     2 - Port                   LPT1:

     3 - Sheet Feeder           None

     4 - Cartridges and Fonts

     5 - Initial Base Font      Courier 10cpi

     6 - Path for Downloadable
           Fonts and Printer
           Command Files




  Selection: 0
```

■**FIGURE A.12:**   *Printer Selection: Edit menu*

5. Press the number corresponding to your printer's port.

Adding cartridges and fonts will be discussed in Appendix B.

6. If you have a sheet feeder, press **3** or **s**, select a sheet feeder from the list that appears, then press Return.

7. Press F7 four times to return to the document.

Changing Printer Definitions   If you later purchase another printer, you have to run INSTALL again to add the printer driver to your program. However, if you copied the .ALL program to your disk, you can add another printer from that file directly within WordPerfect. To do this, press Shift-F7 S A, highlight the printer's name, then press Return six times.

CHANGING PAPER FEED

When WordPerfect installs the printer, it also designates if it feeds paper continuously or manually. In some cases, this setting might not be correct—you may have installed an optional tractor or sheet feeder, or used continuous paper with a printer normally set for manual feed.

To check the feed setting, and change it if necessary, follow these steps.

1. Start WordPerfect.

2. Press Shift-F8 2 7 or select **L**ayout **P**age **P**aper **S**ize to display a list of forms, or page styles, for your printer (Figure A.13). This menu is discussed in detail in Chapter 3. But for now, look at the setting in the LOC column for the Standard form.

   If the setting is correct, press F1 three times—you're ready to use Word-Perfect.

3. If the setting is incorrect, use the arrow keys to highlight the Standard form, then press **5** or **e** to display the Edit Paper Definition menu (Figure A.14).

4. Press **5** or **l** to display the prompt line

   Location: 1 Continuous; 2 Bin Number; 3 Manual: 0

5. Select the type of feed for your configuration. If you select Bin Number, you'll see the prompt

   Bin number:

Enter the number of the paper tray or bin containing the paper you'll be using, then press Return.

6. Press Return four times.

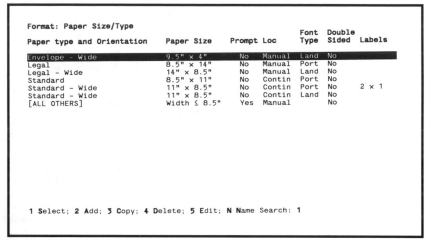

Format: Paper Size/Type

Paper type and Orientation	Paper Size	Prompt	Loc	Font Type	Double Sided	Labels
Envelope – Wide	9.5" x 4"	No	Manual	Land	No	
Legal	8.5" x 14"	No	Manual	Port	No	
Legal – Wide	14" x 8.5"	No	Manual	Land	No	
Standard	8.5" x 11"	No	Contin	Port	No	
Standard – Wide	11" x 8.5"	No	Contin	Port	No	2 x 1
Standard – Wide	11" x 8.5"	No	Contin	Land	No	
[ALL OTHERS]	Width ≤ 8.5"	Yes	Manual		No	

1 Select; 2 Add; 3 Copy; 4 Delete; 5 Edit; N Name Search: 1

■**FIGURE A.13:**   *Paper Size menu*

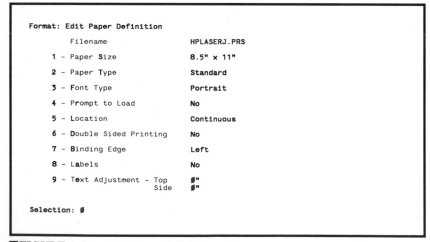

Format: Edit Paper Definition

	Filename	HPLASERJ.PRS
1 –	Paper Size	8.5" x 11"
2 –	Paper Type	Standard
3 –	Font Type	Portrait
4 –	Prompt to Load	No
5 –	Location	Continuous
6 –	Double Sided Printing	No
7 –	Binding Edge	Left
8 –	Labels	No
9 –	Text Adjustment – Top	0"
	Side	0"

Selection: 0

■**FIGURE A.14:**   *Edit Paper Definition menu*

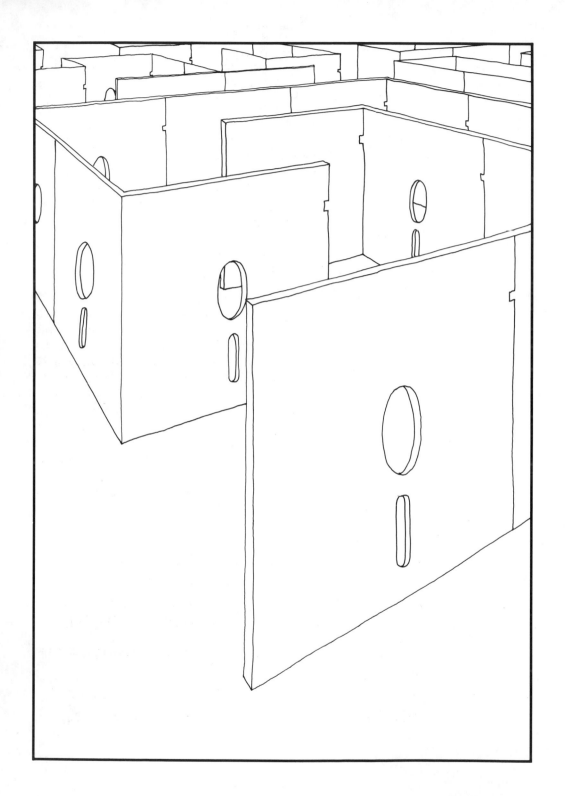

B

INSTALLING FONTS AND TESTING YOUR PRINTER

By using either Appendix A or the Install program, you informed WordPerfect what printer you are using. In most cases, WordPerfect will be able to take advantage of the special features your printer has to offer. In this appendix, we'll see some of your printer's capabilities and learn how to use downloaded fonts.

How your screen appears when you follow the instructions in this appendix depends on your graphics display card and monitor. In most cases, special formats such as superscripts, subscripts, and different type sizes and styles will appear just like normal characters. If you have a color monitor, they might appear in a different color, or if you have a high-resolution card they might actually appear as they will when printed.

So don't be suprised if you see no difference on screen between normal characters and the effects you'll be creating.

You can determine how character attributes appear by using the Setup menu. Setup is discussed in Chapter 5.

TESTING YOUR PRINTER

First, test your printer and see which fonts are available. The process of changing fonts is discussed in Chapter 3. For now, just follow the instructions here.

1. Start WordPerfect. Refer to Chapter 1 if you are not sure how to start the program, then continue here.

2. Type **H**.

3. Press Ctrl-F8 1 to select Size. The prompt line changes to

1 Suprscpt; 2 Subscpt; 3 Fine; 4 Small; 5 Large; 6 Vry Large;
7 Ext Large: 0

4. Press **2** to select a subscripted character.

5. Type **2**.

6. Press → or Ctrl-F8 3 to return the position to normal, then type **0**.

7. Press Return then type **Footnote goes here**.

8. Press Ctrl-F8 1 1 to select a superscripted character.

9. Type **1** then → to move the cursor beyond the Superscript code.

10. Press Return.

11. Press Ctrl-F8 1 3 for fine printing.

12. Type **Fine**, press →, then press Return.

13. Press Ctrl-F8 1 4 to select small printing.

14. Type **Small**, press →, then press Return.

15. Type **Normal** then press Return.

16. Press Ctrl-F8 1 5 to select large printing.

17. Type **Large**, press →, then press Return.

18. Press Ctrl-F8 1 6 to select very large printing.

19. Type **Very large**, press →, then press Return.

20. Press Ctrl-F8 1 7 to select extra large printing.

21. Type **Extra large**, press →, then press Return.

22. Press Shift-F7 1 to print a copy of the test document. Compare your print-out with Figure B.1. Keep in mind that this figure was printed on a LaserJet+ with several downloaded fonts.

23. Press F7 N N to clear the screen.

Note
The appearance of the version 5.1 screen is slightly different, but the steps listed here still apply.

Now let's see what appearances are available.

1. Press Ctrl-F8 2 to display the prompt

1 Bold 2 Undrln 3 Dbl Und 4 Italc 5 Outln 6 Shadw 7 Sm Cap
8 Redln 9 Stkout: 0

2. Press **3** or **d** to select Double Underlining. The position indicator will change color or appearance depending on your computer hardware.

3. Type **Double underline**.

4. Press → or Ctrl-F8 3 to select Normal, turning off the double underline style. Remember, the text may not appear underlined on the screen.

5. Press Return.

6. Press Ctrl-F8 2 4 to select Italic.

7. Type **Italic,** press → once, then press Return. Again, the text may change color or appear in reverse, depending on your system.

8. Press Ctrl-F8 2 5 to select Outline.

9. Type **Outline**, press →, then press Return.

10. Press Ctrl-F8 2 6 to select Shadow.

11. Type **Shadow**, press →, then press Return.

12. Press Ctrl-F8 2 7 to select Small Cap.

13. Type **Small caps**, press →, then press Return.

14. Press Ctrl-F8 2 8 to select Redline.

15. Type **Redline**, press →, then press Return.

16. Press Ctrl-F8 2 9 to select Strikeout printing.

17. Type **Strikeout**, press →, then press Return.

H_2O

Footnote   goes   here[1]

Fine
Small
Normal
Large
Very Large
Extra large

■**FIGURE B.1:** *Sample fonts*

18. Press Shift-F7 1 to print a copy of the test document.

19. Press F7 N Y to exit WordPerfect

Figure B.2 shows a sample printout made with a Hewlett Packard LaserJet+ printer. Notice that even this sophisticated printer doesn't produce outline letters.

Your own printout will show which appearances your printer can produce. Keep it handy so you'll know what's available as you type a real document.

Double underline
Italic
Outline
Shadow
Sₘₐₗₗ ᴄᴀᴘs
Redline
Strikeout

■**FIGURE B.2:** *Sample print styles*

■ LASER PRINTER FONTS

Laser printers are capable of printing in a number of different fonts, or type styles. Some are built into the printer, others are supplied on a cartridge or on a floppy disk. Fonts on disks are called *downloadable,* or *soft,* because they are transferred from the disk to the printer when you need them.

A *type style* refers to the general shape of a character. Some type styles have small cross-strokes at the ends of letters—called *serifs*—and some don't—*sanserif.* If you take all of the letters, numbers and punctuation marks of one type style in one size, you have a font. Fonts are measured in points. There are approximately 72 points to an inch, so a 12-point typeface will fit 6 lines of type in 1 inch of space.

A 12-point font contains all of the characters of a type style in that size. The 12-point bold font of the same type style contains the same letters but in boldface, just as 12-point italic contains all italic characters.

With WordPerfect you can print in all of the type styles and sizes that your printer allows. For some printers, this may mean only one style and one size.

But many dot matrix printers, for example, can print several sizes of characters. And laser printers can print a variety of shapes and sizes.

New Feature
Additional related features in version 5.1 are discussed under "Automatic Font Changes."

The main type style used is called the *base font*. This is the default character style used for normal characters. Other sizes and appearances are just variations on the Base Font. For example, say your base font is Times 12 pt and you have sizes 6 pt., 10 pt., 12 pt., 14 pt., 18 pt., and 24 pt. WordPerfect will match up the fonts and sizes as follows:

This size:	Is this point size:
Fine	6
Small	10
Normal	12 (The base font)
Large	14
Very Large	18
Extra Large	24

If your printer allows, you can change the base font to another style. That way you could have more than one style in the same document. You can change the font size and type style without worrying about the margins.

USING CARTRIDGES AND DOWNLOADED FONTS

If you purchase downloadable fonts on disk, you must tell WordPerfect what and where they are before using them for the first time or selecting one of them as the base font.

Because fonts require a great deal of disk space, you should have a hard disk in order to use them conveniently. So in this section, I'll assume you have a hard disk drive.

First, make a note of the directory that contains your downloadable fonts. Then follow these steps. The figures in this appendix illustrate cartridges and fonts available on a Hewlett Packard LaserJet Plus printer. While your own lists may be different, the same process can be used.

1. Start WordPerfect.

2. Press Shift-F7 S for the Select Printer option.

3. Highlight the name of your laser printer.

4. Press **3** or **e** to select the Edit option. You'll see the Select Printer: Edit menu that you used in Appendix A.

5. Press **5** or **c** to display the Cartridges and Fonts menu (Figure B.3).

   The Quantity column indicates how many cartridge slots you have, or the amount of memory available in your printer to hold downloaded fonts. You can change the amount by using option 2 on the prompt line.

Warning
With version 5.1, press **4** or **c** in step 5.

6. Designate the cartridge(s) you are using. The Cartridge Font selection should be highlighted.

New Feature
Additional related features in version 5.1 are discussed under "Selecting Cartridges and Fonts."

   a. Press Return to display a list of cartridges available for your printer (Figure B.4).

   b. Use the arrow keys to highlight the cartridge you will be using.

   c. Type *.

   d. Repeat this procedure if your printer accepts more than one cartridge at a time.

   e. Press F7 to return to the previous menu.

   Now designate the downloadable fonts you wish to use.

7. Highlight the Soft Fonts option on the Cartridges and Fonts menu (Figure B.3) then press Return. You'll see a list of soft fonts available (Figure B.5). It might take a few seconds for this list to appear.

   You can designate soft fonts as Present or Can be Loaded. WordPerfect

Note
The appearance of the version 5.1 screen is slightly different, but the steps listed here still apply.

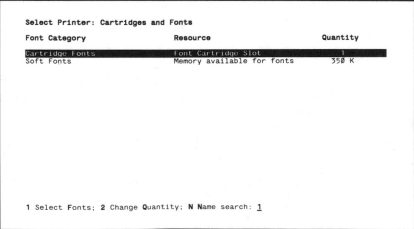

```
Select Printer: Cartridges and Fonts

Font Category                Resource                    Quantity

Cartridge Fonts              Font Cartridge Slot              1
Soft Fonts                   Memory available for fonts     350 K











1 Select Fonts; 2 Change Quantity; N Name search: 1
```

■**FIGURE B.3:** *Cartridges and Fonts menu*

assumes that all fonts marked Present (with an asterisk) have already been downloaded when you start to print a document. (You can download them yourself or have WordPerfect download them for you.) Fonts marked + will be downloaded by WordPerfect when you start to print a document.

8. Scroll through the list and mark each of your fonts with either * (Present) or + (Can be Loaded).

When you mark a font, WordPerfect subtracts the amount of printer memory

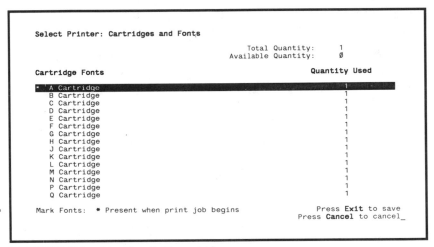

Note

The appearance of the version 5.1 screen is slightly different, but the steps listed here still apply.

■**FIGURE B.4:** *List of available cartridges*

■**FIGURE B.5:** *Soft font list*

it requires from the Available Quantity amount on the top of the menu.

9. Press F7 twice when all of your fonts have been marked. The Edit menu will appear again.

Warning
With version 5.1, press **5** or **f** in step 10.

10. Press **6** or **i** to select the Initial Font option. The list of all available fonts will be displayed.

11. Highlight the font you want to use as the base font, then press Return.

Warning
With version 5.1, press **6** or **d** in step 12.

12. Press **7** or **d** for Path for Downloadable Fonts.

13. Enter the complete path—the disk and directory where the downloadable fonts are stored—then press Return.

14. Press F7 twice to return to the document.

CHANGING BASE FONTS

If you ever want to change your default base font, follow these steps:

1. Press Shift-F7 S 3 to display the Select Printers: Edit menu.

Warning
With version 5.1, press **5** or **f** in step 2.

2. Press **6** or **i** for the Initial Font option. The list of possible fonts will appear on the screen.

3. Highlight the base font using the arrow keys, then press Return four times to return to the document window. That base font will be used as the default whenever you start WordPerfect.

You can also change base fonts temporarily for just the text you are about to type or format.

1. Press Ctrl-F8 4 to display the list of base fonts available.

2. Highlight the base font using the arrow keys, then press Return once to return to the document window.

USING DOWNLOADABLE FONTS

If you plan to use both cartridge fonts and soft fonts, decide which you will use more often. If you don't intend to download fonts every session, then use one of the cartridge or native fonts as the base font. When you want to use a soft font, download the fonts and change to one as the base font temporarily using the instructions just given.

If you marked your soft fonts as Present, WordPerfect will expect them already in your printer (if you selected one as the base font) when you start to print a document. You can either download them with your own utility before starting the program or have WordPerfect download them for you. Press Shift-F7 7 to select the Initialize Printer option and have WordPerfect download each font marked with *.

Fonts marked with + will be downloaded during printing when called for in the text.

Be aware that WordPerfect uses specific file names when downloading fonts—either during initialization or during printing. The program follows the font naming conventions of the printer's manufacturer. If you purchase soft fonts from another source, make sure that they are compatible with those available from your printer's manufacturer and that they use the same naming conventions. If not, try renaming the fonts to match the manufacturer's names and downloading them.

■ VERSION 5.1 FEATURES

AUTOMATIC FONT CHANGES

For printers that use soft fonts or cartridges with various font sizes, WordPerfect matches the font size attribute using these ratios:

Attribute:	Percent of Base Font:
Subscript	60%
Superscript	60%
Fine	60%
Small	80%
Large	120%
Very Large	150%
Extra Large	200%

For example, using a 12-point base font, WordPerfect will use a 24-point font for extra large characters. You can modify these ratios if you'd like other fonts to be used, such as a 30-point font for extra large.

You modify the ratios by using the Setup menus. While customizing Word-Perfect is discussed in detail in Chapter 5, to change the size ratios you follow these steps:

1. Press Shift-F1 4 8, or select **F**ile **S**etup **I**nitial Settings **P**rint Options, to display the Print Options menu (Figure B.6).

   Most of these options determine the default values of settings that are discussed in Chapter 4.

2. Press **6** or **s** to change the size attribute ratios. The cursor moves to the ratio for fine.

3. Type the percentage you'd like to use for that attribute, then press Return or ↓. The cursor moves to the next size attribute. To leave the setting unchanged, just press Return or ↓.

4. Complete the remaining attributes in the same way, then press F7.

SELECTING CARTRIDGES AND FONTS

With version 5.1, the Cartridges and Fonts menu includes the built-in option to select from your printer's internal fonts. Some printers, particularly laser and ink-jet printers, contain several different character sets of the same font. Use the

```
Setup: Print Options

    1 - Binding Offset                    Ø"

    2 - Number of Copies                  1
        Multiple Copies Generated by      WordPerfect

    3 - Graphics Quality                  Medium

    4 - Text Quality                      High

    5 - Redline Method                    Printer Dependent

    6 - Size Attribute Ratios - Fine      6Ø%
        (% of Normal)            Small    8Ø%
                                 Large    12Ø%
                            Very Large    15Ø%
                           Extra Large    2ØØ%
                        Super/Subscript   6Ø%




    Selection: Ø
```

■**FIGURE B.6:** *Print Options menu*

built-in selection to designate which internal fonts you want to use.

In addition, for some laser printers, selecting Soft Fonts will display the Font Group menu (Figure B.7). Highlight the font group you have available, then press Return to display the list of soft fonts within that group.

The soft font list appears as in Figure B.5 with the addition of the * Fonts column to the right of the Total and Available Quantity prompts. The number in Total Fonts is the maximum number of fonts your printer can accept. When you mark a font as Present (with an asterisk) WordPerfect subtracts 1 from the Available Fonts number.

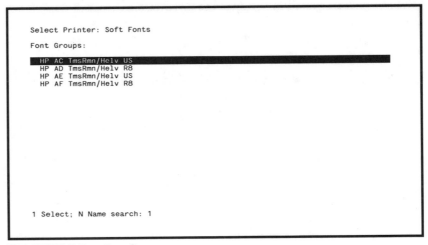

```
Select Printer: Soft Fonts

Font Groups:

    HP  AC  TmsRmn/Helv  US
    HP  AD  TmsRmn/Helv  R8
    HP  AE  TmsRmn/Helv  US
    HP  AF  TmsRmn/Helv  R8

















    1 Select; N Name search: 1
```

■**FIGURE B.7:** *Font Group menu*

USING WORDPERFECT'S DICTIONARY AND THESAURUS

WordPerfect includes both a dictionary and a thesaurus, two excellent tools for improving the quality of your writing. Both programs are started directly from the text window and are as easy to use as they are comprehensive.

The dictionary program, for example, will report if a word in your document is not found in its list of over 100,000 words. It will then display words with the same approximate spelling or words that are pronounced like the misspelled one. You can then select from the list of suggested spellings, and the corrected word will be inserted into the text automatically.

Just like any dictionary, the list may not contain every word in your document. Many technical words and names, for example, will not be found in the dictionary and will be reported as possible misspellings. If the word is indeed spelled correctly, you can add the word to the dictionary so that it will not be reported as incorrect again.

The thesaurus works in a similar manner, except that it locates synonyms and antonyms for the words in your text. You will be shown a list of words with similar and opposite meanings and be allowed to select one to insert into the document. The list often includes synonyms in noun, adjective, and verb forms. For example, looking up the word *test* will show both the noun *examination* and the verb *examine* among the possible choices. You can continue to look up synonyms of suggested choices until you find the proper word.

How you initiate these programs depends on whether you are using a floppy disk system or a hard disk system. Once the programs are started, they operate the same with either type of system.

With a hard disk drive, the dictionary and thesaurus will be installed on the drive during the installation procedure. No special instructions are necessary, and they can be accessed easily.

■ FLOPPY DISK SYSTEMS

Warning
Users of version
5.1 should fol-
low the special
instructions
under "Floppy
Disk Systems.,"
page 674.

Unfortunately, using these word tools with floppy disk drives requires some additional steps. In most cases, you will have the WordPerfect Program disk in drive A and a data disk in drive B. But since the Dictionary and Thesaurus programs use over 335,000 and 215,000 bytes of disk space respectively, there is not enough room to add either of these to the WordPerfect Program disk.

No matter what you do, you will have to swap some disks if you plan to use both programs. The best method is to insert the Dictionary or Thesaurus disk in drive B when you want to use it. But to do so, you must first set up WordPerfect so that it expects to find the dictionary and thesaurus in drive B. Follow these steps:

1. Start WordPerfect.

2. Press Shift-F1 to display the Setup menu.

3. Press **7** to select Location of Auxiliary Files.

4. Press **4** for the Main Dictionary(s) option.

5. Type **B:** then press Return.

6. Press **7** for the Supplementary Dictionary(s) option.

7. Type **B:** then press Return.

8. Press **8** for the Thesaurus option.

9. Type **B:** then press Return.

10. Press Return twice to return to the typing screen.

■ CHECKING SPELLING

You can check the spelling of individual words, blocks of text, pages, or an entire document. All spelling tasks begin by pressing Ctrl-F2.

THE CHECKING PROCEDURE

Here are the steps for checking the spelling in a document:

1. Start WordPerfect and either retrieve a document or type a new one.

2. To check an individual word, place the cursor on or immediately following it. To check a block of text, press Alt-F4 and use the cursor movement keys to highlight the block. To check a page, place the cursor anywhere on the page. To check an entire document, place the cursor anywhere in the document.

3. If you have a floppy disk system, place the Spell disk in drive B.

4. Press Ctrl-F2. The message

   Please Wait

   appears on the screen. Then, unless you have a block highlighted, you see the prompt

   Check: 1 Word; 2 Page; 3 Document; 4 New Sup. Dictionary; 5 Look Up; 6 Count

5. Press *1* to check an individual word, *2* to check all of the words on the current page, or *3* to check the entire document. (Options 4 through 6 will be discussed in the next section.)

This procedure initiates the checking process. If you are checking a block, page, or document, the message

Please Wait

will appear on the status line while the words are compared with those in the dictionary. If you are checking an individual word and the cursor moves to the next word in the document, then the word is spelled correctly. The prompt will remain on the screen. Select another option to continue the checking process or press F1 to stop.

Note
The appearance of the version 5.1 screen is slightly different, but the steps listed here still apply.

If WordPerfect cannot find the word in the dictionary, it will highlight it, and you'll see a screen like the one illustrated in Figure C.1. The double line across the screen and the prompt line will appear first. Then some suggested spellings will appear.

Each of the suggested spellings is labeled with a letter. If the correct spelling appears among the suggestions, press the appropriate letter. That word will replace the one in the document.

When the checking procedure is completed, the number of words checked will be displayed on the status line, and you will be prompted to press any key to return to the document.

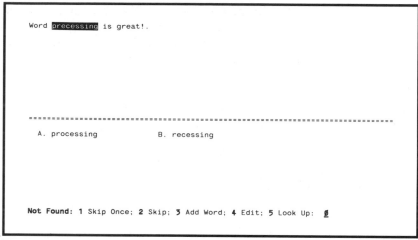

Word `precessing` is great!.

━━

A. processing   B. recessing

Not Found: 1 Skip Once; 2 Skip; 3 Add Word; 4 Edit; 5 Look Up: ▯

■**FIGURE C.1:**   *The screen WordPerfect displays when it cannot find a word in its dictionary*

CHECKING OPTIONS

If none of the suggested words is correct, or none was found in the dictionary, then select one of the following options from the prompt line:

- 1 Skip Once: The word is spelled as you want it to appear in this one instance. WordPerfect will look for the next misspelled word.

- 2 Skip: You want WordPerfect to accept the word as spelled for the remainder of the current checking session. This word will not be highlighted again.

- 3 Add Word: The word is spelled correctly, and since you use it regularly, you want to add it to the supplemental dictionary. Now it will always seem correct to WordPerfect.

- 4 Edit: You want to edit the word. The cursor will appear on the word. You can now use the right and left arrow, Backspace, and Del keys, or type new characters to change the word. (The up and down arrows and other cursor movement keys will not work.) Press F7 to continue the checking process. If the edited word is still misspelled, WordPerfect will highlight it again.

- 5 Look Up: This option allows you to search for a word or word pattern using the wild-card characters * and ?. Each question mark will be replaced by a single character in the search, and each asterisk by any number of characters. So, for example, if you entered *w?n,* you would find *wan, win,* and *won;* and entering *w*n* would display words such as *weatherman* and *woolen.*

In two instances, another prompt will appear on the status line. If WordPerfect finds the same word twice in a row, the prompt changes to

Double Word: 1 2 Skip; 3 Delete 2nd; 4 Edit; 5 Disable Double Word Checking

Enter the appropriate selection:

New Feature
Additional related features in version 5.1 are discussed under "Irregular Cases."

- 1 2 Skip: Keep both words in the text.

- 3 Delete 2nd: Delete one of the pair.

- 4 Edit: Move the cursor to the text for editing.

- 5 Disable double word checking: Ignore paired words throughout the document.

The other prompt appears when WordPerfect finds words that contain numbers, such as *2nd* or *F10.* You will see the prompt

Not Found: 1 2 Skip; 3 Ignore Words Containing Numbers; 4 Edit

Press *1* or *2* to keep the text as is, press *3* to skip any more words containing numbers, or press *4* to move the cursor to the highlighted text for editing.

OTHER SPELLING OPTIONS

In addition to checking a word, block, page, or document, there are three other options on the main Spelling prompt line.

New Sup. Dictionary (option 4) allows you to use a special *supplemental dictionary*—a list of your own words that are not found in WordPerfect's main dictionary. For example, say you often write articles containing technical words. To avoid having these words reported as misspellings, you add them to the supplemental dictionary using the Add Word option when you check spelling. The default supplemental dictionary is called WP{WP}EN.SUP, and it is normally used whenever you check spelling. But since searching this dictionary takes time, why use it when you're writing nontechnical documents that will not contain these words? In this case, create your own supplemental dictionary that you can use whenever you need it as a reference.

To create or use your own supplemental dictionary, select option 4 to display the prompt

Supplemental dictionary name:

Type the name of the supplemental dictionary you'd like to use, or the name of a new dictionary you'd like to create.

The Look Up option (5) works the same as the Look Up option offered when WordPerfect can't find a word in its dictionary. Use it when you simply want to check the spelling of a word before typing it.

The Count option reports the number of words in the current document.

USING THE THESAURUS

The thesaurus will display words whose meanings are similar (synonyms) and opposite (antonyms) to other words. The WordPerfect thesaurus has about 10,000 words, called *headwords*. It is a useful tool for increasing your vocabulary and decreasing the repetition of words throughout a document.

Like the spelling dictionary, the thesaurus requires its own floppy disk. So, if you do not have a hard disk system, you must insert the Thesaurus disk in drive B before using it.

THE THESAURUS PROCEDURE

To use the thesaurus, place the cursor on or immediately following the word for which you would like to find a synonym or antonym, then press Alt-F1. You'll see the Thesaurus screen, along with four lines of text above the selected word, as shown in Figure C.2.

In the sample screen shown in the figure, synonyms are given for the word *help* in both the noun (n) and verb (v) forms, along with several antonyms. The words preceded by dots are other headwords that can be looked up to find more possible substitutions. Press the reference letter next to a headword to see more selections. In our example, pressing *B* (for *aid*) would display the screen shown in Figure C.3. Synonyms for the word *aid* now appear in the second column, and the reference letters are now in that column.

You can continue to search for the proper word by pressing one of the letters next to another headword. If you want to select a word in a column that doesn't have reference letters, you must first shift the letters next to those words by pressing → or ←.

If the original word that you are looking up is not a headword, the message

Word not found

will appear on the status line for a few seconds, then change to

Word:

Type another word with a similar meaning that may be a headword, or press F1 to display the Thesaurus prompt line.

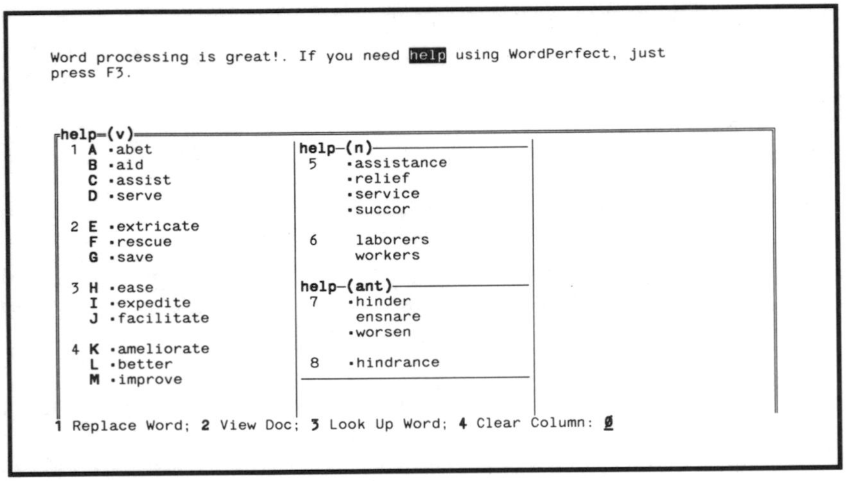

```
Word processing is great!. If you need help using WordPerfect, just
press F3.


┌help—(v)─────────────────┬──────────────────────┬──────────────────────┐
│ 1 A •abet               │help—(n)───────────── │                      │
│   B •aid                │ 5    •assistance     │                      │
│   C •assist             │      •relief         │                      │
│   D •serve              │      •service        │                      │
│                         │      •succor         │                      │
│ 2 E •extricate          │                      │                      │
│   F •rescue             │ 6     laborers       │                      │
│   G •save               │       workers        │                      │
│                         │                      │                      │
│ 3 H •ease               │help—(ant)─────────── │                      │
│   I •expedite           │ 7    •hinder         │                      │
│   J •facilitate         │       ensnare        │                      │
│                         │      •worsen         │                      │
│ 4 K •ameliorate         │                      │                      │
│   L •better             │ 8    •hindrance      │                      │
│   M •improve            │                      │                      │
└─────────────────────────┴──────────────────────┴──────────────────────┘
1 Replace Word; 2 View Doc; 3 Look Up Word; 4 Clear Column: 0
```

■**FIGURE C.2:**   *Thesaurus screen for the word* help

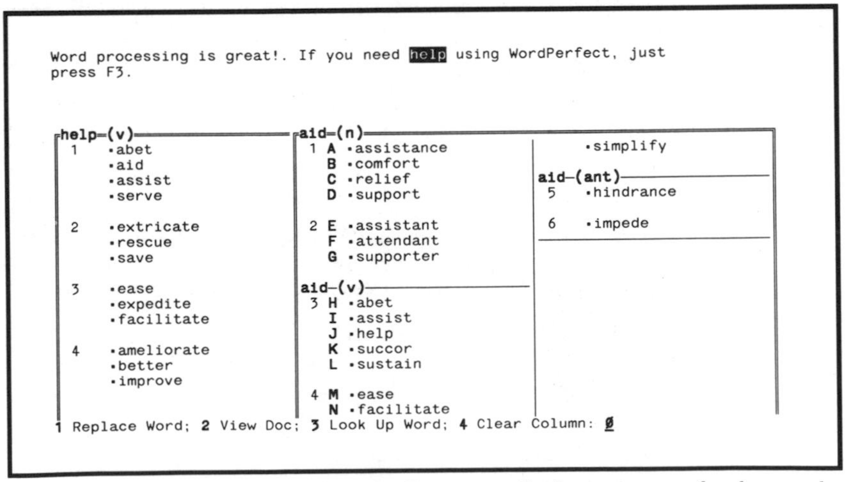

```
Word processing is great!. If you need help using WordPerfect, just
press F3.


┌help—(v)───────────┬aid—(n)──────────────┬────────────────────────┐
│ 1    •abet        │ 1 A •assistance     │      •simplify         │
│      •aid         │   B •comfort        │                        │
│      •assist      │   C •relief         │aid—(ant)────────────   │
│      •serve       │   D •support        │ 5    •hindrance        │
│                   │                     │                        │
│ 2    •extricate   │ 2 E •assistant      │ 6    •impede           │
│      •rescue      │   F •attendant      │                        │
│      •save        │   G •supporter      │                        │
│                   │                     │                        │
│ 3    •ease        │aid—(v)───────────   │                        │
│      •expedite    │ 3 H •abet           │                        │
│      •facilitate  │   I •assist         │                        │
│                   │   J •help           │                        │
│ 4    •ameliorate  │   K •succor         │                        │
│      •better      │   L •sustain        │                        │
│      •improve     │                     │                        │
│                   │ 4 M •ease           │                        │
│                   │   N •facilitate     │                        │
└───────────────────┴─────────────────────┴────────────────────────┘
1 Replace Word; 2 View Doc; 3 Look Up Word; 4 Clear Column: 0
```

■**FIGURE C.3:**   *Selecting* aid *from the first screen displays synonyms for that word*

THESAURUS OPTIONS

You can select an option from the prompt line at the bottom of the screen at any time. The four options are:

- 1 Replace Word: When you find the word that you want to use, make sure that it is preceded by a letter. If not, press the → or ← key until letters appear on that column. Press *1*, and you will be prompted to press the letter for the replacement word.

- 2 View Doc: This option returns the cursor to the document at the top of the screen. You are prompted to press Exit to return to the thesaurus. Use the arrow keys to scroll through the text, then press F7 when you want to return to the thesaurus.

- 3 Look Up Word: Use this option to look up synonyms for words not listed on the screen.

- 4 Clear Column: The Thesaurus screen holds a maximum of three columns. Use the arrow keys to place the letters in a column that you no longer need, then press *4*. The vacated column may be replaced by words that previously could not fit on the screen.

Press Return to select the default 0 option and leave the thesaurus.

VERSION 5.1 FEATURES

FLOPPY DISK SYSTEMS

Follow these steps to set up the drive path when using floppy disk systems.

1. Start WordPerfect.
2. Press Shift-F1 6 or select **F**ile Se**t**up **L**ocation of Files.
3. Press **3** or **t** to select Thesaurus/Spell/Hyphenation.
4. Type **B:**\ then press Return.
5. Type **B:**\ then press Return.
6. Press F7 to return to the typing screen.

You can now insert the Dictionary or Thesaurus disk in drive B when you want to use either program.

IRREGULAR CASES

If a word is found with only the first two letters capitalized, or just the second letter, the prompt changes to

Irregular Case: 1 2 Skip; 3 Replace; 4 Edit; 5 Disable Case Checking

Enter the appropriate selection:

- **1 2** Skip—leaves the work as it appears.

- **3** Replace—capitalizes only the first letter in the word.

- **4** Edit—moves the cursor to the text for editing.

- **5** Disable Case Checking—ignores cases throughout the document.

Index

TO JOIN THE SYBEX MAILING LIST OR ORDER BOOKS
PLEASE COMPLETE THIS FORM

NAME _____ COMPANY _____

STREET _____ CITY _____

STATE _____ ZIP _____

☐ PLEASE MAIL ME MORE INFORMATION ABOUT **SYBEX** TITLES

ORDER FORM (There is no obligation to order)

PLEASE SEND ME THE FOLLOWING:

TITLE	QTY	PRICE
_____	____	____
_____	____	____
_____	____	____
_____	____	____

TOTAL BOOK ORDER _____ $_____

CUSTOMER SIGNATURE _____

SHIPPING AND HANDLING PLEASE ADD $2.00 PER BOOK VIA UPS _____

FOR OVERSEAS SURFACE ADD $5.25 PER BOOK PLUS $4.40 REGISTRATION FEE _____

FOR OVERSEAS AIRMAIL ADD $18.25 PER BOOK PLUS $4.40 REGISTRATION FEE _____

CALIFORNIA RESIDENTS PLEASE ADD APPLICABLE SALES TAX _____

TOTAL AMOUNT PAYABLE _____

☐ CHECK ENCLOSED   ☐ VISA
☐ MASTERCARD   ☐ AMERICAN EXPRESS

ACCOUNT NUMBER _____

EXPIR. DATE _____ DAYTIME PHONE _____

CHECK AREA OF COMPUTER INTEREST:

☐ BUSINESS SOFTWARE

☐ TECHNICAL PROGRAMMING

☐ OTHER: _____

THE FACTOR THAT WAS MOST IMPORTANT IN YOUR SELECTION:

☐ THE SYBEX NAME

☐ QUALITY

☐ PRICE

☐ EXTRA FEATURES

☐ COMPREHENSIVENESS

☐ CLEAR WRITING

☐ OTHER _____

OTHER COMPUTER TITLES YOU WOULD LIKE TO SEE IN PRINT:

_____

_____

OCCUPATION

☐ PROGRAMMER   ☐ TEACHER

☐ SENIOR EXECUTIVE   ☐ HOMEMAKER

☐ COMPUTER CONSULTANT   ☐ RETIRED

☐ SUPERVISOR   ☐ STUDENT

☐ MIDDLE MANAGEMENT   ☐ OTHER:

☐ ENGINEER/TECHNICAL   _____

☐ CLERICAL/SERVICE

☐ BUSINESS OWNER/SELF EMPLOYED

CHECK YOUR LEVEL OF COMPUTER USE

☐ NEW TO COMPUTERS

☐ INFREQUENT COMPUTER USER

☐ FREQUENT USER OF ONE SOFTWARE

PACKAGE:

NAME _____

☐ FREQUENT USER OF MANY SOFTWARE

PACKAGES

☐ PROFESSIONAL PROGRAMMER

OTHER COMMENTS:

_____

_____

_____

_____

_____

_____

_____

PLEASE FOLD, SEAL, AND MAIL TO SYBEX

- -

SYBEX, INC.
2021 CHALLENGER DR. #100
ALAMEDA, CALIFORNIA USA
94501

SEAL

SYBEX Computer Books are different.

Here is why . . .

At SYBEX, each book is designed with you in mind. Every manuscript is carefully selected and supervised by our editors, who are themselves computer experts. We publish the best authors, whose technical expertise is matched by an ability to write clearly and to communicate effectively. Programs are thoroughly tested for accuracy by our technical staff. Our computerized production department goes to great lengths to make sure that each book is well-designed.

In the pursuit of timeliness, SYBEX has achieved many publishing firsts. SYBEX was among the first to integrate personal computers used by authors and staff into the publishing process. SYBEX was the first to publish books on the CP/M operating system, microprocessor interfacing techniques, word processing, and many more topics.

Expertise in computers and dedication to the highest quality product have made SYBEX a world leader in computer book publishing. Translated into fourteen languages, SYBEX books have helped millions of people around the world to get the most from their computers. We hope we have helped you, too.

For a complete catalog of our publications:

SYBEX, Inc. 2021 Challenger Drive, #100, Alameda, CA 94501
Tel: (415) 523-8233/(800) 227-2346   Telex: 336311
Fax: (415) 523-2373

Alphabetic Summary of WordPerfect Commands

Block	Alt-F4	**28**
Boldface print	F6	**54**
Box	Alt-F9	**426**
Cancel	F1	**33**
Cancel printing	Shift-F7 4 1 *	**88**
Center text	Shift-F6	**68**
Center page	Shift-F8 2 1 Return Return	**69**
	(5.1—Shift-F8 2 1 Y Return Return)	
Clear screen	F7 N N	**9**
Column definition	Alt-F7 4 (5.1—Alt-F7 1 3)	**188**
Column off/on	Alt-F7 3 (5.1—Alt-F7 1)	**189**
Copy text	Ctrl-F4	**28**
Cursor movement		
bottom of document	Home Home ↓	**XLI**
bottom of screen	Home ↓	**XLI**
left margin	Home ←	**XLII**
next screen	Home ↓	**XLI**
previous screen	Home ↑	**XLII**
right margin	End	**XLII**
specific page	Ctrl-Home (*page number*) Return	**XLII**
top of document	Home Home ↑	**XLI**
top of screen	Home ↑	**XLI**
Date code	Shift-F5 2	**133**
Date format	Shift-F5 3	**146**
Date text	Shift-F5 1	**133**
Decimal tab align	Ctrl-F6	**207**
Delete to end of line	Ctrl-End	**27**
Delete word	Ctrl-Backspace	**27**
Directory	F5	**26**
Double space	Shift-F8 1 6 2 Return Return Return	**66**
Double underline	Ctrl-F8 2 3	**60**
End Field (^R)	F9	**491**
Exit without saving	F7 N Y	**9**
Flush right	Alt-F6	**69**
Font size	Ctrl-F8 1	**655**
Footnote	Ctrl-F7 1	**315**
Go to page	Ctrl-Home (*page number*) Return	**XLIII**
Graphics	Alt-F9	**426**
Hanging indentation	F4 Shift-Tab	**173**
Help	F3	**XLIV**
Indent, both sides	Shift-F4	**171**
Indent, left	F4	**168**
Insert mode	INS	**6**
Italics	Ctrl-F8 2 4	**60**
Justification off	Shift-F8 1 3 N Return Return	**65**
	(5.1—Shift-F8 1 3 1 Return Return)	
Line numbering	Shift-F8 1 5 Y	**65**
Line spacing	Shift-F8 1 6 *n* Return Return Return	**66**